MCSE Windows NT 4.0 Certification Track Candidates must pass 4 core and 2 elective exams	**MCSE + Internet Windows NT 4.0 Certification Track** Candidates must pass 7 core and 2 elective exams	
CHOOSE 4 CORE & 2 ELECTIVE	**CHOOSE 7 CORE & 2 ELECTIVE**	**CERTIFICATION PRESS STUDY GUIDES**
CORE	CORE	MCSE Windows NT Server 4.0 Study Guide (Exam 70-67) 0-07-882491-5
CORE	CORE	MCSE Windows NT Server 4.0 in the Enterprise Study Guide (Exam 70-68) 0-07-882490-7
CORE	CORE	
CORE	CORE	MCSE Windows NT Workstation 4.0 Study Guide (Exam 70-73) 0-07-882492-3
CORE	CORE	MCSE Windows 98 Study Guide (Exam 70-98) 0-07-882532-6
CORE	CORE	MCSE Networking Essentials Study Guide (Exam 70-58) 0-07-882493-1
ELECTIVE	CORE	MCSE Microsoft TCP/IP on Windows NT 4.0 Study Guide (Exam 70-59) 0-07-882489-3
ELECTIVE	CORE	MCSE Internet Information Server 4.0 with Proxy Server 2.0 and Internet Explorer Administration Kit 1.1 Study Guide (Exams 70-87, 70-79, 70-88) 0-07-882560-1
ELECTIVE	CORE	MCSE Internet Information Server 4.0 with Proxy Server 2.0 and Internet Explorer Administration Kit 1.1 Study Guide (Exams 70-87, 70-79, 70-88) 0-07-882560-1
ELECTIVE	ELECTIVE	
ELECTIVE		
ELECTIVE	ELECTIVE	
ELECTIVE	ELECTIVE	
ELECTIVE	ELECTIVE	
ELECTIVE	ELECTIVE	MCSE System Administration for SQL Server™ Study Guide (Exam 70-28)
ELECTIVE	ELECTIVE	MCSE Exchange Server 5.5 Study Guide (Exam 70-81) 0-07-882488-5
ELECTIVE	ELECTIVE	MCSE Internet Information Server 4.0 with Proxy Server 2.0 and Internet Explorer Administration Kit 1.1 Study Guide (Exams 70-87, 70-79, 70-88) 0-07-882560-1

MCSE NT Server 4.0

Study Guide

(Exam 70-67)

MICROSOFT CERTIFIED SYSTEMS ENGINEER

MCSE NT Server 4.0

Study Guide

(Exam 70-67)

Syngress Media, Inc.

Osborne McGraw-Hill

Berkeley New York St. Louis San Francisco Auckland Bogotá Hamburg London Madrid Mexico City Milan Montreal New Delhi Panama City Paris São Paulo Singapore Sydney Tokyo Toronto

Osborne McGraw-Hill
2600 Tenth Street
Berkeley, California 94710
U.S.A.

For information on translations or book distributors outside the U.S.A., or to arrange bulk purchase discounts for sales promotions, premiums, or fund-raisers, please contact Osborne/**McGraw-Hill** at the above address.

MCSE NT Server 4.0 Study Guide

4567890 DOC DOC 901987654321098

ISBN 0-07-882491-5

Publisher	**Copy Editor**	**Illustrator**
Brandon A. Nordin	Joeth Barlas	Lance Ravella
Editor-in-Chief	**Indexer**	**Series Design**
Scott Rogers	Valerie Robbins	Roberta Steele
Acquisitions Editor	**Proofreaders**	**Cover Design**
Gareth Hancock	Pat Mannion	Regan Honda
Project Editor	Stefany Otis	
Cynthia Douglas	Carroll Proffitt	**Editorial Management**
		Syngress Media, Inc.
Technical Editor	**Computer Designer**	
D. Lynn White	Jani Beckwith	
	Mickey Galicia	
	Roberta Steele	

From Global Knowledge Network

At Global Knowledge Network we strive to support the multiplicity of learning styles required by our students to achieve success as technical professionals. In this series of books, it is our intention to offer the reader a valuable tool for successful completion of the MCSE Certification Exam.

As the world's largest IT training company, Global Knowledge Network is uniquely positioned to offer these books. The expertise gained each year from providing instructor-led training to hundreds of thousands of students worldwide has been captured in book form to enhance your learning experience. We hope that the quality of these books demonstrates our commitment to your lifelong learning success. Whether you choose to learn through the written word, computer-based training, Web delivery, or instructor-led training, Global Knowledge Network is committed to providing you the very best in each of those categories. For those of you who know Global Knowledge Network, or those of you who have just found us for the first time, our goal is to be your lifelong competency partner.

Thank you for the opportunity to serve you. We look forward to serving your needs again in the future.

Warmest regards,

Duncan Anderson
Chief Operating Officer, Global Knowledge Network

January 12, 1998

Dear Osborne/McGraw-Hill Customer:

Microsoft is pleased to inform you that Osborne/McGraw-Hill is a participant in the Microsoft® Independent Courseware Vendor (ICV) program. Microsoft ICVs design, develop, and market self-paced courseware, books, and other products that support Microsoft software and the Microsoft Certified Professional (MCP) program.

To be accepted into the Microsoft ICV program, an ICV must meet set criteria. In addition, Microsoft reviews and approves each ICV training product before permission is granted to use the Microsoft Certified Professional Approved Study Guide logo on that product. This logo assures the consumer that the product has passed the following Microsoft standards:

- The course contains accurate product information.
- The course includes labs and activities during which the student can apply knowledge and skills learned from the course.
- The course teaches skills that help prepare the student to take corresponding MCP exams.

Microsoft ICVs continually develop and release new MCP Approved Study Guides. To prepare for a particular Microsoft certification exam, a student may choose one or more single, self-paced training courses or a series of training courses.

You will be pleased with the quality and effectiveness of the MCP Approved Study Guides available from Osborne/McGraw-Hill.

Sincerely,

Becky Kirsininkas

Becky Kirsininkas
ICV Program Manager
Microsoft Training & Certification

ABOUT THE CONTRIBUTORS

Syngress Media creates books and software for Information Technology professionals seeking skill enhancement and career advancement. Its products are designed to comply with vendor and industry standard course curricula and are optimized for certification exam preparation. Contact them at www.sygress.com.

Cameron Brandon (MCSE, CNE, CNA, MCPS:Internet Systems, A+) is a Network Engineer/Administrator with Computer Systems, and lives in the greater Portland, Oregon, area. His specialty is Windows NT with BackOffice Integration.

Cameron participated in the Intel migration to Windows NT in Oregon, the largest migration of its kind in history. He completed his MCSE, CNE, CNA, MCPS:Internet Systems, and A+ certifications in five months' time, which shows what you can do if you set your mind to it.

Stace Cunningham is a Systems Engineer with SDC Consulting located in Biloxi, Mississippi. SDC Consulting specializes in the design, engineering, and installation of networks. Stace received his MCSE in October, 1996 and is also certified as an IBM Certified LAN Server Engineer, IBM Certified OS/2 Engineer, IBM Certified LAN Server Administrator, Microsoft Certified Product Specialist, IBM Certified LAN Server Instructor, and IBM Certified OS/2 Instructor.

Stace has participated as a Technical Contributor for the IIS 3.0 exam, SMS 1.2 exam, Proxy Server 1.0 exam, Exchange Server 5.0 and 5.5 exams, Proxy Server 2.0 exam, and the revised Windows 95 exam.

His wife Martha and daughter Marissa are very supportive of the time he spends on the computers located throughout his house. Without their love and support he would not be able to accomplish the goals he has set for himself.

Mike Swisher (MCSE) is a 1st Lieutenant in the United States Air Force. He is a communications officer serving at Keesler Air Force Base in Mississippi. His current duties have him designing a networking infrastructure with NT as the primary network operating system for the entire base (more than 10,000 users). He has received numerous awards in his three years in the military. Two years in a row he was selected as the 81st Training Support Squadron Company Grade Officer of the Year. He also distinguished himself by graduating top in his class at the Air Force's Basic Communications Officer Course. He enjoys water skiing and—of course—computers. His hometown is Rock Hill, South Carolina.

Michael D. Kendzierski (MCT, MCSE) works as a Systems Engineer for New Technology Partners, the 1997 Microsoft Solution Provider Partner of the Year. He received his Bachelor's degree from Providence College and has recently completed graduate work at Boston University. He is currently dividing his time between the Midwest and New England, providing consulting, development, and project management for Fortune 100 companies. When he's not fooling around with Visual Basic, he can be found roaming the country searching for a local Starbucks. He welcomes e-mail and can be reached at Mkendzierski@worldnet.att.net

Tony Hinkle (MCSE, CNE) is from southern Indiana, is farm-raised, and holds a Bachelor's degree in Business Accounting from Oakland City University. His accounting career was quickly terminated by destiny, and he moved into the field of computer services. Although he started as a hardware technician, he knew that operating systems and networking would be his fields of excellence. With the assistance of his employer, Advanced Microelectronics, Inc., Tony completed the requirements to become a CNE, an A+ Certified Technician, and an MCSE.

Tony enjoys reading, Frisbee, Scrabble, computing, and participating in most non-contact sports. His claims to fame include being able to chirp like a cricket, knowing the alphabet backward, not owning a television, and knowing how many bytes are in an ATM packet. Tony thanks all of those who have helped to instill in him the knowledge, experience, and self-confidence necessary to excel in his field.

Brian Frederick is an MCSE with more than five years of technical experience. Brian started his computer career at the ripe old age of seven with an Apple II+. Brian attended the University of Northern Iowa and is married with two adorable children. Brian's hobbies include his kids, primarily, as well as little league baseball and web page development. Brian also enjoys other sports, electronics, and multi-player gaming. Brian is involved with MCSE classroom training with a local ATEC.

Sean Wallbridge is a Consultant with NexGen Technologies located in Hamilton, Bermuda. NexGen Technologies is a professional services organization focusing on the design, implementation, and management of sophisticated business solutions which leverage the entire Microsoft BackOffice suite. Sean's qualifications include MCSE+Internet (3.5x/4.x), CNA, MSS and Microsoft Certified Trainer. Specializing in delivering solutions for Microsoft Exchange, SMS, SQL, IIS, Proxy Server and NT, Sean takes pride in building sophisticated BackOffice and Intranet turnkey solutions. Sean can be reached by E-mail at sean@wallbridge.com or by visiting www.wallbridge.com/sean/

Technical Review by:

D. Lynn White is President of Independent Network Consultants, Inc. She is a technical author, editor, trainer, and consultant in the field of networking and computer-related technologies. She has been delivering mainframe, Microsoft Official curriculum, and other networking courses across the country for more than 11 years. Lynn is an MCPS, MCSE and MCT.

From the Classroom sidebars by:

Shane Clawson is a principal in Virtual Engineering, a consulting and engineering firm specializing in network consulting and technology process re-engineering. Shane has more than 20 years' experience as an instructor and in the in networking field. He is a Microsoft Certified System Engineer (MCSE) and a Microsoft Certified Trainer (MCT) who has been working with NT since its inception and teaches for Global Knowledge Network. He specializes in Microsoft networking and BackOffice products. Shane may be reached at ShaneCSE@msn.com.

ACKNOWLEDGMENTS

We would like to thank the following people:

- Rich Kristof of Global Knowledge Network for championing the series and providing us access to some great people and information. And to Patrick Von Schlag, Rhonda Harmon, Marian Turk, and Kevin Murray for all their cooperation.

- To all the incredibly hard-working folks at Osborne/McGraw-Hill: Brandon Nordin, Scott Rogers, and Gareth Hancock for their help in launching a great series and being solid team players. In addition, Cynthia Douglas, Steve Emry, Anne Ellingsen, and Bernadette Jurich for their help in fine-tuning the book.

- Bruce Moran of BeachFront Quizzer, Mary Anne Dane of Self-Test Software, John Rose of Transcender Corporation, Parmol Soni of Microhard Technologies, and Michael Herrick of VFX Technologies.

- Gene Landy of the MIT Enterprise Forum for his support and encouragement, not to mention his incredible legal expertise. And to Tom Warren for handling all our IS needs with a smile.

- And to Holly Heath at Microsoft, Corp. for being patient and diligent in answering all our questions.

CONTENTS

Foreword . . . . *v*

About the Contributors . . . . *ix*

Acknowledgments . . . . *xiii*

Preface . . . . *xxxi*

Introduction . . . . *xxxvii*

I   Introduction to Windows NT Server 4.0 . . . . .   **I**

Certification Objective 1.01
Windows NT Server Overview   2
    Preemptive Multitasking   3
    Multiple Process Management Models   4
    True Multiprocessor Support   6
    Centralized Profiles and Policies   7
    Built-in Remote Access Service (RAS)   8
    Fault Tolerance   9
    Internet Information Server (IIS) and More   14
    Administrative Wizards   16

Certification Objective 1.02
Windows NT Architecture   16

Certification Objective 1.03
User Mode vs. Kernel Mode   17
    User Mode   17
    Kernel Mode   18
    Hardware Abstraction Layer (HAL)   18
    Windows NT Microkernel   19

Certification Objective 1.04
Executive Services   19

Certification Objective 1.05
Windows NT Subsystems   20

Win32 21

MS-DOS 22

Win16 22

OS/2 Subsystem 23

POSIX Subsystem 23

Certification Objective 1.06

Windows NT Memory Organization 23

Virtual Memory 24

Demand Paging 24

Linear 32-bit Address 25

Device Drivers 26

Certification Summary 26

Two-Minute Drill 28

Self Test 30

2 Planning Windows NT 4.0 Installation **33**

Certification Objective 2.01

What's New in NT Server 4.0 34

Administrative Wizards 35

Network Monitor Tool 35

System Policies and Profiles 36

Improved Diagnostics 37

Remote Access Service 37

Friendlier Installation 38

Hardware Profile Support 38

Improved Error Messages 39

Improved Task Manager 39

Improved Protocol (DHCP) 40

Registry Editor 41

Web Browser and "Web-ification" 43

New Printer Folder and UI 43

Certification Objective 2.02

Planning for Installation 44

Certification Objective 2.03

Hardware and Software Compatibility 47

Importance of the HCL 48
Software Compatibility Issues 49
SMP Support 49
Requirements and Recommendations 50

Certification Objective 2.04
Windows NT File Systems 52
File Allocation Table (FAT) 53
CD-ROM File System 54
NTFS 54
Long File Names 58

Certification Objective 2.05
Windows NT Protocols 59
NetBIOS/NetBEUI 60
TCP/IP 60
NWLink (IPX/SPX) 61
AppleTalk 62
Data Link Control (DLC) 62

Certification Summary 63
Two-Minute Drill 64
Self Test 67

3   Installing Windows NT Server 4.0 . . . . **69**

Certification Objective 3.01
Planning the Hard Disk Configuration 70
Per Server vs. Per Seat Licensing 73
Partitions and Fault Tolerance 73
Naming Conventions 74
Preparing for Installation 75

Certification Objective 3.02
Installation Methods 78
Network Installation 79
Network Installation Switches 87
CD-ROM Installation 94
Installing NT on RISC-based Computers 96
Upgrade Installation 96

Unattended Installation 98
Certification Objective 3.03
Server Roles 105
Primary Domain Controller (PDC) 106
Backup Domain Controller (BDC) 107
Member Server 109
Server Promotion Rules 109
Certification Objective 3.04
Removing Windows NT 111
Deleting FAT Partitions 111
Deleting NTFS Partitions 113
Removing Windows NT from a FAT Partition 114
Changing the Boot Loader in an Existing FAT
Partition to MS-DOS 115
Certification Objective 3.05
Troubleshooting the Installation Process 117
Certification Summary 118
Two-Minute Drill 118
Self Test 120

4   Configuring Windows NT 4.0 . . . . **129**

Certification Objective 4.01
Configuring Network Protocols 130
NWLink IPX/SPX-Compatible 130
TCP/IP 130
Certification Objective 4.02
Configuring Peripheral Devices 145
Control Panel 146
Adding SCSI Adapters and CD-ROM Drives 150
Certification Objective 4.03
NT 4.0 Disk Administrator 154
System and Boot Partitions 156
Primary and Extended Partitions 156
Volume Sets 159
Stripe Sets Without Parity 160

Drive Letter Assignment 161

Fault Tolerance (RAID) 161

NT Clients 164

Using the Network Client Administrator 164

Certification Objective 4.04

NT Browser Types 167

Domain Master Browser 167

Master Browser 167

Backup Browser 167

Potential Browser 168

Non-browser 168

Browser Elections 168

Certification Objective 4.05

NT System Registry 169

Hardware Profiles 170

User Profiles 171

Devices 172

Registry Hierarchy 172

Certification Summary 173

Two-Minute Drill 174

Self Test 177

5   Managing Resources **181**

Certification Objective 5.01

User and Group Accounts 182

User Manager 183

Group Administration 193

Local Groups 196

Global Groups 199

Certification Objective 5.02

System Policies 201

System Policy Editor 209

Restriction of Control Panel Options 212

Desktop Customization 213

Network Settings 213

Network Logon 213

Start Menu Options 213

Certification Objective 5.03

User Profiles 214

User Profile Options 214

Types of User Profiles 215

Managing User Profiles 218

Profile Shortcuts 218

Logon Scripts 220

Certification Objective 5.04

Administering Remote NT Servers 221

Network Neighborhood 222

Windows NT Diagnostics 222

Server Manager 223

Printers Utility 226

Certification Summary 226

Two-Minute Drill 227

Self Test 229

6   **Windows NT 4.0 Security** **233**

Certification Objective 6.01

NT Security Model 234

Logon Authentication 235

Account Lockout 238

Certification Objective 6.02

Implementing Permissions and Security 239

Microsoft Object Security Terms 240

Access Control List (ACL) and Access Control

Entries (ACE) 241

Security Account Manager (SAM) 245

Security ID (SID) 245

Access Token 246

Certification Objective 6.03

NTFS Security 246

Permissions When Copying and Moving Files 250

Viewing and Changing Permissions 250

Command Prompt 253

Assigning Rights to Users and Groups 255

Certification Objective 6.04

Shared Server Resources 259

Permissions for Shared Directories 259

Command Prompt 263

Assigning Permissions to Shared Directories 264

Shared Printer Security 265

Certification Objective 6.05

Event Auditing 266

Certification Objective 6.06

Setting Registry Keys 271

Adding a Security Warning Message 272

Disabling the Default Username 272

Disabling the Shutdown Button 273

Certification Summary 273

Two-Minute Drill 274

Self Test 276

7 Windows NT 4.0 Domains **281**

Certification Objective 7.01

The Workgroup Model and the Domain Model 282

Workgroups: Peer-to-Peer Networking 282

Domain Computing 283

Workgroup Model vs. Domain Concept 284

Certification Objective 7.02

Managing Domain Trusts 285

Trusted Domain Concept 285

Trust Relationships Between Domains 285

Number of Trusts 290

Domain Strategies 291

Certification Objective 7.03

Using NT Server Manager 297

Server Properties 297

Monitoring Users 298
Managing Shared Resources 300
Monitoring Resources in Use 301
Monitoring Server Alerts 301
Adding/Removing Computers 302
Promote a BDC to a PDC 304
Synchronize BDCs with PDCs 304

Certification Objective 7.04
Local and Global Groups 305
Setting Up a Global Group 307
Setting Up a Local Group 307

Certification Objective 7.05
NT's Netlogon Service 309
Pass-Through Authentication 310
Configuring Netlogon Service 310
Certification Summary 313
Two-Minute Drill 313
Self Test 315

8   Replication and Data Synchronization **317**

Certification Objective 8.01
Directory Replication 318
Export Server and Import Computers 321
Directory Replicator Service 323
Managing Replication 329

Certification Objective 8.02
Replicating System and Domain Files 333
User Accounts Database 333
Logon Scripts 338
System Policy Files 338
Widely Used Files 340

Certification Objective 8.03
Using My Briefcase to Synchronize Files 341
Certification Summary 344
Two-Minute Drill 345
Self Test 347

9   Printing **351**

Certification Objective 9.01
Overview of Printing Terminology   352
    Printing Devices   352
    Printing Software   352
    Windows NT Print Model   353
    Print Router   356
    Print Spooler   356
    Print Processor   357
    Print Monitors   359
    Print Jobs   360

Certification Objective 9.02
Installing Printers   361
    Creating a Local Printer   361
    Sharing a Printer   362
    Connecting to a Remote Printer   363
    Network Interface Printing Devices   363

Certification Objective 9.03
Configuring Printers   365
    General Tab   365
    Print Test Page   367
    Ports Tab   367
    Scheduling Tab   369
    Sharing Tab   373
    Security Tab   373
    Permissions   374
    Auditing   376
    Ownership   376
    Device Settings Tab   377

Certification Objective 9.04
Managing Print Jobs   378

Certification Objective 9.05
Troubleshooting Printers   379
Certification Summary   381
Two-Minute Drill   382
Self Test   384

10   NetWare Integration **387**

Certification Objective 10.01
Planning NetWare Connectivity   388
   Connectivity Options   390
   NWLink   393
   Using GSNW and CSNW   396
   Migration Tool for NetWare   397
   File and Print Services for NetWare (FPNW)   397
   Directory Services Manager for NetWare (DSMN)   . . .   398
   Migration Strategies   398
Certification Objective 10.02
Gateway Service for NetWare (GSNW)   401
   Installing GSNW   402
   Configuring GSNW   403
   Using Remote Access Service (RAS) with GSNW   409
   Security Issues with GSNW   409
   Connecting to NetWare Services with Explorer   409
   Connecting to NetWare Services with the Command
      Line   411
   NetWare Specific Applications   411
   NetWare Utilities   412
Certification Objective 10.03
The Migration Tool for NetWare   414
   Migrating User Accounts and Groups   414
   Transferring Volumes and Files   415
   Configuring the Migration   415
Certification Summary   421
Two-Minute Drill   421
Self Test   423

11   Remote Connectivity **425**

Certification Objective 11.01
Remote Access Service   426
   Dial-Up Networking for Windows NT and
      Windows 95 Clients   426

Support of LAN and WAN Protocols   427
Support for Connections across PSTN,
    ISDN, X.25, and the Internet   427
Using Multi-Modem Adapters with NT Server
    (Multilink)   428

Certification Objective 11.02
Remote Access Protocols   430
    Serial Line Internet Protocol (SLIP)   430
    Point-to-Point Protocol (PPP)   430
    Windows NT Protocols over PPP   431
    RAS PPTP   432

Certification Objective 11.03
Installing and Configuring Remote Access Service   434
    Configuring RAS Ports   438
    Configuring RAS Network Settings   439

Certification Objective 11.04
Configuring RAS Security   443
    Domain Account Database   444
    Granting RAS Permissions to User Accounts   444
    Callback Security   445
    Encrypted Data Authentication and Logons   446
    Full Audit Capabilities   447
    Support of Third-Party Intermediary Security Hosts . .   448
    PPTP Filtering   448

Certification Objective 11.05
Configuring Dial-Up Networking Clients   449
    TAPI Features of RAS   449
    Defining a Phonebook Entry   450

Certification Objective 11.06
Administering and Troubleshooting RAS   453
    Troubleshooting RAS   455
Certification Summary   457
Two-Minute Drill   457
Self Test   459

12 Backup **463**

Certification Objective 12.01
Backup Strategies 464
    Single vs. Multiple Backups 464
    Hardware for Backups 466
    Backup Software 467
    Backup Schedule 468
    Backup Types 469
    Media Rotation 471
    Storage 472
    Additional Backup Protection 472

Certification Objective 12.02
Windows NT Backup Utility 474
    Hardware for Windows NT Backup 475
    Back Up NTFS or FAT Partitions 476
    Permissions to Perform a Backup 476
    Selecting Files for Backup 477
    NT Backup Options 481
    NT Restore Options 486

Certification Objective 12.03
Performing Backups and Restorations 488
    Performing a Backup 488
    Restoring Data from Backups 490
    Automating Backups 491

Certification Objective 12.04
Windows NT Backup and Recovery Schemes 498
    Disk Administrator 498
    The Emergency Repair Disk 501
    Registry Backups 501

Certification Objective 12.05
Third-Party Backup and Restore Alternatives 504
    Seagate Backup Exec for Windows NT 504
    Stac Replica for Windows NT 505
    ARCserve for Windows NT 506
Certification Summary 506

Two-Minute Drill 507
Self Test 509

13 Windows NT 4.0 Monitoring and
Performance Tuning **511**

Certification Objective 13.01
Performance Tuning 512
    Bottlenecks 513
    Detecting Bottlenecks 513
    Eliminating Bottlenecks 514
    Self-Tuning Mechanisms 514
    Network Tuning *522*

Certification Objective 13.02
Optimizing Applications 524
    Windows NT Task Manager 524
    Foreground Application Performance Boost 527

Certification Objective 13.03
Performance Monitor 530
    Creating a Performance Monitor Chart 534
    Creating a Performance Monitor Alert 535
    Creating a Performance Monitor Report 537
    Creating a Performance Monitor Log 537
    Performance Monitor Capabilities 540
    Processor Performance 541
    Disk Drive Performance 544
    Memory Performance 548

Certification Objective 13.04
Event Viewer 553
    Log Files 553
    Log File Events 555
    Log Event Details 556

Certification Objective 13.05
Windows NT Diagnostics 556
    Version 557

System 557

Display 557

Drives 558

Memory 558

Services 558

Resources 559

Environment 559

Network 559

Certification Objective 13.06

Network Monitor 560

Certification Summary 565

Two-Minute Drill 566

Self Test 568

14 Troubleshooting **571**

Certification Objective 14.01

Installation Problems 572

Certification Objective 14.02

Configuration Errors 575

Boot Failures 575

The Event Viewer 580

Windows NT Diagnostics 581

Certification Objective 14.03

Disk Problems 582

Unknown Volume 583

Extended Partition Problem 584

Certification Objective 14.04

Troubleshooting RAID Problems 584

Regenerating a Stripe Set with Parity 585

Fixing a Mirror Set 586

Fault-Tolerant Boot Disks 587

Certification Objective 14.05

Printing Problems 590

Certification Objective 14.06

Remote Access Service Problems   591

Certification Objective 14.07

Network Problems   594

Certification Objective 14.08

Permission Problems   596

      Taking Ownership of a Resource   597

Certification Objective 14.09

Server Crashes   598

      System Recovery Utility   598

      Task Manager   600

      STOP Error—the "Blue Screen of Death"   601

Certification Objective 14.10

Using Microsoft Resources   604

      Microsoft Web and FTP Sites   604

      Microsoft Service Packs   604

      The Knowledge Base   607

      TechNet CD-ROM   607

      Resource Kits   608

      Help   608

  Certification Summary   609

  Two-Minute Drill   611

  Self Test   613

A   Self Test Answers **617**

Answers to Chapter 1 Self Test   618

Answers to Chapter 2 Self Test   619

Answers to Chapter 3 Self Test   620

Answers to Chapter 4 Self Test   624

Answers to Chapter 5 Self Test   626

Answers to Chapter 6 Self Test   628

Answers to Chapter 7 Self Test   631

Answers to Chapter 8 Self Test   632

Answers to Chapter 9 Self Test   634

Answers to Chapter 10 Self Test 636
Answers to Chapter 11 Self Test 637
Answers to Chapter 12 Self Test 639
Answers to Chapter 13 Self Test 641
Answers to Chapter 14 Self Test 644

B   About the CD **647**

CD-ROM Instructions 648
    Electronic Book 648
    Interactive Self-Study Module 648
    Sample Exams 648

C   About the Web Site **651**

Access Global Knowledge Network 652
    What You'll Find There. 652

Glossary **653**

Index **677**

This book's primary objective is to help you prepare for and pass the required MCSE exam so you can begin to reap the career benefits of certification. We believe that the only way to do this is to help you increase your knowledge and build your skills. After completing this book, you should feel confident that you have thoroughly reviewed all of the objectives that Microsoft has established for the exam.

In This Book

This book is organized around the actual structure of the Microsoft exam administered at Sylvan Testing Centers. Most of the MCSE exams have six parts to them: Planning, Installation and Configuration, Managing Resources, Connectivity, Monitoring and Optimization, and Troubleshooting. Microsoft has let us know all the topics we need to cover for the exam. We've followed their list carefully, so you can be assured you're not missing anything.

In Every Chapter

We've created a set of chapter components that call your attention to important items, reinforce important points, and provide helpful exam-taking hints. Take a look at what you'll find in every chapter:

- Every chapter begins with the **Certification Objectives**—what you need to know in order to pass the section on the exam dealing with the chapter topic. The icon shown at left identifies the objectives within the chapter, so you'll always know an objective when you see it!

- **Exam Watch** notes call attention to information about, and potential pitfalls in, the exam. These helpful hints are written by MCSEs who have taken the exams and received their certification—who better to tell you what to worry about? They know what you're about to go through!

EXERCISE

- **Certification Exercises** are interspersed throughout the chapters. These are step-by-step exercises that mirror vendor-recommended labs. They help you master skills that are likely to be an area of focus on the exam. Don't just read through the exercises; they are hands-on practice that you should be comfortable completing. Learning by doing is an effective way to increase your competency with a product.

- **From the Classroom** sidebars describe the issues that come up most often in the training classroom setting. These sidebars give you a valuable perspective into certification- and product-related topics. They point out common mistakes and address questions that have arisen from classroom discussions.

- **Q & A** sections lay out problems and solutions in a quick-read format:

QUESTIONS AND ANSWERS

I am installing NT and I have HPFS...	Convert it before you upgrade. NT 4 does not like HPFS.

- The **Certification Summary** is a succinct review of the chapter and a re-statement of salient points regarding the exam.

- The **Two-Minute Drill** at the end of every chapter is a checklist of the main points of the chapter. It can be used for last-minute review.

- The **Self Test** offers questions similar to those found on the certification exams, including multiple choice, true/false questions, and fill-in-the-blank. The answers to these questions, as well as explanations of the answers, can be found in Appendix A. By taking the Self Test after completing each chapter, you'll reinforce what you've learned from that chapter, while becoming familiar with the structure of the exam questions.

Some Pointers

Once you've finished reading this book, set aside some time to do a thorough review. You might want to return to the book several times and make use of all the methods it offers for reviewing the material:

1. *Re-read all the Two-Minute Drills,* or have someone quiz you. You also can use the drills as a way to do a quick cram before the exam.

2. *Re-read all the Exam Watch notes.* Remember that these are written by MCSEs who have taken the exam and passed. They know what you should expect—and what you should be careful about.

3. *Review all the Q & A scenarios* for quick problem solving.

4. *Re-take the Self Tests.* Taking the tests right after you've read the chapter is a good idea, because it helps reinforce what you've just learned. However, it's an even better idea to go back later and do all the questions in the book in one sitting. Pretend you're taking the exam. (For this reason, you should mark your answers on a separate piece of paper when you go through the questions the first time.)

5. *Take the on-line tests.* Boot up the CD-ROM and take a look. We have more third-party tests on our CD than any other book out there, so you'll get quite a bit of practice.

6. *Complete the exercises.* Did you do the exercises when you read through each chapter? If not, do them! These exercises are designed to cover exam topics, and there's no better way to get to know this material than by practicing.

7. *Check out the web site.* Global Knowledge Network invites you to become an active member of the Access Global web site. This site is an online mall and an information repository that you'll find invaluable. You can access many types of products to assist you in your preparation for the exams, and you'll be able to participate in forums, on-line discussions, and threaded discussions. No other book brings you unlimited access to such a resource. You'll find more information about this site in Appendix C.

MCSE Certification

Although you've obviously picked up this book to study for a specific exam, we'd like to spend some time covering what you need to complete in order to attain MCSE status. Because this information can be found on the Microsoft web site, www.microsoft.com/train_cert, we've repeated only some of the more important information. You should review the train_cert site and check out Microsoft's information, along with their list of reasons to become an MCSE, including job advancement.

As you probably know, to attain MCSE status, you must pass a total of six exams —four requirements and two electives. One required exam is on networking basics, one on NT Server, one on NT Server in the Enterprise, and one on a client (either Windows NT Workstation or Windows 95 or 98). There are several electives from which to choose. The most popular electives now are on TCP/IP and Exchange Server 5. The following table lists the exam names, their corresponding course numbers, and whether they are required or elective. We're showing you the NT 4.0 track and not the NT 3.51 track (which is still offered).

Exam Number	Exam Name	Required or Elective
70-58	Networking Essentials	Required
70-63	Implementing and Supporting Microsoft Windows 95 or 98	Required (either 70-63/ 70-98 or 70-73)
70-67	Implementing and Supporting Microsoft Windows NT Server 4.0	Required

Exam Number	Exam Name	Required or Elective
70-68	Implementing and Supporting Microsoft Windows NT Server 4.0 in the Enterprise	Required
70-73	Implementing and Supporting Microsoft Windows NT Workstation 4.0	Required (either 70-73 or 70-63)
70-14	Supporting Microsoft System Management Server 1.2	Elective
70-59	Internetworking with Microsoft TCP/IP on Windows NT 4.0	Elective
70-81	Implementing and Supporting Microsoft Exchange Server 5.5	Elective
70-85	Implementing and Supporting Microsoft SNA Server 4.0	Elective
70-87	Implementing and Supporting Microsoft Internet Information Server 4.0	Elective
70-88	Implementing and Supporting Microsoft Proxy Server 2.0	Elective
TBA	System Administration for Microsoft SQL Server X	Elective
TBA	Implementing a Database Design on SQL Server X	Elective

The CD-ROM Resource

This book comes with a CD-ROM full of supplementary material you can use while preparing for the MCSE exams. We think you'll find our book/CD package one of the most useful on the market. It provides all the sample tests available from testing companies such as Transcender, Microhard, Self Test Software, BeachFront Quizzer, and VFX Technologies. In addition to all these third-party products, you'll find an electronic version of the book, where you can look up items easily and search on specific terms. The special self-study module contains another 300 sample questions, with links to the electronic book for further review. There's more about this resource in Appendix B.

How to Take a Microsoft Certification Examination

by John C. Phillips, Vice President of Test Development, Self Test Software
(Self Test's PEP is the official Microsoft practice test.)

Good News and Bad News

If you are new to Microsoft certification, we have some good news and some bad news. The good news, of course, is that Microsoft certification is one of the most valuable credentials you can earn. It sets you apart from the crowd, and marks you as a valuable asset to your employer. You will gain the respect of your peers, and Microsoft certification can have a wonderful effect on your income.

The bad news is that Microsoft certification tests are not easy. You may think you will read through some study material, memorize a few facts, and pass the Microsoft examinations. After all, these certification exams are just computer-based, multiple-choice tests, so they must be easy. If you believe this, you are wrong. Unlike many "multiple guess" tests you have been exposed to in school, the questions on Microsoft certification examinations go beyond simple factual knowledge.

The purpose of this introduction is to teach you how to take a Microsoft certification examination. To be successful, you need to know something about the purpose and structure of these tests. We will also look at the latest innovations in Microsoft testing. Using *simulations* and *adaptive testing*, Microsoft is enhancing both the validity and security of the certification process. These factors have some important effects on how you should prepare for an exam, as well as your approach to each question during the test.

We will begin by looking at the purpose, focus, and structure of Microsoft certification tests, and examine the effect these factors have on the kinds of questions you will face on your certification exams. We will define the structure of examination questions and investigate some common formats. Next, we will present a strategy for answering these questions. Finally, we will give some specific guidelines on what you should do on the day of your test.

Why Vendor Certification?

The Microsoft Certified Professional program, like the certification programs from Lotus, Novell, Oracle, and other software vendors, is maintained for the ultimate purpose of increasing the corporation's profits. A successful vendor certification program accomplishes this goal by helping to create a pool of experts in a company's software, and by "branding" these experts so that companies using the software can identify them.

We know that vendor certification has become increasingly popular in the last few years because it helps employers find qualified workers, and because it helps software vendors like Microsoft sell their products. But why vendor certification rather than a more traditional approach like a college degree in computer science? A college education is a broadening and enriching experience, but a degree in computer science does not prepare students for most jobs in the IT industry.

A common truism in our business states, "If you are out of the IT industry for three years and want to return, you have to start over." The problem, of course, is *timeliness*; if a first-year student learns about a specific computer program, it probably will no longer be in wide use when he or she graduates. Although some colleges are trying to integrate Microsoft certification into their curriculum, the problem is not really a flaw in higher education, but a characteristic of the IT industry. Computer software is changing so rapidly that a four-year college just can't keep up.

A marked characteristic of the Microsoft certification program is an emphasis on performing specific job tasks rather than merely gathering knowledge. It may come as a shock, but most potential employers do not care how much you know about the theory of operating systems, networking, or database design. As one IT manager put it, "I don't really care what my employees know about the theory of our network. We don't need someone to sit at a desk and think about it. We need people who can actually do something to make it work better."

You should not think that this attitude is some kind of anti-intellectual revolt against "book learning." Knowledge is a necessary prerequisite, but it is not enough. More than one company has hired a computer science graduate as a network administrator, only to learn that the new employee has no idea how to add users, assign permissions, or perform the other day-to-day tasks necessary to maintain a network. This brings us to the second major characteristic of Microsoft certification that affects the questions you must be prepared to answer. In addition to timeliness, Microsoft certification is also job task oriented.

The timeliness of Microsoft's certification program is obvious, and is inherent in the fact that you will be tested on current versions of software in wide use today. The job task orientation of Microsoft certification is almost as obvious, but testing real-world job skills using a computer-based test is not easy.

Computerized Testing

Considering the popularity of Microsoft certification, and the fact that certification candidates are spread around the world, the only practical way to administer tests for the certification program is through Sylvan Prometric testing centers. Sylvan Prometric provides proctored testing services for Microsoft, Oracle, Novell, Lotus, and the A+ computer technician certification. Although the IT industry accounts for much of Sylvan's revenue, the company provides services for a number of other businesses and organizations, such as FAA pre-flight pilot tests. In fact, most companies that need secure test delivery over a wide geographic area use the services of Sylvan Prometric. In addition to delivery, Sylvan Prometric also scores the tests and provides statistical feedback on the performance of each test question to the companies and organizations that use their services.

Typically, several hundred questions are developed for a new Microsoft certification examination. The questions are first reviewed by a number of subject matter experts for technical accuracy, and then are presented in a beta test. The beta test may last for several hours, due to the large number of questions. After a few weeks, Microsoft Certification uses the statistical feedback from Sylvan to check the performance of the beta questions.

Questions are discarded if most test takers get them right (too easy) or wrong (too difficult), and a number of other statistical measures are taken of each question. Although the scope of our discussion precludes a rigorous treatment of question analysis, you should be aware that Microsoft and other vendors spend a great deal of time and effort making sure their examination questions are valid. In addition to the obvious desire for quality, the fairness of a vendor's certification program must be legally defensible.

The questions that survive statistical analysis form the pool of questions for the final certification examination.

Test Structure

The kind of test we are most familiar with is known as a *form* test. For Microsoft certification, a form usually consists of 50–70 questions and takes 60–90 minutes to complete. If there are 240 questions in the final pool for an examination, then four forms can be created. Thus, candidates who retake the test probably will not see the same questions.

Other variations are possible. From the same pool of 240 questions, *five* forms can be created, each containing 40 unique questions (200 questions) and 20 questions selected at random from the remaining 40.

The questions in a Microsoft form test are equally weighted. This means they all count the same when the test is scored. An interesting and useful characteristic of a form test is that you can mark a question you have doubts about as you take the test. Assuming you have time left when you finish all the questions, you can return and spend more time on the questions you have marked as doubtful.

Microsoft may soon implement *adaptive* testing. To use this interactive technique, a form test is first created and administered to several thousand certification candidates. The statistics generated are used to assign a weight, or difficulty level, for each question. For example, the questions in a form might be divided into levels one through five, with level one questions being the easiest and level five the hardest.

When an adaptive test begins, the candidate is first given a level three question. If it is answered correctly, a question from the next higher level is presented, and an incorrect response results in a question from the next lower level. When 15–20 questions have been answered in this manner, the scoring algorithm is able to predict, with a high degree of statistical certainty, whether the candidate would pass or fail if all the questions in the form were answered.

When the required degree of certainty is attained, the test ends and the candidate receives a pass/fail grade.

Adaptive testing has some definite advantages for everyone involved in the certification process. Adaptive tests allow Sylvan Prometric to deliver more tests with the same resources, as certification candidates often are in and out in 30 minutes or less. For Microsoft, adaptive testing means that fewer test questions are exposed to each candidate, and this can enhance the security, and therefore the validity, of certification tests.

One possible problem you may have with adaptive testing is that you are not allowed to mark and revisit questions. Since the adaptive algorithm is interactive, and all questions but the first are selected on the basis of your response to the previous question, it is not possible to skip a particular question or change an answer.

Question Types

Computerized test questions can be presented in a number of ways. Some of the possible formats are used on Microsoft certification examinations, and some are not.

True/False

We are all familiar with True/False questions, but because of the inherent 50 percent chance of guessing the correct answer, you will not see questions of this type on Microsoft certification exams.

Multiple Choice

The majority of Microsoft certification questions are in the multiple-choice format, with either a single correct answer or multiple correct answers. One interesting variation on multiple-choice questions with multiple correct answers is whether or not the candidate is told how many answers are correct.

EXAMPLE:

Which two files can be altered to configure the MS-DOS environment? (Choose two.)

Or

Which files can be altered to configure the MS-DOS environment? (Choose all that apply.)

You may see both variations on Microsoft certification examinations, but the trend seems to be toward the first type, where candidates are told explicitly how many answers are correct. Questions of the "choose all that apply" variety are more difficult, and can be merely confusing.

Graphical Questions

One or more graphical elements are sometimes used as exhibits to help present or clarify an exam question. These elements may take the form of a network diagram, pictures of networking components, or screen shots from the software on which you are being tested. It is often easier to present the concepts required for a complex performance-based scenario with a graphic than with words.

Test questions known as *hotspots* actually incorporate graphics as part of the answer. These questions ask the certification candidate to click on a location or graphical element to answer the question. As an example, you might be shown the diagram of a network and asked to click on an appropriate location for a router. The answer is correct if the candidate clicks within the *hotspot* that defines the correct location.

Free Response Questions

Another kind of question you sometimes see on Microsoft certification examinations requires a *free response* or type-in answer. An example of this type of question might present a TCP/IP network scenario and ask the candidate to calculate and enter the correct subnet mask in dotted decimal notation.

Knowledge-Based and Performance-Based Questions

Microsoft Certification develops a blueprint for each Microsoft certification examination with input from subject matter experts. This blueprint defines the content areas and objectives for each test, and each test question is created to test a specific objective. The basic information from the examination blueprint can be found on Microsoft's web site in the Exam Prep Guide for each test.

Psychometricians (psychologists who specialize in designing and analyzing tests) categorize test questions as knowledge-based or performance-based. As the names imply, knowledge-based questions are designed to test knowledge, while performance-based questions are designed to test performance.

Some objectives demand a knowledge-based question. For example, objectives that use verbs like *list* and *identify* tend to test only what you know, not what you can do.

EXAMPLE:
Objective: Identify the MS-DOS configuration files.
Which two files can be altered to configure the MS-DOS environment? (Choose two.)

A. COMMAND.COM

B. AUTOEXEC.BAT

C. IO.SYS

D. CONFIG.SYS

Correct answers: B,D

Other objectives use action verbs like *install, configure,* and *troubleshoot* to define job tasks. These objectives can often be tested with either a knowledge-based question or a performance-based question.

EXAMPLE:
Objective: Configure an MS-DOS installation appropriately using the PATH statement in AUTOEXEX.BAT.
Knowledge-based question:
What is the correct syntax to set a path to the D:\APP directory in AUTOEXEC.BAT?

A. SET PATH EQUAL TO D:\APP

B. PATH D:\APP

C. SETPATH D:\APP

D. D:\APP EQUALS PATH

Correct answer: B

Performance-based question:

Your company uses several DOS accounting applications that access a group of common utility programs. What is the best strategy for configuring the computers in the accounting department so that the accounting applications will always be able to access the utility programs?

    A. Store all the utilities on a single floppy disk, and make a copy of the disk for each computer in the accounting department.

    B. Copy all the utilities to a directory on the C: drive of each computer in the accounting department, and add a PATH statement pointing to this directory in the AUTOEXEC.BAT files.

    C. Copy all the utilities to all application directories on each computer in the accounting department.

    D. Place all the utilities in the C:\DOS directory on each computer, because the C:\DOS directory is automatically included in the PATH statement when AUTOEXEC.BAT is executed.

    Correct answer: B

Even in this simple example, the superiority of the performance-based question is obvious. Whereas the knowledge-based question asks for a single fact, the performance-based question presents a real-life situation and requires that you make a decision based on this scenario. Thus, performance-based questions give more bang (validity) for the test author's buck (individual question).

Testing Job Performance

We have said that Microsoft certification focuses on timeliness and the ability to perform job tasks. We have also introduced the concept of performance-based questions, but even performance-based multiple-choice questions do not really measure performance. Another strategy is needed to test job skills.

Given unlimited resources, it is not difficult to test job skills. In an ideal world, Microsoft would fly MCP candidates to Redmond, place them in a controlled environment with a team of experts, and ask them to plan, install, maintain, and troubleshoot a Windows network. In a few days at most, the experts could reach a valid decision as to whether each candidate should or should not be granted MCSE status. Needless to say, this is not likely to happen.

Closer to reality, another way to test performance is by using the actual software, and creating a testing program to present tasks and automatically grade a candidate's performance when the tasks are completed. This *cooperative* approach would be practical in some testing situations, but the same test that is presented to MCP candidates in Boston must also be available in Bahrain and Botswana. Many Sylvan Prometric testing locations around the world cannot run 32-bit applications, much less provide the complex networked solutions required by cooperative testing applications.

The most workable solution for measuring performance in today's testing environment is a *simulation* program. When the program is launched during a test, the candidate sees a simulation of the actual software that looks, and behaves, just like the real thing. When the testing software presents a task, the simulation program is launched and the candidate performs the required task. The testing software then grades the candidate's performance on the required task and moves to the next question. In this way, a 16-bit simulation program can mimic the look and feel of 32-bit operating systems, a complicated network, or even the entire Internet.

Microsoft has introduced simulation questions on the certification examination for Internet Information Server 4.0. Simulation questions provide many advantages over other testing methodologies, and simulations are expected to become increasingly important in the Microsoft certification program. For example, studies have shown that there is a very high correlation between the ability to perform simulated tasks on a computer-based test and the ability to perform the actual job tasks. Thus, simulations enhance the validity of the certification process.

Another truly wonderful benefit of simulations is in the area of test security. It is just not possible to cheat on a simulation question. In fact, you will be told exactly what tasks you are expected to perform on the test. How can a certification candidate cheat? By learning to perform the tasks? What a concept!

Study Strategies

There are appropriate ways to study for the different types of questions you will see on a Microsoft certification examination.

Knowledge-Based Questions

Knowledge-based questions require that you memorize facts. There are hundreds of facts inherent in every content area of every Microsoft certification examination. There are several keys to memorizing facts:

- **Repetition** The more times your brain is exposed to a fact, the more likely you are to remember it.

- **Association** Connecting facts within a logical framework makes them easier to remember.

- **Motor Association** It is often easier to remember something if you write it down or perform some other physical act, like clicking on a practice test answer.

We have said that the emphasis of Microsoft certification is job performance, and that there are very few knowledge-based questions on Microsoft certification exams. Why should you waste a lot of time learning file names, IP address formulas, and other minutiae? Read on.

Performance-Based Questions

Most of the questions you will face on a Microsoft certification exam are performance-based scenario questions. We have discussed the superiority of these questions over simple knowledge-based questions, but you should remember that the job task orientation of Microsoft certification extends the knowledge you need to pass the exams; it does not replace this knowledge. Therefore, the first step in preparing for scenario questions is to absorb as many facts relating to the exam content areas as you can. In other words, go back to the previous section and follow the steps to prepare for an exam composed of knowledge-based questions.

The second step is to familiarize yourself with the format of the questions you are likely to see on the exam. You can do this by answering the questions in this study guide, by using Microsoft assessment tests, or by using practice tests. The day of your test is not the time to be surprised by the convoluted construction of Microsoft exam questions.

For example, one of Microsoft Certification's favorite formats of late takes the following form:

Scenario: You have a network with…

Primary Objective: You want to…

Secondary Objective: You also want to…

Proposed Solution: Do this…

What does the proposed solution accomplish?

    A. satisfies the primary and the secondary objective

    B. satisfies the primary but not the secondary objective

    C. satisfies the secondary but not the primary objective

    D. satisfies neither the primary nor the secondary objective

This kind of question, with some variation, is seen on many Microsoft Certification examinations.

At best, these performance-based scenario questions really do test certification candidates at a higher cognitive level than knowledge-based questions. At worst, these questions can test your reading comprehension and test-taking ability rather than your ability to use Microsoft products. Be sure to get in the habit of reading the question carefully to determine what is being asked.

The third step in preparing for Microsoft scenario questions is to adopt the following attitude: Multiple-choice questions aren't really performance-based. It is all a cruel lie. These scenario questions are just knowledge-based questions with a little story wrapped around them.

To answer a scenario question, you have to sift through the story to the underlying facts of the situation, and apply your knowledge to determine the correct answer. This may sound silly at first, but the process we go through in solving real-life problems is quite similar. The key concept is that every scenario question (and every real-life problem) has a fact at its center, and if we can identify that fact, we can answer the question.

Simulations

Simulation questions really do measure your ability to perform job tasks. You must be able to perform the specified tasks. There are two ways to prepare for simulation questions:

1. Get experience with the actual software. If you have the resources, this is a great way to prepare for simulation questions.

2. Use official Microsoft practice tests. Practice tests are available that provide practice with the same simulation engine used on Microsoft certification exams. This approach has the added advantage of grading your efforts.

Signing Up

Signing up to take a Microsoft certification examination is easy. Sylvan operators in each country can schedule tests at any testing center. There are, however, a few things you should know:

1. If you call Sylvan during a busy time period, get a cup of coffee first, because you may be in for a long wait. Sylvan does an excellent job, but everyone in the world seems to want to sign up for a test on Monday morning.

2. You will need your social security number or some other unique identifier to sign up for a Sylvan test, so have it at hand.

3. Pay for your test by credit card if at all possible. This makes things easier, and you can even schedule tests for the same day you call, if space is available at your local testing center.

4. Know the number and title of the test you want to take before you call. This is not essential, and the Sylvan operators will help you if they can. Having this information in advance, however, speeds up the registration process.

Taking the Test

Teachers have always told you not to try to cram for examinations, because it does no good. Sometimes they lied. If you are faced with a knowledge-based test requiring only that you regurgitate facts, cramming can mean the difference between passing and failing. This is not the case, however, with Microsoft certification exams. If you don't know it the night before, don't bother to stay up and cram.

Instead, create a schedule and stick to it. Plan your study time carefully, and do not schedule your test until you think you are ready to succeed. Follow these guidelines on the day of your exam:

1. Get a good night's sleep. The scenario questions you will face on a Microsoft certification examination require a clear head.

2. Remember to take two forms of identification—at least one with a picture. A driver's license with your picture, and social security or credit cards are acceptable.

3. Leave home in time to arrive at your testing center a few minutes early. It is not a good idea to feel rushed as you begin your exam.

4. Do not spend too much time on any one question. If you are taking a form test, take your best guess and mark the question so you can come back to it if you have time. You cannot mark and revisit questions on an adaptive test, so you must do your best on each question as you go.

5. If you do not know the answer to a question, try to eliminate the obviously wrong answers and guess from the rest. If you can eliminate two out of four options, you have a 50 percent chance of guessing the correct answer.

6. For scenario questions, follow the steps we outlined earlier. Read the question carefully and try to identify the facts at the center of the story.

Finally, I would advise anyone attempting to earn Microsoft MCSE certification to adopt a philosophical attitude. Even if you are the kind of person who never fails a test, you are likely to fail at least one Microsoft certification test somewhere along the way. Do not get discouraged. If Microsoft certification were easy to obtain, more people would have it, and it would not be so respected and so valuable to your future in the IT industry.

MICROSOFT CERTIFIED SYSTEMS ENGINEER

1

Introduction to Windows NT Server 4.0

CERTIFICATION OBJECTIVES

1.01	Windows NT Server Overview
1.02	Windows NT Architecture
1.03	User Mode vs. Kernel Mode
1.04	Executive Services
1.05	Windows NT Subsystems
1.06	Windows NT Memory Organization

W indows NT Server 4.0 is Microsoft's® latest release of their robust network operating system. In just a few short years of existence, Windows NT has proved to be a premier enterprise networking solution. The modular NT architecture provides for greater stability, performance, and fault tolerance. There are many modular components in the operating system, but the most important components are called the Executive Services, which perform their specific responsibilities while together maintaining the system as a whole. These Executive Services run in privileged mode, also known as Kernel mode, and have direct access to the hardware in the system. The other components are run in User mode and do not have this privilege. The majority of operating system code in Windows NT is run in User mode.

The ability to support high performance hardware, as well as differing processor architectures such as RISC-based processors, makes NT a candidate for even the largest enterprises. The improved memory architecture means you can run more applications at once. This is done by the use of virtual memory, which uses the hard disk to process data when RAM is not available.. The new 32-bit memory architecture supports large amounts of RAM, which is critical to server performance and enables you to run many applications at once. Applications also receive a performance boost, as well as increased stability and protection from misbehaving applications, which can bring down other applications or cause the system to hang. Support for existing applications is provided through the NT Environment Subsystems, which means you do not have to abandon your existing applications to migrate to Windows NT. Application support is critical to NT, and is very important to understand.

CERTIFICATION OBJECTIVE 1.01

Windows NT Server Overview

Windows NT began in 1988 as a project to make a more stable, secure, reliable operating system. After five years in the works, it was finally released as Windows NT 3.1 and Windows NT Advanced Server 3.1 in 1993. It was called 3.1 because of its similarity to the Windows 3.1 operating system that was so popular at the time. Although NT was a significant advancement over Windows 3.1, it did not gain much initial acceptance. However, this changed with the release of Windows NT 3.5, which still had the familiar Windows 3.x user interface but included many enhancements and fixes. One significant change in NT 3.5 was the introduction of new names to differentiate two products: Windows NT Workstation for the workstation operating system and Windows NT Server for the network operating system.

Windows NT 3.51, the next version released, contained significant improvements such as long filename support, Domain Name System (DNS), Windows Internet Name Service (WINS), compression, and performance enhancements. NT 3.51 was the most successful version to date, but the best was yet to come for Windows NT Server.

With the release of Windows 95 and its very popular Start menu, Taskbar, Explorer, and shortcuts, it was no surprise that the Windows 95 user interface would become the interface for the next release of NT Server, entitled NT Server 4.0. Now easier to use, Windows NT 4.0 found a place in the market that challenged its most dominant competitor, Novell NetWare. With an integrated BackOffice suite of products for messaging, system management, database management, and Internet connectivity, NT 4.0 Server quickly started outselling the competition. With the gaining popularity of NT, there also came a demand for skilled, professional administrators and engineers to support the product. By earning the designation of Microsoft Certified Systems Engineer, you will qualify to meet that demand.

Preemptive Multitasking

Windows NT 4.0 uses *preemptive multitasking* to run several applications at once. Although these applications are not being executed at the same time, it appears that they are because the processor is executing *threads* that belong to each program. These threads have different priority levels that determine their order of execution. Threads with lower priorities must yield control to the higher priority task. Threads are also given a time slice of the processor that can expire. In preemptive multitasking, then, the operating system maintains processing control by assigning a *priority* and a *time slice* to each thread.

In previous operating systems the application did not yield control of the processor; this could cause all other active applications to stop responding, or it could even cause the entire system to hang. NT avoids this by preemptive multitasking and by running applications in a special way, as discussed later in the chapter.

The other method for multitasking is *cooperative*, or *non-preemptive.* This is how applications were run on older 16-bit operating systems such as Windows 3.x. The problem with cooperative multitasking is that the applications share an address space, and periodically have to check the message queue for other applications waiting for processing time. When an application fails to yield control of the processor, it can hang the rest of the programs or even the entire system. In order to maintain compatibility with older programs, Windows NT by default cooperatively multitasks these 16-bit applications in a single *Virtual DOS Machine* (VDM), as discussed later in the chapter. Although the 16-bit applications are cooperatively multitasked by default *within* the VDM, they are preemptively multitasked with the rest of the applications running on the system *outside* the VDM.

With NT 4.0 you have the option of overriding this default and running each application in its own memory space. This can prevent interference among currently running 16-bit applications.

Multiple Process Management Models

Let's look at a few concepts that help explain how NT can run so many applications at once—or *multitask* applications—so efficiently. A good way to understand the components of the operating system is to take a look at the information shown in the Windows NT Task Manager. This tool indicates what programs, processes, and threads are currently running on the system. Each of these elements is described in the following paragraphs.

Programs

A *program* is basically the application you are using, such as Microsoft Word or Excel. In Task Manager you can open the Applications tab to view a list of applications (programs) that are currently running. If an application is not responding, you can highlight it and end it.

Tasks

Tasks are more difficult to explain because the term is used to describe many things. However, a task is most often used to refer to a program that is running. The name Task Manager is thus appropriate because it enables you to manage tasks that are running on your computer.

Processes

As you interact with a program, it creates one or more *processes* in order to carry out your instructions. In other words, programs spawn *processes*. Although it appears that a process is the application itself, this is not always true. A program can have more than one process, and each process contains at least one thread. Each process has its own address space so it does not interfere with other processes running on the system. This is not to be mistaken with applications that are run in separate memory with their own address space. The process address space for threads is protected whether or not the application itself is run in separate memory. In other words, you do not have the option of running a process in the same address space or not. This is within the operating system, and cannot be modified. The Process Manager of the Windows NT Executive is responsible for the monitoring of these processes.

You can also use the Windows NT Task Manager to view processes that are currently running on your system. If you suspect an application is not responding, use the Task Manager to see the status of that application. You can also use the Task Manager to end processes that are misbehaving.

Threads

A *thread* is the smallest unit of code. An application can create many threads, and each thread inherits the priority of the process that spawned it. A thread's priority can be adjusted up or down by two levels. For example, let's say a process spawned a thread that inherited the priority of 26. The priority of this thread can be increased to a priority level of 28. (Thread priority in NT ranges from a low of 0 to a high of 31.)

However, a thread cannot have its priority adjusted below its base (initial) priority value. That is, a thread's priority can be adjusted down two levels only if it had previously been increased. When the priority of the thread is increased by two levels by virtue of its being in the foreground, it can then drop two priority levels as it moves from the foreground to the background.

Threads are small so they can be processed quickly. This makes the system appear as if the applications are running simultaneously. If the threads were not small you would be able to see each program execute for a few seconds, then see the system switch to the next application. For even better performance the threads can be executed on any processor of a multiprocessor system, as discussed next.

True Multiprocessor Support

The ability to add more processors to a server as needed is a very welcome feature of the NT Server operating system. This *scalability* allows you to adapt the operating system to the environment in which it will be performing. As shipped from Microsoft, Windows NT Server can support four processors, and OEM versions can support up to 32 processors. If your server requires more processing power you simply add another processor, rather than reinstalling the operating system and applications on another, more powerful server.

There are two categories of multiprocessing:

- Asymmetric Multiprocessing (ASMP)
- Symmetric Multiprocessing (SMP)

Windows NT is an SMP operating system, which is the multiprocessing method of choice. The following paragraphs describe both types of multiprocessing, along with the advantages and disadvantages of each.

ASMP uses one processor for the operating system functions, and any other processors are assigned to handle user threads. Since the operating system resides on a separate processor, it is fairly easy to add more processors, as needed, for application processing. The disadvantage of ASMP (in an example where the system uses two processors) is that one processor can be nearly idle while the other processor is being heavily used. The processor that is idle cannot assist the other processor because it is reserved for one of two functions: either the operating system or the applications.

This problem is resolved with SMP, where threads can be run simultaneously by any processor in the system. In addition, the operating system itself, which can tax system resources because of all the processes it generates, is able to use all available processors. This provides a significant performance increase. If the operating system is performing many executions, it can take advantage of idle processors in SMP. With ASMP, the operating system can only use the processor to which it is assigned.

Centralized Profiles and Policies

When resources such as profiles and policies are centralized, it is much easier for the system administrator to manage them. The domain structure in NT lends itself to centralized administration of these resources through tools such as User Manager for Domains and System Policy Editor.

Profiles

User Manager enables you to create a mandatory user profile for all of your users, or a different profile for each group of users. This can be useful for differentiating the needs of different departments, such as Payroll, Accounting, and Sales. You can tell Windows NT which groups the user belongs to, and NT will apply the corresponding user profile.

You can also employ user profiles to create profiles for different types of systems, because a profile will not work correctly if the system does not support it. For example, let's say you have a user profile that has a Super VGA screen resolution and one of your computers that uses the same profile only supports VGA. In that case the screen will not look correct. The centralized placement of this user profile makes it easier for you to update the profile as needed, rather than updating each user's profile individually. You can make changes to user profiles on a single-user basis, but if you have many users this can become a time-consuming task.

A mandatory user profile prevents users from changing settings, which may be desirable for your organization. If you do not want to restrict users in this way, you can still assign user profiles, but not make them mandatory. This will let users save their changes to the desktop, yet allow other users on the system to receive their own settings when they log on.

Users can also have what is known as a "*roaming*"—or *personal*—user profile, which will maintain their personal settings for every computer they log on to. For example, a user with a roaming profile can log on to a computer that they have never logged on to, and their desktop settings will be identical to the settings on their own computer. Any changes made to the roaming user profile will be incorporated for use the next time they log on.

Policies

The use of the System Policy Editor can restrict what users can do, as well as what they can access on the system. With a system policy in place, the operating system looks in the Netlogon folder on the logon server for a file called NTConfig.pol. If this file is present, the contents are copied to the users' registry. The contents of the NTConfig.pol file overwrite the corresponding parts of the default file. You can have special settings for specific users or you can create groups that receive different settings that you specify. By using a combination of the NT profiles and policies tools, you can greatly customize environments and can restrict access for users and groups on your network.

Built-in Remote Access Service (RAS)

Remote Access Service (RAS) enables users to connect over a phone line to your network and access resources as if they were at a computer connected directly to the network. Once a user is connected and authenticated, the phone line becomes transparent to the user. This is very important for traveling users who must remain in contact with the network for e-mail and transfer of data. They have access to the same file, print, and database servers that they would have at the office. This enables users to work at home, and still submit their files, print reports, and execute database queries. Here are a few features of the RAS:

- Callback ability
- Restrict access from the network to RAS Server only
- Use of integrated NT security
- Encryption

When Windows 95 was introduced, it used the term *Dial-Up Networking* to refer to remote access, and Windows NT 4.0 Server now uses that term. All previous versions of Windows NT referred to it as the RAS client. The two terms are interchangeable.

When working on the client workstation, you will be working with Dial-Up Networking to configure the connection. However, on your NT Server you will be using the Remote Access Administrator to manage the dial-in process. This utility enables you to start and stop the RAS services, send messages, disconnect users, and grant or revoke remote access for users or groups.

You can also grant or revoke access for dial-in by using the User Manager for Domains. This tool enables you to specify three different settings for callback security:

- You can have the RAS server call the user back at a predefined number.

- You can have the user specify the number where they would like to have the server call them back. This is not as secure, but it may be necessary for mobile users who are always at different locations such as hotels and airports.

- The last option is to not call the user back.

There are many types of clients supported through Windows NT RAS: Windows NT, Windows 95, Windows 3.x, MS-DOS, and any other Point-to-Point Protocol (PPP) client. TCP/IP, IPX, and NetBEUI protocols are also supported. If you are using TCP/IP to connect to your RAS server, you can automatically be assigned an IP address. You will learn more about dynamic assigning of IP addresses—and TCP/IP in general—in later chapters of the book. This wide range of support makes it easy to implement RAS in your organization and it is largely responsible for the popularity of RAS. Your laptops can have Windows 95 installed and still be supported, and your home users can have Windows 3.x and still be supported.

Fault Tolerance

With the important role that computers play in today's businesses, downtime or data loss is unacceptable. A business can lose thousands of dollars for every hour that a computer system is not functioning. With this in mind, companies go to great lengths to protect their systems. In mission-critical networks, computers must be fault tolerant. *Fault tolerance* is the ability of a computer to ensure that data and resources remain functional in the event of emergency. This can be achieved with a combination of hardware and/or software techniques, and the solution will vary in price and protection. For example, a fault-tolerant hard drive array will allow a failed hard drive to be removed from the system and replaced while the system is still running. The data from the failed hard drive can even be regenerated without any user intervention. Windows NT provides many built-in fault-tolerant features such as:

- Backup domain controllers
- Multiple network interface cards
- Directory replication
- Recoverable file system
- Hard disk mirroring, duplexing, and striping with parity

These features are described in the following sections.

Backup Domain Controllers

When you are participating in a domain, which is a logical grouping of computers, the presence of Backup Domain Controllers (BDCs) will ensure fault tolerance by having multiple servers available to authenticate users. These domain controllers provide central support for user and resource management. The Primary Domain Controller (PDC) is in charge, and will replicate changes to the BDCs. In the event that a PDC is not available, the BDCs can also be promoted to PDC. If the PDC does not come back online, the BDC can continue as the PDC. If the PDC does come back online, you can demote the second PDC down to BDC again, and continue as you did before. You have the option during installation of NT Server to choose between a PDC, a BDC, or stand-alone server. Make the correct decision, because once you have installed NT as a domain controller, you will have to reinstall the operating system to change it. There is also no way to promote a stand-alone server, sometimes referred to as a member server, into a domain controller without reinstalling NT.

Multiple Network Interface Cards

Multiple network cards in a computer can provide fault tolerance by placing a computer on two segments of a network, or they can be used to connect two networks. Windows NT Server acts as a router that routes packets between the two segments or networks.. This is a common solution for organizations that cannot afford a high quality router, but would still like to route packets to another network. Should one of the other links fail, NT can also be used as an alternate route between two segments or networks. This is most often used with larger network implementations.

exam
ⓦatch

When you take the Networking Essentials exam for your MCSE, you will see scenario questions regarding fault tolerance for networks. For example, if one network connection were to go down in one city, how could you ensure that all cities could remain communicating while the direct connection is restored? This would involve multiple routes between cities. On a smaller scale, you can have multiple routes between segments of the network in your organization to ensure fault tolerance. This could be accomplished by using the NT Server with multiple network controllers.

Directory Replication

The purpose of directory replication is to make an exact copy of a folder and place it on another server. Replicated information could include logon scripts, databases, or any information that is accessed by many users. By replicating this information, you can load balance servers so that one server is not overburdened with excessive traffic. For example, let's say you want to replicate a logon script that you have created and place it on all of the other domain controllers. This is accomplished by placing the information you would like to replicate in the proper export directory, and choosing which servers can import this data. The *Directory Replicator service* will run on both the import and export servers to ensure the replication process goes smoothly.

You can adjust the rate at which replication occurs. If you are replicating a script that is rarely updated, then it would make more sense to increase the amount of time between replications.. If you are replicating a database that must remain consistent, you would decrease the amount of time between replications, to ensure that the latest changes are being copied to the import servers. Replication updates occur automatically. After you set up the replication, the Directory Replicator service maintains the replication process. To replicate a directory, just put the name of the directory you want to replicate in the export box.

Here is the path to the export directory for Windows NT Server 4.0:

C:\systemroot\SYSTEM32\repl\export

Any directory that is found or created under this directory is available for export. You must place the files in a directory *under the export directory* for them to be replicated. You cannot just place files in the export directory.

The import directory for the receiving computer is:

C:\systemroot\SYSTEM32\repl\import

This directory path is created automatically when replication occurs. Check this directory to verify that the replication process went as planned.

Hot Fixes

When an error occurs because of a bad sector, the file system moves the data that was located in this sector (if possible) to another sector, and labels the original sector as bad. This *hot fix* is transparent to the user and to the applications. You will not even be aware that it is taking place. However, there is a possibility that you will lose data. This would never happen on subsequent attempts to access information on this sector because it has been marked as unusable. Hot fixing is a feature of NTFS and SCSI hardware, and is not supported for the FAT file system.

RAID 1 and 5 Support

Redundant Array of Inexpensive Disks (RAID) can be used for fault tolerance within the disk subsystem. RAID technology uses multiple hard drives to provide performance and/or fault tolerance through mirroring or striping data. Windows NT RAID support is done through software support. A hardware RAID implementation produces better results, but it costs more. Notice that there are many levels of RAID support, each with varying degrees of performance and fault tolerance. Windows NT supports three levels of RAID: levels 0, 1, and 5. However, only RAID levels 1 and 5 are fault-tolerant.

■ RAID 1 uses *disk mirroring* to duplicate information to another hard disk. In this method, the operating system writes information to both disks for each operation that is performed. If one of the hard drives fails, the other hard drive is immediately available with the very same information. This provides 100 percent fault tolerance, but only allows you to use fifty percent of your total hard disk space. The other fifty percent is being used for the mirror. That is why this implementation is considered more expensive. You do get a slight increase in performance, because the first available disk is used to service a request.

A technique similar to disk mirroring is *disk duplexing*. This method maintains a mirrored drive, but includes another disk controller, rather than using the same controller for both hard drives. This increases performance and provides fault tolerance against both controller and hard drive failures.

■ RAID 5 uses a method of *striping data* across several hard drives, with parity information also included. This parity information is striped across the drives, rather than being stored on a single hard drive. (Storing information on a single hard drive is the equivalent of RAID level 4.) With the addition of parity, you can re-create the information that was stored on a drive if it were to fail. Just like mirroring, this method is 100 percent fault tolerant. However, you do not waste as much valuable hard disk space as you do with mirroring. Also note that it takes a minimum of three hard disks to implement disk striping with parity. You receive a performance boost with a RAID 5 implementation due to the fact that multiple drives are reading information at the same time. However, it takes more time to calculate the parity information.

exam
Ⓦatch

During the exam you will be asked to choose the correct fault-tolerant strategy for a situation. You must understand the features of each method, and know when it is appropriate to use each. These concepts will be discussed in greater detail throughout the book.

Internet Information Server (IIS) and More

Microsoft has included its Internet Information Server (IIS) with NT Server to make it easy for you to connect your organization to the Internet, or to create an Intranet to browse your organization's internal resources. You have the option of installing IIS 2.0 when you are installing NT Server or any time thereafter. What is unique about the Internet Information Server is that it is free. This may be an effort to convince business that IIS could be used as a low cost (or no cost) alternative to the other Web servers on the market today. Microsoft hopes that you will see the value in their Web server and begin using it. However, IIS will not run on anything other than Windows NT, so you must have an NT Server in order to take advantage of IIS. In addition to providing the basic features of IIS, Microsoft offers additional BackOffice products to enhance its functionality. Microsoft Proxy Server is for connecting your network to the Internet. Microsoft SQL Server is for connecting databases to IIS for viewing and updating information in the database over the network or Internet. You can also read your e-mail through a Web browser with Exchange Server. These are just a few of the possibilities that exist with IIS. Since the popularity of both NT Server and the BackOffice suite has greatly increased, we urge you to become certified in these products. By becoming certified, you demonstrate your ability to support the IIS and the various products that take advantage of it. The following sections describe the features that are part of the IIS and explain the services they provide for NT Server.

Index Server

The Index Server, provided with IIS, enables you to index all HTML documents and other supported formats. It has the ability to find text in HTML documents, as well as Word, Excel, and various other text documents. When you have indexed all of your data, you can query that data using keywords to bring up documents that contain the desired information. This is just like using an Internet search engine to find what you are looking for. (Quite possibly the search engines are also using Index Server to index information.) Once you tell Index Server what information to index, it performs the tasks; it also continues to index new documents as they are added to the server.

FTP Server

You can use the File Transfer Protocol (FTP) server to upload or download information within your company, or outside your company via the Internet. Having an FTP site is useful when outside sources need to send or receive information that is too large to be attached to e-mail. Many organizations provide FTP services along with Web services for making software updates, patches, and drivers available to the public. Although FTP is slowly becoming replaced by the Web, it is by no means dead. FTP still has widespread acceptance in the Internet community, even though it is not as user-friendly as the Web.

Gopher Server

A Gopher server is included with IIS, although the popularity of the World Wide Web has made Gopher nearly extinct. Gopher can be used as an index to look for information on the Internet, or on your own company's Intranet. You can use menus to access text files that are available on the Internet. Gopher is easy to use, has the ability to create links to other computers, and enables you to make your own menus.

Administrative Wizards

NT 4.0 Server includes a number of Administrative Wizards that help you perform common administrative tasks. They do not contain any added functionality—they simply guide those unfamiliar with NT 4.0 Server through the basic operations. After you are comfortable with the Administrative Wizards, you should be ready to venture out on your own. Eight Administrative Wizards are currently available:

- Adding user accounts
- Group management
- Managing file and folder access
- Adding a printer, either local or network
- Add/Remove programs
- Install a new modem
- Network client administrator (installs or updates client workstations)
- License compliance (checks licensing for installed applications)

CERTIFICATION OBJECTIVE 1.02

Windows NT Architecture

Windows NT architecture is unlike any other operating system in Microsoft's arsenal. Many of Microsoft's operating systems—such as MS-DOS or Windows 3.x—require DOS; some argue that Windows 95 stills needs DOS. However, NT has no DOS code at all. This is amazing when you consider that NT can still run DOS and older Windows 16-bit applications. Not only can it run these programs, but in some cases they will run better than in their native environment! If you have been using NT Server since the first version, you may not have seen drastic changes to the architecture with each new version, but NT 4.0 is significantly different from other operating systems. The next sections will describe the architecture that makes NT unique.

User Mode vs. Kernel Mode

An important feature of Windows NT, and one that contributes to the great stability of its architecture, is the use of two types of operating mode. The two modes, User mode and Kernel mode, differ primarily in the amount of privilege assigned to each. *User mode* cannot directly access the hardware, whereas *Kernel mode* can. Figure 1-1 is an overview of the NT architecture, showing the role of User mode and Kernel mode.

User Mode

User mode, often referred to as *non-privileged processor mode*, is where most of Windows NT code is located. This is also where applications and the various subsystems are run. This mode cannot communicate directly with the hardware, and must call upon the operating system to make these calls. This

FIGURE 1-1

User mode versus
Kernel mode

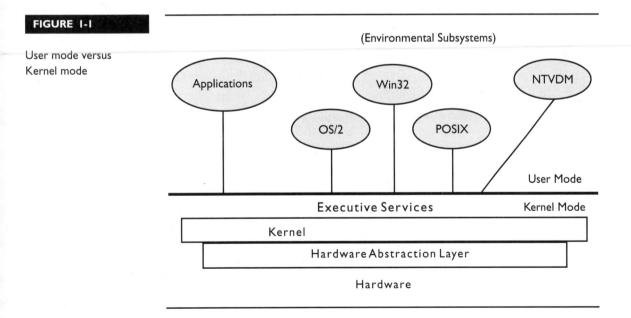

provides stability for the operating system by creating a protective barrier from misbehaving applications, which could possibly bring down the entire operating system.

Kernel Mode

Kernel mode—commonly referred to as *privileged mode*—does have direct access to hardware and software resources in the system. Applications that require hardware functions must be translated into these Kernel mode instructions. The Kernel mode must translate the calls from User mode before the hardware can be accessed, and then must pass the data back to User mode. An important note about the release of NT 4.0 is the fact that some components of NT that used to run as User mode components now run as Kernel mode components. These include the Window Manager, the graphical device interface (GDI), and graphics device drivers. With these components running in Kernel mode, there should be an increase in graphics performance because you no longer need to translate the calls back and forth between the two modes.

Hardware Abstraction Layer (HAL)

The User-mode applications never call the hardware directly, because these calls are handled by the Windows NT Executive. Similarly, the *Hardware Abstraction Layer* (HAL) separates the kernel from the hardware to provide an intermediary layer so that the Windows NT kernel does not have to communicate with the hardware. The HAL is the most common reason why some DOS and early Windows applications are incompatible with NT. These applications expect to communicate directly with the hardware, and will not run if they are not given this privilege. Although this appears to be a disadvantage, it is actually an advantage because the HAL provides increased protection from errant applications. However, the HAL increases system complexity. Not only do you need a separate HAL for each hardware platform, but you need two HALs for each processor architecture—one to support a single processor, and another to support multiple processors.

Windows NT Microkernel

The term *microkernel*, or *kernel*, refers to the core of code in an operating system. This is the most important part of the operating system and is responsible for all functions on the system. However, the kernel cannot do this all by itself. It requires some other components to be responsible for their own functions, leaving the most important tasks to the kernel. As an analogy, think of the CEO of a company. The CEO does not have be a part of every decision that is made at the company, but instead relies on other people such as the President, Vice-President, and various managers of the company. However, when a decision has to be made that will affect the entire company, it is escalated to the CEO, who takes all of the information gathered by the Executives and uses that information to make an appropriate decision. In Windows NT, the operating system kernel calls upon the services of the Windows NT Executive, just as the CEO called upon the corporate executives to provide critical information. NT's modular architecture allows portions of the operating system to be rewritten or replaced as needed. It also facilitates the integration of new components into the architecture.

CERTIFICATION OBJECTIVE 1.04

Executive Services

The NT *Executive Services* (also called *System Services*) provide the operating system services that the kernel is too busy to perform. The kernel is actually part of the NT Executive, and together they are responsible for the entire system. The NT Executive includes the following operating system components:

- Object Manager is responsible for managing objects, which are used to represent resources in the system.

- Security Reference Monitor (SRM) is responsible for enforcing the security policies by verifying credentials for users and groups.

■ Local Procedure Call Facility (LPC) is responsible for processes that share information between each other on the local machine.

■ Process Manager monitors the status and usage of processes and threads.

■ Virtual Memory Manager (VMM) manages the system's virtual memory pool, in which the hard disk is used to simulate RAM.

■ I/O Manager is responsible for all input and output for the file system, I/O devices, and redirectors.

■ Win32 Window Manager and GDI. These components had been in the Win32 subsystem in previous versions of NT, but were moved to the NT Executive in version 4.0.

Figure 1-2 summarizes the Executive Services of Windows NT 4.0.

CERTIFICATION OBJECTIVE 1.05

Windows NT Subsystems

Windows NT maintains compatibility with existing applications through the use of an *environment subsystem* that mimics the environment that the application expects to see. Figure 1-3 illustrates some examples of environment subsystems. If a subsystem for a specific environment were not included in the

FIGURE 1-2

Windows NT Executive Services

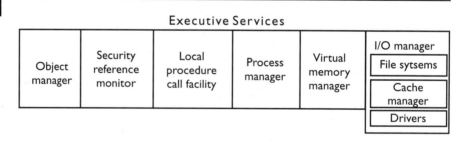

Executive Services					
Object manager	Security reference monitor	Local procedure call facility	Process manager	Virtual memory manager	I/O manager File sytsems Cache manager Drivers

operating system, there would be no backwards compatibility with non-NT applications using that environment. Subsystems for some of the infrequently used environments, such as POSIX and OS/2, can be loaded as needed. This saves memory because they need not be loaded at system startup. However, the Win32 primary subsystem is always created at startup.

Notice that these services are referred to as "subsystems" because they can perform independently of any other subsystem. These subsystems run completely in User mode and each is isolated from other subsystems; this is why they are sometimes referred to as "protected" subsystems.

Win32

As shown in Figure 1-3, Win32 is the primary subsystem for NT, and it is responsible for all user input and output. The Win32 subsystem is also responsible for receiving requests from the other environment subsystems. Win32 used to have the GDI and USER components in the Win32 subsystem, but they have been moved to the NT Executive in the release of NT 4.0. Two subsystems, MS-DOS and Win16, actually belong to the Win32 subsystem. The Win32 subsystem provides a 32-bit, preemptively multitasked environment, where each application receives its own address space for greater stability.

FIGURE 1-3

Windows NT environment subsystems

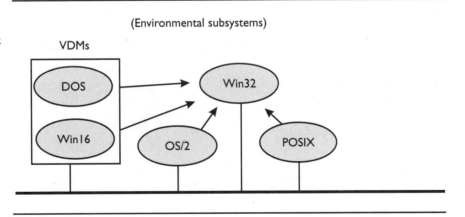

MS-DOS

The MS-DOS subsystem is quite possibly the most important subsystem in NT for compatibility. The DOS environment is called the *virtual DOS machine* (VDM). The VDM fools the DOS application into thinking it is the only application running, just as it was run in the DOS operating system. The VDM is a 32-bit application run in a separate memory space that is capable of being multitasked with other applications (thereby increasing performance). This subsystem will run DOS applications, but it will also run Windows applications that require DOS.

Win16

Since 16-bit Windows applications run over DOS, they must be emulated in this way to work with Windows NT. This is achieved by running the VDM and an emulator called the WOW—short for Win16 on Win32. When a 16-bit application is run, it will have to have the Win16 calls translated into Win32 calls, or vice versa. This is done by a process known as *thunking*. It is much easier to make the Win16 call to Win32 because you just have to add bits, whereas it is much more difficult to go from Win32 to Win16 because you cannot just drop bits.

For 16-bit applications that expect to share address space with other 16-bit applications, the applications are run in a single VDM. Although the 16-bit Windows applications are run in the same memory space by default, they do have the option of being run in a separate memory space. If the applications are run in a shared memory space, there is an increased possibility that one faulty 16-bit application will bring down every application that is sharing the memory space. When the applications are run in their own separate memory space, any application that crashes only affects itself—not other applications currently running outside of the memory space. This is a welcome feature for users of many older 16-bit applications that had trouble with misbehaving applications in the past.

OS/2 Subsystem

The OS/2 subsystem is the most limited of the subsystems provided with NT. There is less need to create a fully functional OS/2 subsystem because support for the OS/2 environment has dwindled. Although the OS/2 subsystem is a 32-bit, multitasking protected subsystem, it can only run character-mode applications; it cannot run graphical applications. Interestingly enough, the OS/2 interface was going to be the primary subsystem for NT until the surprising popularity of the Windows 3.1 operating system. This made the Win32 primary subsystem a more logical choice.

POSIX Subsystem

The POSIX subsystem is included to support open standards, mostly for application support for UNIX platforms. In order to be POSIX-compliant, the software must fulfill certain requirements, such as case-sensitive filenames, hard links (which can be compared to Windows NT shortcuts, in which many entries can point to the same file), and additional time stamping. The POSIX subsystem is a 32-bit, multitasked, protected subsystem; however, you will not have many opportunities to take advantage of it because of the lack of support.

CERTIFICATION OBJECTIVE 1.06

Windows NT Memory Organization

The memory organization of Windows NT is built around three main concepts: virtual memory, demand paging, and a 32-bit flat address space. Each of these methods helps Windows NT provide memory for applications, even when the amount of physical memory has been exceeded.

Virtual Memory

Windows NT uses *virtual memory* to simulate RAM on a computer when more memory is needed. It does this by using the computer's hard disk as needed. Figure 1-4 illustrates how data can be moved from RAM to hard disk. When the computer is not using a portion of data in RAM, the data can be swapped in 4K pages to the hard disk and replaced with data that is currently needed.

Of course, RAM operates much faster than the hard drive, so virtual memory is no substitute for having enough RAM in your system. In older operating systems such as DOS, when you did not have the luxury of virtual memory, the application would not run at all. To accomplish this process, a component of the Windows NT Executive called the Virtual Memory Manager (VMM) is used. The VMM is responsible for mapping the virtual addresses to the physical pages of computer memory. The VMM is also responsible for the actual paging process, which will be described later in this book.

Demand Paging

Demand paging is the process of swapping the information from disk or memory in 4K pages as needed. This process requires the use of the NT paging file, which is an actual file on your hard disk reserved for this use. If your

---

NT memory organization

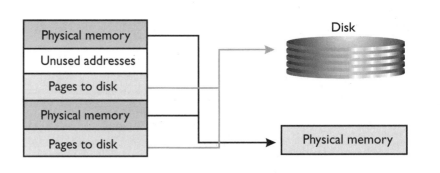

paging file is not large enough, you will see error messages that your system is running low on virtual memory. You will learn more about configuring the paging file in later chapters of the book. For now, you just need to understand that the hard disk will be used when your physical memory is exceeded. You can tell that the hard drive is being used for paging when you hear the hard drive make noise as you switch to another open application. If you had enough RAM, the switch would be instantaneous. Try opening several applications and switching among them to see when your system begins using the page file. You can also bring up the Windows NT Task Manager and view the available physical memory from the Performance tab.

Another term to keep in mind is *thrashing*. Thrashing sounds much worse than paging, and it is. When you have exceeded the amount of physical RAM in the system, and your paging file is becoming full, the system will begin thrashing to look for more available memory. This is a not good for the system, and you should take corrective action, such as adding more physical memory or increasing the size of your paging file.

Linear 32-bit Address

Applications use a 32-bit linear address when they access memory. This is different from the segmented scheme used for MS-DOS and other versions of Windows. With the segmented memory scheme, an application accesses memory by using a segment and an offset; the combination of these two coordinates can identify a memory address. It is comparable to a grid which has rows and columns. To find a location on the grid you find the appropriate row (the segment), then find where it intersects with the column (the offset). The computer required extra time to compute location using this segmented memory scheme; it took even more time for software developers to use this method, because it was difficult and slow.

With the linear 32-bit address, the first address starts at zero, and continues in one-byte increments until the system is out of physical memory. Since memory allocated in this way must use unique addresses, a 32-bit address gives you 4GB of address space. Two gigabytes of this address space are reserved for the applications to use, and the other 2GB are reserved for the system's use. This linear addressing makes NT more compatible with different processor architectures because more RISC processors (and even some CISC processors from Intel) use linear addressing.

Device Drivers

Device drivers enable your system to communicate with the various devices in your system. A driver is basically a small application that the operating system calls when it needs the device to perform a function. A well written driver is important for the stability and performance of your system. A wrong or poorly written device driver will not maximize your performance, and it may cause system problems or just not work at all with the device. Since the driver must communicate with the device to perform a function, you can see how important it is to make sure you have the correct version of the driver. Older drivers for Windows 3.x or Windows 95 will not work with NT, and previous NT versions of drivers may not work either. Microsoft has provided many compatible drivers for use with the operating system, but may not have current drivers for brand new devices. The device vendors may also provide new drivers for NT 4.0 on their Internet Web sites. The good news is that drivers are continually updated. The bad news is that there are still not that many available for NT.

CERTIFICATION SUMMARY

Windows NT Server was created as a high performance network operating system that is optimized for resource sharing. This chapter described the features that increase performance such as *preemptive multitasking* of applications and how the processes spawn threads of differing priority. Priority of these threads is inherited from the parent process, but can be adjusted. Not only can you multitask applications, you can add more processors to the NT system to take advantage of *multiprocessing*. This allows threads to run on any processor in the system. Fault tolerance is supported by the use of *hot fixing*, the use of Backup Domain Controllers, multiple network cards, directory replication, and RAID support. The Redundant Array of Inexpensive Disks offers varying levels of performance and fault tolerance, of which NT supports levels 0, 1, and 5. Levels 1 and 5 are *mirroring* and *disk striping with parity,* respectively. These are both capable of withstanding hard disk failure.

Integrated with Windows NT Server is the Internet Information Server (IIS). This Web server allows you to run your own Web page on the Internet or your company's Intranet. IIS comes with Index Server, and both FTP and Gopher servers.

Under Windows NT architecture, the chapter covered the two modes that portions of code and applications are run in: *User mode* and *Kernel mode.* Kernel mode has direct access to the system resources whereas User mode does not. *The Hardware Abstraction Layer* (HAL) is used as an intermediary between the hardware so the NT kernel does not have to communicate directly with the hardware. The *kernel* is the core of the operating system, and the head of the NT *Executive Services.* The kernel and the Executive Services are responsible for the entire system. Windows NT maintains compatibility with existing applications through the use of an *environment subsystem* that mimics the environment the application expects to see. Examples of environment subsystems are the POSIX, OS/2, and Win32 subsystems. The DOS and Win16 subsystems are actually housed within the Win32 subsystem. Since the DOS and Win16 subsystems are a part of the Win32 subsystem, they also run in User mode. They are also preemptively multitasked with other applications on the system, and protected from each other. They both need to call upon the Win32 subsystem, which is the primary subsystem that handles these requests in NT.

The memory organization of Windows NT is built around three main concepts: virtual memory, demand paging, and a 32-bit flat address space. *Virtual memory* uses the hard drive to simulate RAM as needed. *Demand paging* is the process of swapping pages of memory between the hard disk and memory. The 32-bit flat addressing scheme is an improvement over the segmented memory method. The 32-bit scheme, which allocates addresses in one-byte increments until the physical memory is all gone, allows for 4GB of virtual memory.

✓ TWO-MINUTE DRILL

❑ Preemptive multitasking is the ability to run several applications at once.

❑ Task Manager for Windows NT is a tool that gives you dynamic data for the various programs, processes, and threads that are currently running on the system.

❑ As shipped from Microsoft, Windows NT Server can support four processors, and OEM versions can support up to 32 processors.

❑ There are two categories of multiprocessor support: Asymmetric Multiprocessing (ASMP), and Symmetric Multiprocessing (SMP). Windows NT is a SMP operating system.

❑ Use of the domain structure in NT lends itself to centralized administration of profiles and policies, through tools such as User Manager for Domains and System Policy Editor.

❑ Remote Access Service (RAS) enables users to connect over a phone line to your network and access resources as if they were at a computer connected directly to the network. Features of the Remote Access Service are:

   ❑ Callback ability

   ❑ Restrict access from the network to RAS Server only

   ❑ Use of integrated NT security

   ❑ Encryption

❑ Fault tolerance is the ability of a computer to ensure that data and resources remain functional in the event of emergency.

❑ When you are participating in a domain, which is a logical grouping of computers, the presence of Backup Domain Controllers (BDC) will ensure fault tolerance by having multiple servers available to authenticate users.

❑ Multiple network interface cards in a computer can be used for fault tolerance by placing a computer on two segments of a network, or they can be used to connect two networks.

❑ Replicated information could include logon scripts, databases, or any information that is accessed by many users. Replicating this information allows you to load-balance servers so that one server is not overburdened with excessive traffic.

❑ RAID technology uses multiple hard drives to provide performance and/or fault tolerance through mirroring or striping data.

❑ During the exam you will be asked to choose the correct fault tolerant strategy for a situation. You must understand the features of each method, and know when it is appropriate to use each.

❑ Microsoft has included Internet Information Server (IIS) with NT Server to make it easy for you to connect your organization to the Internet, or to create an Intranet to browse your organization's internal resources.

❑ User mode and Kernel mode differ primarily in the amount of privilege assigned to each. User mode cannot directly access the hardware, whereas Kernel mode can.

❑ Windows NT maintains compatibility with existing applications through the use of *environment subsystems* that mimic the environment the application expects to see. This allows for backwards compatibility with non-NT applications. Some environment subsystems such as POSIX and OS/2 can be loaded as needed, thereby saving memory.

❑ Demand paging is the process of swapping the information from disk or memory as needed. Windows NT has 4K pages.

SELF TEST

The following questions will help you measure your understanding of the material presented in this chapter. Read all the choices carefully, as there may be more than one correct answer. Choose all correct answers for each question.

1. _____ multitasking is the ability to run several applications at once.

2. A _____ is the smallest unit for processing.

3. What is the maximum number of processors that Windows NT can support through OEM versions?

   A. 2

   B. 4

   C. 16

   D. 32

4. When system policies are in place, what file will be in the Netlogon directory?

   A. Config.pol

   B. NTConfig.sys

   C. NTConfig.pol

   D. NTConfig.plo

5. Which is not a RAS security feature?

   A. Calling back a user at a specified phone number

   B. Encrypting authentication information

   C. Auditing

   D. Restricting access to certain phone numbers

   E. Restricting access to the RAS Server only

6. What would be the first step in the replication process if I placed my file to be replicated in this directory? C:*systemroot*\SYSTEM32\repl\export

   A. You have to tell the replication process to begin replicating.

   B. The file would not be replicated because it is not in a subdirectory.

   C. The replication process would begin automatically.

   D. The replication process will begin after you specify the import servers.

7. Which levels of fault tolerant RAID does Windows NT support?

   A. 1-5

   B. 0-5

   C. 1, 5

   D. 0, 1, 5

8. (True/False) RAID level 5 uses a dedicated drive that holds parity information for fault tolerance.

9. (True/False) Environment subsystems are run in the User mode.

10. HAL stands for _____ _____ _____.

11. Which is not a component of the Windows NT Executive?

    A. Security Reference Monitor

    B. I/O Manager

    C. Thread Manager

    D. Process Manager

    E. Object Manager

12. What is the size of the pages that are swapped in and out of memory by the Virtual Memory Manager?

    A. 1 byte

    B. 4 kilobytes

    C. 64 kilobytes

    D. 32 kilobytes

13. With a linear 32-bit address, the address starts at zero, then increments in what size block?

    A. 1 byte

    B. 1 kilobyte

    C. 64 bytes

    D. 64 kilobytes

14. How much virtual memory does the 16-bit addressing scheme support?

    A. 64MB

    B. 128MB

    C. 256MB

    D. 512MB

15. How are 16-bit applications run by default in Windows NT?

    A. Each in a separate memory space, preemptively multitasked with applications *outside* of the VDM.

    B. In the same memory space, cooperatively multitasked with applications *outside* of the VDM.

    C. Each in a separate memory space, cooperatively multitasked with applications *outside* of the VDM.

    D. In the same memory space, preemptively multitasked with applications *outside* of the VDM.

2

Planning Windows NT 4.0 Installation

CERTIFICATION OBJECTIVES

2.01   What's New in NT Server 4.0

2.02   Planning for Installation

2.03   Hardware and Software Compatibility

2.04   Windows NT File Systems

2.05   Windows NT Protocols

T he planning phase for Windows NT 4.0 Server is the most important part of your installation. If you take time to think out and design a strategy for your NT Server installation, you can reduce the amount of downtime caused by installation problems and server upgrades. Since your Windows NT Server is one of the most important parts of your computer network, it makes a lot of sense to take the time to carefully lay out a strategy for your server. There are so many options to consider when doing a Windows NT Server installation that you want to make sure that you do not overlook any important details.

All of the options and features you choose for your Windows NT Server will have a direct effect on the rest of your network. These options include what protocols to install, types of fault tolerance, hardware and software compatibility, and file systems. Each option that you use should be analyzed before installation. This small step can save you a lot of time in the future.

The certification exam for Microsoft Windows NT 4.0 Server will quiz you to make sure you understand every detail of the planning and installation process. For example, you'll need to understand the Hardware Compatibility List and its role during installation. You'll need to understand the advantages of using the NTFS file system or explain why you might need to use a FAT partition. You'll need to select the protocols to be installed on your network and describe the effects they will have on your network. This planning phase will also give you a good understanding of the basics of Windows NT 4.0 Server and provides a smooth transition to the more complicated topics covered in the later chapters.

This chapter begins with a brief section highlighting what's new in NT 4.0 Server, then tackles the issues of planning and installing the system components.

CERTIFICATION OBJECTIVE 2.01

What's New in NT Server 4.0

Although the most notable improvement of Windows NT 4.0 Server is the updated Windows 95 facelift, there are many improved features below the surface that you might not know about.

Administrative Wizards

For those new to Windows NT 4.0, Microsoft has included Administrative Wizards to help guide you through some common administrative duties: adding user accounts, group management, file and folder access, adding printers, installing/removing programs, installing modems, and administering network clients and license compliance. To use the Administrative Wizards tool, open the Start Menu | Programs | Administrative Tools. You'll see the Administrative Wizards screen shown in Figure 2-1. Decide what area of Windows NT administration you need, click on the appropriate icon, and begin.

Network Monitor Tool

Windows NT 4.0 Server now includes the Network Monitor tool, shown in Figure 2-2, which is a scaled-down version of the full network monitoring tool found in Microsoft's Systems Management Server. The main functionality of Network Monitor is to "sniff out" packets on the network and help diagnose

FIGURE 2-1

Administrative Wizards

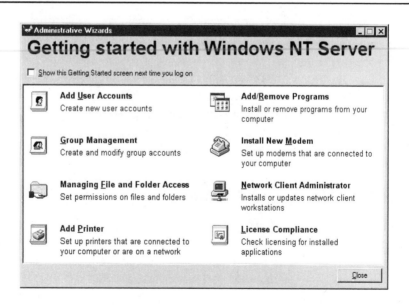

FIGURE 2-2

Network Monitor

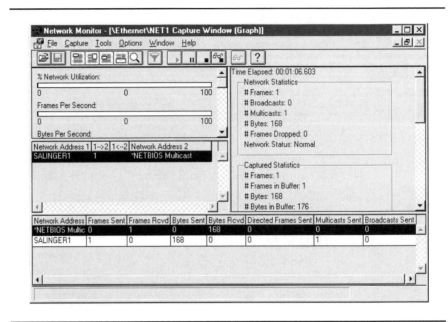

any problems that you are having concerning protocols. It is a very helpful tool when trying to diagnose network traffic, Windows Internet Name Service (WINS), Domain Name Service (DNS) or name resolution issues on your network. The Network Monitor shipped with NT 4.0 Server only provides the ability to capture network packets to and from your own NT Server; it does not enable you to capture packets sent to and from other computers. If you would like the full functional version of Network Monitor, you must install the tool included with Microsoft's Systems Management Server.

System Policies and Profiles

You can maintain and manage users and their desktops by using a combination of system policies and profiles. These enhanced features of NT 4.0 allow the network administrator to set up a specific desktop environment that the user cannot alter. You can set up policies on your server by user, by group, or by computer. For example, a network administrator can effectively lock down the workstation by disabling the Run button on the Start menu, disabling Registry editing tools, or restricting access to the Control Panel. Microsoft has also improved the Task Manager in Windows NT 4.0 Server. You can now monitor the performance of your server, view processes, or end application tasks.

Improved Diagnostics

Windows NT 4.0 enables you to view all of your system information and resources in a single graphical window, using the Windows NT diagnostics tools. Windows NT 3.51 Server had included diagnostics tools, but their functionality is greatly improved in Windows NT 4.0 Server. Now, instead of opening up several applications and windows, you check important diagnostics such as memory, Interrupt Requests (IRQ), network shares, protocols and system information from a single, easy-to-read graphical window. This graphical diagnostic tool also gives the network administrator the ability to look into the system configuration at a moment's notice.

If you are not at the Windows NT machine that you want to analyze, you can use the diagnostics tool remotely from another Windows NT system. This feature is very convenient when you are trying to manage several servers at once and are not on-site.

Remote Access Service

The communication abilities of Windows NT 4.0 have also improved a great deal. To take advantage of multiple phone lines, you have the option of using all of your dial-up lines to achieve better throughput with RAS Multi-Link Channel Aggregation. This will enable you to obtain more bandwidth from analog phone lines by combining the bandwidth of individual lines. Another new feature of NT 4.0 Remote Access Service is Point-to-Point Tunneling Protocol (PPTP), which allows you to set up virtual private networks over public data lines such as the Internet. For a low-cost routing solution, you can add the Multi-Protocol Router service for LAN-to-LAN routing for IPX/SPX, TCP/IP, and AppleTalk. This eliminates the need for an expensive router for small to medium networks.

Depending on your network configuration, you might not need to use all of these features. Whatever your network configuration, these new features of Windows NT 4.0 Server can improve the reliability, performance and flexibility of your network.

Friendlier Installation

Windows NT 4.0 Server includes much-needed improvements in the installation process. First, you now have many different options for installing Windows NT Server. You can run Setup over the network, from CD-ROM or from the /I386 source files. You also have a much more granular control over the Windows NT Setup utility and command-line switches.

An important improvement of the Windows NT 4.0 Server installation process is the autoconfiguration capabilities of the installer. Windows NT 4.0 now supports many different OEM and third-party drivers. You no longer have to search for the driver disks and install your hardware devices yourself. Windows NT 4.0 can recognize your peripherals and configure them for you automatically. A good example of this option is the autoconfiguration of your network card. Microsoft has a list of autoconfigurable network cards located in the document Guide to Automating Windows NT 4.0 Setup. This is an invaluable help when rolling out hundreds or thousands of Windows NT computers using an unattended installation file.

Hardware Profile Support

Flexible hardware profile support is a valuable feature of Windows NT 4.0. Instead of having a single hardware profile, you can set up multiple hardware profiles to support different configurations. This feature comes in especially handy when installing Windows NT 4.0 on laptops. You can have one hardware profile for a "docked" configuration and another for an "undocked" configuration. This means that users need not adjust their hardware devices each time they dock or undock from a workstation. It also gives you more flexibility for testing purposes.

Another important advance is the number of hardware devices supported under Windows NT 4.0. Many vendors now make their hardware devices NT

4.0 compatible. And even if Windows NT does not discover your hardware during installation, you always have the option of adding the necessary drivers manually or after installation. Just make sure that you check the hardware compatibility list before installation.

Improved Error Messages

If you encounter any error messages during installation, NT 4.0 makes it easy to understand and correct your errors. As in Windows NT 3.51, there are two installation modes in Windows NT 4.0—text mode and graphical mode. In previous versions of Windows NT, the Setup process did not log any errors or problems that occurred in the graphical mode of setup. In Windows NT 4.0, Setup logs each change made to the computer during graphical installation to the file Setuplog.txt. This log file is very useful when diagnosing any problems such as IRQ conflicts that have occurred during installation.

One criticism of NT 3.51 was that error messages were too ambiguous and hard to understand. To correct this problem, Microsoft rewrote the error messages to eliminate any confusion they might have caused. For a complete listing of the error messages, you can check the Windows NT 4.0 Resource Kit, where the explanations are more detailed than the screen version.

Improved Task Manager

An improved feature of the Windows NT 4.0 Task Manager is its greater ability to help you monitor performance. Not only can you cut threads and processes directly from Task Manager, but you also can monitor the performance of your processor and memory. Instead of opening the Performance Monitor and searching for the items to be monitored, you can now simply open the Task Manager and take a quick look at your system resources, as shown in Figure 2-3.

The Task Manager's original duty of observing and deleting processes is still available, but it provides a more granular level of detail when looking at processes and threads. You also have the option of removing or setting the priority of individual processes.

FIGURE 2-3

Task Manager

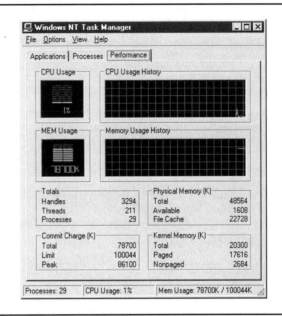

Improved Protocol (DHCP)

Dynamic Host Configuration Protocol (DHCP), added in the Windows NT 3.5 release, is now much easier to use and more reliable. DHCP allows you to dynamically handle TCP/IP addresses and gives you greater flexibility for TCP/IP configuration by using central administration. Instead of changing all of your TCP/IP information on the client, you simply have to change the TCP/IP information at the DHCP server; when clients renew their TCP/IP lease, they are configured with the new information.

Instead of installing a DHCP server on every subnet of your network, you now have the option of using your Windows NT 4.0 Server as a "router" to forward DHCP requests to computers on other subnets. This allows you more flexibility and makes it easier to configure than a system having multiple DHCP servers.

Registry Editor

For those daring enough to explore the Registry, Microsoft has included a new tool for searching the Registry. Both the new tool, Regedit.exe, and the traditional Registry Editor, Regedt32.exe, are included. Some of the new features of Regedit.exe include improved search capabilities and a Windows Explorer interface, shown in Figure 2-4. These features make it much easier to search for keys throughout the Registry. Regedit.exe helps tame some of the awkwardness of the Registry that was inherent in Regedt32.exe. However, with some of the added features, there is some loss of functionality in the new tool. The main feature lost with Regedit.exe is the ability to set permissions on specific keys. To perform this task, you need to open the traditional Registry Editor Regedt32.exe.

FIGURE 2-4

Registry Editor
(Regedit.exe)

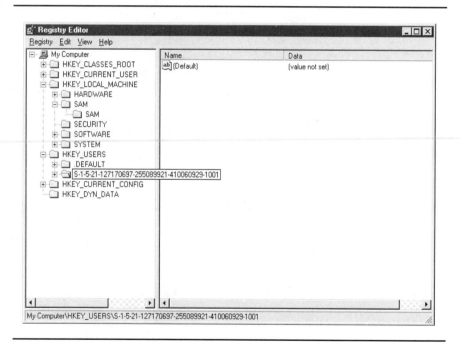

Remember it is always a better idea to perform actions using the Control Panel or other User Interface instead of editing the Registry directly. It is also a lot safer to use the User Interface instead of hacking through the Registry after an unintuitive Registry key. Always make sure that you make an Emergency Repair Disk before you attempt to edit the registry. This gives you a possibility of recovery in case you accidentally delete an important key in the Registry.

During setup, you are asked if you want to create an Emergency Repair Disk (ERD). This step is optional, but it is highly recommended. If you ever have to repair a damaged version of Windows NT, if your computer ever crashes because of a bad installation, a corrupted Registry, a bad boot sector, or if it is unable to start NT Workstation, you'll be glad that you made an ERD. The vital information it contains may help you repair the workstation.

If you decide not to create an ERD during installation, you can create one later by running RDISK.EXE after Windows NT finishes booting. (Just type **RDISK.EXE** at the command prompt.) The information stored in the WINNT\REPAIR folder on your local workstation is copied to the ERD.

Emergency Repair Disk Contents

An ERD contains the following system information that is necessary to rebuild a broken machine. The following files are copied from the Winnt\System32\Repair directory to the Emergency Repair Disk. These files are in compressed form.

- **Autoexec.NT**   Used for MS-DOS applications running the _DEFAULT.PIF

- **Config.nt**   Used for MS-DOS applications running the _DEFAULT.PIF

- **Default._**   Registry key HKEY_USERS\DEFAULT

- **Ntuser.da_**   Copy of User Profiles

- **Sam._**   Registry key HKEY_LOCAL_MACHINE\SAM

- **Security._**   Registry key HKEY_LOCAL_MACHINE\SECURITY

- **System._**   Registry key HKEY_LOCAL_MACHINE\SYSTEM

- **Software._**   Registry key HKEY_LOCAL_MACHINE\SOFTWARE

Web Browser and "Web-ification"

Microsoft is doing its best to integrate the Internet/intranet with your Windows NT 4.0 Server. The plan is to incorporate Internet Information Server (IIS) and Internet Explorer and make them an integral part of the network operating system. The IIS a is a high-performance web server that gives you fast, and easy-to-configure web access. With the inclusion of Service Pack 2, you can also add the functionality of Active Server Pages. The Internet Explorer provides a default web browser incorporated in the Windows NT 4.0 Server package.

Another powerful new addition to Windows NT 4.0 Server is Index Server 1.1. Microsoft's Index Server is installed as part of Internet Information Server and is a web-querying tool. It can be set up as part of your web site to search for files or text by size, author, file type or date. Index Server searches and locates these files located on your web site and creates an HTML-based page with the results of the query.

The Internet is changing the way networks are managed, and Windows NT 4.0 Server is at the cutting edge. Web-based administration means you can administer your Windows NT 4.0 Server from any computer that has a web browser. This feature, by itself, is a very powerful tool. Imagine creating user accounts or troubleshooting printing in San Francisco using one of your servers located in New York. The possibilities of web-based network administration are endless. It is amazing how easily your web server and web browser combine to bring remote network administration to you.

New Printer Folder and UI

Windows NT 4.0 Server makes it a lot easier to create and add printers on your Windows NT network, using the Add Printer Wizard located in your new printer folder. The Add Printer Wizard is a utility that guides you through all of the stages of creating a printer or connecting to one that is already available on your network. All you do is provide the information requested as the Add Printer Wizard runs; Windows NT automatically configures your printer. As in Windows 95, you can set up printers using the Point and Print method. To set up printers using Point and Print, you just click on your print server located in Network Neighborhood and drag the icon over to your printer folder. Windows

NT automatically downloads the necessary print driver and you can begin printing immediately. You can also manage all of your printers from the printer folder interface included with Windows NT 4.0. Each printer is represented as an icon, complete with the properties of all of your printers. You can quickly switch between the printers on your network just by double-clicking on a printer icon.

CERTIFICATION OBJECTIVE 2.02

Planning for Installation

The most important thing that you can do before installing Windows NT 4.0 Server is to make a detailed plan of your server. This includes domains and directory structure, applications that will be installed, protocols, and other layout features. The planning phase of setup is often overlooked because as engineers, we enjoy using technology more than we like thinking or reading about it.

The first order of business is to figure out what your user community is going to be. After you understand the work environment, you can outline an effective plan. Here are some issues you should consider. Are the users going to need strict security guidelines, or will this be a relaxed atmosphere? Will the administrator need to enforce policies and profiles, or should you rely on the users? This aspect is important because your job is to make sure that users can communicate with one another. If you place too many restrictions on them, you could hinder their work environment and have them working against you. However, if you give them too much freedom, you could end up with inadvertent security leaks, or chaos in the network.

Once you have figured out what the user community will be, your next order of business is to figure out what the server usage will be and what applications need to be installed. Server usage will be dependent on hardware, network capacity, and how many users are connected to the server at a time. If your server is configured with the minimum recommended hardware requirements and you have eight hundred users connecting to the server for File and Print services with SQL Server running, you will run into trouble. If you are running a processor and a memory-intensive server application such as Microsoft Exchange you should plan to use and implement serious hardware requirements. In any case, you want to prepare for the worst-case network scenario so that you will not be taken by surprise or have a bottleneck on your network. If you carefully plan your server hardware according to your network layout and leave room for growth, you will be a step ahead of the game.

FROM THE CLASSROOM

Plan Your Installation Now, Avoid Frustration Later

There are many factors to consider when planning the installation of your NT Server. The number one factor that causes trouble at our client shops is the domain structure and the use of domain controllers. Although you have not yet learned about NT domains (you will read more about them in Chapters 3 and 7), it is important to include.

How you set up your NT domains is critical. NT domains are the security building blocks of your network; if you get it wrong, there may be no end to the trouble you have. Another reason to get your domain model correct from the start is that it will be very difficult to change later. In some cases, you can actually box yourself into a nice little corner with no doorway out. Microsoft classifies domains into four types. Select the best domain model for your organization after careful planning and assessment of your needs. Pay particular attention to the future requirements of your

organization—not just what the organization looks like today. You may have to look into your crystal ball to see the shape of things to be.

If you are new to NT domains, a natural tendency is to set up one domain, just to get a feeling for domains. Then you set up another —just to understand the relationships between domains. This will go on for awhile, one domain leading to another. The point is that you never intended for this to go on, it just seemed to happen. Before you could plan your domain model, your organization was actually using domains, and perhaps not the ones you might have chosen! Too late now to plan and too late to recover.

The next planning decision is which NT Servers to set up as domain controllers and which to set up as member servers. This is a frequent issue at our clients', and one that is the source of considerable frustration. Your server's role is set at time of installation and cannot be

FROM THE CLASSROOM

changed later. Once you make a server a domain controller, it must always be a domain controller. Likewise, if you install a server as a non-domain controller, there is no way later to then make it a domain controller. The only way to change these roles is completely reinstall the operating system.

The number one "I did not understand that" issue from our clients and students is that a domain controller may *never* leave the domain into which it was installed. To state it another way, if you install a domain controller into Domain A, and then decide you want it to now be part of Domain B you can only do that if you re-install NT into a new directory. So plan now where your domain controllers will go, and save yourself work and frustration later.

—By Shane Clawson, MCT, MCSE

Before installing hardware or software applications you need to make sure that your system can support them. To ensure compatibility, use the guidelines for hardware and software described in the following section. Planning your hardware and software requirements is critical to your success.

After you have done the research for your hardware and software requirements, you have to establish naming conventions for your Windows NT Servers. You will want to select NetBIOS-compatible computer names that are intuitive and easy to recognize, even on a wide area network. For example, if you are placing a print server in Boston, MA, why not call the server something easy to recognize like "NT_Boston1t" instead of B-994-X83? This first name is easy to recognize and easy to understand. You always have the option of naming your Windows NT Servers by facility, location, function, or ownership. Sometimes cute server names are nice, but they can get confusing once the number of servers begins to grow. Just use common sense when naming your NT Servers and you should not have any problem.

One of the most overlooked points of security is passwords and password education. Passwords are the most common form of security failure. As a network administrator, you should try to restrict the chance that a hacker or curious employee can compromise security. Here are a few simple guidelines that should be followed to protect you, the server, and the user data. First, Microsoft recommends renaming the Administrator account. If the hacker knows the name of an administrator-level account, half the battle is lost. Also, hackers can attempt to crack into the default administrator account as many times as they want without being locked out, because the default administrator account cannot be locked out. It is also a good idea to have your users change their password every thirty days to restrict the ability for passwords to be exchanged.

Windows NT Security is a heavily debated issue with network administrators, IS managers, and end users. Everyone wants to know: Just how secure is Windows NT? The security of the server depends on how much the network administrator decides to lock down the networking environment.

Physical security should always be the first point of business when locking down a server. Make sure that only the right personnel can get to your server. To be safe, the server should be in an air-conditioned, locked room. Once that step is taken care of, you can think about the advantages that Windows NT offers.

Windows NT 4.0 Server provides many tools to help lock down your server. These include using NTFS partitions, policies, mandatory profiles, file and directory security, auditing, as well as password education and security. All of these tools can give you a secure and stable computing environment. A very good web site to check out that outlines the proper steps for locking down your server can be found at http://www.ntsecurity.com.

It is always a good idea to double-check your Windows NT security by logging on to your network as a Domain-User to verify that all of your components are secured. Sometimes even the most competent Windows NT administrators can miss a vital piece of security.

CERTIFICATION OBJECTIVE 2.03

Hardware and Software Compatibility

Today's network servers are more powerful and reliable than ever before. Just a few years ago it was unthinkable that a server could handle the workload of

File and Print requests while running various server applications. However, this quick explosion in technology comes at a price—namely, the extensive hardware requirements that networking operating systems such as Windows NT 4.0 Server impose. If you try to run Windows NT 4.0 Server with the minimum hardware, you lose a lot of functionality and performance. The hardware configuration for your server also depends on the number of applications and users you plan to connect. As stated earlier, if you are planning to run Microsoft Systems Management Server and SQL Server on the same Windows NT Server, you will need extensive processing power and memory to run all of the server services and still crunch all of the data.

Before selecting hardware for your Windows NT Server, you should check the Hardware Compatibility List (HCL). High-end server hardware is generally expensive, so you do not want to make the mistake of buying incompatible equipment. You can also save yourself a lot of time in the future by checking the HCL before you try any hardware upgrades or installations on your server. If your hardware devices appear on the HCL, your installation should run smoothly. If you skip this step and install Windows NT Server 4.0 on untested and unsupported hardware, you could run into serious problems. The following sections have more information about the Windows NT HCL.

Just as you made sure that your hardware devices will work with Windows NT 4.0, it is also a smart idea to check that your server software is compatible. Most current 32-bit applications will run on your Windows NT 4.0 Server with no problem at all. However, some 16-bit legacy applications, which try to access the hardware directly, might have trouble running because Windows NT 4.0 limits access to the kernel.

Importance of the HCL

As you already know, the Hardware Compatibility List is a detailed inventory of all supported hardware for Windows NT 4.0. Microsoft updates the HCL periodically, as new and updated hardware passes their compatibility testing.

The HCL is readily available in several different spots. For starters, you can find it on the Windows NT 4.0 Server CD-ROM. However, if you use this option there is a good chance it might not include the latest hardware. For the latest, most up-to-date version of the HCL you can check out Microsoft's web site. Those using CompuServe can find an HCL there on a forum strictly devoted to Windows NT. Those who subscribe to Microsoft TechNet can find a monthly updated version of the HCL located under the MS Windows NT Server section of the CD-ROM. Whatever version of the HCL you decide to use, try to verify that it contains the latest updates. *The use of supported devices will save you time and headaches in installing and running Windows NT 4.0 Server.*

If for some reason your hardware device does not appear on the HCL, it does not necessarily mean that your hardware is incompatible with Windows NT 4.0. Sometimes it takes time for new hardware devices to appear on the HCL. You can always check for the latest drivers on the vendor's web site or use the hardware drivers that were distributed from the hardware vendor

Software Compatibility Issues

Which software applications are right for your NT Server and your network? Some network software applications are just not compatible with different pieces of hardware and network operating systems. One way of checking software's compatibility with Windows NT is to see if your software applications have the "Designed for Microsoft BackOffice" logo on the software package. To qualify for this logo, the software must meet Microsoft's strict product testing with Windows NT and the rest of the Microsoft BackOffice suite. This logo guarantees that, when you install the software application on your Windows NT Server, you will not encounter any software incompatibility issues.

SMP Support

As discussed in Chapter 1, Windows NT 4.0 Server is a Symmetric Multiprocessing (SMP) network operating system, which can take advantage of having more than one processor do all of the work. As an SMP operating system, Windows NT Server uses multiple processors to help balance the workload for both the operating system and the software applications. Windows NT currently supports up to 32 processors in OEM builds from other manufacturers. SMP support is utilized best when it is processing multiple queries from applications such as SQL Server or IIS, where the server is doing many tasks at once. Symmetric multiprocessing allows the NT Server to handle more processes at once instead of sharing the processor on each individual thread.

Requirements and Recommendations

You can either run Windows NT Server 4.0. with the minimum requirements or the recommended requirements. Your choice of hardware will have a direct effect on the performance that you achieve. The minimum requirements Microsoft recommends for NT Server are baselines that will boot up the operating system and allow for minimal server functionality. Windows NT will work with these minimum requirements, but performance will be very limited; depending on the number of users connected, throughput will be very slow. The minimum requirements for Windows NT 4.0 Server *x*86 are as follows:

- Intel Processor 486/33 or higher (Pentium, Pentium-Pro, Pentium II)
- 16MB of RAM
- 125MB of free hard disk space
- CD-ROM drive (or have access to a network share or CD-ROM)
- VGA or higher resolution graphics card
- Microsoft mouse or compatible pointing device

Windows NT 4.0 Server offers a multitude of choices to customize your Windows NT Server to your network requirements. You can install all types of backup devices, modems, ISDN adapters, and multiple network interface cards. The options available to the user are virtually endless. If you are using Remote Access Service for remote connectivity, you can customize your NT Server by installing several modems or ISDN adapters. If you want to use your Windows NT Server as a router, you have the option of installing more than one network card. Besides adding several different hardware peripherals to your server, you can increase performance by installing more memory and possibly adding another processor. If you decide to do this, you should see a serious increase in performance over the minimum requirements.

Here is a list of hardware recommendations for a Windows NT 4.0 member server that will be running regular File and Print services along with SQL Server.

- Because you are going to be doing heavy number crunching, you want to make sure that you will have enough processing power. A good suggestion would be a dual Pentium Pro 200MHz. This will allow both processors to share the workload on your server. For memory, I wouldn't use less than 160MB of RAM. With all of the application services loaded, the memory will be used up very quickly. You can always add more if you see a performance degradation.

- Because hard disk space is so inexpensive nowadays, it makes sense to use multiple SCSI drives and take advantage of both RAID 5 fault tolerance and the performance benefits of disk striping with parity. You might see some decrease in performance with RAID 5, but the dual processors will be able to handle the extra workload.

- With the advent of 100MB EtherNet switches, you want to make sure that your network cards are at least 100MB compatible. This will increase your network performance as long as there is enough available bandwidth.

- Last but not least, you need to provide for data backup. A common and effective choice is the use of standard 8mm tape backup. Tape drives are becoming quicker and are capable of backing up gigabytes of data in a relatively short time. Those with larger pocketbooks might want to consider optical-magneto, a special type of optical CD-ROM disks that can back up gigabytes in seconds.

Since we have talked about the different types of hardware requirements for your server, let's see if you can make recommendations for these different scenarios.

QUESTIONS AND ANSWERS

Your server will be configured to run SQL and SMS at the same time being a domain controller. Do you want to use the minimum requirements?	No way. If you are going to be running complex server applications on your NT Server, you will need to configure a quick processor to run SQL and will need a lot of memory to deliver packages with SMS.
You have a 1000 node network that requires your server to handle file and print services. What kind of hardware requirements should you use?	Since your computer will not be doing too much work, a dual or quad processor is not required. You might want to use at least 128MB of RAM to process the handling of files on your network.
You just got in a new computer from your buddy who makes them using extra parts from old computers. It is configured with 64MB of RAM, Pentium 133 and a 2GB hard disk. You try installing Windows NT 4.0 Server on the computer, but it will not load. What is the problem?	Even though you have the right "hardware requirements," you have to make sure that each hardware device is on the HCL. This is what is prohibiting the computer from correctly installing.

CERTIFICATION OBJECTIVE 2.04

Windows NT File Systems

Windows NT 4.0 recognizes and is compatible with many different types of file systems such as FAT, NTFS, and CDFS. This lets Windows NT 4.0 Server communicate with many different types of platforms and gives the users many different options to choose from. For backward compatibility with other MS-DOS, Windows 3.x and Windows 95 computers, Windows NT recognizes the FAT (File Allocation Table) system used in those operating systems. The FAT file system has been around for quite a while and is an industry standard. The NTFS file system was specifically designed to take advantage of many features in Windows NT 4.0, such as security, fault tolerance and quick performance with large partitions. Another supported file system is the Compact Disk File System (CDFS), normally used by

CD-ROMs and marked read-only. The High Performance File System (HPFS) in OS/2 is no longer supported with Windows NT 4.0 Server. If you are installing Windows NT 4.0 on a HPFS partition, you must first either delete the HPFS partition or convert the partition to NTFS. After you have converted or deleted your HPFS partition, you can continue with your installation.

For those experimenting with FAT-32, beware! Windows NT 4.0 does not recognize the FAT-32 file system. It cannot install on a FAT-32 partition or use FAT-32 for storage space. If you encounter FAT-32 partitions, you will have to reformat the partition as FAT-16. FAT-32 will not be recognized by Windows NT, until Windows NT 5.0 is released. Until then, you're out of luck!

File Allocation Table (FAT)

The FAT file system is predominantly used for other operating systems such as Windows 3.*x* and Windows 95. To support backward compatibility, Windows NT fully supports the FAT file system. This is also due to FAT's universal acceptance and accessibility through other operating systems. Here are some characteristics of FAT file systems: they are good with hard disks under 511MB; they require the 8.3 naming scheme (eight-character filename with a three-character extension); they lack file-level security. If you are going to use a RISC computer such as an Alpha or MIPS, it will require you to have a 2MB FAT partition for your system files. The characteristics of FAT files are summarized here.

- Good for smaller hard disks of 200 – 400MB because of overhead.
- Files are not protected by the security features of Windows NT. No file and directory security.
- Good if you need to be accessible through DOS or OS/2. Easily fragmented.
- Can accept partitions up to 2GB.
- Universally accepted as a file system.

- Necessary if you wish to dual boot between NT and DOS or OS/2.

- Cannot take advantage of fault tolerance.

- Needed for dual-boot capability with MS-DOS and Windows 95.

CD-ROM File System

Windows NT 4.0 Server recognizes CDFS (the CD-ROM file system) as a read-only file system. On a CDFS volume, the files are burned into the volume or marked read-only. This means that you cannot make any changes to the files located on the CD-ROM. Files can be copied from the CD-ROM and changed thereafter, but there is no support for changing files on a CDFS volume. CD-ROM drives are normally shared on the network to allow multiple users to access the data or software applications located on the CD-ROM.

NTFS

New Technology File System (NTFS) is the file system of choice for Windows NT 4.0 Server. By installing Windows NT onto an NTFS partition, you can take advantage of the many benefits that NTFS provides for Windows NT.

One of the greatest benefits of NTFS is the compliance with the Windows NT security model, which allows excellent control of network access. Unlike FAT, NTFS allows you to set both file and directory permissions on your Windows NT Server. Figure 2-5 shows the Windows NT screen used to control network access.

NTFS also allows you to set up security auditing, to keep track of File and Object access on the NTFS partitions. To allow easy recovery, the NTFS partitions log all transactions to the file system in case of failure.

Two other advantages of the NTFS file system are the large partition size and the file compression capability. Incorporating NTFS partitions with Windows NT 4.0 Server defeats the FAT partition size restriction of 2GB. NTFS allows partition sizes of up to 16 exabytes and the use of Long File Names of up to 255 characters. File compression, while not a recommended option because of performance issues, yields very good results on NTFS partitions. The advantages of NTFS partitions are summarized next.

FIGURE 2-5

NTFS file security

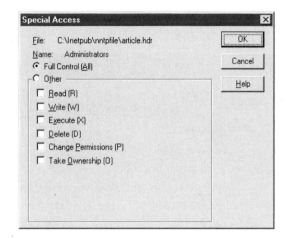

- Better for hard disks over 500MB. Less overhead.

- File and directory security that allows the user to specify access.

- Supports complete Windows NT security, so administrator can specify who is allowed various kinds of access to a file or directory with auditing.

- Recognized only by Windows NT. When the computer is running another operating system (such as MS-DOS or OS/2), that operating system cannot access files on an NTFS partition on the same computer.

- Allows the expansion of partitions on hard disks over 2GB. Supports files and partitions as large as 16 exabytes (2 to the 64th).

- 255 characters per filename.

- Fast access, recoverable and secure.

NTFS Implementation Issues

Implementing NTFS into your environment can be done any number of ways. When installing your Windows NT 4.0 Server you can either create an NTFS partition during installation or you can convert an existing FAT partition to NTFS once installation is completed. You also have the option to create an

NTFS partition with the Disk Administrator tool located in the Administrative Tools Common Group.

If your Windows NT 4.0 Server is installed on a FAT partition, you can always convert this partition to NTFS using the command line utility Convert.exe. After you have converted the file system to NTFS, the computer asks you to reboot. During the initial boot-up phase Windows NT converts the partition to NTFS. It is important to remember that once a FAT partition is converted to NTFS, it cannot be converted back to FAT or any other file system.

As mentioned earlier, Windows NT 4.0 does not support the HPFS file system. If you are installing your Windows NT 4.0 Server on an HPFS partition, you will have to delete the existing partition or convert the partition to NTFS. Previous versions of Windows NT supported HPFS, but Windows NT 4.0 does not.

EXERCISE 2-1

Converting an Existing FAT Partition to NTFS

If you want to take advantage of the NTFS file system after you have installed Windows NT on a FAT partition, you can convert your FAT partition to NTFS. This will allow you to take advantage of the NTFS file system while using Windows NT 4.0.

1. Log on to your computer as Administrator.

2. Click the Start Menu | Programs | Command Prompt.

3. At the command prompt, use the conversion utility Convert.exe. Type

   ```
   C:\Convert D: /FS:NTFS
   ```

   This converts the D: partition to NTFS.

4. Once you have completed this step you will have to reboot in order for the file system to be created. This is because you do not have exclusive rights to the file system (NT cannot access the hardware directly). The file system begins converting to NTFS during the boot process.

NTFS Runtime File Compression

If you are having trouble finding disk space on your server, Windows NT 4.0 Server allows both file and directory compression on NTFS partitions. The size of your file or directory ultimately determines what type of compression ratio it will attain. If you decide to use NTFS compression, you might see some performance degradation on your server. When a compressed NTFS file is copied, it is uncompressed first and then recompressed into a brand new file. This takes processing power to accomplish and ultimately slows down your server. When transferring a compressed file from your server to another computer on the network, the file is transferred in an uncompressed state that will limit bandwidth. If you decide to use NTFS compression, you will receive a performance hit because the operating system must uncompress the file each time it is accessed. If you multiply this over hundreds of files, you will see a decrease in performance.

Moving and Copying Files

If you move a file from one folder to another on the same partition, the file "attribute" is retained. This "attribute" is retained no matter what the state of the destination folder. If you move an uncompressed file to a compressed folder, the file will remain uncompressed after the move. However, if you decide to copy a file from one folder to another, the compression is changed so that the copied file inherits the attributes of the destination directory. Files moved from a FAT partition to an NTFS partition always inherit the compression attributes of the destination folder. Any compressed files moved from an NTFS partition to a FAT partition are uncompressed or lose their "attribute" on the FAT partition. Here is a chart to help explain the effects for moving and copying files on NTFS and FAT partitions.

Copy	Same Partition	Inherited
	Different Partition	Inherited
Move	Same Partition	Retained
	Different Partition	Inherited

The only time that the compress bit is retained is when the user moves a file to a folder on the same partition.

If you try to move or copy a compressed file to an almost full NTFS partition, you may see unexpected error messages. This occurs because

Windows NT wants to make sure that there is enough room on the partition in case the file is ever uncompressed. If the file is uncompressed on a full partition you will see error messages stating that there is no room left on the partition.

File and directory compression has some advantages, but in the real world you are taking unneeded risks by using compression. Hard disks and storage are too inexpensive to warrant compression on your server. File compression is just another operation that can go wrong and ultimately cause you to lose your data. To be safe, it is a better idea to upgrade your server with more hard disk space than to attempt to save disk space using file compression.

Long File Names

Long File Names were not possible in the 16-bit computing world that used operating systems such as MS-DOS and Windows 3.*x*. With the introduction of 32-bit operating systems, Long File Names became a reality. Like Windows 95, Windows NT 4.0 Server supports Long File Names on both NTFS and FAT partitions.

In a large computing environment you may be accessing hundreds or even thousands of files, directories, or share points. The Long File Name capability frees you from the restrictive 8.3 naming scheme that was a part of previous versions of Windows. With longer filenames, you can adopt a more intuitive naming structure that makes it easier to identify files. Navigating is also easier because longer filenames make it easier to describe the points of reference on your network.

LFN Capabilities

Long File Names can have 255 characters per name for each individual file, directory, or share point. This should alleviate any problems that you have had with the truncated MS-DOS 8.3 naming schemes. If you are working with a FAT partition with Windows NT, Windows NT automatically generates a truncated version of the Long File Name so that the long filename will be accessible from an MS-DOS or Windows 3.*x* workstation. This is a transparent change and allows backward compatibility with all of the 16-bit operating systems.

Truncated Filenames

While Windows NT supports Long File Names on both FAT and NTFS partitions, MS-DOS cannot recognize long filenames. Whenever you create a file on a FAT partition using Windows NT, the operating system automatically creates a truncated or shortened version of the filename so that MS-DOS workstations can recognize that file. MS-DOS workstations can only read files with the 8.3 extension. To allow for backward compatibility, Windows NT automatically truncates the Long File Names to the 8.3 MS-DOS standard. This allows MS-DOS computers to recognize the same file, directory or share point as the Windows NT computer that is using the long filename. If two filenames have the same beginnings or extensions, Windows NT will separate the two files by using numbers. For example, if you have two files named ReviewsForMicrosoft.doc and ReviewsForOracle.doc, Windows NT will truncate the filenames by adding the number 1 and number 2 as part of the truncation.

CERTIFICATION OBJECTIVE 2.05

Windows NT Protocols

Windows NT 4.0 uses different types of protocols to communicate with other workstations and computers on the network. The protocols installed on your Windows NT Server determine what type of computers your NT Server can communicate with. To allow for the widest range of communication, Windows NT Server offers many different types of protocols that can be installed, including NetBEUI, TCP/IP, IPX/SPX, DLC, AppleTalk or PPTP. Each of these protocols has individual advantages and disadvantages that make it unique. For example, some protocols such as NetBEUI are not routable or cannot talk to other networks on the other side of a router. Two protocols that are routable are TCP/IP or IPX/SPX. TCP/IP is regularly used on the Internet and IPX/SPX is primarily used to communicate with Novell Networks.

Depending on the specific needs of your networks, you will need to install some of these protocols. It is important to note that installing several protocols on your Windows NT Server will cause more traffic than installing only one protocol.

NetBIOS/NetBEUI

The NetBEUI protocol was introduced to communicate on Windows networks. NetBEUI is a very fast protocol on a Local Area Network (LAN), but there are some serious limitations to its performance on a Wide Area Network (WAN). Its primary limitation is that it is not a routable protocol, which means that it cannot talk to other computers or networks on the other sides of a router. This limitation restricts its use to small local area networks (about 20 to 200 workstations).

TCP/IP

TCP/IP stands for Transmission Control Protocol/Internet Protocol. It is an industry-standard suite of protocols designed for local and wide-area networking. TCP/IP was developed in 1969, in a Defense Advanced Research Projects Agency (DARPA) research project on network interconnection. Formerly a military network, this global area network has exploded and is now referred to as the Internet.

TCP/IP has gained most of its popularity through its wide use for Internet communication. Connecting computers together throughout the world, it is known for being both reliable and routable, and for being able to talk to foreign networks.

Windows NT TCP/IP allows users to connect to the Internet as well as any machine running TCP/IP and providing TCP/IP services. This includes some applications that require TCP/IP to function. The advantages of the TCP/IP protocol are summarized next.

- Provides connectivity across operating systems and hardware platforms.

- This protocol is the backbone of the Internet. If you need to connect to the Internet, you will need TCP/IP.

- TCP/IP is routable. This means that you can talk to other networks through routers.

- Very popular. Think of all of the computers on the Internet.

- Some applications need TCP/IP to run.

- Provides connectivity across operating systems and hardware platforms. Windows NT can FTP to a UNIX workstation.

- Simple Network Management Protocol (SNMP) support. Used to troubleshoot problems on the network.

- Dynamic Host Configuration Protocol (DHCP) support. Used for Dynamic IP addressing.

- Windows Internet Name Service (WINS) support. Resolves Windows NetBIOS names on the network.

NWLink (IPX/SPX)

The NWLink Protocol is most commonly used to connect to Novell Networks. You should also select this protocol if you will be using any applications that use IPX/SPX—for instance, if you are running any client/server applications such as SQL Server. When selecting IPX/SPX, it is important to make sure that you pick the correct frame type. This is often a problem when using NWLink. The protocol will default to auto-detect the frame type, but you should choose it manually to be certain it is correct. To access files or printers on a NetWare server, you must have Microsoft's Client Services for NetWare (CSNW) installed or Novell's NetWare Client for Windows NT. You can also use IPX/SPX to gain access to an NT Server that has Gateway Services for NetWare installed or a SQL Server that is using the NWLink protocol to communicate. The characteristics of IPX/SPX are summarized next.

- Connects to Novell Networks.

- Remember to pick the correct frame type. Do not let IPX/SPX auto-detect the frame type.

- You might need this protocol to connect to an application server running IPX/SPX.

- You need Client Services for Netware to gain access to files and printers that reside on a NetWare server.

exam
ⓦatch

A common problem with using NWLink (IPX/SPX) is that it will default to auto-detect the frame type. Make sure that you choose the correct frame type when you are configuring the protocol.

AppleTalk

This protocol is used to communicate with Macintosh networks. Generally, an NT Server with Services for Macintosh uses this protocol to communicate with the Macintosh clients.

Data Link Control (DLC)

Unlike most protocols, DLC is not mainly used for communication between computers. The main function for DLC is to allow connectivity to Hewlett-Packard printers. By installing the DLC protocol on your server, you can let your network clients communicate with the HP printer. The DLC protocol does not need to be installed on the network clients, only on the server. However, you do not necessarily always need DLC to connect to HP printers. You can give your HP printer a TCP/IP address and connect to the printer via TCP/IP printing in Windows NT 4.0.

Besides connecting NT servers to HP printers, DLC also is used to connect to mainframe computers to run 3270 applications.

exam
ⓦatch

A frequent test question asks you to identify the principal function of the DLC protocol. DLC is used primarily to connect to a Hewlett-Packard printer.

Now that you have a grasp of the different types of protocols available with Windows NT, let's see if you can answer these questions.

QUESTIONS AND ANSWERS

You are connecting to a Novell NetWare server and have Gateway Services for NetWare installed. What protocol do you want?	NWLink. If you are connecting to a NetWare server, NWLink is required.
You have a small LAN of about 15 workstations in a workgroup environment. You want a quick protocol compatible with Windows computers. What protocol do you want?	NetBEUI. It is a quick, non-routable protocol that is predominantly used for small networks.
You will be connecting to the Internet to allow people to come to your web site and buy from your online store. What protocol do you want?	TCP/IP. It is the standard protocol of the Internet.
You have a few Hewlett-Packard printers that are using HP Jet-Direct cards installed on your network. What protocol should you install to allow your clients to connect to the printers?	DLC, which enables computers to connect to HP printers and also enables workstations to connect to mainframe computers.

CERTIFICATION SUMMARY

The information covered in this chapter is directly related to the material you will be tested on in the Windows NT 4.0 Server exam. The detailed explanations and exercises in this book should make you better prepared to pass the exam. The information presented here is taken directly from the requirements listed on the exam preparation page of Microsoft's web site. Our approach is to explain what will be covered on the exam and to summarize the key points you'll need to understand when taking the exam.

A straightforward, but often overlooked, section of the exam covers the hardware requirements for Windows NT 4.0 Server. The minimum hardware requirements for installing an Intel-based server are a: 486/33 processor, 16MB of RAM and 120MB of hard disk space. When installing NT 4.0 Server, you must remember to select hardware that's listed on Microsoft's HCL. If you don't, you have no guarantee that the hardware will work. Worse yet, you have no guarantee that Microsoft will support the system.

You will be asked to choose the appropriate file system to use in a given situation: NTFS, FAT or HPFS. The NTFS file system was developed especially for Windows NT. By using NTFS on your partitions you can take advantage of its file and directory security, as well as its auditing, transaction logging, and partition size features. You will also need to understand the role of the FAT file system, which will probably be part of your system if you use 16-bit operating systems with NT. Remember that FAT partitions do not allow you to set file permissions or use auditing. Finally, you need to remember that OS/2 (the HPFS file system) is no longer supported with Windows NT 4.0. You must either delete the HPFS partition or convert the partition to NTFS during setup.

You will also have to know how Windows NT 4.0 Server handles Long File Names on both FAT and NTFS partitions. Long File Names can be up to 255 characters in length. On a FAT partition, Windows NT automatically creates an alias for the long filename so that MS-DOS machines can recognize them. Windows NT truncates the long filename to the 8.3 standard, with eight characters for the filename and three for the extension. If two or more files in the same directory would have identical names when truncated, they're designated filenam~1.ext, filenam~2.ext, and so forth.

Finally, you will be asked to choose a communication protocol for various situations. You will have to choose among TCP/IP, NWLink IPX/SPX Compatible Transport and the NetBEUI protocol. Remember that TCP/IP is used to connect to the Internet, is routable, and can be used to run applications over the network. NWLink is commonly used to connect to Novell NetWare Networks, to connect to other servers that are running Gateway Services for NetWare, and to connect to other servers running applications such as SQL Server.

TWO-MINUTE DRILL

❑ Windows NT 4.0 Server includes a series of Administrative Wizards to guide the novice user through basic network administration tasks.

❑ NT 4.0 Server includes a basic Network Monitor tool that enables you to "sniff out" packets on the network and help diagnose any problems you are having with protocols.

❑ The Windows NT diagnostics tools enable you to check important diagnostics like memory, IRQ, network shares, protocols and system information from a single, easy-to-read graphical window.

❑ You can set up policies on your server by user, by group, or by computer. For example, a network administrator can effectively lock down the workstation by disabling the Run button on the Start menu, disabling Registry editing tools, or restricting access to the Control Panel.

❑ The Task Manager enables you to monitor the performance of your server, view processes, or end application tasks.

❑ NT 4.0 Remote Access Service includes Multi-Link Channel Aggregation, which enables you to obtain more bandwidth from analog phone lines by combining the bandwidth of individual lines.

❑ RAS Point-to-Point Tunneling Protocol (PPTP) allows you to set up virtual private networks over public data lines such as the Internet.

❑ For a low-cost routing solution, you can add the Multi-Protocol Router service for LAN-to-LAN routing for IPX/SPX, TCP/IP, and AppleTalk. This eliminates the need for an expensive router for small to medium networks.

❑ Windows NT 4.0 Server installation process has improved autoconfiguration capabilities that now supports many different OEM and third-party drivers.

❑ Windows NT 4.0 Server includes Regedit.exe, a new tool for searching the Registry.

❑ Internet Information Server (IIS) and Index Server (IS) are powerful new additions that support improved Internet/intranet access for Windows NT 4.0 Server.

❑ The most important thing that you can do before installing Windows NT 4.0 Server is to make a detailed plan of your server. This includes domain and directory structure, applications that will be installed, protocols and other layout features.

❑ Before recommending any hardware for your Windows NT Server, you should first check the Hardware Compatibility List (HCL). Microsoft wants you to use the hardware on the HCL because these devices have been tested with Windows NT 4.0.

❑ Microsoft's "Made for Microsoft BackOffice" logo eliminates any confusion by the software vendor over software compatibility with Windows NT.

❑ As an SMP operating system, Windows NT Server can utilize multiple processors to help balance the workload for both the operating system and the software applications.

❑ Windows NT 4.0 recognizes and is compatible with many different types of file systems such as FAT, NTFS and CDFS.

❑ The FAT file system is predominantly used for the other operating systems such as Windows 3.x and Windows 95.

❑ Windows NT 4.0 Server recognizes CDFS (the CD-ROM file system) as a read-only file system.

❑ NTFS (New Technology File System) is the file system of choice for Windows NT 4.0 Server. It provides security for both files and directories as well as auditing and transaction logging.

❑ Windows NT 4.0 Server allows both file and directory compression on NTFS partitions.

❑ Like Windows 95, Windows NT 4.0 Server supports Long File Names on both NTFS and FAT partitions.

❑ Windows NT Server offers many different types of protocols that can be installed including NetBEUI, TCP/IP, IPX/SPX, DLC, AppleTalk or PPTP.

❑ NetBEUI is a very fast protocol on a Local Area Network (LAN), but there are some serious limitations to its performance on a Wide Area Network (WAN). The limitation of NetBEUI is that it is not a routable protocol.

❑ TCP/IP is an industry-standard suite of protocols designed for local and wide-area networking.

❑ A common problem with using NWLink (IPX/SPX) is that it will default to auto-detect the frame type. Make sure that when selecting IPX/SPX that you select the correct frame type.

❑ The DLC protocol is used to connect to a Hewlett-Packard printer.

❑ Dynamic Host Configuration Protocol (DHCP) allows you to dynamically handle TCP/IP addresses.

SELF TEST

The following questions will help you measure your understanding of the material presented in this chapter. Read all the choices carefully, as there may be more than one correct answer. Choose all correct answers for each question.

1. Huey's boss wants him to install Windows NT 4.0 Server onto some legacy hardware. What choices does Huey have to install Windows NT 4.0 Server?

    A. 386/20, 48MB of RAM, 2.3GB hard disk

    B. 486/33, 24MB of RAM, 1.0GB hard disk

    C. 266 Pentium II, 256MB of RAM, 16.5GB hard disk

    D. Pentium 166, 12MB of RAM, 3.0GB hard disk

2. Elliot wants to check the HCL before he installs his Windows NT 4.0 Server. Where can he find the HCL?

    A. Microsoft web page

    B. Tech-Net

    C. Windows 95 CD-ROM

    D. Microsoft TV

3. J.D. wants to install a protocol to connect up to a client-server database on a Novell NetWare 3.11 server. What must be installed in order for him to use the database?

    A. Client Services for NetWare

    B. NWLink Protocol

    C. Gateway Services for NetWare

    D. Novell GroupWare

4. Milton wants to let his users connect to a Hewlett-Packard printer that has a HP Direct-Jet card installed. What protocol should he have installed on his server in order for his users to access the printer?

    A. Point-to-Point Tunneling Protocol (PPTP)

    B. DLC

    C. Streams

    D. Infrared

5. What new functionality does the Task Manager provide in Windows NT 4.0?

    A. Printer management

    B. View processor and memory usage

    C. Add users

    D. Scripting tool

6. Steve S. wants to convert his server's boot partition to a secure file system that enables auditing and transaction logging. What file system should he use?

    A. HPFS

    B. CDFS

    C. NTFS

    D. NFS

7. Michael has never used Windows NT 4.0 Server before and is required to create some

new printers for his job. What utility will help Michael to do his job?

   A. Windows NT Diagnostics

   B. Migration Tool for NetWare

   C. Server Manager

   D. Administrative Wizards

8. Paul and Laurie are building a web server on their Windows NT 4.0 Server. What new components are included?

   A. Network Monitor

   B. SNA Server

   C. Internet Information Server

   D. Index Server

9. Convert the following Long File Names to the MS-DOS 8.3 standard. (This is a common question on many of the Microsoft exams.)

   A. Accounting101397.doc

   B. ExpenseReport46.xls

   C. ExpenseReport47.xls

   D. MikesFavoriteBooks.doc

   E. SystemsMS.db

10. (True or False) Symmetric Multiprocessing (SMP) takes advantage of the multiple processors in your computer by having each processor share the workload.

11. (True or False) The version of Network Monitor included with Windows NT 4.0 Server allows the user to capture network packets from any computer on the network.

12. (True or False) Regedit.exe allows you to set security permissions on individual keys of the Registry.

MICROSOFT CERTIFIED SYSTEMS ENGINEER

3

Installing Windows NT Server 4.0

CERTIFICATION OBJECTIVES

3.01   Planning the Hard Disk Configuration

3.02   Installation Methods

3.03   Server Roles

3.04   Removing Windows NT

3.05   Troubleshooting the Installation
        Process

A s discussed in the previous chapter, planning and preparation are an important part of the Windows NT Server installation process. In this chapter you will learn more about hardware requirements that need to be considered, the type of file system to be used, and type of licensing to choose. The bulk of the chapter describes two methods you can use to install Windows NT Server 4.0: across the network using a network share, or from a local CD-ROM. After a step-by-step description of the installation process, the chapter considers some special situations such as installation on a RISC computer, procedures for upgrading from a Windows NT 3.51 installation, and unattended installations.

As you complete the installation, you'll need to know what protocol(s) the network will use for communication. Windows NT Server supports three protocol standards: TCP/IP, NWLink, and NetBEUI.

Another major section of this chapter deals with server roles, particularly the use of primary domain controllers (PDCs) and backup domain controllers (BDCs) for domain management. The final sections describe methods for removing Windows NT from a server and troubleshooting an installation.

CERTIFICATION OBJECTIVE 3.01

Planning the Hard Disk Configuration

Before you begin to install Windows NT 4.0, you *must* plan your hard disk partitioning scheme. Make sure to have a minimum amount of space available on the partition where you are installing Windows NT Server. You can set up a partition scheme prior to installation if you want to, or you can configure the partition scheme during installation. After the operating system is installed, system administrators can make changes to partitions using Disk Administrator—except that the *system* partition must be configured during the installation process, and cannot be changed without reinstalling.

Windows NT 4.0 Server requires a minimum amount of free space on the system partition (the partition where you install Windows NT Server). The absolute minimum recommended by Microsoft for Intel *x*86-type computers is 124 MB, but for satisfactory performance most networks require more space.

Two types of partitions are involved in Windows NT 4.0 installations: The *system* partition and the *boot* partition. It is interesting (and sometimes confusing) that the "system" partition is where the operating system boots from, and the "boot" partition is where the system files are stored. These aren't the only partitions available with Windows NT Server. Many other partitions can be set up for storing data and applications.

File System Considerations

You also need to decide how you want your file system configured. You can install Windows NT Server either with the traditional FAT (file allocation table) file system used for DOS, Windows 95, Windows 3.1, and Windows for Workgroups 3.11, or you can use NTFS, the new technology file system developed specifically for Windows NT. Certain hardware dictates the choice of file type. For instance, you can install Windows NT on a RISC-based system, but you must use a FAT partition for the system files.

NTFS allows the administrator to set up permissions that specify who can and cannot access files or directories (folders) on the drive. In other words, selecting NTFS allows the administrator to take full advantage of Windows NT's security features, and the FAT file system does not. If security is important in your corporate environment, NTFS is the preferred file system for Windows NT Server installations.

If you decide to use NTFS for your system partition, remember that the FAT file system is kept intact until the installation is completed. The setup program does not format a new partition to NTFS. The system partition is converted to NTFS on the first boot of the server after a successful installation. If you install Windows NT Server on a FAT file partition, you have the option of converting the partition later on, using a CONVERT utility included with NT 4.0 Server that runs from a DOS session prompt.

You also need to consider whether the computer you are installing will be a "multiboot" system. Generally a Windows NT Workstation is more likely to have a multiboot configuration than an NT Server is. Operating systems such as Windows 95 and DOS cannot access NTFS drives. If you need to share information between operating systems on a multiboot computer, FAT would be the appropriate file system choice. If you do install Windows NT as an NTFS partition, be sure that the system partition is set up as FAT so the other operating systems can boot properly. You can make a separate NTFS partition for your data by using Disk Administrator within Windows NT.

As mentioned earlier, if information security is essential in your company, then it's smart to take advantage of the NTFS security features. This also prevents someone from getting at the files on your server by using a DOS boot disk.

As you are studying for the Windows NT Server exam, it's a good idea to create a dual-boot installation, with Windows 95 in one partition and NT Server 4.0 in another partition. This will give you a hands-on experience with the installation process. Remember, Windows NT can be installed on an existing partition. For example, let's say that you have a computer with Windows 95 already installed and want to install Windows NT Server. You can install to the same partition, but you cannot install Windows NT into the same directory as Windows 95! In addition, if you have multiple instances of NT Server or NT Workstation on one computer you must install them in separate subdirectories. The installation program will automatically update the boot loader menu.

If you have MS-DOS and Windows 3.1 or Windows for Workgroups, you can install NT Server in the same Windows subdirectory. This has the advantage that the automatic setup of icons and programs that already exist under Windows 3.1 or Windows for Workgroups. However, if you install Windows NT Server in the same subdirectory as Windows 3.1 or Windows for Workgroups the original operating system will no longer be available. With Windows 95 and other NT operating systems (4.0 or greater) you must reinstall all your applications so they are accessible from each operating system on your hard disk.

Most of the options mentioned above can be decided during the installation process. However, it is best to prepare and plan ahead of time. Planning your installation will save time and reduce the possibility of mistakes.

Per Server versus Per Seat Licensing

Another factor to consider is how your licensing will be configured. Licensing is important because it affects the cost of your network installation. Part of the planning process presented in Chapter 2 is network layout and design. The license arrangement is part of this design.

Windows NT comes with two licensing options: Per Server or Per Seat licensing. These options provide different types of client access.

With Per Server licensing, your license depends upon the number of concurrent connections. If you have 100 workstations accessing your server, you would need 100 client access licenses and a server set up with Per Server licensing. This is ideal for networks that only have one server because each workstation needs a separate client access license for each server it accesses. The server itself controls the number of connections. If you have Per Server licensing set up and a 100-client access license for Windows NT Server, workstation 101 will not be able to log on when all the licenses are in use.

With Per Seat licensing you can set up your server so that each client has an access license for as many servers as it can access. In this case, the server doesn't control logons. Instead, you are licensed for the number of computers on the network, but the clients are not limited to one server. Each workstation can concurrently use multiple servers even though it only has one license.

During the installation process you must specify whether you want Per Server or Per Seat licensing. You can take advantage of the Licensing option in your Control Panel (see Figure 3-1) to tell Windows NT Server how many licenses you have. If you are unsure about which type of licensing is best for your organization, select Per Server. If Per Seat turns out to be what you need, you can make a one-time switch from Per Server licensing to Per Seat licensing.

exam
ⓦatch

You may see one or two questions about Per Seat and Per Server licensing. Be sure to keep in mind that you can make that one-time switch only from Per Server to Per Seat. You cannot switch in the other direction.

Partitions and Fault Tolerance

When planning partitions—especially your system or boot partition—you should also consider fault tolerance and what methods you plan to use.

Control Panel
Licensing option

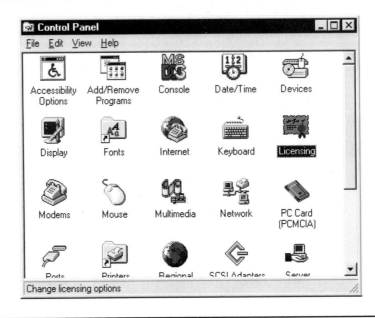

Remember that mirroring, in which the data on one disk is exactly duplicated on a separate disk, is the only fault-tolerant scheme that can be used on the system or boot partitions. If you need more information about RAID (Redundant Array of Inexpensive Disk) techniques for fault tolerance, refer to Chapter 4 of this book.

To set up effective fault tolerance you need to keep data and fault tolerant information on a separation partition and/or disk. A good rule of thumb is to set up one partition for the system files and then keep the remaining data on a separate partition. This enables you to set up the appropriate fault tolerant scheme that you choose.

Naming Conventions

When installing Windows NT 4.0 Server, it is important to understand the naming conventions. Microsoft uses a NetBIOS form of a UNC, or a

Universal Naming Convention. Everything in Windows Networking relates to naming conventions. Each computer in the domain or workgroup is given a "friendly name." Windows NT converts the friendly name into the TCP/IP address, MAC address, or other identifiable means of routing the information. The syntax for the UNC name is *computername\sharename*. Because the server name is determined during the installation process, make sure to give the server a name that makes sense. Often administrators will name the server something in relation to its responsibilities. The NetBIOS name of a computer can be 15 characters in length. For example, a Backup Domain Controller in the New York office for a company named Acme might be 'AcmeNewYorkBDC'. Share names, on the other hand, can be up to 255 characters in length. An example of a share name might be NT40CDROM. In this case the UNC name would be \\AcmeNewYorkBDC\NT40CDROM. The slashes are important. Be sure to use the '\' (backslash) and not the '/' (forward slash). The server (or computer) name in Windows Networking should be preceded by two backslashes, with one backslash separating the server (computer) name and share name.

Preparing for Installation

In the following exercises, you will prepare your hard disk for Windows NT 4.0 Server installation. *PLEASE BE WARNED that these exercises will delete the entire contents of your hard disk. Be sure to use a computer where you can clear the hard disk!*

During the pre-installation process you can use FDISK and FORMAT from a DOS boot disk to partition and format the hard disk. For this exercise you will need a DOS boot disk with FDISK and FORMAT as well as the installation CD and boot disks.

<table>
<tr><td>EXERCISE 3-1</td><td></td></tr>
</table>

Preparing the Hard Disk Before the Installation Process

1. For this first exercise, use the DOS boot disk that contains FDISK and FORMAT. Insert this disk into your floppy drive and boot your new computer. Before you begin the exercise, the hard disk should have no partitions on it.

2. When you get to an A:> prompt type **FDISK**.

3. You will see a menu of options. Select Option 1, Create DOS Partition or Logical DOS Drive. (See Figure 3-2.)

FIGURE 3-2

FDISK main menu

Microsoft Windows 95

Fixed Disk Setup Program

(C) Copyright Microsoft Corp. 1983-1995

FIDISK Options

Current fixed disk drive: 1

Choose one of the following:

1. Create DOS partition or Logical DOS Drive

2. Set active partition

3. Delete partition or Logical DOS Drive

4. Display partition information

5. Change current fixed disk drive

Enter Choice: [1]

Press Esc to exit FDISK

---

4. On the second menu select option 1, Create Primary DOS Partition.

5. The program asks if you want to use the entire available space on that drive to create the partition. Answer No. For this exercise, use 50% of the available space.

6. After the partition is created, leave the DOS boot disk in the drive and reboot.

7. This time when you see an A:> prompt, type **FORMAT C:**.

8. You will be asked if you're sure you want to format that drive, as it will destroy all data. Answer Yes.

9. After a few minutes, the drive should format. You are now ready to start Windows NT setup and installation.

Alternatively you can partition the hard disk during the Windows NT 4.0 Server installation process. Exercise 3-2 shows you how to do that.

<table>
<tr><td>EXERCISE 3-2</td><td></td></tr>
</table>

Preparing the Hard Disk During the Installation Process

1. For this exercise, use the Windows NT Server boot disks and CD-ROM. Insert the first boot disk into the floppy drive and boot the computer.

2. Insert the CD-ROM into your CD-ROM drive while disk 1 is booting up. A series of drivers loads and you will be prompted for the second disk.

3. Insert the second disk. When the option comes up, select ENTER to install Windows NT Server.

4. The second screen shows what other devices were detected on the system. Your CD-ROM information should show up here. If not, you cannot continue installation unless you have the manufacturer's driver disk.

5. If you have the driver disk from the manufacturer and your CD is not showing in the list, press the S key to specify additional devices. From the device list, select the option that requires a disk from the OEM manufacturer. Insert your disk and the program should load the appropriate driver into memory.

6. When you are satisfied with the choices in the additional devices list, press ENTER to continue.

7. You should now see the License Agreement screen. Scroll down to the end, then press F8 to agree to the license information.

8. Next you see a summary screen containing information about your system configuration. You should see display information, keyboard information, pointing device, and so forth.

9. The next screen is the key screen in this exercise. This is where you select the partition where you want to install Windows NT. If partitions are already created (and of course if space permits), you can select one of them.

10. If you see free space without a partition type, you can select that free space, then select what type of format to apply. Your options in Windows NT are FAT and NTFS. For this exercise select FAT.

11. After a few minutes, the drive should format. You are now ready to start Windows NT setup and installation.

CERTIFICATION OBJECTIVE 3.02

Installation Methods

When installing Windows NT Server 4.0 there are various methods one can use to configure the server. Windows NT Server comes with three boot disks and one CD. The installation files are no longer available on floppy disks. The CD contains just over 600MB of information, which would require more than 420 high density disks! Most new computers now come with a CD-ROM drive. If not, you can add one for less than $100.

You can install over the network or from the CD. The CD install can be done one of two ways.

■ The Windows NT Server 4.0 CD is a bootable CD-ROM. If your server's BIOS supports it, you can boot directly from the CD and start the installation process that way.

- If not, the three floppy disks that come with Windows NT Server are boot disks designed to allow users to start the installation process without a bootable CD-ROM drive.

The reason the "boot" process is so important is that the installation program runs on a low-level version of Windows NT. The installation can start in DOS, but certain related files load to allow the system to reboot and start the NT operating system.

The following sections first describe the network installation option, then examine the CD installation process.

Network Installation

In a network installation, files are made available (shared) from another network computer, such as another server or workstation. With a network boot disk, you access the shared directory to run the setup utility. Files are then transferred across the network to the local hard disk during the installation process. Figure 3-3 illustrates this process.

This isn't necessarily the best way to install across the network. Most network administrators would recommend copying the installation subdirectory (\i386) to the local computer and then executing the setup file to start installation.

You can use Windows NT Client Administrator to create a network boot disk for a target computer. Exercise 3-3 shows you how to configure Windows NT Client Administrator so it will install the client files and set up the share. You need to have the Windows NT Server CD in the CD-ROM drive to perform this exercise.

FIGURE 3-3

Network installation

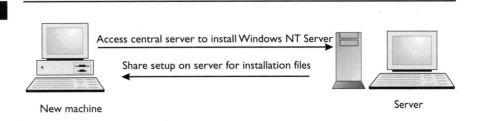

Access central server to install Windows NT Server

Share setup on server for installation files

New machine

Server

Configuring Microsoft Network Client Administrator

1. From the Start menu, select Programs | Administrative Tools (Common).

2. Click the icon for Network Client Administrator.

3. When it opens, Network Client Administrator displays a screen showing four options (see Figure 3-4). The option Make Network Installation Startup Disk should be selected by default. Click OK.

4. A screen displays (see Figure 3-5) that gives you the option to specify the path to the client files on the Windows NT CD. The destination directory where the files will be installed is also shown, as well as the name of the share.

5. The files on the CD are in the "clients" subdirectory. Most administrators use this path on their hard disk as well. The default share name is Clients.

6. Click OK. The program copies the Windows NT Client Administrator files from the CD to the hard disk and configures a network share.

Now, in Exercise 3-4, you will create an Installation Startup Disk. This is sometimes confused with an Installation Disk Set, which is a complete set of disks used to install the network client software on a PC. The Installation Startup Disk is a single bootable disk that contains the network client software and allows you to access the network share and proceed with the installation.

FIGURE 3-4

Network Client
Administrator

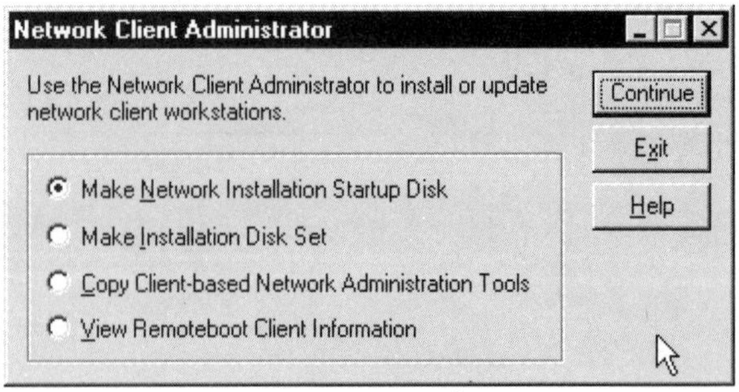

Setting up Network Client
Installation Files for client
installs

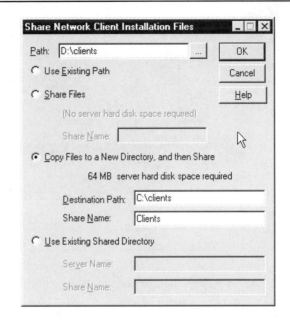

To complete this exercise you will need at least one blank floppy disk. You
should have also completed Exercise 3-3, which installs the client files and sets
up the share on the central server.

Creating a Network Boot Disk Using the Windows NT Client Administrator

1. Once the files are copied (in Exercise 3-3), you are prompted for
   what type of boot disk you want to make. The options are Network
   Client 3.0 for DOS and Windows or a Windows 95 boot disk (see
   Figure 3-6). For this exercise, select the Network Client 3.0 for DOS
   and Windows.

2. Make sure you have the appropriate network card selected and that
   your floppy disk is in the drive. Then click OK.

FIGURE 3-6

Target Workstation
Configuration

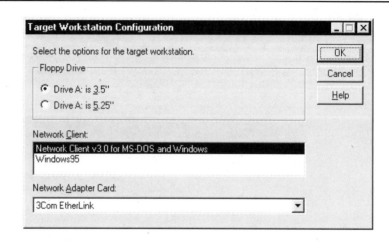

3. The next screen (see Figure 3-7) allows you to specify the computer
   name, domain, and protocol in use on the network. This is also where

FIGURE 3-7

Network Startup Disk
Configuration

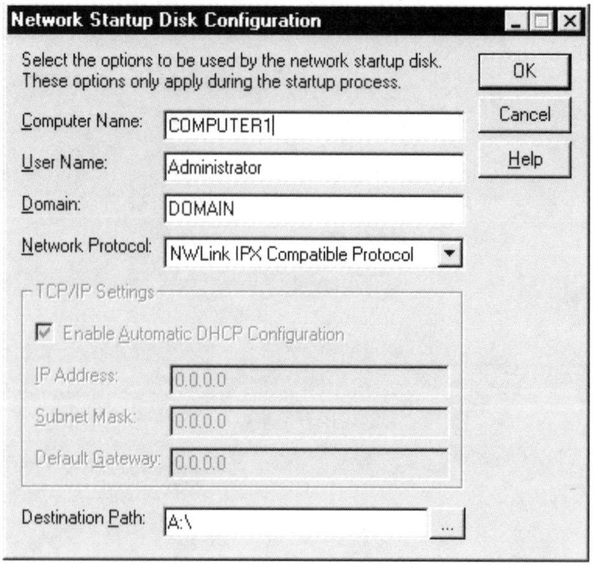

you specify the default user name to use—a name that automatically displays in parentheses during the boot process of the disk. (If you are using TCP/IP, the TCP/IP setting will not be grayed out as in Figure 3-7. If you are not using DHCP—Dynamic Host Configuration Protocol, described in Chapter 2—you will have to specify the TCP/IP information.)

4. When you have entered the settings you want to use, click OK. Network Client Administrator configures the disk as a boot disk that loads the network drivers, connects to the server, allows you to log on to the domain, and allows you to access shared resources.

Once the boot disk is created, you'll go to the computer where you are installing the network operating system, and connect to the network. However, you must first set up a share on a central Windows NT 4.0 file server, as shown in Exercise 3-5, so the new computer can access the appropriate files.

For this exercise, you will need the Windows NT Server CD. At the file server, the administrator needs to share the CD-ROM so the installation files can be accessed from a remote computer. The administrator also needs a boot disk that loads network drivers on the new computer so it can connect to the shared resource.

| EXERCISE 3-5 | **Creating a Network Share on a Central Windows NT 4.0 File Server** |

1. Make sure you are on a Windows NT 4.0 Server computer. You will need to log on as administrator in order to set up a share.

2. Double-click the My Computer icon.

3. Find the drive letter that corresponds to your CD-ROM drive (in this exercise we use D:).

4. *Right-click* on the CD-ROM drive letter and you should see a pop-up menu, as shown in Figure 3-8.

5. Select the Sharing option on the menu to open the Sharing window. Two options display: Not Shared and Shared As.

6. Select the option and enter the name of your share. For this exercise, type **NT40CD**.

FIGURE 3-8

Sharing your CD-ROM
drive in Windows NT
server

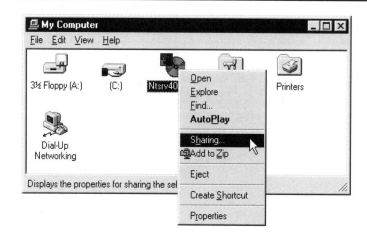

7. Click OK. Record the computer name of the server and the share
   name you just created. You will need this information when installing
   the target computer with the network boot disk. (If you don't know
   the computer name of the server, you can find it by opening the
   Control Panel and selecting the network option. Click the Network
   Properties icon and the General Tab. The computer name and domain
   name should be displayed there.)

When setting up the share on the server, some people suggest copying the
entire contents of the CD to a directory on the hard disk and then sharing
that, rather than using the CD. This can provide a faster response, due to the
fact that hard disks have faster seek times than CD-ROM drives.

Once your network boot disk is created and you have a share set up on a
central file server, you can use the floppy disk to access the share and then
install Windows NT 4.0, as shown in the remaining exercises in this section.

Exercise 3-6 shows how to connect to the network drive share that contains
the distribution files. For this exercise, you will need the network boot disk
created in Exercise 3-4. You also need to have a share set up on a central server,
as discussed in Exercise 3-5.

EXERCISE 3-6

Connect to the Network Drive Share that Contains the Distribution Files

1. Insert the network boot disk created in Exercise 3-4 into the floppy drive on the new computer.

2. As the computer boots, you should see the network drivers load and you should see a prompt that shows you a user name. You can press ENTER to use the default user name or specify a new user name at this point.

3. After you enter your user name, you will have to supply a password just as if you were logging on to the server in the graphical user interface (GUI).

4. Upon proper connection and logon, you should see the message, "This command completed properly." This tells you that you are connected.

5. At the A:> prompt, type **net use [drive letter]: \\servername\ sharename of Windows NT Server 4.0 CD**. (Specify whatever drive letter you want; the net use command maps a drive letter to the share set up on the server.) Also make sure there is a space between the colon after the drive letter and your \\servername\sharename.

6. This should connect a network drive to whatever drive letter you specified. Change to that drive and type **dir**.

7. You should see the directory of the Windows NT 4.0 Server CD.

Once you have made your share on a central server and connected to that share via the network boot disk, you are ready to start the installation process on the target computer, as shown in Exercise 3-7. For this exercise, you should have completed Exercise 3-6, where you connect to a network drive to obtain the installation files.

EXERCISE 3-7

Starting a Network Share Installation Process

1. If you are on an Intel computer, you will want to copy the entire \i386 subdirectory from the CD prior to running the setup program.

2. Make a directory on your local drive called i386. Change back to your local drive and type **md i386** from the root.

3. Then type **copy [networkdriveletter:]\i386*.***
   [localdriveletter:]\i386*.* /s. (The /s switch is an instruction to
   include all subdirectories.)

4. After all the files are copied to your local i386 directory, change to
   your local i386 directory.

5. Type **winnt /b** at the command prompt. (The /b switch indicates the
   install will not use floppy disks.) This starts the installation process.

You can run the setup program across the network, but the recommended
procedure is to copy the files locally, then run the install. The reason for this is
to prevent excess activity on the network that will affect other users. Copying
the files to your local directory is faster and it does not put as much strain on
the file server.

To run setup from the file server, you would complete Exercise 3-6 first.
Then, instead of copying files as in Exercise 3-7, you would change to the i386
directory on the network drive and then type **winnt /b** there.

Exercise 3-8 takes you through network installation, step by step. To
perform this exercise you need to make sure, at the dedicated server, that the
CD or directory containing the files is a shared resource. If necessary, refer to
Exercises 3-5 to do this. Also make sure that you have a network boot disk that
contains the MS-DOS Network Client 3.0; the disk should be set up with the
appropriate network drivers for your new computer. If necessary, refer to
Exercises 3-3 and 3-4 to complete this task.

EXERCISE 3-8

Network Installation of the Windows NT 4.0 Server

1. Insert the disk into the floppy drive of the new computer and boot up
   the machine.

2. Refer to Exercise 3-6 to log on and set up a network drive connection
   to the shared directory on the server.

3. Next, you will want to copy the installation files to the local drive.
   Refer to Exercise 3-7 for information on how to copy the files and
   start the setup program.

4. Once the setup program starts, you should be prompted for the
   location of the Windows NT Server installation files. Confirm the
   default on the screen and press ENTER.

There will be instances where as an administrator you may have to re-create the three installation boot disks. This can be done by using the Windows NT 4.0 CD. You can use various switches in conjunction with the setup file, as shown in Table 3-1 later in this chapter. You can create the boot floppy disks from a working computer (either DOS, Windows 95, or Windows NT) with the Windows NT Server CD in the CD-ROM drive. From the command prompt you would type **Winnt /ox.** (The /ox switch tells the winnt.exe file to only create the boot floppy disks and not to continue with the remaining part of the installation.)

Exercise 3-9 shows how to re-create the Windows NT boot floppy disks. For this exercise, you will need three blank, formatted high-density floppy disks.

EXERCISE 3-9

Re-creating Windows NT Boot Floppy Disks

1. On a working DOS, Windows 95, or Windows NT computer (either server or workstation), insert the Windows NT 4.0 Server CD into your CD-ROM drive.

2. At the command prompt, type the driver letter of your CD-ROM drive. For example, type **D:** if your CD-ROM drive letter is D.

3. Change to the subdirectory of the computer type you will be installing. In this exercise type **cd i386**. (This is for an Intel-type computer.)

4. From the command prompt type **winnt /ox**.

5. Follow the prompts on the screen. The setup program should prompt you for each of the three blank disks.

Notice that the setup program creates the disks in reverse order. The third disk is created first and the first disk is created last. The setup program tells you this, but many people overlook it. *Be sure to label the disks accordingly.*

Network Installation Switches

When you install Windows NT in a network installation setting, there are various switches that can be used (see Table 3-1). These switches can make a network installation go more smoothly and quickly. In most cases the '/b' switch is used in a network installation. This switch controls whether or not floppy disks are needed during the installation. In most cases, an administrator would not want to use the floppy disks if they were installing over the network.

TABLE 3-1

Switches Available for Winnt.exe or Winnt32.exe

Switch	Result
/b	Floppyless install
/c	Tells setup not to check for free disk space on setup boot floppy disks
/e	Specifies command to execute when setup is finished
/i	Specifies the name of the setup information file
/f	Tells setup to not verify files as they are copied to setup boot floppy disks
/ox	Creates the boot floppy disks only. Doesn't actually install Windows NT Server
/r or /rx	Specifies optional directory to be installed; the /RX denotes optional directory to be copied
/s	Lets the administrator specify the location of the source files (for example, winnt /s:location or \\server\share\[path:])
/t	Tells setup where to put the temporary installation files (for example, winnt /t:location). This must be a local drive
/u	This is used for Unattended Installations; requires /s
/udf	Specify the Uniqueness Database File to use for unattended installation
/x	Do not create boot floppy disks

exam
ⓦatch

You may see one or two questions about the switch combinations on the exam. Be sure to look over Table 3-1 before you take the exam.

The setup program contains two parts. The installation process starts in text mode, and the second part uses the Windows NT GUI. The text part of the progam:

- Identifies correct hardware
- Confirms selection of partitions

■ Confirms file system to be used for Windows NT

■ Confirms the directory where Windows NT Server will be installed

■ Copies essentials files to hard disk so setup can start NT upon reboot

Exercise 3-10 shows you how to use the text portion of the setup process.

EXERCISE 3-10

Using the Text Part of the Windows NT Setup Program

1. When you start the Windows NT Server setup process, the first screen shows the setup program loading various drivers.

2. The next screen identifies all hardware in your system. Your options are:

F1	Get help on installation (good for first-time installers)
ENTER	Set up Windows NT Server
R	Repair a damaged Windows NT Server install
F3	Quit without installing

3. Press ENTER to continue. You will see a list of drives that Windows NT setup detects. You can press the S key if you need to specify additional CD-ROM drives or SCSI adapters. (Note: If no CD-ROM drive is displayed, setup cannot continue unless you specify more devices by pressing S. You'll need the driver disks from your CD/SCSI manufacturer to install these devices.) Once you have installed the necessary devices, press ENTER to continue to the next screen.

4. The next screen shows the License Agreement. Scroll down to the bottom of the agreement and press F8 to continue. F8 is the equivalent of agreeing to the License Agreement. If you don't agree with the agreement, you can press ESC; in that case, setup will not continue.

5. On the next screen you should see a summary display of components on your system, including computer type, display, keyboard, keyboard layout, pointing device, and so forth. If everything looks okay, choose Accept. If something needs to be changed, use the arrow keys to scroll up to the option and make the change. When all the necessary changes have been made, press ENTER.

6. The next screen allows you to specify information about the various partitions. *Be very careful on this screen: Pressing D will delete the highlighted partition!* The F1 help on this section is good.

7. Once you select a partition, the setup program asks what you want to do with the partition. The options are: Format the partition (you can select from FAT or NTFS); Select a different partition; Convert a selected FAT partition to NTFS (if you are installing to an existing volume); Leave the current file system intact. This is a good choice, especially if you are installing for the first time.

8. The next screen asks you to specify the directory where you want to install Windows NT 4.0 Server.

9. Next you have an opportunity to run exhaustive diagnostics on the drive you are installing to. If you press ENTER the setup program will perform an exhaustive test of the hard disk. If you press ESC, it performs a short test of the drive and setup continues.

10. In the final screen of the text section, the program copies files to the specified path. After the files are copied, setup prompts you to remove floppy disk from disk drives and the CD from the CD-ROM drive.

Once all the temporary files have been copied to the appropriate subdirectories, the system reboots and the setup program continues to the graphical portion of the installation, where all the important configuration items are chosen. The graphical portion uses the Windows NT Setup wizard, which divides the installation into three sections. The first is called the Information Gathering, the second is Installing Windows NT Networking, and the final phase is Finishing Setup. Although the Windows Setup wizard proceeds directly through the three sections, we describe each section in a separate exercise for convenience.

Information Gathering

Exercise 3-11 guides you through the first section of the GUI setup, Information Gathering.

EXERCISE 3-11

Using the NT Setup Wizard—Information Gathering

1. When the wizard displays, click Next to proceed. The first screen you see asks you to enter your name and organization. The NAME field is

required, but the ORGANIZATION field is optional. Click Next to continue.

2. In the next screen you have to select how you want your server licensing set up. You have two options: Per Server or Per Seat. Refer to the discussion of licensing in the first section of this chapter if you need to review these options.

3. The next screen asks you to enter the CD key, which is a portion of the software serial number. The CD KEY, as on most Microsoft software, is located on the back of the CD sleeve or back of the CD jewel case. Enter the CD key and click Next to continue.

4. The next step is vital to the future of your server. This screen allows you to specify the name of the server computer. Enter the server name, then click Next to continue.

5. The next screen also contains an important decision-making step. You need to choose which server role you want your server to fulfill. Refer to the section on Server Roles near the end of this chapter if you need to examine these options.

6. Next, you need to enter the Administrator password. *Be sure to keep this information in a secure location in case you should forget it!* You will have to enter the password twice. The password must be 14 characters or less. Click Next to continue.

7. Next you must choose whether or not you want a repair disk. A repair disk is recommended for fixing crashed servers. If you don't create a repair disk now, you can use the RDISK utility at a later time to create or update a repair disk. (Chapter 14 covers Windows NT repair disks.) Click Next to continue.

8. In the next screen, you need components for the final installation, including:

   ■ **Accessories** 13 components—calculator, screen savers
   ■ **Communications** 3 components—chat, Hyperterminal
   ■ **Games** 4 components—FreeCell, Solitaire
   ■ **Multimedia** 9 components—CD Player, sound schemes
   ■ **Windows Messaging** 3 components—Internet Mail

Choose the components you want to install, then click Next to proceed.

9. A transition screen shows that you are now entering the second section of the GUI setup: Installing Windows Networking.

Installing Windows NT Networking

Exercise 3-12 guides you through the second section, Installing Windows NT Networking.

EXERCISE 3-12

Using the NT Setup Wizard—Installing Windows NT Networking

1. The first screen asks if your server will be wired directly to the network or be accessing the network remotely. In most cases your server will be wired directly to the network. Choose the appropriate option, then click Next to continue.

2. The next screen is the Install Microsoft Internet Information Server screen. This option is not needed unless your domain is wired directly to the Internet and you will use IIS to run your Web site. This can also be used for your company intranet, if you have one.

3. Next you need to select the type of network adapter to be used. You can choose Start Search to have the program look for an adapter card, or choose Select from list to identify the card in use. Once you have identified the appropriate card, click Next to continue.

4. Next you must tell Windows NT Server what protocols the network will use to communicate. Windows NT Server can communicate with the following protocols: TCP/IP, NWLink (IPX/SPX-compatible), and NetBEUI (NetBIOS Enhanced User Interface). You can use the Select from List option to install some other protocols including DLC, PPTP, and Streams. When you finish this task, click Next to continue.

5. The next screen allows you to install Network Services such as DNS Server, Windows Internet Names Service, or Remote Access Server. Choose the services you want, then click Next to continue.

6. The next screen deals with the copying of network components. You may see one of several screens, depending on what protocols you selected previously.

■ If you selected NWLink (IPX/SPX-compatible transport), you will be prompted for the frame type you want to use.

■ If you selected TCP/IP, you will see a question about DHCP as well as a screen to specify the TCP/IP properties.

Answer the questions, then click Next to proceed.

7. Next you see a screen on network bindings. In most cases, the defaults are fine unless you need to remove or add something specific. Click Next to continue.

8. Now you have two choices. You can click Next to start the network and continue setup or you can click Back to stop the network if it is running. You have to choose Next to complete setup. If Windows NT Server is successful in starting the network, the setup program will continue to copy files. If starting the network is unsuccessful, you will be prompted to change to configuration of the network adapter—for instance, its IRQ (interrupt request identifier) or base port address.

9. The next screen varies according to the type of server you are installing. If you are installing a Primary Domain Controller, you simply have to specify the Computer Name and the Domain Name. If you are installing a Backup Domain Controller or a Stand Alone Server, you will have four fields to complete: Computer Name, Domain Name, Administrator User Name, and Administrator Password. You need the administrator's user name and password so the Backup Domain Controller can be added to the domain. If the username and password you specify do not have administrator privileges, the computer will not be added to the domain.

10. A transition screen shows that you will now enter the third phase of the graphical portion of setup: Finishing Setup.

Finishing Setup

Exercise 3-13 guides you through the final section of the wizard, Finishing Setup.

EXERCISE 3-13

Using the NT Setup Wizard—Finishing Setup

1. During this final phase you will see a series of screens that show the copying of files, setup of program groups, etc.

2. If you installed Internet Information Server 2.0, you will be prompted to verify the directory names for this application.

3. Next you will be asked to set up the time, time zone, and date information.

4. Next you will have an oppotunity to adjust your display properties. The setup program should check your system for the appropriate video adapter and install the driver. You may find that the setup program installs a standard VGA driver. If this occurs, all you have to do is change it after setup is completed.

5. The next screen you see depends on whether you chose to create a repair disk earlier in the setup process. If so, this is the place where the disk is created. If not, you can still create the repair disk at a later time with the RDISK utility.

6. Next you see the final copying of files for Windows NT Server.

7. Finally, Windows NT Server setup configures Windows Messaging and saves the final configuration. (Note: If you decide to install Windows NT Server on a NTFS partition you will see the format and installation take place on a FAT partition. After a successful installation Windows NT Server converts the partition to NTFS. The setup program ensures that everything was successful before it continues.) You should see a successful message, then the system reboots.

CD-ROM Installation

If the computer you are configuring has the option, you can boot directly from the Windows NT Server CD-ROM. The option to boot from the CD-ROM drive is configured from within the computer's BIOS. If you are installing directly from the CD you should make sure that the CD-ROM drive is compatible with Windows NT. If the CD-ROM drive is not supported, you could run into problems later on if you try to configure Windows NT and the operating system prompts you for the CD. If your CD is unsupported under Windows NT Server 4.0, you should copy the contents of the appropriate subdirectory to your hard disk prior to installation and run the setup program from there.

Exercise 3-14 shows how to start a CD-ROM installation without floppy disks. For this exercise, you will need the Windows NT 4.0 Server CD.

EXERCISE 3-14

Starting a CD-ROM Installation Without Floppy Disks

1. Be sure that the computer you are installing has the CD-ROM drive set up as a bootable device. In order to work properly, this drive should be ahead of your hard disks in the boot order.

2. With the CD in the CD-ROM drive, reboot or turn on your computer.

3. Upon booting from the CD the installation program will start automatically.

QUESTIONS AND ANSWERS

I want to install Windows NT Server. I do not have a bootable CD-ROM drive and one of my boot disks is giving me a read error consistently.	On a working computer with a CD-ROM drive, use the winnt.exe setup utility to re-create the floppy disks by using the /ox switch.
I am getting ready to install Windows NT Server 4.0 on a computer with Windows 95 already on it. I want to keep Windows 95 available as a boot option and allow the Windows 95 operating system to view the contents on my NT 4.0 Server drives created with Disk Administrator. What do I have to do?	In this scenario you need to use FAT for two reasons. The first reason is to enable Windows 95 to boot. If you install NT into an existing FAT partition, you want to retain the FAT partition so the original OS can still boot. Windows 95 can only read FAT partitions. If you were to create a new drive letter from within Windows NT Disk Administrator using NTFS, Windows 95 would not be able to read the contents of that drive.
I am installing across the network and do not want the setup program to even mention using the boot floppy disks. What command or switch do I need to use in this instance?	In this instance you would use the /b switch.
I want to create a network boot disk with Network Client Administrator (NCA). I've never run NCA before. In which subdirectory of the Windows NT Server 4.0 CD are the files kept? What is the default share name specified upon first-time setup?	\Clients and Clients
I am setting up a new computer and I want to name it NEWSALESCOMPUTER12A. I consistently get errors when I try to name the computer. Why?	NetBIOS names are limited to 15 characters.
I have only 80MB of free space left on my main hard disk in my Intel computer and I want to install Windows NT Server 4.0. Can I install it?	You need at least 124MB of free space to install Windows NT Server 4.0. It is recommended that you have more, but 124MB is the bare minimum.

Installing NT on RISC-based Computers

One of the nice things about Windows NT Server is the fact that you can install it on multiple platforms. You can install Windows NT on a RISC-based system, but you must use a FAT partition for the system files. With RISC-based systems, the partitions must be set up ahead of time. Windows NT cannot set up and configure RISC partitions.

Upgrade Installation

If you currently have a server running Windows NT 3.51, you can install NT 4.0 Server as an upgrade. You can also upgrade from DOS, Windows 3.1, Windows for Workgroups 3.11, and Windows 95. One important note: later releases of Windows 95 use the FAT32 file format, so make sure you are not trying to upgrade in a FAT32 environment. Windows NT 4.0 cannot access the FAT32 file system.

To upgrade from a previous version of Windows NT, you run the Winnt32.exe file. The first part of the upgrade process is the same as the normal installation. The setup program copies files from the CD into temporary directories on the hard disk (see Figure 3-9).

Once the files are copied to the temporary directory, you will be prompted to reboot or stay in the current version of Windows NT (see Figure 3-10).

You will have the option to overwrite the existing operating system or install a dual-boot computer. If you choose to have a dual-boot machine, the boot loader menu will have a selection that allows you to choose the original operating system.

Of course, when upgrading you want to be sure and have a complete server backup available—in case the setup fails to complete and you have to revert to the original version. The following case study recounts an instance where a known good backup saved a company thousands!

A medical center had a Microsoft Windows NT 3.51 Server with various NT Workstations and Windows for Workgroups clients. This particular server was a Compaq ProLiant with a built-in CD-ROM drive and a Plextor 8 CD attached to it. An upgrade was scheduled for Saturday. Halfway through the installation, the server rebooted and the drive letters changed—which caused

FIGURE 3-9

Windows NT Upgrade
copies file to temporary
directory on hard disk

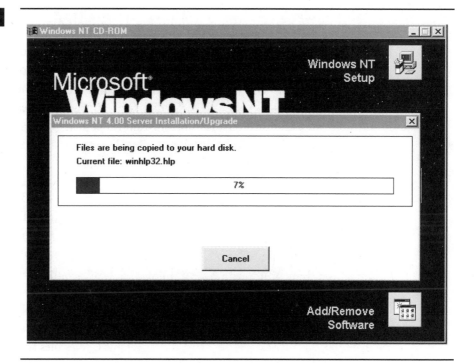

the entire upgrade to come to a screeching halt. Trying to reboot the server
into Windows NT 3.51 did not work.

The only option was to reinstall Windows NT Server 3.51, then restore
from backup. Then we started over on the upgrade. However, this time we

FIGURE 3-10

Rebooting during the
upgrade

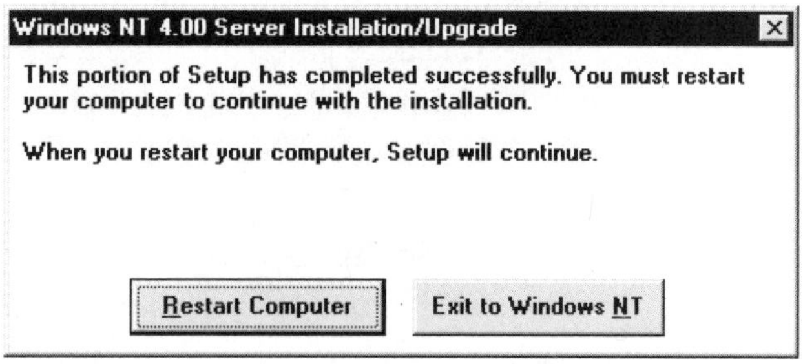

Windows NT 4.00 Server Installation/Upgrade ☒

This portion of Setup has completed successfully. You must restart
your computer to continue with the installation.

When you restart your computer, Setup will continue.

[**R**estart Computer]   [Exit to Windows **NT**]

disconnected the Plextor so that no drive letters would be changed in the middle of the installation process!

When upgrading from Windows NT 3.51 to Windows NT 4.0 you should be aware that the two products do not use the same default directory. By default, Windows NT 3.51 is installed in the \NT351 directory and Windows NT 4.0 uses the \WINNT directory. However, to maintain desktop, applications, and user information it is a good idea to put the upgrade files into the directory where the original version of NT had been located on that computer (in other words, in directory \NT351, *not* \WINNT). If you do not specify this directory when upgrading, you will end up with a dual-boot computer.

Of course the other big change with the transition from Windows NT 3.51 to Windows 4.0 is the GUI. The desktop and the product "look and feel" of Windows NT 4.0 is more like Windows 95. The change is similar to going from Windows 3.1 or Windows for Workgroups 3.11 to Windows 95. If your organization is used to the Windows 3.1 look of NT 3.51 it is essential to plan some training before the upgrade, to make end users comfortable with the new interface.

Unattended Installation

If you are deploying a large network with many servers and workstations, an unattended installation can make the operation much more efficient. Windows NT Server gives you the option to create an unattended answer file. Windows NT Server 4.0 CD contains a utility in the support\deptools\ <computer type> subdirectory called SETUPMGR (see Figure 3-11). This is a GUI program that will help you set up answer files for unattended installation.

There are three groups of options: General Setup, Network Setup, and Advanced Setup. The following sections describe how to set the options in each category.

General Setup Options

The General Setup Options screen covers basic information about the installation. The first tab is the User Information tab, shown in Figure 3-12, which includes User Name, Organization, Computer Name, and Product ID.

FIGURE 3-11

Setup Manager

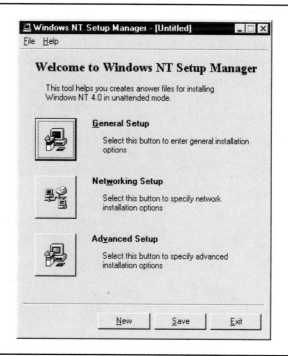

The General tab includes basic information about how setup will run in unattended mode. For example, you can specify that you want setup to confirm hardware during setup and you can list upgrade options. You can even specify that you want to run a program during setup.

On the Computer Role tab you choose one of the following as a role for the computer:

- Primary Domain Controller
- Backup Domain Controller
- Stand Alone Server in Domain
- Stand Alone Server in Workgroup
- Workstation in Domain
- Workstation in Workgroup

FIGURE 3-12

General Setup Options
window in SETUPMGR

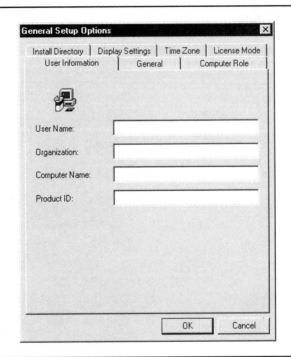

Along with the computer role you can specify the Workgroup name, if applicable, or the Account Name, if appropriate.

The License Mode lets you specify the license mode if the Computer Role tab indicates the computer is being set up as a Server or Domain Controller. If you have Workstation in a Workgroup or Domain you do not need to complete the License Mode tab.

The Time Zone tab is self-explanatory: it lets you select the time zone where the computer is located.

The Display Settings tab enables you to configure Display Properties during installation. You can set up refresh rate, horizontal and vertical resolution, bits per pixel, and various flags.

The Install Directory tab lets you specify where the installation files will be located. Choices here include: Use default directory, Prompt user for installation directory, and Specify installation directory now.

Networking Options

The Networking Options area includes information on network adapter card configuration, bindings, protocols, Internet, and modem. The General tab, shown in Figure 3-13, allows you to specify whether you want a manual network installation or an unattended network installation. As part of the Unattended option, you can ask setup to detect and install the first network adapter it finds or you can ask it to detect specific adapters. Alternatively, you can bypass the detection stage and specify what adapters to install.

On the Adapters tab, you can specify the network adapters to install.

On the Protocols tab, you can specify what protocols to load and install. Only the three basic Windows NT networking protocols are listed in this section: TCP/IP, NetBEUI, and NWLink (IPX/SPX-Compatible Transport).

FIGURE 3-13

General tab of Networking Options window in SETUPMGR

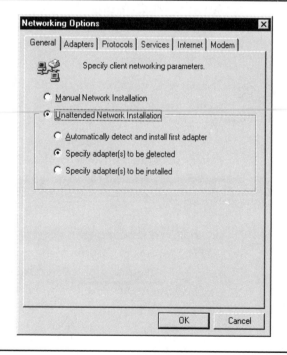

The Services tab allows you to specify which network services to install. The available options by default include SNMP (Simple Network Management Protocol), Client Services for NetWare, and RAS (Remote Access Service).

The Internet tab is accessible only if the computer role in the General Setup section is set up as a server. If it is, this tab tells the setup program to install Internet Information Server (IIS) and gives configuration information for it. For example, you can tell setup where to install IIS and what subdirectories to set up for FTP, WWW, and Gopher. You can choose which options you want installed: Internet Service Manager (ISM), HTMLA (an HTML version of ISM), and sample Web pages. You can also specify the guest account username and password to set up.

The Modem tab must be completed only if the Remote Access Service is selected in the Services tab. You can specify the COM port, modem type, manufacturer, provider, as well as the driver to install.

Advanced Options

The Advanced Options window allows advanced users to specify additional information for the unattended installation process. The General tab in the Advanced Options, shown in Figure 3-14, lets you specify information on the Hardware Abstraction Layer (HAL), the keyboard layout, whether or not to reboot after text and graphic setup sections, and whether to skip the Welcome Wizard page and Administrator Password wizard.

The File System tab allows you to select whether you want to leave the current file system intact or convert the file system to NTFS. You also have the option here to extend the partition beyond two gigabytes (a FAT limitation), if you convert to NTFS.

The Mass Storage tab allows you specify additional mass storage devices to install drivers for during installation.

The Display tab, Pointing Device tab, and the Keyboard tab all let you specify display drivers for the installation process.

The Advertisement tab lets you customize the banner text, logo, and background information for your installation. This is a spot where network administrators can gratify their egos by personalizing an unattended installation.

The Boot Files tab allows you to specify a list of boot files.

FIGURE 3-14

General tab of Advanced
Options window in
SETUPMGR

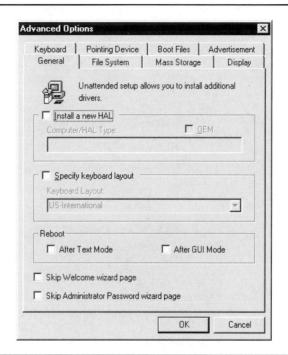

Once you've supplied the appropriate information, click the Save button in
the main SETUPMGR window. You can give the file any name you want; it
will have a .txt extension. There is also a New button on the main window,
which clears all the information in the highlighted section so you can start
over.

Exercise 3-15 describes how to create an unattended answer file.

EXERCISE 3-15

Creating an Unattended Installation Answer File

1. To become familiar with the SETMGR, use the following scenario to
   create an answer file that will set up a server in a domain:

   ■ **Username** Bill Byttes

   ■ **Organization** Acme Inc.

   ■ **Computer Name** Bill's Machine

   ■ Be sure to confirm the hardware during setup

- Use the default install directory
- Configure the graphics device at logon
- Have setup choose the Bogota, Lima time zone
- Convert the existing file system to NTFS
- Add a 3COM Etherlink III Adapter
- You need to have TCP/IP and NWLink IPX/SPX loaded
- Be sure to skip the Welcome Wizard page
- Set up Per Server licensing with 100 licenses
- You have Novell workstations on your network, so be sure to add Client Services for Netware

2. Save the file, then try using it in an unattended installation. Remember to use the /u switch.

Once you've created the answer file, you have to tell setup where to get the file when the installation process begins. As mentioned earlier, the switch to use for an unattended answer file is: /u. For example you would type:

winnt /u:unattend.txt /s:{source}

Unattended Setup and the Uniqueness Database File

When deploying large networks, the unattended answer file is a great tool for speeding up the installation process. When you have ten or more machines to set up and install on your network, creating an answer file for each can be tedious. Windows NT allows the creation of what is called a Uniqueness Database File (UDF).

A UDF allows an administrator to specify information for each individual workstation or server that is being installed. Items such as computer name, IP address (in a static IP environment), time zone, and other information can be specified on a per-machine basis. To use a UDF, a valid answer file must already exist.

The UDF is created as a text file that contains information to be merged into the default answer file. This is done through the use of specific switches with winnt.exe or winnt32.exe.

An example of a command line use:

winnt /u:unattend.txt /s:d:\ /t:c: /udf:useridl,z:\udf.txt

e x a m
ⓦa t c h

This information is not presented in depth in the exam. But be sure to understand the difference between the /u and /udf switches and their respective purposes.

CERTIFICATION OBJECTIVE 3.03

Server Roles

One of the most common concepts you will hear throughout your studies will be that of the *domain*. A domain, as shown in Figure 3-15, is a group of computers containing domain controllers that share account information and have one centralized accounts database. An administrator needs to determine what role the server or servers will play in the domain model. This is an important step in the installation process. A server can belong to only one domain.

The Windows NT operating system has various roles a server can play. Remember, each server can only fulfill one role. The three possibilities are: Primary Domain Controller (PDC), a Backup Domain Controller (BDC), or Member Server (MS). Choosing whether the server will be a domain controller is a very important decision in the installation process. At the beginning of an installation, you must choose a role for the server you are setting up. If you make a mistake, you will have to restart the installation process.

Security is an important consideration when designing your network. An important role of domain controllers is to maintain security information— accounts information and the accounts database—for the domain. Domain controllers share a common security policy. The domain can also contain stand-alone (member) servers that do not maintain account and security information.

FIGURE 3-15

Simple domain model
showing various
server roles

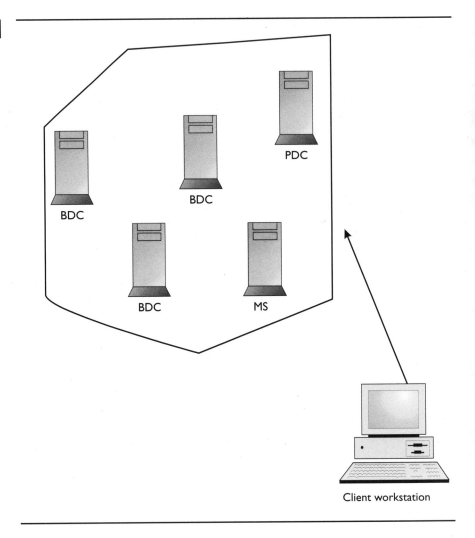

Client workstation

Primary Domain Controller (PDC)

A PDC is the central server in the network. There must be one—and only one—PDC per domain. If the server you are installing is the first computer in the domain, it will be installed as a PDC. If you are not installing a PDC, another PDC must already be connected to the network.

When installing the PDC you have the opportunity to name the domain. This is an important step, because it affects how the remaining servers and workstations will be named. When other servers and workstations are added to the domain, the domain name—the name you assigned when you set up the PDC—will become part of each server or workstation name.

The master accounts database resides on the PDC. Synchronization is the process of copying the security information (accounts and permissions) to the BDC's and performing periodic updates to keep the information up-to-date. This database is synchronized on the BDC's only. The domain administrator sets up synchronization and specifies how often it will occur.

Backup Domain Controller (BDC)

A BDC serves multiple purposes in a Windows NT Domain. The rule of thumb is to have at least one BDC per domain. As mentioned in the preceding paragraph, the BDC is responsible for helping maintain user account database information. When installing the BDC you must know the name of the domain to which you are assigning it. Whoever installs the BDC must have administrative privileges in the domain. Since BDC's cannot be added to the network prior to installation, administrative privileges are needed to add machines to the network.

When a non-domain controller computer starts up, it goes through a process called *discovery*. That means the workstation looks across the network for a domain controller in its domain (and in all "trusted" domains; refer to the section "Trust Relationships" in Chapter 7). Once the workstation locates a domain controller, it uses that BDC or PDC for subsequent authentication.

BDC's can authenticate users when they log on to the domain. If the BDC fails to authenticate the user, then the logon request is passed to the PDC for authentication.

Another function of the BDC is to back up the PDC in the event of a PDC crash. Promotion of a BDC to a PDC by the domain administrator allows the BDC to take over the primary roll in the domain. This is the only type of server within Windows NT that can be changed without reinstalling.

FROM THE CLASSROOM

The Number One Problem in Installing BDCs

Once you have your planning done, and have made sure that your hardware is compatible (or that you have all of the OEM diskettes you might need to install any hardware that isn't on the distribution CD-ROM), NT installation is pretty straightforward.

Then you come to the dialog box that asks you to set the role for the server. You have three choices: PDC, BDC and member server. In the classroom, we frequently pretend that the students are servers, and set them up in domains. One student is the PDC, others are BDCs or member servers. We make a point of emphasizing that anyone who is a BDC must wait until the PCD is completely installed before they can perform their installation. In every class, there are several students who ask for help because they get hung up when they try to select a role. This is because the installation cannot find the PDC. Of course not—their domain partner has not yet completed the installation of the PDC!

The same problem arises at our clients' sites, where the environment is not so tightly controlled. There are two situations when it can occur. The first is when IP subnetting is in place. The administrator is attempting to install a BDC on one subnet and the primary is on another subnet with no gateway (router) between them. Of course the BDC cannot find the PDC, and installation cannot continue. A more mysterious variation of this same theme occurs when the PDC is on one subnet and the BDC is on another and a router *does* exist between the subnets. The problem is solved, right? So why does the setup program return an error saying that the BCD cannot locate the PDC? If you find the answer to this question, please let us know!

The second situation occurs when the client is installing the BDC at a remote site and the PDC is on the net connected by a WAN link. Can you anticipate the problem? You guessed it! In our scenario, the administrator has planned a one-day trip to the remote site, many miles away, and arrives to find that the WAN link is down. Of course, the administrator discovers this during the installation. And the WAN provider promises the link should be up shortly—a story that's right up there with "the check is in the mail." For the next two days, the WAN link "bounces" up and down. If only you could predict the "up" times, you might be able to finish the installation! Too often, in this case, we get a request for support from the administrator who explains the symptoms to us,

Member Server

A member server (sometimes referred to as a stand-alone server) is not a domain controller. Member servers have no responsibility in the accounts database and security information. They are used for application servers, print servers, or SQL servers. They are dedicated to process high-end searches, and non-security type functions. They help take the load off your domain controllers, which can concentrate on security and account information processing.

Server Promotion Rules

When something happens to the PDC, such as a crash or being taken offline for an upgrade, then the administrator must decide how the domain will function. If the PDC will be offline for an extended period, a BDC can be promoted to a PDC to take over the domain. When you try to bring a PDC back online, it will check the domain. If another BDC has been promoted to PDC, the original PDC will not be able to log on to the network. The administrator will have to use the Server Manager to demote the original PDC. (The Promote option on the Computer menu in Server Manager changes to a Demote option if the original PDC is highlighted on the list of computers in the domain.)

Stand-alone servers cannot be promoted or demoted. The only way to change the role of a member server is to reinstall Windows NT Server on the machine. The same applies to PDC's and BDC's. If an administrator wants to change an existing domain controller to a member server, the operating system must be reinstalled on that particular machine.

When promoting a BDC to a PDC there are two distinct possible scenarios. The BDC can be promoted while the existing PDC is still online or it can be done after the PDC has been taken offline.

If administrators know the current PDC will be offline, they can promote a BDC to a PDC to keep the domain alive. This is only recommended if the PDC will be down for an extended period. The master accounts database is synchronized on the BDC being promoted. When the BDC is promoted, the operating system automatically "demotes" the PDC, since there can't be multiple PDC's in the domain.

If a PDC is in danger of crashing, the domain administrator must decide how to maintain the domain. If the BDC is promoted while the PDC is already offline, the BDC uses the most recent update it has for the account database. If a domain synchronization hasn't been done for a while and users have been added at the PDC, *those users will be lost*. When the original PDC returns to service, it will have to be demoted before it can return to the domain. This is done with the Demote option on the Computer menu of the Server Manager utility, shown in Figure 3-16. Remember, the user who performs this activity must have domain administrator permissions.

exam
ⓦatch

Make sure you have a clear understanding of the promotion/demotion process. A Backup Domain Controller can be promoted to a Primary Domain Controller if the current PDC is going to be taken offline or if it has already been taken offline. If taken offline, the original PDC will have to be demoted before it can return to the domain. If the PDC is online when the BDC is promoted, the demotion takes place automatically. If the PDC is already offline when the BDC is promoted, the system administrator will have to use the Server Manager utility to demote the old PDC. Stand-alone or member servers cannot be changed to a domain controller without reinstalling Windows NT Server. Similarly, a domain controller cannot be converted to a member server without reinstalling.

FIGURE 3-16

Server Manager with
Promote to PDC
highlighted

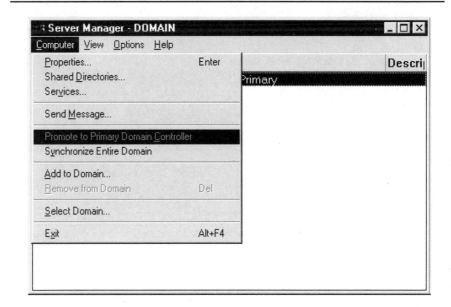

CERTIFICATION OBJECTIVE 3.04

Removing Windows NT

If you replace your server, you may want to remove Windows NT Server from
the hard disk of the old server. There are a couple of ways to do this. You can
delete the partition or you can simply delete the system files. The second
method is better since it keeps other data intact.

Deleting FAT Partitions

You can use FDISK from DOS or Windows 95 to delete a FAT partition.
Some administrators think they can use Windows NT Disk Administrator to
remove the system partition. This is incorrect. Disk Administrator lets you
delete partitions, but *not* the system partition. Excercise 3-16 shows you how
to delete a FAT partition.

EXERCISE 3-16	**Deleting a FAT Partition**

1. Boot your server with a DOS or Windows 95 boot disk that contains FDISK.EXE and FORMAT.COM.

2. When you see the A:> prompt, type **FDISK**.

3. You will see a menu that looks like Figure 3-17.

FIGURE 3-17	

FDISK Menu (Windows 95 version)

```
              Microsoft Windows 95

          Fixed Disk Setup Program

      (C) Copyright Microsoft Corp. 1983-1995



                  FIDISK Options

      Current fixed disk drive: 1


      Choose one of the following:


      1. Create DOS partition or Logical DOS Drive

      2. Set active partition

      3. Delete partition or Logical DOS Drive

      4. Display partition information

      5. Change current fixed disk drive




      Enter Choice: [1]



      Press Esc to exit FDISK
```

4. Choose option number 3: Delete partition or Logical DOS drive. You will see a list of partitions currently on your drive.

5. When you select a partition to remove, you will be prompted for the partition name, to make sure you selected the appropriate one.

6. Once the partition is removed you need to reboot so the changes will take effect. Keep the floppy disk in the drive and reboot to the boot machine.

7. When you get to the A:> type **FDISK** to get back into FDISK. This time you will have to select option number 1 to create a new DOS partition to replace the old one. You will have to reboot one more time.

8. When you are back at the A:> prompt, type **Format <driveletter>:**.

9. You will be prompted to be sure that you want to destroy all data on that drive.

10. After the drive is formatted it will be blank. You can now install a different operating system on it.

Deleting NTFS Partitions

You cannot use the FDISK utility from the DOS and Windows 95 operating systems to delete NTFS partitions because DOS and Window 95 do not recognize NTFS partitions. A utility such as DELPART, found in the Windows NT Resource Kit CD, can be used. DELPART is also available for download from the Internet. Use one of the major search engines, such as Yahoo or Excite, to locate it.

One other option for deleting an NTFS partition is to use the OS/2 version of FDISK. You can use the /D option to delete a partition.

If installing MS DOS 6 or later, you can go through the installation process to remove Windows NT and set up a new master boot record. Boot with the first disk of the installation set. When prompted, choose the Remove files option.

One final way to delete an NTFS partition is to initiate a new Windows NT Server installation and choose Delete partition in the text portion of the setup process.

Removing Windows NT from a FAT Partition

If you don't want to destroy the data on your drive but want to remove Windows NT Server 4.0, you can delete certain system files. There are hidden, read-only system files on the drive root that you need to remove. You also need to remove some files in the Windows NT root (the subdirectory where you installed Windows NT Server—the default location is c:\WINNT). This procedure, described in Exercise 3-17, will work only if the partition is FAT, not NTFS.

EXERCISE 3-17

Deleting the System Files to Remove Windows NT from a FAT Partition

1. Boot to a DOS boot disk that has ATTRIB.EXE, SYS.COM, and DELTREE.EXE from DOS or Windows 95.

2. Once you are at the A:> prompt, type **DELTREE c:\WINNT** If WINNT is the Windows NT root (the directory where you installed Windows NT 4.0 Server).

3. There will probably be a file named pagefile.sys on the drive root. This file will also have to be deleted. Type **DEL c:\pagefile.sys**.

4. There are a handful of other files you need to delete as well, but they are hidden system files. Type **ATTRIB c:\<FILENAME> -h -r -s**. This will have to be done for the following files:

   ■ NTLDR

   ■ BOOT.INI

   ■ BOOTSECT.DOS

   ■ NTBOOTDD.SYS

   ■ NTDETECT.COM

5. Once you have changed the attributes of the files listed above, then you can go ahead and delete them. Type **DEL c:\<FILENAME>** for each of the above files, to delete it.

6. The final step to uninstalling Windows NT Server is to restore the DOS Master Boot Record. Type **SYS c:** and reboot.

7. Upon rebooting, you should see a C:> prompt where you can load your new operating system.

Changing the Boot Loader in an Existing FAT Partition to MS-DOS

When Windows NT Server installs the master boot record on the drive is changed. In the event that a server needs to be set up with a different operating system, you need to make sure that the master boot record is rewritten for the operating system you have chosen. There are a couple of ways to do this. The first is shown in Exercise 3-18, which shows you how to change the boot loader in an existing FAT partition to MS-DOS.

EXERCISE 3-18

Changing the Boot Loader in an Existing FAT Partition to MS-DOS

1. Use a DOS/Windows 95 boot disk and the SYS utility to configure the master boot record.

2. Insert the boot disk in the drive. Be sure that this disk has the file SYS.COM.

3. At the A:> prompt type **SYS C:**.

4. Reboot the machine. Now you should boot to a C:> prompt.

If you do not want to remove Windows NT Server and simply want to make MS-DOS your default operating system, you can change the startup process within Control Panel. The procedure for doing this is described in Exercise 3-19.

EXERCISE 3-19

Setting MS-DOS as your Default Operating System

1. Select Start | Settings | Control Panel.

2. In Control Panel, select the System icon.

3. In the System properties window, select the Startup tab.

4. In this windows select MS-DOS in the startup box and enter the number 0 in the Show List for box.

QUESTIONS AND ANSWERS

I want to set up a server that will not be bothered with maintaining account information. What do I want to install?	You should set up a member server, which has no responsibility with the user account database.
My PDC just crashed and I need to keep the domain running. What do I do?	Use Server Manager to promote a BDC to PDC.
As a new member of Technical Support, I got a call from an Administrator who said that she was having a problem setting up a second PDC in her Domain Ajax. What should I tell her?	Only one PDC is allowed per domain.
I am the administrator of a domain that has one PDC and one BDC designated for each satellite office, but they are located in our local office. 15,000 client workstations are spread across the country in various satellite offices. (On the exam you will see questions that have network scenarios as big or bigger than this.) Users complain that it takes a very long time to log on. The satellite offices are connected via T1 connections. What can I do to remedy this situation?	This question leans toward the Windows NT Server in the Enterprise exam, but it is still relevant here. An efficient way to speed logons in a WAN environment is to locate a BDC in the remote office. Logging on across the WAN link can slow the process considerably.
I am the administrator of a Windows NT network that has one PDC and no BDC's. The PDC has crashed and will not boot. The last known good backup is from yesterday. What can I do to bring the server back online?	Without a BDC to promote to PDC, your only choice is to reinstall Windows NT Server 4.0 and then restore from backup. Any changes between the backup and the server crash will be lost.
I am about to start the installation process with the boot disks. As I boot the machine, what do I have to type to get the installation process started?	Nothing. When you use the boot disks or CD-ROM drive for installations, the setup process starts automatically as the machine boots.
I have a machine whose CD-ROM drive is not compatible with Windows NT. What can I do to install Windows NT Server?	Copy the installation file to your hard disk and run the installation from there. Until you obtain an NT-compatible CD-ROM drive, you cannot install Windows NT Server from a CD-ROM.
I want to create an answer file for unattended installation. What utility is available to help me do this?	SETUPMGR on the Windows NT Server CD-ROM. You'll find it in the Support/Deptools/i386 subdirectory.

Troubleshooting the Installation Process

During installation you may have to do some troubleshooting if your installation doesn't go smoothly. Here are some of the most common troubleshooting problems.

Faulty media is a common problem. The boot disks may have one bad disk or the CD itself may not be functioning correctly. There have also been many documented cases of insufficient disk space problems. These simple problems can cause financial headaches for companies, because it can take hours to track them down and resolve them.

Another item that can cause problems with configuration is an incompatible SCSI device, or a third-party drive like a Zip or Jaz drive. SCSI adapters devices (which is what most hard drives in servers are) can be one of the more challenging devices to get to work with Windows NT. The recommended method, of course, is to consult the latest edition of the Hardware Compatibility List (HCL). Microsoft Technical Support will not support you if you are having a problem with a device that is not on the HCL.

Another simple mistake—such as a wrong username, domain name, or protocol—can make it seem that the machine you are configuring is not connecting. Oversights such as usernames and domain names, if not checked, can be mistaken for hardware problems. It's much more economical to spend 15 minutes troubleshooting the basic network configuration than it is to buy a new NIC and toss the old one out.

Here's a real-life example.

A network engineer, when setting up a new PDC and various workstations, named the domain MainOffice1. In the course of setting up the network, one of the workstations was also named MainOffice1. This network is part of a WAN environment, with other domain controllers set up in trusted relationships. When finalizing all the machines and rebooting the PDC and workstations, the engineer encountered an error message. What do you think it was?

Right: duplicate names. This is a classic case of mere oversight. You always have to make sure that any and all names are unique. Whether it is a domain name or a computer name, it must be unique in the network.

CERTIFICATION SUMMARY

As part of the certification process you will need to be proficient in hands-on exercises; you'll also have to apply your knowledge to complex scenarios. The installation process for Windows NT Server accounts for about 10% of what you need to know on the exam and 40% of what you need to know in real life.

Be sure to know the hardware requirements for installing Windows NT Server 4.0. A good understanding of hard disk partitioning and planning is also important. Knowledge of basic NT administrative tasks, such as re-creating the installation disks and the switches available for WINNT.EXE and WINNT32.EXE is also important. Be sure you have a good handle on the different security roles a server can have. You need to know how to maintain the domain environment, especially in the event of a PDC failure. When a Windows NT 4.0 Server installation fails, a good administrator can work through problems to get the server back online and restore proper functioning. Being able to troubleshoot the installation process is essential to the administration of your domain.

These items may be a small percentage of the entire exam, but they are invaluable for real-world situations. A good installation, with proper planning and preparation, can make domain administration a much easier process.

TWO-MINUTE DRILL

- ❑ Windows NT Server supports three protocol standards: TCP/IP, NWLink, and NetBEUI.
- ❑ The absolute minimum recommended by Microsoft for Intel *x*86-type computers is 124MB.
- ❑ The syntax for the UNC name is *computername**sharename*.
- ❑ You can install Windows NT on a RISC-based system, but you must use a FAT partition for the system files.

❑ With RISC-based systems, the partitions must be set up ahead of time. Windows NT cannot set up and configure RISC partitions.

❑ Windows NT 4.0 cannot access the FAT32 file system.

❑ By default, Windows NT 3.51 is installed in the \NT351 directory and Windows NT 4.0 uses the \WINNT directory.

❑ The SETUPMGR utility in the support\deptools\<computer type> is a GUI program that will help you set up answer files for unattended installation.

❑ The Uniqueness Database File (UDF) allows an administrator to specify information for each individual workstation or server that is being installed.

❑ A PDC is the central server in the network. There must be one—and only one—PDC per domain.

❑ Member servers are used for application servers, print servers, or SQL servers. They are dedicated to process high-end searches, and non-security type functions.

❑ Stand-alone servers cannot be promoted or demoted. The only way to change the role of a member server is to reinstall Windows NT Server on the machine.

SELF TEST

The following questions will help you measure your understanding of the material presented in this chapter. Read all the choices carefully, as there may be more than one correct answer. Choose all correct answers for each question.

1. What is the file to start the installation process that you type at the command prompt on a DOS machine?

    A. setup.exe

    B. install.exe

    C. winnt.exe

    D. winnt32.exe

2. You want to install Windows NT Server 4.0 and have all available security options accessible. What file system type do you want to choose during the installation?

    A. HPFS

    B. FAT32

    C. NTFS

    D. FAT

3. How many PDC's can a domain have?

    A. unlimited

    B. no more than 15

    C. only 2

    D. only 1

4. Your server name is SERVER and you share with the Windows NT 4.0 Server installation files is called NTCD. What do you type at the command prompt to

connect to the network share when using a network boot disk?

    A. net use g: \\SERVER\NTCD

    B. net use g:=//SERVER/NTCD

    C. net connect g:\\SERVER\NTCD

    D. connect g:=\\SERVER\NTCD

5. You promote your BDC to a PDC while the PDC is off the network. What will happen if you reinsert the old PDC into the network?

    A. The administrator must first demote the old PDC to a BDC.

    B. You can't use it again, because only one PDC can exist within a domain.

    C. You get error #45132: Duplicate computer name on network

    D. None of the above

6. What switch do you use to re-create the setup boot floppy disks?

    A. /OD

    B. /RC

    C. /FD

    D. /OX

7. What method allows you to install across the network successfully on an MS-DOS workstation?

    A. Use an Installation Startup Disk to connect to the Server with a share set up and run the setup.exe file to start the installation process.

B. Use a Network Boot disk to connect to the Server with a share set up and run the winnt32.exe file to start the installation process.

C. Use an Installation Startup Disk to connect to the Server with a share set up and run the ntsetup.exe file to start the installation process.

D. Use an Installation Startup Disk to connect to the Server with a share set up and run the winnt.exe file to start the installation process.

8. In which subdirectory on the Windows NT 4.0 Server CD-ROM are the installation files for an Intel machine located?

A. \intel

B. \386

C. \i386

D. \mips

E. \windowsnt

9. You have a BDC you want to make a member server. What do you have to do?

A. Reinstall Windows NT Server.

B. Demote the BDC to a member server.

C. Rename the BDC and change its server type in Server Manager.

D. Use the Server Setup option in Control Panel.

10. Which switch tells setup not to look for or create the floppy disks when starting setup?

A. /F

B. /C

C. /B

D. /D

11. You need to set up and configure three new BDC's for your WAN. What is the quickest and most efficient way to do this?

A. Boot each machine with the floppy disks and proceed with the installation with one machine one step behind the other.

B. Boot each machine with a separate CD and proceed with the installation with one machine one step behind the other.

C. Boot with a network boot disk and connect to a network share point with the installation files.

D. Boot with another server's hard disk and copy the files over to the new drive in a master/slave relationship.

12. You are setting up a new Windows NT server on the network. This server will be a member server in the Finance department. You want to name this computer for the department where it is located. All servers, domain controllers, or non-domain controllers are set up and named in this fashion. The Finance department already has a BDC installed. What problems will you run into with this installation?

A. You cannot have a member server in the same domain as a domain controller.

B. Member servers must be installed prior to domain controllers.

C. The installation will result in a duplicate computer name on the network.

D. All servers must be set up at the same time before workstations can be added.

13. What is the default network protocol for Windows NT?

A. TCP/IP

B. NetBEUI

C. NWLink

D. DLC

14. You have installed Windows NT Server 4.0 and now want to set up fault tolerance on your hard disk. Which of the following fault-tolerance methods can the system files be part of?

A. mirror set

B. stripe set without parity

C. stripe set with parity

D. volume set

15. A machine in your organization was formerly a Windows NT server. Now you find that you need this machine as a extra workstation. While logged on locally to the machine, you open the Disk Administrator and try to delete the main system partition. What will happen in this instance?

A. Disk Administrator will ask you to confirm your choice. When you click Yes, the partition information will be deleted.

B. Disk Administrator will ask you to confirm your choice, then show a message explaining the change that will take effect when the server is shut down.

C. Disk Administrator will ask you to confirm your choice, then shut down the server and remove the partition when you click Yes in the confirmation window.

D. Disk Administrator will return an error message saying that the operation cannot be performed.

16. When installing Windows NT Server, you selected Per Seat licensing. You find now that you should have chosen Per Server. What can you do in this instance?

A. Use the Convert.exe utility to convert the server from Per Seat to Per Server licensing.

B. Use the Control Panel Licensing option to change the licensing from Per Seat to Per Server.

C. You can't change it unless you reinstall Windows NT Server 4.0.

D. You can change it, but you must contact Microsoft at licensing@microsoft.com.

17. When installing Windows NT Server you selected Per Server licensing. You find now that you should have chosen Per Seat. What can you do in this instance?

A. Use the Convert.exe utility to convert the server from Per Server to Per Seat licensing.

B. Use the Control Panel Licensing option to change the licensing from Per Server to Per Seat.

C. You can't change it unless you reinstall Windows NT Server 4.0.

D. You can change it, but you must contact Microsoft at licensing@microsoft.com.

18. You are installing a multiboot system containing Windows 95, Windows NT Server, and Windows NT Workstation. You want to be able to share files and data among the three operating systems. What file system should you choose?

A. NTFS

B. FAT

C. HPFS

D. FAT32

19. You are upgrading from Windows NT Server 3.51 that was installed with default settings. You want to maintain the icons, desktop settings, and basic Windows NT information. How would you accomplish this?

A. Use the winnt.exe utility and install into the WINT35 directory.

B. Use the winnt32.exe utility and install into the WINNT directory.

C. Install into the WINNT35 directory using the winnt32.exe file.

D. Install into the WINNT directory using the WINNT32.EXE file.

E. None of the above

20. What Server Manager menu do you open to get the option to promote the BDC?

A. Computer

B. View

C. Options

D. Help

21. You are getting ready to start the installation process and decide to boot from the CD. When you put the CD in the CD-ROM drive and boot the machine, the computer still boots from the hard disk. What is a possible cause of this? (Select all that apply.)

A. The computer you are setting does not have a bootable CD-ROM drive.

B. The Windows NT Server CD is not bootable.

C. The boot sequence on the machine is set to: Hard Drive, Floppy, and then CD-ROM.

D. The BIOS is not configured to include CD-ROM boot as part of the regular boot process.

22. Where is the SETUPMGR utility installed by default?

A. SETUPMGR is not installed by default, but it is located on the Windows NT CD-ROM in the [CDDRIVE]:>SUPPORT\ DEPLTOOLS\I386\.

B. SETUPMGR is located in the Windows NT subdirectory on the hard disk after a default installation.

C. SETUPMGR is only available on certain versions of Windows NT prior to 4.0.

D. SETUPMGR must be downloaded from www.microsoft.com\ deployment\tools\i386\ SETUPMGR.MGR

23. You've just installed a new server in a domain. You've verified that there are no evident errors on boot up. You check the domain name, and the name on the PDC

matches the name on the server. You verify that you have a valid username and password. For some reason you cannot connect to the network. You check the Protocols tab in Network Properties on the new server and see the information shown in Figure 3-18. You check the same tab on the PDC and see the information shown in Figure 3-19. Why won't the computers communicate?

A. Each server must be part of its own respective domain.

FIGURE 3-18

Protocol setup on new server

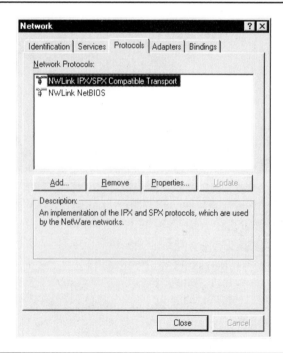

FIGURE 3-19

Protocol setup on PDC

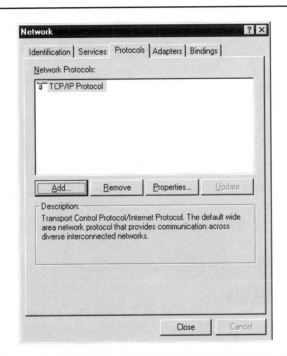

B. There is a protocol mismatch between the two computers.

C. The frame type on the new server must match the IP address of the PDC.

D. You need to add the DLC protocol so the two computers will be able to communicate.

24. You are installing a BDC and encounter an error when the computer is being added to the network. Why is this happening?

   A. The new BDC is using the wrong protocol.

B. The computer name is not valid for the domain.

C. The username/password you are using doesn't have permission to add computers to the domain.

D. The maximum number of BDC's in the domain has been exceeded.

25. You are installing Windows NT Server to be a member server. This machine is a dual-boot machine with Windows 95 OEM Service Release 2 already installed on it. You install Windows NT 4.0 Server in its own partition. You make sure to install the Windows NT partition as a FAT partition

so Windows 95 can access the information on it. When you are in Windows NT you cannot access the drives that contain the Windows 95 information. You open Disk Administrator and see the screen shown in Figure 3-20. After reviewing the information in Disk Administrator, what conclusion do you reach?

A. The Windows 95 partitions were deleted and that is why they are showing Unknown.

B. The Windows 95 partitions are HPFS partitions which are not compatible with Windows NT 4.0 Server.

C. The Windows 95 partitions were formatted during the installation process and therefore show Unknown.

D. The Windows 95 partitions are FAT32 partitions, which are not compatible with Window NT 4.0 Server.

26. You have just installed Windows NT Server and realize you forgot to install Windows Messaging. Now you want to add it. What

---

FIGURE 3-20

Disk Administrator on a dual boot machine

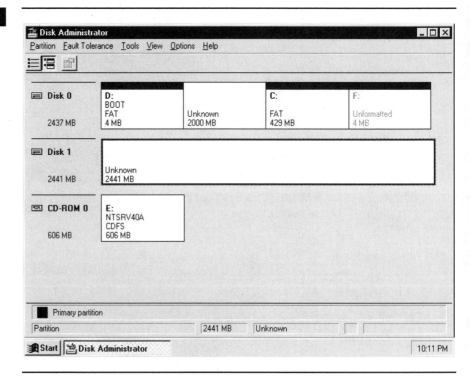

icon do you open in Control Panel (see Figure 3-21) to do this?

A. Network

B. Add/Remove Programs

C. Server

D. Internet

27. Which switch tells setup not to check for free disk space on floppy disks when creating them?

A. /F

B. /C

C. /D

D. /OX

FIGURE 3-21

Control Panel

4

Configuring
Windows NT 4.0

CERTIFICATION OBJECTIVES

4.01	Configuring Network Protocols
4.02	Configuring Peripheral Devices
4.03	NT 4.0 Disk Administrator
4.04	NT Browser Types
4.05	NT System Registry

I n order to pass the exam you'll need to know how to configure various components within NT. This chapter will discuss configuring network protocols and various peripheral devices to include tape backup devices, SCSI adapters, and display adapters. It will teach you how to use Disk Administrator to manage your hard disk partitions—including how to set up software RAID levels 0, 1, and 5. You'll also need to know the various clients that are available for NT. Finally, you'll learn about the NT system registry and how it is organized.

CERTIFICATION OBJECTIVE 4.01

Configuring Network Protocols

For the exam you'll need to know which protocols can be configured. TCP/IP must be configured and NWLink can be configured if needed. NetBEUI doesn't need configuration.

NWLink IPX/SPX-Compatible

NWLink does not require any configuration. By default it uses Auto Detect to detect the frame type. However, if a Novell network uses more than one frame type, you may need to specify which frame type to use. To specify the frame type, open Network Properties and choose the Protocols tab. Double-click the NWLink IPX/SPX Compatible Transport. In the next dialog box, open the drop-down menu for frame type. There will be four frame types to choose from: 802.2, 802.3, II, and SNAP. NetWare version 2.2 and 3.1 use Ethernet type 802.3 as the standard frame type. NetWare version 4.0 and above uses 802.2.

TCP/IP

TCP/IP requires configuration, unless you have a DHCP server assigning TCP/IP information. (Dynamic Host Configuration Protocol—DHCP— is explained later in this chapter.) First you'll need to open the network properties and choose the Protocols tab. Then double-click the TCP/IP protocol. If your server is multihomed (in other words, if it has more than one network connection), you'll need to select the adapter where you want to configure on the IP Address tab; otherwise, the appropriate adapter is already selected. You'll need to specify an IP address, subnet mask, and default gateway. A default gateway may not be necessary if your computer doesn't need to communicate outside its local subnet. However, since TCP/IP is usually used in a routed environment, a default gateway is usually necessary. Figure 4-1 shows the IP Address tab filled out properly. If your network has more than one gateway, you can use the Advanced button to configure the additional gateway(s).

If you plan to connect your server to the Internet, you'll need to configure the DNS (Domain Name System) tab. Under Host Name fill in your computer's host name (be sure to follow proper Internet naming conventions). In the Domain field you'll enter your Internet domain name. This is not the same thing as an NT domain. The Internet domain name should look

FIGURE 4-1

IP Address tab

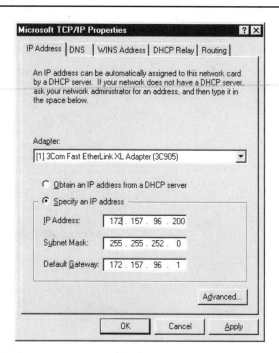

something like this: microsoft.com or your.companyname.net. Click the Add button under the DNS Service Search Order to add DNS servers. Finally, click the Add button for the Domain Suffix Search Order. Add any domain suffixes you want to add. Using a domain suffix can slow your system down when trying to connect to network resources. It appends the suffixes to the end of every failed connection. So if you mistakenly type WWW.mcirosoft.com, NT will try to connect to WWW.mcirosoft.com—then it will add your domain suffixes to the end of the search and try to connect to those sites. It will time out only after all suffixes have failed. Figure 4-2 shows a properly configured DNS tab.

If you use WINS for name resolution on your network, you'll need to configure the WINS Address tab. As with the IP Address, you'll need to select the proper adapter if you have a multihomed machine. Enter at least a Primary WINS Server IP address. If you have two WINS servers on your network, you should fill in the Secondary WINS Server text box. On this tab you can Enable

FIGURE 4-2

DNS tab

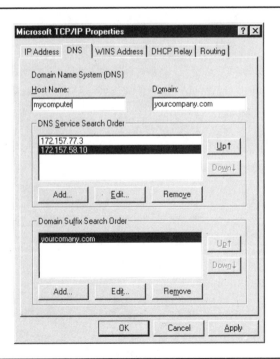

DNS for Windows Resolution. If you check this box, a DNS server will be used to resolve your Windows network names. Since DNS (unlike WINS) is not dynamic, it will be too difficult to manage a large Windows network using only DNS. If you only have a couple of Windows-based computers on your network, there are some advantages to using DNS for Windows Resolution. First, you won't have to install a WINS server, which uses resources on the server where it is installed. Second, you can enable LMHOSTS Lookup. To use an LMHOSTS file, make sure the Enable LMHOSTS Lookup check box is marked, then click Import LMHOSTS. Choose the LMHOSTS file you want to import and click Open. Finally, you can set a Scope ID. All computers must have the same scope ID to communicate on a TCP/IP network. If you change the Scope ID of your server, all computers on your network must be changed to have the same scope ID. Figure 4-3 shows a fully configured WINS Address tab.

FIGURE 4-3

WINS Address tab

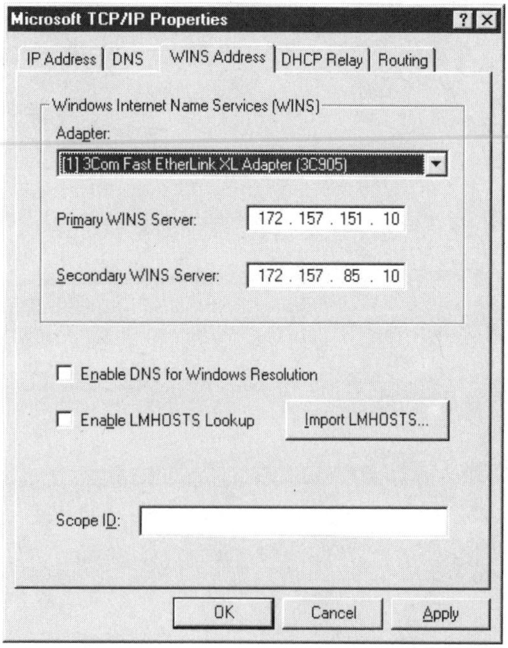

The DHCP Relay tab is used to forward DHCP request through a router. If your router isn't able to forward DHCP requests, you can use this service to broadcast the request to other subnets. This service only supports clients on the local physical subnet. Simply click the Add button and enter the IP address of the DHCP server. If the Add button isn't an available option, you first must install the DHCP Relay Agent. The DHCP Relay tab is shown in Figure 4-4.

The Routing tab (shown in Figure 4-5) has only one check box. If you have a multihomed computer and you want to use static IP routing between the two NIC's, you need to check this box.

NT TCP/IP Services

NT ships with several TCP/IP services, allowing NT to host many common UNIX server-based services. DHCP, WINS, and IIS services included with Windows NT Server 4.0 are described in the following sections.

FIGURE 4-4

DHCP Relay tab

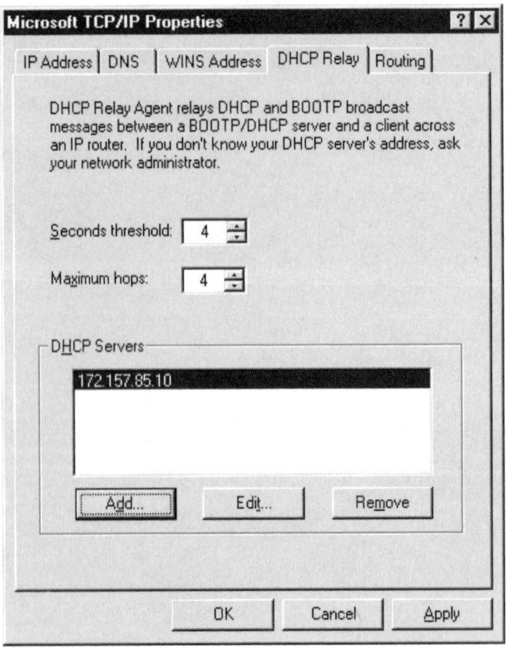

FIGURE 4-5

WINS Routing tab

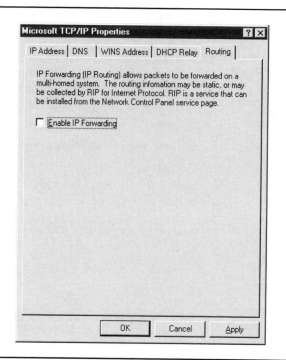

FIGURE 4-5

WINS Routing tab

DYNAMIC HOST CONFIGURATION PROTOCOL (DHCP)

As mentioned earlier, DHCP is used to assign TCP/IP configuration parameters on networked clients. DHCP is similar to BootP, except it leases IP addresses instead of giving out a new address every time the computer boots. The DHCP server administrator configures a *scope* for which a set of valid IP addresses are assigned. Each physical subnet that uses DHCP must have an active scope for that subnet if it is using DHCP. The routers also must be configured to broadcast DHCP requests.

When configuring a scope you need to enter the following items:

- A range of unique IP addresses (called a pool of IP addresses)
- A valid subnet mask for each pool of IP addresses
- Excluded IP addresses from the pool
- Duration of the lease (default 3 days)

Creating a DHCP scope

1. Open DHCP Manager.

2. Double-click the server you want to manage. Even if the server you want to manage is listed, you'll need to highlight it and add it.

3. Click Scope | Create.

4. Enter the IP Address Pool Start Address and End Address.

5. Enter the Subnet Mask of that IP Address Pool.

6. Exclude any addresses from the IP Address Pool by typing in the Exclusion Range then clicking Add. Repeat for each range that you want to exclude.

7. Set your Lease Duration.

8. Enter the Name of your scope.

9. Enter a Comment if necessary.

10. Click OK.

11. After clicking OK, you'll be asked if you want to activate the scope. Answer Yes. In order for a scope to give out IP addresses, it must be activated.

exam
ⓦatch

Be careful when setting the lease duration. You should set a lease duration that best meets your needs. If you have a lot of IP addresses but relatively few computers, you can set a long lease duration. Conversely, if you have only a few IP addresses and many computers you should set a short lease. If you have many IP addresses you may be tempted to choose Unlimited, that isn't recommended because DHCP not only assigns IP addresses, but also client configuration information. If you set the lease duration to Unlimited, your clients won't ever update their configuration information if it changes, unless you manually update DHCP at each client.

DHCP can also be used to set the configuration information for the clients. The following configuration information is commonly set for Windows-based networking clients:

■ Router (Default Gateway) is mandatory

■ WINS/NBNS Servers

■ WINS/NBT node type (must be set to 0x8 [h-node])

■ DNS Servers

■ Domain name

DHCP options can be set for Global or Scope. Global settings apply to all the scopes on the DHCP server and a Scope setting applies to the selected scope. Exercise 4-2 teaches you how to configure Global and Scope options for a DHCP Server.

EXERCISE 4-2

Configure DHCP Options

1. Open DHCP Manager.

2. Double-click the server you want to manage.

3. Select the scope you want to configure.

4. Click DHCP Options | Scope.

5. Choose Router under Unused Options.

6. Click Add.

7. Highlight Router under Active Options.

8. Click Value.

9. Click Edit Array.

10. Add the New IP Address for the Router. This will be the default gateway for that subnet.

FROM THE CLASSROOM

Configuring NT to Avoid Problems

The number one fallacy and misunderstanding among NT administrators surrounds something called NetBIOS—what it is and what to do with it. In NT, NetBIOS is extremely important (even critical, you might say). It must be present if you want NT to function on the network. The perceived fallacy is that NetBIOS is a transport protocol—that NetBIOS is NetBEUI or that NetBEUI is NetBIOS (or some kind of an enhanced version of it).

FROM THE CLASSROOM

Let's take these misconceptions one at a time. NetBIOS is not a transport protocol inside NT. NetBIOS, as it applies to NT is a set of 19 API calls at various levels in the NT networking model. *We repeat, it is not an NT transport protocol.* Unfortunately, some LAN network operating systems (NOSs) use a transport protocol called "NetBIOS." In fact, an early Microsoft/IBM NOS used a transport protocol called NetBIOS, *but this is not it.*

That brings us to the transport protocol called NetBEUI. Interestingly enough, the acronym NetBEUI stands for NetBIOS Enhanced User Interface. So that makes NetBIOS just a subset of NetBEUI, which is a transport protocol. Which by inference (if A=B and B=C, then A=C) makes NetBIOS a transport protocol within NT, right? WRONG! Read on, MacDuff.

Microsoft ships three transport protocols with NT: NetBEUI, NWLINK, and TCP/IP. When you install any of these protocols, each installs its appropriate NetBIOS layer automatically. Remember that NetBIOS is a set of API calls. This layer must be present with each protocol stack that you install. You do not want to disable this.

OK, next fallacy. The reasoning goes, "if we must have the NetBIOS layer and if NetBEUI is sort of NetBIOS (which it is not; read the previous paragraphs if you are unsure), then we must have NetBEUI protocol always installed. Right? WRONG! We cannot tell you how many certified technicians—who claim to be NT-literate—have told us this. We go to sites where clients are running both TCP/IP and NetBEUI protocols. When we ask why, we get the above explanation. To demonstrate the fallacy, we remove the NetBEUI protocol and ask the administrator to show us what doesn't work after it is removed. We actually have an administrator at one client who still insists, two years later, that something is missing, but he just hasn't found it yet!

Yes, you do need the NetBIOS layer. No, NetBIOS and NetBEUI are not the same thing, although the names are misleading. Yes, the NetBIOS layer is loaded for each transport protocol stack you load. You now know more than many MCSEs.

—By Shane Clawson, MCT, MCSE

·WINDOWS INTERNET NAMING SERVICE (WINS) WINS resolves computer names to IP addresses on a windows based network. WINS performs the same role as DNS, except it is dynamic. Whenever a client computer starts, it registers its name and IP address with the WINS Server. Then, when a client tries to locate another computer, it asks the WINS database to resolve the requested name to an IP address. WINS uses several configuration parameters to govern the WINS client behavior. Table 4-1 describes each configuration option. Table 4-2 describes each advanced configuration option.

exam
ⓦatch

When using DHCP and WINS, your WINS renewal interval must be at least one-half the time of the DHCP lease. This ensures that the registered computer names have the proper IP addresses assigned to them.

INTERNET INFORMATION SERVER (IIS) IIS provides FTP, Gopher, and Web services. When you install NT you are asked if you want to install IIS. You can also install IIS from the Network Control Panel Services

TABLE 4-1		
	Option	**Description**
WINS Configuration Options	Renewal Interval	Specifies how often a client registers its name. Default is six days.
	Extinction Interval	When it is marked it specifies the interval between an entry marked as released and extinct. Default is six days.
	Extinction Timeout	Specifies the interval between an entry marked extinct and when it is deleted (scavenged) from the database. Default is six days.
	Verify Interval	Specifies the interval in which the WINS server must verify that names owned by another WINS server are still active.

TABLE 4-2

WINS Advanced
Configuration Options

Advanced Option	Description
Logging Enabled	Turns on logging of the J50.log files.
Log Detailed Events	Turns on verbose logging. Events are written to the system event log. This requires a lot of computer resources.
Replicate Only with Partners	Only allows your WINS server to replicate with its configured push-and-pull partners. This prevents unauthorized/unwanted WINS servers from pushing or pulling to your database.
Backup on Termination	Backs up the database whenever WINS stops, but not when the system is shut down.
Migrate On/Off	Specifies that static unique and multihomed records in the database are treated as dynamic when they conflict with a registration or replica.
Starting Version Count	Used to fix a corrupted database. Enter a higher version number than what appears for a version number on all replication partners. This only needs to be set if you have a corrupt database.
Database Backup Path	Specifies a local directory where the WINS database is backed up. If a path is specified, WINS automatically backs up the database every 24 hours.

tab. After installing IIS you configure it using Internet Service Manager (ISM). You can find ISM through the program group, Microsoft Internet Server (Common). Figure 4-6 shows the Internet Service Manager.

After starting ISM you can have it search your network for other computers running IIS. If you have proper rights to these computers you can manage them from your computer using ISM. To configure a service, simply double-click the service you want to modify. Exercise 4-3 teaches you how to configure the World Wide Web Service.

FIGURE 4-6

Internet Service Manager

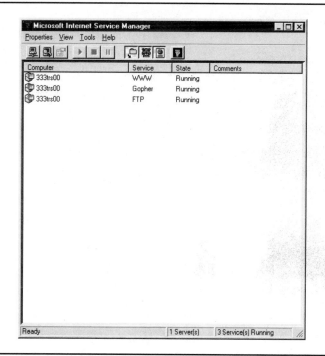

EXERCISE 4-3

Configuring the WWW Service on IIS

1. Open ISM.

2. Double-click the WWW service.

3. Under the Service tab (shown in Figure 4-7) you can change the following:

   ■ **TCP Port**   You should leave this at 80 since it is the standard port that Web browsers use; if you need to change it for security reasons, just enter a new port number.

   ■ **Connection Timeout**   The amount of time that the client can remain idle before the service kills the connection.

FIGURE 4-7

WWW Service tab

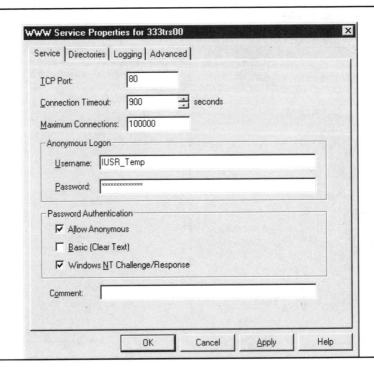

■ **Maximum Connections** Change this number to set the maximum number of computers than can connect to your server through the WWW service at a single time.

■ **Anonymous Logon** The text boxes will specify the user account and password for anonymous logons.

■ **Password Authentication** You can choose Allow Anonymous, which doesn't require a logon account; Basic (Clear Text), in which anyone with a sniffer program can intercept your passwords; and Windows NT Challenge/Response, a more secure way of authenticating users.

■ **Comment** Use this space to describe your service on the network to other administrators.

4. Click the Directories tab (shown in Figure 4-8) to configure the following:

FIGURE 4-8

WWW Directories tab

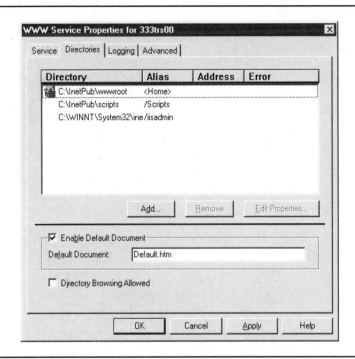

- **Directory**   Lets you specify the directories that the service has access to.
- **Enable Default**   Document: Allows you to use a default file name for the directory so the user doesn't have to type in the entire URL.
- **Directory Browsing Allowed**   Allows users to browse the directory via his Web browser.

5. Click the Logging tab (shown in Figure 4-9) to configure the following:

- **Enable logging**   Lets you specify the type of log file, how often to start a new log, and the directory where the log files are stored.
- **Log to SQL/ODBC Database**   Lets you log directly to a database by providing a proper User ID and password.

FIGURE 4-9

WWW Logging tab

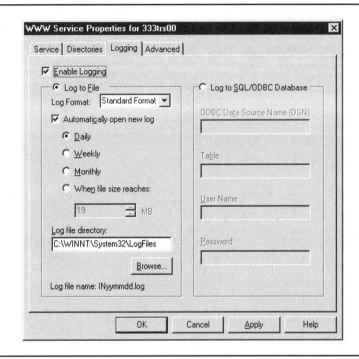

6. Click the Advanced tab (shown in Figure 4-10) to configure the following:

- **By default, all computers will be**   Granted Access or Denied Access, which allows you to specify how access is to be granted. By using the list box, you can allow only certain IP addresses access or you can deny only certain IP addresses access.

- **Limit Network Use by all Internet Services on this computer**   Lets you specify the amount of network use (in KB/Sec) that this service can use.

FIGURE 4-10

WWW Advanced tab

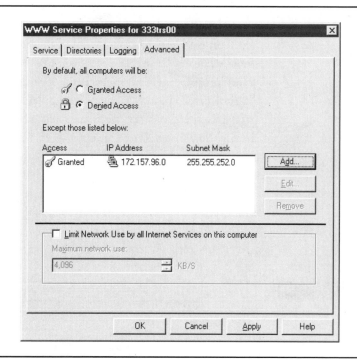

CERTIFICATION OBJECTIVE 4.02

Configuring Peripheral Devices

Most peripheral devices can be configured with the Control Panel; however, some may require a vendor-specific setup program.

Control Panel

The Control Panel has many applets that control device drivers. Figure 4-11 shows what our Control Panel looks like. As you add programs to your system, your Control Panel may change in appearance because some programs add Control Panel applets. Some of the applets are user-specific and others are computer-specific. User-specific applets allow each user to set NT to operate the way they prefer. The computer-specific applets affect all users and can only be changed by an administrator. The Control Panel accomplishes this by interacting with the registry. The user-specific applets control HKEY_CURRENT_USER subtree and the computer-specific applets interact with the HKEY_LOCAL_MACHINE subtree. We'll discuss the registry and subtrees in more detail later in this chapter. The following are user-specific applets: Display, Accessibility Options, Internet, Telephony, Console,

FIGURE 4-11

Control Panel

Regional Settings, Keyboard, Mouse, Printers, Sounds, Dial-up Monitor, and certain parts of the System application.

Changing Display Adapter Settings

The following exercises step you through using these applications. Each exercise starts by assuming you have the Control Panel open on your desktop. The first, Exercise 4-4, teaches you how to change your display adapter, resolution, and color depth.

EXERCISE 4-4

Changing the Display Adapter

1. In the Control Panel, double-click the Display icon.
2. Choose the Settings tab.
3. Click the Display Type button.
4. Click the Change button.
5. Select the appropriate driver from the list. If the driver you need isn't listed, you'll need to click Have Disk and type the path to the vendor-supplied driver.
6. Click OK.
7. When your computer has copied the drivers, you need to restart your system so the change can take affect.
8. Open the Display applet and choose the Settings tab.
9. Set the Desktop Area slider bar to the resolution you want to use. The resolution you can choose depends on your video card and your monitor.
10. Choose the color depth you want to use in the drop-down menu under Color Palette. After choosing your color depth your resolution may change. This occurs because your video card can't support that number of colors at the resolution you had picked.
11. Click Test.
12. Click OK to the message box telling you that NT is testing your new configuration.

13. If everything goes well you should see a colorful pattern of boxes on your screen. After 5 seconds NT asks you if you saw the test bitmap properly. Click Yes if you saw the pattern. If you didn't see the pattern, go to step 15.

14. Click OK to accept your new configuration and end the exercise.

15. If you didn't see anything click No. NT resets to your previous display configuration. Repeat steps 9 through 14.

Removing NT Components

You use the Add/Remove Programs applet to remove NT components. Exercise 4-5 shows you how to remove WordPad from your computer.

EXERCISE 4-5

Removing a Windows NT application

1. Double-click Add/Remove Programs.

2. Select the Windows NT Setup tab.

3. Highlight Accessories.

4. Click Details.

5. Scroll down to WordPad and remove the check mark.

6. Click OK.

7. Click OK.

Splitting the Paging File

You can increase the performance of your machine by spreading your page file out across several disks, especially if you have more than one disk controller or a controller that performs concurrent I/O. To spread you page file across multiple disks follow the steps in Exercise 4-6.

EXERCISE 4-6

Splitting the Paging File across Multiple Physical Disks

1. Double-click the System icon.

2. Choose the Performance tab (shown in Figure 4-12).

FIGURE 4-12

System Performance tab

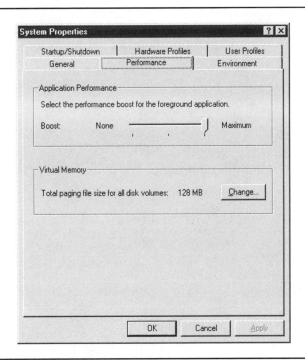

3. Click the Change button, as shown in Figure 4-13.

4. Highlight the partition where you want to add a paging file.

5. Enter the Initial Size and the Maximum Size.

6. Click Set.

Adding Tape Backup Drives

NT supports tape back-up drives for disaster recovery purposes. Adding a tape device is simple. Follow Exercise 4-7 to add a tape device.

EXERCISE 4-7

Adding a Tape Device

1. In Control Panel, double-click the Tape Devices icon

2. Select the Drivers tab (shown in Figure 4-14).

3. Click the Add button.

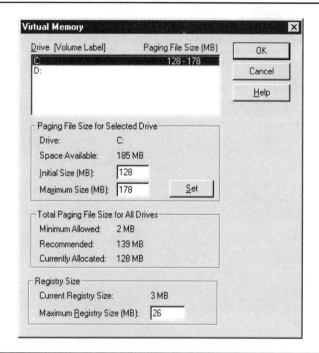

FIGURE 4-13

Modifying the page
file drive

4. Select the appropriate driver from the list. If the driver you need isn't
   listed, click Have Disk and type the path to the vendor-supplied driver.
5. Click OK.

Adding SCSI Adapters and CD-ROM Drives

The SCSI Adapters Control Panel applet is used to install SCSI adapters, but
it is also used to install IDE CD-ROM drivers. This may confuse you when
you are adding an IDE CD-ROM device and need to find the proper Control
Panel applet to execute. Just remember to use the SCSI Adapters applet for
both SCSI and IDE devices.

EXERCISE 4-8

Adding a SCSI Adapter

1. Open the SCSI Adapters Control Panel applet.

FIGURE 4-14

Adding a tape
device driver

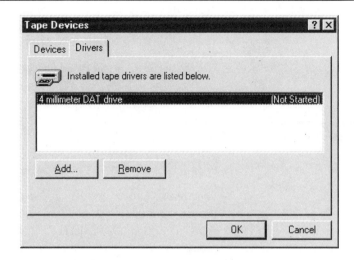

2. Choose the Drivers tab (shown in Figure 4-15).

3. Click the Add button.

4. Select the appropriate driver from the list. If the driver you need isn't
   listed, click Have Disk and type the path to the vendor-supplied driver.

FIGURE 4-15

Adding a SCSI adapter
driver

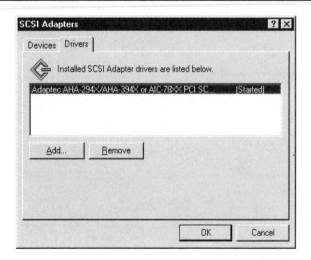

    5. Click OK.

Adding Modems

You use the Modems Control Panel applet to add and remove modems. Exercise 4-9 teaches you how to add a modem.

EXERCISE 4-9

Adding a Modem to Windows NT

1. Open the Modems Control Panel applet, as shown in Figure 4-16.

2. Click Add.

3. Click Next, if you want NT to detect your modem. If you want to choose from the list or add a modem that's not listed, click the following option: Don't detect my modem; I will select it from a list check box.

FIGURE 4-16

Adding a modem

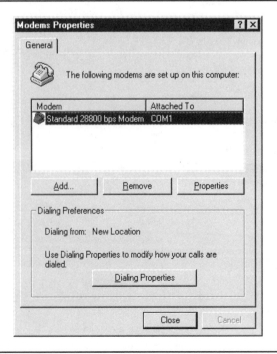

4. After selecting the appropriate modem click Next, or click the Have Disk button if you're installing a modem that's not listed.

5. Choose the port the modem will use.

6. Click Next.

7. Click Finish.

Adding Uninterruptible Power Supplies (UPSs)

An UPS is an important part of fault tolerance. If you have an UPS you can use NT's UPS Control Panel applet to configure it. Before you can configure it you'll need to have a serial cable connected to your computer and the UPS. By configuring the UPS you can have NT automatically shut down when power is lost, execute a command, and notify all connected users. Figure 4-17 is the UPS Control Panel applet screen.

The first step in configuring a UPS is to click the check box next to the option: Uninterruptible Power Supply is installed on. Choose the port it's connected to in the drop-down box. Configuring the rest of the UPS depends

FIGURE 4-17

UPS Control Panel applet

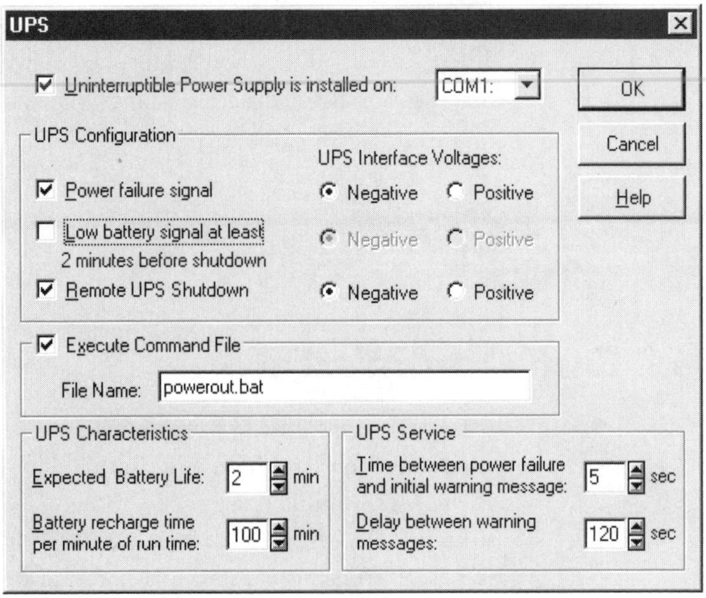

on the type of UPS you have and how the manufacturer has designed it. In the UPS Configuration group box , you can choose whether a negative or positive signal is sent during an active state. In other words, the signal you choose is the type that's normally sent; it changes when a power failure occurs. You'll need to use the Owner's Manual that comes with your UPS to obtain the correct values.

You can have NT run a command file when a power failure occurs. Just click next to the Execute Command File check box and type the name of the file you want to execute when the power fails. The command file must execute completely within 30 seconds, or NT terminates the command. Therefore, your command file shouldn't contain any dialog boxes because they require user intervention and would probably take more than 30 seconds to complete. The command file must be placed in your %systemroot%\System32 folder and be an executable file type (.exe, .com, .cmd, .bat).

The UPS Service group box enables you to set the duration of power outage that triggers a message to connected users, as well as the time interval that should pass before subsequent warning messages are issued.

The UPS Characteristics group box enables you to set the battery run time (Expected Battery Life) and the recharge rate (Battery recharge time per minute of run time). If you set the Expected Battery Life too long and your UPS doesn't support a Low battery signal, your UPS may not shut down in time. Be careful when setting your expected battery life.

CERTIFICATION OBJECTIVE 4.03

NT 4.0 Disk Administrator

If you're familiar with MS-DOS, you have probably used FDISK.EXE in the past to partition your hard disk. Rather than FDISK.EXE, NT uses a program called Disk Administrator, shown in Figure 4-18, to create and manage partitions. Disk Administrator is considerably easier to use than FDISK.EXE. Exercise 4-10 helps you start Disk Administrator for the first time. After

FIGURE 4-18

Disk Administrator

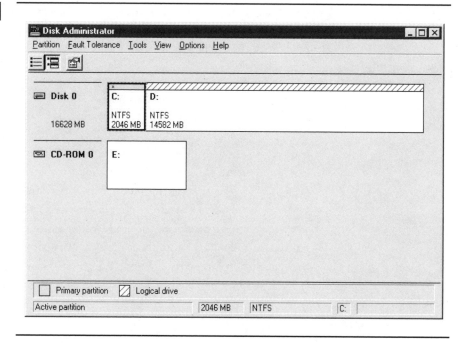

starting Disk Administrator, you can create and delete partitions; you can also manage stripe sets, volume sets, stripes sets with parity, and mirror sets.

EXERCISE 4-10

Launching Disk Administrator

1. Log on using an account that has administrator privileges.

2. Click Start | Programs | Administrative Tools (Common) | Disk Administrator.

3. You will see the following message:

```
No signature found on Disk 0. Writing a signature is a
safe operation and will not affect your ability to access
this disk from other operating systems, such as DOS.
If you choose not to write a signature, the disk will be
inaccessible to the Windows NT Disk Administrator
program.
Do you want to write a signature on Disk 0 so that the
Disk Administrator can access the drive?
```

4. Click Yes to write a 32-bit signature that uniquely identifies the disk written to the primary partition. This is done so that even if you change the disk controller or identification, NT will still recognize the disk.

System and Boot Partitions

NT uses two special partitions called the *system* and *boot* partitions for its start-up procedure. The definition of these partitions may sound backwards, but it is correct. The *system* partition contains the boot files such NTLDR and BOOT.INI. The *boot* partition contains system files such as the WINNT folder and the SYSTEM32 folder. The system partition can be set to active. When the system partition is set to active your computer will boot from that partition. If you have more than one system partition you can change the active partition—thereby changing which partition you boot from. Exercise 4-11 shows how to change the active partition of your system.

EXERCISE 4-11

Changing the active partition

1. Open Disk Administrator.

2. Right-click the partition you want to make active (it must be a primary partition).

3. Select Mark Active.

4. Choose Partition | Commit changes now from the menu bar.

Primary and Extended Partitions

Before you can access your hard disks, they first must be partitioned. You can create either *primary partitions* or *extended partitions*. A primary partition can be used as a system partition (set to active). Each hard disk can have up to four primary partitions. If you use an extended partition on a disk, you can only have three primary partitions on that disk. The key is you are only allowed to have a total of four partitions (not including logical drives) on a disk. A *logical drive* is a method of subdividing an extended partition. Unlike a primary partition, an extended partition can be divided into many logical drives. This enables you to have many more than four drive letters per disk.

Figure 4-19 shows a computer configured with two hard disk drives (Disk 0 and Disk 1) and one CD-ROM. Disk 0 has one primary partition (C:) and one extended partition that contains three logical drives (E: to G:). Disk 1 has one primary partition (D:), one extended partition with four logical drives (I: to L:), an Unknown partition (it's a partition that runs the Linux operating system, a version of UNIX that you don't need to know for the test), and 502 MB area of free space. You'll notice that drive C: has an * above it, which means it's marked as active (the system partition).

Exercises 4-12 through 4-14 show how to manage and configure partitions using Disk Administrator.

EXERCISE 4-12

Deleting a partition

1. Open Disk Administrator.

2. To select the partition you want to delete, right-click it and select delete.

3. Click Yes when asked if you are sure you want to delete the partition.

FIGURE 4-19

Primary and extended partitions

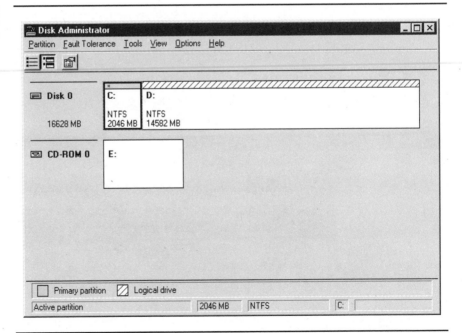

4. Choose Partition | Commit changes now from the menu bar. Commit changes now actually makes your changes take place. After step 3 you could have recovered the partition simply by exiting Disk Administrator and not saving the changes when prompted.

EXERCISE 4-13

Creating an extended partition with logical drives

1. Open Disk Administrator.
2. Right-click an area of free space.
3. Choose Create Extended.
4. Enter the size of the partition.
5. Click OK.
6. Choose Partition | Commit changes now from the menu bar.
7. Right-click the same area of free space.
8. Choose Create.
9. Enter the size of the logical drive.
10. Click OK.
11. Repeat steps 6-10 to create more logical drives.
12. Choose Partition | Commit changes now from the menu bar.

EXERCISE 4-14

Formatting a partition

1. Open Disk Administrator.
2. Right-click a partition.
3. Choose Format.
4. In the Format dialog box, select a file system.
5. Enter a Volume label if you want to name your partition.
6. Check Quick Format if you don't want to scan for bad sectors while formatting (this is much quicker).
7. If you chose NTFS as the file system, you can enable compression on the entire drive.
8. Click Start.

9. Click OK when you see the warning message that all data on the disk will be erased.

Volume Sets

Volume sets combine 2 to 32 areas of free space on one or multiple hard disks. Use volume sets to combine different sized areas of free space as a single volume (drive letter) from any type of hard disk (IDE, SCSI, or ESDI). Volume sets don't provide any fault tolerance or performance gains. They are simply used to combine multiple areas of free space as one logical drive. You can also extend your volume set if you format it using NTFS. If your volume set is formatted with the FAT file system, you'll need to convert it to NTFS if you want to extend it. Extending a volume set allows you to format more areas of free space into an existing volume set without destroying the data. Although you can increase the size of a volume set, you can never decrease it. Exercise 4-15 teaches you how to create a volume set and Exercise 4-16 shows you how to increase the size of your volume set.

EXERCISE 4-15

Creating a Volume Set

1. Open Disk Administrator.

2. Select the areas of free space you want to include. You'll need to hold down the CTRL key to select multiple areas of free space.

3. Choose Partition | Create Volume Set from the menu bar.

4. Enter the size of the volume set.

5. Click OK.

6. Choose Partition | Commit changes now from the menu bar.

7. Format the volume set.

EXERCISE 4-16

Extending a volume set

1. Make sure the volume set is formatted with NTFS.

2. Open Disk Administrator.

3. Select the volume set and the area of free space you want to add.

4. Choose Partition | Create Volume Set from the menu bar.

5. Enter the size of the new volume set.

6. Click OK.

7. Choose Partition | Commit changes now from the menu bar.

Stripe Sets Without Parity

Stripe sets without parity are like volume sets except they provide performance gains. They can combine 2 to 32 areas of free space as a single logical drive; however, the free space must be on different hard disks and each hard disk must contain the same amount of free space. If you have two disks—Disk 1 one with 100MB free and Disk 2 with 200MB free—you can use 100MB free space from each disk, and ignore the remaining 100MB available on Disk 2.

The data is written to a stripe set in 64KB blocks, going disk by disk. If you use multiple controllers or if your controller supports concurrent I/O, you can see significant speed improvements because you can access your data by reading from more than one drive at a time. However, stripe sets without parity have a disadvantage: when a hard disk fails, all your data is lost. Since each disk contains a portion of the data, you lose all the data if any one disk fails. Exercise 4-17 teaches you how to create a stripe set without parity. This exercise requires you to have at least two hard disks with an equal area of available free space.

EXERCISE 4-17

Creating a stripe set

1. Open Disk Administrator.

2. Select at least two areas of free space, each on a different hard disk.

3. Click Partition | Create Stripe Set.

4. Enter the size of the stripe set you want to create.

5. Click OK.

6. Choose Partition | Commit changes now from the menu bar.

7. Format the stripe set using the file system of your choice.

Drive Letter Assignment

Assigning drive letters is easy in NT. You use Disk Administrator to assign or change drive letters. Be very careful when changing drive letters on drives that are already in use. Although the drive letter changes, the registry settings for programs that are set up on that drive are not updated and users may lose access to files. Exercise 4-18 shows how to change the drive letter for your CD-ROM drive.

EXERCISE 4-18

Assigning drive letters

1. Open Disk Administrator.
2. Right-click the CD-ROM drive partition.
3. Choose Assign Drive Letter.
4. Change the current drive letter to an unused letter (obviously, you can't assign a letter that is already in use).
5. Answer Yes when asked if you want to continue.
6. Click OK.
7. Close Disk Administrator.

Fault Tolerance (RAID)

If you've worked with computers for very long, you probably already know that they break. In fact the hard disk is one of the most commonly broken components in a computer. In order to increase your computer's uptime (the amount of time it is online) you should consider using RAID (Redundant Array of Inexpensive Disks). NT Supports software RAID levels 0, l, and 5, in which the operating system controls how the data is written to the physical drive. Hardware redundancy is more expensive, but it provides better performance. Windows NT HCL contains a list of hard disks supported for software RAID. RAID level 0 is a stripe set without parity, which was just discussed. This is the only level of RAID that *doesn't* provide fault tolerance, because it doesn't include a parity bit that can be used to reconstruct the data set.

Mirroring

Raid level 1 is disk mirroring, in which two hard disks contain identical information. If one drive fails, the other drive can still be accessed; since it contains identical information, no data is lost. Software RAID 1 can be used on the system and boot partition, whereas software RAID 5 can't be used on these partitions. Exercise 4-19 shows you how to create a mirror set and Exercise 4-20 shows how to repair a damaged mirror set using Disk Administrator.

EXERCISE 4-19

Creating a Mirror Set

1. Open Disk Administrator.

2. Select the partition that you want to mirror. Press CTRL and select free space on another drive that is the same size or larger than the partition you want to mirror.

3. Click Fault Tolerance | Establish Mirror.

EXERCISE 4-20

Repairing a Damaged Mirror Set

1. Open Disk Administrator.

2. Select the mirror set that is damaged.

3. Click Fault Tolerance | Break Mirror.

4. Replace or repair the damaged disk.

5. Recreate the mirror set as outlined in Exercise 4-19.

Duplexing

Disk duplexing is exactly like mirroring except that it uses two disk controller cards. This provides redundancy in case one of the controllers fails. Duplexing eliminates the single point of failure that comes with using a single controller card.

Striping with Parity

RAID 5, also called a stripe set with parity, uses 3 to 32 drives with the same size partition. It manages the data just like a stripe set, except it writes a parity bit across all the disks. Table 4-3 shows the order in which data is written to a stripe set with parity. RAID 5 uses this parity bit to reconstruct the data on a disk if that disk fails. If more than one disk fails, there isn't enough

TABLE 4-3

Stripe Set with Parity

	Disk0	Disk1	Disk2	Disk3
Stripe1	Parity 1	1	2	3
Stripe2	4	Parity 2	5	6
Stripe3	7	8	Parity 3	9
Stripe4	10	11	12	Parity 4

information to reconstruct the missing data; therefore, you shouldn't rely on RAID 5 alone—you'll also need to perform regular backups. The more disks you include in a stripe set with parity, the more economical it is. The amount of space lost to parity is 1/n (where n is the number of disks in the set). Unlike mirroring, software RAID 5 can't be used on the system or boot partitions. Exercise 4-21 shows you how to create a stripe set with parity and Exercise 4-22 shows how to repair a stripe set with parity.

EXERCISE 4-21

Creating a stripe set with parity

1. Open Disk Administrator.
2. Choose at least three areas of free space on separate disk drives (you can't choose more than 32 areas of free space).
3. Click Fault Tolerance | Create Stripe Set with Parity.
4. Enter the size of the stripe set with parity you want to create.
5. Click OK.

EXERCISE 4-22

Repairing a damaged stripe set with parity

1. Replace the damaged disk.
2. Open Disk Administrator.
3. Select the stripe set with parity by clicking on it.
4. Select an area of free space on the newly added hard disk (it must have an area of free space as large as the other disks in the stripe set).
5. Click Fault Tolerance | Regenerate.
6. Close Disk Administrator and restart NT.

NT Clients

One reason NT has been so successful is because of its support for many different clients. NT can communicate with MS-DOS with Network Client 3.0, Windows 95, Windows 3.11 for Workgroups, NT Workstation, OS/2, LAN Manager, Macintosh, NetWare, and UNIX clients.

Not all clients operate in the same way with NT. Table 4-4 shows the network protocols supported by the clients. Table 4-5 shows the supported TCP/IP protocol-related services.

Using the Network Client Administrator

The Network Client Administrator tool gives administrators the ability to customize the way they install networking clients. You can make a network installation startup disk or an entire installation disk set, copy client-based network administrative tools, and view Remoteboot client information. The Network Client Administrator tool, shown in Figure 4-20, is located in the Administrative Tools program group.

| TABLE 4-4 | | Supported Network Client Protocols | | |

Client	NetBEUI	IPX/SPX Compatible	TCP/IP	DLC
MS-DOS Network Client 3.0	X	X	X	X
Windows 95	X	X	X	
Windows 3.11	X	X	X	
LAN Manager 2.2c for MS-DOS	X		X	X
LAN Manager 2.2c for OS/2	X		X	
Windows NT Workstation	X	X	X	X
NetWare 3.11		X		

	Client	DHCP	WINS	DNS
TABLE 4-5				
TCP/IP Related Protocol Services	MS-DOS Network Client 3.0	X		
	Windows 95	X	X	X
	Windows 3.11	X	X	X
	LAN Manager 2.2c for MS-DOS	X		
	Windows NT Workstation	X	X	X

Make Network Installation Startup Disk

This option allows you to create a bootable floppy disk that will connect to an NT Server and download the files necessary for installing the selected operating system. Windows NT Workstation, Windows 95, and Microsoft Network Client 3.0 for MS-DOS are all supported.

Make Network Client Installation Disk Set

This option makes a complete installation disk set for the selected network operating system. You can make installation disks for Microsoft Network Client 3.0 for MS-DOS, LAN Manager 2.2c for MS-DOS Client, LAN Manager 2.2c OS/2 client, and Windows 95.

FIGURE 4-20

Network Client Administrator

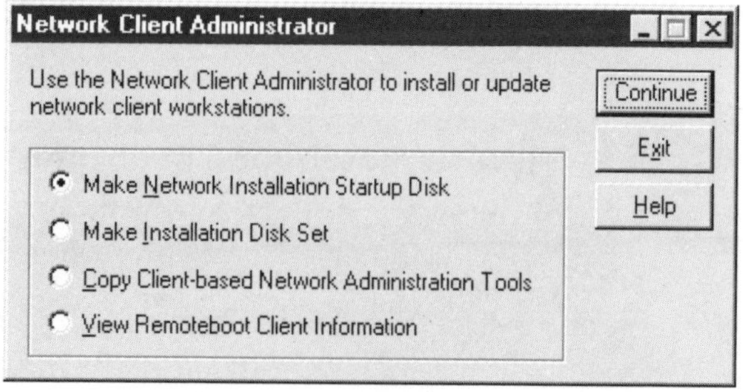

Copy Client-based Network Administration Tools

This option makes the NT administration tools available via the network. The list of tools you can execute depends on which operating system you are running.

The Windows NT Workstation tools are as follows:

- Server Manager
- DHCP Manager
- WINS Manager
- User Manager for Domains
- Remoteboot Manager
- Services for Macintosh
- System Policy Editor
- RAS Administrator

The tools for Windows 95 are as follows:

- Server Manager
- Event Viewer
- User Manager for Domains
- User Manager extensions for NetWare Services
- NTFS File permissions tab
- Print Security tab

View Remoteboot Client Information

Allows an administrator to view the remoteboot information provided by an NT Server running the Remoteboot service. Remoteboot service boots MS-DOS and Windows-based computers via the network.

NT Browser Types

NT uses a computer browser service to locate other computers on the network. Each protocol you have installed takes up resources in the computer browser service because each one must have its own browse list. There are four types of browsers: domain master browser, master browser, potential browser, and non-browser.

Domain Master Browser

The *domain master browser* is responsible for maintaining a list of master browsers on all subnets. It combines each subnet's master browser's list into one list for the entire domain. This list is forwarded back to the master browser on each subnet. By default, the PDC serves as the domain master browser.

Master Browser

Each subnet for the domain or each workgroup has a computer, known as the *master browser*, responsible for maintaining the browse list. Every time a computer starts, it registers itself with the master browser. The master browser records all registered computers in a list and forwards it to the domain master browser.

Backup Browser

The *backup browser* helps the master browser by giving its browse list to clients who request it. The master browser gives its browse list to a backup browser so the backup browser can give the list to local clients. Whenever a master browser goes offline, a backup browser becomes the master browser.

Potential Browser

A *potential browser* is a computer that isn't acting as a browser, but can do so if requested.

Non-browser

No matter what, this computer can't serve as a browser.

Browser Elections

Browser elections occur whenever a client or backup browser can't find a master browser. The browser election tries to find the most robust computer to be the master browser. A computer initiates an election by sending an election datagram out to the network. When a browser receives an election datagram, it examines the election criteria set on that datagram. If the browser has better election criteria it sends out its own election datagram. This continues until no more election datagrams are broadcast. When a browser can't send an election datagram because it doesn't have better criteria, it attempts to find the new master browser. Some of the criteria used to determine the master browser are:

- **Operating system** NT Server scores higher than Workstation; Workstation gets a higher score than Windows 95; and Windows 95 higher than 3.11.

- **Version** NT Server 4.0 scores higher than NT Server 3.51; and NT Server 3.51 higher than 3.5.

- **Current Browser Role** Backup browser gets a higher score than a potential browser.

You can use the MaintainServerList parameter in the registry to tell your server whether it should always try to become the master browser, never become the master browser, or be a potential browser. Edit the registry key:

HKEY_LOCAL_MACHINE\System\CurrentControlSet\Service\Browser\
Parameters MaintainServerList (set to Yes, No, or Auto)

Setting the MaintainServerList parameter to Yes forces your server to always try to become the master browser. The value No causes the computer to never become the master browser, and Auto sets it to be a potential browser.

NT System Registry

First, a warning: Editing the registry can severely damage your NT configuration. It's not like an .INI file where you can go back and correct your mistakes. If you damage your registry by editing the wrong key by mistake, you may have to reload NT. Before editing your registry, you should run the RDISK utility to make sure you have a current Emergency Repair Disk.

The registry contains all your system and program configuration parameters. It is a very powerful database that controls your computer. The registry is a much better way to maintain configuration information about your computer than .INI files were. First of all, .INI files were flat and couldn't contain subcategories within sections, whereas the registry can. Also .INI files couldn't apply security as the registry can. The registry offers a centralized place for configuration information, whereas .INI files were far from centralized—remember WIN.INI and SYSTEM.INI? Finally, the registry is very flexible. .INI files could only hold ASCII text, but the registry can hold binary values, hexadecimal values, and even executable code.

However, the registry does have its critics. It's very hard to navigate and understand. It's very easy to get lost in the plethora of directories and subdirectories. The registry is also a very deadly tool because one mistake can wipe out your entire system.

You should try to avoid editing the registry with regedt32.exe. You can save yourself a lot of trouble by using the proper tools designed for editing the registry. The Control Panel is a common tool used for editing the registry. When you change values using a Control Panel applet you are usually changing registry values. You can also use the administrative tools that come with NT to edit the registry: User Manager, Event Viewer, and Server

Manager. If you *must* edit the registry, Exercise 4-23 and Exercise 4-24 teach you how to get started.

Editing the Registry

1. Click Start | Run.
2. Type **REGEDT32**.
3. Click OK.
4. Choose the registry subtree you want to edit by clicking on its title bar (choose HKEY_LOCAL_MACHINE).
5. Expand the branches of the registry to get to the key you want to edit. Let's edit the key that configures the browser service. Go to the following key: HKEY_LOCAL_MACHINE\System\CurrentControlSet\Service\ Browser\Parameters.
6. Double-click MaintainServerList in the right-side pane.
7. Change the value listed from Auto to Yes (if it is already set to Yes change it to Auto).
8. Click OK.

Finding occurrences of a word in the registry

1. Start the registry editor.
2. Select the HKEY_CURRENT_USER subtree.
3. Click the highest directory (HKEY_CURRENT_USER).
4. Click View | Find Key.
5. Type **winlogon** in the Find What text box.
6. Click Find Next.

Hardware Profiles

Hardware profiles allow you to boot your computer using different configurations—most commonly laptops and docking stations. If the laptop is docked, it has one type of hardware configuration; when it isn't docked, it has a different configuration. By using hardware profiles you can specify which configuration to use when your system boots. NT uses the registry key HKEY_CURRENT_CONFIG to maintain the information about the hardware profile you selected at startup. You can create or edit hardware profiles using the Hardware Profiles tab in the System applet of the Control Panel.

User Profiles

User profiles store configuration information for a specific user. Users can choose many of their own environment settings without changing the environment for other users. Different environment settings for user profiles are stored in different files and locations within NT. The file NTUSER.DAT contains most of the registry information for a user profile; however, much of the information is also stored in folders located in %winnt%\profiles folder. This folder contains information such as recently used files, shortcuts, startup programs, and desktop configuration.

There are two types of user profiles: roaming and local. Roaming profiles allows users to log on to any NT Workstation or Server and have the same user profile. To set a roaming profile you need to set a profile path in User Manager. Roaming profiles can be mandatory. A mandatory profile doesn't allow the user to change his environment. To create a mandatory profile, you must specify a profile path in User Manager. Then copy a profile to the users profile directory using the Copy To button in the System applet. After the profile is copied, rename the file NTUSER.DAT to NTUSER.MAN. The .MAN extension makes the file read-only so that any changes the user makes to his environment won't be saved when the user exits.

A local profile resides on the local machine. Any changes made to the profile are updated locally. The first time a user logs on, NT uses the local default user profile to create a profile for the new user, unless the user has a roaming profile. If a user has a roaming profile, it is downloaded to the local machine.

Devices

You can configure the startup value of the devices on your system by using the Devices applet in Control Panel. There are five types of device you can configure:

- **Boot**   Has a start value of 0 in the registry; devices assigned this value start as soon as the kernel is initialized. Examples: tape and disk devices.

- **System**   Has a start value of 1; these devices start after the boot devices have finished starting and after the HKEY_LOCAL_MACHINE subtree is built. Examples: CD-ROM, serial mouse, and video drivers.

- **Automatic**   Has a start value of 2; these devices start just before the WINLOGON dialog box appears. Examples: parallel and serial ports.

- **Manual**   Has a start value of 3; these devices never start without an administrator to manually start the device.

- **Disabled**   Has a start value of 4; these devices can't be started without first changing their startup type.

Registry Hierarchy

The registry is made up of a hierarchy that can be visualized as a tree. At the top of the hierarchy is the subtree. Each subtree appears in its own window when using REGEDT32. There are five subtrees:

- HKEY_LOCAL_MACHINE
- HKEY_USERS
- HKEY_CLASSES_ROOT
- HKEY_CURRENT_USER
- HKEY_CURRENT_CONFIG

The next order in the hierarchy is the *hive*—a collection of registry keys which has a corresponding file saved on the hard disk. This gives the registry fault-tolerance. If the registry is corrupt, it can read the affected hive from a file on the hard disk. The registry keys appear as folders when using the registry-editing tool. A key is a category that can contain subkeys. At the bottom of the hierarchy are the values.

Data Types

There are five different types of data value that you can store in the registry.

- **REG_BINARY**   Indicates that the data is binary.
- **REG_DWORD**   Indicates that the data is stored in a word (four-byte number).
- **REG_SZ**   Indicates that the data is a string (text).
- **REG_MULTI_SZ**   Indicates the data is a multiple string (list).
- **REG_EXPAND_SZ**   Indicates the data is an expandable string (variable).

CERTIFICATION SUMMARY

This chapter had many exercises in it. In order to pass the exam you'll need to know how to perform all these tasks, so if you skipped any of the exercises be sure to go back and complete them before taking the exam.

The chapter began with instructions to configure TCP/IP. You need to know that TCP/IP must be configured, and that you can use DHCP to automatically configure your clients. DHCP and WINS are two services that you'll probably use on a Microsoft TCP/IP network. DHCP Server can automatically assign IP addresses and configuration information on your clients. WINS is used to resolve computer names to IP addresses dynamically.

The chapter contains many exercises that use Disk Administrator. One common element in all of the exercises was the fact that you had to commit your changes before applying new modifications to your partitions. NT forces you to do this, so that you can always undo your changes in case you make a mistake. The chapter also discussed RAID levels 0, 1, and 5. RAID level 0, a stripe set without parity, does not provide fault tolerance. RAID level 1, disk mirroring, uses two disk drives and keeps the exact same information on each disk. RAID level 1 can be used for boot and system partitions. RAID level 5, a stripe set with parity, can't be used on system and boot partitions. It uses 3 to 32 disks to provide fault tolerance by writing a parity bit that is spread across all the disks in the set. This parity bit is used to reconstruct the data if one of the disks fails.

You'll need to know how various clients can connect to NT via which protocols. The Network Client Administrator is used to install network shares for client installations and NT Administrative Tools. It can also be used to view the Remoteboot client information for networks that boot clients from a server.

Finally, the chapter discussed the registry and its subtrees. The registry can be visualized as a tree. Each window in the tree (called a subtree) has branches called keys. These branches eventually end with leaves, which are the actual data values.

TWO-MINUTE DRILL

- ❑ NWLink does not require any configuration. By default it uses Auto Detect to detect the frame type.

- ❑ If you use WINS for name resolution on your network, you'll need to configure the WINS Address tab.

- ❑ All computers must have the same scope ID to communicate on a TCP/IP network. If you change the Scope ID of a server, all computers on the network must be changed to have the same scope ID.

- ❑ The DHCP Relay tab is used to forward DHCP request through a router.

- ❑ If you have a multihomed computer and you want to use static IP routing between the two NIC's, you need to check the box in the Routing tab.

- ❑ DHCP is used to assign TCP/IP configuration parameters on networked clients.

❑ DHCP is similar to BootP, except it leases IP addresses instead of giving out a new address every time the computer boots.

❑ The DHCP server administrator configures a *scope* for which a set of valid IP addresses are assigned. Each physical subnet that uses DHCP must have an active scope for that subnet if it is using DHCP.

❑ WINS resolves computer names to IP addresses on a Windows-based network. WINS performs the same role as DNS, except it is dynamic.

❑ The computer-specific applets affect all users and can only be changed by an administrator.

❑ You can increase the performance of your machine by spreading your page file out across several disks, especially if you have more than one disk controller or a controller that performs concurrent I/O.

❑ The SCSI Adapters Control Panel applet is used to install SCSI adapters, but it is also used to install IDE CD-ROM drivers.

❑ NT uses two special partitions called the *system* and *boot* partitions for its start-up procedure.

❑ Volume sets combine 2 to 32 areas of free space on one or multiple hard disks. Use volume sets to combine different sized areas of free space as a single volume (drive letter) from any type of hard disk.

❑ A primary partition can be used as a system partition (set to active). Each hard disk can have up to four primary partitions.

❑ If you use an extended partition on a disk, you can only have three primary partitions on that disk.

❑ A *logical drive* is a method of subdividing an extended partition.

❑ Disk duplexing is exactly like mirroring except that it uses two disk controller cards. This provides redundancy in case one of the controllers fails.

❑ The *domain master browser* is responsible for maintaining a list of master browsers on all subnets.

❑ Each subnet for the domain or each workgroup has a computer, known as the *master browser*, responsible for maintaining the browse list.

❑ The *backup browser* helps the master browser by giving its browse list to clients who request it.

❑ Whenever a master browser goes offline, a backup browser becomes the master browser.

❑ The file NTUSER.DAT contains most of the registry information for a user profile.

❑ There are two types of user profiles: roaming and local.

❑ A *hive* is a collection of registry keys which has a corresponding file saved on the hard disk.

SELF TEST

The following questions will help you measure your understanding of the material presented in this chapter. Read all the choices carefully, as there may be more than one correct answer. Choose all correct answers for each question.

1. You have two SCSI drives, each with a 2GB partition and its own disk controller. You want fault tolerance and you want to be able to continue to use one of the drives should the other fail. What type of fault tolerance should you use?

   A. Volume set

   B. Disk duplexing

   C. Stiped set with parity

   D. Raid Level 5

2. You have an NT Server computer. You install the client Network Administration Tools on your Windows 95 computer. How can you remotely manage file and directory permissions?

   A. Server Manager

   B. Windows Explorer

   C. NET USE commands

   D. User Manager for Domains

3. You have two network cards you want to configure with TCP/IP in the same server. How can you do this? (Choose all that apply.)

   A. Use DHCP.

   B. Manually assign IP addresses.

   C. Use an LMHost file to point to the second card.

4. You have NetBEUI and TCP/IP installed on your server. Most of your clients have TCP/IP installed on their systems as the default protocol. You've noticed that clients with TCP/IP as the default protocol take longer to connect to your server. How can you fix the problem?

   A. Move TCP/IP higher in the binding order.

   B. Remove NetBEUI from the server.

   C. Install two network cards.

   D. Upgrade to an ATM network.

5. Your users have a mandatory profile with a .man extension assigned. They are logging on to the system for the first time, but the server with the mandatory profile is offline. What will happen?

   A. They will be logged on using the default profile.

   B. They can't log on because the mandatory profile is unavailable.

   C. NT uses a cached mandatory profile to log the user on.

   D. They can log on, but changes to the current profile won't be saved.

6. You are creating a stripe set with parity on four disk drives, each with a 100MB partition. What's the largest size stripe set with parity you can create?

A.   300MB

B.   400MB

C.   200MB

7.   You are creating a stripe set with parity on four disk drives, each with a 100MB partition. What's the largest amount of data that can be saved to the stripe set with parity?

A.   300MB

B.   400MB

C.   200MB

8.   You have four hard disks. Drive 1 has 100MB of free space, Drive 2 and Drive 3 each has 200MB of free space, and Drive 4 has 500MB of free space. What's the largest size stripe set you can create?

A.   500MB

B.   1GB

C.   600MB

D.   400MB

9.   What service should you use to provide IP address configuration information to Windows clients?

A.   WINS

B.   LMHOSTS

C.   DHCP

D.   Simple TCP/IP Services

10.   What are the required parameters for a TCP/IP configured server in a routed environment? (Choose all that apply.)

A.   IP address

B.   Subnet mask

C.   Default gateway

D.   DHCP Server

E.   WINS Server IP address

11.   How would you install Win95 over a network? (Choose all that apply.)

A.   Share the Windows 95 installation files using the Network Client Administrator tool.

B.   Make an Installation startup disk with the Network Client Administrator tool.

C.   Install using a network startup disk.

D.   Install using the disk set.

12.   You have four physical disks, each with 250MB of free space. You want to create a stripe set. What will be the largest stripe set you can create?

A.   250

B.   500

C.   750

D.   1000

13.   You are administering a Windows NT Server computer from a Windows 95 client computer. You install client-based Network Administrative Tools on the Windows 95 computer. You want to share a CD-ROM that is attached to the Windows NT Server computer. What must you use on the Windows 95 computer to do this?

A.   Server Manager

B.   Disk Adminstrator

C.   Explorer

D. NET USE commands

14. You configure a stripe set without parity on three physical disks. One of the disks fails. What can you do to recover data that was stored on the stripe set?

    A. Break the stripe set and recover the data by choosing Regenerate in Disk Administrator.

    B. Install a new hard disk to replace the failed disk and choose Regenerate from the Fault Tolerance menu in the Disk Administrator.

    C. Run the Command RECOVER /FS from a command prompt, then reboot your computer.

    D. Restore the lost data from a tape backup.

15. Your network uses NWLink IPX/SPX Compatible transport protocol. Half of the client computers use 802.3, the other half use 802.2 frame type. You are adding a Windows NT Server computer to the network. This server has one network adapter. What must you do on the new server so it can communicate with all the clients?

    A. Install RIP for NWLink IPX/SPX Compatible protocol.

    B. Use Auto Frame Detection in NWLink IPX/SPX Compatible protocol.

    C. Configure NWLink IPX/SPX compatible protocol to use Manual Frame Type detection. Add the 802.3 and 802.2 frame type.

    D. Install the driver for the network adapter twice, once for each frame type. Configure each instance of the driver to support one of the required frame types.

16. Your server has six disks, each with two partitions. On the first disk are the boot and system partitions. How can you optimize the pagefile?

    A. Place a pagefile on each disk except the first.

    B. Place the pagefile on any disk except the first.

    C. Place the pagefile on the first disk.

    D. Place the pagefile on the largest available partition.

17. What is the startup value of a boot device in the registry?

    A. 0

    B. 1

    C. 2

    D. 3

    E. 4

18. What is the file name of a mandatory profile?

    A. NTUSER.DAT

    B. NTUSER.PRO

    C. NTUSER.MAN

    D. NTUSER.POL

19. You want to use WINS on your routed network as the only way for name resolution across the router. Your clients consist of 100 Windows 95 computers, 50 Windows NT

Workstations 4.0, 3 NT Servers 4.0, and 5 LAN Manager 2.2c for MS-DOS clients. Will this work?

A. Yes, because they are all Microsoft products.

B. Yes, because WINS is an Internet standard as specified in RFC 302.

C. No, because not all the clients can support WINS.

5

Managing Resources

CERTIFICATION OBJECTIVES

5.01   User and Group Accounts

5.02   System Policies

5.03   User Profiles

5.04   Administering Remote NT Servers

This chapter deals with a very challenging aspect of administering a Windows NT network: managing resources. Resources can mean a lot of things in Windows NT, such as users, groups, workstations, servers, disks, and memory, but for this chapter we are going to narrow the scope to users and groups. Without users to use the resources there would not be such a demand for people like us to manage them. They are the reason we have been hired. We know how to use Windows NT and make life easier for these users by giving them access to resources that they require to do their jobs. We also know how to group users according to function, so we can better manage them. When these users are grouped in a logical fashion, it makes administration easier. We can easily apply restrictions and polices to the group, without having to modify each user account. Having the option of controlling access on a per-user basis is very powerful. Not only can we create policies for groups, we can create them for specific users, to control what we want them to see and do on the network. Although this sounds restrictive, we can use these conventions to make the user's life easier through the use of profiles and logon scripts, which can customize a user's computer environment to access his resources more efficiently. We close the chapter with some discussion on managing server resources that are not discussed in other chapters.

User and Group Accounts

Let's face it: if not for the users, we would not have much to do on the network as administrators. Everything we do as administrators revolves around the user in some way. Next time you are having fun configuring that RAID array, remember that its purpose is to increase the performance for the user. Since everything revolves around the user, it makes sense to begin the discussion of managing resources with the user account.

The user account is what gives a user access to the network. If you do not have a user account, you aren't allowed to log on to the network. Since the account is based on the user, it makes sense that a new account must be created for each user. This can be time-consuming, but it is necessary. Once the user account is created and configured, you don't have to do much housekeeping with the user accounts, unless their situation changes, or they get locked out of the system. At the time of creation, the user account should be placed in the proper groups.

Group accounts are for grouping together users who perform the same function or require access to the same resources. If it were not for group accounts, you would have to grant access to resources on a per-user basis. It is entirely possible to use group membership for resource access without having to grant access on a per-user basis, but it's nice to know you can grant or deny access down to the user level.

Your grouping should mirror the way users are logically grouped in your organization. Say you have an organization with a sales force, support engineers, and technicians. If you group the users according to their job function, it makes it easier to do things such as granting access to resources and sending notifications to group members. You can send a memo to the sales force informing them of sales-related information, which would not be of interest to your engineering staff. Perhaps the sales staff is the only group you would like to give Internet access to.

User and group accounts seem very logical, but we see later in the chapter how this can quickly become confusing for administrators. It's just like a computer to go and make things more confusing than they need to be!

User Manager

The User Manager is where most of your user and group management takes place. From here you create, modify, and delete accounts, and assign rights. This is one of the most important utilities to the administrator of a network. You will be here every day. In this chapter, we cover everything you need to know to become efficient at managing users and groups within User Manager. User Manager is located in the Administrative Tools under the name User Manager for Domains in Windows NT Server, and the name User Manager in Windows NT Workstation.

Figure 5-1 shows the user accounts and groups on a domain. You can tell by looking at the icon next to the group whether the group is local or global. An icon of two users and a computer is a local group. An icon of two users and a globe is a global group. You might specify whether a group is local or global in the group name, such as Sales Local. This is so other users can place

FIGURE 5-1

User Manager icons
show whether a group is
local or global

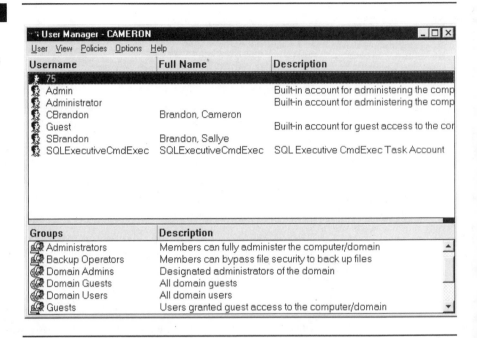

accounts accordingly. You learn more about local and global groups later in
the chapter.

User Accounts

User accounts represent users who access the resources on the domain. User
accounts do not have to represent individuals; they can also be accounts for
services, such as the SQL Server account I have in my list of user accounts.
You should have a naming convention in place if you are just starting your
domain, or you should adhere to the convention already in place if you are
administering an established network. The most common naming convention
is the first initial and full last name, such as GCramer for Garth Cramer.
However, this naming convention is not a good security practice, so it is not
recommended. If a hacker can figure out your username, he is halfway to
cracking your account.

In Figure 5-2 you notice the full name has been in the last name, first name
format. This is to facilitate searching by last name. User Manager for Domains

FIGURE 5-2

In the New User window,
enter last name first in the
Full Name field

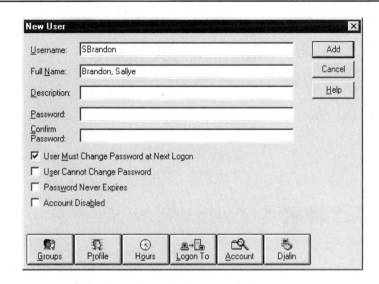

can display users by their username, such as SBrandon, or by their full name. If
you entered the full name as Sallye Brandon, you won't find it with a search of
last names. This is extremely important if you have a large number of users in
your domain.

EXERCISE 5-1

Creating a New User Account

In this exercise we add a new account to the domain. If you are using User
Manager from Windows NT Workstation rather than NT Server, you are
creating a local machine account.

1. Open up User Manager for Domains in the Administrative Tools
   program group.

2. Select the User pull-down menu.

3. Select New User.

4. Type in a username. Adhere to the naming conventions that you
   created, or the conventions that were already in place.

5. Type in a full name for the user with the last name first.

6. Type in a description, such as position or location to make it easier to
   identify the user.

7. Type in a password for the user, and confirm the password. (If this is a new user, it is common to use *password* as the password, and have the person change it to a password of their choice. This is not a good security practice, because someone can log on to their account if they know *password* is commonly used for the password.)

8. Select the User Must Change Password at Next Logon if you entered a temporary password, and would like to give the user a chance to change it at the next logon.

9. Check the User Cannot Change Password, or Password Never Expires boxes if you prefer.

EXERCISE 5-2

Copying a User Account

If you have already made a user account that you would like to use as a template for subsequent users, you can make use of the copy feature. This feature does not copy the Password, Full Name, or Username, but it does copy the password settings. It also copies the Description, Groups, Profile, and Dialin information.

1. Highlight the user account you would like to copy.

2. Select Copy from the User menu, or press the F8 key.

3. Type in a username.

4. Type in the full name.

5. Type in a password and confirm it.

6. Change any information that you do not wish to be copied.

EXERCISE 5-3

Disabling a User Account

Disabling a user account is a function to be used when a person has not logged on to the system recently, but may still be a part of the company. You should disable, rather than delete, the account, just in case the user returns. We use a third-party utility at our company to tell us when the user logged on last. If the last logon has been longer than three months, the account is disabled. If the last logon has been longer than six months, the account is deleted. You want to minimize the risk of others accessing the network through these unused accounts.

1. Double-click the user account you would like to disable.

2. Check the Account Disabled box.

<table>
<tr><td>EXERCISE 5-4</td></tr>
</table>

Deleting a User Account

You need to delete an account if a user is no longer with the company, or will no longer be needing network access. Make certain it is safe to delete the account, because it cannot be re-created with the existing rights and permissions. You can re-create the name, but that does not undelete all of the prior user's information. This is because accounts are created with a security identifier (SID). You cannot re-create this SID for security reasons. The new account may have the same name, but the SID is different, therefore the account is different. This provides security against someone trying to re-create an account that had been deleted and gaining access to all of the existing information.

1. Highlight the account you would like to delete and press the DELETE key, or select Delete from the User menu.

2. Confirm your intentions by selecting OK at the prompt, and then selecting Yes to make sure.

<table>
<tr><td>EXERCISE 5-5</td></tr>
</table>

Renaming a User Account

Renaming an account is especially useful if a user is replaced by another person, who must retain the same security settings. To illustrate the usefulness of renaming an account with existing permissions, we will make this exercise more extensive.

1. Have a user already in place that we can rename.

2. Open Windows Explorer and right-click a folder.

3. Select Properties, and then the Security tab.

4. Click the Permissions button.

5. Click Add and select the user that you have in place from step 1.

6. Give the user any access to the folder that you wish.

7. Verify that the user is listed in the Directory Permissions dialog box.

8. Click OK twice to exit back to Windows Explorer.

9. Open User Manager for Domains and highlight the user that you gave directory permissions to in the preceding steps.

10. Select Rename from the User pull-down menu.

11. Enter the new name for the user account.

12. Open Windows Explorer and right-click the folder that you gave permissions to in step 2.

13. Select Properties, and then the Security tab.

14. Click the Permissions button.

15. Notice the permissions for this folder reflect the user that we just renamed.

The User Environment Profile dialog box, shown in Figure 5-3, is for managing profiles, as well as a user's home directory. It is accessed by clicking the Profile button on a user's account in User Manager for Domains.

There is nothing in the User Environment Profile dialog box that is mandatory; it is all optional.

EXERCISE 5-6

Creating User Directories

In this exercise we create user directories for users to store their personal information. In this example we use a directory at the local computer, rather than a network share.

1. Open up User Manager for Domains.

2. Double-click the user you would like to create a user directory for.

3. Click the Profile button.

4. In the Local Path under the Home Directory section, type in the path you would like to store the user's information. If the path is not found, User Manager creates it for you. You can also use the %username% variable to substitute the name of the user account that logs on. This is effective for automatically assigning a new user a directory for storing information. Here is the syntax:

   C:\WINNT\USER\%username%

With User Manager, you can limit the hours a user is able to access the domain. This is to prevent misuse, or to clear the network for events such as tape backup. The Logon Hours dialog box, shown in Figure 5-4, can be accessed by clicking the Hours button for the specific account in User Manager for Domains. The configuring of logon hours is only available on a domain controller.

FIGURE 5-3

The User Environment Profile dialog box is for managing profiles, as well as a user's home directory

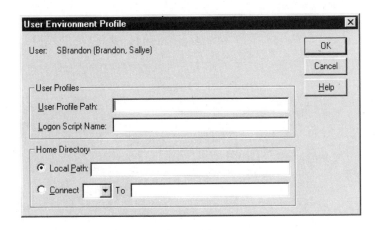

FIGURE 5-4

At Logon Hours, you can limit the hours a user is able to access the domain

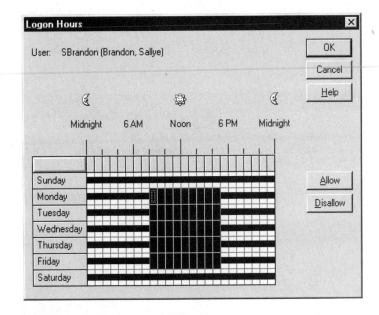

EXERCISE 5-7

Setting Logon Hours

In this exercise we specify the times users are allowed on the network.

1. Open up User Manager for Domains.

2. Select the user you would like to set new logon hours for.

3. Click the Hours button.

   By default the user is allowed access at all hours. We will give our user access to the network only during business hours Monday through Friday.

4. Click Sunday, and the entire row is highlighted.

5. Click the Disallow button.

6. Repeat this with Saturday.

7. Highlight the cell for Midnight on Monday. Click and drag to 8 AM.

8. Click the Disallow button.

9. Highlight the cell for 5 PM on Monday. Click and drag to Midnight.

10. Click the Disallow button.

11. Continue this for the remaining days that you are disallowing access.

Another impressive feature of Windows NT security is to disallow users to log on from machines other than their own. At the Logon Workstations dialog box, shown in Figure 5-5, you can allow users to log on to all workstations, which is the default, or specifically restrict a user to one or more workstations.

FIGURE 5-5

At Logon Workstations
you can allow users to
log on to all workstations,
or restrict them to one
or more

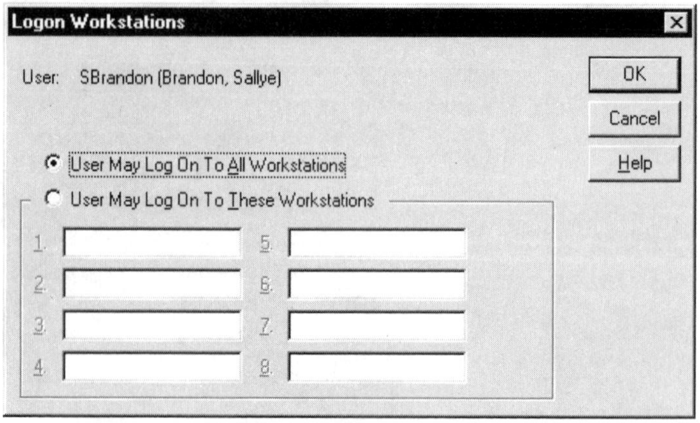

The Account Information dialog box, shown in Figure 5-6, is useful for granting temporary accounts for consultants or contractors that require temporary access to the network. For maximum security you can have this account expire after a contract has expired. You also can specify the account type, which is global by default. You should specify a global account if this user is a member of another domain, or if the account will be used in another domain. Specify a local account if you know the user will not require access to other domains.

In order for users to access the network via Remote Access, they have to be given permission. This can be done either from the Remote Access Service Manager, or User Manager for Domains. See Figure 5-7 for the Dialin Information dialog box. When permission is granted, a choice is made among three options regarding the Call Back feature:

- The user does not get called back.

- The user gets called back at the number he specifies. This option is convenient for travelling users, who call from different locations.

- The user gets called back at a predetermined number. This option is the most secure, because the phone number is entered by the administrator.

FIGURE 5-6

At Account Information you can grant temporary accounts for consultants or contractors that require temporary access to the network

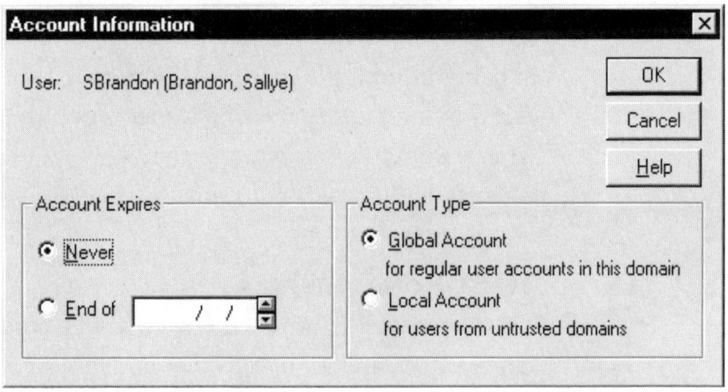

At Dialin Information,
choose from three
options regarding the
Call Back feature

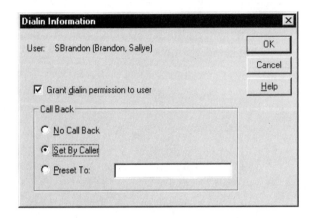

Modifying Dialin Information

1. Open up User Manager for Domains.

2. Double-click the user you would like to modify the dialin information for.

3. Click the Dialin button.

4. Check the box to give them dialin permission.

5. Click the radio button that corresponds to the call back settings you prefer.

Group Accounts

The Group Memberships dialog box, shown in Figure 5-8, is used to modify the groups that the user is a member of. The user inherits more rights by virtue of being in multiple groups. However, if a user is a member of a group that has access to a resource, and of another group that does not have access to that same resource, access is not given. This should be taken into consideration when assigning users to groups.

Trust Relationships

Trust relationships are a very complicated issue for Windows NT domains. Luckily, they are not covered in depth on the Windows NT Server exam. (They are covered in extreme detail in the Windows NT Server on the Enterprise

At Group Memberships,
add or remove a user from
a group

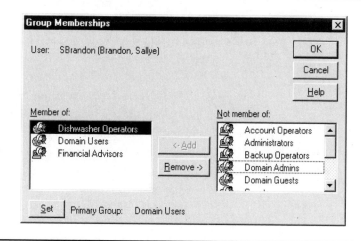

exam.) For now, we will discuss a few things concerning rudimentary trust
relationships and how they relate to user and group administration.

In order to access resources from another Windows NT domain, there must
be a trust relationship between the two domains. This can be a one-way trust, or
a two-way trust relationship. When the trust relationship is in place, users from
one domain can access resources in the other domain. Trust relationships are
added and removed in User Manager for Domains. Later in this chapter you
learn which user and group accounts can access resources in other domains.

Group Administration

Now that you realize the importance of using groups for administration, you
need to understand some techniques for proper group administration, and for
making sure users are placed in the right groups. Users are placed in groups
according to their function and your overall group strategy.

Local Groups vs. Global Groups

Understanding the difference between local and global groups requires
knowledge of the Windows NT domain structure. If you are unfamiliar
with domains in general, you may benefit from reviewing their purpose

before continuing further into this section. It's a subject that can quickly become confusing.

Place users in a local group for resource access within the domain. If you have created a local group called Marketing, you can place users from within the same domain into this group and everything will be fine. You cannot take this group and give them access to resources on another domain. This is why it is called a local group. Just remember that local groups are local to the domain.

Global groups can be created to access resources, not just within the domain, but outside of the domain as well. This is the type of group you would use if you had a multiple-domain model, and were giving access to resources outside of the domain.

exam
ⓌatchW

Local and global groups (as well as trust relationships) are not covered in much depth during the Windows NT Server 4.0 exam. They are covered in great depth in the Windows NT 4.0 Server on the Enterprise exam. However, it is very important to understand the differences between the two. It will also make studying easier for the next exam, when you will need this background. Local and group administration can be a very complex issue, especially when Microsoft gets their hands on it for the exam.

Group Administration Strategies

Now is an opportune time to explain a strategy for group administration that is often discussed in MCSE newsgroups. The tip to remembering the local versus group method is this acronym: AGLP.

A = Accounts.
G = the Global group, in which accounts are placed.
L = the Local group, where the global group is placed.
P = Permissions are set for the local group.

Global groups are to organize the users, and local groups are to assign permissions and rights.

With that in mind, follow along with this guide to making decisions about group assignments:

QUESTIONS AND ANSWERS

I only have one domain and I need to assign permissions or rights...	Use a local group. This is the correct group if you only have one domain. You can add users, and also other global groups if you need to give permissions to members of another domain later.
I need to place a group within...	Use local. Only local groups can contain a global group. In fact, that is the only way one group can be placed in another group.
I need to give users permissions on workstations or member servers...	Use a global group. You cannot create a global group on a member server or workstation, but you can add this global group to the member server or workstation's local group. You can then grant permissions to the local group.
I need to group users so they can access resources from another domain...	Use a global group. Global groups can be placed in the other domain's local groups. The other domain can then grant permissions to the local group.
I need a group to include users from other domains...	Use a local group. Although the group cannot be used outside the local domain, it can be used to hold global groups that contain users from other domains.

Groups within Groups

When it comes to placing groups within groups, you can only place global groups within local groups. This is the only way you can use nested groups. Here is what is *not* accepted when it comes to nested groups:

- Local groups cannot be placed in local groups.
- Global groups cannot be placed in global groups.
- Local groups cannot be placed in global groups.

In order to understand the nested group rule, let's create a scenario involving two domains. One domain is your local domain called BRANCH1. This contains a group of users known as SALES_LOCAL. This group contains user accounts from your domain. Since you are a branch office, you have a corporate domain called CORPORATE. There is a global group on the CORPORATE domain called SALES_GLOBAL, which contains users from the

CORPORATE domain. If members of the SALES_GLOBAL group are coming to your BRANCH1 domain to train your users, you can quickly place the SALES_GLOBAL group within your local SALES_LOCAL group, to give them access to the resources that have been given to the SALES_LOCAL group.

Creating and Managing Groups in User Manager

Here is a rundown of the options you have in User Manager for Domains concerning groups:

- Double-click the group to see the members and to add or remove members.

- Double-click the user and click the Groups button to add or remove them from groups.

- Select New Global Group from the User pull-down menu to create a new Global group.

- Select New Local Group from the User pull-down menu to create a new Local group.

- To delete a group, highlight it and press DELETE, or select Delete from the User pull-down menu.

Local Groups

Local groups, as we have discussed, are for resource access within your domain. If you know beyond the shadow of a doubt that you will not be accessing resources in another domain, then go ahead and use local groups for everything. Place global groups and users from your domain directly into a local group. This can be helpful if you do find yourself needing to give access to groups from other domains. You will have to make new global groups for granting access to resources in other domains, if you find yourself with more than one domain.

You may not have to create many groups, because Windows NT comes equipped with built-in groups to help organize users with various tasks. Of course, it doesn't come with built-in groups like Sales or Marketing, but it includes some groups to relieve the administrative burden. Before we discuss the built-in groups, let's demonstrate the creation of a new group. Refer to Figure 5-9 for the New Local Group dialog box.

EXERCISE 5-9

Creating a Local Group

This exercise creates a local group on the domain. If you are using Windows NT Workstation, this is the only type of group you can create.

1. Open up User Manager for Domains.

2. Select New Local Group from the User pull-down menu.

3. Enter the name of the local group, and a description, if necessary. This is a good time to specify whether the group is local or global, for future reference.

4. Click the Add button to show a list of users and groups that can be placed in this local group.

5. Highlight the user you would like to add, and click the Add button.

6. Select OK twice to save the changes. You should now see your local group in the bottom portion of the dialog box.

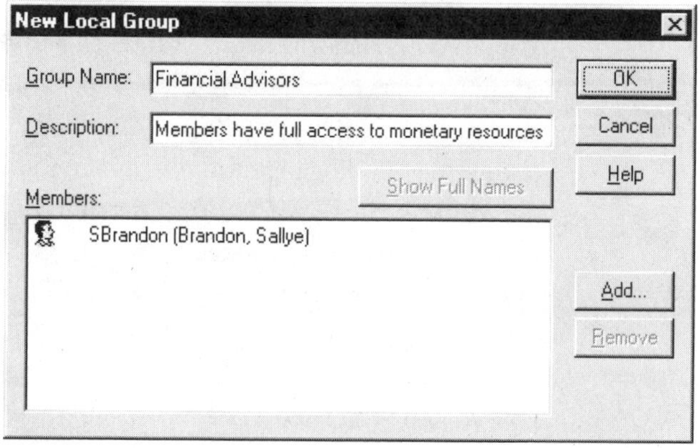

FIGURE 5-9

At the New Local Group dialog box, create a local group on the domain

Administrators

The Administrators local group is the most powerful of all of the groups. As you would expect, you have full control of the computer by virtue of being in this group. For this reason, only those trusted with this great responsibility should be members of this elite group. By default, the Domain Admins global group is a member of the local Administrators group. You can remove this global group if you desire.

Users

The Users local group has enough rights for users to get work done at their workstations, but not much else. Users don't have the right even to log on at a Windows NT Server. The Domain Users global group is a member of the Users local group by default, but can be removed.

Guest

The Guest group is even more limited than the Users group. It should be used for one-time, or temporary access to resources. Users can log on using the built-in workstation Guest account, or by using the domain built-in Guest account. Either way, they are restricted in the tasks that they can perform. The Domain Guests global group is by default a member of the Guest local group, but you can remove it.

Server Operators

The Server Operators group is intended to relieve the burden on the administrator. Members of this group can shut down servers, format server hard disks, create and modify shares, lock and unlock the server, back up and restore files, and change the system time. Although its purpose is to decrease the administrator's workload, it may increase his paranoia. Members of this group should be well trained in Windows NT, because they have rights that can be very damaging to the network. The Server Operators group only exists on a domain controller.

Print Operators

Print Operators have the ability to create, delete, and modify printer shares. These will most likely be on print servers, which the members of the Print

Operators group can log on to, and shut down if need be. The Print Operators group only exists on a Domain Controller.

Backup Operators
Members of the Backup Operators local group can back up and restore on the primary and backup domain controllers. Just like the Print Operators, they can log on to, and shut down the server, if needed.

Account Operators
Account Operators have permissions to add, modify, and delete most user and group accounts in User Manager for Domains. They do not have the ability to modify any of the default groups just mentioned, nor can they modify any member that belongs to any of these groups. They can also use Server Manager to add computers to the domain. The Account Operators group only exists on a domain controller. Members have the right to log on at domain controllers, and also have the right to shut them down. I once was an Account Operator at Intel, and I didn't even work there! I was a contractor for another company.

Replicator
The Replicator group contains the Replicator user account for the replication services. This group should not be used for any other purpose. In other words, users other than your replicator service account should not be added here.

Global Groups

Global groups give users access to resources in other domains. Global groups were designed to move the people to the resource, since you can't move the resource to all the people. This is accomplished by adding the global group to the local group where the resource is located.

You have now seen the purpose of global groups, and learned when they should be chosen over local groups. If you are using Windows NT Workstation rather than Windows NT Server, you don't have the option of creating global groups.

Creating a Global Group

1. Open up User Manager for Domains.

2. Select New Global Group under the User pull-down menu.

3. Enter the name of the group, and give the group a description if necessary. This may be a good time to specify whether the group is local or global, for future reference.

4. Click the Add button to show a list of users that can be placed in this global group.

5. Highlight the user you would like to add, and click the Add button.

6. Select OK twice to save the changes. You should now see your global group in the bottom portion of the dialog box.

Domain Administrator

The Domain Admins global group is a member of the Administrators local group on every computer in the domain by default. (Actually, this is just for computers running Windows NT, because operating systems like Windows 95 do not use groups to administer the local machine.) Having the Domain Admins global group in the Administrators local group by default gives an administrator full control to modify computers in the domain. You can revoke this right by removing the Domain Admins group from the Administrators local group on the machine.

Domain Users

The Domain Users global group contains all subsequent accounts created in the domain. This gives users the ability to access resources in other domains. The Domain Users global group is by default a member of the Users local group on every Windows NT computer in the domain. This gives users the ability to access non-domain controller computers and workstations in the domain. If you do not wish them to have this ability, remove the Domain Users group from the Users local group on the specific machine.

Domain Guests

The Domain Guests global group is intended to provide limited and/or temporary access to the domain. By default, the Domain Guests global group is a member of the Guests local group.

System Policies

In this section we focus on the ways you can implement policies on your domain for activities such as account restrictions, desktop settings, and network settings. Using these policies you can fine-tune users' access and abilities on the network. Although system policies are very effective in what they accomplish, they can add more work for the administrator of the network. Not only must the administrator learn the various utilities for system policy, he must decide what to restrict, verify that the restrictions work, and explain to users why they have been restricted.

Most system policy restrictions are considered optional, but one that should always be adjusted is the Account Policy found in User Manager for Domains. This feature, illustrated in Figure 5-10, contains settings for passwords and lockout features for security, and should not be ignored. You have to determine which settings are appropriate for your organization. The more policy restrictions you implement on your network, the angrier users get. For example, the password restrictions, such as expiration and password uniqueness, are sure to upset users over time. At my company, where the computer remembers an employee's last six passwords, and passwords expire every month, not a day goes by that I don't hear users complaining about the inconvenience of these restrictions. I have to explain that these settings apply to everyone, from the president of the company right down to the hourly employees. NT should let us differentiate account policy for groups, rather than the entire domain.

The Account Policy dialog box is reached through User Manager for Domains by selecting Account from the Policies pull-down menu.

EXERCISE 5-11

Changing Account Policies

In this exercise we adjust some important settings for the Account Policy.

1. Open up User Manager for Domains if you have not already.

2. Select Account from the Policies pull-down menu.

FIGURE 5-10

The Account Policy
dialog box contains
settings for passwords
and lockout features

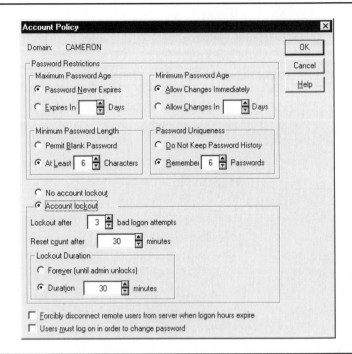

3. In the Minimum Password Age portion, have the password expire after a certain period of days. This is usually a month to three months, depending on the security needs of your organization. The less time before password changes, the more secure your network is.

4. In the Minimum Password Length portion, enter a value of five or larger. This makes it more difficult to guess passwords.

5. In the Password Uniqueness portion, have NT remember a few passwords. This prevents a user from using the same password over and over. The more the system remembers, the more upset your users get.

6. Enable the Account Lockout feature. This locks out an account temporarily or permanently after a certain number of incorrect password attempts.

7. Lock out the account after three or more password attempts. This gives the user enough chances to type the password correctly.

8. For the Lockout Duration, select a duration of thirty minutes to an hour. If you lock the account out forever, the administrator has to be called whenever a user locks himself out of the account.

Another area for adjusting policy is through the User Rights Policy, illustrated in Figure 5-11. This is also found in User Manager for Domains. Administrators don't make adjustments to most of these rights, with the exception of two: Log on Locally, and Access This Computer From Network. We will adjust these settings in the next exercise.

EXERCISE 5-12

Modifying User Rights

1. Open up User Manager for Domains if you have not already.

2. Select User Rights under the Policies pull-down menu.

3. Find the Log on Locally right and select it. This setting is to specify which users are allowed to sit at this computer and log on. This is a very effective way to restrict users from logging on to certain computers.

4. If there are users you would like to remove, highlight them and click the Remove button. If there are users you would like to add, click the Add button.

FIGURE 5-11

The rights most commonly adjusted in User Rights Policy are Log on Locally and Access This Computer From Network

---

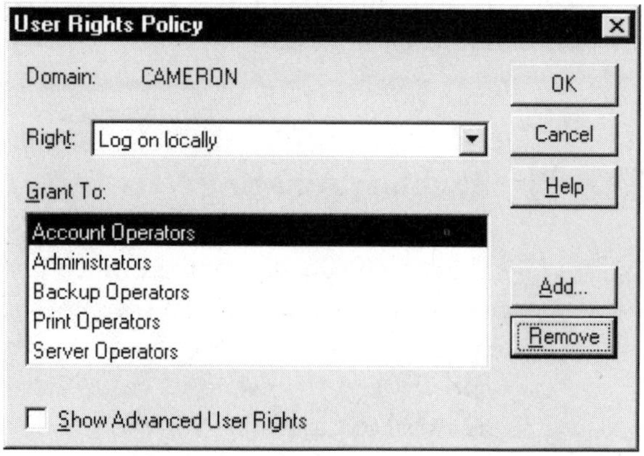

5. Highlight the group you would like to add, or select the Show Users button to see available users.

6. Highlight the user and select Add.

7. Click OK to return to the User Rights Policy dialog box.

8. Find the Access This Computer From Network right and select it. This setting is to specify which users are allowed to connect to this computer from the network. This is also an effective way of restricting users from accessing a specific computer.

9. If there are users you would like to remove, highlight them and click the Remove button. If there are users you would like to add, click the Add button.

10. Highlight the group you would like to add, or select the Show Users button to see available users.

11. Highlight the user and select Add.

12. Click OK to return to the User Rights Policy dialog box.

13. Click OK again to exit.

Here are some examples of situations where you have to modify these system policies. If a user calls you and tells you he got a message saying, "the local policy of this system does not allow you to log on interactively," you know you have to adjust the Log on Locally setting for the computer. At my own company, Access This Computer From Network was once stopping our backup program from attaching to a user's computer and backing up a folder on their hard disk.

Enabling Auditing

In this exercise, we will enable auditing, which logs events that we specify in the Security portion of the Event Viewer. This feature lets you determine who succeeded or failed at accessing resources. The more events you log, the larger the log file grows, and the more work it is for you, the administrator, to sort through the events. It would be wise to spend some time auditing events as a trial to determine whether or not you would benefit from those events being logged. Try to find a good balance of useful information against administrative and log file overhead. Be careful, because the audit settings are

8. At the main Directory Permissions dialog box, check the box to Replace Permissions on Subdirectories or Existing Files.

Here is an important bit of advice: Do not check Replace Permissions on Subdirectories unless you know what you are doing! I once spent a couple of hours untangling a mess, because a user with full control over a directory checked this box after giving someone else access to the directory. This option doesn't just give the user permissions to subdirectories underneath; it replaces the permissions on every folder under it with what you see in the dialog box. All of the custom permissions you might have made deeper in the directory are replaced.

FROM THE CLASSROOM

Managing Users, or the Really Hard Things Made Easy

Here are three things students find the most difficult to grasp—and a thumbnail explanation of each.

- Deleting vs. disabling a user's account
- User rights and permissions
- Local and global groups

DELETING VS. DISABLING A USER'S ACCOUNT When you create an account a unique identifier, called a SID, is assigned to the account. Whenever rights are given and permissions assigned, the administrator uses the "username" and NT uses the SID. When you delete an account, you remove the SID from all

rights and objects. Even if you later re-create the user's account using the same username and password, NT will create a new SID. Think about it: if you wanted to give the original user access to all the objects they could access before you deleted the first account, you would have to hunt down each object and reassign permissions. Imagine trying to do this with 60GB of data spread across 44 servers! By disabling the account, you render it unavailable for log on authentication, but do not disturb rights and permissions.

Most administrators are faced with the issue of an employee who resigns from the organization. What do you do with the account—delete it or disable it? At first glance,

FROM THE CLASSROOM

deleting the account may seem the answer. However, consider the merits of an alternative approach. Consider disabling the account for some period of time (say 30 days) and then delete the account. Then, if you want access to the account (for whatever reason), you will save many hours of re-creating permissions.

USER RIGHTS AND PERMISSIONS

Different operating systems may use the same words to mean different things. In the NT world, the word "rights" does not mean the same thing as it does in the NetWare world. In NT, a *right* is the ability to perform a task such as "Log on locally" or "Change system time." On the other hand, a *permission* is the authority to access an object such as a file or a printer. Permissions are grouped into different categories, such as Read or Write.

Rights and permissions are not related. Each is set—either for individual users or for groups—independently of the other. Understanding the differences will help greatly in your administrative tasks and with passing the certification exam.

LOCAL AND GLOBAL GROUPS

One of the more difficult concepts to grasp and to apply is the difference between local and global groups. At first, these can be quite confusing. But if you will remember a few simple guidelines, it all falls into place.

Remember, global groups only exist in the context of a domain. No domain, no global groups. Pretty simple. You create global groups in the domain's directory service database and you put user accounts in the global groups. Global groups are available to all NT computers in the domain.

Most networks have other NT servers (the so-called *member servers*, which are not domain controllers) that are used as applications servers, file servers, print servers, mail servers and so forth. These servers are collectively referred to as *resource servers* because that's where the resources are.

You create local groups at the resource servers and assign permissions to the local groups. Then you put the global groups from the domain into the local groups. Thereby the users, who are in the *global* group, which is in the *local* group, will be able to use the resource for which the local group had permission. When you need to create a new user, you add them to the global group. In this single step, they will have all the access needed, because their global group is a member of the appropriate local groups, which have permissions.

—By Shane Clawson, MCT, MCSE

System Policy Editor

With the System Policy Editor you can create a policy that restricts users, groups, or computers on the local domain. If you do not have the System Policy Editor icon in your Administrative Tools program group, check in your WINNT directory. If you still do not see it there, it can be found on the Windows NT Server CD-ROM, under CLIENTS\SRVTOOLS\WINNT \I386\POLEDIT.EXE.

Creating a system policy is simple with the graphical System Policy Editor. Most of the settings are self-explanatory, or have a description of what the restriction implies. In order to make sure we understand the System Policy Editor, and can take advantage of its features, we will, in the next exercise, implement a policy for our user account. Refer to Figure 5-12 for an illustration of the Policies tab. Hopefully, your NT Server is set as a domain controller.

EXERCISE 5-16	**Hiding the Network Neighborhood Icon**

1. Open the System Policy Editor.
2. By default no policy template should be displayed. Click the New Policy icon on the toolbar, or select New Policy from the File menu.
3. Click the Add User button on the toolbar, or select Add User from the Edit menu.
4. If you know the name of the account you are currently logged on as, go ahead and type it, or select the Browse button to locate it.
5. When you have added your current user account, it is visible in the System Policy Editor window. Double-click this icon to set the new policy.
6. Click the plus sign next to Shell to expand it.
7. Click the plus sign next to Restrictions to expand it.
8. Check the box next to Hide Network Neighborhood.
9. Click OK to accept the changes.
10. Select Save As from the File menu.

FIGURE 5-12

At the Policies tab, you can create a policy that restricts users, groups, or computers on the local domain

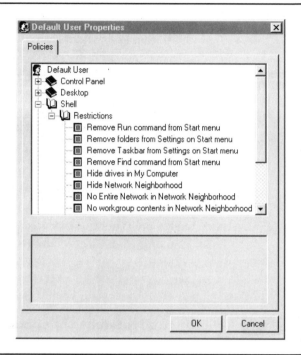

11. Open the Network Neighborhood icon, and select your computer. If your computer is a domain controller, you should see the Netlogon folder. Save the policy file as Ntconfig.pol in this folder.

12. Close all programs and log back on to the system.

13. When your system is finished booting, you will notice that the Network Neighborhood icon is no longer visible.

Of course the Network Neighborhood icon is important, so you may want to uncheck the box in the System Policy Editor to retrieve the icon. Feel free to experiment with the other options available in the System Policy Editor. You may find some settings that are appropriate for members of your family, or for users on your network. One setting that I found especially useful was No Entire Network in Network Neighborhood. We had a problem with a user who browsed another domain, found some games on a remote machine, and e-mailed every user on the network with the shortcuts to the games. Needless to say, the president of the company was not impressed with that e-mail. With an adjustment to the System Policy Editor, this need never happen again.

Registry Mode

If you open the System Policy Editor in Registry mode, you can edit the Registry of the local computer by selecting the Open Registry option under the File menu. You don't have all the options you would see with Regedit or Regedt32, since you can only edit the values that are present in the System Policy Editor. In other words, if you do not see the setting you would like to modify for the local Registry within System Policy Editor, you cannot modify it using this tool. You must use the Registry editors. Think of Registry mode as a limited graphical Registry Editor.

Policy File Mode

When you open System Policy Editor in Policy File mode, you are creating a policy that overwrites a user's Registry values with the ones you have specified. This policy file that you create can be used for as many users as you like. If you want the policy file to be downloaded automatically when a user logs on, call the policy NTconfig.pol and place it in the Netlogon share on a domain controller. Windows NT automatically applies the appropriate information if this file is found.

Templates

A System Policy Template file (.ADM) presents you with the available categories that you can configure for your policy file. You can see which template files are in use on your computer by selecting Policy Template from the Options menu.

- The COMMON.ADM template is for options common to both Windows 95 and Windows NT 4.0 machines.
- The WINNT.ADM template is for Windows NT 4.0 machines only.
- The WINDOWS.ADM contains settings specific to Windows 95.

Policy Order

It is important to understand the order in which policies are applied to users and groups, especially those users belonging to multiple groups. The groups are listed from top to bottom in order of priority, as shown in Figure 5-13.

■ Members of the Domain Admins group receive all of the settings for each group. Settings are applied from lowest priority (bottom) to highest priority (top). Any settings that appear in a higher-priority policy overwrite the lower-priority policy. The settings for the Domain Admins policy override any other policies.

■ Members of the Finance group receive the settings of the Domain Users group, then they receive the settings for their own group. The Finance settings, if any, overwrite the Domain Users settings.

■ The Domain Users group receives only this policy.

Restriction of Control Panel Options

When you select a user (and not a machine) in the System Policy Editor you have the option to hide display settings for the user or group. These include every tab that is visible in the Display applet, such as Background, Screen

| FIGURE 5-13 |

In the Group Priority window, groups are listed in order of priority

Saver, Appearance, and Settings. Hiding these settings restricts a user from changing any of the settings, and so maintains a uniform desktop throughout the organization.

Desktop Customization

With the Desktop settings (also by selecting a user and not a machine) you can select a wallpaper to appear on all users' desktops. You can also set a color scheme that the user will not be able to modify.

Network Settings

When you select a machine rather than a user, you can modify network settings for the machine. These include the capability to create hidden drive shares for server and workstation, as well as the update method for your system policies. If you select the Automatic Update mode, the policy file should be located in the default folder, which is the Netlogon folder. If you select the Manual Update mode, you have to enter the path to the policy file that you created.

Network Logon

You can adjust a number of settings for the network logon. These might include something like creating a custom logon banner to warn users that unauthorized access will not be tolerated. You also can specify whether the Shutdown button is visible during logon. It is visible by default in NT Workstation, but not for NT Server. It is too risky to enable a shutdown button on NT Server that anyone can click. You have the option of not displaying the username of the last user logged on to the system, although this option may be an annoyance to a person who uses the same machine all day. He would have to retype his username at every logon.

Start Menu Options

There are many options for restricting Start menu features and icons. These options are accessed by clicking a user, expanding the Shell tree, and then expanding the Restrictions tree. Applying most of these options can cripple a machine. For example, you can remove the Run and Find commands from the Start menu, as well as the Shut Down command. This makes it less likely that a user will shut down or restart your system.

User Profiles

User Profiles contain the preferences for each user logged on to the system. Since NT requires a user account for every user that logs on to the system, a User Profile is created for every user. These profiles can be located on the local machine, or stored on a server. You can have a different User Profile for each computer that you log on to. Each user retains his custom settings, even though many other users log on to the same machine. If he has not logged on to this specific computer before, the settings for the default are used to create the new User Profile. While the user is logging off, the User Profile is copied and saved.

User Profile Options

When you are creating a User Profile for a user or a group of users, you should know what options you have that are configurable. This allows you to create a snapshot of the environment to be applied to the default or mandatory profile. The following is a list of settings saved in the User Profile:

- Program Manager groups, items, and properties
- Printer connections and settings
- Window position and arrangement
- Screen colors
- Network connections and settings
- Application settings
- General desktop appearance
- Online Help bookmarks

Types of User Profiles

User profiles are how users retain their current desktop and network settings when they log off the machine. There are a number of User Profile types that can be used to suit your administrative needs, including the option to let the user customize the profile.

System Default

The System Default profile is what is used when no user is currently logged on to the computer. This profile is stored in the WINNT\SYSTEM32\CONFIG \DEFAULT folder. You have to edit the Registry to make adjustments to this profile. You should experiment with the System Default profile, because you may be asked to create a screen saver to be used when no one is logged on.

User Default

The User Default profile is used as a template for any subsequent users that log on to the system. This profile does not affect users that currently have a profile on the system. To create a User Default profile, log on to a sample account, such as CONFIG, and configure the environment as you wish. Log on as the administrator and use the User Profile tab in the System applet to copy the account that you just created to the NETLOGON folder of the PDC. Here is an example of the path you would type:

\\myserver\netlogon\default user

When you specify the User Default folder, it is created automatically, and the NTUSER.DAT file is stored there.

Local

A local profile is local to the computer that is being used. Any changes to this profile are not reflected if a user logs on to another machine. The user just creates another separate local profile on the other machine. If you want the changes to be reflected on every machine you use, you must enable a server-based, or roaming, profile.

Server-based

A server-based (or roaming) profile is stored on a server, so it is available to the user regardless which machine the user logs on to. Any changes to a roaming profile are saved to the server, to be retained for the next logon.

exam
ⓦatch

For the exam, make sure you know how and why to configure a roaming profile.

EXERCISE 5-17

Creating a Roaming User Profile

In the next exercise we create a roaming user profile. It may not appear as if we are creating a roaming profile, but when you check the System applet in the Control Panel you will notice NT automatically makes our profile roaming. You have the option of changing it back to local if you prefer.

1. Open up User Manager for Domains.

2. Select the user account that you would like to create a User Profile for.

3. Click the Profile button.

4. In the User Profile Path box, type in the path to your User Profile. I am logged on as Administrator, so here is the path to my User Profile as an example:

   \\133\PROFILES\ADMINISTRATOR

   First start with the two backslashes, and then type the server name where the profile is located. You can see that my computer's name is 133. Next is the Profiles folder name. Do not use the true path of winnt\profiles, because PROFILES is a shared directory. (We will create a shared directory later in the exercise.)

5. Click the OK button twice to close User Manager.

6. Open Windows Explorer.

7. Under the partition that has Windows NT installed (it will probably open under that partition by default) find the WINNT folder and expand the tree.

8. Right-click the Profiles folder and select Sharing.

9. Share the folder with the name you specified in step 4, most likely the share name of Profiles.

10. Close all programs and log on as the user you specified in this exercise to test the profile.

    If everything goes according to plan, no dialog box appears. You know it did not work if you get a dialog box upon starting that says your roaming profile could not be found.

11. If you received no error, go to the System applet of the Control Panel.

12. Click the User Profiles tab and see if your account is now specified as roaming and not local.

You will learn more about local and roaming profiles later in the chapter.

In the User Environment Profile dialog box, you also have the option to specify logon scripts for users. Enter the name of the logon script in the field provided. For the logon script to work, there has to be a logon script of that exact name in a certain directory. Specify the name of a batch file you would like to use for a logon script, such as SCRIPT.BAT. If you use the name SCRIPT.BAT, then there must be a batch file called SCRIPT.BAT in the default location for logon scripts, which is C:\WINNT\SYSTEM32\REPL\ IMPORT\SCRIPTS. Your system root may not be C:\, as mine is. Please note that your logon script does not have to be called SCRIPT.BAT. To test the logon script, create a simple batch file such as one that contains just the word *pause*, and then close all programs and log on again to see whether the prompt that verifies your logon script works correctly.

Mandatory

When a user cannot change the settings in his profile, it is called a mandatory user profile. You can specify a user or group of users that are restricted by the mandatory user profile. These profiles can be stored on the local machine, but more commonly they are stored on a server, where they can be accessed by a number of users, and give the administrator centralized access to configuring these profiles. Here is a list of the items you can restrict with mandatory profiles:

- Explorer settings
- Control Panel

- Taskbar
- Accessories
- Network Neighborhood
- Printers
- Desktop
- Favorites

You may be asked how the mandatory profile reacts in the event of a server crash. If for some reason the server that contains your mandatory profile is not on the network, one of two things will happen:

- *If you have never logged on to the domain before, the default User Profile is used.*

- *If you have successfully logged on to the domain before, the local cache profile on your computer is used.*

Managing User Profiles

User Profiles can be managed from the System applet in the Control Panel, as well as User Manager for Domains, as you saw earlier in the chapter. As you can see from Figure 5-14, you can delete, copy, and change the profile type for a user. You can change a profile from local to roaming, or vice versa.

- If you do not want to use a local or roaming profile for a user anymore, delete the profile path within User Manager for Domains.

- If you want to delete the entire User Profile, use the User Profiles tab in System Properties.

Profile Shortcuts

Earlier in the chapter you saw how you could copy a user account in User Manager for Domains to simplify account creation. You can copy User Profiles

FIGURE 5-14

At the User Profiles tab, you can delete, copy, and change the profile type

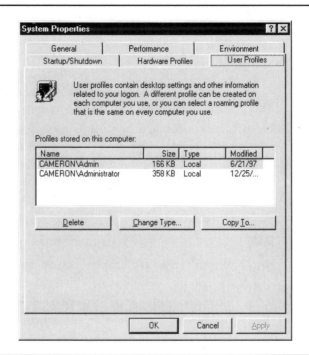

to other users in this same fashion, but this procedure is not performed in User Manager. It is done through the System applet in the Control Panel. When you copy a profile to another user, he receives the identical profile the first time he logs on. After the initial logon, the settings are saved to the new user's profile. In the next exercise, we copy a User Profile to another user.

EXERCISE 5-18

Copying a User Profile

1. Open the System applet in the Control Panel.

2. Select the User Profiles tab.

3. Highlight the local or roaming profile you would like to copy to the other user.

4. Click the Copy To button.

5. Enter the UNC pathname to the user's profile directory. Here is an example:

\\Server\share\profile_directory

You can also click the Browse button and use Network Neighborhood to select the computer, and find the user's profile directory. It should be under the SYSTEMROOT\WINNT\PROFILES\PROFILE_DIRECTORY.

6. Click the Change button to specify the users who are allowed to use this profile.

7. Click OK to copy the profile.

8. Click OK to close the System applet.

Logon Scripts

Logon scripts can be used to start applications or set environment variables for a computer upon startup. They are optional, and can be implemented on a user, group, or entire network basis. If you are using logon scripts, you have to enable and configure the replication service to replicate the logon scripts to all domain controllers. Logon scripts increase administrative overhead while being created, especially if they are customized for individual users. They do, however, provide a number of advantages that should be considered:

- **Backward Compatibility**   In most cases a user's logon script can still be used.

- **Limited Management**   Once the scripts are created, there is little administrative overhead.

- **Ease of Use**   Logon scripts can be simple to create.

- **Personal Profiles Needed for Common Settings**   You can customize scripts for individual users.

- **Residence of Scripts**   Logon scripts are located and replicated to domain controllers.

Logon scripts are enabled in User Manager for Domains, as described earlier in the chapter.

Administering Remote NT Servers

There are a number of ways to remotely administer your Windows NT Servers. Microsoft's System Management Server greatly increases your ability to administer remote servers, but Windows NT Server has built-in utilities for some remote administration. These utilities are not located in one area, which is unfortunate. Here are a number of ways you can administer remote servers.

- The Event Viewer in Administrative Tools lets you open the Event Logs of remote computers.

- Server Manager lets you view the properties of remote computers by letting you open files and resources, create alerts, and remotely disconnect users. Server Manager also lets you create, modify, and delete shares, as well as adjust the number of users allowed, and the permissions associated with the shares. You can stop and start services as if you were directly in front of the machine. The remote computer's Services dialog box appears exactly as your local services utility, with no features disabled.

- The Registry Editor lets you connect to remote computers to modify Registry values.

- Windows Explorer enables you to map to remote drivers to add, modify, or create files and directories.

- System Policy Editor can modify the Registry on remote computers.

For clients other than Windows NT, you can use the client administration tools provided with Windows NT. With these tools you have access to User Manager, Server Manager, and Event Viewer from your 16-bit Windows-based client. There are two ways to give users access to the client administration tools:

- You can share the server tools directory from the Windows NT Server CD-ROM.

- You can use Network Client Administrator to copy the server tools to a share on the server's hard disk.

The option you would choose from the Network Client Administrator is Copy Client-based Network Administration Tools. Then specify a path to the tools to share, or copy those files to a new share. You then have to run the SETUP.EXE from the client that you would like the tools to be placed on.

When using the client administration tools, you accomplish the same tasks from the client (Windows 95 or Windows NT) as you would with the NT Server administration tools.

exam
⚠atch

A number of people who have taken the NT Server exam reported being asked how to change file permissions on a Windows NT Server from a Windows 95 machine. One of the answers provided is Server Manager, which is part of the client administration tools, but this is not the correct answer. It seems tricky, but you use Windows Explorer to assign file permissions.

Network Neighborhood

The Network Neighborhood icon on the desktop is where you view computers in the workgroup or domain, and access the resources they are sharing. Double-clicking the globe for Entire Network displays other networks and domains that you can access. Once you share a folder on your computer, if a user clicks your computer the share will be visible, and may or may not be accessed, depending on the permissions you configured for the share.

Windows NT Diagnostics

This Windows version of Microsoft Diagnostics displays most of what you need when it comes to configuration. Windows NT diagnostics does not allow you to configure devices; it is read-only. Many of the settings displayed in Windows NT Diagnostics are available elsewhere, such as the various Control Panel applets. There are a few bits of information located here that you should be aware of:

- The Resources tab devices have settings such as IRQ, DMA, I/O port, and memory address.

- The Display tab has video subsystem information that can also be viewed from the Display applet in the Control Panel.

- The Memory tab has information on physical memory, usage, and paging file information that can also be viewed form Task Manager.

- The Environment tab has current environment information that can also be viewed from the System applet in the Control Panel.

- The Services tab has the same information as the Services Control Panel applet, except for the fact you cannot stop or start services.

- The Network has detailed information not located anywhere else, regarding network usage and settings.

Become familiar with the Windows NT Diagnostics utility, because it is the central repository for information that you can quickly access. You can be sure of its accuracy, because the information is coming directly from the Registry.

Server Manager

Server Manager is a utility not only for managing servers, but for managing workstations and the domain. Server Manager is located in Administrative Tools with the other administrative utilities. When you first start Server Manager you see the servers and workstations in your domain. You have the option of displaying only servers, displaying only workstations, or displaying both. You can see the status of each server or workstation by looking at the icon next to the computer. If the icon is transparent, the computer is not currently on the network. This is helpful for eliminating computers that are no longer active on the network. I usually have to delete computers from this utility on a weekly basis, because their names have been changed, or the computer has permanently been taken off the network. Be careful, because laptops can appear as transparent icons, also. This can mean the laptop is not currently on the network, so care must be taken when deleting computer accounts.

When you would like to see the properties of a selected machine, just double-click it and bring up a dialog box just like the one you see in the Control Panel when you click the System icon. You can also highlight the computer and select Properties from the Computer pull-down menu. This dialog box displays shared resources, the users connected to them, open resources, alerts, and replication information. These properties can be helpful when you need to see who is connecting to the computer, without having to be seated in front of it.

When you highlight the selected computer and select Shared Directories from the Computer pull-down menu, you see shared resources that resemble the Properties dialog box. However, you have greater control of these shared directories. You can quickly see which directory is the source for the shared directory. This may seem obvious when you have a share like C or D, but it can quickly become confusing when you have a share called NETLOGON, that maps to the source directory of WINNT\SYSTEM32\REPL\IMPORT\ SCRIPTS. From this dialog box, you can also create new shares by clicking the Add button, or delete a share by clicking the Stop Sharing button. If you were to double-click the shared directory, or highlight the shared directory and select Properties, you can make a comment for the share, or set a maximum number of users allowed. Clicking the Permissions button allows you to add, modify, or delete users and groups that have permission to access this shared directory.

Managing services for remote computers is probably the most useful of the features provided by Server Manager. By highlighting a computer and selecting Services from the Computer pull-down menu you bring up a list of services on the machine. These services may be started, and you can see how they are configured for startup: disabled, manual, or automatic. If you wanted to start a service on the remote computer, just highlight the service and select Start. Follow the same procedure for stopping a service, except you select Stop. If you would like to change the way a service is started, select the service and click the Startup button. You can change the startup type to disabled, manual, or automatic, and also select the user account used for the service. This can be the internal system account, or another account of your choice. If the computer has hardware profiles, you can choose which services are to be started and how they are started for each profile specified. You can also specify parameters to be used when the service starts up by entering them in the Startup Parameters portion.

Starting and stopping of services remotely came in very handy for our company when we were troubleshooting the BackOffice product, Systems Management Server. We had a few computers that would not inventory themselves correctly. We had to map a drive to the computer and adjust a setting in an .INI file, then stop and restart the service for the change to take effect. This computer was in another building, and would have taken up too much valuable time to go there and stop and start the service.

You also use Server Manager to add and delete computers from the domain—another common activity for an administrator. If you are creating accounts for the computers to use, you would enter them here. When you begin installing Windows NT or Windows 95 you select the name that you previously entered in Server Manager for the machine name. This way you can enter the names in advance (with your administrative rights) and instruct the users to use that name when they configure their computer name, so it can join the domain. If you are the one installing and configuring Windows NT on the workstations, you specify your administrative name and password to create an account in the domain during installation when it asks you for the computer name. It is for security that only administrators, or those users and groups that have the Add Workstation to Domain right, can join the domain.

- If you highlight the Primary Domain Controller in the Server Manager window, you have the option of synchronizing this computer with the entire domain from the Computer pull-down menu.

- If you highlight a backup domain controller in the Server Manager window, you have the option to Promote to Primary Domain Controller, or synchronize with the primary domain controller.

- If you highlight a workstation or stand-alone member server, you don't have any of these options.

You are not restricted to managing just servers and workstations in this domain. From the Computer pull-down menu, you can also select another domain to administer.

Printers Utility

I had no idea that, as a network administrator, I would be spending as much time with printers as I do. But, second to the phone line going out, the worst thing for users is a printer being down. Users get very upset when they cannot print, and even get upset when they have to walk some distance to another printer. You are expected to fix the problem, no matter what it is. Fortunately, the printers utility can fix many problems.

Start by selecting Printers from the Control Panel, or by opening My Computer and selecting Printers. If you have any printers installed, either local or remote, they are visible here. You also see the Add Printer option. To see the status of a printer, double-click it. This shows you the print queue and any documents that are waiting to be printed. If you select Properties from the Printer menu, you have the option of changing many of the device settings. The General tab is where Print Test Page is located, which allows you to verify the correct installation and configuration of the printer.

CERTIFICATION SUMMARY

You witnessed in this chapter just how many options you have for user and group management. It may seem overwhelming, but most of the other options, such as logon scripts, roaming and mandatory profiles, and system policy settings are not required on your network. However, a strong knowledge of creating, modifying, and deleting user and group accounts is very important. You should become familiar with User Manager for Domains and Server Manager, as these two are your first choice for user, group, and computer resource management. Become familiar with the capabilities of the optional methods for user and group management, because you may find yourself in a situation where you have to restrict user access, or require a standard desktop. With a grasp of these options, you will know how to implement these policies.

The various utilities for administering your computers remotely, such as Server Manager, Event Viewer, and the client-based administration tools, make your life as an administrator easier, and save you time. However, you must know what each utility is capable of. Spending time with these utilities now will save you time in the future when you are administering your own Windows NT domain.

✓ TWO-MINUTE DRILL

❑ The user account is what gives a user access to the network.

❑ Group accounts are for grouping together users who perform the same function or require access to the same resources.

❑ The User Manager is where most of your user and group management takes place. From here you create, modify, and delete accounts, and assign rights.

❑ In order for users to access the network via Remote Access, they have to be given permission.

❑ Local and global groups (as well as trust relationships) are not covered in much depth during the Windows NT Server 4.0 exam. They are covered in great depth in the Windows NT 4.0 Server on the Enterprise exam. However, it is very important to understand the differences between the two.

❑ Local groups are for resource access within your domain.

❑ Global groups give users access to resources in other domains.

❑ Using System Policies you can implement policies on your domain for activities such as account restrictions, desktop settings, and network settings.

❑ With the System Policy Editor you can create a policy that restricts users, groups, or computers on the local domain.

❑ User Profiles contain the preferences for each user logged on to the system.

❑ For the exam, make sure you know how and why to configure a roaming profile.

❑ On the exam, you may be asked how the mandatory profile reacts in the event of a server crash.

❑ User Profiles can be managed from the System applet in the Control Panel, as well as User Manager for Domains.

❑ Logon scripts can be used to start applications or set environment variables for a computer upon startup.

❑ Windows NT Server has built-in utilities for some remote administration.

❑ A number of people who have taken the NT Server exam reported being asked how to change file permissions on a Windows NT Server from a Windows 95 machine. One of the answers provided is Server Manager, which is part of the client administration tools, but this is not the correct answer. It seems tricky, but you use Windows Explorer to assign file permissions.

❑ The Network Neighborhood icon on the desktop is where you view computers in the workgroup or domain, and access the resources they are sharing.

❑ Become familiar with the Windows NT Diagnostics utility, because it is the central repository for information that you can quickly access.

❑ Server Manager is a utility not only for managing servers, but for managing workstations and the domain.

❑ The printers utility can fix many printing problems.

SELF TEST

The following questions will help you measure your understanding of the material presented in this chapter. Read all the choices carefully, as there may be more than one correct answer. Choose all correct answers for each question.

1. You would like to create a template called USER_TEMPLATE for making new user accounts easier. What is the correct way to do this?

    A. It will automatically create the new user based on these settings.

    B. Make the new user, and then copy the settings of the USER_TEMPLATE to the new account.

    C. Copy the USER_TEMPLATE account and enter the new user information.

    D. Create a global group called USER_TEMPLATE and place the new user in this group.

2. The manager for the Sales department has left the company. He has an immediate replacement. What is the best way to give the new user access to the resources the previous manager had?

    A. Copy the previous user's account from User Manager for Domains, and then delete the old account.

    B. Rename the previous user's account with the new user's name.

    C. Use the System applet in the Control Panel to copy the profile to the new user's account.

    D. Create the new user, and copy the permissions from the old manager to the new manager.

3. Members of the Human Resources group have a mandatory user profile. Everything was fine for each user until one day, the server that holds the mandatory user profile went down. What will happen when a user from the Human Resources group attempts to log on?

    A. The default user profile will be used.

    B. The locally cached profile will be used.

    C. A profile from another group will be used.

    D. The user will not be able to log in.

4. A user calls you and tells you he just received a message about his account expiring. What should you do to give him access again?

    A. Assume he meant his account was locked out, and unlock it from User Manager for Domains.

    B. His account will become disabled as a result, so clear the check box next to Account Disabled in User Manager for Domains.

    C. Set a later date for the expiration of the user account in the Account

Information dialog box in User Manager for Domains.

   D. This is a security feature of Windows NT. You have to re-create his account.

5. (True/False) Everything in the User Environment Profile dialog box is optional.

6. What is the default location to place logon scripts?

   A. WINNT\SYSTEM32\REPL\

   B. WINNT\SYSTEM32\REPL\SCRIPTS\

   C. The NETLOGON folder on all domain controllers.

   D. WINNT\SYSTEM32\REPL\ IMPORT\SCRIPTS

7. What is the difference between local and global groups? Choose all that apply.

   A. You can only create global groups on the primary domain controller.

   B. You cannot create global groups on Windows NT Workstation.

   C. You cannot place users in local groups.

   D. You cannot place local groups in global groups.

   E. You cannot place global groups in local groups.

8. (True/False) To create a new local group in User Manager for Domains, you would select New Local Group from the File pull-down menu.

9. The _____ global group is a member of the Administrators local group

on every Windows NT computer in the domain by default.

10. A user would like to log on to any computer in the network and see the same desktop. How do you go about doing this?

   A. On the domain controller, go to the System applet and copy the user profile to his user account.

   B. On the domain controller, go to the System applet and copy the user profile to his home directory.

   C. Assign a home directory in User Manager for Domains. A roaming profile will then be created.

   D. Assign a UNC path to the profile for the user account.

11. You are going to shut down the server for repairs, but before you do you need to disconnect users. Which utility is the best way to accomplish this?

   A. The System applet in the Control Panel.

   B. Server Manager.

   C. User Manager for Domains.

   D. The Services applet in the Control Panel.

12. Where do you adjust the Log On Locally setting?

   A. Select Policies from the User menu in User Manager.

   B. Select User Rights from the Policies menu in User Manager.

   C. Select Policies from the User Rights menu in User Manager.

D. Double-click the user and select Policy.

E. Double-click the user and select User Rights.

13. (True/False) You can audit a user's attempt to change his password.

14. When Windows NT logs a user on, what is the name of the policy file it automatically looks for and applies for the user?

A. CONFIG.POL

B. NTCONFIG.ADM

C. CONFIG.ADM

D. NTCONFIG.POL

15. Which action is not possible in Server Manager?

A. Stopping a remote computer's service.

B. Sending a message to a remote computer.

C. Disconnecting a user on a remote computer.

D. Shutting down a remote computer.

16. (True/False) The WINDOWS.ADM System Policy Template file is for options that are common to both Windows 95 and Windows NT.

6

Windows NT 4.0 Security

CERTIFICATION OBJECTIVES

6.01   NT Security Model

6.02   Implementing Permissions
        and Security

6.03   NTFS Security

6.04   Shared Server Resources

6.05   Event Auditing

6.06   Setting Registry Keys

S ecurity is a key element of a networked operating system, especially if the system can be accessed from the Internet. If you have a networked computer that's vital to your company's mission, you need to use the right level of security. Hackers break into computer systems every day; the United States, which has the most computer systems, is the biggest target. Often administrators don't think security is important until something happens—then it's too late. Unfortunately, many supervisors think you are doing a good job if you catch break-ins after they occur, but that is the wrong type of thinking. A good administrator will implement security that doesn't allow break-ins. Of course, it's always possible to break into a networked system, but you should still take reasonable steps to stop intruders.

Making the system secure is only part of the equation. Meeting the mission is equally important. If you apply too much security, so it is impossible for your users to do their jobs, you've failed to apply the proper security. Security is an art form. You need to know how much is required to secure the system and at what level your mission suffers. This chapter explains NT security and the steps you should take to secure your system. The amount of security you implement depends on your company's policies and your ability to sell the need for security.

CERTIFICATION OBJECTIVE 6.01

NT Security Model

The NT security model has four main components: logon processes, Local Security Authority (LSA), Security Account Manager (SAM), and the Security Reference Monitor. I'll give a brief explanation of each component, then explain their functions in more depth. Logon processes include interactive logons at the computer console and remote network logons. The logon process gives the user access to the system. The Local Security Authority is the heart of the security subsystem. It creates security access tokens, authenticates users, and manages the local security policy. The SAM database maintains all user, group, and workstation accounts in a secure database, and Local Security Authority validates user logons against the SAM database. Finally, the Security

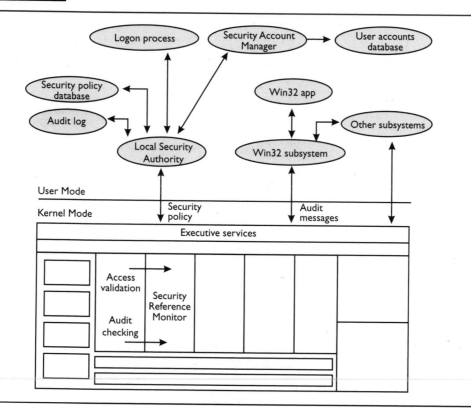

FIGURE 6-1   NT security components

Reference Monitor verifies that the user has permission to access the requested object, then performs the requested action. It also provides audit messages when needed. Figure 6-1 is a graphical representation of the security model.

Logon Authentication

NT supports four types of logons: local, remote, domain, and pass-through authentication. Use Figure 6-1 and Figure 6-2 to help you follow the logon process described in the next paragraphs.

The first type of logon we'll discuss is a local logon. A local logon occurs when you're logging on to a computer from that computer's console. NT

FIGURE 6-2

Winlogon process

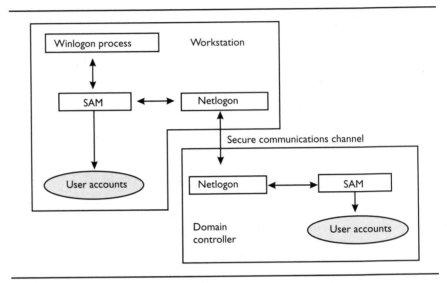

Workstation security starts at logon. Before any user can get onto your system, they must provide a username and a password. The exact process starts when the user presses CTRL-ALT-DEL to activate the winlogon process. The winlogon process prompts for a username and password, and lets you choose whether to log in to the local machine or a specific domain.

If you choose to log in to the local machine, winlogon passes the username and password you supply to the security subsystem. At the heart of the security subsystem is the *Local Security Authority* (LSA). The LSA generates access tokens, manages the local security policy, and provides interactive user authentication services. The LSA also controls audit policy and logs the audit messages generated by the Security Reference Monitor. The security subsystem verifies your username and password against the *Security Account Manager* (SAM) database. The SAM is actually a hive in your Registry where all user account information is stored. If your information passes verification, the security subsystem creates an access token and passes it back to the winlogon process. Winlogon calls the Win32 subsystem to create a new process and provides the access token, which is attached to the newly created process. The access token is then used as your "ID card," so your username and password are no longer needed.

The next type of logon we'll discuss is remote logon. A remote logon occurs when someone accesses your computer via the network. Your workstation receives an encrypted username and password from the requesting computer via the netlogon service. Then your workstation's security subsystem processes the request just as if it were a local logon. The one exception is that the netlogon service replaces the winlogon process.

When you log on to a domain, you must choose the domain you want to log on to when you enter your username and password. If your workstation is a member of that domain, it logs on using the domain logon method; otherwise, it uses pass-through authentication. Domain logon starts when you submit your username, password, and a domain name to the winlogon process. Winlogon identifies your request as going to the network, so it passes it to the netlogon service. The netlogon service establishes a secure communications channel with the first available domain controller that recognizes the workstation as a member of its domain. The netlogon service on the domain controller passes the request to the domain controller's security subsystem, where the username and password are verified against the domain's SAM database. If the username and password are correct, the domain controller creates an access token and informs your workstation of a successful match.

The final type of logon you need to know is pass-through authentication. Pass-through authentication occurs when you choose a domain to log on to from your NT Workstation, but your workstation doesn't have an account in that domain. When your workstation starts (before the winlogon process even begins) it creates a secure communications channel with the domain controller for which it is a member. The connection provides the winlogon process with the list of domains available to the workstation. Only the member domain and all trusting domains are displayed in the initial logon list box. This is the same domain controller that responds to the logon request to the domain in which your workstation is a member. However, it serves a different role when you choose to log on to a *trusted domain*. When logging on to a trusted domain, your request is passed from the domain controller where your secure communications channel exists to the trusting domain's domain controller. That domain controller then processes the logon and returns a token to your domain controller for you. Logon then occurs just as it does in domain logon between the *trusted and trusting domains*, except that another step occurs, in which your member domain controller notifies your workstation of a successful logon.

Account Lockout

You can set NT to lock out an account after a certain number of unsuccessful logon attempts. (Three bad attempts is a common choice.) This prevents hackers from breaking into your account with a hacking program. Hackers have programs that use wordlists and brute strength password crackers on accounts. If you don't set NT to lock out accounts after a number of bad attempts, the hacker is free to run a program to attack your accounts. You can set the account to be locked out forever, which requires the administrator to unlock the account, or you can have it automatically reset after a certain period of time.

EXERCISE 6-1

Changing Account Lockout Settings

This exercise teaches you how to change the account policy on NT.

1. Start User Manager (click the Start button, and select Programs| Administrative Tools|User Manager (for Domains, if on a domain controller).

2. On the menu bar choose Policies | Account. The Account Policy dialog box opens (Figure 6-3).

3. Check the Account Lockout option button in the middle of the window.

4. "Lockout after" option sets the number of bad attempts. Three is a good number to use.

5. "Reset count after" option sets the amount of time that must pass before the counter resets to zero. Simply put, if you log on with a bad password, NT will remember that you entered a bad password for the amount of time set in this option. Set it to 30 minutes.

6. Lockout Duration can be forever or it can be set for a certain amount of time. Set this to 30 minutes. Lockout Duration goes into effect after the required number of bad attempts occurs.

FIGURE 6-3

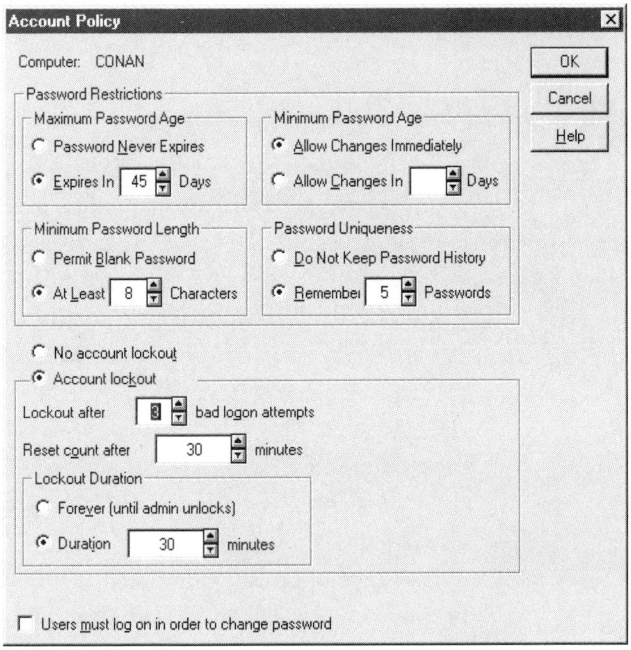

Account Policy dialog box

CERTIFICATION OBJECTIVE 6.02

Implementing Permissions and Security

NT implements security by placing controls on objects. Security is an attribute on an object. NT uses *Access Control List* (ACL) and *Access Control Entries* (ACE) attributes to secure objects. Once a user is logged on they receive an access token. This access token (also known as a security token) is used to identify the user to the operating system whenever requests are made. The access token is compared against the ACL to ensure the user has permissions to that object. If they do, access is granted. If the user doesn't have sufficient permissions, access is denied. Remember, if at any point an object has a NO ACCESS attribute, access permissions will not be granted to that object.

Microsoft Object Security Terms

To really understand NT security you need to understand objects. In NT just about everything is an object. A file is an object and so is a window. NT controls access to objects. A program asks the NT operating system to perform specific tasks to objects. For example, if you open a text file in Notepad called HELP.TXT, Notepad makes a request to NT to open the object HELP.TXT. NT then verifies your access permissions and, if you have the proper permissions, it opens HELP.TXT. Programs are *not* allowed to directly access the hardware. This is why many MS-DOS programs won't work on NT. The most common type of object is a file object, but just about everything you can think of is an object; named pipes and processes are also objects.

The type of object you are setting permissions for determines the type of permissions that may be set. For example, you can read, write, and delete a file; however, on a printer you can manage documents, purge documents, and view the printer queue.

There are two classes of objects: container objects and noncontainer objects. A container object can contain other objects; a noncontainer object doesn't contain other objects. A container object can inherit permissions from its parent container. This will be explained in more detail later in this chapter.

Any object that can be secured has a security descriptor. The security descriptor, which describes the security attributes for the object, has four parts.

- **Owner security ID**   Identifies the owner of the object, which allows that person to change the permissions for the object.
- **Group security ID**   Only used by the POSIX subsystem.
- **Discretionary Access Control List (ACL)**   Identifies the groups and users who are allowed and denied access. Owners control the discretionary ACL.
- **System ACL**   Controls the auditing of messages the system will create. The security administrators set system ACLs.

Access Control List (ACL) and Access Control Entries (ACE)

ACLs and ACEs were mentioned earlier; now let's look at how they work. ACL stands for an Access Control List, which is comprised of Access Control Entries (ACE). The ACE specifies auditing and access permissions for a given object for a specific user or group of users.

There are three different types of ACEs: AccessAllowed, AccessDenied, and SystemAudit. AccessAllowed and AccessDenied are discretionary ACEs which grant and deny access to a user or group of users. SystemAudit is a system security ACE which logs security events to the Event Viewer. The access validation process is summarized in Figure 6-4.

Every ACE must have an access mask. An access mask tells the ACE which attributes are available for a particular object type. The ACE can then grant permissions based on that mask. For example, a file can set Read, Write, Execute, Delete, Take Ownership, and Change Permissions because an access mask defines these attributes.

FIGURE 6-4

Access validation

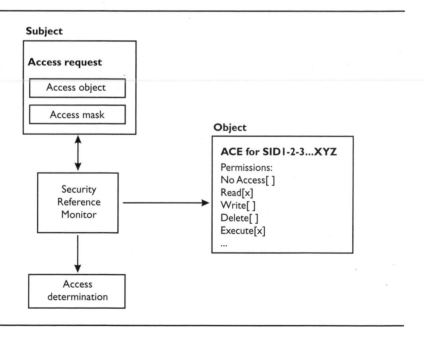

Whenever an ACL is evaluated, every ACE is processed and evaluated in the following order:

1. AccessDenied ACEs are processed before AccessAllowed ACEs. The security ID in the user's security token is evaluated against the security ID in the ACE. If no match occurs the ACE is not processed.

2. If access is denied, the security subsystem checks to see if the original desired access mask contained a ReadControl or a WRITE_DAC. If it does, the system will also check to see if the user is the owner. If both evaluate to true, access is allowed.

3. For an AccessDenied ACE, the ACE access mask and the desired access mask are compared. If there are any accesses in both masks, processing stops, and access is denied. Otherwise, the next ACE is processed.

4. For an AccessAllowed ACE, the ACE access mask and the desired access mask are compared. If all accesses in the desired access mask are matched by the ACE, processing stops, and access is granted. Otherwise, the next ACE is processed.

5. If the contents of the desired access mask are not completely matched when the end of the ACL is reached, access is denied.

To understand this difference, look at two different examples.

In the first example, a user, MikeS, wants to delete a file called J:\JESSE\HELP.TXT. Figure 6-5 shows the groups MikeS belongs to and the discretionary ACL applied to the file.

In Figure 6-5 the desired operation of delete is not carried out. The user MikeS wants to delete the file J:\JESSE\HELP.TXT. NT reads the discretionary ACL and evaluates it in the following way:

1. NT reads MikeS's desired access mask of Delete for the file HELP.TXT.

2. NT reads the AccessDenied ACE to Sales. AccessDenied by default is placed at the front of the discretionary ACL. Once an AccessDenied is processed, further processing of the ACL halts.

FIGURE 6-5   Delete request denied

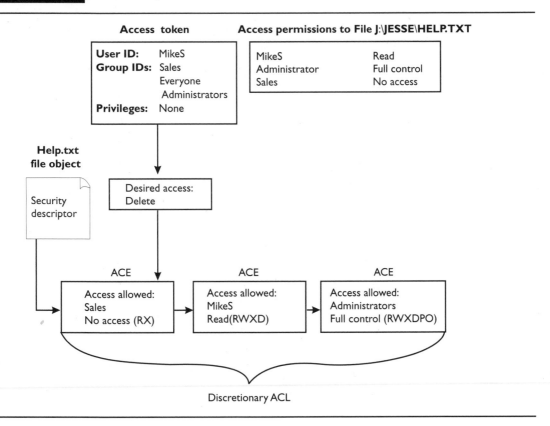

In Figure 6-6 user MikeS is granted access to delete the file HELP.TXT.

3. NT reads MikeS's desired access mask to delete the file HELP.TXT.

4. NT processes the request by first looking at MikeS' ACE. No match is found.

5. NT then processes the group Sales and matches the Delete request. Further processing of the ACL halts since the proper access is matched.

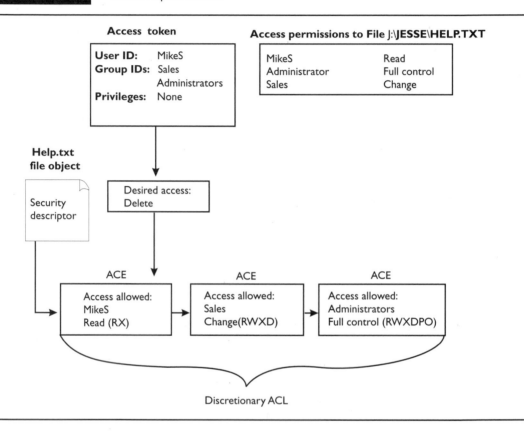

FIGURE 6-6 Delete request allowed

Since NT stops processing the ACL as soon as the desired access mask is matched, it is important that the No Access ACE is always processed first.

exam
⚠ atch

Permissions are cumulative, except for No Access. This may confuse people because you don't have to belong to a group that has all the proper permissions. If your account has read access and you belong to a group with write access you will be granted read and write access.

Security Account Manager (SAM)

The SAM (also called *user account database*) is a database that maintains all user, group, and workstation accounts in a secure database. The local security authority validates user logons against the SAM database, and the security subsystem verifies your username and password against the SAM database. The SAM is actually a hive in your Registry where all user account information is stored. If you run Regedt32 and look at HKEY_LOCAL_MACHINE, you'll see a key named SAM. Inside that key is a subkey—also called SAM— which is grayed out. It's grayed out because it is secured from all users, even administrators. When you create an Emergency Repair Disk, a compressed copy of your server's SAM is placed on the disk. This is why you must protect your Emergency Repair Disk just as if it were a server.

Security ID (SID)

A SID is used to uniquely identify each user, NT Workstation, and Server on the network. NT creates a new SID for each user that is added to your system. The SID is never changed and can never be re-created. Because a SID can never be re-created, you need to be very careful when deleting user accounts. In fact, it is common practice to disable accounts for a period of time before you delete them. This saves you time later if you really didn't need to delete the account. For example, let's say that Betty, a receptionist in Marketing, gets mad one day and tells her boss that she quits. Her boss notifies you that her account must be deleted immediately since it has access to sensitive information. You immediately follow your customer's order and delete her account. The next day Betty's replacement, Robert, comes in and needs access to all the same information that Betty had access to. So you create a new account and try to assign him to the same groups and rights that Betty had. This could be a considerable task. What should you have done instead of deleting Betty's account? You should have disabled the account. This would prevent Betty from logging in and doing unsavory things to her boss's sensitive files. When her replacement came in, you should have renamed the account, changed the password, and then enabled the account. This would give Robert the same access that Betty had, and it would have kept your system secure by preventing Betty from logging on.

Access Token

An access token is created every time a user logs on to your computer, whether via the network or console. Once the user is validated, an access token is created containing the user's security ID (SID) and the SIDs of the Everyone group and other groups to which the user belongs. It also contains user rights (to be discussed later) assigned to the collected SIDs. If a user is logged on to your server when you change his group and rights to your system, the changes won't take effect until the user logs off and then logs on again.

exam
ⓦatch

This can be tricky if you see it on the test. The key to assigning and removing a user to a group is that the user must be logged off before the change can take effect. If the user isn't logged on when the change is made, the change will reflect the next time the user logs on. If the user is logged on when the change is made, he must first log off, then log back on to apply the changes.

CERTIFICATION OBJECTIVE 6.03

NTFS Security

The type of file system you choose determines what level of file security you can use on NT. FAT will not allow folder or file permissions, whereas NTFS will allow permissions on folders and individual files. If you're concerned about security, NTFS is the file system to use—unless you have a RISC processor. RISC systems require the system partition to be formatted with NTFS; however, other partitions may also be formatted with NTFS. For RISC systems you can secure the system partition with Disk Administrator to allow only administrators access to the system partition.

As previously mentioned, NTFS allows folder- and file-level access permissions. The owner can set the following permissions for file-level permissions:

- **No Access**   The user isn't able to access the file at all. This takes precedence over all other permissions. If a user is assigned to a group which is allowed Read Access and a group with No Access, the user will not be able to read the file because No Access always takes precedence.

- **Read**   Allows the user to read or execute the file. No modifications may be made to the file.

- **Change**   Allows the user to read, write, execute, or delete the file.

- **Full Control**   Allows the user to read, write, execute, delete, change permissions, and take ownership of the file.

- **Special Access**   Allows the owner to choose individual access permissions to read, write, execute, delete, change permissions, and take ownership of the file.

Table 6-1 summarizes the file-level permissions available with NTFS.

The owner can also set folder-level permissions. The following permissions are available:

- **No Access**   Completely restricts the user from accessing the folder and its files. No Access takes precedence over all other permissions set for the user.

TABLE 6-1		
File-Level Permissions	**Access Level**	**Permissions**
	No Access	None
	Read	RX
	Change	RWXD
	Full Control	RWXDPO
	Special Access	Custom
	Permissions Key: (R)ead, (W)rite, e(X)ecute, (D)elete, change (P)ermissions, take (O)wnership	

- **List**   Allows the user to view the files and folders list within the directory, but the user cannot access the files and folders.

- **Read**   Allows the user to read files within the folder but doesn't allow the user to save changes.

- **Add**   The user can't list or read the files in the folder, however, the user can write new files to that folder.

- **Add and Read**   Allows the user to list, read, and write new files within the folder. The user can read, but not save changes to existing files.

- **Change**   Allows the user to list, read, write new files, modify, and delete existing files within the folder. The user can also change attributes and delete the folder.

- **Full Control**   Allows the user to list, read, change, and delete the folder and the files within the folder. The user can also take ownership and change permissions of the folder and its files.

- **Special Directory Access**   Allows the owner to set custom access to the directory.

- **Special File Access**   Allows the owner to set custom access on the files within the folder.

Table 6-2 summarizes the folder-level permissions available with NTFS.

exam
ⓌatcH

There is one more permission type called File Delete Child. File Delete Child is a POSIX function that allows a user who has Full Control of a folder to delete a top-level file within that folder, even though the user doesn't have permissions to delete that file. Let's say you have full control of a folder called "Sales Reports." Within that folder there is a file called "Mary's SALES.XLS" in which you have No Access permissions assigned. Since you have full control of the "Sales Reports" folder you can delete the file "Mary's SALES.XLS" even though you don't have access to that file.

Who is the owner of a file or folder? Each NTFS file and folder has one user account designated as its owner. The owner is the person who created the file or folder. By default, the owner of a resource is the only account that has the

TABLE 6-2
Folder-Level Permissions

Access Level	Folder Access Permissions	File Access Permissions
No Access	None	None
List	RX	N/A
Read	RX	RX
Add	WX	N/A
Add and Read	RWX	RX
Change	RWXD	RWXD
Full Control	RWXDPO	RWXDPO
Special Directory Access	Custom	
Special File Access	Custom	Custom
Permissions Key: (R)ead, (W)rite, e(X)ecute, (D)elete, change (P)ermissions, take (O)wnership		

right to access a resource, modify its properties, and secure it from outside access. The file's owner can give an administrator no access to a file; however, an administrator can always take ownership of the file. Once the administrator is the owner he has full control of that file. Normally a user is the owner of a resource, except when that user is an administrator. When a user with administrator privileges owns a file, the group Administrators is the owner of that resource. Ownership can only be taken; it can never be forced on someone. This helps protect people from malicious administrators.

The person who created the file or folder is the owner and is responsible for securing those files and folders. It isn't only the administrator's job to ensure security of files and folders. This type of access control is called *discretionary access*.

EXERCISE 6-2

Taking Ownership of a File or Folder

1. Right-click on the file or folder and choose Properties.
2. Choose the Security tab.
3. Click the Ownership button.
4. Click the Take Ownership button.

exam
ⓦatch

Many people think an administrator can do anything. That isn't true—especially when it comes to resource ownership. Remember that once you take ownership you can't give it back to the previous owner. In order for the previous owner to become the owner, he will need to follow the four steps just mentioned.

Permissions When Copying and Moving Files

You must be careful when copying and moving files on NTFS partitions. The permissions will change depending on the type of operation being performed. When you copy a file or folder, the new copy inherits the permissions of its parent folder. As previously mentioned, a container object can inherit permissions from its parent container; this is known as *inherited permissions*. For example, when you copy a file from a directory with full control to a directory with read permission, the copied file will have read permission only. This also applies when creating new files and folders. However, it isn't quite as easy when moving files and folders. When you move a file or folder from one partition to a different partition, the file or folder will inherit the parent folder's permissions. But here's the twist—if you move a file or folder within the same partition it keeps its previous security permissions. This doesn't occur when you move a file between partitions because NTFS copies the file to the new partition then deletes the old file. When NTFS moves a file within the same partition it simply changes the master file table (MFT), which does not affect the permissions of the file. The MFT is a special file that points to all other files on the NTFS volume. NTFS uses the MFT to locate all other files on the partition.

exam
ⓦatch

This may seem simple at first, but when you are taking the test you may get the MOVE and COPY commands mixed up. It may be helpful for you to test it out. Create two NTFS partitions on your system and try out the different possibilities.

Viewing and Changing Permissions

In the next exercise you will learn how to change permissions on a directory. You will remove the Everyone group from the directory and give your user account full control. Before you begin you must have an NTFS-formatted volume on your system. If you don't have an NTFS volume you must run the command:

```
CONVERT drive: /FS:NTFS
```

where `drive:` is the letter of the drive you want to convert to NTFS.

Changing Access Permissions for a Directory

1. Once you have an NTFS volume, right-click on a folder in that volume and choose Properties.

2. Next select the Security tab and click the Permissions button. The Properties dialog box opens (Figure 6-7).

3. Click the Remove button to remove the group Everyone from having access to this directory. Warning—make sure the directory isn't part of the NT system directory. Then click the Add button. The Directory Permissions dialog box opens (Figure 6-8).

4. Click on the Show Users button. Then select your username and click the Add button. On the Type of Access drop-down menu choose Full Control, as shown in Figure 6-9 and click OK.

FIGURE 6-7

Security tab

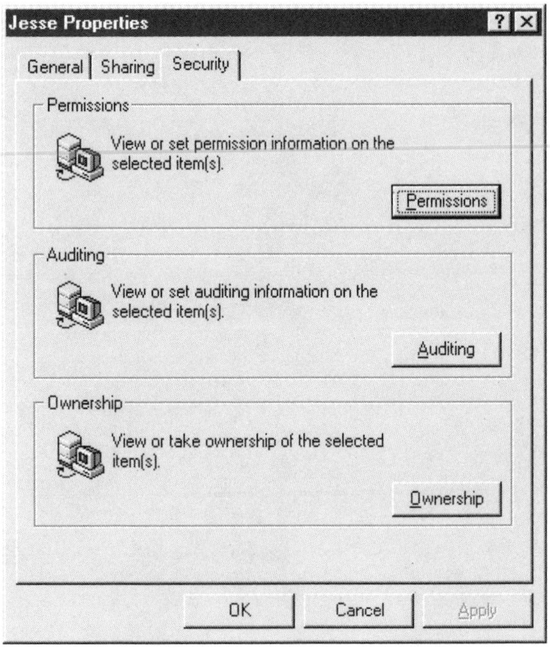

Jesse Properties
General | Sharing | Security

Permissions
View or set permission information on the selected item(s).
[Permissions]

Auditing
View or set auditing information on the selected item(s).
[Auditing]

Ownership
View or take ownership of the selected item(s).
[Ownership]

[OK] [Cancel] [Apply]

FIGURE 6-8

Directory Permissions
dialog box

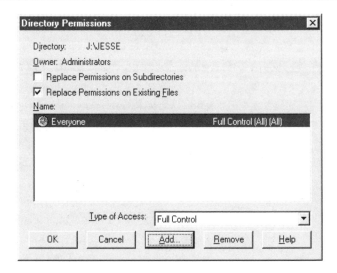

FIGURE 6-9

Add Users and Groups
dialog box

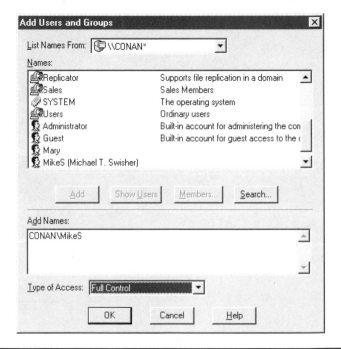

5. The Directory Permissions dialog box (Figure 6-10) offers the option to Replace Permissions on Subdirectories or to Replace Permissions on Existing Files (the default). For this exercise just choose the default.

Command Prompt

You can also use the command prompt for changing permissions on directories. The NT command shell has a built-in command called CACLS.EXE. The following are the available switches:

```
CCACLS filename [/T] [/E] [/C] [/G user:perm] [/R user
[...]] [/P user:perm [...]]
            [/D user [...]]
  filename     Displays ACLs.
  /T           Changes ACLs of specified files in the current
               directory and all subdirectories.
  /E           Edit ACL instead of replacing it.
  /C           Continue on access denied errors.
  /G user:perm Grant specified user access rights.
               Perm can be: R Read
                            C Change (write)
                            F Full control
```

Directory Permissions
dialog box

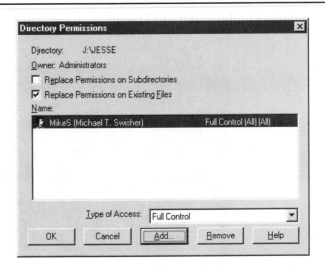

```
/R user      Revoke specified user's access rights (only
                valid with /E).
/P user:perm Replace specified user's access rights.
                Perm can be: N None
                             R Read
                             C Change (write)
                             F Full control
/D user      Deny specified user access.
```

The completed command prompt is shown in Figure 6-11.

Using CACLS to Change Access Permissions

Now let's change back the permissions on the folder you changed in the previous exercise. You will need to remove your username and put the Everyone group with full control on the desired folder.

1. C:\>CACLS J:\JESSE /E /R MikeS /G Everyone:F

2. C:\>CACLS J:\JESSE*.* /E /R MikeS /G Everyone:F

Notice that this is a two-step process. Step 1 changes the permissions on the folder. In order to change the permissions on every file in that directory you must use wild card characters. That is step 2. If you used the /T switch it would replace the permissions on the files, but it would also replace permissions on all files and subfolders under that directory.

FIGURE 6-11

Command prompt

```
E:\WINNT\System32\cmd.exe                                          _ □ ✕
E:\>cacls.exe
Displays or modifies access control lists (ACLs) of files

CACLS filename [/T] [/E] [/C] [/G user:perm] [/R user [...]]
               [/P user:perm [...]] [/D user [...]]
   filename      Displays ACLs.
   /T            Changes ACLs of specified files in
                 the current directory and all subdirectories.
   /E            Edit ACL instead of replacing it.
   /C            Continue on access denied errors.
   /G user:perm  Grant specified user access rights.
                 Perm can be: R  Read
                              C  Change (write)
                              F  Full control
   /R user       Revoke specified user's access rights (only valid with /E).
   /P user:perm  Replace specified user's access rights.
                 Perm can be: N  None
                              R  Read
                              C  Change (write)
                              F  Full control
   /D user       Deny specified user access.
Wildcards can be used to specify more that one file in a command.
You can specify more than one user in a command.

E:\>
```

Assigning Rights to Users and Groups

User rights are used to control the actions a user can perform. If the computer is a domain controller, the rights are allowed on all domain controllers. If the computer is a member server, the rights are computer-specific. Rights are different from permissions because they apply to the system as a whole, not just certain objects on the system. Rights can override permissions. If you deny access to a file for a specific user, but that user is also a backup operator with the rights to back up your system, the user is still able to back up your system including the denied access file. This is possible because backup rights take precedence over all file permissions. You manage user rights using User Manager if your server is a member server, or User Manager for Domains if it is a domain controller. Figure 6-12 shows you what User Manager should look like (except for the user and group accounts that I've created) and Figure 6-13 depicts the User Rights Policy dialog box.

FIGURE 6-12

User Manager window

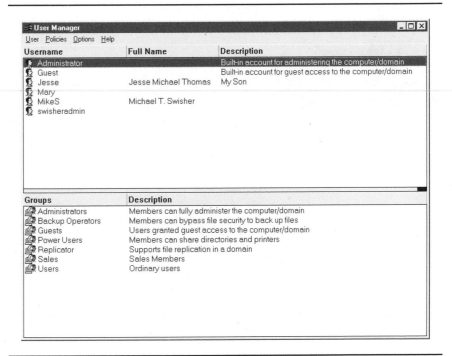

FIGURE 6-13

User Rights Policy
dialog box

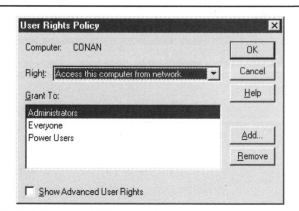

Table 6-3 describes the basic user rights you can manage using the User Rights Policy and Table 6-4 describes the advanced user rights.

In the next exercise you'll learn how to modify the user right "log on locally." By default NT allows users to log on to the server locally (except for domain controllers, which only allow server operators and administrators to log on by default). In order to make your system more secure you should only

TABLE 6-3 Basic User Rights

User Right	Permits User to	By Default Assigned to
Access this computer from network	Connect over the network to the computer.	Administrators, Server Operators, Everyone
Add workstations to domain	Add a workstation to the domain, allowing the workstation to recognize the domain's user and global group accounts.	Administrators, Server Operators
Back up files/directories	Back up files and directories. This right takes precedence over file and folder permissions.	Administrators, Backup Operators
Change system time	Set the time for the computer's clock.	Administrators, Server Operators
Force remote shutdown	A user to shut down a remote computer.	Administrators
Load/unload device drivers	Install and remove device drivers.	Administrators

TABLE 6-3	Basic User Rights (continued)	
User Right	**Permits User to**	**By Default Assigned to**
Log on locally	Log on at the computer's console.	Administrators, Backup Operators, Guests, Server Operators, Users
Manage audit and logs	Specify what to audit, but doesn't allow the user to turn auditing on and off—only an administrator can turn auditing on and off. View and clear the security log.	Administrators
Restore files/directories	Restore files and directories. This right takes precedence over file and folder permissions.	Administrators, Backup Operators
Shut down the system	Shut down NT.	Administrators, Backup Operators, Server Operators, Users
Take ownership of files or objects	Take ownership of files, folders, and other objects on the computer.	Administrators

TABLE 6-4	Advanced User Rights	
User Right	**Permits User to**	**By Default Assigned to**
Act as part of operating system	Perform as a secure, trusted part of the operating system. Some subsystems are granted this right.	None
Bypass traverse checking	Change folders and travel through a directory tree, even if the user has no permissions for those directories.	Everyone
Create pagefile	Create a pagefile.	Administrators
Create a token object	A user or program can create access tokens. Only the local security authority can do this.	None
Create permanent shared objects	Create special permanent objects, like \\Devicename.	None
Debug programs	Debug various low-level objects such as threads and processes.	Administrators

TABLE 6-4   Advanced User Rights (*continued*)

User Right	Permits User to	By Default Assigned to
Generate security audits	A user or program to generate security audit log entries.	None
Increase quotas	Reserved for future use.	N/A
Increase scheduling priority	Boost the priority of a process.	Administrators, Server Operators
Lock pages in memory	Lock pages in memory so they cannot be paged out to a backing store, such as PAGEFILE.SYS.	None
Log on as a batch job	Reserved for future use.	N/A
Log on as a service	A process to register with the system as a service.	None
Modify firmware environment values	Modify system environment variables stored in nonvolatile RAM on systems that support this type of configuration.	Administrators
Profile single process	Perform profiling (performance sampling) on a process.	Administrators, Server Operators
Profile system performance	Perform profiling (performance sampling) on the system.	Administrators
Replace process-level tokens	Modify a process' security access token. This is a powerful right, used only by the system.	None

give the right to users who need to log on to your system that right. Let's remove all users and groups who can log on to your server, except administrators.

EXERCISE 6-5   **Modifying User Rights**

1. Start User Manager.

2. On the file menu choose Policies | User Rights.

3. Click the right drop-down menu.

4. Select Log on Locally.

5. Remove all groups except the Administrators group.

Shared Server Resources

Share-level security is used to give other users access to your hard drive via the network. Any file system that is available on NT can use share-level security. You can share folders many different ways, but using Explorer or My Computer is probably the easiest. In order to share a folder on a Windows NT workstation computer you must be a member of the Administrators or Power Users group. This is one right that can't be modified. You can't grant any other groups the ability to share folders, nor can you take away the power users' ability to share folders. A user must also have permission to list the directory contents to share it. This only applies to NTFS formatted partitions.

Permissions for Shared Directories

Permissions for shared directories are much like NTFS file permissions, but not as granular. You can't set special permissions on shares as you can in NTFS. The four types of share permissions are No Access, Read, Change, and Full Control.

- **No Access**   The user is allowed to connect to the share, but no files or folders are listed. They receive the message "You do not have permissions to access this directory."

- **Read**   Allows the user to read or execute files or folders in that shared folder.

- **Change**   Allows the user to read, write, execute, or delete files and folders in that shared directory.

- **Full Control**   Allows the user to read, write, execute, delete, change permissions, and take ownership of the files and folders in that share. Change permissions and take ownership of the file only applies to shares on NTFS partitions.

Table 6-5 summarizes the folder share-level permissions.

TABLE 6-5

Folder Share-
Level Permissions

Access Level	Permissions
No Access	None
Read	RX
Change	RWXD
Full Control	RWXDPO
Permissions Key: (R)ead, (W)rite, e(X)ecute, (D)elete, change (P)ermissions, take (O)wnership	

Let's set up a shared directory. Use the same directory you used for changing permissions. Assign your user account Read access via a network share.

EXERCISE 6-6

Sharing a Directory for the First Time from the Desktop

1. Right-click on the folder and choose Properties. The Properties screen shown in Figure 6-14 is displayed.

FIGURE 6-14

Properties screen with
Sharing tab open

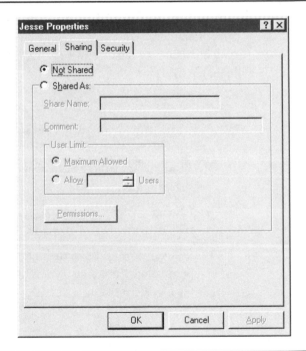

2. Choose the Shared As: option button. The name of the folder will default to the share name. Change the User limit to 1. On NT Workstation the max users are 10. You should change it to 1 because your account is the only one that will be given access, so there is never any need for more than one connection. This helps improve security by thwarting hackers trying to get into that directory while you are logged on. You will also be alerted of a problem if you try to connect to the share and you can't because someone else is connected. Then click the Permissions button (Figure 6-15).

3. Remove the Everyone group (shown in Figure 6-16). Then click the Add button.

4. Click the Show Users button (Figure 6-17) and select your name from the list. Click the Add button. Make sure the Type of Access is set to Read. Then click OK.

5. Your screen should look similar to Figure 6-18. Click OK.

FIGURE 6-15

Completed Sharing tab

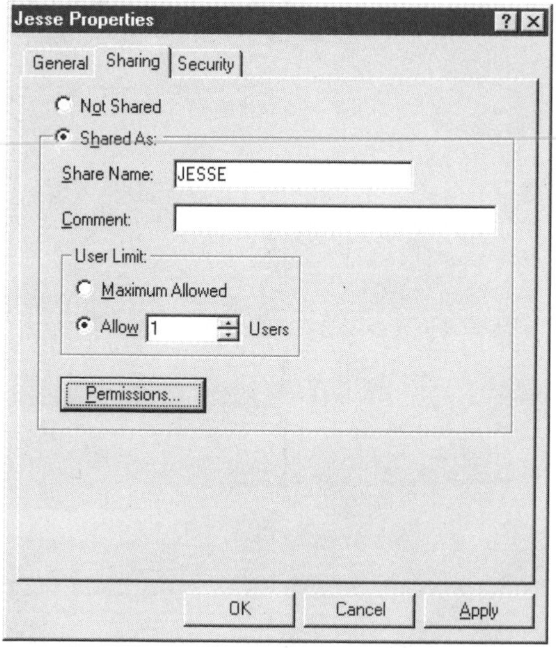

FIGURE 6-16

Access Through Share
Permissions dialog box

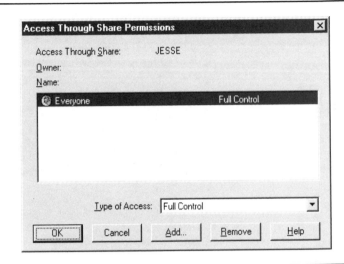

FIGURE 6-17

Add Users and Groups
dialog box

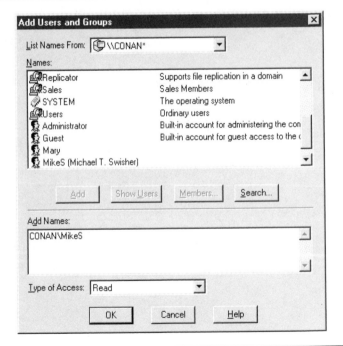

FIGURE 6-18

Completed Access
Through Share Permissions
dialog box

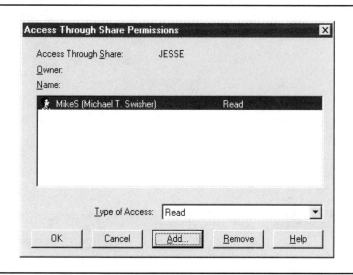

Command Prompt

You can also share a directory via the command prompt. To do so you must use the NET SHARE command.

```
NET SHARE sharename
        sharename=drive:path [/USERS:number | /UNLIMITED
                        [/REMARK:"text"]
        sharename [/USERS:number | /UNLIMITED]
                [/REMARK:"text"]
        {sharename | devicename | drive:path} /DELETE
```

The proper command for sharing the same directory as this is:

```
E:\>net share jesse=J:\jesse /USERS:1
```

This shares the directory for one user but it puts it at the default Everyone group with full control.

To delete a share via the command prompt, type:

```
E:\>net share jesse /Delete
```

Assigning Permissions to Shared Directories

If you share a directory on an NTFS partition you can get more granular with your permissions. You're still stuck with the four types of share permissions, but you can change permissions on the files and folders for added security.

Let's say you need to share a program on your NTFS formatted hard drive, which surveys your customers. Everyone with access to your computer via the network is your customer. In order to conduct your survey you need to give all the users Read, Write, and Execute permissions. How can you do this without allowing users to delete the files in that directory?

Assigning Directory Permissions

1. Create a directory on you NTFS formatted hard drive. Let's call it "survey."

2. On the folder, set the NTFS security permissions for Add and Read. Be sure that you check the boxes to change the permissions on all subdirectories and files.

3. Share that directory with change permissions to the Everyone group.

e x a m
ⓦ a t c h

Be sure to understand which permissions are applied when a user connects through a network share. The most restrictive permission always take place. If a user is granted Full Control on an NTFS directory, and accesses the files in that directory through a Read permission share, that user will only be allowed to read the files. If the permissions were the opposite, user granted Read permission on NTFS and Full Control permission on the share, he would still only be able to read the files.

There are several ways to connect to a shared resource. You can map a drive using Explorer or the NET USE command. You can also access shared folders via Network Neighborhood or the Start | Run button. For the next exercise we'll connect to a shared resource by mapping a drive via Explorer. You'll need two computers networked together—at least one running NT Server and the other Windows 95, NT Server or Workstation.

EXERCISE 6-8

Connecting to a Shared Resource

1. Share a folder as just described with the share name survey.
2. On the client computer start Explorer (if the toolbar isn't showing, go to View | Toolbar).
3. Click on the Map Network Drive icon.
4. Choose the drive letter you wish to assign.
5. In the path block type **\\\\computername\\survey**.
6. Click OK.

You can also share a directory using Server Manager. If you are an administrator who needs to share a directory on a server to which you don't have physical access, you should use Server Manager to share the directory.

EXERCISE 6-9

Creating a Network Share Using Server Manager

1. Start Server Manager.
2. Select the computer on which you want to share a directory.
3. On the menu bar, choose Computer | Shared Directories.
4. Click New Share.
5. Type in the Share Name and the Path (use the path as if you were at that console).
6. Set up the number of connections and permissions.

Shared Printer Security

You can share printers on the network much like you can share directories, but the permissions you can assign are different. There are four types of permissions allowed for sharing printers: No Access, Print, Manage Documents, and Full Control. By default, the creator is the owner of his own document; therefore, users can delete their own print job. Table 6-6 describes the permissions allowed for printers.

TABLE 6-6   Printer Permissions

	No Access	Print	Manage Documents	Full Control
Print documents		X		X
Control settings for documents			X	X
Pause, resume, restart, and delete documents			X	X
Pause, resume, purge printer				X
Change printer properties				X
Delete printer				X
Change printer permissions				X
Change print order of documents				X

CERTIFICATION OBJECTIVE 6.05

Event Auditing

After learning about directory and file security, you now have your system file permissions secured as required, but there is one major step missing. You need to audit who is accessing your sensitive files. NTFS allows you to audit access to your files and directories. Auditing allows you to trace which users accessed files on your system. This is a good way to ensure your permissions are properly set up on your system.

Before you can audit events in NT you first must turn on auditing. Exercise 6-10 shows you how to enable auditing on your system. To activate auditing, you must be a member of the Administrators group.

EXERCISE 6-10

Auditing Attempts to Take Ownership

1. Open User Manager.
2. Choose Policies Audit to open the Audit Policy dialog box (Figure 6-19).
3. Click the Audit These Events option button.

FIGURE 6-19

Audit Policy dialog box

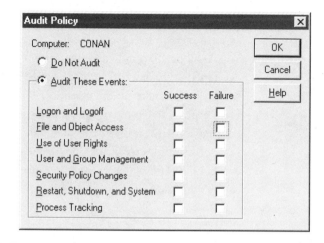

4. Choose which events you want to audit.
5. To audit file and directory events, check the File and Object Access check boxes. To see which users accessed audited files or directories, you must use the Security Login Event Viewer.

Table 6-7 explains all the events you can audit.

TABLE 6-7   Audit Events

Event	Definition
Logon and Logoff	Logs all logons and logoffs both local and remote.
File and Object Access	Logs successful actions to file, folder, and printer objects. Must be on NTFS to audit file and folder objects.
Use of User Rights	Use of anything requiring user rights.
User and Group Management	Any user accounts or groups created, changed, or deleted. Any user accounts that are renamed, disabled, or enabled. Any passwords set or changed.
Security Policy Changes	Any changes to user rights or audit policies.
Restart, Shutdown, and System	Logs all shutdowns and restarts of the local system.
Process Tracking	Tracks program activation, handle duplication, indirect object access, and process exit.

Auditing isn't a substitute for virus protection; however, it can assist you in identifying a virus. If you are auditing write processes to a drive and you notice an unusual amount of writes to it, you should check to see if it could be a virus. You'll still need a good virus protection program, but new viruses are being developed every day and auditing can be a useful tool for identifying viruses.

You should take careful consideration when planning your audit policy. How much you should audit depends on your security requirements. If you have no security requirements at all you don't need to audit, but if you have very sensitive files requiring great security you should audit every applicable event. Be careful when auditing because it slows your system down and it causes your hard drive to fill up with audit logs.

EXERCISE 6-11

Auditing Attempts to Take Ownership

In this exercise we are going to audit for anyone taking ownership on J:\JESSE\ HELP.TXT file. You'll see how to turn auditing on and how to check if someone takes ownership of the file.

1. In User Manager turn on auditing for Successful Use of User Rights.

2. Access the Security tab of the file J:\JESSE\HELP.TXT (or any file you wish to audit on an NTFS partition) by going to the file's property sheet.

3. Click the Auditing button.

4. In the File Auditing dialog box (Figure 6-20), set the properties to match the screenshot.

5. Now log on with a different username (make sure the user has the right to Take Ownership).

6. Repeat steps 1 and 2.

7. Click the Ownership button.

8. In the Owner dialog box (Figure 6-21) click the Take Ownership button.

9. Now run Event View and look at Security log (Figure 6-22).

10. Look at Event ID: 578.

FIGURE 6-20

File Auditing dialog box

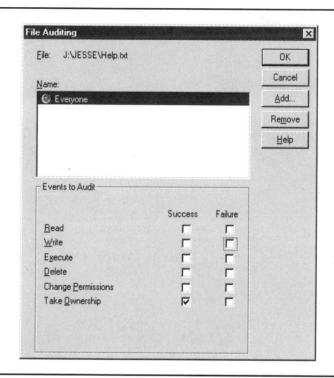

FIGURE 6-21

Owner dialog box

FIGURE 6-22

Event Detail dialog box

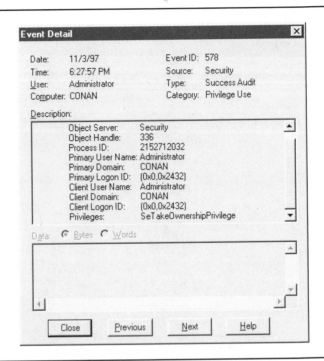

FROM THE CLASSROOM

The Top Three Auditing Mistakes

Three mistakes pop up time and time again in the classroom, as well as at clients' sites. A student will call our attention to their Security log, which is disturbingly empty. "Why is this?" they ask. The solution is often simple: "Have you turned on auditing in User Manager?" we ask. "Ha, we did that!" they say. "OK, fine. Did you actually select any events to audit?" we ask.

This often invokes a blank stare by the students and a quiet, "Oh." It is a common oversight. The administrator enabled auditing but did not go to the lower half of the dialog box and select the events they wanted to audit.

Or we may get a call from an administrator saying that someone is deleting files and they would like to know who is doing it. When they

FROM THE CLASSROOM

open the Properties page of the folder and select the Security button, the audit boxes are grayed out. But auditing is enabled. What is the problem? Again, it's pretty simple. The administrator has not checked the File and Object Access box in the Audit Policy dialog box. It is a two-step process to audit who is doing what to files and folders. First you must enable auditing and check File and Object Access. Then you must use the object properties sheet and select the users you want to track (for example, the Global group Domain Users).

The third problem area has to do with audit policies. Generally speaking, it may be advisable to audit by exception rather than by rule. On busy servers, auditing for all information all of

the time can generate megabyte-size records in a short time. What do administrators do when presented with reams of information that stretches from here until tomorrow? Our observation is such data is mostly ignored—often because it is too overwhelming. You might set it aside with the best intention of getting to it tomorrow (except tomorrow brings its own information deluge). So ask yourself, how valuable is information that you might never look at? Might it be better to audit for a few key items, and spot check other items that don't generate so much information?

—*By Shane Clawson, MCT, MCSE*

CERTIFICATION OBJECTIVE 6.06

Setting Registry Keys

In order to make your system more secure you need to edit the Registry. Be very careful when editing the Registry—you can make your system unstable if you make a mistake. By editing the Registry you can enhance physical security by adding a security warning message, disabling the default user name, and disabling the shutdown button.

Adding a Security Warning Message

You can have NT give a security notice before logging on to your system. This is important if you want to prosecute charges against a hacker. The government lost a case against a computer hacker because the logon screen said Welcome. Exercise 6-12 explains how to enter a security notice.

Changing the WinLogon Security Notice

1. Click on Start | Run.

2. Type **regedt32** and press ENTER.

3. Select the Registry key. HKEY_LOCAL_MACHINE\SOFTWARE\ Microsoft\Windows NT\CurrentVersion\Winlogon.

4. Double-click on the value LegalNoticeCaption.

5. In the string box type a caption you want to appear in your title bar. "Warning: this is a Private System" is a good example.

6. Double-click on the value LegalNoticeText.

7. In the string box type in a legal notification like "This is a private system owned and operated by Swisher Enterprises. By logging on you consent to monitoring. Any illegal activity may and will be reported to law enforcement officials. If you don't have official use on this system you are violating the law."

Disabling the Default Username

Another security measure is to not display the username of the last user who logged on. You need two things to break into an account: a username and a password. Security is improved when the intruder has to guess both a username and a password. Exercise 6-13 shows how to disable the default username.

Disabling the Default Username

1. Click on Start | Run.

2. Type **regedt32** and press ENTER.

3. Select the Registry key. HKEY_LOCAL_MACHINE\SOFTWARE\ Microsoft\Windows NT\CurrentVersion\Winlogon.

4. On the menu bar choose Edit, Add Value.

5. In the Value box enter DontDisplayLastUserName.

6. In the string box enter 1.

Disabling the Shutdown Button

By default NT Workstation allows users to press CTRL-ALT-DEL and shut down the system. You can disable this by editing a Registry key. You may be thinking, "Why would I want to disable the shutdown button?" Well, let's say you have a computer where your sales team enters data on the sales floor. You can lock the CPU and power supply up in a cabinet to keep customers from turning it off, but what if they can just press CTRL-ALT-DEL and click Shutdown. By disabling this feature you can help protect your system against unauthorized shutdowns.

EXERCISE 6-14

Disabling the Winlogon Shutdown Button

1. Click on Start | Run.

2. Type **regedt32** and press ENTER.

3. Select the Registry key. HKEY_LOCAL_MACHINE\SOFTWARE\ Microsoft\Windows NT\CurrentVersion\Winlogon.

4. Double-click on the value ShutdownWithoutLogon.

5. In the string box enter 0.

CERTIFICATION SUMMARY

This chapter described the NT security model and its four components. It also explained how logons occur and the role that the Local Security Authority plays in the logon process. You learned about the four logon types: local, remote, domain, and pass-through. You also learned about ACLs and ACEs and how they interact with access tokens.

File and directory security is an important topic that you will continuously apply as you use NT. This is how you protect your most common shared resources on the network. There are various levels of permissions for files and directories, but you need an NTFS formatted partition to use them. Another type of security is shared security. It can be applied to any type of file system. Sometimes you need to combine shared security with NTFS file and directory security to get the right level of permissions assigned for sharing files on the network.

Finally, we discussed auditing and making your system more secure by editing the winlogon Registry key. Take what you've learned in this chapter with you after you pass the exam. As the Internet grows and more companies put their networks on the Internet, the more our systems are vulnerable to attack. We must apply security to our systems *before* we are attacked; otherwise it is too late.

TWO-MINUTE DRILL

- ❑ The NT security model is made up of four main components: logon processes, Local Security Authority, Security Account Manager (SAM), and the Security Reference Monitor.
- ❑ There are four types of logons that NT supports: local, remote, domain, and pass-through authentication.
- ❑ You can set NT to lock out an account after a certain number of unsuccessful logon attempts.
- ❑ NT uses Access Control List (ACL) and Access Control Entries (ACE) attributes to secure objects.
- ❑ The ACE specifies auditing and access permissions for a given object for a specific user or group of users.
- ❑ There are three different types of ACEs: AccessAllowed, AccessDenied, and SystemAudit.
- ❑ Permissions are cumulative; except for No Access.
- ❑ Local Security Authority validates user logons against the SAM database.
- ❑ A SID is used to uniquely identify each user, NT Workstation, and server on the network.
- ❑ An access token is created every time a user logs on to your computer, whether via the network or console.
- ❑ The key to assigning and removing a user to a group is that the user must be logged off before the change can take effect.

❑ NTFS will allow permissions on folders and individual files. If you're concerned about security, NTFS is the file system to use.

❑ File Delete Child is a POSIX function that allows a user who has Full Control of a folder to delete a top-level file within that folder, even though the user doesn't have permissions to delete that file.

❑ Container objects can inherit permissions from their parent container; this is known as *inherited permissions*.

❑ If you move a file or folder within the same partition, it keeps its previous security permissions.

❑ User rights are used to control the actions a user can perform. If the computer is a domain controller, the rights are allowed on all domain controllers. If the computer is a member server, the rights are computer-specific.

❑ Rights are different from permissions because they apply to the system as a whole, not just certain objects on the system. Rights can override permissions.

❑ Share-level security is used to give other users access to your hard drive via the network.

❑ The four types of share permissions for shared directories are: No Access, Read, Change, and Full Control.

❑ There are four types of permissions allowed for sharing printers: No Access, Print, Manage Documents, and Full Control.

❑ NTFS allows you audit access to your files and directories. Auditing allows you to trace which users have accessed files on your system.

❑ Be very careful when editing the Registry—you can make your system unstable if you make a mistake.

SELF TEST

The following questions will help you measure your understanding of the material presented in this chapter. Read all the choices carefully, as there may be more than one correct answer. Choose all correct answers for each question.

1. The _____ creates security access tokens, authenticates users, and manages the local security policy.

    A. Local Security Authority

    B. SAM

    C. ACL

    D. ACE

2. What maintains the database of all user, group, and workstation accounts?

    A. Local Security Authority

    B. SAM

    C. ACL

    D. HKEY_LOCAL_MACHINE

3. NT supports which of the following logons? (Choose all that apply.)

    A. local

    B. pass-through authentication

    C. remote

    D. domain

4. Why must you press CTRL-ALT-DEL to log on to NT?

    A. Reboot the system to refresh the memory.

    B. Reboot the system to clear the Security logs.

    C. Prevent trojan horse viruses.

    D. Erase the last username from the logon dialog box.

5. Which of the following are objects? (Choose all that apply.)

    A. file

    B. window

    C. process

    D. keyboard

6. A _____ is used to uniquely identify each user account.

    A. SID

    B. GUID

    C. Group ID

    D. ACL

7. If you delete a user account how can you get it back?

    A. You can't undelete an account. You must create a new account.

    B. Choose undelete from the file menu.

    C. Run the command ACCOUNT / UNDELETE.

    D. Use the recycle bin.

8. Which tool should you use to share a folder on a remote computer? (Choose all that apply.)

    A. My Computer

    B. Server Manager

C. User Manager

D. Permissions property page

9. User JesseS belongs to the local group marketing. The permissions on the file DICTIONARY.DOC are as follows: JesseS has Change (RWXD) permission and the marketing group has No Access permissions. When user JesseS tries to read the file what access will he be granted?

A. Change

B. Read

C. Read and Execute

D. No Access

10. Which ACE does NT process first?

A. AccessAllowed

B. ReadControl

C. WriteDenied

D. AccessDenied

11. User MaryS is assigned to the local group sales. Mary has Read permissions for all files on your system. The group sales has special permissions of Write on all the files in the folder called reports. If Mary requests Read and Write permissions at the same time what will happen?

A.. Access will be denied because she doesn't have enough access in any individual group.

B. Access can't be resolved.

C. Access will be granted.

D. Access will be granted, but an administrator must approve it first.

12. If you want to limit the people who can access a folder on your system while they are using the console, how must your hard disk partition be formatted?

A. NTFS

B. FAT

C. HPFS

D. CDFS

13. Why is there a special utility to secure the boot partition of RISC computers?

A. RISC computers can't be physically secured, so it requires extra protection.

B. RISC computers are more secure than Intel-based computers because they can access more security subsystems.

C. RISC systems must boot on a FAT partition.

D. Microsoft just hasn't compiled the utility for other systems yet.

14. What command allows the user to change file permissions from a command shell?

A. NET PERMISSIONS

B. SET FILE

C. CACLS

D. ACE

15. If you want audit access to files stored on your NTFS formatted hard drive, what must you do first?

A. Turn on auditing using User Manager.

B. Turn on auditing for the folder by using Explorer.

C. Do nothing; NT automatically audits all file access once NTFS is installed.

D. Use the program Security Manager to enable auditing.

16. If you change a user's rights on a domain controller, which of the following statements are true? (Choose all that apply.)

A. The user's rights will only be applied to the server you used to apply the changes.

B. All domain controllers will be modified to reflect the new rights.

C. All domain controllers and member servers will be modified to reflect the new rights.

17. Who is the owner of a new file on a FAT partition?

A. Administrator

B. System

C. Whoever created the file

D. FAT doesn't support owners

18. Who is the owner of a new file on an NTFS partition?

A. Administrator

B. System

C. Whoever created the file

D. NTFS doesn't support owners

19. (True/False) Only administrators can give someone ownership of a file.

20. When moving a folder from drive c: to drive d: what permissions will the folder have? (Assume both drives are formatted with NTFS.)

A. The folder will keep its original permissions.

B. The folder will inherit the permissions of drive D:.

C. NTFS will reset the folder to Everyone Full Control.

D. NTFS doesn't support permissions between drives.

21. Which file systems support share-level security?

A. FAT

B. NTFS

C. CDFS

D. All of the above

22. Which one is *not* a type of share permission on an NTFS partition?

A. Read

B. No Access

C. Full Control

D. Special Access

E. None of the above

23. How can you share a folder on the network to allow everyone to read, write, and execute files, but not delete any files?

A. You can't.

B. Give everyone group Change share permissions.

C. Give everyone group Read, Write, and Execute share permissions.

D. Give everyone group Change share permissions and Read, Write, Execute Special File permissions on NTFS.

24. Which of the following are negative results from auditing all file object accesses on your system? (Choose all that apply.)

    A. Slows your computer's processor down

    B. Creates more disk access

    C. Fills your Security log up too fast

    D. None of the above

25. What auditing function must be turned on to allow you to audit writes to your NTFS directories?

    A. Logon and Logoff

    B. File and Object Access

    C. Use of User Rights

    D. Process Tracking

26. User RyanB is given share-level access of Full Control to share SalesRPT; however, the NTFS permissions are set to Read for the group sales. RyanB is a member of the group sales. When he connects to the share SalesRPT what type of access will he have?

    A. Full Control

    B. Read

    C. No Access

    D. None of the above

27. User MarcieJ is a member of Domain Users. She attempts to log on to a domain controller at the console, but she can't be validated. Whenever she tries to access the server through the network, she connects without any problems. What is the most likely cause of this problem?

    A. She is using an incorrect password.

    B. She doesn't have an account on the domain.

    C. Her account is locked out because of too many bad logon attempts.

    D. She doesn't have the right to log on locally.

MCSE
MICROSOFT CERTIFIED SYSTEMS ENGINEER

7

Windows NT 4.0 Domains

CERTIFICATION OBJECTIVES

7.01   The Workgroup Model and the Domain Model

7.02   Managing Domain Trusts

7.03   Using NT Server Manager

7.04   Local and Global Groups

7.05   NT's Netlogon Service

This chapter discusses the NT workgroup and domain models. We'll discuss which domain model is appropriate for given situations. In order to completely understand all the domain models, we'll explain what a trust is and how it relates to the domain models. Once a domain model is decided upon you'll need to manage user accounts by combining them into groups. You'll learn about local and global groups and when it's appropriate to use each type. Then we'll discuss Server Manager and how to use it to manage your NT domains and servers. Finally, we'll tell you how to configure the netlogon service so you can optimize it for your network needs.

The Workgroup Model and the Domain Model

All NT computer systems participate in either a workgroup or a domain. The biggest difference between the two is where the user accounts are located. If the user accounts are located locally (except for domain controllers), the computer is part of a *workgroup*. If the user accounts are located on a remote server, the computer is part of a *domain*.

Workgroups: Peer-to-Peer Networking

A workgroup is an organizational unit that groups computers together if they don't already belong to a domain. A computer that participates in a workgroup is responsible for keeping track of its users and groups. This information is maintained by the local computer and not shared with other computers in the workgroup. Because of this feature, users in a workgroup must have a user ID and password for every NT computer they need to access. This is good for small networks, but can become impossible to manage if many computers are involved. Since there is no central user accounts database in a workgroup, all computers are considered to be peers. This is known as *peer-to-peer networking*. No one computer has authority over any other computer; all computers are equal.

Domain Computing

A domain is a group of computers that share a common user accounts database and security policy. A Windows NT Server can act either as a domain controller or a member server to a domain. Domain controllers (either primary or backup) maintain a copy of the directory service database. Servers that don't maintain a copy of the directory service database are called member servers. NT Workstation can also be part of a domain, but it can't maintain a copy of the directory service database. By being part of the domain, a computer allows the domain to provide security validation for its users. Logon requests are processed by domain controllers for all computers participating in a domain.

A domain doesn't refer to a single geographic location. A domain can consist of computers on a LAN or WAN. The computers can be connected by many types of physical connections that allows them to communicate, including ISDN, EtherNet, Token-Ring, satellite, leased lines, ATM, dial-up adapters, etc.

As mentioned earlier, a server can either be a domain controller or a member server. A member server is much like a workstation on the domain. It relies on the domain controllers for user authentication. There are two types of domain controllers: primary domain controllers (PDC) and backup domain controllers (BDC). There must be one and only one PDC per domain. The PDC is responsible for tracking changes made to the directory service database, then distributing these changes to the BDCs. The PDC is the only server that can accept changes to the directory service database. If you try to change a user's password when the PDC is unavailable you'll get an error message stating that the PDC for the domain can't be found.

A BDC contains a copy of the directory service database. The BDC's directory service database is automatically synchronized with the PDC. The BDC is used to authenticate user logons and it can be promoted to be the PDC in case the PDC fails. You can use multiple BDCs to load balance your network by placing BDCs near many users. The number of BDCs that are required depends on your network. You have to consider the number of workstations on your network, the physical location of the workstations, and the connection speed to all areas of your network. Table 7-1 shows the

TABLE 7-1	Number of Workstations	Number of BDCs
	<5,000	1
Number of BDCs per	5,000	2
Number of Workstations	10,000	5
	20,000	10
	30,000	15

Microsoft recommended number of BDCs per number of workstations. Since you'll still need a PDC for each domain, the total number of domain controllers is the number of BDCs plus one. These numbers were calculated using a 486/66 computer with 32MB of RAM. As the hardware performance increases, you can decrease the number of recommended BDCs.

Workgroup Model vs. Domain Concept

The workgroup model has one advantage in that it doesn't require central administration. Since all computers are peers, every computer can have its own administrator. In small LANs that don't require central security/administration that's an advantage; however, in larger LANs it's a disadvantage. The more computers you manage, the more you need to use a domain.

Domains offer several advantages over workgroups. First, domain controllers create a single administrative unit, which allows administrators to manage only one account for each user. This centralized network administration gives a view of the entire network from any workstation in the domain. It gives administrators the ability to manage users, groups, and resources in distributed network. Second, since there is only one account per user, each user only needs to remember one password and user ID. Single user logon allows users to access any server in the domain for which he has proper permissions with only one logon. The third advantage ties in with the second, universal access to resources. One logon allows users to access multiple servers within the domain. The account validation is extended to allow seamless user access to multiple servers throughout the domain or other trusted domains.

Managing Domain Trusts

At this point you're probably asking, "What is a trust?" A *trust* is a link that combines two separate domains into one administrative unit that can authorize access to resources on both domains. To put it another way, validated users in domain X can access resources in domain Y if a trust relationship is established. To manage trusts you use User Manager for Domains.

Trusted Domain Concept

A trust allows administrators to manage multiple domains as a single administrative unit. Each trust has a trusting domain and a trusted domain. The trusted domain is the domain that can perform administrative tasks in the other domain. User accounts created in the trusted domain can access resources in the trusting domain (if proper permissions are assigned). The trusting domain trusts another domain to manage its user, group, and resources. To put the two concepts together, the trusting domain allows the trusted domain to manage its users, groups, and resources. Although a trust exists, administrators in the trusting domain can still manage their own local resources and users; however, they can't manage users in the trusted domain.

Trust Relationships Between Domains

You can create a one-way or a two-way trust relationship. In a one-way trust relationship, one domain trusts the users in the other domain to use its resources. In other words, validated users of domain X can access resources in domain Y, but domain Y users cannot access resources in domain X. If users in domain Y need access to domain X, you'll need to create a two-way trust. Two-way trusts are actually two separate one-way trusts. It allows users from either domain to access resources in the other domain. Figure 7-1 shows a one-way trust in which the Sales domain trusts the Marketing domain. Figure 7-2 shows a two-way trust where Sales trusts Marketing and Marketing trusts

FIGURE 7-1

One-way trust

Sales. Notice the direction of the arrows. They may appear backwards, but they're not. The arrow should point from the trusting domain to the trusted domain. In Figure 7-1, Sales trusts Marketing, so it points at Marketing for its security provider. You may think the arrow should point the opposite direction because the users from Marketing can get into Sales. Well, that's not correct, although it makes sense. Microsoft has defined arrows as pointing from the trusting domain to the trusted domain.

exam
ⓦatch   *Be sure to know which way the arrows point for trusts. You may see several diagrams with arrows representing trusts on your test. If you forget that the arrows point from the trusting domain to the trusted domain, you'll probably miss the question.*

The following exercises teach you how to use trusts and manage them in various situations. First let's create a one-way trust. Follow Exercise 7-1 to create a one-way trust between two domains. We'll establish a one-way trust between the domain Sales and the domain Production where Sales is the

FIGURE 7-2

Two-way trust

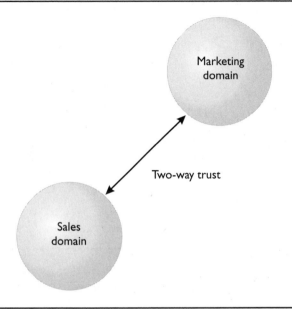

trusted domain. For this exercise you'll need to have administrator rights to two NT domains.

EXERCISE 7-1

Creating a One-Way Trust Relationship

1. In the Sales domain (the trusted domain), open User Manager for Domains.

2. Click Add Button for the Trusting Domains.

3. Enter the name of the trusting domain (Production), as shown in Figure 7-3.

4. Enter a password and confirm the password by entering it a second time. The trusting domain uses this password to establish the one-way trust.

5. Click OK.

6. In the Production domain (the trusting domain) open User Manager for Domains.

Adding Production as a
trusting domain

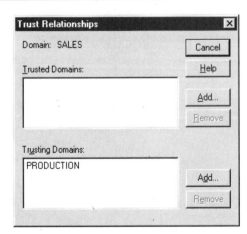

7. Click Add Button for the Trusting Domains.

8. Enter the name of the trusted domain (Sales), as shown in Figure 7-4.

9. Enter the password you used in step 4.

10. Click OK.

Adding Sales as a trusted
domain

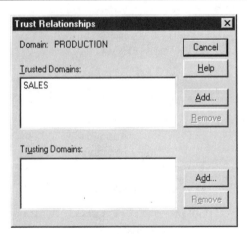

Exercise 7-2 shows you how to give users permissions to a shared directory in a resource domain.

EXERCISE 7-2

Using the Trust Relationship

1. Log on to a server in a resource domain. (You must have at least server operator or power user privileges.)
2. Share the folder on the network.
3. Add a user from the master domain by selecting the master domain in the List Names From drop-down menu box.
4. Notice how all the groups from the master domain appear when you select the master domain as the List Names From domain. To view the users, click the Show Users button.

Exercise 7-3 shows you how to identify the trust relationships on a domain.

EXERCISE 7-3

Identifying the Trust Relationships on Domain B

1. Open User Manager for Domains.
2. Click User | Select Domain.
3. Double-click on domain B (or whatever domain you want to view).
4. Select Policies | Trust Relationships.
5. You can now view the trust relationships established for domain B.

Terminating a trust is easy. Exercise 7-4 shows how to do it.

EXERCISE 7-4

Terminating a Trust Relationship

1. Open User Manager for Domains.
2. Click User | Select Domain.
3. Double-click on domain B (or whatever domain you want to view).
4. Select Policies | Trust Relationships.
5. Select the domain you want to stop trusting.
6. Click Remove.

exam
Watch

After removing a trust from one domain you can't simply add it back by using the same password you used to establish the trust. After both domains establish a trust relationship, NT changes the password used to create the trust. This is done so that you won't have to re-create trusts after your administrator leaves the company. Since the password is changed, you won't have to worry about an ex-administrator hacking into your system via the trusts.

Number of Trusts

Before version 4.0, NT had a recommended limit of 128 trusts per domain. NT 4.0 has increased the number of possible trusts to unlimited. It also increased the number of LSA secrets significantly higher than the previous limit of 256. (You use one LSA secret for each trust you establish.) Another limiting factor was the nonpaged pool size of the domain controllers on which the resource domains are stored. Whenever a domain controller starts, it sends a message to each domain in an attempt to discover domain controllers in all trusted domains. Each domain controller in every trusted domain responds with a message to the starting domain controller. The response is temporarily stored in the nonpaged pool until netlogon can read it.

NT 4.0 provides a large default nonpaged pool size, which provides for a substantially higher number of trusted domains than earlier versions did. The default nonpaged pool size depends on the amount of physical RAM on your server. Table 7-2 lists the default nonpaged pool size that is configured when NT Server is installed on computers with different amounts of physical memory. If necessary, you can use the Registry editing tool Regedit to increase the size of your nonpaged pooled memory size. Edit the following key to increase the nonpaged pooled memory size:

HKEY_LOCAL_MACHINE\SYSTEM\CurrentControlSet\Control\
Session Manager\Memory Management

TABLE 7-2	Nonpaged Pool Size	# of Trusted Domains	Total Physical Memory
	1.2MB	140	32MB
Default Nonpaged Pool Size Vs. Physical Memory	2.125MB	250	64MB
	4.125MB	500	128MB

Domain Strategies

Now that you understand trust relationship, we can discuss Microsoft's recommended domain models. There are four recommended domain models: single, master, multiple master, and complete trust.

Single Domain Model

Let's start by discussing the simplest domain model—the single domain model. The single domain consists of one domain; therefore, no trusts are set up. All user and group accounts are located in this domain. Figure 7-5 depicts the single domain model. Notice how all user accounts and resources are located in one domain. A single domain can handle up to 26,000 users, but that really depends upon the type of hardware and number of servers in the domain. The single domain is good for central administration and small networks.

Master Domain Model

The master domain model is also good for central administration. As in the single domain, all user accounts are located in a single domain, which is called the *master domain*. Resources, like printers and files, are shared in other domains called *resource domains*. This provides for organizational grouping of your network resources, but still allows central administration. The master domain model can handle about 30,000 users depending on the number of

FIGURE 7-5

Single domain model

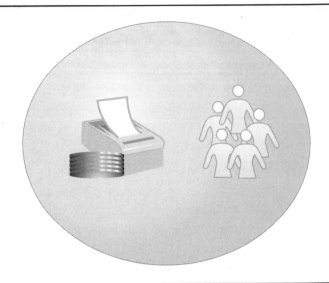

servers and type of hardware. This model is a very common model to be used in the real world. It gives departments the ability to manage their own resources. As an administrator you'll quickly find that inter-department politics will definitely play a role in choosing a domain model. This model is used to allow departments to control their own resources while allowing a central administrator to manage user accounts. This is a good compromise between the single domain model and the full trust model (which we'll discuss a little later).

Figure 7-6 depicts the master domain model. Users log on to the master domain called MyCompany. Resources are then shared to those users in other domains. The resource domains Sales, Marketing, and Production can each have their own administrators to manage their resources.

The master domain model is good for:

- Centralized account management. User accounts can be centrally managed; add/delete/change user accounts from a single point.

- Decentralized resource management or local system administration capability. Department domains can have their own administrators who manage the resources in the department.

FIGURE 7-6

Master domain model

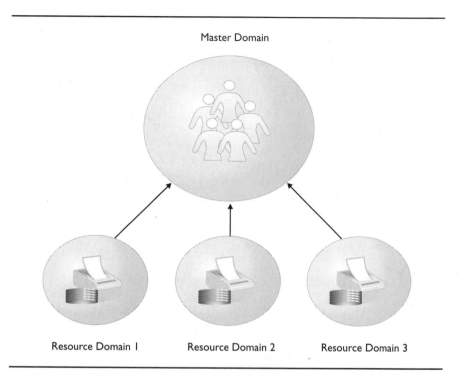

Master Domain

Resource Domain 1   Resource Domain 2   Resource Domain 3

■ Resources can be grouped logically, corresponding to local domains.

Multiple Master Domain Model

The multiple master domain model is managed much like the master domain model, except it can handle more users. The multiple master domain is actually two or more master domain models joined by a two-way trust. Figure 7-7 shows the trusts that are needed to create a multiple master domain.

The multiple master domain has the same benefits of the master domain model plus the following:

■ Organizations of more than 40,000 users. The multiple master domain model is scalable to networks with any number of users.

■ Mobile users. Users can log on from anywhere in the network, anywhere in the world.

FIGURE 7-7

Multiple master
domain model

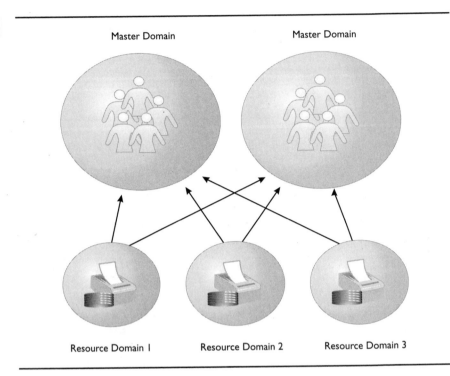

- Centralized or decentralized administration.
- Organizational needs. Domains can be configured to mirror specific departments or internal company organizations.
- BDCs can be distributed between sites to facilitate LAN-WAN interactions.

Complete Trust Model

This model doesn't fit in with the other models. This model is generally used when a company cannot decide on a central place for administration. Since there is no central administrator, each domain is a complete entity unto itself. In order to facilitate communication between domains, a two-way trust is established between every domain participating in this model.

This model can scale to more than 30,000 users. In fact, like the multiple master domain model, it can scale to an unlimited number of users. You'll just need to create a new domain and establish the proper trusts for that domain for every 30,000 users. This model is 100 percent decentralized management. Each domain has its own administrator. Resources can be shared to users in other domains because of the two-way trust arrangement.

This model requires many trusts to be established. The formula for determining the number of trusts is n(n-1) = total number of trusts; where n is the number of domains. If you have 7 domains you'll need 42 trusts. Add one more domain and you need 56 trusts. This can get out of hand very quickly.

Figure 7-8 shows the complete trust model for four domains. Notice that each domain has to have a two-way trust established with every domain.

Complete trust domain model

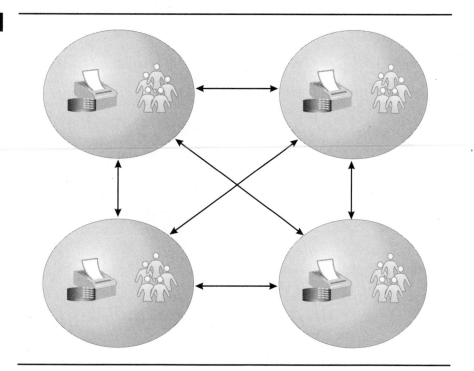

FROM THE CLASSROOM

Trust Relationships Between Domains: Who Do You Trust?

Trust relationships may be tough to understand at first. In simplest terms, a trust relationship allows administrators to preserve the "one user, one account" design goal. That is, any user should be able to go anywhere in the enterprise, log on with the same account, and still have access to the same resources—without the need for multiple accounts in different domains.

One of the most confusing things for students to understand is the "trusted/trusting" terminology. This may simply have to be memorized.

■ The "trusted" domain has the user accounts.

■ The "trusting" domain has the resources that the users want to access.

In other words, the domain with the resources is going to "trust" the security system of the domain with the user accounts. Stated another way, the resource domain (the one with the stuff the user wants to get at) will be "trusting" the authentication of the user's account done by the accounts domain—the "trusted" domain.

Microsoft documentation says that you may set up either side of the trust first, and then complete the other side. Experience in both the classroom and at client sites suggests that if you set up the "trusted" side first and the "trusting" side next, it will be easier for you to determine that the trust relationship was established. This is because only the "trusting" side receives a message indicating success or failure. If you try to set up this side first, you will always get an error message stating that the trust could not be verified at this time. That is simply because the trusted side has not been set up.

If you start with the trusted side first and then do the trusting side, the message will report that the trust has been successfully established. While you can do it either way, one way could lead to confusing messages.

—*By Shane Clawson, MCT, MCSE*

Using NT Server Manager

The Server Manager utility allows you to manage servers and computers in your domain. You can use Server Manager to:

- Select a domain, workgroup, or computer for administration
- Manage a computer by viewing a list of connected users, viewing shared and open resources, managing services, managing shared directories, and sending messages to connected users
- Manage a domain by promoting a BDC to the PDC, synchronizing BDCs with its PDC, and adding or removing computers from the domain

Server Manager has many of the same functions as the Server and Services applets in the Control Panel, but Server Manager allows you to manage both the local computer and remote computers. Exercise 7-5 shows how to launch Server Manager.

EXERCISE 7-5

Launching Server Manager

1. Click Start on the taskbar.
2. Choose Programs | Administrative Tools (Common) | Server Manager.

Server Properties

By double-clicking on the computer you want to manage, you will cause the Properties dialog box for that computer to display (see Figure 7-9). You can use Server Manager to monitor:

- **Sessions**   Total number of users remotely connected to the computer
- **Open Files**   Total number of open files currently accessed via the network
- **File Locks**   Total number of file locks placed by remote users against the open files
- **Open Named Pipes**   Total number of open named pipes between the computer and remote clients

Server Manager allows you to enter a description of your computer, which will appear whenever users view your computer using Server Manager. You can do more than just look at the open connections; you can also manage the connections using the control buttons located at the bottom of the Properties windows.

There are five buttons on the Properties window, but in this chapter we'll only discuss four of them: Users, Shares, In Use, and Alerts.

Monitoring Users

The Users button opens the User Sessions dialog box. The User Sessions dialog box allows you to view a list of all the network users connected to the

Server Manager properties for server CONAN

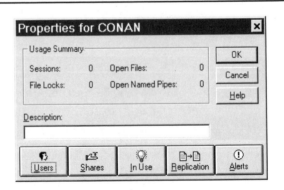

computer, and list all the resources opened by a selected user. Optionally, you can disconnect one or all of the users connected to the computer. Exercise 7-6 teaches you how to disconnect one user from your computer. Although you can disconnect the user while accessing a shared folder, the client connections are persistent. In other words, the client will keep attaching to the shared resource even after you disconnect the user. To prevent the user from connecting again you'll have to stop sharing the resource with that user.

EXERCISE 7-6

Disconnecting a User Session

1. Open Server Manager.
2. Double-click on the server you want to manage.
3. Click Users. You'll see the display shown in Figure 7-10.
4. Select the user you wish to disconnect.
5. Click Disconnect.
6. Click Close.

FIGURE 7-10

User sessions on server CONAN

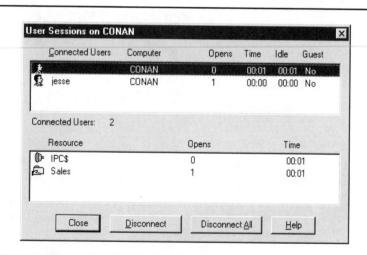

Managing Shared Resources

The Shares button opens the Shared Resources dialog box. Use this dialog box to view list of the shared resources available on the computer and for a selected resource list of connected users. Optionally, you can disconnect one or all of the users connected to the share. Use Exercise 7-7 to disconnect a user accessing a shared directory.

EXERCISE 7-7

Disconnecting a User on a Shared Directory

1. Open Server Manager.

2. Double-click on the server you want to manage.

3. Click Shares. You'll see the display shown in Figure 7-11.

4. Choose the share you wish to manage under Sharename.

5. Select the user you want to disconnect.

6. Click Disconnect.

7. Click Close.

FIGURE 7-11

Shared resources on server CONAN

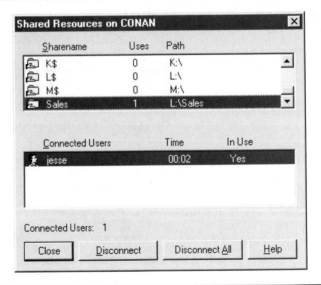

Monitoring Resources in Use

The In Use button opens the Open Resources dialog box. Use this dialog box to view a list of the computer's open shared resources, as shown in Figure 7-12. You can also close one open resource or all open resources by selecting the resource that is open and clicking Close Resource.

Monitoring Server Alerts

Server Alerts are used to send notification messages to users or computers. Server Alerts are generated by the system, and relate to server and resource use. They warn about security and access problems, user session problems, printer problems, and server shutdown because of power loss when the UPS service is available. It's a good idea to have a message sent to both the administrator and the administrator's workstation. See Exercise 7-8 to manage Server Alerts.

<table>
<tr><td>EXERCISE 7-8</td><td>

Managing Server Alerts

1. Open Server Manager.

2. Double-click the computer name you want to manage.

3. Click Alerts. You'll see the display shown in Figure 7-13.

</td></tr>
</table>

<table>
<tr><td>FIGURE 7-12</td><td></td></tr>
<tr><td>Open resources on server Conan</td><td>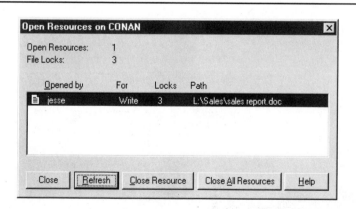</td></tr>
</table>

FIGURE 7-13

Alerts on server CONAN

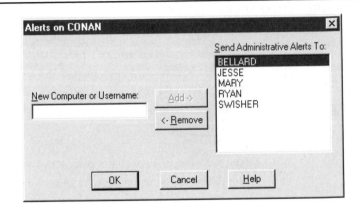

4. To add a user or computer to the list of alert recipients, enter the username or computer name in New Computer or Username, then click Add.

5. To remove a user or computer from the list of alert recipients, select the username or computer name in Send Administrative Alerts To, then click Remove.

6. Click OK.

7. Stop and restart the Server and Alerter services to put your changes into effect.

Adding/Removing Computers

There are two ways to add NT Servers and Workstations to a domain. You can use the Network Control Panel on the computer that you want to add to the domain. This method requires an administrator's password to create the computer account. A server operator can also use Server Manager to add computers to the domain. Exercise 7-9 shows you how to add a computer to your domain.

EXERCISE 7-9

Adding a Computer to a Domain

1. Open Server Manager.

2. Click Computer | Add to Domain. You'll see the display shown in Figure 7-14.

3. Select either Windows NT Workstation or Server or Windows NT Backup Domain Controller.

4. Enter the Computer Name.

5. Click Add. An account for that computer name is added to the domain directory database.

6. Click Close. The computer is added to the Server Manager's list.

7. After a computer has been added, instruct the user of that computer to join the domain.

Exercise 7-10 shows you how to delete a computer from a domain.

EXERCISE 7-10

Deleting a Computer from a Domain

1. Open Server Manager.

2. Select a computer from the list in the Server Manager window. Do not select the primary domain controller, because it cannot be removed.

3. Click Computer | Remove from Domain.

4. Instruct the user of that computer to remove this domain name in the Network Control Panel and to enter a different domain name or workgroup name.

FIGURE 7-14

Adding a computer to a domain

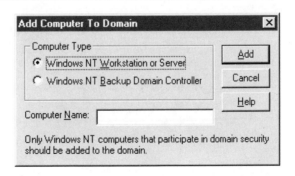

Promote a BDC to a PDC

When a PDC fails, a BDC must be promoted to fulfill the role of the PDC. After the failed PDC is fixed and before it comes back online, it must be demoted from the role of PDC. (After it is demoted it can later be promoted to the PDC role.) Exercise 7-11 shows how to promote a BDC to a PDC.

EXERCISE 7-11

Promoting a BDC to a PDC

1. Open Server Manager.

2. Select a backup domain controller from the list of computers in the Server Manager window. Be sure to choose a computer that is capable of handling the increased network load.

3. Click Computer | Promote to Primary Domain Controller. If the PDC is still online and functioning properly, it will automatically be demoted to a BDC.

Exercise 7-12 shows how to demote a recovered PDC to a BDC.

EXERCISE 7-12

Demoting a Recovered PDC to a BDC

1. Open Server Manager.

2. Select the former primary domain controller from the list of computers in the Server Manager window.

3. Click Computer | Demote to Backup Domain Controller.

Synchronize BDCs with PDCs

Synchronization is usually done automatically by the system, but if the domain directory database on a computer running Windows NT Server becomes unsynchronized or if a BDC is unable to establish network connections due to password failure you'll need to manually synchronize the BDC. You can either manually synchronize one BDC or all the BDCs. Exercise 7-13 teaches you how to manually synchronize domain controllers.

| EXERCISE 7-13 | **Manually Synchronizing a BDC with the PDC** |

1. Open Server Manager.
2. Select the BDC from the list in the Server Manager window.
3. Click Computer | Synchronize with Primary Domain Controller.

Exercise 7-14 teaches you how to synchronize all BDCs with the PDC.

| EXERCISE 7-14 | **Manually Synchronizing all BDCs with the PDC** |

1. Open Server Manager.
2. Select the PDC on the list in the Server Manager window.
3. Click Computer | Synchronize Entire Domain.

CERTIFICATION OBJECTIVE 7.04

Local and Global Groups

This can get confusing. Global groups can only be created on domain controllers, whereas local groups can be created on domain controllers, member servers, and workstations. Since global groups are exclusive to domain controllers, you should add users to global groups. Then on the resource servers you should add global groups to local groups and give local groups permissions to the shared resource.

You treat a local group as a single security object that can be granted access to many objects in a single location (domain, workstation, or member server) rather than having to edit the permissions on all those objects separately. Using global groups, you can group user accounts that might be granted permissions to use objects on multiple domains and workstations.

With more than one domain, you can use global groups to allow other trusting domains to add them to their local groups. Global groups can pass through trusts, whereas local groups cannot. To allow groups to be granted permissions in resource domains, create a global group to hold the user accounts and then add the global group to a local group in a trusting domain.

When using a single domain you should still follow this model. In the future you may create a trust in which you can then add the global groups from the trusted domain to your domain's local groups. The same is true for the other domain. Your global groups can be given permissions in the trusting domain via that domain's local groups.

Domain global groups can also be used for administrative purposes on computers running Windows NT Workstation or on member servers running Windows NT Servers. For example, the Domain Admins global group is added by default to the Administrators built-in local group on each workstation or member server that joins the existing domain. Membership in the workstation or member server local Administrators group enables the network administrator to manage the computer remotely by creating program groups, installing software, and troubleshooting computer problems.

Table 7-3 provides guidelines for using global and local groups.

TABLE 7-3   Global and Local Group Guidelines

Purpose	Type	Remarks
Group users of this domain into one common entity for use in a trusting domain or user workstations.	Global	Other domains or workstations can place global groups into their local groups.
Need permissions and rights only in one domain.	Local	The local group can contain users and global groups from this and other domains.
Need permissions on computers running NT Workstation or on member servers.	Global	A domain's global groups can be given permissions on these computers, but a domain's local groups cannot.
Contain other groups.	Local	The local group can contain only global groups and users; however, no group can contain other local groups.
Include users from multiple domains.	Local	The local group can be used in only the domain in which it is created. If you need to be able to grant this local group permissions in multiple domains, you will have to manually create the local group in every domain in which you need it.

Be sure to understand local and global groups. When you create a local group on a domain controller, it can only be used on other domain controllers within the same domain. The local group created on a domain controller can't be used on member servers and workstations. A global group created on a domain controller can be used on member servers, workstations, and in other domains.

Setting Up a Global Group

Creating a new global group is easy. However, once you create a global group you can't rename it. In order to rename the group you'll need to create a new group with the name you want to use and assign permissions and users as appropriate. To create a new global group follow Exercise 7-15.

EXERCISE 7-15

Creating a New Global Group

1. Open User Manager for Domains.
2. Select the domain to which you want to add a global group.
3. Click User | New Global Group.
4. Enter the Group Name and a Description.
5. Select the members you want to add to the group in the right side pane.
6. Click Add.
7. Click OK. You'll see the screen shown in Figure 7-15.

Setting Up a Local Group

Unlike global groups, local groups can be created on a domain controller, member server, or a workstation. Therefore, you can use User Manager for Domains or User Manager to create the group. Like global groups, local groups can't be renamed. Follow Exercise 7-16 to create a local group.

EXERCISE 7-16

Creating a New Local Group

1. Open User Manager for Domains or User Manager.
2. Select the domain or computer to which you want to add a local group.

FIGURE 7-15

New global group

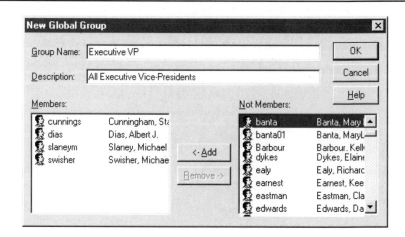

3. Click User | New Local Group.

4. Enter the Group Name and a Description. Figure 7-16 shows the screen used to enter this information.

5. Click Add.

6. Select the groups and users you want to add to the group. You can select users from your local machine or trusted domain. Figure 7-17 shows the screen used to enter this information.

FIGURE 7-16

New local group

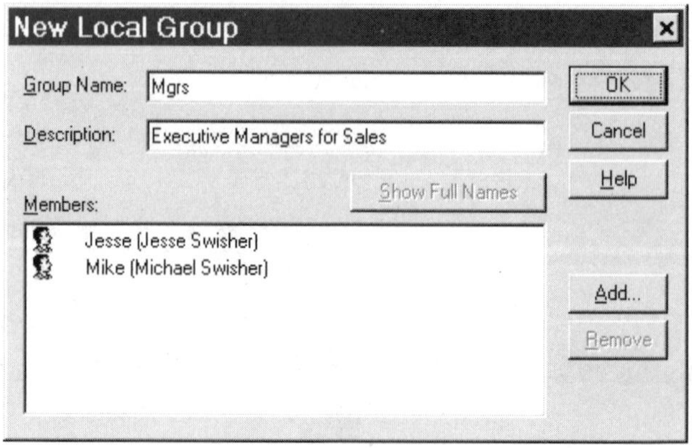

FIGURE 7-17

Adding users and groups to
a local group

7. Click OK.

8. Click OK.

CERTIFICATION OBJECTIVE 7.05

NT's Netlogon Service

The netlogon service used in Windows NT 4.0 Server domain computing
is described in the first section of Chapter 6. When you log on to the network
from a remote location, the netlogon service establishes a secure communications
channel with the first available domain controller that recognizes the computer as
a member of its domain. The netlogon service on the domain controller passes the
request to the domain controller's security subsystem, where the username and
password are verified against the domain's directory service database. If the
username and password are correct, the domain controller creates an access
token and informs you of a successful match.

Pass-Through Authentication

Pass-through authentication occurs when you choose a domain to log on to from your NT computer, but your computer doesn't have an account in that domain. When your computer starts it creates a secure communications channel with the domain controller for which it is a member. The connection provides the winlogon process in your local computer with the list of domains available to the workstation. Only the member domain and all trusting domains are displayed in the initial logon list box. This is the same domain controller that responds to the logon request to the domain in which your computer is a member. However, it serves a different role when you choose to log on to a trusted domain.

When logging on to a trusted domain, your request is passed from the domain controller where your secure communications channel exists to the trusting domain's domain controller. That domain controller then processes the logon and returns a token to your domain controller. Logon then occurs just as it does in domain logon between the trusted and trusting domains, except that another step occurs, in which your member domain controller notifies your computer of a successful logon.

Configuring Netlogon Service

The netlogon service not only helps authenticate users, it also manages changes to the directory service database. Use the following key to configure the netlogon service:

HKEY_LOCAL_MACHINE\SYSTEM\CurrentControlSet\Services\
Netlogon\Parameters

Configurable options are discussed in the following paragraphs.

Pulse

The interval after which the netlogon service looks for new changes to the database and sends a pulse (change notice) to the BDCs (default: 5 minutes).

PulseConcurrency

The number of backup domain controllers that pulses are sent concurrently. A higher number increases the amount of network bandwidth required at each synchronization (default: 10).

PulseMaximum

The interval after which the netlogon service will send a pulse to the BDCs to verify the synchronization level, whether or not there are new changes to the database (default: 2 hours).

PulseTimeOut1

Defines how long (in seconds) the PDC waits for a non-responsive BDC. When a BDC receives a pulse, it must respond within this time period. If not, the BDC is considered to be non-responsive. A non-responsive BDC is not counted against the PulseConcurrency limit, allowing the PDC to send a pulse to another BDC in the domain. If this number is too large, a domain with a large number of non-responsive BDCs will take a long time to complete a partial replication. If this number is too small, a slow BDC may be falsely accused of being non-responsive. When the BDC finally does respond, it will partially replicate from the PDC—unduly increasing the load on the PDC (default: 5 seconds).

PulseTimeOut2

Defines how long (in seconds) a PDC waits for a BDC to complete partial replication. Even though a BDC initially responds to a pulse (as described for PulseTimeout1), it must continue making replication progress or the BDC will be considered non-responsive. Each time the BDC calls the PDC, the BDC is given another PulseTimeout2 seconds to be considered responsive. If this number is too large, a slow BDC (or one that has its replication rate artificially governed) will consume one of the PulseConcurrency slots. If this number is too small, the load on the PDC will be unduly increased because of the large number of BDCs doing a partial sync.

This parameter only affects the cases where a BDC cannot retrieve all the changes to the directory service database in a single RPC call. This will only happen if a large number of changes are made to the database (default: 300 seconds).

Randomize

Specifies the BDC backoff period (in seconds). When the BDC receives a pulse, it will back off between zero and Randomize seconds before calling the PDC. The pulse is sent to individual BDCs, so this parameter should be small. Randomize should be smaller than PulseTimeout1. Consider that the time to replicate a directory service database change to all the BDCs in a domain will be greater than:

[(Randomize/2) * NumberOfBDCsInDomain] / PulseConcurrency

When this value is not specified in the Registry, netlogon determines optimal values depending on the domain controller's load (default: 1 second).

ReplicationGovernor

Limits the amount of bandwidth the domain synchronization process can consume. Forces the netlogon service to sleep between calls and use smaller buffers to allow other network traffic to pass. This is usually configured for slow WAN links, so that directory service database replication won't consume all your bandwidth. Setting ReplicationGovernor to 50 percent will use a 64K buffer rather than a 128K buffer and will only have a replication call outstanding on the net a maximum of 50 percent of the time. Do not set the ReplicationGovernor too low, or replication may never complete. A value of 0 will cause netlogon to *never* replicate. The directory service database will be allowed to get completely out of sync. (default: 100 percent of available bandwidth).

The ReplicationGovernor is set on BDCs only, not on the PDC.

CERTIFICATION SUMMARY

In order to pass the NT Server 4.0 Core Technologies exam, you need to fully understand the four different NT domain models: single domain, master domain, multiple master domain, and complete trust domain. Be sure to understand the trust relationships involved with each model and which users and groups can be granted access to different domains. Another item to remember is how to configure the netlogon service, especially the ReplicationGovernor. The ReplicationGovernor is used to limit the amount of bandwidth used for synchronizing domains, usually over a slow WAN link.

TWO-MINUTE DRILL

❑ All NT computer systems participate in either a workgroup or a domain.

❑ If the user accounts are located locally (except for domain controllers), the computer is part of a *workgroup*. If the user accounts are located on a remote server, the computer is part of a *domain*.

❑ Peer-to-peer networking means no one computer has authority over any other computer; all computers are equal.

❑ A domain is a group of computers that share a common user accounts database and security policy.

❑ There are two types of domain controllers: primary domain controllers (PDC) and backup domain controllers (BDC).

❑ A *trust* is a link that combines two separate domains into one administrative unit that can authorize access to resources on both domains.

❑ NT 4.0 has increased the number of possible trusts to unlimited.

❑ There are four recommended domain models: single, master, multiple master, and complete trust.

❏ The single domain consists of one domain; therefore, no trusts are set up. All user and group accounts are located in this domain.

❏ All user accounts are located in a single domain, which is called the *master domain.*

❏ Resources, like printers and files, are shared in other domains called *resource domains.*

❏ The multiple master domain is actually two or more master domain models joined by a two-way trust.

❏ The Server Manager utility allows you to manage servers and computers in your domain.

❏ Server Manager has many of the same functions as the Server and Services applets in the Control Panel, but Server Manager allows you to manage both the local computer and remote computers.

❏ Server Alerts are used to send notification messages to users or computers. Server Alerts are generated by the system, and relate to server and resource use.

❏ Global groups can only be created on domain controllers, whereas local groups can be created on domain controllers, member servers, and workstations.

❏ Pass-through authentication occurs when you choose a domain to log on to from your NT computer, but your computer doesn't have an account in that domain.

Self Test

The following questions will help you measure your understanding of the material presented in this chapter. Read all the choices carefully, as there may be more than one correct answer. Choose all correct answers for each question.

1. Domain A trusts domain B. What needs to be done so that the administrator in domain A can be an administrator of domain B?

   A. Create a local group in domain A

   B. Create a local group in domain B

   C. Add the Administrators local group in domain A to domain B's Domain Admins global group

   D. Add the Domain Admins group in domain A to domain B's local Administrators group

2. You changed the ReplicationGovernor on a BDC to a lower value. What effect does this have? (Choose all that apply.)

   A. Lowers buffers on BDC and lowers frequency of call to the PDC

   B. Limits the available bandwidth for domain synchronization

   C. Reduces the wait time for the PDC to timeout

   D. Increases the number of BDC that can concurrently synchronize

3. You have two domains, Sales and Marketing. You want all users in both domains to have access to a resource in the Sales domain. You also only want to use one group to manage access to the resource. What three steps must you perform?

   A. Create a local group in Sales

   B. Create a local group in Marketing

   C. Add all users to a local group in Marketing

   D. Add all users to a local group in Sales

   E. Make Sales the trusted domain and Marketing the trusting domain

   F. Make Marketing the trusted domain and Sales the trusting domain

4. Ten Scientists each work on their own computer. Each user is responsible for security and backing up of their own computer's information. When they need to share information they must ensure only the intended person has access. Which model should you use?

   A. Single domain

   B. Master domain

   C. Complete Trust

   D. Workgroup

5. Which variable in the Registry do you change to slow down replications of accounts?

   A. ReplicationGovernor

   B. PulseConcurrency

   C. PulseMaximum

   D. Pulse

6. User Sally in domain A needs to access a share in domain B. Domain B trusts domain A. What needs to be done to let

Sally access the share? (Choose the best answer.)

A. Put Sally's account in a local group with permissions in domain B

B. Put Sally in a global group in domain A, add that global group to a local group in domain B, then give the local group permissions to the share

C. Put Sally in a global group in domain B, add that global group to a local group in domain B, then give the local group permissions to the share

D. Put Sally in a local group in domain A, add that local group to a global group in domain B, then give the local group permissions to the share

7. In a corporate office you have 150 users with five servers in a centralized office. MIS wants to keep complete control of user accounts and resources. Which model should you use?

A. Single domain

B. Master domain

C. Multiple master domain

D. Complete trust domain

8. In a corporate office you have 2,000 users spread out over three buildings. MIS wants to keep complete control of user accounts, but wants the departmental manager to control local resources. Which model should you use?

A. Single domain

B. Master domain

C. Multiple master domain

D. Complete trust domain

9. Domain Production trusts domain Sales. You create a local group in domain Production. What can this group contain? (Choose all that apply)

A. Users from Production

B. Global groups from Sales

C. Global groups form Production

D. Users from Sales

10. What's the maximum number of trusts available in NT 4.0?

A. 128

B. 256

C. 512

D. unlimited

11. What's the total recommended number of domain controllers for a single domain with 10,000 users?

A. 3

B. 4

C. 5

D. 6

MICROSOFT CERTIFIED SYSTEMS ENGINEER

8

Replication and Data Synchronization

CERTIFICATION OBJECTIVES

8.01	Directory Replication
8.02	Replicating System and Domain Files
8.03	Using My Briefcase to Synchronize Files

I n a Windows NT domain, it is imperative that the data, such as the user accounts database, be synchronized between the Primary Domain Controller (PDC) and all Backup Domain Controllers (BDCs) to maintain smooth operation throughout the domain. It is also important that data such as the user login scripts and profiles be replicated so they can be readily available when a user logs into the domain. This chapter examines methods by which this can be accomplished—including directory replication and domain synchronization. It also describes the use of My Briefcase to transfer updated files from one computer to another.

CERTIFICATION OBJECTIVE 8.01

Directory Replication

Directory replication is a service of Windows NT that allows you to set up and automatically maintain identical directory trees on many computer systems. Updates made to the files within the directories on the export server are periodically replicated to import computers. (Export servers and import computers are described in more detail later in the chapter.) Using replication in this manner means you only have to maintain one up-to-date copy of the files that are within the export directories, rather than having to update each copy on all the machines where it may exist.

Replication can be very useful, especially for load balancing among servers. For example, if a file is used by several users and it is located on a single server, that server could become overburdened and slow user access. However, if identical copies of the file are located on multiple servers, the load is spread as users access the file.

If possible, replication should be used for read-only information, to prevent replication of any files that are open for revision. Furthermore, because the import computer directories that contain the replicated files are overwritten each time replication occurs, any changes made to files in those directories will be lost the next time replication from the export server occurs.

Replication can occur between computers in different domains. The export server can export to a domain name and the import computers can import from that domain name. This method is very convenient in cases where many computers are involved in the replication process; you only need to specify a domain name for export or import, instead of using a long list of computer names.

Before you can use the Directory Replicator service, you must create a special user account required by the Directory Replicator service. The Directory Replicator service on each participating computer uses the same user account. Figure 8-1 shows the User Manager for Domains window where you will create this account.

Figure 8-2 displays the New User dialog box where you will create the Directory Replicator service account. Be sure to place a check next to the Password Never Expires block when you create this account.

Figure 8-3 shows the group membership for the dReplicator account. When you create this account, be sure to put it in both the Replicator and the Backup Operators groups.

FIGURE 8-1

User Manager window with Username accounts

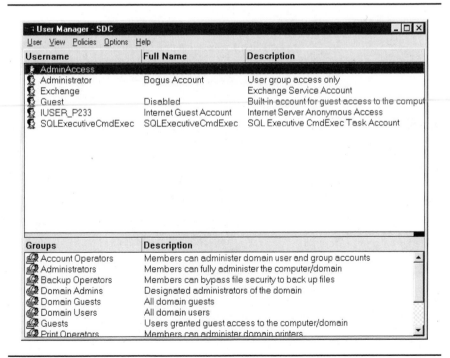

FIGURE 8-2

New User dialog box for
the dReplicator account

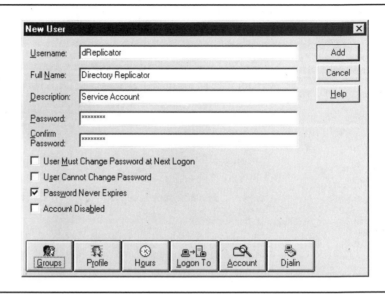

*You can name the replicator service account by any name that you
want, with the exception that it cannot have the same name as a group.
That is the reason it is named dReplicator—not just Replicator—
because a group by that name already exists.*

FIGURE 8-3

Group Memberships for
the dReplicator account

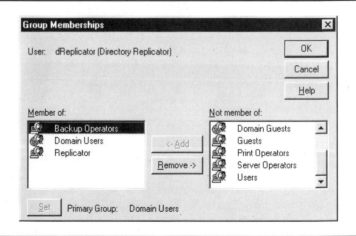

In Exercise 8-1 you'll create the Directory Replicator account that you will use for the rest of this chapter.

Adding a Directory Replicator Account

1. Log on to your Windows NT Server as an Administrator.

2. Click the Start button and choose Programs | Administrative Tools | User Manager for Domains.

3. Select the User menu and choose New User.

4. Fill in the following properties.
   Username: dReplicate
   Full Name: Directory Replicator
   Description: Service Account
   Password: drep1024password
   Confirm Password: drep1024password
   User Must Change Password At Next Logon: Check box cleared
   Password Never Expires: Check box marked

5. Click the Groups button and select the Backup Operators group from the Not Member of box and click the Add button. Select the Replicator group from the Not Member of box and click the Add button. Click the OK button.

6. Click the Hours button and make sure that all logon hours are allowed. Click the OK button.

7. Click the Add button. You have now successfully created the service account that the Directory Replicator service will be using.

Now that you have created the necessary service account, let's move on to see what else is required for successful replication.

Export Server and Import Computers

The three main components needed for replication are: the export server, import computer(s), and export and import directories. Figure 8-4 shows an example of an export/import scenario with the default directories used.

FIGURE 8-4

Export server and
import computers

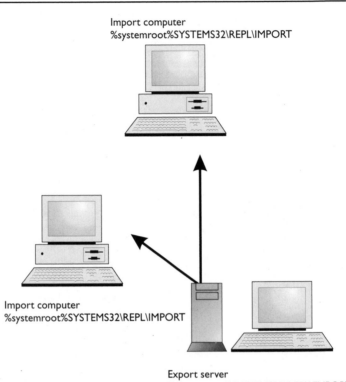

Import computer
%systemroot%SYSTEMS32\REPL\IMPORT

Import computer
%systemroot%SYSTEMS32\REPL\IMPORT

Export server
%systemroot%SYSTEMS32\REPL\EXPORT

Export Server

The *export server* is the computer that provides the directories to be replicated.
The selected directories can be replicated from the export computer to any
number of specified computers or to other domains.

exam
Ⓦatch

*Only computers that are running Windows NT Server can be configured
as export servers. The Windows NT Server does not have to be a domain
controller to be used in this configuration.*

Import Computers

Systems that receive the replicated files and directories from the export server
are called *import computers*. Import computers can be Windows NT domain

controllers and servers or Windows NT Workstations. If the import computer is not part of the export server's domain or trusting domain, it will need to create a replication user account as illustrated in Exercise 8-1. The account must have permission to access the export server's REPL$ share, as discussed in the following paragraph.

Export and Import Directories

By default, the *export server* keeps the directories that will be replicated in an export directory located at %systemroot%SYSTEM32\REPL\EXPORT. You can create as many subdirectories as necessary beneath this directory structure for all the files that you want to replicate to the import computers. A file is replicated when it is first added to an export directory, then replicated again every time the file on the export server is saved (such as when changes are made). Replication occurs automatically once the Directory Replicator service is enabled and fully functional. The %systemroot%SYSTEM32\REPL\ EXPORT directory is shared as REPL$ after the Directory Replicator service is started. REPL$ is the single directory tree that contains the main directory "export" and up to 32 subdirectories.

Each system that has been configured to be an *import computer* contains an import directory. By default, the import directory is located at %systemroot%SYSTEM32\REPL\IMPORT. Imported files and subdirectories are automatically placed under this directory. Subdirectories are created during replication, so there is no need for you to worry about creating them prior to replication.

Now that we have discussed the main components needed for replication, let's get the Directory Replicator service functioning.

Directory Replicator Service

The Directory Replicator service has to be configured and started in order for replication to occur. You can have your export server and import computers set up, but replication will not occur unless the Directory Replicator service is configured and running on each system. Figure 8-5 shows the Services dialog box for a system. You can see that the Directory Replicator is set for manual startup and has not been started.

FIGURE 8-5

Services on P233
dialog box

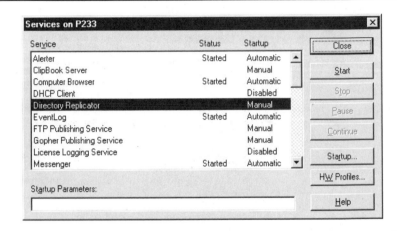

Figure 8-6 displays the Directory Replicator service startup parameters. This is where you modify the Directory Replicator service so it will start up automatically and use the service account you created in Exercise 8-1.

FIGURE 8-6

Directory Replicator
service startup parameters

Exercise 8-2 leads you through the steps needed to configure your system for the Directory Replicator service. The exercise assumes you have a machine named Computer1 on your network. You'll need to change the name Computer1 to the actual name of a system (one for which you have administrator privileges) on your local network. Exercise 8-2 must be performed for each system you intend to use as either an export server or an import computer.

EXERCISE 8-2

Configuring the Directory Replicator Service

1. Log on as an Administrator.
2. Click Start and select Programs | Administrative Tools | Server Manager.
3. Highlight Computer1 and choose Services from the Computer menu.
4. Under Service select Directory Replicator and then choose Startup.
5. Under Startup Type, select Automatic.
6. Under Log On As, select This Account.
7. In the This Account dialog box, type **dReplicator.**
8. The Password and Confirm Password boxes will be filled in automatically. If you run into any "access denied" problems, you can return to this point and enter a known good password.
9. A Server Manager dialog box reports that the account dReplicator has been granted the right to Log On As A Service. Click OK.
10. Click the Close button.

The Directory Replicator service has now been configured to automatically start at system initialization using the dReplicator service account. But you haven't actually started the service, you have only configured it.

Now you need to start the service so replication can begin. In Exercise 8-3 you'll designate a system to be the export server, configure the export directories, and then start the Directory Replication service. The exercise assumes you have a machine named Computer1 on your network. Again, change the name Computer1 to the actual name of a system (for which you have administrator privileges) on your local network.

Starting the Directory Replicator Service on the Export Server

1. Log on as an Administrator.

2. Click Start and select Programs | Administrative Tools | Server Manager.

3. Highlight Computer1 and choose Properties from the Computer menu.

4. Click the Replication button.

5. Select the Export Directories radio button.

6. Under Export Directories, choose the Add button.

7. From the Select Domain dialog box, select the domain your system belongs to and then click the OK button. You could also go down your domain list and pick out several machine names, but it's quicker just to pick the domain name.

8. The Service Control status box reports that it is starting the Directory Replicator service.

9. Click the OK button to close the Properties dialog box.

Figure 8-7 shows how the export server looks on our system. SDC is the domain name where this export server is located. If you do not specify

FIGURE 8-7

Directory Replication export directories

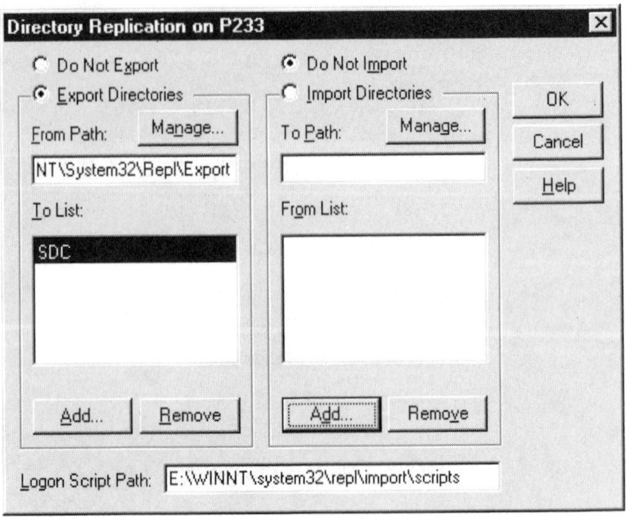

computer names or a domain in the To List, directories will be exported to all import computers in the local domain.

In Exercise 8-4 you'll designate a different system to act as an import computer, configure the import directories, and then start the Directory Replication service. The exercise assumes you have a machine named Computer2 on your network. Change the name Computer2 to the actual name of a system (one for which you have administrator privileges) on your local network.

EXERCISE 8-4

Starting the Directory Replicator Service on the Import Computer

1. Log on as an Administrator.
2. Click Start and select Programs | Administrative Tools | Server Manager.
3. Highlight Computer2 and choose Properties from the Computer menu.
4. Click the Replication button.
5. Select the Import Directories radio button.
6. Under Import Directories, choose the Add button.
7. From the Select Domain dialog box, select the domain your system belongs to and click the OK button.
8. The Service Control status box reports that it is starting the Directory Replicator service.
9. Click the OK button to close the Properties dialog box.

Figure 8-8 shows how the import computer looks on our system. SDC is the domain name where this particular import computer is located. If you do not specify computer names or a domain in the From List, the computer will import from all export servers in the local domain.

You may want to consider setting up your export server as an import computer as well, depending on what files and directories you may be exporting. As you'll see later in the chapter, this is necessary if your export server is the PDC or a BDC. Once completed, the Directory Replication dialog box for your export server should look like the one in Figure 8-9.

Now you have created export directories on the export server. As mentioned earlier, import directories are automatically created on the import computers.

FIGURE 8-8

Directory Replication import directories

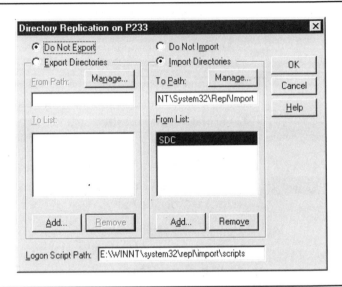

FIGURE 8-9

Directory Replication showing export and import directories

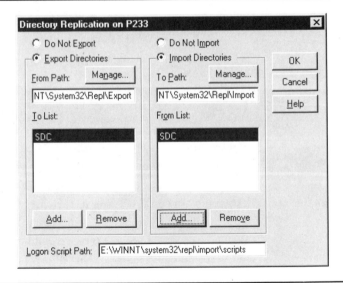

But how do you really know if data is being replicated? Exercise 8-5 gives you the opportunity to verify that replication has really occurred. The exercise assumes you have machines named Computer1 and Computer2 on your network. Change the names Computer1 and Computer2 to the names you used in Exercises 8-3 and 8-4.

Verifying Directory Replication

1. Log on as Administrator to Computer1.

2. Click Start and choose Programs | Windows NT Explorer.

3. Go to %systemroot%SYSTEM32\REPL\EXPORT and create a subdirectory called TEST.

4. Navigate to the TEST directory and create a text file called TEST.TXT. Close Windows NT Explorer and log off Computer1.

5. Log on as Administrator to Computer2.

6. Click Start and choose Programs | Windows NT Explorer.

7. Go to %systemroot%SYSTEM32\REPL\IMPORT and verify that a directory called TEST with the file TEST.TXT exists. Now you know that the Directory Replicator service is working properly on your network.

Now that the Directory Replicator service is working, you've done everything necessary—right? Let's hope you answered No to that question, because you still need to manage the replication process.

Managing Replication

Let's look at what you do to manage the replication process. First, you can use Server Manager to control what directories are replicated from the export tree and what directories are copied into the import tree. You can also control a variety of export server functions from the Server Manager, as described in the following list.

■ **Locks** Prevents a directory from being exported. You may want to use a lock when you are working on files in a directory and do not want the directory replicated until you have completed all the work. You activate this function by clicking the Add Lock button.

■ **Stabilize** Shows whether the files in the export directory will wait two minutes or more after changes before being exported. You would use this function to help prevent the premature replication of a directory that is currently being changed (and thus might not contain complete data). To activate this function, place a check mark in the box next to Wait Until Stabilized.

■ **Subtree** Shows whether the entire subtree will be exported. To activate this function, place a check mark in the box next to Entire Subtree.

■ **Locked Since** Shows the date and time a lock was placed on a directory.

Figure 8-10 shows the Manage Exported Directories dialog box you use to control these functions.

Exercise 8-6 gives you some practice in managing directories on the export server. The exercise assumes you have a machine named Computer1 on your network. Change the name Computer1 to the name of the system you set up as the export server in Exercise 8-3.

| EXERCISE 8-6 | **Managing a Replication** |

1. Log on as Administrator.
2. Click the Start button and choose Programs | Administrative Tools | Server Manager.
3. Highlight Computer1 and choose Properties from the Computer menu.
4. Click the Replication button.

| FIGURE 8-10 |

Manage Exported Directories dialog box

5. Under Export Directories, click the Manage button.

6. Under Sub-Directory, select Scripts and click the Add Lock button. The Scripts subdirectory will no longer be replicated to the import computers.

7. Click the OK button to return to the Directory Replication dialog box.

8. Click the OK button to return to the Properties dialog box.

9. Click the OK button to return to the Server Manager.

10. Exit from the Server Manager.

Figure 8-11 shows the Manage Imported Directories dialog box. You can control a variety of functions for the import computer by using the Server Manager.

■ **Locks**   Prevents a directory from being imported. You activate it by clicking the Add Lock button.

■ **Status**   Shows the status on receiving updates from the export server. There are four possible items you may see here:

■ **OK**   Regular updates are being received from the export server and the data being imported is identical to the data exported.

■ **No Master**   Updates are not being received from the export server. This could be caused by the export server not running or it might have stopped exporting updates.

■ **No Sync**   This shows that updates have been received, but the data is not up-to-date: it can happen if there are open files on the import computer or export server, if access permissions to the export server are not available to the import computer, or if the export server has malfunctioned.

■ **[empty]**   The status block is empty if replication has never occurred for the directory. This can be caused if replication has not be properly configured for the export server, this import computer, or both.

■ **Last Update**   Date and time the last update was made to a file in the import directory.

FIGURE 8-11

Manage Imported
Directories dialog box

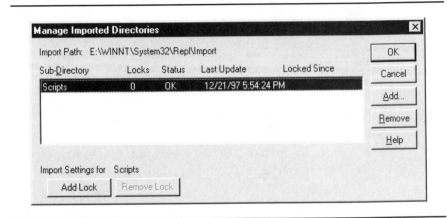

EXERCISE 8-7

Viewing Directory Replication Status

1. Log on as Administrator.
2. Click the Start button and choose Programs | Administrative Tools | Server Manager.
3. Highlight Computer2 and choose Properties from the Computer menu.
4. Click the Replication button.
5. Under Import Directories, click the Manage button.
6. View the status of the imported Scripts directory. It should display "No Sync"—indicating that it is no longer up-to-date. This was caused by placing the lock on the Scripts directory in Exercise 8-6.
7. Click the OK button to return to the Directory Replication dialog box.
8. Click the OK button to return to the Properties dialog box.
9. Click the OK button to return to the Server Manager.
10. Highlight Computer1 and choose Properties from the Computer menu.
11. Click the Replication button.
12. Under Export Directories, click the Manage button.
13. Under Sub-Directory, select Scripts and click the Remove Lock button.
14. Click the OK button to return to the Directory Replication dialog box.

15. Click the OK button to return to the Properties dialog box.

16. Click the OK button to return to the Server Manager.

17. Exit from the Server Manager.

Replicating System and Domain Files

Now that you've seen how to use the Directory Replicator service to replicate directories, let's look at some other replications that occur on a Windows NT domain. One of the most important items that needs to be replicated when you have one or more BDC's in your network is the user accounts database. This section also describes the use of replication in the management of logon scripts, system policy files, and widely used files.

User Accounts Database

The user accounts database is synchronized automatically by Windows NT Server. This communication is managed by the netlogon service. Based upon the PulseConcurrency value in the Registry, the PDC sends out notices that signal the BDC's to request database changes from the PDC. (Table 8-1 explains the PulseConcurrency value.) To keep bandwidth usage down, the notices are staggered so all BDC's do not request changes at the same time. A BDC does not request changes if it is up-to-date. When the BDC requests a change, it informs the PDC of the last change it received.

Changes requested by BDC's may consist of any new or changed passwords, new or changed user and group accounts, or any changes in their group memberships or user rights. The changes are stored in the *change log*. The number of changes that can be held in the log depends upon its size. The default log size is 64KB and each change is approximately 32 bytes in size. This allows about 2000 changes to fit into the log. When the log is full, the oldest change is overwritten as a new change is added. Changes that occurred since the last synchronization are copied to the BDC when the BDC requests changes. If a BDC does not request changes in a timely manner, the entire user accounts database must be synchronized to that BDC. For example, if a BDC on a busy domain is offline for a day for scheduled maintenance, more changes will occur during that time than can be stored in the change log.

Partial and Full Synchronization

As discussed in the preceding paragraphs, a *partial synchronization* is the automatic, timed replication to all domain BDC's of only those directory database changes that have occurred since the last synchronization. You can use the Server Manager to force a partial synchronization to all BDC's in the domain. For example, if you add a new user (who happens to be your boss) to the domain and you want to get the new account added to all the BDC's quickly, you can perform a partial synchronization to get the account added to all BDC's as soon as possible.

It is also possible to use Server Manager to force a partial synchronization of a particular BDC with the PDC. This can be useful if the BDC has been offline for a few minutes and you don't want to wait for automatic partial synchronization to occur.

As seen in Table 8-1, it is possible to control synchronization information by modifying the following Registry key:

```
\HKEY_LOCAL_MACHINE\SYSTEM\CurrentControlSet\Services\
NetLogon\Parameters
```

It is important to note that if a value is not present in the registry, the default value is in effect.

In a *full synchronization,* the PDC sends a copy of the entire user accounts database to a BDC. However, a full synchronization can be a bandwidth hog because user accounts databases can be as big as 40 megabytes! If changes have been overwritten from the change log before replication occurs, full synchronization is performed automatically. Full synchronization also occurs when a new BDC is added to the domain.

Normally, a full synchronization will not be required because the netlogon service, by default, sends out updates every five minutes and, as mentioned earlier, the change log holds about 2000 changes.

TABLE 8-1	Synchronization Control Parameters

Name of Value	Description
Pulse	The pulse frequency in seconds. All changes made to the user accounts database since the last pulse are compiled; when the pulse time expires, a pulse is sent to each BDC that needs the changes. A pulse is not sent to a BDC that does not need the changes. Default value: 300 (5 minutes); value range: 60 (1 minute) - 3600 (1 hour)
PulseConcurrency	The maximum number of simultaneous pulses the PDC will send out to BDC's. The netlogon service sends pulses to individual BDC's, which in turn causes the BDC's to respond by asking for any database changes. The PDC will have only the number of pulses specified in PulseConcurrency out at any one time. This feature is designed to control the maximum load placed back on the PDC. If you increase PulseConcurrency, the PDC has an increased load. However, when you decrease PulseConcurrency, it takes longer for a domain with a large number of BDC's to send a change to all the BDC's. Default value: 20; value range: 1-500
PulseMaximum	The maximum pulse frequency in seconds. Regardless of whether a BDC's user accounts database is up-to-date it is sent at least one pulse at the frequency reflected by this parameter. Default value: 7200 (2 hours); value range 60 (1 minute) - 86400 (1 day)
PulseTimeout1	This is how long, in seconds, the PDC will wait for a BDC that is not responding. If the BDC does not respond within this time period, it is not counted against the PulseConcurrency limit. This allows the PDC to send a pulse to another BDC in the domain. A partial synchronization can take a long time to complete if this number is too large and the domain has a large number of BDC's that do not respond. The load can be increased on the PDC if this number is too small and a slow BDC is not responding fast enough. This is because after the BDC finally does respond, it still has to receive a partial synchronization from the PDC. Default value: 5 (5 seconds); value range 1 (1 second) - 120 (2 minutes)
PulseTimeout2	This is how long, in seconds, a PDC will wait for a BDC to complete partial synchronization. Synchronization progress has to continue even though a BDC has initially responded to a pulse. A slow BDC will consume one of the PulseConcurrency slots if this number is too large. On the other hand, if this value is set too small the load on the PDC could be increased because of the number of BDC's that are doing a partial synchronization. Default value: 300 (5 minutes); value range: 60 (1 minute - 3600 (1 hour)
Randomize	Specifies the BDC backoff period, in seconds. After receiving a pulse the BDC will back off some number of seconds between zero and the Randomize value before calling the PDC. The Randomize value should always be smaller than the PulseTimeout1 value. Default value: 1 (1 second); value range: 0 - 120 (2 minutes)

Synchronizing Domain Controllers

When using Server Manager to synchronize domain controllers, the Computer menu command chosen for synchronizing changes depends on whether you select the PDC or BDC.

When the PDC is selected, the Synchronize Entire Domain command is available on the Computer menu. When this command is issued, the latest changes to the user accounts database are immediately copied from the PDC to all the BDC's in the domain. The command does not wait for any synchronization currently in progress to complete.

When a BDC is selected, the Synchronize With Primary Domain Controller command is available on the Computer menu. This command copies the latest user accounts database changes only to the selected BDC.

Domain Synchronization Over a Slow Wide Area Network (WAN) Link

A parameter exists in the Windows NT Server Registry to help increase the performance of replication over a slow WAN link. That parameter is called the ReplicationGovernor. A BDC uses the ReplicationGovernor to increase the performance of domain synchronization by defining both the size of the data transferred on each call to the PDC and the frequency of the calls.

A BDC can take advantage of the ReplicationGovernor parameter by adding it to the following key in its Registry:

```
\HKEY_LOCAL_MACHINE\SYSTEM\CurrentControlSet\Services\
NetLogon\Parameters
```

Assign a type of REG_DWORD and a value from 0 to 100 (the default is 100). As mentioned earlier, the value defines both a percentage for the amount of data transferred on each call to the PDC and the frequency of the calls to the PDC. For example, if the value of the ReplicationGovernor were set to 75 percent, it would use a 96KB buffer instead of the default 128KB buffer. Also the BDC would have an outstanding synchronization call on the network for only a maximum of 75 percent of the time. If you want to decrease the value of ReplicationGovernor, you need to increase the size of the change log. The new value does not take effect until you stop and restart the netlogon service.

The ReplicationGovernor value should be used only when necessary, because synchronization may never complete if it is set too low. If synchronization is set below 25 percent, the user account database may become completely out of sync.

Now that you are familiar with different automatic synchronization parameters you can adjust how your domain will replicate. Exercise 8-8 shows you how to modify your registry in order to change the synchronization interval within your domain.

Setting Synchronization Intervals (PDC to BDC's)

1. Log onto your PDC as an Administrator.

2. Click Start and choose Run.

3. Type REGEDT32 to start the Registry Editor.

4. Maximize the HKEY_LOCAL_MACHINE window if it isn't already maximized.

5. Navigate to the SYSTEM\CurrentControlSet\Services\NetLogon\ Parameters folder. This is where you add the Pulse parameter to override the default value of 300 seconds (5 minutes).

6. Choose Add Value from the Edit menu.

7. Type **pulse** in the Value Name dialog box.

8. Select REG_DWORD in the Data Type dialog box and click the OK button.

9. Select Decimal from the Radix dialog box.

10. Type **60** in the Data dialog box and click the OK button. The Pulse value appears in the Parameters folder using the hexadecimal notation of 0x3c.

11. Exit from the Registry Editor.

12. Click Start and choose Programs | Administrative Tools | Server Manager.

13. Highlight the PDC and choose Services from the Computer menu.

14. Select NetLogon and click the Stop button.

15. Click the Yes button when prompted, if you are sure you want to stop the service.

16. After the service has stopped, click the Start button.

17. Click Close to return to the Server Manager.

18. Exit from the Server Manager. The PDC will now send a pulse every 1 minute instead of the default of 5 minutes.

Logon Scripts

User accounts can be assigned *logon scripts*. Every time a user logs on, the logon script assigned to that user is run. An administrator can use the logon script to affect the user's environment without trying to manage all aspects of it. When the PDC or a BDC processes a logon request, it locates the logon script by combining a filename specified in User Manager for Domains with a path specified in Server Manager.

If you plan to use logon scripts in a domain that has a PDC and at least one BDC, you should replicate the logon scripts to all the domain controllers. The master copy of each logon script should be stored in the export tree of the export server. The export server might be the PDC, but it is not required to be. Copies of the master logon scripts should be replicated to each import computer that participates in authenticating logons for the domain. If this is done, only one copy of each logon script needs to be maintained, but every system that participates in authenticating domain logons will have an identical copy of all the user logon scripts.

As mentioned earlier, replication is configured so that Windows NT Server computers export subdirectories and logon scripts from the directory %*systemroot*%SYSTEM32\REPL\EXPORT\SCRIPTS, and import subdirectories and logon scripts to the directory %*systemroot*%SYSTEM32\ REPL\IMPORT\SCRIPTS. We have added the SCRIPTS subdirectory to specifically be used for logon scripts. For the PDC and every BDC, the path to imported logon scripts must be entered in the Logon Script Path dialog box of the Directory Replication dialog box shown in Figure 8-12.

exam
Ⓦatch

The logon script path cannot be changed for member servers. You need to store logon scripts in %systemroot%SYSTEM32\REPL\IMPORT\ SCRIPTS or in subdirectories of that path.

System Policy Files

You can define a specific user's settings or the settings for a group of users by using a system policy file. A single policy file can contain the registry settings

FIGURE 8-12

Logon script path location

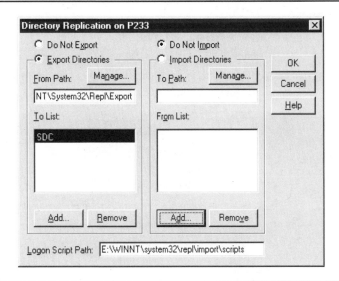

for all users, groups, and computers. There is no need to use separate policy files for each user, group, or computer.

If you create a system policy file that will be automatically downloaded from validating domain controllers, you should name the file Ntconfig.pol for Windows NT users and config.pol for Windows 95 users.

When a user of a Windows NT 4.0 system logs onto the network, the system conducts a check of the *netlogon share* on the validating domain controller for the NTconfig.pol file. By default, the netlogon share is %systemroot%SYSTEM32\REPL\IMPORT. If the system finds the file, it downloads it, scans it for the user, group, and computer policy data, and applies it if appropriate.

When you implement a system policy file for Windows NT or Windows 95 users and computers, make sure that directory replication is working properly among all domain controllers that share in user authentication. By default, the course of action is for the system that is logging on to check for a policy file in the *netlogon share* of the validating domain controller. If directory replication to a domain controller fails and the system logging on does not find a system policy file on that domain controller, then no policy will be applied and the existing settings will remain. In that case, users may have more capabilities than you intended for them to have.

Widely Used Files

While replication can be a very handy feature to use on your Windows NT network, you must use it with caution so that it doesn't backfire on you. The following guidelines should help you determine when a file should be replicated and when it should not be. If a file is one that is commonly read by several users on your network, but not updated, then you should replicate it out. If a file is changed by only one person and widely read, then you should probably replicate it. If a file is updated by many people, many times per day, you may not want to replicate it out because the most current version may not be the one replicated—especially across a slow link. Speed of the link is a valid point to consider when considering replication of files. If the file is only accessed once per day across a slow link, but updated three times a day, then it's best not to replicate it. However, if the files are accessed several times per day over a slow link and only changed once, you should replicate the file over the slow link so users can access it faster via their local network.

FROM THE CLASSROOM

To Replicate or Not To Replicate: That is the Question

There are some limitations to the directory replication service that can lead to problems if you are not familiar with them. Directory replication is a holdover from the old LAN Manager days. Today, it is almost exclusively used to replicate policy files and logon scripts among domain controllers. You may find other uses of it to be unsatisfactory.

The number one problem in setting up directory replication is a logon failure of the service account. Directory replication must be set up in a tediously exact fashion. We make a point of this to the students, yet we can still rely on several of them to make mistakes. This allows us to demonstrate to the class the error and its fix—without having to script the failure in advance. Two things are important. First the service account must be a member of both the Replicators and Backup Operators Local group. Second, the password specified when you created the account must match the password you supplied when you configured the Directory Replication service in the Services applet.

One of the limitations to the service is that it can not be scheduled. Directory replication happens on its own schedule. This is not the

FROM THE CLASSROOM

kind of service where you can make massive changes and expect them to replicate during off hours, or come in a few minutes early one morning to make some policy changes and expect them to replicate across your domain controllers by the time users start logging on.

Another limitation, in terms of file distribution, is that directory structure on the import computers will be made to be identical to the directory structure of the export server. This is the job of the import computer. When the export server announces changes, the import computer looks at the directory structure of the

export server and then creates an identical directory structure. This enables files on the export server to be brought to the import computer. Unfortunately, it also means that files that are on the import computer *but are not on the export server* will be deleted from the import computer! What happens if you modify a file on the import computer? Remember, the import computer will create a directory structure (including all files) that is identical to that of the export server.

—By Shane Clawson, MCT, MCSE

CERTIFICATION OBJECTIVE 8.03

Using My Briefcase to Synchronize Files

You probably need to keep the most up-to-date files on the computer you are currently using, regardless of whether you are connected to a network or if you use multiple computers such as a notebook system and a desktop system. Transferring these files can be a very tedious process, in which you have to compare file dates and copy files from one machine to another. This is a job for My Briefcase, which tracks relationships between file versions on different computers—either on the network or stand-alone. It helps to eliminate problems that are caused by manually trying to keep files synchronized. My Briefcase provides file-level synchronization. It has no clue about the format the file is in and it doesn't care. Figure 8-13 shows what My Briefcase looks like when it is first initialized. Exercise 8-9 leads you through the steps of creating your own My Briefcase.

FIGURE 8-13

My Briefcase when
first initialized

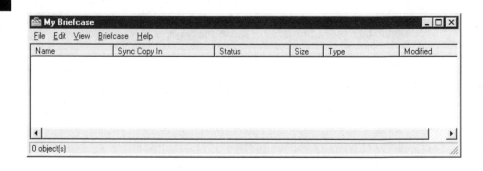

EXERCISE 8-9

Enabling My Briefcase

1. Click the Start button and choose Programs | Windows NT Explorer.

2. Open the folder where you want to create a new My Briefcase icon.

3. On the File menu, select New, then select Briefcase from the pop-up menu.

To use My Briefcase, make sure it is on your notebook system, then simply drag and drop the files and directories that you want to track onto the briefcase icon. It doesn't matter whether you make changes to the files inside My Briefcase or to the original files in other directories of the computer. Exercise 8-10 shows you how to add some of your own documents to My Briefcase.

EXERCISE 8-10

Adding Documents to My Briefcase

1. Click the Start button and select Programs | Windows NT Explorer.

2. Locate the file or folder that you want to add to My Briefcase.

3. Left-click the file or folder, then drag it to My Briefcase and drop it onto the icon.

4. If you prefer, you can use your right mouse button to drag the file or folder, then drop it on the My Briefcase icon. You will see a menu of available options.

When you put your notebook back on the network, you can instruct My Briefcase to update the unmodified files, whether they are on another system on the network or on your notebook system. There are a couple of ways My Briefcase can do this.

Here's the quickest and easiest way: if *either* the original file *or* the one in My Briefcase has changed, then My Briefcase suggests that the newer version of the file be copied to the original location and to My Briefcase.

However, if *both* the original file *and* the one in the Briefcase have changed, then My Briefcase has two options to consider. First it checks to see if a reconciliation handler for the file is available. If it is, My Briefcase passes synchronization control to the application. If there is no reconciliation handler, My Briefcase doesn't change either copy of the file, but instead notifies you so that you can choose to keep both files or else select the latest version. Exercise 8-11 shows you how to keep your files synchronized using My Briefcase.

| EXERCISE 8-11 | **Synchronizing Files Through My Briefcase** |

1. Click the Start button and select Programs | Windows NT Explorer on the system that contains My Briefcase.

2. Copy files from shared directories on your "main" computer to the directory that has My Briefcase.

3. Change data in any one of the files in My Briefcase and save the changes you have made.

4. Double-click the My Briefcase icon.

5. From the Briefcase menu, click Update All.

6. My Briefcase synchronizes the file by replacing the old version with the most current one.

When you look at the contents of My Briefcase, you'll notice information such as the location of the sync copy and the status for each document as seen in Figure 8-14.

My Briefcase, with
additional file information

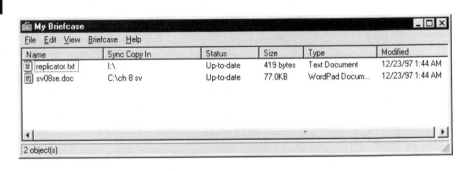

CERTIFICATION SUMMARY

The Directory Replicator service enables you to set up and automatically maintain identical directory trees on multiple computer systems. With directory replication, you can maintain a single master copy of a file but have it available for use on other systems. Updates made to the files in directories on the export server that have been set up for replication are periodically copied to import computers. Directory replication is useful for load balancing. To successfully implement the Directory Replicator service, you must create a special service account for it to use. The Server Manager is used to configure most of the Directory Replicator.

The user account database is an example of a replication that does not use the Directory Replicator service. If you have a PDC and one or more BDC's in the same domain, then at predetermined intervals the user account database is synchronized among them. The synchronization can be either a partial synchronization or a full synchronization. Several parameters can be changed in the Registry to control how synchronization will occur within a domain.

My Briefcase enables you to keep the most up-to-date files on the computer you are currently using—regardless of whether you are connected to a network or if you use multiple computers such as a notebook system and a desktop system. My Briefcase tracks relationships between file versions on different computers. My Briefcase provides file-level synchronization and does not recognize the format any file is in.

✓ TWO-MINUTE DRILL

❑ Directory replication is a service of Windows NT that allows you to set up and automatically maintain identical directory trees on many computer systems.

❑ Before you can use the Directory Replicator service, you must create a special user account required by the Directory Replicator service.

❑ You can name the replicator service account by any name that you want, with the exception that it cannot have the same name as a group. That is the reason it is named dReplicator—not just Replicator—because a group by that name already exists.

❑ The three main components needed for replication are: the export server, import computer(s), and export and import directories.

❑ Only computers that are running Windows NT Server can be configured as export servers. The Windows NT Server does **not** have to be a domain controller to be used in this configuration.

❑ The Directory Replicator service has to be configured and started in order for replication to occur.

❑ Use Server Manager to control what directories are replicated from the export tree and what directories are copied into the import tree.

❑ One of the most important items that needs to be replicated when you have one or more BDC's in your network is the user accounts database.

❑ Based upon the PulseConcurrency value in the Registry, the PDC sends out notices that signal the BDC's to request database changes from the PDC.

❑ A *partial synchronization* is the automatic, timed replication to all domain BDC's of only those directory database changes that have occurred since the last synchronization.

❑ In a *full synchronization,* the PDC sends a copy of the entire user accounts database to a BDC.

❑ User accounts can be assigned *logon scripts.* Every time a user logs on, the logon script assigned to that user is run.

❑ The logon script path cannot be changed for member servers. You need to store logon scripts in *%systemroot%*SYSTEM32\REPL\IMPORT\SCRIPTS or in subdirectories of that path.

❑ You can define a specific user's settings or the settings for a group of users by using a system policy file.

❑ My Briefcase tracks relationships between file versions on different computers—either on the network or stand-alone.

SELF TEST

The following questions will help you measure your understanding of the material presented in this chapter. Read all the choices carefully, as there may be more than one correct answer. Choose all correct answers for each question.

1. In order for replication to fully function, what computers need to be running the Directory Replicator service?

    A. PDC and 1 BDC

    B. PDC and all BDC's

    C. Export computer and import servers

    D. Export server and import computers

2. (True/False) It is best to replicate files that are modified by several people on a daily basis.

3. What is the purpose of My Briefcase?

    A. To track files to make sure that you do not use a pirated copy

    B. To track relationships between file versions on different computer platforms

    C. To track files to make sure that they do not catch a virus

    D. To track relationships between file versions on different computer systems

4. A company has asked you to consult for them. They have decided they want to use logon scripts for half of their users. The company has more than one domain controller that is validating users. How can you make sure that the logon script will be available for the users who require it?

    A. Create a logon script on the PDC and configure it to be an export server. Configure each domain controller that validates users as an import computer.

    B. Create a logon script on the PDC and configure it to be an import computer. Configure each domain controller that validates users as an import computer.

    C. Create a logon script on the PDC and configure it to be an export server. Configure each domain controller that validates users as an export server.

    D. Create a logon script on the PDC and configure it to be an import computer. Configure each domain controller that validates users as an export server.

5. (True/False) By default, the netlogon share is %systemroot%SYSTEM32\REPL\ EXPORT.

6. The Directory Replicator service account is used by the_____ .

    A. export server

    B. server manager

    C. import computers

    D. user manager

7. The PDC in your domain becomes overloaded each time it notifies the BDC's of changes in the user account database.

What parameter should be changed in the Registry?

- A. The PulseMaximum should be decreased.
- B. The PulseMaximum should be increased.
- C. The PulseConcurrency should be decreased.
- D. The PulseConcurrency should be increased.

8. (True/False) The ReplicationGovernor parameter is used by the PDC.

9. A new vice president has arrived at your company and you create her user account. How can you make sure it gets replicated out to all seven of the validating domain controllers quickly?

- A. Use Server Manager, select PDC and choose the Synchronize With Primary Domain Controller menu item.
- B. Use Server Manager, select BDC and choose the Synchronize With Primary Domain Controller menu item.
- C. Use Server Manager, select BDC and choose the Synchronize Entire Domain menu item.
- D. Use Server Manager, select PDC and choose the Synchronize Entire Domain menu item.

10. (True/False) By default, a full replication of the user accounts database occurs every five minutes.

11. What is the default import directory path?

- A. %Systemroot%SYSTEM\REPL\ IMPORT
- B. %Systemroot%SYSTEM\IMPORT\ REPL
- C. %Systemroot%SYSTEM32\REPL\ IMPORT
- D. %systemroot%SYSTEM32\IMPORT\ REPL

12. While managing exported directories, you see that the Script directory has Yes under the word Stabilize. What does this mean?

- A. It indicates that the files will be exported immediately after they have been changed.
- B. It indicates that the files will be imported after waiting two minutes or more after changes have been made.
- C. It indicates that the files will be exported after waiting two minutes or more after changes have been made.
- D. It indicates that the files will be imported immediately after they have been changed.

13. When you create the service account for use by the Directory Replicator service, what group(s) does it need to belong to?

- A. Administrators
- B. Backup Operators
- C. Guest
- D. Replicator

14. It will take you approximately 30 minutes to make changes to several files located in your Script export directory. What can you do to prevent replication from occurring until you have completed your work?

    A. Place a check mark in the box next to the Entire Subtree option.

    B. Place a lock on the Script directory.

    C. Remove the lock from the Script directory.

    D. Change the status of the update.

15. The default size of the change log is _____ .

    A. 32KB

    B. 64MB

    C. 32MB

    D. 64KB

9

Printing

CERTIFICATION OBJECTIVES

9.01   Overview of Printing Terminology

9.02   Installing Printers

9.03   Configuring Printers

9.04   Managing Print Jobs

9.05   Troubleshooting Printers

T his chapter describes how printing takes place on an NT Server. First, it will cover terminology, because NT uses a definition for printers and print queues that is a little different from what you may be used to. We'll take a look at the NT print model and see how it uses print drivers and print processors. Then we will discuss how to create, share, and connect to printers. After explaining how to create a printer, we'll explain the configuration options in depth and show how to edit the registry to change some settings. Finally, we'll take a look at how you can troubleshoot some print problems.

CERTIFICATION OBJECTIVE 9.01

Overview of Printing Terminology

Microsoft defines printing terms in a slightly different way from definitions you have probably seen in the past. To begin a discussion about NT printing you should first understand some of their definitions.

Printing Devices

Printing devices are what you commonly refer to as printers. The term refers to the actual hardware that prints the document. Why did Microsoft change the term? Because when they refer to a printer, they are referring to the software that manages the printing devices.

Printing Software

Printing software is the printer. As mentioned in the previous paragraph, a *printer* is the software that manages a specific printing device (or devices, in the case of printer pooling). The printer determines how the print job gets to the printing device. Does it go directly to the parallel port, the serial port, or via the network? One printer can manage one or more printing devices. NetWare refers to this as the *print queue*, but Microsoft considers the print queue to be the actual *documents* that are waiting to be sent to the printing device via the printer. Remember, a printer is not the hardware device, but the software interface.

Windows NT Print Model

Here are the steps in the Windows 4.0 NT Print sequence:

1. The user at an NT server prints a document. The Windows application calls the graphics device interface (GDI). The GDI calls the print driver for the selected printing device. Using the print device information from the print driver and the document information from the application, the GDI renders the print job in the appropriate language.

2. The print job is sent to the spooler. The client side of the spooler makes an RPC to the server side spooler, which makes a direct application programming interface (API) call to the router. The router passes the print job to the local print provider, which then spools it.

3. The local print provider polls the print processors. Once the print processor recognizes the job's data type it receives the print job and modifies it, if necessary, according to its data type.

4. Control of the print job passes to the separator page processor. If configured to do so, this processor adds a page to the front of the print job.

5. The job is despooled to the print monitor. If the printing device is not bi-directional, the job goes directly to the port monitor, which transmits the print job to the printing device. If the printing device is bi-directional, the monitor is a language monitor, which handles bi-directional communications with the printer and then passes the job to the port monitor.

6. The print device produces the printed document.

Figure 9-1 is a graphic depiction of the NT print model.

Graphics Device Interface (GDI)

The GDI controls how graphics are displayed on the monitor and printers. It provides a set of standard functions that let applications communicate with graphics devices without knowing anything about the devices. From an application point of view, the GDI enables application code to be independent

FIGURE 9-1

Overview of the
printing process

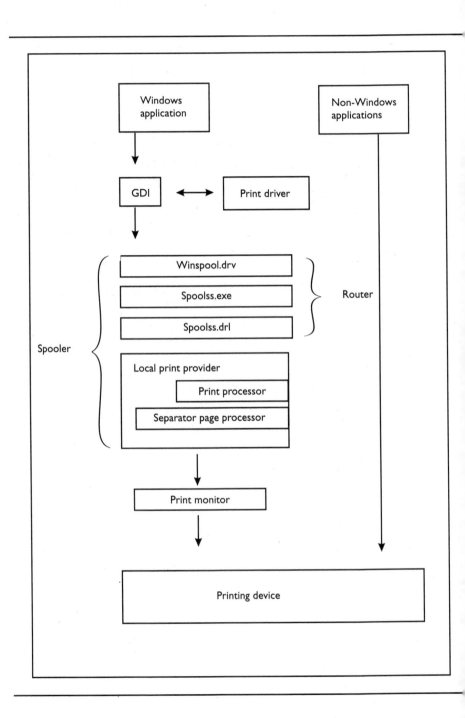

of the hardware devices and their drivers. Hardware vendors only have to write a minidriver to interact between the GDI and their hardware. The application sends commands to the GDI and the GDI uses the minidriver to send commands to the hardware.

Print Driver

Print drivers are the software that allows an application to communicate with printing devices. Print drivers contain three files, which act together as a printing unit. If the client printer is point-and-print capable (Windows NT and Windows 95) the version of the driver on the client is compared to the version on the server before sending the print job. If the server has a newer driver, the client's driver is automatically updated with the server's driver as the newer driver is downloaded to the client.

PRINTER GRAPHICS DRIVER   The printer graphics driver, which is always called by the GDI, provides the rendering portion of the printer driver. In other words, it translates print data into a form that the printing device can read, as described later in this chapter.

PRINTER INTERFACE DRIVER   The printer interface driver provides the user interface for configuration management of the print driver. It converts output from the application to a format understood by the print device.

CHARACTERIZATION DATA FILE   The characterization data file contains all the printing device specific information, such as page protection, graphics resolution, memory, paper size and orientation, printing on both sides of the paper, etc. The printer interface and the printer graphics driver use this file whenever they need printing device specific information.

Print drivers are usually not binary compatible. This means that each different type of operating system and hardware platform that needs to print to the printing device has to have a print driver compiled for it. Thus you can't use a Windows 95 print driver on a Windows NT machine, nor can you use a Windows NT 3.51 print driver on a Windows NT 4.0 machine. Because the NT 4.0 workstation and the NT 4.0 server have identical core components, the two operating systems can use the same print drivers. However, they must have the same hardware platform; for example, Intel print drivers can't be used for an Alpha.

Windows NT provides three generic print drivers, one to support each of the three basic types of print devices: raster, PostScript, and plotter. The three generic print drivers are:

- Universal print driver (unidriver), also known as the raster driver because it provides raster graphics printing. The unidriver carries out requests on most types of printers. Each hardware vendor writes a printing device minidriver that operates with the unidriver to communicate with its print devices.

- PostScript print driver uses Adobe version 4.2 compatible PostScript printer description (ppd) files. The PPD files are the only printer driver files that are binary-compatible across operating systems.

- HP-GL/2 plotter driver supports several different plotters that use the HP-GL/2 language. It doesn't support the HP-GL language.

Print Router

The print router routes the print job from the spooler to the appropriate print provider.

Print Spooler

The print spooler is a service that actually manages the print process. It's responsible for:

- Tracking which print jobs are going to which printing device
- Tracking which ports are connected to which printing device
- Routing print jobs to the proper port
- Managing pooled printers
- Prioritizing print jobs

The spool file folder's default location is the %systemroot%\ system32\ spool\printers folder. To stop and start the spooler service, you can use the control panel service application or use the NET START SPOOLER or NET STOP SPOOLER command.

Print Processor

The print processor completes the rendering process if necessary and returns the job to the spooler. *Rendering* is the process of translating print data into a form that a printing device can read. Since each type of client creates print jobs differently, different print server services are required to receive and prepare the jobs. The print processor performs different tasks depending on the data type. The default data type is Enhanced Metafile for PCL printers and RAW for PostScript printers. Exercise 9-1 explains how to change the default data type.

EXERCISE 9-1

Changing the Default Data Type for a Printer

1. Click Start | Settings | Printers.
2. Right-click the printer for which you wish to change the default data type.
3. Click Properties.
4. Click the General tab.
5. Click the Print Processor button to open the Print Processor dialog box shown in Figure 9-2.
6. In the Default Datatype list box choose the data type.
7. Click OK.

Windows NT provides two print processors: Windows print processor and Macintosh print processor. Printing device vendors can develop a custom print processor if needed.

FIGURE 9-2

Print Processor dialog box

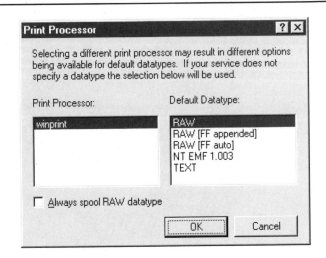

Windows NT Print Processor

WINPRINT.DLL is the primary Windows NT print processor. It supports five data types:

1. **EMF** Print jobs received from NT clients are Enhanced Metafiles (EMF). Unlike the RAW printer data generated by the printer driver, EMF information is generated by the GDI before spooling. After the EMF is created, control returns to the user. The EMF is interpreted in the background on a 32-bit printing subsystem spooler thread and sent to the print driver. The EMF has two advantages: (1) it returns control of the application to the user immediately, without waiting for printer calls to be interpreted by the print driver; and (2) EMF files can be printed on any printing device.

2. **RAW** Raw files are fully rendered print data, which require no processing from the print processor. Encapsulated PostScript (EPS) is an example of a raw data type because it doesn't need print processor interpretation. EPS files are sent directly to the spooler for routing to the graphics engine.

3. **RAW (FF Auto)** This data type tells the spooler to append a form feed character to the end of each job if it isn't already present. This is

used to print the last page on a PCL printing device if the application doesn't send a form feed.

4. **RAW (FF Appended)**   Like RAW (FF Auto), this data type appends a form feed character to the end of the job. However, it always adds a form feed character—even if one is already present.

5. **TEXT**   Raw text with minimal formatting. The print job is in ANSI text. It uses the printing device's factory defaults for printing the document. This is used for printing devices such as PostScript printers that can't accept simple text jobs.

Macintosh Print Processor

This print processor (SFMPSPRT) is installed when Services for Macintosh is installed. It supports the PSCRIPT1 data type. It indicates that the print job is level 1 PostScript code, but the printing device isn't a PostScript printer. The images are converted into monochrome raster graphics for printing to the printing device.

Print Monitors

The print monitor controls access to the printing device, monitors the status of the device, and communicates with the spooler—which relays device information via the user interface. The print monitor controls the data going to a printer port by opening, closing, configuring, writing, reading, and releasing the port.

The print monitors supplied with the NT operating system are:

- **Local Port**   LPT1, LPT2, Com1, Com2, and so forth.
- **Digital Network Port**   Supports both TCP/IP and DECnet protocols for digital network printing devices. The DECnet protocol doesn't ship with NT.
- **Lexmark DLC Port**   Supports Lexmark DLC printing devices.
- **Lexmark TCP/IP Port**   Supports Lexmark TCP/IP printing devices.
- **LPR Port**   Supports printing to UNIX LPD printing devices.
- **Hewlett-Packard Network Interface**   Supports printing to HP JetDirect enabled printers using DLC protocol.

lpr

The lpr command is used to print to UNIX print servers and LPD capable network interface printing devices. To use this service you must install the network service Microsoft TCP/IP Printing from the network control panel. After installing this service you can submit print jobs to LPD print servers using the following case-sensitive syntax:

```
lpr -S <server name> -P <printer name> <filename>
```

Windows NT can also act as an LPD print server for UNIX clients. First, you must install Microsoft TCP/IP Printing from the network control panel. Second, you need to start the TCP/IP Print Server service via the services control panel applet or use the command NET START LPDSVC.

Hewlett-Packard Network Port Print Monitor (Hpmon.dll)

Hpmon.dll sends print jobs to HP JetDirect adapters. JetDirect cards can communicate using different protocols, including DLC, IPX, TCP/IP, and AppleTalk; however, the Hpmon.dll must use DLC. Since Hpmon.dll requires the DLC protocol you must have DLC loaded on your system before using the HP network port print monitor. In fact, you won't even be given the option to use the HP network port print monitor unless DLC is installed.

Hpmon.dll can only manage printers over one network adapter, which must be adapter 0 or adapter 1. If your server is printing to multiple JetDirect cards and your server has multiple network cards, you must have all the JetDirect enabled printers connected to only one of the cards. In other words, they must be on the same physical subnet.

Print Jobs

Print jobs are source code consisting of both data and commands for print processing. All print jobs are classified into data types. The data type tells the spooler what modifications need to be made to the print job so it can print correctly on the printing device.

Installing Printers

You can create printers two ways in NT. You can use the Add Printer wizard or you can use Point and print. To manage printing you use the Printers folder. The Add Printer wizard is located inside the Printers folder. There are three ways to access the Printers folder:

- Click Start | Settings | Printers.
- In Control Panel, double-click the Printers folder shortcut.
- In My Computer, double-click Printers folder.

Creating a Local Printer

A local printer can be a print device connected directly to a port on your computer or to the network. Don't confuse a printing device directly connected to the network with a shared network printer. A printing device connected directly to the network may be a local printer if your spooler can send jobs directly to the printing device. Exercise 9-2 teaches you how to create a local printer.

EXERCISE 9-2

Creating a Local Printer

1. Open the Printers folder.
2. Double-click the Add Printer wizard.
3. Choose the My Computer option button, then click Next.
4. Click the check box for the port your printer is connected to (probably LPT1), then click Next.
5. Choose the printer driver by selecting the manufacturer from the left window pane, then selecting the correct model. If your model doesn't

appear on the list, you'll need to click the Have Disk button and supply the path to the driver. Click Next.

6. Give your printer a name (up to 32 characters) and choose whether or not you want it to be the default printer. Click Next.

7. You can share your printer, but for now make sure Not Shared is chosen. Click Next.

8. Choose Yes to print a test page, then click Next.

9. Make sure your NT Server CD is in your CD-ROM drive, then click Finish.

Sharing a Printer

Sharing a printer on the network allows other users to print to a printing device connected to your computer. Users' workstations will first spool the print job to their spooler, then send the job to the server's spooler for final processing and printing. If the local computer doesn't support local spooling, the print job will be sent directly to the server's spooler.

You can share the printer when you create it locally or later after it has been created. Exercise 9-3 shows you how to share a printer on the network after it's been created locally on your system.

EXERCISE 9-3

Sharing a Printer on the Network

1. Click the Sharing tab in the Printer Properties dialog box.

2. Give the printer a share name (the default is the first 8 characters of the printer name).

3. Choose any other operating systems that will print to this printer. This tells NT to load the drivers for each of the selected operating systems; when users point and print, the correct driver will automatically be copied to their system.

4. Click OK.

Connecting to a Remote Printer

To connect to a remote shared printer on another NT server, you only need to double-click the printer icon; that printer is automatically installed on your system (assuming the correct driver is loaded). This is called *point and print.* You can also use the Add Printer wizard to connect to a remote shared printer. Exercise 9-4 shows how to connect to a remote printer using point and print. To do this exercise, you'll need to have a printer shared on another Windows NT 4.0 server. (Refer to Exercise 9-3 if you need to set up a shared printer.) If the printer has a different hardware platform, the appropriate driver for your system must be installed on the shared printer's server.

EXERCISE 9-4

Connecting to a Shared Printer

1. Browse the network neighborhood and double-click the computer that has the shared printer you want to connect to.

2. Double-click on the printer you want to connect to. NT will start the Add Printer wizard to install the printer on your system.

Network Interface Printing Devices

A network printer is a printer that attaches directly to your network. It isn't connected to a computer's serial or parallel port. NT supports Hewlett-Packard JetDirect cards using the DLC protocol, DEC network printing devices using DECnet or TCP/IP protocols, Lexmark network printing devices with DLC or TCP/IP protocols, and any other device that supports LPD using TCP/IP. You can set printers on all your workstations to print directly to a network interface printing device; however, it is common practice to set up a print server to print to the network interface printing device and share that printer out using NT network shares. This improves the performance of the workstations because additional protocols do not need to be loaded on the clients.

exam
Watch

Be sure to understand that Hewlett-Packard JetDirect cards require the DLC protocol to be loaded on your system. Because DLC is not a routable protocol, the print server and the printing device must be on the same side of a router.

FROM THE CLASSROOM

Problems Printing to Network Attached Printers

NT makes a dandy print server for HP JetDirect type devices. Configuration is typically straightforward until you come to a point where you must select a port. Students often complain they can't find the Hewlett-Packard port. Here's the trick. By default, there is no Hewlett-Packard facility: it is installed when you install the DLC protocol. If you do not see the HP facility, check to insure that DLC is installed.

Another problem can occur when you start to add a new port and are presented with a list of the MAC addresses of the attached HP devices. To select the appropriate printer, you need to know its MAC address. You can get this information by printing a test page at each printer. Don't forget to label the page to indicate the printer it came from! This might seem trivial, but it happened to us. We were helping a client reconfigure their network, which included setting up printer servers for their HP printers. Of course, the client did not have the MAC addresses for the devices and asked a technician to print a test page from each printer and collect the addresses. After some

time, the technician returned and dropped 60 test print pages on the desk. Unfortunately, there was nothing to indicate which test page came from which printer, so we had no way to tie the MAC addresses to a particular printer. The tech had to repeat his work—this time marking the test sheets with the printer locations!

Here's an even knottier problem: When you are setting up new printer servers, NT displays a list of all MAC addresses on the network—even those that have been assigned to use a different NT computer as the print server. If you tell NT to configure a second NT computer as a print server for a previously assigned MAC address (regardless of whether you do it deliberately or accidentally), NT will accept your request. You now have two printer servers attempting to serve the same printing device. This will probably insure that **no** print job will get printed at the printer. The moral to this story is: "Keep track of which MAC addresses are configured at which NT print servers."

—By Shane Clawson, MCT, MCSE

CERTIFICATION OBJECTIVE 9.03

Configuring Printers

The options you can configure depend on the printing device you have and the driver that manages it. Some printers allow printing on both sides, printing from different paper trays, different fonts, and various other options. These options are configured using the Device Settings tab. Although some options vary according to the driver, there are several common options that can be configured on all printers. To configure the common options you use the following tabs: General, Ports, Scheduling, Sharing, and Security.

General Tab

The General tab shown in Figure 9-3 is used to identify the driver you want to use, describing the printer and telling network users where it's located. It also allows you to select a separator page, change the print processor, and print a test page. The key item here is the ability to change the printing device driver.

Separator Page

The separator page is used to identify the start of a print job. It helps users identify where their print job stops and the next one begins. A separator page is also used to switch between PostScript and PCL printing. The Separator Page dialog box is shown in Figure 9-4.

By default NT does not print a separator page; you must first configure a separator file. NT provides three separator files (located at %systemroot%\system32) or you can write your own.

- **PCL.SEP**   Switches Hewlett-Packard printers to PCL mode for printers not capable of auto-switching. It also prints a separator page before each document.

- **PSCRIPT.SEP**   Switches Hewlett-Packard printers to PostScript mode for printers not capable of auto-switching.

- **SYSPRINT.SEP**   Prints a separator page for PostScript printers.

FIGURE 9-3

General tab

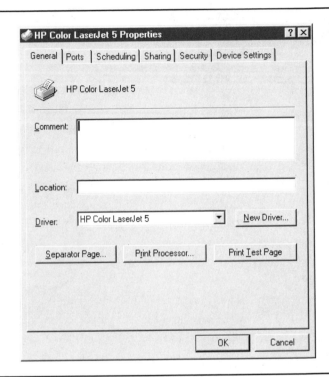

FIGURE 9-4

Separator Page dialog box

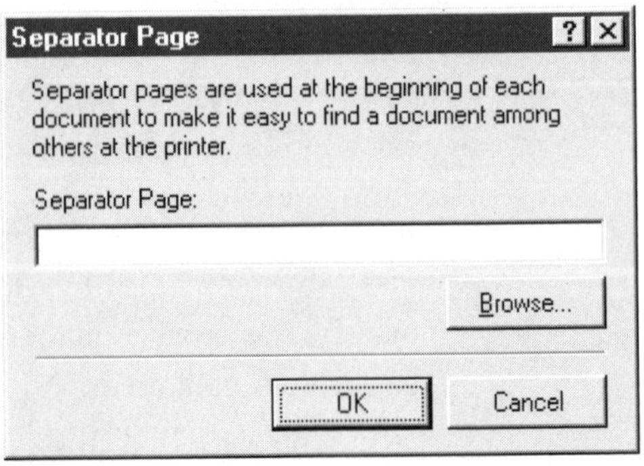

You don't have to use one of the Microsoft predefined separator pages. You can create you own if you like. Use the escape codes listed in Table 9-1 to create your customized separator page.

Print Test Page

Printing a test page prints a document to the printing device. The document lists the .dll files used by the print driver. Windows NT asks you if the document printed correctly. If you answer No, a step-by-step help feature assists you in troubleshooting the problem.

Ports Tab

The Ports tab shown in Figure 9-5 lets you choose a port for the printer, and it allows you to add or delete ports from your system. This is also where you

TABLE 9-1	Code	Action
	\\<number\>	Skips specified number of lines (1-9)
Separator Page Escape Codes	\B\S	Prints text in single-width block mode
	\B\M	Prints text in double-width block mode
	\U	Turns block mode off
	\W\<width\>	Sets width of page (must not exceed 256)
	\E	Eject page
	\F\<filename\>	Print a file
	\H\<code\>	Send hexadecimal ASCII code
	\I	Print job number
	\L\<text\>	Print specified text
	\N	Print username of owner
	\D	Print current date
	\T	Print current time

FIGURE 9-5

Ports tab

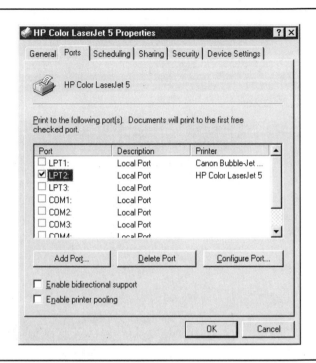

enable printer pooling. The Configure Port button lets you specify the Transmission Retry Timeout setting. This is the amount of time that a printer is allowed to not respond before NT sends the user notification.

Printer Pooling

Printer pooling is an efficient way to streamline the printing process. It sends print jobs to a pool of printing devices, and the first available device actually prints the document. In order to use printer pooling you need at least two printing devices that can use the same print driver. The printing devices should be located next to each other since users aren't notified which device is printing the document.

Exercise 9-5 shows you how to create a printer pool. In this exercise you'll connect two HP LaserJet 5 printers equipped with JetDirect Cards to your Server. Before starting this exercise be sure DLC protocol is enabled on your JetDirect enabled printers and print a test page to get the MAC address of the JetDirect Card.

EXERCISE 9-5 **Creating a Printer Pool**

1. Open the Network Control Panel and select the Protocols tab.

2. Check to see if DLC is listed as a protocol. If it isn't, choose Add, then select DLC from the next screen. You'll need to reboot your system for the changes to take effect.

3. Click Start | Settings | Printers | Add Printer wizard icon.

4. Choose My Computer, then click Next.

5. Check Enable printer pooling.

6. Click Add Port.

7. Double-click on the Hewlett-Packard Network Peripheral Port.

8. Enter the MAC address of the first printer in the address block.

9. Enter a name for the port. Let's call the first port Jet1 and the second Jet2.

10. Repeat steps 7-9 to enable the second printer port.

11. Click Close.

12. Make sure both printer ports have check marks on them, then click Next.

13. Select the print driver that will manage both printers, then click Next.

14. Give the printer a name. Let's call it HP5 pool. Click Next.

15. Share the printer on the network. Click Next.

16. Click Finish.

Scheduling Tab

The Scheduling tab shown in Figure 9-6 lets you specify the times the printer is available to print documents, and it allows you to set the printer's priority. This tab also provides you a way to change the way the printer spools.

Priority

The priority setting tells NT which printer gets to print to the printing device first. Printers with higher priority print before printers with a lower priority. The printer priority ranges from 1 (the default) to 99. This does not affect the document priority. It is only useful when you have more than one printer

Scheduling tab

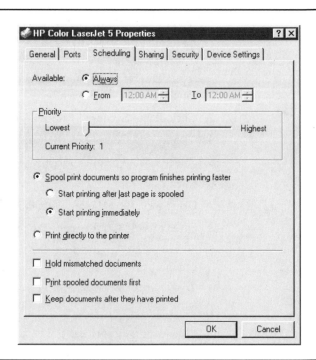

printing to the same printing device. A good use of printer priority would be to give the most important users a printer with the highest priority. For less important users, you could create another printer that has a lower priority. Set the proper permissions (discussed later) and the important people will be given access to the printing device first.

exam
Watch

Be sure to understand that changing the priority of a printer doesn't affect the priority of the print queue. When you have two printers printing to the same printer device, a printer with a higher priority will print to the device, when it's available, before a printer with a lower priority. If the lower priority printer is busy printing a document, it will finish printing the job before releasing control to a higher priority printer.

Exercise 9-6 teaches you how to create two printers that have different priorities and available times. We'll create two different printers printing to the same printing device. One will be for regular office users available from 8:00 A.M. until 6:00 P.M. The other printer will be for management and will be available 24 hours per day.

EXERCISE 9-6

Enabling Printer Priorities

1. Create two printers printing to the same printing device. (See Exercise 9-2 to create a new printer.) Name the first printer "Regular" and the second printer "Management."

2. Right-click the "Regular" printer and choose Properties.

3. Click the Scheduling tab.

4. Choose the Available From option button and set the times from 8:00 AM to 6:00 PM.

5. Make sure priority is set to 1.

6. Click OK.

7. Right-click the "Management" printer and choose Properties.

8. Click the Scheduling tab.

9. Choose the Available Always option button.

10. Set the priority to 50.

11. Click OK.

To administer these priorities, you need to share the printers on the network. You also need to make sure that only managers are allowed to print to the Management printer.

Spooling Options

You can change the spooling options to troubleshoot or speed up your print jobs. The default is optimized for typical print jobs.

SPOOL PRINT DOCUMENTS VS. PRINT DIRECTLY TO THE PRINTER   Spooling is the process of copying the print job to the spool folder located in %systemroot%\system32\spool\printer. "Spool print documents" is the default and shouldn't be changed to "Print directly to the printer". However, if you are troubleshooting a print problem, it may help to print directly to the printer. If you can print directly to the printer but can't print when you spool, you probably have a spooling problem. Spooling is more efficient than printing directly to the printer, because the printer and the computer don't have to wait for each other. When you select spooling you can have the print job start immediately (default) or after the last page is spooled. Printing after the last page is spooled may seem like a better choice than starting immediately, but if a user is sending a big print job it may take a long time before the printer starts printing. It is more efficient to start printing immediately.

HOLD MISMATCHED DOCUMENTS   If a print job is sent to a printer that doesn't match the printing device's configuration, it can cause the printer to hang with an error. To prevent this, choose the "Hold mismatched documents" check box. This tells NT to examine the configuration of the print job and the printing device, to make sure that they are in sync, before sending the print job to the printing device.

PRINT SPOOLED DOCUMENTS FIRST   By default NT prints documents on a first-come, first-served basis. By checking the "Print spooled documents first" box, you can have NT print documents that are completely spooled while another document is still spooling—even when the spooling document arrived first.

KEEP DOCUMENTS AFTER THEY HAVE PRINTED   The option to "Keep documents after they have printed" holds the document in the printer's queue window, even after the document has been printed. This allows all users to see what print jobs have been run.

Sharing Tab

The Sharing tab shown in Figure 9-7 is used to share your printer on the network. This tab also enables you to add other drivers to your server. By adding drivers for other operating systems, you allow them to use point and print functionality.

Security Tab

The Security tab shown in Figure 9-8 enables you to set permissions for users who will print to your printer. It also allows you to enable auditing (if you have auditing turned on in User Manager) and it allows you to take ownership of the printer if you have the proper permissions to do so.

FIGURE 9-7

Sharing tab

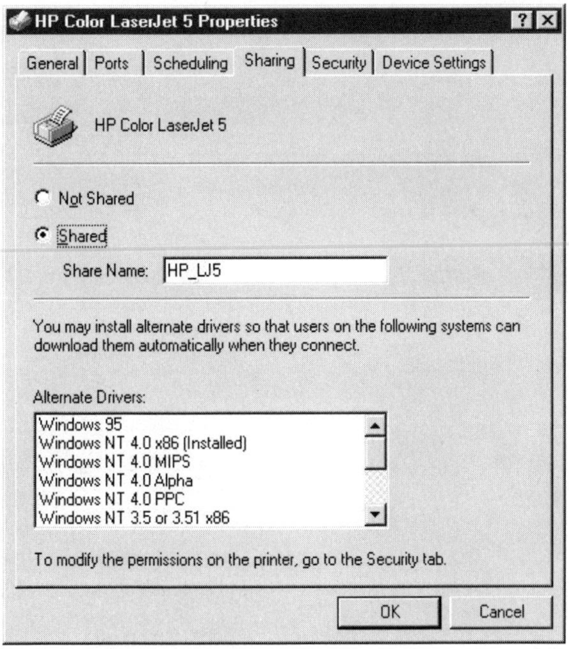

Security tab

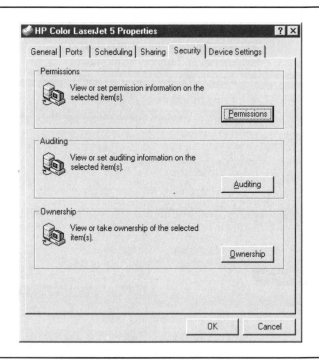

Permissions

Printers are objects that have access control lists. To set permissions, a user must be the owner, have full control permissions or be a member of the Administrators, Power Users, Server Operators, or Printer Operators group. Figure 9-9 shows the Printer Permissions dialog box.

You can assign four types of permissions to printer objects:

- **No Access**   The user isn't able to access the printer at all. This takes precedence over all other permissions. If a user is assigned to a group, which is allowed Print Access, and a group with No Access, the user will not be able to print because No Access always takes precedence.

FIGURE 9-9

Printer Permissions
dialog box

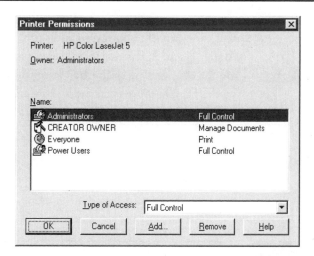

- **Print** Allows users to print and control the setting and print status of their own print jobs.

- **Manage Documents** Allows the user to print and to control the settings and print status for all print jobs.

- **Full Control** Allows the user to print and to control the settings and print status for all print jobs including the printer itself. Users with full control can share, stop sharing, change permissions, take ownership, and delete the printer.

The default permissions for printers, both local and shared, are as follows:

Administrators	Full Control
Creator Owner	Manage Documents
Everyone	Print
Power Users	Full Control

Auditing

Click the Auditing button to audit print events. Figure 9-10 shows the Printer Auditing screen. To enable auditing, you simply highlight and add the users or groups you want to audit, then select the events you want to audit. Before you can audit, you must open the User Manager and turn on the auditing function. Audit events are reported in the Event Viewer Security Log.

Ownership

To take ownership of a printer just click the Ownership button, then click the Take Ownership button. Once you take ownership you can't give it back. You must be a member of the Administrator group to take ownership of resources in NT.

Device Settings Tab

The Device Settings tab is used to assign forms to paper trays so the users don't have to worry about where the form is located. This tab has different options depending on the print driver you are using. Figure 9-11 shows the Device Settings tab for an HP LaserJet 5 and Figure 9-12 shows the Device Settings tab for a Canon BJC-4100.

FIGURE 9-11

Device Settings tab for
HP LaserJet 5

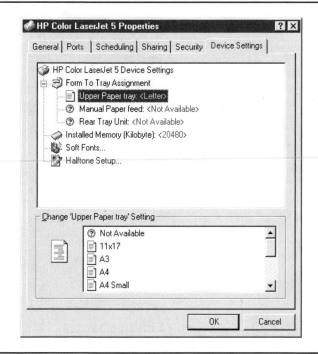

FIGURE 9-12

Device Settings tab for
Canon BJC-4100

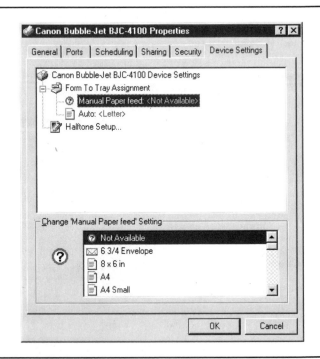

CERTIFICATION OBJECTIVE 9.04

Managing Print Jobs

By default creator owners of a print job can manage their own print job.
Figure 9-13 depicts what the screen looks like when you manage a print queue.
Exercise 9-7 teaches you how to manage a print queue.

EXERCISE 9-7

Managing Print Jobs

1. In the Printers Folder, double-click the printer you want to use.

2. In the menu bar for your printer, choose Printer | Pause Printing (this enables print jobs to remain in the queue for this exercise).

3. Use Notepad to open a text document on your hard drive.

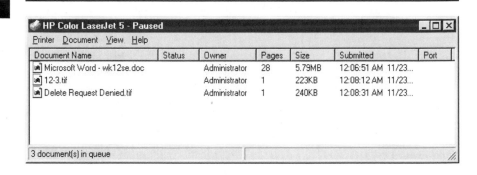

FIGURE 9-13

Managing print jobs

4. Print the document four times.

5. Double-click the printer icon on the lower-right corner of Task Manager to display the print queue.

6. Click the second document in the list.

7. On the File menu, choose Document | Pause.

8. Resume the print job by choosing Document | Resume.

9. To remove the print job, click Document | Cancel.

10. To pause all print jobs in the queue, select Printer | Pause Printing. (This is the same thing you did in step 2.)

11. Repeat step 8 on all jobs in the queue to end this exercise.

CERTIFICATION OBJECTIVE 9.05

Troubleshooting Printers

Troubleshooting printers can be very painful. NT handles printing extremely well, but problems can still arise. Use the following guidelines to help isolate printing problems.

1. Check the printer cable connection to the computer. This is an obvious step that is often skipped. You can waste valuable time trying to diagnose a problem that could be fixed in seconds.

2. Ensure the application is printing to the proper printer by checking to see what printer is selected in the print dialog box.

3. Verify that the correct print driver is being used. Try reinstalling the print driver or loading a new driver, if necessary.

4. Try printing from another client via the same server. If you can print from a different client machine, the print problem is more than likely located on the troubled client. If you can't print from a different client, the problem is probably on the server.

5. Check the amount of disk space on the drive where the spooler is located. Move the spooler or increase available hard disk space if needed.

6. Try to print using another application. If the problem is only with certain applications, check the appropriate subsystem.

7. Print the document to a file. Then copy the output to a printer port. If this works, your spooler is the problem. If this doesn't work, the problem is related to the driver or application driver.

One common printing problem is that the printer spool file—located in the folder %systemroot%\system32\printers—runs out of disk space. To prevent this, make sure the drive that contains the spooler has plenty of available space. You should also defragment your hard drive. Because NT doesn't provide a defrag utility, you'll need to purchase a third party program.

You can move the default spooler location by editing the registry. Use extreme caution when editing the registry. Add the value called DefaultSpoolDirectory with type REG_SZ set to <spool path> at the following registry location.

HKEY_LOCAL_MACHINE\System\CurrentControlset\Control\ Print\Printers

You can also change the spool directory for a specific printer by adding the value

SpoolDirectory with type REG_SZ set to <spool path> in the following registry key:

HKEY_LOCAL_MACHINE\System\CurrentControlset\Control\ Print\Printers\<printer>

where <printer> is the name of the printer you want to change. After making these changes you'll need to restart the spooler service.

If your system crashes while it has a print job in its spooler, it tries to complete the print job after the computer restarts. When a system crashes the spooled file sometimes becomes corrupt and remains in the spool directory. When this happens you'll need to stop the spooler service, then go to the spooling directory and delete the files that won't print. You should check the time date stamps to determine which files are old.

If NT Server is acting as a print server and it appears to be running slowly, you can increase the priority of the spooler service. By default NT Server assigns a priority of 9 to the spooler service. To change the priority for the spooler service you'll need to edit the registry. Add a value called PriorityClass with type REG_DWORD with the value of the priority you want to the following registry key:

HKEY_LOCAL_MACHINE\System\CurrentControlset\Control\Print

You can also use the Print Troubleshooter wizard. To start this wizard, print a test page and answer No to the question, "Did the test page print correctly?"

CERTIFICATION SUMMARY

In this chapter you learned that NT refers to printers as the software that manages the process of sending print jobs to the printing device. You learned how the spooler service manages the process of printing. You also learned about print monitors, print drivers, print processors, print routers, and print jobs.

You learned how to create a local printer and how to connect to a remote printer. You also learned about the difference between a network printer, which attaches directly to the network, and a shared network printer, which prints via a share on an NT Server.

You learned how to configure printers to use a separator page, how to change the default data type, and how to share a printer on the network. You also learned how to apply permissions security and audit printing.

Finally, the chapter explained some troubleshooting techniques you can use to identify print problems, such as changing the default spooling folder.

TWO-MINUTE DRILL

- ❑ Printing devices are what you commonly refer to as printers.
- ❑ Printing software is the printer.
- ❑ The Graphics Device Interface (GDI) controls how graphics are displayed on the monitor and printers.
- ❑ Print drivers are the software that allows an application to communicate with printing devices.
- ❑ The print router routes the print job from the spooler to the appropriate print provider.
- ❑ The print spooler is a service that actually manages the print process.
- ❑ Rendering is the process of translating print data into a form that a printing device can read.
- ❑ WINPRINT.DLL is the primary Windows NT print processor. It supports five data types: EMF, RAW, RAW (FF Auto), RAW (FF Appended), and TEXT.
- ❑ The print monitor controls access to the printing device, monitors the status of the device, and communicates with the spooler.
- ❑ Print jobs are source code consisting of both data and commands for print processing.
- ❑ You can create printers two ways in NT. You can use the Add Printer wizard or you can use Point and print. To manage printing, use the Printers folder.

❑ A local printer can be a print device connected directly to a port on your computer or to the network. Don't confuse a printing device directly connected to the network with a shared network printer.

❑ Sharing a printer on the network allows other users to print to a printing device connected to your computer.

❑ A network printer is a printer that attaches directly to your network.

❑ Be sure to understand that Hewlett-Packard JetDirect cards require the DLC protocol to be loaded on your system. Because DLC is not a routable protocol, the print server and the printing device must be on the same side of a router.

❑ To configure the common printing options, use the following tabs: General, Ports, Scheduling, Sharing, and Security.

❑ Printer pooling is an efficient way to streamline the printing process. It sends print jobs to a pool of printing devices, and the first available device actually prints the document.

❑ Be sure to understand that changing the priority of a printer doesn't affect the priority of the print queue. When you have two printers printing to the same printer device, a printer with a higher priority will print to the device, when it's available, before a printer with a lower priority. If the lower priority printer is busy printing a document, it will finish printing the job before releasing control to a higher priority printer.

❑ You can assign four types of permissions to printer objects: No Access, Print, Manage Documents, and Full Control.

❑ To enable auditing, you simply highlight and add the users or groups you want to audit, then select the events you want to audit.

❑ To take ownership of a printer just click the Ownership button, then click the Take Ownership button.

❑ By default creator owners of a print job can manage their own print job.

❑ One common printing problem is that the printer spool file—located in the folder %systemroot%\system32\printers—runs out of disk space.

SELF TEST

The following questions will help you measure your understanding of the material presented in this chapter. Read all the choices carefully, as there may be more than one correct answer. Choose all correct answers for each question.

1. What are two advantages of the EMF data type? (Choose two.)

    A. It requires less bandwidth to print over the network.

    B. It returns control of the application to the user more quickly.

    C. EMF files can be printed on any printer.

    D. EMF files are in PSCRIPT1 format.

2. What are the two types of print processors shipped with NT?

    A. Windows Print Processor (WINPRINT.DLL)

    B. PostScript Print Processor (PSCRIPT1.dll)

    C. Macintosh Print Processor (SFMPSPRT)

    D. UNIX Print Processor (LPD)

3. If you want to add an HP JetDirect networked printer to your computer, what two things must you do?

    A. Install DLC protocol on your computer.

    B. Configure the DLC protocol address on the printer.

    C. Print a test page to get the MAC address of the JetDirect Card.

    D. Install AppleTalk on your computer.

4. You shared an HP LaserJet 5 on an NT server for everyone in your department to use. When users try to connect to the printer using Windows 95 they get the following error message: "The server on which the printer resides does not have a suitable driver installed. Click on OK if you wish to select a driver to use on your local machine." What should you do to prevent users from receiving this error message?

    A. Install the Client for Netware Services.

    B. Give them the proper access permissions.

    C. Install an appropriate Windows 95 print driver on the server.

    D. Change the default data type to RAW.

5. (True/False) A local printer must have a port on the local computer.

6. You want to set up a printer pool using two printers. Neither printing device can use a common driver. How can you enable both printing devices to be in a printer pool?

    A. You can set up a printer for each printing device, then add a third printer to manage the two independent printers.

    B. Install DLC protocol to bridge the printing drivers.

C. Add both printing devices to the ports property page and check Enable printer pooling.

D. You can't because they have to share a common driver.

7. Your boss needs to print to her secretary's printer, but she doesn't want to wait for her print job behind anybody else's print job. How can you share the printer and give your boss a higher priority?

A. Share the printer and give her full control of the printer.

B. Set the printer to print directly to the printer.

C. Create two printers. On one printer give your boss permissions to print and set the priority to 99. On the second printer give everyone permissions to print and set the priority to 1.

D. Create one printer, but share it out twice. On one share give your boss permissions to print; on the other share, give everyone permissions to print.

8. User JamieS sent a print job to an NT print server. When he went to the printer to pick up the print job he noticed a 200-page report was printing out. He didn't want to wait on his print job, so he printed the document on a different printer. Because JamieS is environmentally conscious, he doesn't want to waste paper printing the first print job. How can he delete the first print job? (Choose the best answer.)

A. Double-click on the printer icon, select his print job, then choose Delete.

B. Ask the administrator to delete the print job for him.

C. There's nothing he can do to delete the first print job.

D. Turn off the printer as soon as the 200-page report has been printed.

9. To what group(s) must you add users so they can manage other people's print jobs? (Choose all correct answers.)

A. Administrators

B. Creator Owner

C. Power Users

D. Users

10. Drive C: has 10MB of available disk space on it. Drive D: has 300MB of disk space available. Windows NT is installed on Drive C: which is almost out of space. Sometimes when you print your computer locks up and you need to restart your system. What should you do to prevent this problem in the future?

A. Use Disk Administrator to combine the two drives into one logical drive.

B. Use Explorer to move your WINNT directory to the D: drive.

C. Move the printer spooler to the D: drive.

D. Move the print monitor to the D: drive.

11. Print jobs are stuck in the queue. What is the best thing you can do to fix the problem?

    A. Wait until the queue is auto-flushed.

    B. Restart the print server.

    C. Stop and restart the spooler service on the print server.

    D. Delete all the jobs in the print queue.

12. You want to allow a printer to be used only during normal working hours (9:00 A.M. to 6:00 P.M.) What is the best way to implement this requirement?

    A. On the Scheduling tab of that printer's property page, make it available from 9:00 A.M. until 6:00 P.M.

    B. On the Scheduling tab of that printer's property page, make it unavailable from 6:01 P.M. until 8:59 A.M.

    C. Turn the printer off when you don't want people to use it.

    D. Use the AT Scheduler to stop and start the spooler service at the required times.

13. What command do you use to print to a UNIX print server?

    A. LPD

    B. lpr

    C. net print

    D. \\computername\sharename

14. (True/False) NT can act as a UNIX print server.

MICROSOFT CERTIFIED SYSTEMS ENGINEER

10

NetWare Integration

CERTIFICATION OBJECTIVES

10.01   Planning NetWare Connectivity

10.02   Gateway Service for NetWare (GSNW)

10.03   The Migration Tool for NetWare

Windows NT Server includes a number of tools, services, and protocols to facilitate migrating from NetWare, as well as existing peacefully with it. Networks maintaining both NetWare and Windows NT Server will benefit greatly from the well-planned use of these NetWare interoperability components included with Windows NT Server. These components are covered in this chapter, which includes the following topics:

CERTIFICATION OBJECTIVE 10.01

Planning NetWare Connectivity

Whether you are migrating from NetWare to Windows NT Server or you are adding Windows NT Servers to a NetWare network, your implementation will be much more enjoyable for all parties involved if it is carefully planned. Unfortunately, network administrators are often given deadlines that do not allow adequate time for planning. In addition to time, good planning requires a thorough understanding of the network's needs, and the tools available to meet those needs. Although your network's specific needs cannot be addressed in this book, the Windows NT Server tools that can be used in your environment are covered.

Passing the Windows NT Server exam is not the only reason you need to learn about these tools. At some point in your career, you may be faced with a project deadline that does not allow ample time for researching both the needs and the solutions. If you already understand the NetWare integration capabilities of Windows NT Server, a significant part of the research is done before you even get the project. This will enable you to spend more time developing an implementation plan. In turn, your project will be more successful than it would have been if you hadn't known about the NetWare tools included with Windows NT Server.

There are as many reasons to use both NetWare and Windows NT servers as there are organizations using them—and that's a lot! Some examples are:

- A government office has been required to migrate from NetWare to Windows NT in order to implement C-2 security.

■ Two companies, one using Windows NT Server and one using NetWare, have merged; management decides not to convert either network, due to major application software changes that would be necessary.

■ A school has been using NetWare for file and print services, but an administrative software package built on SQL Server, which runs only on Windows NT Server, is being implemented.

■ A firm's critical time-reporting system requires a NetWare server, but Windows NT was selected to establish an Internet firewall and proxy server.

NetWare servers have been successfully providing file and print services to millions of users for a number of years. NetWare is a very mature product that was designed to deliver file and print services with speed. Network administrators and managers are not going to discount the established performance of NetWare and migrate to Windows NT just because Windows NT has a graphical user interface (well, not all of them, anyway). However, Windows NT Server has several features, besides the GUI, that set it apart from NetWare and make it the network operating system of choice for many applications. Table 10-1 shows a comparison of the capabilities of NetWare and Windows NT Server.

As you can see, Windows NT Server can easily find its way into many NetWare environments, especially since it is less costly than NetWare. While some networks are migrating from NetWare to Windows NT so that they can benefit from the added functionality of Windows NT while having only one network operating system to manage, others are opting to keep the NetWare

TABLE 10-1		NetWare	Windows NT Server
NetWare and Windows NT Server comparison	**File and Print**	Fast, Reliable, Mature	Reliable, Easy, Flexible
	Application Server	Crash-prone, Few apps	Stable, Many apps
	Messaging Server	Good for small entity	Scales to enterprise
	Internet/Intranet	Difficult, Weak	Easy, Strong
	Remote Access	Add-on package	Built-in
	Faster CPUs	Supports Intel only	Supports Intel and Alpha

servers for file and print services permanently. Network administrators in both environments need to understand and use the NetWare tools provided by Windows NT Server.

Connectivity Options

Client-to-server connectivity in a mixed Windows NT and NetWare environment can be approached in three ways:

1. Load two network redirectors on each client PC. This enables clients to directly access both Windows NT and NetWare resources.

2. Configure Windows NT Server as a gateway to NetWare servers. This allows Microsoft Networking clients to access NetWare servers through a Windows NT Server.

3. Set up Windows NT Server to emulate NetWare servers. This permits NetWare clients to use resources on Windows NT servers.

Since each network's environment and needs are different, there are dozens of ways in which these three methods can be applied. You may find that you need to use the second or third method for the short-term, as you work to implement the first. You might also find it best to use method #2 for some users, while using method #1 for others.

Method #1: Two Redirectors on Each Client

Client computers participating in an environment where NetWare and Windows NT Server are permanent residents may need client software for both types of networks. Windows for Workgroups, Windows 95, and Windows NT are all designed to enable two network clients to be used simultaneously. The memory limitations of DOS make it impractical at best to use both NetWare and Microsoft network clients at the same time. The additional resources required to run two redirectors will also very likely have a significant negative impact on the performance of Windows for Workgroup computers. Windows 95 and Windows NT, however, should have no trouble, except in instances where the computer has only the minimum required RAM to run the operating system.

Although each client system has to use precious resources to run a second redirector, this method of integration should result in the best performance for users, since each client computer can directly access each type of server. The other options require Windows NT Server to emulate or act as a gateway to NetWare servers. These server-side processes cause responses from the server to be slower than if the client is communicating with the NetWare server natively.

The NetWare client redirector that comes with Windows NT is called Client Service for NetWare (CSNW) and is included with both Windows NT Workstation and Windows NT Server. CSNW is installed on Windows NT Server by installing the Gateway Service for NetWare (GSNW). Windows NT computers with CSNW installed are able to log on to NetWare servers to use file, print, and application services.

Although the two-redirector method results in the best overall performance, it also requires the greatest amount of time to implement and maintain. Each PC must be configured to use both network redirectors, and may need to have additional protocols installed and configured as well. Each user must also have an account on each network, which doubles account creation and maintenance chores.

Method #2: Windows NT Server as a Gateway to NetWare

With GSNW, Microsoft Network clients can access files and printers on NetWare servers through gateway shares on Windows NT Server computers, without using any NetWare-compatible protocol or client. With this method of connectivity, only one network redirector, Client for Microsoft Networks, is necessary on client computers, and it is not necessary to load NWLink on client PCs. Clients only need one protocol in common with the Windows NT GSNW server to make use of the server's gateway shares.

Another benefit of this method is that each user has only one user account to create and maintain. The disadvantages of GSNW include increased network traffic that may adversely affect NetWare connectivity performance to the extent that users notice, and the significant resources on the gateway server required to run GSNW.

If your physical network's bandwidth utilization is already high, implementing GSNW may cause serious problems, since each gateway file transfer and print job hits the network twice. Likewise, if a Windows NT Server computer is already straining under its workload, using it as a host for GSNW could cause performance problems in some circumstances. While GSNW can be installed and configured in a very short time, a poorly planned implementation has the potential to turn a precarious situation into a disastrous one. Due to the performance and utilization issues, GSNW is not considered a good permanent solution for most mixed environments. It is typically used as a short-term solution while method #1 is being implemented.

Method #3: Windows NT Server Emulating NetWare

The third method employs the use of Windows NT Server's File and Print Services for NetWare (FPNW). FPNW is a part of Microsoft Services for NetWare, an add-on package available for Windows NT Server. To NetWare clients, a Windows NT Server with FPNW looks and acts just like a NetWare server, and client computers need only one network redirector, a NetWare client, in order to access NetWare servers and Windows NT servers running FPNW. See Figure 10-1 for a diagram of this setup.

Like GSNW, FPNW is not considered to be a good permanent solution. It is, however, helpful in NetWare to Windows NT migration environments. When the first Windows NT server is brought online, FPNW can be installed

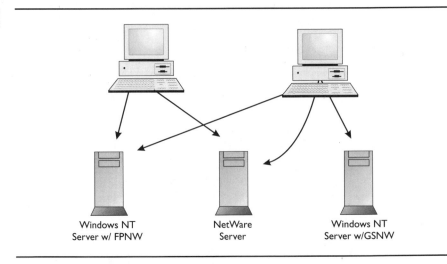

FIGURE 10-1

Client connectivity options with one redirector

Windows NT Server w/ FPNW | NetWare Server | Windows NT Server w/GSNW to enable all NetWare clients to use files and printers on it immediately. When all of the NetWare servers have been converted to Windows NT, the Client for Microsoft Networks can be loaded on each client and then FPNW can be removed from the Windows NT servers.

NWLink

Windows NT computers must use NWLink, an IPX/SPX-compatible transport protocol, to communicate with NetWare servers. Since it is merely a transport protocol, loading NWLink by itself does not enable client PCs to use NetWare file and print services. NetWare Core Protocol (NCP) is the file and print sharing language of NetWare, while NWLink is simply the delivery agent for NCP messages between NetWare clients and servers.

NWLink is a relatively fast and efficient protocol and should always be considered as an option when determining which protocol is best for a given network. Since IPX/SPX is routable, NWLink can also be used to communicate across WANs.

NetWare connectivity services on Windows NT are completely dependent on NWLink. If it is not already present, NWLink will be installed automatically when any NetWare component is installed, and attempts to remove NWLink without first removing NetWare components will be unsuccessful.

Installing and Configuring NWLink

NWLink is installed from the Protocols tab in the Network Properties dialog box. NWLink is very easy to install and requires no configuration at the time of installation. NWLink NetBIOS also appears as an installed protocol when NWLink is installed on a computer.

NWLink NetBIOS enables Windows NT computers to use Novell NetBIOS to communicate with Novell servers and other Windows NT machines using NWLink. The NWLink NetBIOS item cannot be removed separately from NWLink or configured in any way. Microsoft's NWLink NetBIOS includes some features not available in Novell's IPX/SPX NetBIOS. Consequently, these features are not used when a Windows NT machine communicates with a NetWare server.

EXERCISE 10-1

Installing NWLink

1. Go to the Network Properties dialog box by right-clicking Network Neighborhood and selecting Properties, or by double-clicking the Network icon in Control Panel.

2. Select the Protocols tab and click the Add button.

3. Select NWLink IPX/SPX Compatible Transport and click OK.

4. Enter the path to the Windows NT Workstation 4.0 source files, if necessary, and click OK.

Configuring the Ethernet Frame Type and IPX Network Number

NetWare has a number of different frame types that can be used with Ethernet, and while Windows NT can automatically detect which one is in use, it may be necessary at times to force a certain frame type to be used. If the frame type specified on the computer does not match the frame type in use on the network, communication fails. The following four frame types can be selected if you wish to manually configure NWLink:

- Ethernet 802.2
- Ethernet 802.3
- Ethernet II
- Ethernet SNAP

When Auto Frame Type Detection is selected, Windows NT listens for each frame type in the order listed above. If none of these is detected, Windows NT uses the Ethernet 802.2 frame type by default.

In the NWLink IPX/SPX Properties dialog box, you can't see which frame type was detected and used when Auto Frame Type Detection is selected. To see this information you must use the IPXROUTE CONFIG command which tells you which frame type(s) is being used, and to which network adapters each frame type is bound. The IPXROUTE command has other functions as well, such as displaying the Service Advertising Protocol (SAP) table and viewing IPX statistics. You can see the available options by entering IPXROUTE /? from the command line.

Frame types, network numbers, and the internal network number can be changed from the NWLink IPX/SPX Properties dialog box. It is possible to use more than one frame type at once, and doing so is a rather common practice. However, just as the use of multiple protocols diminishes network performance, using two or more frame types also causes network performance degradation. Windows NT Server can also be enabled to route IPX/SPX traffic between networks.

The IPX network number is an eight-digit hexadecimal number used to identify uniquely the physical network segment attached to the computer, so that IPX traffic can be routed. Each physical network segment in an IPX environment must have one or more unique network numbers. Windows NT Server automatically detects the IPX network number in use on the attached segment, if Auto Frame Type Detection is selected or 0 (zero) is entered as the network number.

The internal network number, also an eight-digit hexadecimal number, is a number that must be unique for each NetWare server in a given network. Windows NT Server uses 00000000 as the default, so you need to change this if you have more than one Windows NT Server using NWLink, or if 00000000 is already in use by a NetWare server.

EXERCISE 10-2

Configuring NWLink

1. Select the Protocols tab in the Network Properties dialog box.

2. Select NWLink IPX/SPX Compatible Transport and click the Properties button. This brings up the screen in Figure 10-2.

3. Enter a unique number from 00000000 to FFFFFFFF in the Internal Network Number field.

4. To manually configure frame types and network numbers, select the Manual Frame Type Detection radio button and click the Add button. You now see the dialog box in Figure 10-3.

5. Select the desired frame type in the drop-down list, enter the network number, and click Add.

6. Click Add to configure each additional frame type and click the OK button to finish.

FIGURE 10-2

Configuring NWLink. The
Internal Network Number
shown is the default

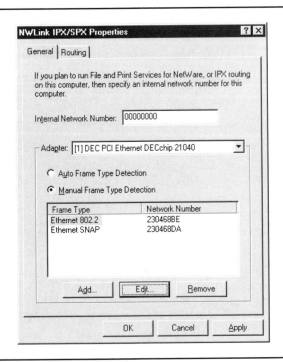

Using GSNW and CSNW

The Gateway Service for NetWare (GSNW) is an important tool that comes
with Windows NT Server and is installed as a network service. This service

FIGURE 10-3

Adding frame types
to NWLink

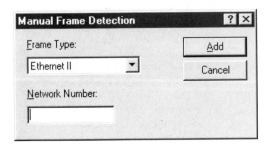

enables administrators to create shares on the Windows NT Server for files and print queues that exist on NetWare servers. Microsoft network clients that are not using NWLink or a NetWare client can then access files and print queues on NetWare servers through gateway shares created on a Windows NT Server running the GSNW. GSNW is completely dependent on NWLink. If it is not already present, NWLink is automatically installed when GSNW is installed. Attempts to remove NWLink without first removing GSNW will be unsuccessful.

GSNW also includes the client functionality of Windows NT's Client Service for NetWare (CSNW), which enables a Windows NT computer to access NetWare servers to use files and print queues. When GSNW is installed, the service selection reads "Gateway (and Client) Services for NetWare." CSNW enables Windows NT computers to connect to NetWare services, while GSNW provides the ability to share the NetWare connections to Microsoft clients.

Migration Tool for NetWare

The Migration Tool for NetWare is a powerful tool included with Windows NT Server that can copy user accounts, groups, and data from NetWare servers using bindery services. It is a copy mechanism only and does not modify the files or user account information on the NetWare servers. The Migration Tool doesn't work with Novell Directory Services objects. Used in conjunction with FPNW or GSNW, the Migration Tool can make the immense tasks of creating new user accounts and copying data much less of a chore.

File and Print Services for NetWare (FPNW)

File and Print Services for NetWare is part of Microsoft Services for NetWare, an add-on package available for Windows NT Server. FPNW enables Windows NT servers to emulate NetWare servers so that NetWare clients, using only NetWare client software, can use files and printers on the FPNW server.

Memory and processor requirements for FPNW to run on Windows NT Server are quite significant, so you'll need a faster CPU and more memory to get acceptable performace. Putting FPNW on a server that has minimal memory or a slow processor, or that is already highly utilized, is not considered a good idea.

A Windows NT server running FPNW cannot completely replace a NetWare server. For example, NetWare Loadable Modules (NLMs) will not work on a Windows NT Server, nor will Transaction Tracking System (TTS). While FPNW does a good job of emulating NetWare for basic file and print services, counting on it for much more than that is not recommended.

e x a m
ⓦ a t c h
Knowing the exam material isn't the only thing necessary to pass certification exams. Being relaxed and focused during the exam enables you to apply your knowledge to the exam questions. Learn some relaxation and focusing exercises, and use them before and during the exam.

Directory Services Manager for NetWare (DSMN)

Directory Services Manager for NetWare is the second component of Microsoft Services for NetWare. DSMN copies user accounts from NetWare servers to Windows NT servers and then propagates any password changes back to the NetWare servers. This allows user accounts on both networks to be administered from a single database. DSMN works with binderies on NetWare 2.*x* and 3.*x* servers and must be installed on a Windows NT primary domain controller. Using DSMN to manage user accounts facilitates a single authentication, not only for Microsoft and NetWare networks, but for NetWare servers as well.

Migration Strategies

Many entities are migrating to Windows NT Server from NetWare, each for its own reasons. For the smallest networks, migration might require only a few minutes of planning, while larger ones benefit from several weeks of planning and preparation. A number of factors come into play to determine the best

FROM THE CLASSROOM

Are We Being Served?

Some of our most stimulating classroom discussions involve comparisons of Microsoft's Gateway Services for NetWare (GSNW) and their File and Print Services for NetWare (FPNW). Each service accommodates a particular situation, and interestingly enough, one scenario is the inverse of the other. Let's consider them both.

Here's one scenario. You have your users' machines configured with the Microsoft network client. Your network has acquired a NetWare file server and you'd like your users to connect to it, but you don't have time to reconfigure their computers with the NetWare client. How can you get them attached to the NetWare server? The answer is to install Microsoft's GSNW service and configure it to allow the users attached to the NT server to use it as a gateway to the NetWare server. Two important points must be made:

- You must also configure the NetWare server.

- Using GSNW for a large number of users will prove to be slow, perhaps to the point of being unacceptable.

The second scenario is the inverse of the first. Here the users' computers are configured with the NetWare clients and you plan to introduce an NT file server into the environment. You do not want to reconfigure the users' machines with the Microsoft client, but you still want them to attach to the NT Server. What could you do? Install Microsoft's FPNW service. Unlike GSNW, which is included on the NT Server distribution CD, FPNW is a separate product that you must buy from Microsoft. FPNW sets up easily and, when configured, it enables NetWare client machines to see the NT server as another NetWare server. The limitation of FPNW is that it will only emulate a bindery mode server.

The two scenarios have common themes:

- The users' computers have one network client.

- You do not want to reconfigure the client computers.

- You want the users to be able to access the server.

When studying for the test, keep straight which service allows for what. You will most likely see questions on it. When you're more focused on implementation, remember that GSNW is included with NT Server, but you have to buy FPNW.

—By Shane Clawson, MCT, MCSE

migration strategies for different networks. These include, but are not limited to, the following:

- The size of the network and the number of servers to migrate
- Deadlines for completion
- Administrative and support personnel available for the project
- Hardware available for temporary and permanent use
- Network performance during the migration
- Security concerns
- Funds available for additional software purchases
- Additional requirements dictated by management

Having few simple plans from which to choose suffices for small networks, while large networks require custom plans unique to each environment. The same basic migration plans used for small networks, however, can be the basis for planning large migration projects. Regardless of the plan you have at the start of your migration, it should be constantly evaluated and modified to meet the goals of the project.

Data First, Users Second

One migration method is to move all data from NetWare servers to Windows NT servers running FPNW, and then install the Client for Microsoft Networks on the client PCs as you remove the NetWare client software. After all of the clients have been converted, remove FPNW from the Windows NT servers. User accounts must be created on the Windows NT network before you can start moving data, of course, and can be copied from the NetWare servers using the Migration Tool or integrated with DSMN.

Users First, Data Second

Creating user accounts on Windows NT with the Migration Tool or DSMN is the first step in this method, as well. One or more Windows NT servers configured with GSNW can be built, and as client PCs are converted to the Microsoft networking model, they can access the data on the NetWare servers via GSNW. After all of the client computers are migrated, data can be moved from the NetWare servers to the Windows NT servers. If you plan carefully, you can keep the new native share names the same as the old gateway share names, so that client drive mappings remain valid.

Two Redirectors on Client Computers

While this method offers the most flexibility, it also requires the most administration. As with the other two methods, user accounts are created on the Windows NT network as the first step. The Client for Microsoft Networks is then added to the client computers, enabling them to access both NetWare and Windows NT servers natively. After all the data is moved, network clients must be touched again to remove the NetWare client software. This method is labor-intensive, but it provides better performance, data availability, and server stability than the other techniques.

CERTIFICATION OBJECTIVE 10.02

Gateway Service for NetWare (GSNW)

The Gateway Service for NetWare included with Windows NT Server enables files and print queues on NetWare servers to be shared through Windows NT Server computers. While the benefits that can be derived from this capability may be obvious, the liabilities are not. For this reason, it is not recommended that GSNW be used as a permanent solution for providing NetWare connectivity to network clients. The following points should be kept in mind when considering the use of GSNW on your network:

- The translation of protocols that is necessary for GSNW to operate have a negative impact on the performance of activity between the clients and the NetWare server.

- Each request using GSNW creates twice as much network traffic, since the client communicates with the Windows NT Server, which then communicates with the NetWare server. The NetWare server then responds to the Windows NT Server, which then responds to the client.

■ Since client requests must be translated from Microsoft's SMB to Novell's NCP, a Windows NT Server with GSNW is busier than one might expect. A server that is already experiencing high CPU utilization should not be configured with GSNW.

■ Each gateway directory share requires a drive letter on the server, so the number of gateway shares on each Windows NT server is limited to 26 minus the number of physical drives.

Installing GSNW

GSNW is easy to install and configure; the most difficult part is the long NDS path names required for directories on NetWare 4.*x* servers. A GSNW gateway could be installed and configured in a matter of minutes. Creating gateway shares and assigning permissions takes only a few minutes more. A network administrator's total time to install, configure, and go live with the first GSNW shares could be well under an hour.

Removing NetWare Redirectors

Before attempting to install GSNW, it is necessary to remove any other NetWare client software that might be on the Windows NT Server computer. Novell develops and distributes its own NetWare client software for Windows NT; if any version of this is already installed, Windows NT informs you that it must be removed, and the computer rebooted, before you can install GSNW.

Installing GSNW on Windows NT Server

GSNW is installed from the Services tab in the Network properties dialog box. As mentioned earlier, CSNW is installed automatically as a part of GSNW. NWLink, Windows NT's IPX/SPX-compatible transport protocol, is also installed automatically when GSNW is installed, if it is not already present.

EXERCISE 10-3

Installing Gateway Services for NetWare

1. Go to the Network Properties dialog box by right-clicking Network Neighborhood and selecting Properties, or by double-clicking the Network icon in Control Panel.

2. Select the Services tab and click the Add button.

3. Select Gateway (and Client) Services for NetWare and click the OK button.

4. Enter the path to the Windows NT Server source files, if necessary, and click OK.

5. Reboot. You are now ready to configure GSNW.

exam
ⓦatch

Be sure to install GSNW and take a look at the interface. Even if you don't have a NetWare server, you can still get a feel for the GSNW interface. Installing it and checking out the different options will help you to remember them. Running the Migration Tool is helpful as well, but you need a NetWare server to explore all its capabilities.

Configuring GSNW

After the GSNW service is installed, Windows NT prompts each user for preferred logon information the first time they log on. A GSNW icon, which invokes the GSNW dialog box, is also added to the Control Panel. (See Figure 10-4 for an illustration of this icon.) This is where you can change the preferred logon information after the first logon and configure gateway shares.

Configuring the Preferred Logon

Configuring the preferred logon for GSNW is exactly like configuring the preferred logon for CSNW in Windows NT Workstation. The only difference is that the icon in Control Panel says GSNW instead of CSNW.

The GSNW icon added to Control Panel

Configuring the Preferred Logon

1. Once you have installed GSNW, the Select NetWare Logon dialog box appears after you log on to the computer. This dialog box, shown in Figure 10-5, can also be invoked after the first logon by double-clicking the GSNW icon that is added to the Control Panel. The Overview button on this dialog box brings up the CSNW Help file, which contains lots of good information.

2. If you want to use a bindery logon to a specific server, select the Preferred Server radio button and choose in the Select Preferred Server field the server to which you wish to log on at startup.

3. If you are logging on to an NDS tree, select the Default Tree and Context radio button and complete the Default Tree and Context fields accordingly.

4. Check the Run Logon Script check box if you want the NetWare logon script to execute at the time of authentication.

FIGURE 10-5

Configure the logon
at Gateway Service
for NetWare

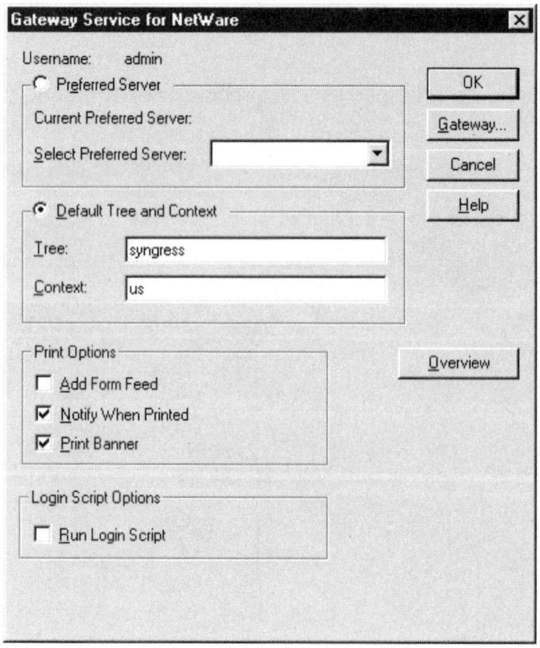

The username and password used for your Windows NT logon are passed to the preferred server or tree. If a user account with the same password exists on the NetWare server or tree, you are logged on accordingly. If the username does not exist, or if the password supplied by Windows NT is incorrect, you are prompted to supply the correct information to complete the logon.

Configuring the NetWare Server

Before you can successfully create a gateway share, a group named NTGATEWAY must exist on the NetWare server or NDS tree to which you are logging on. A user account that you want to use as the gateway account must be a member of this group. The group and user can be created with the SYSCON utility or NWAdmin, depending on whether your NetWare servers are using bindery services or NDS.

There are no restrictions on the name of the gateway account, and you can use the admin or supervisor accounts if you wish. Whatever account you use, it must have appropriate permissions to the files or print queues that are going to be accessed via the gateway share on the Windows NT server.

Enabling the Gateway

Windows NT needs to know the name of the gateway account that you created on the NetWare network as well as the password for that account. Once Windows NT has this information, it authenticates to the NetWare network with these credentials to retrieve files and submit print jobs for clients who are using the gateway shares. You will notice that a Gateway button appears on the GSNW properties dialog box. Except for this button, the GSNW properties dialog box is identical to the CSNW properties dialog box in Windows NT Workstation.

Creating Gateway Shares to NetWare Directories

To create a gateway share to a NetWare directory, you must be logged on to the NetWare network with an account that has permissions to the NetWare resources the gateway share will access. This is in addition to the gateway account that is used by the Gateway Service.

EXERCISE 10-5

Creating a Gateway Directory Share

1. Double-click the GSNW icon in the Control Panel and click the Gateway button.

2. Check the Enable Gateway check box to activate the dialog box shown in Figure 10-6.

3. Enter the gateway account that is a member of the NTGATEWAY group on the NetWare network.

4. Enter the password for the gateway account in the Password and Confirm Password fields.

5. Click the Add button to create a new gateway share.

6. Enter a name for the share in the Share Name field. This is the name of the share that will be created on the Windows NT server.

7. Enter the path to the directory you wish to share in the Network Path field, for example, \\SERVER\VOLUME\DIRECTORY.

8. Enter a comment in the Comment field if you would like to record additional information about the gateway share that you are creating.

FIGURE 10-6

Configuring the
gateway service

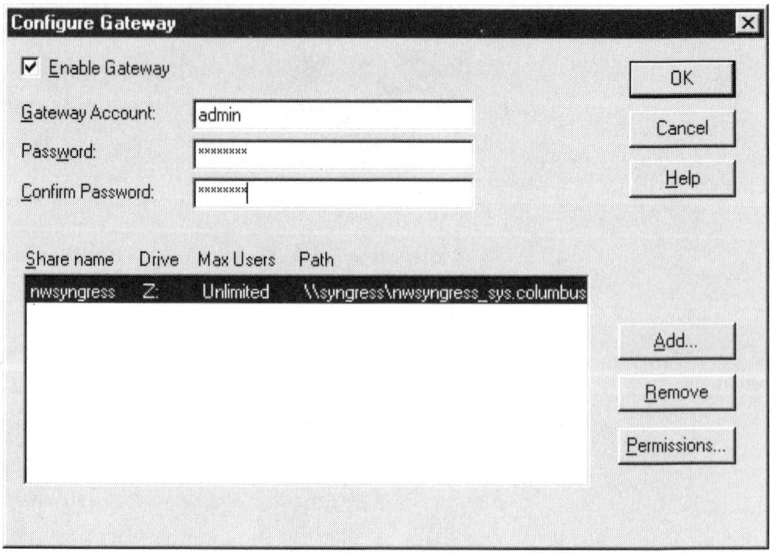

9. Select a drive letter in the Use Drive drop-down list. Windows NT must assign a drive letter to the NetWare connection in order to share it as a gateway share.

10. If you wish to limit the number of sessions for this gateway share, click the Allow radio button and enter the appropriate number.

11. Click OK.

Creating Gateway Shares to NetWare Print Queues

Setting up a gateway share to a NetWare print queue is very similar to sharing a Windows NT printer. It involves setting up a NetWare print queue as you would for normal use, and then clicking one radio button to share it. The Enable Gateway check box in the Configure Gateway dialog box must be checked before gateway print shares can be created.

EXERCISE 10-6

Creating a Gateway Printer Share

1. Double-click the Printers icon in Control Panel and then double-click the Add Printer icon.

2. Select Network Printer Server and click Next.

3. Browse the Share Printers list and double-click the NetWare printer for which you want to create a gateway share.

4. Click Yes to install a printer driver if necessary, then indicate whether the printer is to be set as the default and click Next.

5. Click Finish to create the printer connection.

6. Right-click the printer just created and select Properties.

7. Select the Sharing tab and click the Shared radio button. Change the Share Name field, if you so desire, and click OK.

Setting Permissions for Gateway Shares

Setting permissions on gateway shares is very similar to setting permissions on native Windows NT shares. The only difference is the location of the Permissions button for directory shares. Default permissions for directory and print queue gateway shares are the same as the default permissions for native Windows NT directory and printer shares.

Setting Permissions on Directory Gateway Shares

1. Double-click the GSNW icon in the Control Panel, click the Gateway button, and check the Enable Gateway check box.

2. Select the gateway share in the bottom window on which you want to change permissions, and click the Permissions button.

3. If you wish to change the type of access for any of the listed users or groups, click the user or group, and then select the appropriate permission from the Type of Access drop-down box.

4. To add a user or group to the access list, click Add, select the appropriate domain and user(s), click Add, select the desired access in the Type of Access drop-down list and click OK.

5. Click OK to finish.

Setting Permissions on Print Queue Gateway Shares

1. Double-click the Printers icon in Control Panel.

2. Right-click the printer on which you want to change permissions.

3. Select the Security tab and click the Permissions button.

4. If you wish to change the type of access for any of the listed users or groups, click the user or group and then select the appropriate permission from the Type of Access drop-down box.

5. To add a user or group to the access list, click Add, select the appropriate domain and user(s), click Add, select the desired access in the Type of Access drop-down list and click OK.

Accessing Gateway Shared Resources

After the gateway shares are created, users can map network drives to gateway directory shares and set up network printers in the same way they use native Windows NT shared resources. The only thing that might tip a user off to the fact that the files are on a NetWare server is that the Security tab does not appear when a file or directory's properties are viewed with a Windows NT computer. Users would not be able to distinguish the difference between a native Windows NT printer and a gateway printer.

When clients access a NetWare server directly, they can map network drives to any subdirectory on the server, since NetWare shares every directory by default. When a Windows NT Server gateway share is used, however, the client can only map a drive to the share name, since Windows NT does not share all the subdirectories below a share.

Using Remote Access Service (RAS) with GSNW

Clients connecting to the network with RAS can use gateway shares just as if they were connected to the network locally. Remote clients do not need any additional protocols or services beyond what is necessary to use native Windows NT shares on the gateway server.

Security Issues with GSNW

Since the Gateway Service connects to the NetWare server with just one user account, the gateway account, permissions for gateway users can't be controlled on the NetWare server. Share-level security at the Windows NT Server computer is the only point of security configuration, and since share-level security is less extensive than NetWare's file permissions you lose some granularity in the level of access you can permit. Additionally, since a Windows NT server can only host about 23 gateway shares, you can only provide that many users with secure home directories through gateway shares. Due to this limitation, you should plan to move user home directories to a Windows NT server as soon as your migration plan can allow.

Since the gateway account on the NetWare server must have access to all of the data that is accessed through the Windows NT Server gateway, keeping the account name and password secure is a must. This is by far the most important security concern regarding GSNW.

Connecting to NetWare Services with Explorer

Mapping network drives and browsing files on a NetWare server with Windows NT Explorer is the same as mapping drives and browsing files on a Windows NT Server. The most significant difference is that NetWare servers appear under the NetWare Compatible Network in the Network Neighborhood, while Windows NT Servers appear under the Microsoft Windows Network.

EXERCISE 10-9

Connecting to a NetWare Directory

1. Double-click the Network Neighborhood. If the server you wish to connect to is present, go to step 4.

2. Double-click Entire Network and then double-click NetWare or Compatible Network. If the server you are connecting to is present, go to step 4.

3. Double-click the NDS tree that contains the server you are connecting to. Continue browsing through the organizational units until you see the server.

4. Double-click the server and then right-click a folder and select Map Network Drive to connect a network drive to the folder, or just double-click the folder to browse its contents.

Connecting to NetWare print queues is just like connecting to shared printers on Windows NT computers. Three print queue configuration options are available in the GSNW dialog box, which is started with the GSNW icon in the Control Panel. If you want to eject a page at the end of each print job, check the Add Form Feed option; choose Notify When Printed to receive notification that your document has been printed; and select Print Banner for a banner page to be printed before each print job. The options selected apply to all NetWare printers used by the Windows NT computer.

EXERCISE 10-10

Connecting to a NetWare Printer Queue

1. Double-click the Network Neighborhood. If the server you wish to connect to is present, go to step 4.

2. Double-click Entire Network and then double-click NetWare or Compatible Network. If the server you are connecting to is present, go to step 4.

3. Double-click the NDS tree that contains the server you are connecting to. Continue browsing through the organizational units until you see the server.

4. Double-click the server. The contents of the server contain printer icons for each available print queue on the server.

5. Double-click on the print queue that you wish to use. Continue setting up the printer by specifying make and model to install the appropriate drivers, and naming the printer.

Connecting to NetWare Services with the Command Line

Mapping network drives and connecting to print queues on NetWare servers with the command line is different depending on whether the server is using bindery services or NDS. Listed below are examples of how to use command-line utilities to make drive and printer connections with either bindery or NDS servers.

NetWare Specific Applications

Most NetWare-aware applications operate correctly running on Windows NT Server, although they may require extra steps for setup and configuration. They typically require the NetWare dynamic link libraries (.DLL files) that are included with the NetWare client for Windows. To get these NetWare-aware applications to operate correctly, install the NetWare client for Windows onto a Windows NT Server computer, copy the .DLL files from the NetWare client directory to the Windows NT system32 directory, and then delete the

QUESTIONS AND ANSWERS

I want to use the command line to map a drive to a NetWare server using bindery services...	NET USE G: \\SERVER\VOLUME\DIRECTORY
I want to use the command line to map a drive to a NetWare server using NDS...	NET USE G: \\TREE\VOLUME.ORGUNIT.ORGUNIT
I want to use the command line to connect to NetWare print queue using bindery services...	NET USE LPT1 \\SERVER\PRINTQUEUE
I want to use the command line to connect to a NetWare print queue using NDS...	NET USE LPT1 \\TREE\PRINTQUEUE.ORGUNIT.ORGUNIT

NetWare client directory. The NWDOC.HLP file contains documentation for a few common MS-DOS and Windows NetWare-aware applications, including Btrieve and Lotus Notes.

As Windows NT becomes more common as a network client, software developers are recognizing the need to provide Windows NT-compatible software and documentation. Before attempting to make an application work on Windows NT, consult the software documentation and any technical support from the software vendor. It is likely that step-by-step instructions are available to solve the problems you are encountering. Checking for a newer version of the software is always a good idea also. Many software companies are requiring any new software they release to be compatible with Windows NT. Much of the PC software released prior to 1995 was not developed for, or tested on, the Windows NT platform. The latest version of any software is more likely to be compatible with Windows NT than an earlier version of the same software.

NetWare Utilities

NetWare provides command-line utilities for connecting to NetWare resources and managing NetWare servers. Novell designed these utilities for computers using DOS or OS/2 and the NetWare clients that Novell provides for those platforms. Since Windows NT does a good job of emulating DOS, most of the utilities operate as expected on Windows NT computers.

Supported Utilities

Almost all of the file and server management utilities provided with NetWare function with no problem with Windows NT. Only two utilities, SESSION and VOLINFO, have specific problems when used. When executed from a Windows NT Server computer, the SESSION command does not support search mapping and always maps as root, and the VOLINFO command runs very slowly if the update interval is set to five.

Some NetWare utilities do not function properly unless a network drive is mapped to the NetWare SYS/PUBLIC directory. If you plan to use NetWare utilities it's a good idea to use a logon script to map a drive accordingly.

A Windows NT Help file states that the NetWare RCONSOLE command has some known problems running on Windows NT Server. However, the RCONSOLE command functions normally with Windows NT, and you should have no problems with it. The following is a list of supported NetWare commands:

CHKVOL	COLORPAL	DSPACE
FLAG	FLAGDIR	FCONSOLE
FILER	GRANT	HELP
LISTDIR	MAP	NCOPY
NDIR	PCONSOLE	PSC
PSTAT	RCONSOLE	REMOVE
REVOKE	RIGHTS	SECURITY
SEND	SESSION	SETPASS
SETTTS	SLIST	SYSCON
TLIST	USERLIST	VOLINFO
WHOAMI		

Unsupported Utilities

Four NetWare commands are not supported on Windows NT. Everything that is accomplished with these NetWare commands, however, can be done in Windows Explorer or from the command line with the NET command. Table 10-2 presents the four inoperative NetWare commands and the equivalent Windows NT command. The specific syntax to use can be found by using the /? switch after the command (for example, NET LOGON /?).

TABLE 10-2

NetWare utilities not supported on Windows NT

NetWare Command	Windows NT Command
Login	net use device: \\server\path /user:*username*
Logout	net use device: /delete
Attach	net use device: \\server\path
Capture	net use lpt1: \\server\queue

The Migration Tool for NetWare

The Migration Tool for NetWare is automatically installed when GSNW is installed on Windows NT Server. The Migration Tool copies data, users, and groups from NetWare 2.*x* and 3.*x* servers to Windows NT servers. Once you have the Client for Microsoft Networks loaded on workstations, you are ready to use the Migration Tool to quickly copy the users and data from NetWare servers to the Window NT environment.

One of the best features of the Migration Tool is the ability to execute a trial migration. Logs are created which enable you to see any errors encountered during the trial migration, so they can be addressed before the real migration is attempted.

Migrating User Accounts and Groups

User and group accounts are copied to the Windows NT server from the NetWare server, and group memberships are retained in the process. Passwords, however, cannot be migrated. The Migration Tool allows you to set the password for migrated users to blank, the username, something else you wish to specify, or to use a mapping file to create unique passwords for each user. You can also set an option to force each new user to change his password the first time he logs on to the Windows NT server.

Account policies in effect on the NetWare server can also be transferred by selecting the Use Supervisor Defaults option on the Defaults tab in the User Options dialog box. This option is the only one in the Migration Tool that is quite misleading. All other options are plainly labeled and easily understood.

If you want to migrate the users and groups to a trusted domain, the Migration Tool allows you to do this, too. This enables you to migrate the files to a server in a resource domain and create the accounts in a master domain, if that best suits your needs.

Transferring Volumes and Files

The Migration Tool allows you to select which volumes and files on the NetWare server you want to migrate. It automatically creates a share on the Windows NT server to which it copies the data from the NetWare server. The path for this share can be changed within the Migration Tool, or you can choose to move the data to an existing share on the server.

Files transferred to an NTFS partition retain the effective rights they were assigned on the NetWare server. The translation of NetWare directory rights to Windows NT permissions is given in Table 10-3, and NetWare file rights converted to NT permissions are shown in Table 10-4. Basic file attributes are retained as indicated in Table 10-5, but file attributes unique to NetWare's file system are ignored.

Configuring the Migration

Once you have determined your strategy for passwords, file migration, account polices, and any other issues, you can run the Migration Tool, configure the migration, and execute a trial migration. After you review the logs from the trial, you can change any parameters necessary to achieve the desired results, and test your new configuration. It probably won't take more than two or

TABLE 10-3 NetWare Directory RightsTranslated to NT Permissions	NetWare Directory Rights	NT Folder Permissions
	Supervisor (S)	Full Control (All)
	Read (R)	Read (RX)
	Write (W)	Change (RWXD)
	Create (C)	Add (WX)
	Erase (E)	Change (RWXD)
	Modify (M)	Change (RWXD)
	File Scan (F)	List (RX)
	Access Control (A)	Change Permission (P)

TABLE 10-4

NetWare File Rights Translated to NT Permissions

NetWare File Rights	NT File Permissions
Supervisor (S)	Full Control (All)
Read (R)	Read (RX)
Write (W)	Change (RWXD)
Erase (E)	Change (RWXD)
Modify (M)	Change (RWXD)
Access Control (A)	Change Permission (P)
Create (C)	Not Transferred
File Scan (F)	Not Transferred

TABLE 10-5

NetWare File Attributes Translated to NT Attributes

NetWare File Attributes	NT File Attributes
Read Only (Ro)	Read Only (R)
Archive (A)	Archive (A)
System (Sy)	System (S)
Hidden (H)	Hidden (H)
Read Write (Rw)	None
Copy Inhibit (C)	Not Transferred
Delete Inhibit (D)	Not Transferred
Execute Only (X)	Not Transferred
Indexed (I)	Not Transferred
Purge (P)	Not Transferred
Rename Inhibit (R)	Not Transferred
Read Audit (Ra)	Not Transferred
Shareable (SH)	Not Transferred
Transactional (T)	Not Transferred
Write Audit (Wa)	Not Transferred

three trials to get your migration configured for success, and then you are ready to start the migration.

The options available in the Migration Tool are relatively straightforward, except for the account policies option mentioned earlier. Walking through each step of Exercise 10-11 will familiarize you with the options available and make you comfortable with the tool. Use the Help buttons to get additional information on the options available in each dialog box.

EXERCISE 10-11

Migrating a NetWare Server to Windows NT Server

1. Run the Migration Tool for NetWare, found under Programs | Administrative Tools in the Start menu. You should see the dialog box in Figure 10-7.

2. Click the ... button to select a NetWare server for the From NetWare Server field. Select the NetWare server you wish to migrate and click OK.

3. Click the ... button to select a Windows NT server for the To Windows NT Server field. Select the Windows NT server that will receive the migration data and click OK.

4. Click OK to continue. If you are not currently logged on with a user account that has administrative privileges on the NetWare server, you are prompted for those credentials.

5. Click the User Options button to bring up the window in Figure 10-8, and check the Transfer Users and Groups check box. Check the Use Mappings in File check box if you want to create, edit, or use a mapping file to change user names, group names, or user passwords as they are migrated.

FIGURE 10-7

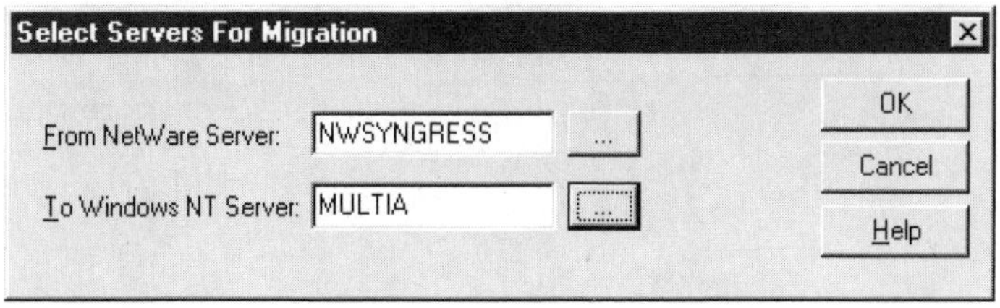

Selecting source and destination servers for migration

FIGURE 10-8

Configuring user and group
options for migration

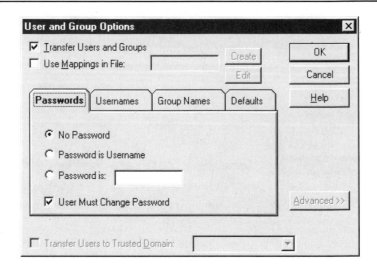

6. Select the Passwords tab and click the radio button of your choice to
   set the password options for the new accounts created on the
   Windows NT server. Checking the User Must Change Password check
   box sets the User Must Change Password at Next Logon option on the
   new Windows NT account.

7. Click the Usernames tab and select the desired option for what you
   want to happen when the Migration Tool encounters duplicate
   usernames on both servers.

8. Click the Group Names tab and select the desired option for what you
   want to happen when the Migration Tool encounters duplicate group
   names on both servers.

9. Select the Defaults tab and check Use Supervisor Defaults to migrate
   account policies from the NetWare server to the Windows NT server,
   if you wish. If you want the members of the NetWare Supervisors
   group to be placed in the Administrators group on the Windows NT
   server, check Add Supervisors to the Administrators Group.

10. Click the Advanced button if you wish to add the migrated accounts to a trusted domain. Check the Transfer Users to Trusted Domain check box and select the desired domain from the drop-down list.

11. Click OK and click the File Options button on the Migration Tool for NetWare window, bringing up the window in Figure 10-9.

12. Select a file system, if you wish to modify which directories get migrated, and click the Files button. Check the directories you wish to have migrated. If you wish to migrate system and hidden files, check those options under the Transfer menu. Click OK to close the Files To Transfer window.

13. Click Modify, if you want to change the share on the Windows NT server to which the files are copied. If you wish to use a share other than the default, you must create the share outside of the Migration Tool. To change where the default share is created, click the Properties button, enter the desired path, and click OK.

14. Click OK to finish setting File Options.

FIGURE 10-9

Configuring file options for migration

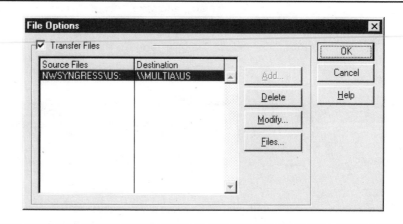

15. Click the Logging button, which brings up the dialog box in Figure 10-10, and select the options you want, then click OK.

16. Click the Trial Migration button to perform a test of the procedure. After the trial is completed a dialog box appears that lets you view the log files created. The logs show you how many duplicate users and groups are encountered, if the destination file system has enough free space for the data to be migrated, the new account policies, and other information.

17. Make any changes that are necessary for the migration to be successful, and run as many trials as necessary to make sure everything is ship-shape.

18. After you are satisfied with the migration configuration, click the Start Migration button. If you've got nothing better to do, you can sit back and watch, but you might be better off taking a nap.

19. When it is finished, you may want to print the log files for future reference.

    Unfortunately, you cannot save the log files from the LogView applet, but you can highlight all of the text in a log and press CTRL-C to copy it to the clipboard. You can then paste it into Notepad or a word processor, and save it from there.

20. Click OK to close the Transfer Completed windows, and click Exit to close the Migration Tool.

FIGURE 10-10

Logging options in the migration tool

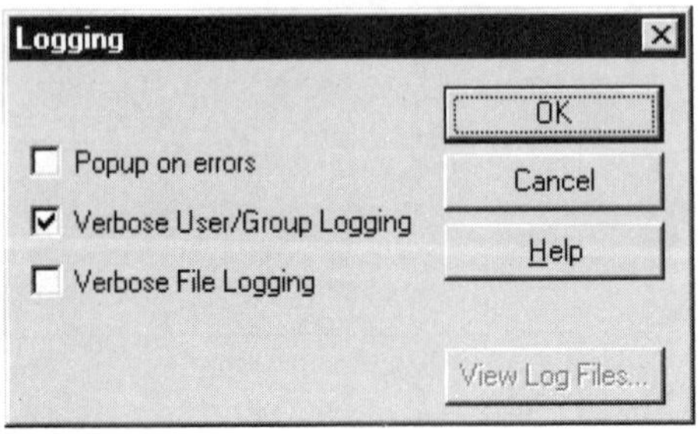

CERTIFICATION SUMMARY

Windows NT Server has two NetWare integration components included with the operating system: GSNW and the Migration Tool for NetWare. GSNW has the functionality of CSNW and enables gateway shares to be created that access files and print queues on NetWare servers. The Migration Tool copies user accounts, groups, and data from NetWare 2.*x* and 3.*x* servers to Windows NT servers, and has a number of configuration options to optimize the process. NWLink is the IPX/SPX-compatible protocol that Windows NT uses to communicate with NetWare servers. Frame types, network numbers, and the internal network number can all be manually configured, or Windows NT can automatically detect the frame type and network number, which is the default setting.

Microsoft Services for NetWare is an add-on package available for Windows NT Server that includes FPNW and DSMN. FPNW enables a Windows NT server to emulate a NetWare server, while DSMN creates a user account database, which it incrementally propagates to selected NetWare 2.*x* and 3.*x* servers, enabling centralized administration of user accounts on both networks from a Windows NT domain. This enables network administrators to provide users with a single logon for the Windows NT domain and NetWare servers in their environment.

Careful planning and a working knowledge of the Windows NT tools available enables a migration project to move quickly, while keeping data available to users. The smallest migration projects may not need to use any of the tools, but large migrations benefit greatly from their use.

TWO-MINUTE DRILL

- ❏ The NetWare client redirector that comes with Windows NT is called Client Service for NetWare (CSNW) and is included with both Windows NT Workstation and Windows NT Server.
- ❏ CSNW is installed on Windows NT Server by installing the Gateway Service for NetWare (GSNW).

❏ Loading two network redirectors on each client PC enables clients to directly access both Windows NT and NetWare resources.

❏ Configuring Windows NT Server as a gateway to NetWare servers allows Microsoft Networking clients to access NetWare servers through a Windows NT Server.

❏ Setting up Windows NT Server to emulate NetWare servers permits NetWare clients to use resources on Windows NT servers.

❏ Windows for Workgroups, Windows 95, and Windows NT are all designed to enable two network clients to be used simultaneously.

❏ Windows NT Server's File and Print Services for NetWare (FPNW) is a part of Microsoft Services for NetWare, an add-on package available for Windows NT Server.

❏ Directory Services Manager for NetWare (DSMN) copies user accounts from NetWare servers to Windows NT servers and then propagates any password changes back to the NetWare servers.

❏ Each gateway directory share requires a drive letter on the server, so the number of gateway shares on each Windows NT server is limited to 26 minus the number of physical drives.

❏ GSNW is installed from the Services tab in the Network properties dialog box. CSNW is installed automatically as a part of GSNW.

❏ Before you can successfully create a gateway share, a group named NTGATEWAY must exist on the NetWare server or NDS tree to which you are logging on.

❏ When executed from a Windows NT Server computer, the NetWare SESSION command does not support search mapping and always maps as root, and the NetWare VOLINFO command runs very slowly if the update interval is set to five.

SELF TEST

The following questions will help you measure your understanding of the material presented in this chapter. Read all the choices carefully, as there may be more than one correct answer. Choose all correct answers for each question.

1. (True/False) Windows NT will successfully migrate all NetWare file attributes with the Migration Tool for NetWare.

2. Which of the following functions are features of GSNW?

    A. Enables Windows NT Server to emulate NetWare servers.

    B. Enables Windows NT Server to transfer user and group information from NetWare servers.

    C. Enables Windows NT Server to share resources that are located on NetWare servers.

    D. Enables Windows NT Server to use file and print services on NetWare servers.

3. Microsoft Services for NetWare includes which two products?

    A. GSNW

    B. FPNW

    C. DSMN

    D. CSNW

4. (True/False) Loading two network redirectors on client PCs is the only way users can access both Windows NT and NetWare servers.

5. What is the name of the group that must be created on the NetWare server for GSNW to operate?

    A. GSNW

    B. NWGATEWAY

    C. GATEWAY

    D. NTGATEWAY

6. (True/False) GSNW and FPNW do not create much load on the server, or traffic on the network.

7. (True/False) The Migration Tool for NetWare allows you to copy users and groups, but account policies cannot be migrated.

8. (True/False) Remote users cannot access gateway shares when they dial in through RAS.

9. (True/False) An unlimited number of gateway shares can be created on a Windows NT Server with GSNW.

10. (True/False) NetWare file permissions are an effective way to restrict GSNW users from accessing each other's data.

11. (True/False) NWLink is not necessary for GSNW if the NetWare server is using TCP/IP.

12. (True/False) Permissions cannot be set on gateway shares, so security is greatly compromised when using GSNW.

13. Passwords for migrated accounts can be set to which of the following with the Migration Tool?

    A. The username

    B. Blank

    C. A password entered in the Migration Tool

    D. Passwords associated with user accounts in a mapping file

14. (True/False) The Migration Tool can only copy entire volumes. You cannot select specific directories to be migrated.

15. (True/False) Windows NT and NetWare offer pretty much the same functionality, and there isn't much reason to choose one over the other.

11

Remote
Connectivity

CERTIFICATION OBJECTIVES

11.01	Remote Access Service
11.02	Remote Access Protocols
11.03	Installing and Configuring Remote Access Service
11.04	Configuring RAS Security
11.05	Configuring Dial-Up Networking Clients
11.06	Administering and Troubleshooting RAS

Y ou are already familiar with how Windows NT Servers provide network services such as file and print over a local area network (LAN). This chapter explores the ability to use a Windows NT Server as a dial-in client, a dial-up server and an Internet gateway server. In the new global office, almost any local area network (LAN) you implement will undoubtedly have users requesting access to their e-mail and other network resources while at home or on the road. Installing the remote access service (RAS) on a Windows NT server can effectively meet those needs and more by making use of the Internet, phone lines, or digital communications.

CERTIFICATION OBJECTIVE 11.01

Remote Access Service

Windows NT Server and Windows NT Workstation include a powerful communications feature called the Remote Access Service. Usually referred to as RAS (pronounced raz), or as a RAS Server, the remote access service provides computers with wide area network (WAN) inbound and/or outbound connectivity to your server and/or network. RAS supports connections across Public Switched Telephone Networks (PSTN), Integrated Services Digital Networks (ISDN), and X.25 (a type of packet-switching network). New to version 4.0, Windows NT can also be deployed as an Internet gateway server via new Point-to-Point Tunneling Protocol (PPTP) technology.

exam
ⓦatch
Although Windows NT Workstation and Server have identical implementations of the RAS, Windows NT Server allows a whopping 256 simultaneous inbound connections while Windows NT Workstation allows only one.

Dial-Up Networking for Windows NT and Windows 95 Clients

In Microsoft Windows NT version 4.0, the Remote Access Service (RAS) client has been renamed to Dial-Up Networking (often referred to as DUN) and has been given a new look to be consistent with Microsoft Windows 95. This enhancement enables users to connect via DUN in Windows 95 or Windows NT 4.0, without having to learn and understand different interfaces.

DUN allows you to connect to any dial-up server using the Point-to-Point protocol (PPP) as a transport mechanism allowing for TCP/IP, NetBEUI, or

IPX/SPX network access over your analog modem, ISDN, or X.25 Pad devices. Windows NT can also be configured as a SLIP client connecting to a third-party SLIP server. By default, DUN setup is initiated after you install a modem on your computer. During configuration you will be prompted to create a phonebook entry that you can then use to store your connection settings for future use.

Windows NT version 4.0 has also added a check box so that you can log on via DUN when you enter your CTRL+ALT+DEL key sequence. When you check this box, the program displays the DUN phonebook where you can select an entry to dial, in order to log on. DUN then establishes a connection to the RAS server, to reach a domain controller for the specified domain to validate your logon request.

Support of LAN and WAN Protocols

As an integrated service within Windows NT, RAS supports the TCP/IP, IPX/SPX, and NetBEUI protocols. When you configure a RAS server in Windows NT to allow network traffic from your dial-up clients, you can enable use of one or all of these protocols.

Support for Connections across PSTN, ISDN, X.25, and the Internet

The Remote Access Service allows for connections across several media. The most common of these is the Public Switched Telephone Network (PSTN). PSTN is the technical name for the medium you use every day to make phone calls and send faxes. Hardware requirements for RAS over PSTN are any combination of analog modems supported on the Windows NT Hardware Compatibility List (HCL) placed at the originating and receiving ends of an asynchronous connection. Most RAS connectivity you will be supporting in your networks will be over PSTN. Almost every new laptop or desktop computer nowadays comes pre-configured with a modem—just as every home, office, and hotel is equipped with a phone line.

ISDN (Integrated Services Digital Networks) connections take place over digital lines and provide faster and more reliable connectivity. ISDN has been a very successful and popular choice in some areas, but it has not caught on at all in others. The primary benefit of ISDN is its speed and reliability. ISDN is commonly found in two speeds: 64kbps and 128kbps. Connection speed is determined by how many 'B' channels your telephone company or Internet Service Provider (ISP) is willing to give you and/or how much you are willing to pay. A 'B channel' allocates 64KB of bandwidth and the lesser-known 'D channel' allocates a small amount of bandwidth for error-correction and transmission verification. Often you will hear someone refer to his or her ISDN implementation as 2B+D which would indicate a 128kbps ISDN connection. However, ISDN hasn't caught on everywhere, primarily due to its cost and limited availability.

X.25 networks transmit data with a packet-switching protocol, bypassing noisy telephone lines. Clients can access an X.25 network directly by configuring DUN to use an X.25 PAD (packet assembler/disassembler). For more information on X.25, see your Windows NT documentation, the Windows NT Resource Kit, and Microsoft TechNet.

New to Windows NT 4.0 is the ability to utilize the new PPTP in your organization. Now, instead of having your organization absorb the costs of creating, managing, and maintaining a large RAS server or servers, including all of the necessary modems and other hardware, you can implement PPTP. PPTP provides a secure method to outsource the hardware and support portion of remote network access to Internet Service Providers (ISP). With the implementation of PPTP, a company needs only to set up a RAS server with Internet access and manage user accounts and permissions. The company can then use a dedicated service provider, such as a telephone company or local ISP, to manage the dial-in lines, modems, ISDN cards, and so on. For example, a user would dial a modem pool maintained by their local service provider. Once connected to the Internet, the user would then establish a second DUN session, requesting the TCP/IP address of your RAS server across the Internet. This connection will provide them with the equivalent remote network access you would have had by directly calling the RAS server—all at greatly reduced hardware and support cost. PPTP is also an excellent solution for minimizing long distance charges and eliminating the need for an 1-800 number.

Using Multi-Modem Adapters with NT Server (Multilink)

RAS Multilink combines two or more physical links, most commonly analog modems, into a logical "bundle." This bundle acts as a single connection to increase the available bandwidth/speed of your link. Multilink requires that you have multiple WAN adapters installed on both the client and the serving computer and that both are configured to use Multilink. For example, if ISDN were not available in your area and you required more bandwidth than a typical 28.8 modem could provide, you could combine four 28.8kbps modems on your workstation and four modems on the receiving RAS server for a whopping combined bandwidth of 115.2kbps bundled aggregate. It's a reasonable solution indeed, considering the next option is an expensive and sometimes unavailable 128kbps 2B+D ISDN link. Now imagine being able to Multilink multiple ISDN lines. You can! RAS performs PPP Multilink dialing over multiple ISDN and modem lines.

If a client is using a Multilinked phonebook entry to dial to a server that is enforcing callback (discussed later under RAS Security), only one of the Multi-linked devices will be called back. Only one callback number can be stored in a user's RAS permissions, allowing only one device to connect. All other devices will fail to complete the connection, and the client loses Multilink functionality. Multilink is callback-compatible *only* if the Multi-linked phonebook entry uses both channels for ISDN and both channels are using the same phone number.

QUESTIONS AND ANSWERS

ISDN is not available in our locality. What can we do to increase our bandwidth to those kinds of speeds without spending lots of money?	Install additional modems on your clients and servers and take advantage of Multilink which will allow you to bundle together multiple modems into one connection.
I want to have users connect through an ISP and then establish a connection to my network through the Internet.	Use PPTP. Configure a RAS PPTP server and enable PPTP on your DUN client computers. If the ISP has PPTP configured, you don't need to configure PPTP on your RAS server.
I have a Windows NT Workstation that I want to install a RAS server on. I expect to have up to ten simultaneous users connecting to it. What are my options?	Windows NT Workstation only supports one inbound RAS connection. You will need to install a RAS server on a Windows NT Server or reinstall Windows NT Server on your NT Workstation.

Remote Access Protocols

RAS connections to your network are established over the Serial Line Internet Protocol (SLIP) or the Point-to-Point Protocol (PPP). PPP is an improvement over the original SLIP specification and is the primary choice for most Microsoft RAS implementations. PPP is fully supported by the Remote Access Service in both a server and client role. SLIP is only supported under Windows NT as a dial-up client to a third party or UNIX SLIP server.

Serial Line Internet Protocol (SLIP)

The Serial Line Internet Protocol (SLIP) was developed to provide TCP/IP connections over low-speed serial lines. Plagued by limitations such as lack of support for WINS and DHCP, Microsoft has chosen PPP for their Remote Access standard. However, Microsoft has also provided SLIP support for Windows NT dial-up networking, giving clients access to TCP/IP and Internet services through a SLIP server. Often, SLIP connections rely on text-based logon sessions and require additional scripting by a host or Internet Service Provider (ISP) to automate the logon process. This, combined with a lack of support for NetBEUI and IPX/SPX, has been the primary reason for the popularity of PPP and the decrease in SLIP connectivity in Microsoft networks.

Point-to-Point Protocol (PPP)

PPP enables DUN clients and RAS servers to interoperate in complex networks. PPP supports sending TCP/IP, NetBEUI, IPX/SPX, AppleTalk, and DECnet data packets over a point-to-point link. The Microsoft RAS implementation of PPP supports the standard Windows NT protocols: TCP/IP, NetBEUI, and IPX/SPX.

Windows NT Protocols over PPP

RAS and TCP/IP

With the booming popularity of the Internet, the Transmission Control Protocol/Internet Protocol (TCP/IP) is commonly found in most new and existing networks. On a TCP/IP network, unique TCP/IP addresses are given to every host. This also applies to all hosts connecting through RAS. Typically, any computer connecting to a RAS server via PPP on a Microsoft TCP/IP network is automatically provided an IP address from a static address pool provided by the RAS server or allocated dynamically from a DHCP server. A RAS administrator may also choose to permit users to request a specific address by entering a valid IP address in their DUN configurations.

As in any TCP/IP LAN, most users do not want to have to remember all sorts of complicated IP addresses. Name resolution for IP addresses helps ease network naming in a TCP/IP environment. All name resolution methods available on a Windows NT network are also available to clients connecting through RAS. A RAS server can take advantage of the Windows Internet Name Service (WINS), broadcast name resolution, the Domain Name System (DNS), HOSTS and LMHOSTS files. DUN clients are assigned the same WINS and DNS servers that are assigned to the RAS server unless you modify the registry to override them. DUN clients are also able to select their own WINS and DNS servers by specifying them in their DUN settings. If WINS or DNS is not available on your network, DUN clients can use HOSTS or LMHOSTS files configured locally for name resolution.

RAS and NetBEUI

NetBEUI is a small and fast network protocol commonly found in small, local area networks with 1 to 200 users. Like TCP/IP and IPX/SPX, NetBEUI is supported by RAS allowing NetBEUI packets access through your RAS server to your network. Once installed, the only additional configuration NetBEUI requires is making the decision to allow remote users to access your entire network or just the RAS server the user is connecting to. The RAS server NetBEUI Configuration screen is illustrated in Figure 11-1.

RAS and IPX

IPX is the protocol introduced by Novell and implemented in most Netware environments. Like TCP/IP, it is a routable protocol—making it very popular for large enterprise-wide networks. A Windows NT RAS server behaves as an IPX router and Service Advertising Protocol (SAP) agent for DUN clients. Once RAS is configured with IPX, file and print services, as well as the use of Windows Sockets applications, are available to DUN clients.

When a DUN client connects to an IPX network through a RAS server, an IPX network number is provided to the client by RAS and SAP services are provided by the RAS server. The IPX network number can be automatically generated by the RAS server using the Netware Router Information Protocol (RIP). Manual IPX network number assignments can also be configured within RAS. However, when assigning an IPX network number to a RAS server, be sure not to select any numbers already in use on your network. A single network number can be assigned to all DUN clients on your RAS server to minimize RIP announcements.

RAS PPTP

Windows NT 4.0 introduces direct remote access support to the Internet with the implementation of the Point-to-Point Tunneling Protocol (PPTP). Using PPTP, a user can establish a connection to the Internet through a local ISP

The RAS server NetBEUI Configuration screen

(Internet Service Provider). Once connected to the Internet, the user initiates a connection to your network by requesting the IP address of the RAS server. This is referred to as Virtual Private Networking (VPN). PPTP offers the following advantages over other WAN solutions:

- **Lower Transmission Costs**   Connections made over the Internet will be cheaper for users outside your local area. A user simply connects to an ISP anywhere in the world and connectivity is then carried out over the Internet. Local ISP charges are far more reasonable than long-distance rates or a dedicated 800 number.

- **Lower Hardware Costs**   For the server side of a RAS PPTP implementation, a server needs only to have a connection to the Internet, eliminating the need for large modem pools.

- **Lower Administrative Overhead**   Because Internet Service Providers take over the costs of ownership of dial-up connections, your only considerations as network administrator are maintaining user accounts, security, and RAS dial-in permissions.

- **Security**   PPTP filtering can process TCP/IP, IPX, and NetBEUI packets. PPTP acts as a secure, encrypted tunnel allowing for safe transportation of your data over the Internet.

Installing the PPTP on your server is a three-step process. First, establish connectivity to the Internet with your RAS server. Next, install the PPTP as you would any other protocol in Windows NT and indicate the number of Virtual Private Networks you want to implement. Finally, apply any PPTP filtering you require to the TCP/IP protocol by choosing the Advanced button in the TCP/IP protocol settings. Enabling PPTP filtering will effectively remove all other protocol support on that adapter, securing your network from intruders.

Once PPTP is installed on the server, you will be able to establish a connection to it over the Internet with a PPTP enabled client, such as Windows NT Workstation. To initiate a VPN, a user will first need to use DUN to dial an ISP and establish an Internet connection. The user would then use DUN again to 'Dial' the RAS server using the IP address of your RAS server as the phone number and the Virtual Private Network number as the port.

QUESTIONS AND ANSWERS

I have clients currently using third-party SLIP client software to connect to an existing UNIX server at my site. I want to replace the UNIX dial-up server with a Windows NT RAS server. Are there any additional considerations I should make?	If you implement a Windows NT Server as your dial-up server, you will need to install PPP client software on your users' workstations. RAS does not provide a SLIP server component. If your users are using Windows 95 or Windows NT Workstation, consider installing DUN on those machines.
Users on my network currently connect to my RAS server using the NetBEUI protocol. I want these users to be able to browse Internet web sites through my network's current Internet gateway.	Install TCP/IP on the users' workstations. TCP/IP is the language we speak on the Internet and users will need it if they want to browse Internet resources.

CERTIFICATION OBJECTIVE 11.03

Installing and Configuring Remote Access Service

A RAS server can be installed during the installation of Windows NT or at any other time by adding it as a network service. Prior to installing RAS, you should be aware of the following:

- Verify that the modems you are using are supported on the Windows NT Hardware Compatibility List (HCL). Make sure you have the current driver software for those modems.

- Know the role of the RAS server and its port configurations. Will this server be used to dial in, dial out or both?

- Know what protocols you require for network support and install them on your server prior to installing RAS.

- Consider any security settings such as callback and RAS user permissions.

Before installing RAS you may also want to consider installing your modems first. If your modems are working prior to the installation of RAS, you can eliminate most hardware issues when troubleshooting RAS connectivity problems.

Installing a RAS device

1. To install a modem in Windows NT, double-click the Modems icon in the Control Panel.

2. If a modem is already present on your system, the Modems Properties screen will open. If no modems are currently installed, the Install New Modem wizard (shown in Figure 11-2) will open.

3. Choose Next to have Windows NT attempt to detect your modem.

4. If Windows NT finds your modem, you can choose Finish to complete the setup of your modem. If a modem was not detected, you can then choose to install a modem from the list of Windows NT supported modems. You can also choose to load drivers for your modem from the disk (illustrated in Figure 11-3).

5. Once you have selected a modem click Next. You then have the opportunity to choose what port you want to install the modem on.

6. Click Finish to exit the modem installation screen. You will be returned to the Modem Properties screen (shown in Figure 11-4) where you can add another modem or modify your current selections.

FIGURE 11-2

The Install New Modem wizard screen

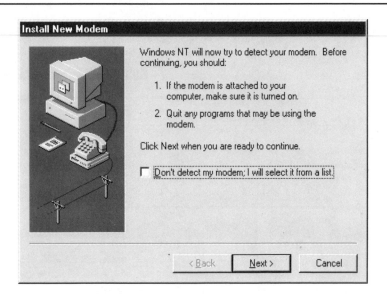

FIGURE 11-3

The Install New Modem
screen. You can select your
modem make and model
from this list or install
supported drivers from a
vendor-supplied disk.

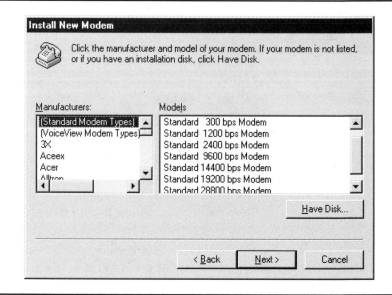

FIGURE 11-4

Modem Properties/
General tab

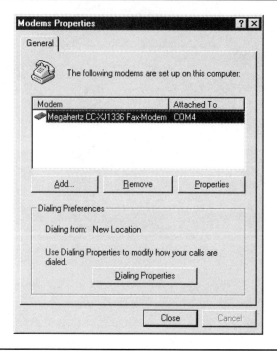

If your modem is not listed in the supported modems list, you can modify the MODEM.INF file and create your own modem type. Simply add the name of your modem in brackets followed by any modem initialization strings that your particular modem requires. These commands are commonly found in your modem's documentation.

Installing the RAS

1. To install RAS, double-click the Network icon in the Control Panel. This will open the Network Settings screen.

2. Select the Service tab and press the Add button.

3. In the Select Network Service screen, choose Remote Access Service and click OK.

4. The program will request the location of your Windows NT Server or Workstation setup files. Insert your Windows NT CD-ROM and supply the information needed to access it. Click OK.

5. After the files required for RAS have been copied to your system, the RAS setup program will prompt you for the first device you want RAS to initialize. If you don't already have a RAS-capable device (such as a modem) installed, you can select the Install Modem or Install X.25 Pad buttons to configure new devices. When you select the Install Modem button, the Install New Modem wizard will walk you through the modem hardware installation.

6. Once RAS setup has a valid device configured for use with RAS, you may configure each RAS port as shown in Figure 11-5, adding support for the network protocols you require.

After you have successfully installed RAS, you will need to restart your system for the changes to take effect.

Removing/Uninstalling RAS

1. If you later decide to change the role of your server or workstation and want to remove RAS from the system, double-click the Network icon in Control Panel to open the network Configuration screen.

2. Select the Services tab, select Remote Access Service from the list of installed services and click the Remove button. Choose Yes to accept the warning that RAS will be permanently removed from your system.

3. Click Close. When prompted to restart your computer, click Yes.

FIGURE 11-5

The Remote Access Service Setup screen. From here you can add and remove ports, configure port usage and alter network configuration properties.

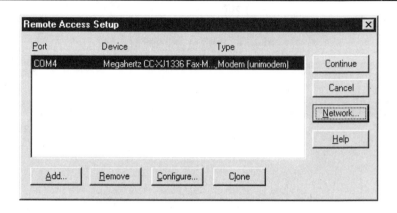

Removing the Remote Access Service will not remove any modems you may have installed. You can remove modems by selecting the Modems icon in Control Panel, selecting a modem, and pressing the Remove button. If you remove a modem from your system, you will be prompted to reconfigure DUN.

Configuring RAS Ports

After you have installed a modem, ISDN device or X.25 PAD, you can configure the RAS port for each device. To configure a port, open RAS setup, choose a port and press the Configure button. You can also install a new modem directly from this dialog box by selecting the Add button. Once the ports have been configured for RAS you can then identify which role each port will play. Ports can be configured for dialing out, receiving calls, or both, as shown in Figure 11-6. If you set the port to receive calls, you may specify whether to give callers access to the entire network or restrict access to the RAS server only.

Configuring port usage

1. In the Port Usage Configuration screen (Figure 11-6), specify how the port is to be used. Options are: dial out only, receive calls only, or both.

2. Click OK when you are finished. Calls cannot be received on a port until RAS has been started.

FIGURE 11-6

The Port Usage Configuration screen. Each port can be configured here to be used as a dial-out client, as a server (receive calls), or both.

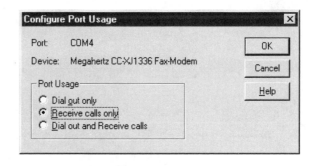

EXERCISE 11-5

Configuring an ISDN adapter

1. To configure or install a new ISDN adapter, choose the Network icon in Control Panel or right-click the Network Neighborhood icon on your desktop and choose Properties.

2. Choose the Adapters tab and click Add to install a new adapter or click Properties to modify your current adapter.

3. Configure your new ISDN port for dial out only, receive calls only, or dial out and receive calls.

Configuring RAS Network Settings

When configuring RAS network settings such as protocol usage or encryption settings, keep in mind that any configuration settings you make will apply to all RAS operations for all RAS-enabled ports (see Figure 11-7). For example, if you were to enable NetBEUI support for Dial-Out settings on your server, all RAS capable devices on that server will support NetBEUI. The Remote Access Service, when installed on a RAS computer, can access a LAN as a server and as a client. For each role, you must configure how you want each port to be utilized. When configuring Dial-Out protocols, keep in mind that any protocols you do not enable in RAS Network Configuration will be unavailable to you when you later configure a phone book entry for dialing out. When setting up RAS to service remote clients, you must configure each protocol carefully so that RAS protocol settings don't conflict with communications on the rest of your network. When choosing an encryption

The RAS Network
Configuration Screen

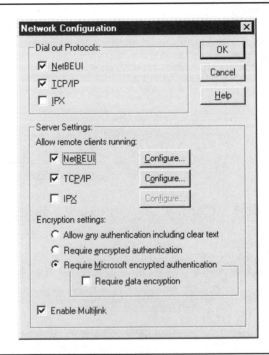

method, always apply the highest level of encryption possible, keeping in mind
the encryption capabilities of your clients.

EXERCISE 11-6

Configuring a RAS server with TCP/IP

1. When configuring a RAS server to use TCP/IP for network
   connections, open the Control Panel and double-click the Network
   icon to start the network setup program.

2. On the Services tab, select the Remote Access Service and click the
   Properties button.

3. In the Remote Access Setup dialog box, click the Network button.

4. In the Server Settings box, make sure the TCP/IP check box is selected
   (if TCP/IP is installed) and then click Configure. See Figure 11-8 for an
   illustration of the RAS Server TCP/IP Configuration screen.

FIGURE 11-8

The RAS server TCP/IP
Configuration screen

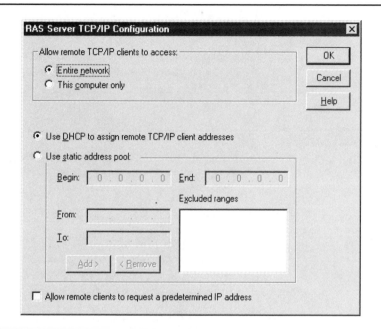

5. In the RAS Server TCP/IP Configuration dialog box, select whether to allow TCP/IP clients to access the entire network or the RAS server only.

6. If a DHCP server is available on your network, select 'Use DHCP to assign remote TCP/IP addresses.' This service dynamically assigns valid TCP/IP addresses to your dial-up clients.

7. If a DHCP server is not available, select Use static address pool. To configure a pool of valid and available addresses for your network, enter the beginning and ending range of TCP/IP addresses that you wish to allocate to your dial-up clients. You must assign at least two addresses. If you assign a large range of addresses, you can reserve some addresses from this list by adding them to the excluded ranges list.

8. If you prefer to have users specify a TCP/IP address in their DUN configuration, select the Allow remote workstations to request a predetermined IP address check box.

9. Click OK.

10. In the Network Configuration dialog box, click OK.

11. In the Remote Access Setup dialog box, complete any additional port configurations and then click Continue. You must restart your server for these changes to take effect.

Configuring a RAS server with IPX/SPX

1. To configure a RAS server to use IPX for network connections, open Control Panel and double-click the Network icon.

2. The network setup screen will appear. On the Services tab, select the Remote Access Service and then click the Properties button.

3. In the Remote Access Setup dialog box, click the Network button.

4. In the Server Settings box, make sure the IPX check box is selected (if IPX is installed) and then click Configure. (See Figure 11-9 for an illustration of the RAS Server IPX Configuration screen.)

5. In the RAS Server IPX Configuration screen, select whether to allow IPX clients to access the entire network or the RAS server only.

FIGURE 11-9

The RAS Server IPX
Configuration screen

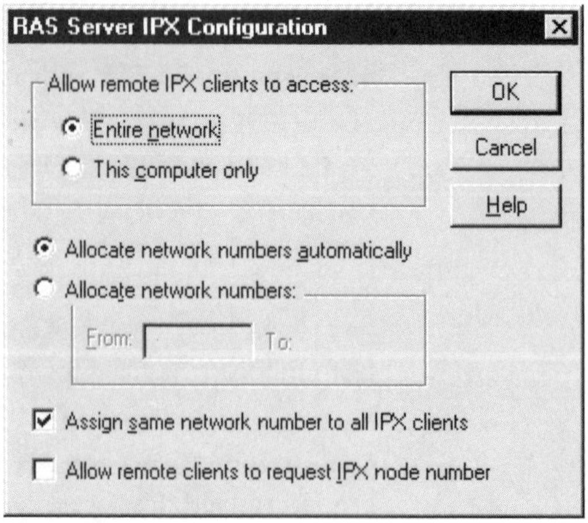

6. Choose 'Allocate network numbers automatically' if you want to allow RAS to use the Router Information Protocol (RIP) to determine an IPX network number that is not in use on your IPX network. If you want more control over IPX network number assignments, choose 'Allocate network numbers' and type your first network number in the From box. RAS will automatically determine the number of available ports and insert the ending network number for you.

7. Select 'Assign same network number to all IPX clients' if you want to assign the same network number to all connected IPX clients.

8. Select the 'Allow remote clients to request IPX node number' check box to allow the remote client to request its own IPX node number in its DUN configuration rather than use the RAS server-supplied node number.

9. Click OK.

10. In the Network Configuration dialog box, click OK. You must restart your server for these changes to take effect.

exam
ⓦatch

Gateway Services For NetWare (GSNW) is a Windows NT Server network service that changes SMB packets to NCP packets so NetWare computers can receive them. Files, print queues, and some NetWare utilities on NetWare servers are then available to all clients, even though they may not be running a NetWare-compatible protocol or client. This applies as well to DUN clients dialing in to a RAS server.

CERTIFICATION OBJECTIVE 11.04

Configuring RAS Security

To connect to a RAS server, clients will always need a valid Windows NT user account and RAS dial-in permission enabled. The integrated Domain security designed into Windows NT, as well as individual RAS user permissions, callback security, data encryption, auditing, support for third-party intermediary security hosts, and PPTP filtering combine to provide additional RAS security and functionality.

Domain Account Database

The single point of logon implementation of Windows NT extends to RAS users. Access to RAS can be granted to all Windows NT user accounts. The ability to use resources throughout the domain and any trusted domains is business as usual after Windows NT authentication occurs. Let's look at a brief scenario. By day, Wendy is connected locally to the network with her laptop via an installed network card and patch cable. By night, she connects with her laptop, by modem, through RAS to the network. In either situation, once she gives her Windows NT username and password, she is granted access to all network services.

Granting RAS Permissions to User Accounts

After installing RAS on your server, you will need to grant RAS permission to your users. To grant RAS permission, you can use either User Manager for Domains or the Remote Access Admin utility. When using the Remote Access Admin utility, permissions are set by choosing the Permissions option from the Users drop-down list. This opens the Remote Access Permissions screen shown in Figure 11-10. When using User Manager for Domains, permissions for RAS are granted or denied by selecting the properties of a user and pressing the Dialin button. This will open the Dialin Information screen for that user, as shown in Figure 11-11). The callback feature can also be configured here.

<table>
<tr><td>EXERCISE 11-8</td></tr>
</table>

Assigning RAS user permissions

1. Start the Remote Access Admin from the Administrative Tools group.
2. Select the Remote Access Server you want to administer.
3. Select Permissions from the Users drop-down list.
4. Enable the checkbox 'Grant Dialin Permision to User' to grant dialin permission for individual users or select the 'Grant All' or 'Revoke All' buttons to grant or remove permissions for all users on the RAS server.
5. Apply any callback security options.
6. Click OK.
7. Exit the Remote Access Admin program.

FIGURE 11-10

The Remote Access
Permissions screen is
opened from within the
Remote Access Admin
program. This screen
allows you to assign users
the permission to use RAS
and configure individual
callback settings.

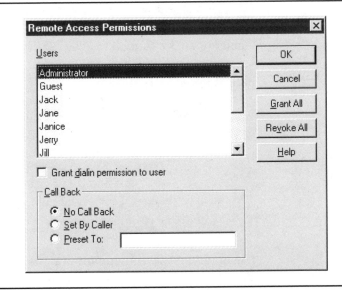

Callback Security

Another security feature implemented within RAS is callback. When a user is
configured to use callback and dials in to a RAS server, the server disconnects

FIGURE 11-11

The Dialin Information
screen is presented when
you select a user in User
Manager for Domains and
select the Dialin button.
You can allow or revoke
the ability for a user to use
RAS and assign individual
callback settings here.

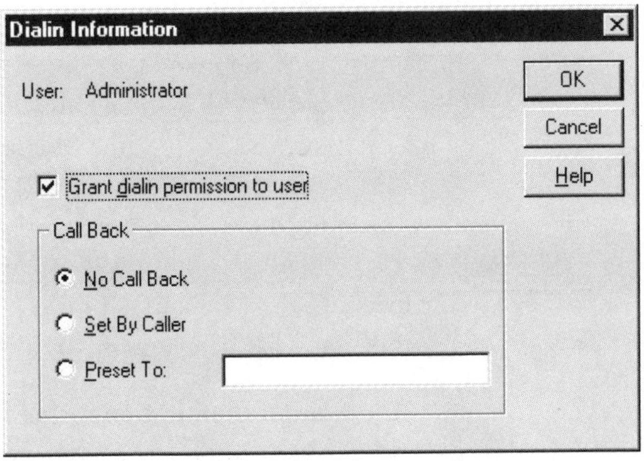

the session, and then calls the client back at a preset telephone number or at a number provided during the initial call. Callback gives you as the administrator the comfort of knowing that successful connections to your RAS server are only coming from trusted sites, such as a users home. There are three options for callback:

- **No call back**   No callback is required for the user.
- **Set by Caller**   The server prompts the user to type in a number at which to be called back.
- **Preset To**   The administrator determines the number where the user will be reached. This type of callback provides an additional level of security by ensuring that the user is calling from a known location.

If a client is Multilink-enabled and they are configured for callback on the RAS server, the call will go to only one of the Multilink devices. The RAS Admin utility allows the administrator to store only one number for callback, so Multilink functionality is lost.

Encrypted Data Authentication and Logons

The Remote Access Service supports a number of methods to encrypt logons and the subsequent connections to your network. Encrypted authentication methods include the simple Password Authentication Protocol (PAP) which permits clear-text passwords and the Shiva Password Authentication Protocol (SPAP) used by Windows NT workstations when connecting to a Shiva LAN Rover. SPAP can also be used by Shiva clients when connecting to a Windows NT RAS server. MS-CHAP is the Microsoft implementation of the Challenge Handshake Authentication Protocol (CHAP) which provides encrypted authentication and can also be configured to provide data encryption. MS-CHAP is used by Microsoft RAS servers and clients to provide the most secure form of encrypted authentication.

The following RAS encryption selections are shown in Figure 11-12:

- **Allow any authentication including clear text**   This option permits users to connect using any authentication method requested by the

FIGURE 11-12

The Network
Configuration screen allows
you to select the dial-in and
dial-out protocols you want
to implement and their
specific settings. Also
configured here are
encryption methods and
Multilink capability.

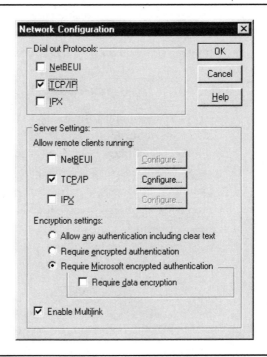

client including MS-CHAP, SPAP, and PAP. It is most commonly
used when you have dial-up clients using non-Microsoft client software.

- **Require encrypted authentication**   This option permits connections
  using any authentication method requested by the client except PAP
  and requires encrypted passwords from all clients.

- **Require Microsoft encrypted authentication**   This option permits
  connections using the MS-CHAP authentication method only.
  Selecting the Require data encryption check box will also ensure that all
  data sent over the wire is encrypted.

Full Audit Capabilities

You will find system, application, and security events recorded in the
Windows NT Event Viewer. As an integrated component of Windows NT,
RAS also makes use of this utility. The Remote Access Service uses Event

Viewer to log hardware malfunctions, service starts and stops, port problems, and failed or successful login attempts by users. All events can be viewed in Event Viewer from anywhere on the network, assuming proper privileges have been granted.

Support of Third-Party Intermediary Security Hosts

RAS can also support the use of a third-party security host machine that intercepts connection attempts between a DUN client or clients and the RAS server—providing yet another layer of security. Microsoft RAS supports a number of third-party intermediary devices (security hosts and switches) including modem-pool switches and security hosts. The US standard for protecting against password discovery is implementation of DES encryption. Another popular standard is MD5. Note, however, that MD5 can only be negotiated by Microsoft DUN clients and not by Microsoft RAS servers.

PPTP Filtering

When using RAS as an Internet gateway for PPTP connectivity, you should enable PPTP Filtering on the network adapter. This will ensure all other protocols on the adapter are disabled. PPTP filtering adds another layer of security for your corporate network, preventing unwanted threats while your RAS server is connected to the Internet. You can use the Network program in Control Panel to enable PPTP filtering.

QUESTIONS AND ANSWERS

What methods can I implement to make my RAS server more secure?	A secure physical facility with a locked door is a basic necessity. You can also implement callback so you can confirm where calls are being made from, monitor Windows NT auditing, apply PPTP filtering if required, and implement a third-party intermediary device if you want more security than RAS itself provides.
If MS-CHAP is the best encryption method available to me in RAS, why wouldn't I always use it?	MS-CHAP is supported by Microsoft Windows clients but is not widely adopted by many other types of clients. Therefore, if you have UNIX hosts on your network or third-party dial-up clients, you will need to select another encryption method for those clients.

Configuring Dial-Up Networking Clients

As noted earlier, DUN is the new terminology for describing RAS client connectivity within Windows NT. The interface for the client side of RAS has changed dramatically to reflect the improvements made in the original Windows 95 DUN program. DUN is comprised of RAS client support, Phonebook entries, and TAPI features such as storing location and Calling Card Information.

TAPI Features of RAS

Communications applications can control functions for data, fax, and voice through the Windows NT Telephony API (TAPI). TAPI allows you to configure your computer with common dialing parameters such as your local area code. TAPI also manages all communication between the computer and the connected telephone network, providing the basic functions of answering and terminating telephone calls. Included in the TAPI specification is the ability to provide features such as hold, conference, and transfer found in most common PBXs (Private Branch Exchanges), ISDN and other telephone systems. TAPI can also store location information, outside line access codes, and Calling Card information. See Figure 11-13 for a preview of the TAPI Dialing Properties screen.

EXERCISE 11-9

Configuring DUN

1. Installing DUN in Windows NT is very similar to the setup in Windows 95. Start by double-clicking the My Computer icon on your desktop.

2. Double-click the DUN icon and press the Install button. (Keep in mind that since Dial Up Networking is a Windows program, there may not be an icon on your desktop. To install it, use the Add/Remove Programs option from the Control Panel and select the Windows setup tab.)

3. If a dialog box returns asking you for Files Needed, insert the Windows NT CD-ROM and click OK.

FIGURE 11-13

The Dialing Properties screen allows you to specify the local area code, Calling Card information, and any additional dialing settings required

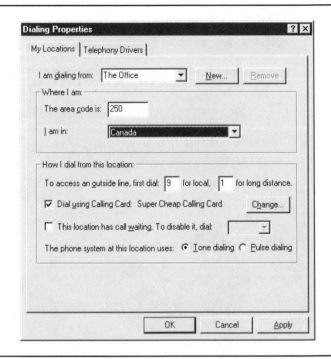

Once DUN has been installed on your system, you will be prompted to configure a new modem (if you haven't already). You will then be prompted to enter your dialing location (for example, The Office) and other TAPI information. After DUN has been installed, you will need to restart your computer for these changes to take effect.

Defining a Phonebook Entry

Phonebook entries store the information required to connect to a remote network. Entries are stored as individual dial-up connections in a phonebook file. To edit existing phonebook entries or to create a new entry, you modify DUN through My Computer or by selecting the DUN icon in the Accessories menu located within the Programs group on the Start menu. The first entry you make in the phonebook initiates the New Phonebook Entry wizard shown in Figure 11-14. Subsequent entries in the phonebook can be made by cloning

The New Phonebook Entry
wizard walks you through a
simple DUN configuration
session

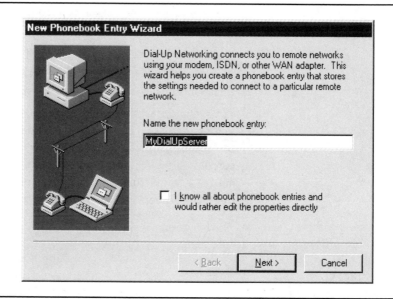

an existing entry and modifying it—or by clicking on the Make New
Connection icon to start the Phonebook Entry wizard again.

Creating a Phonebook entry

1. To create a Phonebook entry in Windows NT, double-click the DUN
   icon in My Computer. DUN returns a message stating that the
   Phonebook is empty.

2. Click OK. The New Phonebook Entry wizard appears.

3. In the 'Name the new Phonebook entry' box, type a descriptive name
   that will identify which dial-up host you are going to be connecting to.
   Click Next.

4. The Server settings dialog box appears. These check boxes will
   pre-configure default server and encryption information if required.
   Make sure all check boxes are cleared and press Next.

5. Enter the phone number of your dial-up server. You can also enter
   alternate phone numbers, if there are any. Alternate numbers will be

tried if you get a busy signal or if communication can't be established at the first number.

6. Select the Use Telephony Dialing Properties if you need to enter an area or country code for this phonebook entry. Select Next.

7. Click Finish to exit the New Phonebook Entry wizard.

8. You will be presented with the DUN screen, pictured in Figure 11-15. With this utility, you can configure additional server information, user preferences, logon preferences, and clone new entries from your current entry. This is the same screen you will see when you want to initiate a connection with DUN to a dial-up server. Click Close to exit the DUN screen.

FIGURE 11-15

The Dial-Up Networking program can be used to create new Phonebook entries, edit and delete existing entries, and initiate a DUN session

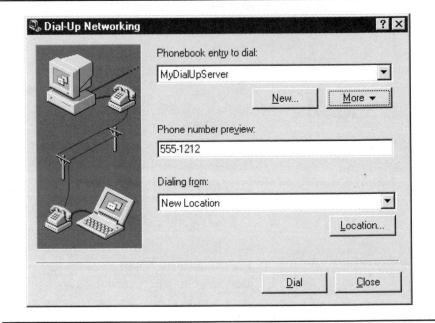

CERTIFICATION OBJECTIVE 11.06

Administering and Troubleshooting RAS

As the administrator of a RAS server, your role will include maintaining strict security of your LAN from potential intruders, maintaining ports and connections, and troubleshooting RAS problems. The Remote Access Admin program can be found in the Administrative Tools Common Group on the Start Menu. The Remote Access Admin program can be used to disconnect attached users; start, stop, and pause the RAS service; monitor port usage; and assign RAS user permissions. Figure 11-16 shows the Remote Access Admin program options.

exam
⚲atch

For specific information on the Remote Access Admin program, open the Help menu item. Specific information for every feature of this program is provided here and is often where Microsoft exam questions come from. Information is specific and to-the-point. Reading the help of all dialogs within Windows NT Server is not a lengthy task and is well worth the time.

FIGURE 11-16

The Remote Access Admin program can be used to monitor port usage, start and stop the RAS service, disconnect users, and assign user permissions

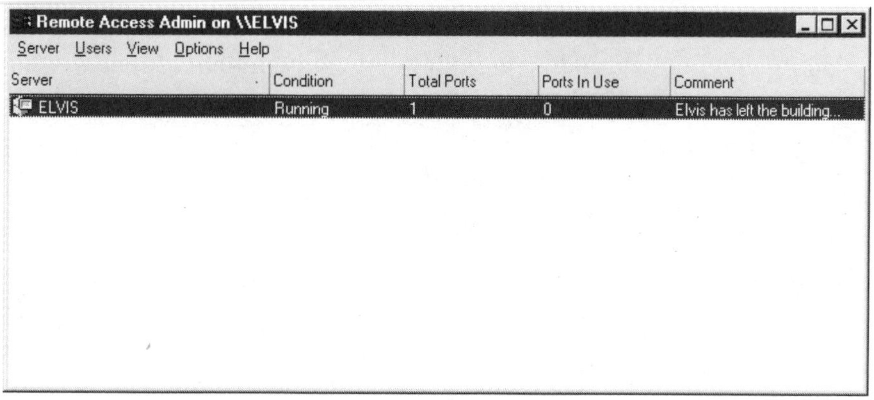

Remote Access Admin on \\ELVIS				
Server Users View Options Help				
Server	Condition	Total Ports	Ports In Use	Comment
ELVIS	Running	1	0	Elvis has left the building...

EXERCISE 11-11

Disconnecting a RAS session

1. Start the Remote Access Admin program.

2. On the Users menu, click Active Users.

3. On the Remote Access Users dialog box, select the account name of the user you want to disconnect.

4. Click Disconnect User.

5. The Disconnect User dialog box displays the account name of the user that will be disconnected when you click OK.

6. You can revoke the user's remote access permission as you disconnect them by selecting the Revoke Remote Access Permission check box.

FROM THE CLASSROOM

Where Are All the RAS Administration Features I really Want?

Many of the features not provided in RAS are available for free for use in your RAS implementations. Get yourself a copy of the Windows NT Server 4.0 Resource Kit CD-ROM. On the CD you will find an installation option that allows you to install Remote Access Manager, by Virtual Motion. Remote Access Manager allows you to perform typical RAS administrative tasks such as displaying RAS server port status, disconnecting RAS sessions for any port, and enabling and disabling RAS privileges for any user. Some of the added features it provides are enhanced security control, enabling you to restrict RAS access based on group memberships, and added control of RAS access based on the time of day. Also, an administrator can limit the number of connections per day, define the maximum amount of time a user can remain connected, and monitor RAS with features such as server and port resource utilization bar graphs, billing reports, and user accounting.

The files required to install Remote Access Manager can be found in the \APPS\RASMGR folder on the Windows NT Server 4.0 Resource Kit CD.

—By Sean Wallbridge, MCT, MCSE

Troubleshooting RAS

Event Viewer

Windows NT Event Viewer can be useful in diagnosing RAS problems. Many RAS events, including service failures and driver problems, are logged in the Event Viewer System Log.

DEVICE.LOG

The DEVICE.LOG file is often used to help determine common RAS problems by maintaining a record of the conversations between RAS and your modems. Setting the value of Logging to 1 in the system registry in the following subtree enables the DEVICE.LOG file:

HKEY_LOCAL_MACHINE\System

   \CurrentControlSet

      \Services

         \RasMan

            \Parameters

Once enabled, the DEVICE.LOG file is created and can be found in the \<winnt_root>\SYSTEM32\RAS directory. The file is flushed anytime a RAS component is restarted and all other RAS components have been stopped.

DUN Monitor

The DUN Monitor program is started by double-clicking the Dial-Up Monitor icon in Control Panel (see Figure 11-17). Duration of calls, the amount of data transmitted and received, and the number of errors that have occurred are all shown in this program. Multilink line utilization can also be observed in Dial-Up Monitor.

exam
ⓦatch

You will find that most questions concerning registry entries and where they should be placed will most likely find their way into the HKEY_LOCAL_MACHINE subtree. HKEY_LOCAL_MACHINE contains configuration information about the local computer system, including hardware and operating system data.

FIGURE 11-17

Dial-Up Monitor shows the
status of your current
DUN session

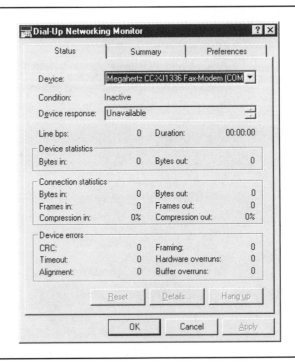

QUESTIONS AND ANSWERS

Is there a way to start or stop RAS from a command prompt?	Yes. RAS is a service and can be started with the NET START function. To start the Remote Access Service, type: **NET START "REMOTE ACCESS SERVER"** To stop the RAS service, type: **NET STOP "REMOTE ACCESS SERVER"**.
What other methods can I use to start and stop the RAS service?	The RAS service can be started and stopped with the Services icon within Control Panel or with the Remote Access Admin program.

CERTIFICATION SUMMARY

DUN and the Remote Access Service comprise the basic components of remote client to LAN communications in the Microsoft networking environment. The RAS client portion of Windows NT is now similar in style to Windows 95 and shares the same DUN name. DUN includes many powerful features, including support for dialing up to SLIP and PPP servers, phonebook entries, support for Windows NT protocols, simplified modem installation, and other communications wizards. Dial-Up Monitor has also been included for easy viewing of communications statistics.

The server side of the Remote Access Service, usually referred to as a RAS server, includes powerful PPP support for dial-up clients. It offers the ability to combine multiple communications devices with Multilink, secure encryption methods including MS-CHAP data encryption, callback security, and remote access administration tools. Also new to Windows NT 4.0 is the implementation of PPTP, which allows for secure communications within an encrypted tunnel allowing for Internet connectivity by clients that use an ISP. PPTP offers an excellent alternative for dial-up clients and administrators, almost eliminating hardware support and long-distance costs by placing connectivity issues in the hands of third-party ISPs.

TWO-MINUTE DRILL

- ❑ Remote Access Services provides computers with wide area network (WAN) inbound and/or outbound connectivity to your server and/or network.

- ❑ DUN allows you to connect to any dial-up server using the Point-to-Point protocol (PPP) as a transport mechanism allowing for TCP/IP, NetBEUI, or IPX/SPX network access.

- ❑ The primary benefit of ISDN is its speed and reliability. ISDN is commonly found in two speeds:64kbps and 128kbps.

- ❑ If WINS or DNS is not available on a network, DUN clients can use HOSTS or LMHOSTS files configured locally for name resolution.

❑ A RAS server can be installed during the installation of Windows NT or at any other time by adding it as a network service.

❑ When choosing an encryption method, always apply the highest level of encryption possible, keeping in mind the encryption capabilities of your clients.

❑ To grant RAS permission, you can use either User Manager for Domains or the Remote Access Admin utility.

❑ Encrypted authentication methods include the simple Password Authentication Protocol (PAP) which permits clear-text passwords and the Shiva Password Authentication Protocol (SPAP) used by Windows NT workstations when connecting to a Shiva LAN Rover.

❑ Communications applications can control functions for data, fax, and voice through the Windows NT Telephony API (TAPI).

❑ TAPI allows you to configure your computer with common dialing parameters such as your local area code.

SELF TEST

The following questions will help you measure your understanding of the material presented in this chapter. Read all the choices carefully, as there may be more than one correct answer. Choose all correct answers for each question.

1. Which of the following configurations are valid using Windows NT RAS?

   A. A Windows 95 SLIP client accessing a Windows NT SLIP server

   B. A Windows NT SLIP client accessing a Windows NT SLIP server

   C. A Windows NT PPP client accessing a Windows NT PPP server

   D. A Windows NT SLIP client accessing a UNIX SLIP server

2. When you select 'Require Microsoft encrypted authentication' what authentication methods are used to achieve connectivity?

   A. SPAP, PAP, and MS-CHAP

   B. MS-CHAP only

   C. MS-CHAP and PAP

   D. SPAP only

3. Users are complaining about the difficulty of connecting to your RAS server. From the information you receive, you determine that the problem may be hardware-related. What actions should you take? (Choose two.)

   A. Enable the DEVICE.LOG file by selecting the 'Enable modem log file'

   checkbox in the Remote Access Admin utility.

   B. Enable the DEVICE.LOG file by making the appropriate entry in the HKEY_CURRENT_CONFIG system registry.

   C. Enable the DEVICE.LOG file by making the appropriate entry in the HKEY_LOCAL_MACHINE system registry.

   D. Analyze the DEVICE.LOG file in the root directory of the system partition.

   E. Analyze the DEVICE.LOG file found in \<winnt_root>\SYSTEM32\RAS.

4. Which of the following files can be modified to add RAS support for a non-supported modem?

   A. RAS.INF

   B. DEVICE.LOG

   C. DEVICE.INF

   D. MODEM.INF

5. When configuring a port for RAS usage, which of the following are true?

   A. A RAS port can be configured so that only dialing in is possible.

   B. A RAS port can be configured so that only dialing out is possible.

   C. A RAS port can be configured so that both dialing in and out are possible.

D. RAS ports cannot be configured. By design all ports are always configured to provide dialing in and dialing out.

E. RAS ports cannot be configured. Only dialing in is possible.

6. Which protocols are supported by RAS?

A. DLC

B. NetBEUI

C. TCP/IP

D. IPX/SPX

E. AppleTalk

7. Which of the following security features are available when using RAS?

A. DES encryption

B. MD5 on the RAS server

C. Callback security

8. You have three Windows NT Servers with the Remote Access Service installed on three different TCP/IP network segments. Windows NT workstations dial into these servers. What method would you use to minimize time required to resolve NetBIOS names?

A. Configure an LMHOSTS file on the RAS server.

B. Configure an LMHOSTS file on each workstation.

C. Disable the NetBIOS interface.

D. Install WINS servers on all workstations.

9. What new option has been added to the Windows NT 4.0 logon dialog box?

A. Start Dial-up Networking

B. Shutdown

C. The option to log on via Dial-Up Networking

D. The option to use Dial-Up Networking without logging on to Windows NT

10. What is true of using PPTP?

A. Short connect time

B. Lower transmission cost

C. Lower speed connections

D. Higher transmission cost

11. With PPTP filtering enabled, which of the following does a Windows NT Server 4.0 RAS accept?

A. Accepts IPX only

B. Accepts PPTP only

C. Accepts SLIP only

D. Does not accept anything

12. Your RAS server has two internal modems. Remote users report that when they try to dial in to the RAS server, they are being disconnected immediately. How can you diagnose this problem?

A. Use the Registry Editor to enable device logging.

B. Use Performance Monitor to view RAS connection details.

C. Use the RAS Admin utility to view the port status.

D. Use Network Monitor.

13. What utilities can you use to grant users permission to log in to your RAS server?

A. User Manager for Domains

B. Remote Access Admin

C. RUSER.EXE

D. DIAL-UP NETWORKING

14. You have a RAS server to which Windows 95 clients dial in. They have Client for Microsoft Networks and IPX/SPX installed. You also have a Netware server from which you want to allow these users to access resources. What should you install on the Windows NT RAS server?

A. CNSW

B. GSNW

C. RIP

D. OSPF

15. You have been providing Multilink remote access ability to your users for the last six months without problems. When your manager insisted that you implement tighter security, you chose to implement callback security. Now users complain about dramatic drop in speed when they connect to RAS? Why is this happening?

A. Callback performs extensive error checking which absorbs lots of bandwidth.

B. Your modems are not supported by callback.

C. The RAS server is only able to call back one of the Multilink devices.

D. RAS does not support callback security.

16. Identify three ways you can manually start and stop RAS.

A. From a command prompt using the Net Start and Net Stop commands

B. In the Network Configuration screen

C. With the Service utility in Control Panel

D. With the Remote Access Admin program

E. With the Network Client Administrator program

17. You want to provide Internet connectivity to your corporate LAN. What should be implemented to help secure your server from Internet-related threats?

A. PPTP filtering

B. SLIP

C. IPX/SPX

D. Callback security

E. Multilink

12

Backup

CERTIFICATION OBJECTIVES

12.01   Backup Strategies

12.02   Windows NT Backup Utility

12.03   Performing Backups and Restorations

12.04   Windows NT Backup and Recovery
         Schemes

12.05   Third-Party Backup and Restore
         Alternatives

Y ou have just had a system failure of a critical Windows NT Server that holds the entire inventory and customer database of the company you work for. What do you do? Is it time to panic and look for a new job? Or is it time to show your boss how smart you were for implementing a sound, reliable backup plan that allows you a quick recovery from this catastrophe? By applying the strategies and techniques presented in this chapter, you should be able to keep your job and even win a compliment or two.

The chapter starts with a discussion of various backup strategies, including media types and storage considerations. Then it presents an in-depth discussion of the Windows NT Backup utility. Normal backups and restorations using Windows NT Backup are considered, as well as some methods for backing up unique data using techniques other than the Backup utility. The last section describes third-party backup alternatives.

CERTIFICATION OBJECTIVE 12.01

Backup Strategies

There are many strategies to consider when creating a backup plan for your organization. In this section we will discuss many of them—starting with single versus multiple backups, then moving to hardware considerations. We'll also look at the kinds of backup schedule that can be used and the different types of backups that are available for your use.

Single vs. Multiple Backups

You need to consider several factors when deciding whether you want to conduct your backups from a single location or have multiple backup locations.

Budget Factor

First, consider the budget you have to work with. Obtaining the hardware required to support multiple backup locations can put a serious dent into an information systems budget if not planned for properly.

Size Factor

The size of the location will also dictate whether you need to use a single, central location or multiple locations. For example, if you have one server and three client machines located in the same building, then it would probably be fine to back them all up from a single location. However, if you had fifty servers located across several different buildings, it would probably be best to have multiple backup locations.

Control Factor

The amount of control needed will also determine whether you choose a single or multiple backup strategy. For example, it is possible that you will have a location, such as the research and development department, that needs to control their own backups to ensure that no confidential information is released inadvertently.

Speed Factor

The speed factor can be critical when backing up data. If you have a bandwidth problem, you may want to consider backing up to multiple locations by keeping the backup traffic segmented to local subnets—thereby alleviating congestion on your backbone.

Completeness Factor

How complete must the backed up information be? This can affect your decision to choose a single or multiple backup strategy. For example, it is possible that you will have a location, such as the accounting department, that needs to make backups every couple of hours while another department—say the clerical department—may only need to make a backup at the end of each work day.

It is important to know when you need to add another tape drive to your network and where it should be located.

Hardware for Backups

Windows NT Server provides support for magnetic tape which is the most common medium used for performing backups. Tape remains popular because it has the ability to store a great capacity of data at a relatively low cost.

Common Media Types

There are a variety of media types available and the data capacity varies with each type. Four of the most common types are listed here.

- **Digital Linear Tape (DLT)**   DLT is the new kid on the block. It has the capability to store 70 gigabytes of data on a single tape. DLT breaks the tradition of other types of tape media by recording and reading multiple channels simultaneously. DLT segments tape media into parallel, horizontal tracks and records data by running the tape past a stationary head. DLT is faster than most other types of tape, achieving transfer rates of up to 5Mbps.

- **Quarter-Inch Cartridge (QIC)**   QIC is the oldest of the tape formats presented here. Capacity can range from 40 megabytes to 5 gigabytes. QIC tapes are among the most popular tapes used for backing up personal computers but rarely used for backing up network servers. QIC tapes are divided into two general classes: full-size and minicartridge. QIC uses sequential access. Sequential access refers to reading or writing data records in sequential order—that is, one record after the other. To read record 24, for example, you would need to wind the tape past records 1–24.

- **Digital Audio Tape (DAT)**   DAT is a high-speed format most commonly seen in the 4mm variety. DAT uses a process called helical scan to record data. A DAT cartridge is slightly larger than a credit card and can hold from 2 to 24 gigabytes of data. It can support data transfer rates of about 2Mbps. Like other types of tapes, DATs are sequential-access media. The most common format for DAT cartridges is digital data storage (DDS).

■ **8mm Cassette** 8mm cassettes can store between 1 gigabyte to 5 gigabytes of data. It uses helical-scan cartridges but requires a relatively expensive tape drive. They also have relatively slow data transfer rates.

Interface Type

The two most common interface types you will encounter in a tape drive are *Integrated Drive Electronics* (IDE) and *Small Computer Systems Interface* (SCSI). IDE is mainly used in the slower and lower-capacity QIC-style tape drives while you will find SCSI in the high-capacity, high-performance DAT and DLT drives. The main reason for this is the SCSI's higher operating speed. A secondary reason for using SCSI is the fact that more devices can be placed on the SCSI bus than on the IDE bus.

exam
ⓦatch

Make sure you know the procedure for adding a tape drive to your system.

Selection and Purchasing

When deciding which tape drive hardware you need to purchase, check the latest Windows NT Server Hardware Compatibility List (HCL) to make sure the drive you are considering is listed. If not, make sure that third-party drivers are available for Windows NT Server 4.0.

Backup Software

There are several factors that need to be considered with respect to the software you may be considering. Depending on your situation, some of the following factors may weigh more heavily in your decision than others.

■ **Network Enabled** Does the software have the capability to back up only the server it resides on or can it back up other network drives? Depending on your needs, this may or may not be critical, especially when deciding on a single or multiple backup locations.

■ **Automation and Scheduling**   Does the software have the capability to schedule the time a backup will occur, such as at midnight each night when usage is at a minimum? If the software does not have this capability, it could ruin your night if you had to go in to manually start a backup at midnight.

■ **Individual Element Selection or Exclusion**   Does the software have the capability to include or exclude individual items or must you do a complete backup of your entire hard drive? This could be a very time-consuming process if you needed to only back up an individual 62 kilobyte file but had to wait for the entire 4 gigabyte drive to be backed up.

■ **Report, Progress, History, and Status Logs**   Do you need detailed logs that reflect the progress or history of backups? Some backup software may not include any of these features.

■ **Error Correction and Data Verification**   How important is it to you that the data you are backing up has its integrity verified by the backup software? If you perform a backup and do not verify that it is good then you may be in for a rude surprise if you ever need to use the backup tape.

■ **Security Measures**   What type of security measures does the software provide? Is it possible that anyone getting the tape can recover data from it easily?

■ **Restoration Options and Requirements**   When you restore from tape can you restore a single file or directory or are you forced to restore the entire archive?

Backup Schedule

Now that you have decided what media to use and have picked out the backup software that meets your needs, you have another question to answer. What kind of schedule should you use to perform your backups? There are two factors to consider in determining your backup schedule.

■ **How often**   The frequency at which you create the backups depends on how much the data changes and how valuable the data is to you.

■ **Time of day**   The time of day can also be determined by how much data changes and how valuable the changing data is to you. Normally you should try to do your backups at a point in time when it will cause minimal interruption on your network and also when bandwidth does not need to be considered. Midnight is often used, because few files are being used. If people using the network had files open, the backup tape might not reflect the true status of the network.

Backup Types

There are five backup types available for you to use. Your situation will help determine which type or types are most suitable. You may find that your backup plan uses a combination of the different types.

Normal
Another name for the normal backup is a full backup. A full backup copies all selected files and marks each as having been backed up. Files can be restored quickly from a normal backup because the most current files are on the last tape.

Incremental
An incremental backup will back up only those files created or changed since you performed the last normal or incremental backup. The incremental backup will mark files as having been backed up. If you use a combination of normal and incremental backups, you must start with your last normal backup and then working through all the incremental tapes when you restore.

Differential
A differential backup copies files that have been created or changed since the last normal or incremental backup. The differential backup does not mark files as having been backed up. If you are doing normal and differential backups, restoring requires only the last normal and last differential backup tape. If you perform two differential backups in a row, the files backed up during the first backup will be backed up again, even if they have not changed. This is because files are not marked as having been backed up.

Copy

Using a copy backup copies all the files you select but it will not mark each file as having been backed up. This can be useful if you want to back up files between normal and incremental backups; copying will not alter any setting that would invalidate these other backup operations.

Daily

A daily backup copies all (specified) files that have been modified during the day you perform the daily backup. The backed up files will not be marked as having been backed up. While this may not sound especially useful, it can be helpful if you want to take work home and need a quick way to select all the files that you worked on that day.

Of the five backup types, the most commonly used are normal, incremental, and differential. Table 12-1 shows you some of the advantages and disadvantages of each of these three common backup types.

TABLE 12-1   Advantages and Disadvantages of Common Backup Types

Backup Type	Advantage	Disadvantage
Normal	You can easily find files because they are always on the current backup of your system. Only one tape set is required for recovery.	Backups are redundant if files do not change very often. Most time-consuming backup type.
Incremental	The least time-consuming backup type. Uses the least amount of data storage space.	It can be difficult to locate a file because it could be located across several different tapes.
Differential	Uses less time than a normal backup does. Only the last normal backup tape and the last differential tape are required for recovery. Also, it is quicker than an incremental backup.	Recovery takes longer than a normal backup if files were located only on a single tape. If data changes frequently, then backups can take more time than an incremental.

Media Rotation

It does not take hundreds of tapes to keep a good backup of your system. By using a sound media rotation plan you can get maximum benefit from only a few tapes.

- **Reuse of tapes** With proper planning you can reuse tapes over and over again without having to constantly purchase new tapes. Of course, the life cycle of a tape will depend on the manufacturer of the tape and the conditions in which the tape is stored.

- **Reduction of media costs** By alternating backup tapes you lower the total backup cost. It is possible to use only 19 tapes over the course of one year of backups as shown in Figure 12-1.

FIGURE 12-1

A typical one-year backup plan using media rotation

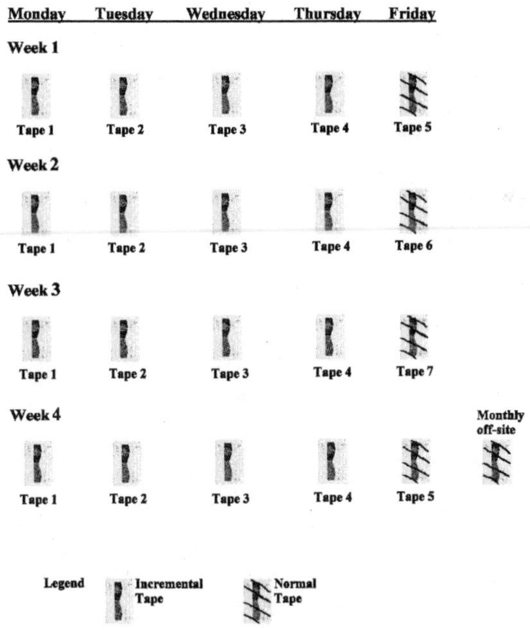

In Figure 12-1, four tapes are used Monday through Thursday for incremental backups, and three tapes are used for weekly normal backups which are performed each Friday. The remaining 12 tapes are used for monthly normal backups and are stored off-site. We will discuss off-site storage in the next section. There are many other ways for you to use media rotation. This is only one example.

Storage

Now that you have seen how to put a good media rotation plan in use, let's discuss how and where you should store the tapes created from your backups.

Off-site

You must find an off-site location for storage of backup tapes. This way, if something causes your building to catch fire or otherwise become unusable you can at least be reassured that your data can be recovered. The location can be a vault, a safe deposit box at a local bank or a fireproof safe at home. If you decide to use a fireproof safe, make sure it is specifically designed to protect magnetic media.

Protection from Hazards

No matter which off-site area you choose for storage of your tapes, make sure that it can protect the tapes from fire, water, theft, and other hazards. You can increase the life of your tapes by storing them in cool, humidity-controlled locations. Your storage area should also be free of magnetic fields, such as those found near telephones and the back of computer monitors.

Additional Backup Protection

Additional backup protection is provided by verification, multiple complete sets, and document backups.

Verification

A *verify* operation is used to compare files on the hard disk to files that have been backed up to tape. It occurs after all the files are backed up and will take about as long as the backup procedure itself. You should perform a verify operation after every backup, even though it extends the overall time of the backup. It is better to spend some extra time now, when you can afford to, than to find out that your latest backup does not function when you really need it. Remember the scenario presented at the beginning of this chapter. If you try to restore from tapes that were not verified, there is a chance they may not work; now it *is* time to start looking for another job! It is also advisable to perform verification after a file recovery—to make sure that everything recovered properly.

If a file verification fails, check to see when that file was modified last. The verify procedure will fail if someone has changed a file between a backup and the verify operation. Log files are one area where this will happen.

Multiple Complete Sets

Normally you should keep three complete copies to protect against tape failure or loss. If you implement the one-year media rotation plan described earlier, you will always have three complete copies of your data.

Documenting Backups

In order to find information on your backup tapes quickly, it is essential that you accurately maintain backup records, especially if you have collected a large number of tapes. Your records should include tape labels, which can be accompanied by a log book, catalogs, or log files.

The following information needs to be included on the tape labels: the date of the backup, what type of backup is on the tape (normal, incremental, or differential), and information about the contents of the tape. It is very important that you indicate the type of backup used for the tape; if you are restoring from differential or incremental backup tape, you will have to locate the last normal backup tape and either the last differential tape or all incremental tapes created since the last normal backup. Another method you can use is to label tapes sequentially and keep a log book of tape contents.

The majority of backup software packages include a tool for cataloging files that it has backed up. Catalogs are created within the backup application for each backup set and normally they cannot be printed or saved to disk.

Along with the backup software catalog, information about the backup can be logged to a text file. The log file can include the names of all files and directories that have successfully been backed up or restored.

CERTIFICATION OBJECTIVE 12.02

Windows NT Backup Utility

Windows NT comes with its own utility to perform backups of your system. The Backup program provides a convenient GUI you can use to back up and restore local and remote disk drives—including the Registry of the local machine. This section surveys what the Windows NT Backup utility has to offer you. Figure 12-2 shows the Drives window of the Backup program.

FIGURE 12-2

The Drives window of the Windows NT Backup utility

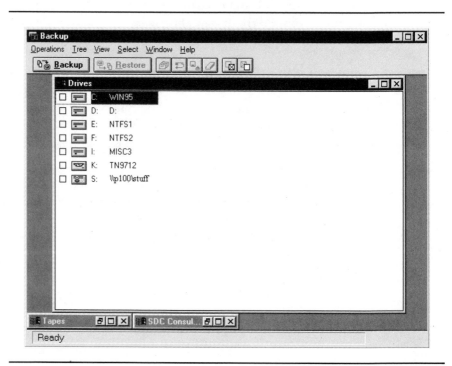

Hardware for Windows NT Backup

Windows NT Server automatically checks for a tape drive when it starts and it will initialize the hardware each time you start Backup. The tape drive must be hooked to the system you are running Backup from and the tape drive must be turned on before starting Windows NT Server to ensure the drivers load properly. If you have not configured a tape drive for your system prior to starting Backup you will see the screen illustrated in Figure 12-3.

If you receive this error, you need to make sure that the drive is connected properly, power for the drive is on, and that the correct tape device driver has been installed.

Currently Windows NT Server supports high-capacity SCSI tape drives such as 4mm DAT, 8mm cassette, and QIC and also the lower capacity minicartridge drives.

FIGURE 12-3

Tape drive error detected
dialog box

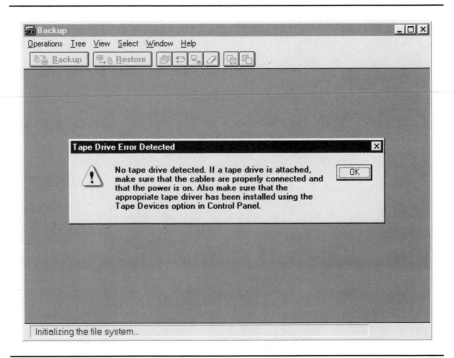

If you try using a higher-density tape than what the tape drive can use, you may receive the message "Tape Drive Error Detected" which will prevent the tape from being ejected until you close the Backup program.

Back Up NTFS or FAT Partitions

Windows NT Backup allows you to back up either NTFS or FAT partitions. It also allows you to back up information from one file system and restore it to another file system. For example, you could back up NTFS files to tape and restore them to a FAT file system. Of course, all file and directory security would be lost, because FAT does not support file permissions.

Permissions to Perform a Backup

Unless specific user rights have been granted, the only files and directories that can be backed up using the Backup utility are those that a user normally has access to. Any user or group of users that has been given the right to *Backup Files and Directories* will be able to circumvent the security provided by normal file permissions when backing up those files and directories. The right to *Restore Files and Directories* allows a user or group of users to disregard normal file permission problems and overwrite files when restoring files and directories. Although backup and restore rights are independent of each other, it is recommended that you grant backup rights along with the restore rights. Be very careful when you grant restore rights because normal file permissions are ignored during restoration. Existing files can be overwritten, with disastrous results!

If users have not been granted specific rights, they cannot back up or restore files and directories that they do not have access to unless they are a member of the Administrators or Backup Operators group. The Administrators and Backup Operators groups are granted these rights by default. It is normal to put users who will be conducting regular backups into the Backup Operators group since the group already has the proper user rights.

Selecting Files for Backup

By drilling down through the directory structure you can get very granular when selecting the files that you need to back up. Figure 12-4 shows that the E: drive has been drilled down to the WINNT directory. WINNT and all subdirectories have been tagged to be backed up, but nothing else on the E: drive has been selected.

It is easy to tell whether the whole drive has been marked to be backed up or if only portions of the drive has been marked as shown in Figure 12-5. If portions of the drive have been marked, the box will show an X and be grayed out, or ghosted, like the E: drive. If the entire drive is to be backed up, the box will only contain an X as shown by drive F:.

FIGURE 12-4

Selecting files to be backed up with the Backup utility

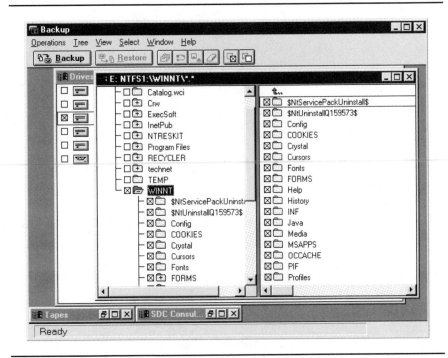

FIGURE 12-5

Drive windows showing a
partial drive and full drive
backup

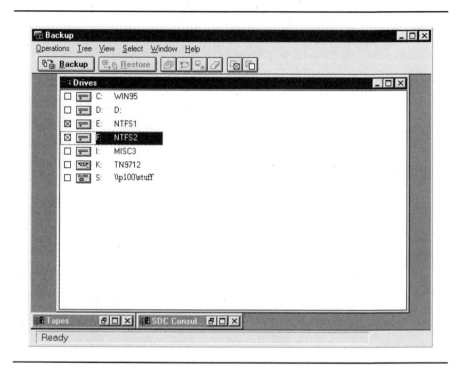

Review Full Catalog of Backup

After inserting a tape to be restored, only information for the complete backup
set will appear in the Tapes window as shown in Figure 12-6. If you do not
want to restore the entire tape, you will need to load the catalog from the tape
to show a list of any other backup sets and files. This can be accomplished by
selecting the set from the tape whose catalog you want to load from the Tapes
window and double-clicking the set's icon. Figure 12-7 shows the catalog of a
recent backup.

Span Multiple Tapes

Depending on the size of your backup media and the amount of data that
must be backed up, you may need to use several tapes in order to successfully

FIGURE 12-6

Tapes window from
Windows NT Backup

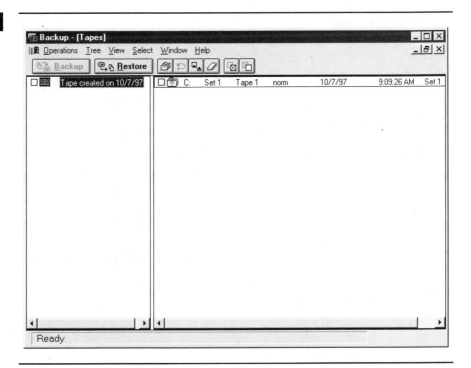

complete the backup. Luckily this is not a problem. It is possible to span
multiple tapes with the Backup utility because there is no file-size restriction.

Control Restoration Destination

It is possible to control the destination that files will be restored to by
specifying a different directory location instead of the original directory. One
of the reasons that you may want to do this is to compare the restored files to
the original files already on the disk drive.

Verification and Logging

The Windows NT Backup utility has the capability to perform verification of
the backups and restores it accomplishes to ensure the integrity of your data. It
is highly recommended that you verify every backup that you perform.

Catalog from a recent tape backup

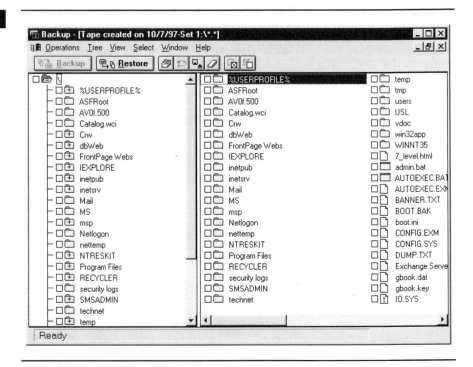

Logging is also possible within the Backup utility and the level of logging you need to use is dependent on your situation. The various levels of logging are discussed later in this chapter.

Files Not Backed Up with the Backup Utility

There are some files that are not backed up automatically by the Windows NT Backup utility for a variety of reasons. The following is a list of files that will not be backed up:

- **Files that the user does not have permission to read** As discussed earlier, only users with the Backup Files and Directories user right can copy files they do not own.

- **Paging file** The PAGEFILE.SYS file is a temporary file that is used to represent virtual address space and is only a temporary holding space for data in use or recently in use.

- **Registries on remote computers** Windows NT Backup can only back up the Registry on the local machine.

- **Any file that has been exclusively locked by application software** Windows NT Backup cannot copy files locked by application software. However, if Windows NT Backup encounters a file that has been opened in share/read mode, it will back up the last saved version of the file.

Files Not Restored with the Backup Utility

Windows NT Backup will restore all files automatically except for the following:

- Files on tape that are older than files that are on the disk drive. The Backup utility will ask you to confirm replacement if this situation occurs.

- If you try to restore a file into an area to which you do not have access. Of course, this condition will not apply if you have restore rights to the area.

NT Backup Options

In this section we will look at specific options available to you while using the Windows NT Backup utility. After you select files or drives to back up and click the Backup button, the Backup Information window opens, as shown in Figures 12-8 and 12-9. You can refer to these figures to locate the options as they are discussed.

Backup Set Information

The Backup Set Information is located in the middle of the Backup Information window. Some information cannot be changed at this point:

Backup information for a
local disk drive

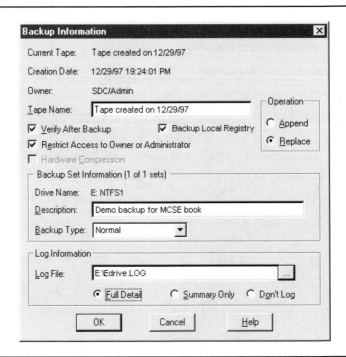

for example, the number of the set being backed up and the drive name
that is being backed up. Other information can be changed: for example, the
description for the backup set and the type of backup to conduct.

Backup Type

The Backup Type option allows you to choose whether you are going to create
a normal, incremental, differential, daily, or copy. The options are available in
a drop-down box located in the Backup Set Information section of the Backup
Information window. The advantages and disadvantages of the different
backup types were discussed earlier.

Tape Name

If the tape was previously used for a backup, the existing name will be in the
Tape Name section. If it is a new tape, it will be blank. You can use up to 32
characters to name the tape. The default tape name is the current date.

FIGURE 12-9

Backup information for a
remote disk drive

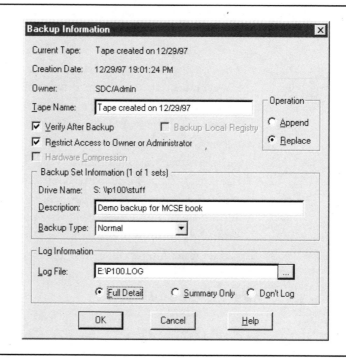

Append or Replace

The Append or Replace radio buttons are located on the right side of the
Backup Information window situated under the Operation heading.

Selecting the Append radio button causes Backup to add the backup set(s)
to the end of the last backup set on the tape that is in the tape drive. Two
options will not be available if you select the Append radio button: the Tape
Name and Restrict Access to Owner or Administrator.

Selecting the Replace radio button causes Backup to overwrite all the
information on the current tape. Before the information is overwritten, you will
have a chance to confirm the choice. If you do not confirm the choice, you receive
another message that gives you the choice of appending to the tape instead.

Verify After Backup

Verify After Backup gives you the opportunity to specify whether or not to
perform a verification comparison of the files that are written to tape and the

files on the disk drive after the backup has completed. This will almost double the time it takes for your backup to complete, but it is time well spent. I cannot emphasize enough the value of performing a verification. One time I did not verify a backup that I had done because I was in a hurry to leave for the weekend. As fate had it, the drive crashed and I got called in Sunday night to fix it. I thought it would be a quick matter since I had just done the normal backup on Friday. Most of the backup went without a hitch but two files would not restore from the tape correctly. They were .DLL files for an application that controlled billing cycles. Luckily, the files were available on the original CD-ROM disc; after some tense moments spent trying to locate the disc, the files were easily recovered. However, the incident pointed up the value of doing a verification of the data on backup tapes. What if the corrupted data had been part of the Registry, such as the directory service database? One thing is clear: no one wants to be in that situation!

Back Up Local Registry

If you are backing up from a local drive that contains the Registry, you can include a copy of it in the backup set. Keep in mind that this option is only available if the drive containing the Registry is selected for backup. Windows NT Backup will not back up the Registry or Event Logs located on remote systems. If it is possible for you to back up the Registry then Backup Local Registry on the Backup Information window will not be ghosted as shown in Figure 12-8. If you are backing up a disk drive on a remote computer, the Backup Local Registry will be ghosted as shown in Figure 12-9.

exam
ⓦatch
Windows NT Backup can be used to back up the Registry which includes security settings and user account information while the system is running.

Restrict Access to Owner or Administrator

It is possible for you to provide some security for the backup tapes you create by choosing the Restrict Access to Owner or Administrator option. If this option has a check mark in the box, only the tape owner or a member of the Administrators or Backup Operators group can read, write, or erase the tape using the Backup utility. If the tape owner needs to restore it to another system in the same domain, they must be logged on with the same user account name. The exception to this rule is that members of the Administrators or Backup Operators group can read, write, or erase a tape on any computer in any domain.

Although this option does provide access security, you still need to keep the tape physically secure. If a normal user on your domain can get access to one of your backup tapes, it is possible for them to take it home, for example, where they might be running Windows NT Server. If they are running Windows NT Server at home, you can be sure that they belong to the Administrators group there! That means they can recover information such as the user accounts database from your tape. Then they could try to crack other users' passwords, including the Administrator's account or equivalent, at their leisure.

Hardware Compression

If the tape drive that you use to conduct your backups supports hardware compression, this option will not be ghosted. As shown in Figure 12-7, the choice was ghosted because the tape drive used to conduct that backup did not support hardware compression. Enabling hardware compression will cause the tape drive to compress the data onto the tape media, which can nearly double the amount of data you can store on each tape. However, you don't want to select this option if the remotest possibility exists that you will need to move the tape to another tape drive that does not support hardware compression. Even if you move it to another brand of drive that does support compression, you could receive an error message. Some of the messages you may see are "Tape Drive Error Detected," "Tape Drive Not Responding," or "Bad Tape."

Log Options

The lower section of the Backup Information window is dedicated to Log Information. A log file of backup operations can be generated to capture the operations that take place during the backup. The log file is stored as a normal text file that can be read with your favorite text editor such as Notepad. There are three options, depending on the level of activity that will be written to the log file.

- **Full Detail**   If you choose this option, information for *all* operations, including the names of all the files and directories that are backed up will be written to the log file.

- **Summary Only**   If you choose this option, only the major operations, such as loading a tape, starting backup, and failing to open a file will be written to the log file.

- **Don't Log**   If you choose this option, no information will be written to the log file.

NT Restore Options

In this section we will look at specific options available to you while using the Windows NT Backup utility. After selecting the files or drives to restore and clicking the Restore button the Restore Information window will appear as shown in Figure 12-10. You can refer to this figure to locate the options as they are discussed.

The first section provides information about the backup sets on the loaded tape and indicates the number of tapes in that set. As seen in Figure 12-9 the data is the same as the information used during the backup shown in Figure 12-7 from the previous section.

Restore to Drive

You must specify the drive to which you want the information restored. Normally this will be the same drive from which the information was backed up.

Alternate Path

It is also possible to specify an alternate directory path to place the files into that is different than the original location that they were backed up from. You might do this if you want to compare the backed up files to the files on the disk drive. You can use the ellipsis button at the end of the Alternate Path dialog box to help you locate the path you want to use.

FIGURE 12-10

Windows NT Backup
utility Restore Information
window

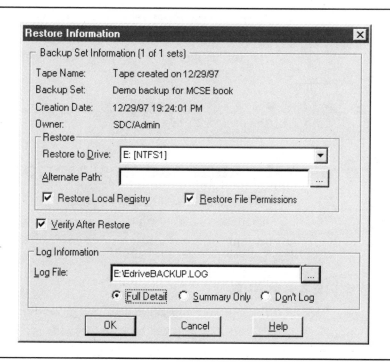

Restore Local Registry

If you need to restore Registry files, select the Restore Local Registry box.
Restart the system to make sure that the restored registry information takes
effect. If you have made any configuration changes since the last Registry
backup then they will be lost.

Restore File Permissions

If you are restoring to a NTFS partition and want the system to restore the
security information along with the files, you need to select the Restore File
Permissions box. If this box is not selected and you restore to an NTFS
partition, the files will inherit the security permissions of the directory into
which they were restored. Remember that to restore security permissions, you
have to originally back the files up from an NTFS partition.

Verify After Restore

If you need to compare the contents of the restored files against the files on tape, you need to select the Verify After Restore box.

Performing Backups and Restorations

In this section you'll have an opportunity to perform a backup and restoration of your system. You will also be introduced to a method of automating your backups.

Performing a Backup

You'll be able to practice performing two different backups in this section. In Exercise 12-1 you will back up the entire partition and in Exercise 12-2 you will back up a directory of data.

EXERCISE 12-1

Backing Up a Partition

1. Make sure your tape drive has power and that a writeable tape has been inserted into the tape drive.

2. Log on to your system as Administrator.

3. Click the Start button and select Programs | Administrative Tools | Backup.

4. Maximize the Drives window, if it is not already maximized. Click on the box next to your C: drive.

5. Click the Backup button.

6. Select the Replace radio button.

7. Place a check mark in the boxes to the left of Verify After Backup, Restrict Access to Owner or Administrator, and Backup Local Registry.

8. Select Normal as the Backup Type.

9. Name the log file as C:\CNORMAL.LOG and click the full Detail radio button.

10. Click OK.

Now sit back and relax as your C: drive is backed up and verified. After the backup has completed, you may want to examine the log file that was created as CNORMAL.LOG in the root of your C: drive.

Next, imagine that you only needed to back up a single directory structure and not the entire disk drive. For example, you might want to do this prior to performing an upgrade that would modify files in that directory structure. Exercise 12-2 leads you through this procedure.

EXERCISE 12-2

Backing Up Data with NT Backup

1. Make sure your tape drive has power and that a writeable tape has been inserted into the tape drive. Be sure to use a different tape than the one used for Exercise 12-1.

2. Log on to your system as Administrator.

3. Click the Start button and select Programs | Administrative Tools | Backup.

4. Maximize the Drives window, if it is not already maximized. Double-click the C: drive icon. A directory layout of the drive will display. Scroll down until you see the directory named WINNT. Place an X in the box to the left of WINNT. This marks the entire WINNT directory structure, including all subdirectories, to be backed up. Click the X in the upper-right corner of the dialog box to return back to the Drives window. You can see that the C: drive now has an X in the box but that it has a gray background. This signifies that only a portion of the drive has been selected to be backed up.

5. Click the Backup button.

6. Select the Replace radio button.

7. Place a check mark in the boxes to the left of Verify After Backup, Restrict Access to Owner or Administrator, and Backup Local Registry.

8. Select Normal as the Backup Type.

9. Name the log file as C:\WINNTBACKUP.LOG and click the Full Detail radio button.

10. Click OK.

Notice that this backup is much quicker than the backup conducted in Exercise 12-1. Sometimes you may only need to back up a single directory depending upon your needs.

Restoring Data from Backups

Now that you have two verified backups, practice restoring them to your system by performing Exercises 12-3 and 12-4.

You discovered that when you installed a new application it overwrote everything in your WINNT\SYSTEM32\REPL directory. To fix this problem, perform Exercise 12-3 which allows you to restore only a portion of the directory of data that you backed up in Exercise 12-2.

EXERCISE 12-3

Restoring Data with NT Backup

1. Make sure your tape drive has power and that the tape you used for Exercise 12-2 has been inserted into the tape drive.

2. Log on to your system as Administrator.

3. Click the Start button and select Programs | Administrative Tools | Backup.

4. Maximize the Tapes window if it is not already maximized. Double-click the tape icon that is displayed. Double-click the SYSTEM32 directory and place an X in the box to the left of Repl. This selects it to be restored. Click the X in the upper-right corner of the dialog box to return back to the Tapes window.

5. Click the Restore button.

6. Place a check mark in the boxes to the left of Restore File Permissions and Verify After Restore.

7. Name the log file as C:\REPLRESTORE.LOG and click the Full Detail radio button.

8. Click the OK button.

After the restore operation completes, you will have the same WINNT\
SYSTEM32\REPL directory that you had when you made the backup tape.

You've been having all sorts of problems today. Now you discover that your
C: drive is full of corrupted data. By performing Exercise 12-4, you will fix the
problem. by restoring the entire partition that you backed up in Exercise 12-1,

EXERCISE 12-4

Restoring a Backed-up Partition

1. Make sure your tape drive has power and that the tape you used for
   Exercise 12-1 has been inserted into the tape drive.

2. Log on to your system as Administrator.

3. Click the Start button and select Programs | Administrative Tools |
   Backup.

4. Maximize the Tapes window if it is not already maximized and click and
   place an X to the left of the tape icon that is displayed.

5. Click the Restore button.

6. Place a check mark in the boxes to the left of Restore Local Registry,
   Restore File Permissions, and Verify After Restore.

7. Name the log file C:\CRESTORE.LOG and click the Full Detail
   radio button.

8. Click OK.

These two exercises gave you practice for the inevitable day when you will
need to complete a restoration operation.

Automating Backups

While performing a backup is not an overly complex task it can get very
boring when you must do it on a daily basis. Luckily there is a way for you to
automate the process. You cannot use the GUI to automate backups; instead,
you must run NTBACKUP.EXE from a command file. In this section you

will discover how to automate your backups using the Schedule service, NTBACKUP.EXE, a .CMD file, and the AT command.

Using Schedule Service

The Schedule service must be running in order to use the AT command discussed in this section. Exercise 12-5 shows you how to start the Schedule service, if it is not already running on your system.

Starting the Schedule Service

1. Log on to your system as Administrator.

2. Click the Start button and select Settings | Control Panel | Services.

3. Highlight Schedule and click the Start button.

4. If you plan to use automated backups all the time and the Schedule service is not set to start automatically, click the Startup button and under Startup Type select Automatic. If you don't want the Schedule service to start automatically, skip to step 5.

5. Click the Close button.

6. Log off the system.

Creating a .CMD File

Now that you have the Schedule service running, the next to complete is the creation of the command file. NTBACKUP.EXE has many command line switches that can be used in the command file. The syntax for the NTBACKUP command is:

```
ntbackup operation path [/a][/v][/r][/d "text"][/b][/hc:{on
| off}] [/t {option}][/l "filename"][/e][/tape:{n
```

Table 12-2 defines the purpose of the different parameters that can be used by NTBACKUP.EXE.

Using the parameters described in Table 12-2, you can create a command line that can be placed in a .CMD file using your favorite text editor. An example is:

TABLE 12-2

Parameters for
NTBACKUP.EXE

Parameter	Purpose
operation	Specifies the operation to perform; *backup* or *eject*.
Path	Specifies one or more paths to the directories to be backed up.
/a	Causes backup sets to be added or appended after the last backup set that is on the tape. If the /a is not specified, NTBACKUP will overwrite all existing data. If more than one drive is specified but /a has not been used, NTBACKUP overwrites the contents of the tape with data from the first drive selected and appends the backup of the remaining drives.
/v	Performs a verification of the backup.
/r	Restricts access. However, /r will be ignored if /a has also been specified.
/d "text"	Specifies a description of the backup.
/b	Specifies that the local Registry be backed up.
/hc:on /hc:off	Indicates whether hardware compression is turned on or off.
/t {option}	Specifies what type of backup will be performed. The valid options are *normal, incremental, differential, copy,* and *daily*.
/l "filename"	Specifies the name of the backup log file.
/e	Specifies that the backup log file include exceptions only.
/tape:{n}	Specifies the tape drive to which the files will be backed up to. {n} is a number from 0–9 that equals the number the tape drive was given when the tape drive was initially installed.

```
ntbackup backup C: D: E: /t Normal /v /r /d "Full Backup of
drives C, D, and E" /b /l C:\LOG\CDEFULL.LOG"
```

From the previous example you can conclude:

■ All files on the C: D: and E: drives will be backed up using the Normal option.

- If any files exist on the tape they will be overwritten.

- Verification will be completed after the backup.

- Access will be restricted to the owner or an administrator.

- One backup is created, which will contain all three drives and have the label of "Full Backup of drives C, D, and E."

- The local Registry will be backed up.

- All backup information will be logged to the file CDEFULL.LOG located in the C:\LOG directory.

Launching the Automated Execution of .CMD

Now that you are familiar with how to create a .CMD file, let's find out how to automate the use of the file. This is where the AT command comes into the picture. The AT command schedules commands and programs to run on a computer at a specified date and time. The syntax for the AT command is:

```
AT [\\computername] [ [id] [/DELETE] | /DELETE [/YES]]
```

or

```
AT [\\computername] time [/INTERACTIVE] [ /EVERY:date[,...]
| /NEXT:date[,...]] "command"
```

The second syntax is the one you need to use for automating backups. Table 12-3 explains the parameters that are available using the AT command.

Using the parameters described in Table 12-3, you can create an AT command that will execute a .CMD file An example is:

```
AT 23:59 /every:M,W,F BACKMEUP.CMD
```

From the previous example you can conclude that every Monday, Wednesday, and Friday at 23:59 the contents of the BACKMEUP.CMD file will execute.

There is one caveat to be wary of when using the AT command. If you use it without the interactive parameter and it encounters an error when running the Windows NT Backup utility (for example, if there is no tape in the tape drive), then the Backup utility stops responding. You will not be able to run

TABLE 12-3

Parameters for the
AT Command

Parameter	Purpose
\\computername	Specifies a remote computer. Commands are scheduled on the local computer if this parameter is omitted.
Time	Specifies the military time when command is to run.
/INTERACTIVE	Allows the job to interact with the desktop of the user who is logged on at the time the job runs.
/EVERY:date[,...]	Runs the command on each specified day(s) of the week or month. If date is omitted, the current day of the month is assumed.
/NEXT:date[,...]	Runs the specified command on the next occurrence of the day (for example, next Thursday). If date is omitted, the current day of the month is assumed.
"command"	Is the Windows NT command, or batch program to be run.
ID	Is an identification number assigned to a scheduled command.
/DELETE	Cancels a scheduled command. If ID is omitted, all the scheduled commands on the computer are canceled.
/YES	Used with CANCEL ALL JOBS command when no further confirmation is desired.
Note that you can also use numeric values for the /Every and /Next switches.	

Windows NT Backup again until you reboot your Windows NT Server. To prevent this situation from occurring you should use the interactive parameter. If any errors occur, you will be able to correct them and continue or quit the Backup utility.

Now that you have all the pieces it takes to automate a backup, let's practice. Exercise 12-6 shows you how to automate the backup process.

EXERCISE 12-6

Automating a Backup

1. Log on to your system as Administrator.

2. Click the Start button and select Settings | Control Panel | Services and make sure the Schedule service is running. If it isn't, perform Exercise 12-5.

3. Open your favorite text editor and add the following line: **ntbackup backup c: /v /r /t Normal /d "My Automated Full Backup of the C: Drive" /b /l "C:\Cfullbackup.log".** Save the file as C:\CFULL.CMD.

4. Click the Start button and select Settings | Programs | Command Prompt.

5. Type the following AT command into the Command Prompt: **AT 0100 /INTERACTIVE /every:m,f C:\Cfull.CMD.** Your system will now be backed up automatically every Monday and Friday at 0100 if there is a tape in the tape drive.

6. Close the Command Prompt window and log off.

FROM THE CLASSROOM

Making Your Backups Work for You, or When You're Popping Corn, Cover the Pot!

NT 4.0 Server includes a reasonably complete backup program. It is good for backing up the local server and has a nice GUI interface. However, there are two limitations to this program. One is easy to overcome and the other is not.

The first limitation is that you cannot schedule an unattended backup from the GUI interface. *Unattended backup* means the backup program launches at a scheduled time, does the specified backup, then terminates. This is an important capability because many servers get backed up at night when few files are open. (Open files do not get backed up.) Fortunately, you can make the backup run as a scheduled

operation by using the AT Schedule service. The Schedule service is a basic (perhaps lightweight) job scheduler. While it may lack the sophistication of other job scheduler programs, for the purpose of backups, it will work fine.

You will need to create an account for the Schedule service and the account will need to be a member of the Local Backup Operators group. Then you will need to configure the Schedule service through the Control Panel. Don't forget to set the startup mode to automatic and get the password correct. Then you will need to create a batch file, using Notepad or some other editor that will launch

FROM THE CLASSROOM

the backup program and do the backup. Windows NT Online Help can show you how to do this. Also, you will need to schedule the job, using the AT command from the command prompt. Again, review the Online Help (type **AT /?**) for more details. If you do not want to use the command line, the NT Resource Kit has a nice GUI utility for the AT Scheduler. The net result is this: at the scheduled time, the Schedule service will launch the backup program in your absence. In other words, it's an unattended backup.

Here's the other limitation: the backup program that ships with NT will not allow you to back up the Registry of a remote NT computer. You can back up the Registry of the local computer without a problem. And you can reach out over the network and back up the drives of a remote server. However, since the Registry files are open at the remote server, they will not be backed up. If you need to restore the Registry of the remote server, you will not be able to do this. We use a class exercise to demonstrate this limitation to the students. There are third-party programs that address this limitation, but they'll cost you extra money. There is a workaround that is not elegant, but it

will allow you to get a safety copy of the Registry on the remote server. This also involves the AT Schedule service, which must be running on the remote server as well, and the RDISK.EXE program. Schedule the command "RDISK.EXE /s" to run at the remote server several minutes before the backup job is sent across the network to back up the drive(s) on the remote server. The RDISK command with the /s parameter will copy the registry files into the <WINROOT>\REPAIR directory at the remote server. Be sure to include this directory in your backup and then you will have a "backed up copy" of the Registry file of the remote server.

To use these files to recover a Registry, you must first restore them from tape to the <WINROOT>\REPAIR folder, run the emergency repair procedures and press ESC when prompted to search the hard drive for the repair files. Yes, yes, it's not pretty or elegant, but it will save the cost of a backup program, if that's important to you. On the other hand, you've already spent $18,000 on your server— perhaps another $695 for an enterprise-scale backup program is a worthwhile investment.

—By Shane Clawson, MCT, MCSE

CERTIFICATION OBJECTIVE 12.04

Windows NT Backup and Recovery Schemes

It is possible to back up portions of your system without having to use the Backup utility. This section describes some of the other alternatives that are available for your use.

Disk Administrator

The first alternative to examine is the Disk Administrator. Figure 12-11 shows us what the Disk Administrator looks like when it has been opened.

FIGURE 12-11:

Disk Administrator

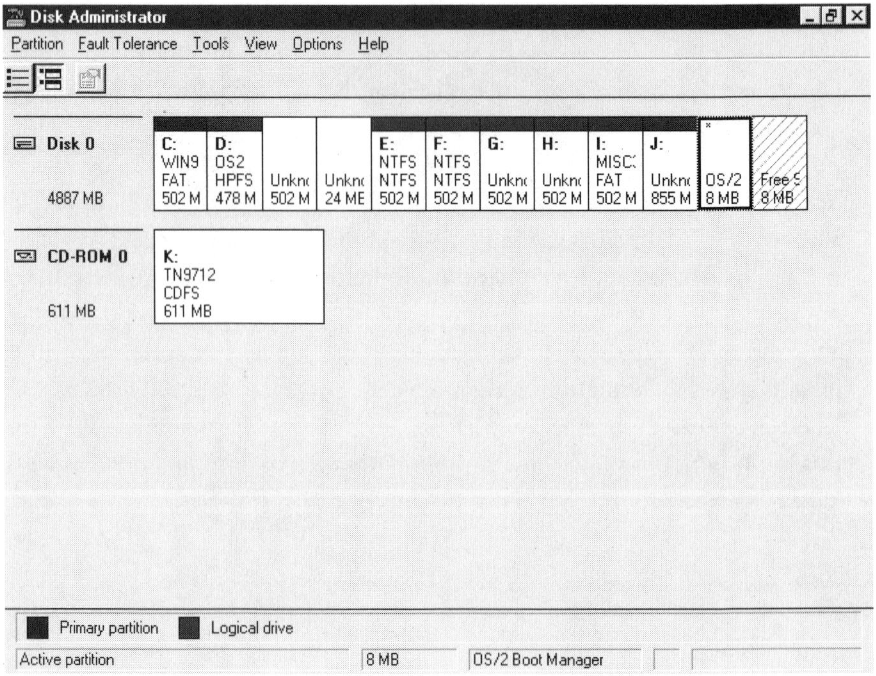

At this point you may be wondering how the Disk Administrator can help you back up your system. The \HKEY_LOCAL_MACHINE\SYSTEM key contains the configuration information about your currently defined drive letters, volume sets, stripe sets with parity, and mirror sets. This key can be saved by using the Disk Administrator. The unique feature of saving the key using Disk Administrator is that it will always save the key to a floppy disk.

Backup Drive Configuration

When you back up the drive configuration you will see the dialog box shown in Figure 12-12. Exercise 12-7 shows you how to use Disk Administrator to save the configuration information that deals with your disk drives.

EXERCISE 12-7

Backing Up the Disk Configuration with the Disk Administrator

1. Log on to your system as Administrator.

2. Click the Start button and select Programs | Administrative Tools | Disk Administrator.

3. From the Partition menu select Configuration, then Save.

4. Insert a formatted floppy disk in your A: drive and click OK. The information from \HKEY_LOCAL_MACHINE\SYSTEM will be written to your floppy disk.

5. Exit the Disk Administrator program.

FIGURE 12-12

Insert Disk dialog box during disk configuration backup

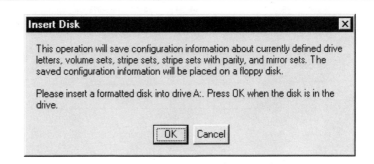

FIGURE 12-13

Dialog box asking for confirmation of the restoration

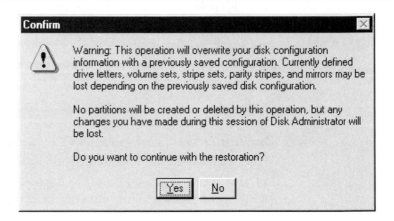

Restore Drive Configuration

If you ever need to restore information pertaining to your disk drives—and your configuration disk is current—then you should have no problem restoring your system. As you are restoring, you will be prompted by the two dialog boxes shown in Figures 12-13 and 12-14. Windows NT wants to make sure that you really want to restore the SYSTEM key. Exercise 12-8 shows you how to restore your disk configuration.

FIGURE 12-14

Insert Disk dialog box during disk configuration restoration

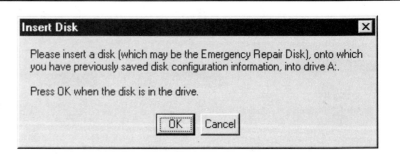

EXERCISE 12-8

Restoring the Disk Configuration with the Disk Administrator

1. Log on to your system as Administrator.

2. Click the Start button and select Programs | Administrative Tools | Disk Administrator.

3. From the Partition menu select Configuration, then Restore.

4. Click Yes.

5. Insert the floppy disk that was created during Exercise 12-7 into your A: drive and click OK.

6. Information will be written to your Registry. Reboot your system so it will take effect.

The Emergency Repair Disk

The Emergency Repair Disk is another way to back up vital system information. If you recall, Figure 12-13 stated that you could insert the Emergency Repair Disk (ERD) to complete the operation. This is because the ERD holds Registry information, including the disk configuration information. The ERD will be covered in more depth when we discuss troubleshooting in Chapter 14.

Registry Backups

Another alternative to using Backup is to use one of the two Registry Editors that are included with Windows NT Server 4.0. Of the two editors, we recommend Regedit because it can back up the entire Registry, whereas Regedt32 can only back up individual Registry keys. Figure 12-15 shows Regedit and Figure 12-16 shows Regedt32

In the following two exercises you will use Regedit to back up and restore the entire Registry. Exercise 12-9 gives you an opportunity to back up your complete Registry.

FIGURE 12-15

Windows NT Regedit

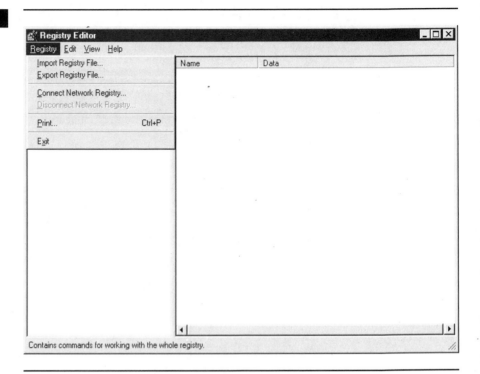

Backing Up the Registry with the Registry Editor

1. Log on as Administrator.

2. Click the Start button and select Run.

3. Type **Regedit** and click OK.

4. Click the Registry menu and select Export Registry File.

5. Type **BACKUP.REG** in the Filename box and click Save. Your Registry file will be saved to the file BACKUP.REG in your root directory.

It is possible to back up only branches of the Registry if you so desire. You just have to change the export range from all to a selected branch when you are in the Export Registry File window.

FIGURE 12-16

Windows NT Regedt32

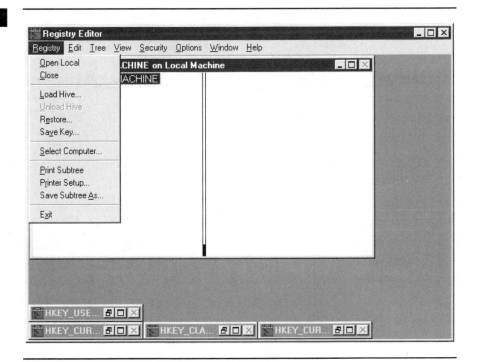

Now that you have successfully backed up your registry, try restoring it using Regedit. Exercise 12-10 shows you how to accomplish the task.

EXERCISE 12-10

Restoring the Registry with the Registry Editor

1. Log on as Administrator.

2. Click the Start button and select Run.

3. Type **Regedit** and click OK.

4. Click the Registry menu and select Import Registry File.

5. Select BACKUP.REG from the Import Registry File window and click the Open button. A progress bar fills as the file is imported.

6. Reboot your system for the imported Registry to be fully effective.

CERTIFICATION OBJECTIVE 12.05

Third-Party Backup and Restore Alternatives

While Windows NT Backup is a capable backup utility, there are many third-party backup and restore utilities on the market with even more coming into the channel daily. This section will briefly describe some of the alternatives available to you.

Seagate Backup Exec for Windows NT

Seagate Backup Exec, now in its fifth version, allows you complete control of your backups by providing 24-hour network-wide scheduling, administration, monitoring, device and media management.

Some of the main features of Seagate Backup Exec are:

- **Intelligent disaster recovery** Recovery time can be minimized with a point-in-time, rapid-recovery system for fast, dependable Windows NT Server recovery.

- **Microsoft compatibility** Provides 100 percent data interchange with the Windows NT Backup utility.

- **Performance optimization** Maximizes performance, minimizes network traffic/backup time using an exclusive technology that allows distributed processing/source compression.

- **Integrated crystal reports** Create user-defined and predefined reports for network-wide administration, monitoring and management.

- **Advanced device and media management** Maximizes backup performance by utilizing drive pooling, dynamic load balancing, drive cascading, fault-tolerant processing and media overwrite protection.

Stac Replica for Windows NT

Stac's Replica for Windows NT offers complete, secure disaster recovery and tape backup protection for businesses or branch offices. Replica is currently in its third version. Figure 12-17 shows the Replica 3 interface.

Some of the main features of Stac Replica 3 are:

■ **Advanced technology permits ultra fast replication** Replica's unique technology supports full read and write access to your server during replication. This allows you to not have to utilize complex incremental backup schemes.

Stac Replica 3 for
Windows NT

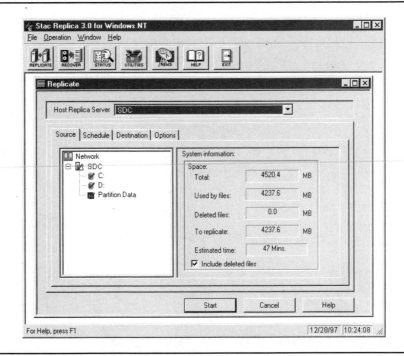

- **Complete system backup** In the event of a disaster, Replica can restore the complete server including the boot volume, disk partitions, Registry, NT operating system, user files and files that were open during replication.

- **Individual files easily recovered from any desktop** Stac's Replica includes a feature that mounts tapes as NT volumes so that users can recover individual files themselves, using tools like File Manager and Explorer. Since all security objects are also replicated, users can only see those files that they had access to on the original server.

ARCserve for Windows NT

ARCserve, currently at version 6.5, provides a comprehensive, integrated storage management platform for Windows NT. It delivers high-performance backup, restore and distaster recovery for small LAN's and heterogeneous enterprises.

Some of the main features of ARCserve are:

- **Parallel streaming** ARCserve can back up and restore data simultaneously, to or from a maximum of 32 devices.

- **Quick file access** ARCserve maintains the location of files on a tape in its online database. This enables very fast access to a file on tape without the need to scan through the whole tape.

- **Automated tape drive configuration** ARCserve will identify SCSI tape drives in use and automatically set the correct configuration parameters.

- **Centralized administration** Monitor and manage multiple ARCserve servers from any Windows NT server or workstation.

CERTIFICATION SUMMARY

The strategy you use for backups can be determined by several different factors, such as the size of the backup and the speed at which it needs to be completed. Other factors that need to be considered are the type of media that you use for the backups and what software to use. Software will be determined by the features that you require. After determining the software to use, you need to determine how often you will back up and what type of backup to use. The backup type can be normal, incremental, differential, copy, or daily. A decision also needs to be made regarding media rotation and sufficient off-site storage for the backups that are created.

Windows NT comes with a Backup utility that you can use to start backing up your data immediately. The Backup utility works from a GUI and supports backups and restores to tape only. Backup looks for a tape drive as soon as it starts and generates an error if it does not find one. In order to utilize Backup, you must have permission to access the data you are trying to back up.

It is possible to back up and restore the entire partition or only certain files that have been selected. In order to make it easier to back up, you can create a .CMD file and use it in conjunction with the AT command and the Schedule service.

Several other tools enable you to back up and restore selected pieces of data. The Disk Administrator can be used to back up information that deals with drive letters, volume sets, and more. The Emergency Repair Disk can also be utilized to repair Registry information. Regedit and Regedt32 are also available to back up and restore Registry data. Regedit is the more flexible tool, because it can back up and restore the entire Registry while Regedt32 can only save individual Registry keys.

There are a significant number of other software packages on the market that can back up and restore your Windows NT Server. A few of the titles are Seagate Backup Exec for Windows NT, Stac Replica for Windows NT, and ARCserve for Windows NT.

✓ TWO-MINUTE DRILL

- ❑ The two most common interface types you will encounter in a tape drive are *Integrated Drive Electronics* (IDE) and *Small Computer Systems Interface* (SCSI).

- ❑ IDE is mainly used in the slower and lower-capacity QIC-style tape drives while you will find SCSI in the high-capacity, high-performance DAT and DLT drives.

❑ Any user or group of users that has been given the right to *Backup Files and Directories* will be able to circumvent the security provided by normal file permissions when backing up those files and directories.

❑ Another name for the normal backup is a full backup. A full backup copies all selected files and marks each as having been backed up.

❑ An incremental backup will back up only those files created or changed since you performed the last normal or incremental backup.

❑ A differential backup copies files that have been created or changed since the last normal or incremental backup.

❑ Using a copy backup copies all the files you select but it will not mark each file as having been backed up.

❑ A daily backup copies all (specified) files that have been modified during the day you perform the daily backup.

❑ A *verify* operation is used to compare files on the hard disk to files that have been backed up to tape.

❑ The Windows NT Backup utility has the capability to perform verification of the backups and restores it accomplishes to ensure the integrity of your data.

❑ It is possible for you to provide some security for the backup tapes you create by choosing the Restrict Access to Owner or Administrator option.

❑ *Unattended backup* means the backup program launches at a scheduled time, does the specified backup, then terminates.

❑ The \HKEY_LOCAL_MACHINE\SYSTEM key contains the configuration information about your currently defined drive letters, volume sets, stripe sets with parity, and mirror sets.

SELF TEST

The following questions will help you measure your understanding of the material presented in this chapter. Read all the choices carefully, as there may be more than one correct answer. Choose all correct answers for each question.

1. In order to successfully back up your Windows NT Server you need to use _____ .

   A. a software backup utility

   B. a RAID controller

   C. tape media with an approved tape drive

   D. WINS Manager

2. (True/False) Windows NT Backup can back up to floppy disks.

3. You need to back up the Registry on your PDC to tape without taking it offline. The tape drive is located on your BDC. What must be done to perform the backup?

   A. Select Backup Local Registry from the Backup Information window so that the PDC's Registry can be successfully backed up

   B. Nothing: it is impossible to back up the Registry on the PDC

   C. Use Server Manager to back up the PDC's Registry

   D. Add a tape drive to the PDC and select Backup Local Registry from the Backup Information window

4. To make a full backup of your entire partition you would use a _____ .

   A. daily backup

   B. copy backup

   C. incremental backup

   D. differential backup

   E. normal backup

5. You have one tape drive located on your PDC. It is responsible for backing up a BDC and 18 client machines. Through careful monitoring, you have found that the backup is interfering with users getting their work accomplished (it has not been completed when they start work). What can you do to ensure that backup is done before users arrive at work?

   A. Add a bigger tape drive to the PDC

   B. Use hardware compression on the tape drive

   C. Add a tape drive to the BDC and split the backup load equally

   D. Add a tape drive to the BDC to back up only itself

   E. Move the tape drive to the BDC and back up all machines from there

6. You need to back up 30 gigabytes of data from your network. What type of medium would be best to use for this backup?

   A. QIC

   B. DAT

C. 8mm

D. DLT

7. (True/False) A differential backup marks files as having been backed up.

8. (True/False) It is possible to complete backups for one year using only 19 tapes.

9. A user is attempting to back up a partition but the system does not allow him to back up everything. What could be the problem?

   A. The user has permissions to all directories.

   B. The user is not a member of the Replicator or Print Operator groups.

   C. The user is not a member of the Administrators or Backup Operators groups.

   D. The user does not have a tape drive that is on the HCL.

10. If your backup strategy consists of completing backups for one year using 19 tapes, what type of method(s) should be used?

    A. Normal

    B. Copy

    C. Daily

    D. Differential

    E. Incremental

11. You can successfully back up the entire partition on your system; however, you run into difficulties when you try to restore the partition. What can cause this problem?

    A. You do not have Restore Local Registry selected

    B. You do not have Verify Restore selected

    C. You do not have the Backup Files and Directories user right

    D. You do not have the Restore Files and Directories user right

12. It is recommended that you have _____ complete backup sets in case of tape failure or loss.

    A. 4

    B. 3

    C. 2

    D. 1

13. (True/False) You should not store the tape backups off-site as this causes a delay if you need to use them for restoration.

14. (True/False) The Windows NT Backup utility cannot back up all the files on your system.

15. You want to back up only your complete Registry. What tool should you use?

    A. Server Manager

    B. Disk Administrator

    C. Regedit

    D. Regedt32

13

Windows NT 4.0 Monitoring and Performance Tuning

CERTIFICATION OBJECTIVES

13.01	Performance Tuning
13.02	Optimizing Applications
13.03	Performance Monitor
13.04	Event Viewer
13.05	Windows NT Diagnostics
13.06	Network Monitor

O ne might ask, "Why do you need to tune your automobile?" One might just as well ask," Why do you need to tune your Windows NT Server system?" Just as you tune your vehicle for maximum efficiency, you should also optimize your Windows NT system to maximize its potential.

Before optimizing your Windows NT system, you must be able to recognize where bottlenecks may exist. The first part of this chapter will examine what a bottleneck is and suggest some methods for detecting and eliminating them. It will describe some self-tuning mechanisms that Windows NT Server can use to optimize its own performance and network performance.

The next part of the chapter describes the Performance Monitor application—a very valuable tool in assisting you with diagnosing bottlenecks within your system. The remaining sections describe other tools that Windows NT Server provides for monitoring your system and network: Event Viewer, Windows NT Diagnostics, and Network Monitor.

CERTIFICATION OBJECTIVE 13.01

Performance Tuning

Performance tuning Windows NT Server is the art of taking your existing configuration and maximizing its performance to achieve the optimal outcome. It is a systematic approach that starts by locating the primary process that is hindering your system and resolving it. However, tuning your system does not stop there: it is an ongoing process.

This section will examine what a bottleneck is, then describe ways to detect and eliminate bottlenecks. It will also explore some specific mechanisms Windows NT Server provides to help your machine run smoothly.

Bottlenecks

Just as the neck is the narrowest part of a bottle, which restricts the flow of the bottle's contents, a computer bottleneck is the component that impedes the system as a whole from operating at its maximum potential. One useful way to define a bottleneck is to locate the resource that consumes the most time while a task is executing. You know you have a bottleneck if one resource has a high rate of use while other resources have relatively low usage.

Detecting Bottlenecks

All computer systems have bottlenecks that impede their performance capabilities. Depending on how you use your system, you may never notice what your bottlenecks are. If you routinely use your system as a stand-alone server, it may perform quickly enough that you do not notice a problem. On the other hand, if you use your system as the primary domain controller for a 15,000-node network and it slows down immensely while validating client logons, you will definitely notice that you have a bottleneck.

However, just knowing that your system is running slowly does not help you to identify the resource responsible. Is it the physical memory, hard disk drive, processor, or possibly a Windows NT service or application? If you have to constantly fetch data from your paging file, is the hard drive causing the problem or is it a lack of memory in your system? If your system slows to a crawl, is it due to processor-intensive calculations or an application that is stealing processor time? At this point only a psychic could guess the reason, because any of these items could be slowing your system.

To locate a bottleneck in your system you must evaluate a set of metrics based upon the number of requests for service, the arrival time of the requests, and the amount of time requested. Typically the resource with the lowest maximum throughput capability becomes the bottleneck when it is in high demand. It is important to realize that a resource need not be at 100 percent utilization for a bottleneck to occur. Later in this chapter, when we begin using the performance monitor, we will discuss different levels of utilization that typically indicate a bottleneck.

Eliminating Bottlenecks

Once you recognize that a bottleneck exists, you are halfway to solving your problem and speeding up your system. The steps you take to eliminate the bottleneck will vary, depending on what type of bottleneck you have. In various situations you may need to add more memory to the system, add a faster hard drive, or add more processors.

Once you have eliminated the most significant bottleneck in your system, try to find the next bottleneck and eliminate that one. Performance tuning is a constant cycle of improvement; there will always be some bottleneck to overcome unless your system becomes so fast that you do not perceive any slowdowns.

Self-Tuning Mechanisms

Windows NT Server provides several mechanisms to help optimize your system performance automatically. These include:

- Methods to avoid fragmentation of physical memory
- Methods to utilize multiple pagefiles
- Multiprocessing capability
- Thread and process prioritization
- Caching disk requests

Methods to Avoid Fragmentation of Physical Memory

Windows NT Server utilizes two types of memory, *physical memory*, which is the actual RAM (random access memory), and *virtual memory*, which is hard drive space acting as though it is additional RAM. Virtual memory is used when the amount of physical memory is not enough to run the current applications, processes, and threads. Data is transferred transparently between physical memory and virtual memory under the control of the *virtual memory manager*, which swaps unused data from RAM to the hard drive and from the hard drive to RAM so that it can be accessed faster.

The smallest portion of memory that can be managed is 4KB (kilobyte). This 4KB section of memory is called a *page*. Both physical memory and virtual memory (the file stored on the hard drive is called *PAGEFILE.SYS)* have the same page size. This allows the virtual memory manager to manipulate data that is being moved either from physical memory to virtual memory or vice versa in standard data blocks. Any available space in physical memory or virtual memory can be used for the transferred page without fear of fragmentation. Fragmentation occurs when there is unused space within contiguous pages. If there is sufficient fragmentation in a system, it has areas of memory that cannot be used by other applications. This means that memory is wasted.

Other operating systems use much larger pages—up to 64KB in size. Let's compare data storage using a Windows NT 4KB page and another operating system that has a 64KB page size. If there were 3KB of information stored using 64KB pages, then 61KB of that memory will be wasted. However, if that same 3KB of data were stored in Windows NT pages, there would only be 1KB of unused memory. Or take another example where a *thread* (which allows a process to run different portions of its program concurrently) that needs 26KB of memory is executing. On Windows NT it uses 7 pages ($7 \times 4KB = 28KB$), leaving only 2KB being unused. On the operating system that uses 64KB pages, this single thread wastes 38KB of memory. Keep in mind that this example is for only one thread; normally there are numerous threads running on a system, so the waste would be multiplied.

By optimizing the size of the pages in this manner Windows NT Server leaves more physical memory available for your application, but it does not have to do as much swapping to virtual memory. It is still important to have as much physical memory in your system as possible to reduce the page swapping that the virtual memory manager will have to perform.

Methods to Utilize Multiple Pagefiles

It is not always possible to add more memory to your system to reduce paging, but the virtual memory manager within Windows NT can recognize more than one pagefile. When you first launched the Windows NT Setup program, it created a file called PAGEFILE.SYS on the physical drive where the operating system was being installed. The default size of PAGEFILE.SYS is the amount of physical RAM or, if the system has less than 22MB of physical RAM, the PAGEFILE.SYS is 22MB or the amount of available space, whichever is less.

If you have multiple logical or physical drives, it is possible to have more than one pagefile. Windows NT supports up to a maximum of 16 pagefiles per system. There can be one pagefile per logical disk but, for maximum efficiency you should create additional pagefiles (one per physical disk). By placing the additional pagefiles on separate physical drives, you can significantly increase levels of I/O (input/output) if your hard drive controller is capable of reading and writing to multiple hard drives at the same time. If you place additional pagefiles on logical drives, you may notice a slowdown in your system because the drive head is having to move between the multiple pagefiles on the physical drive that hosts the logical drives. Exercise 13-1 shows you how to split your paging file among multiple hard drives. Keep in mind that to perform this exercise you must have more than one physical drive in your system.

EXERCISE 13-1

Splitting the Paging File Among Multiple Disks

1. Right-click the My Computer icon.
2. Select Properties from the pop-up menu.
3. Select the Performance tab.
4. Open the Virtual Memory section and click the Change button.
5. Select the primary volume on the first drive.
6. Set Initial Size to 8MB.
7. Set Maximum Size to 16MB.
8. Click the Set button. The settings you just made are now reflected in the Drive window.
9. Select the primary volume on the second drive.
10. Set Initial Size to 8MB.
11. Set Maximum Size to 16MB.
12. Click the Set button.
13. Click the OK button.

14. Click the Close button.

15. Answer Yes to restart the system so the changes you have made will take effect.

Figure 13-1 shows multiple pagefiles in use on a Windows NT Server system. Notice that the minimum pagefile size Windows NT allows is 2MB.

Multiprocessing Capabilities

Windows NT is an operating system that can increase the performance of your system by taking advantage of more than one processor in a system. In a single-processor system, only one thread can be executed at a time. In a multiprocessor system, each processor can handle one thread—thereby improving performance.

Multiprocessing systems are not all created equally. A multiprocessing system can fit into one of two different categories—asymmetric or symmetric.

FIGURE 13-1

Multiple pagefile settings

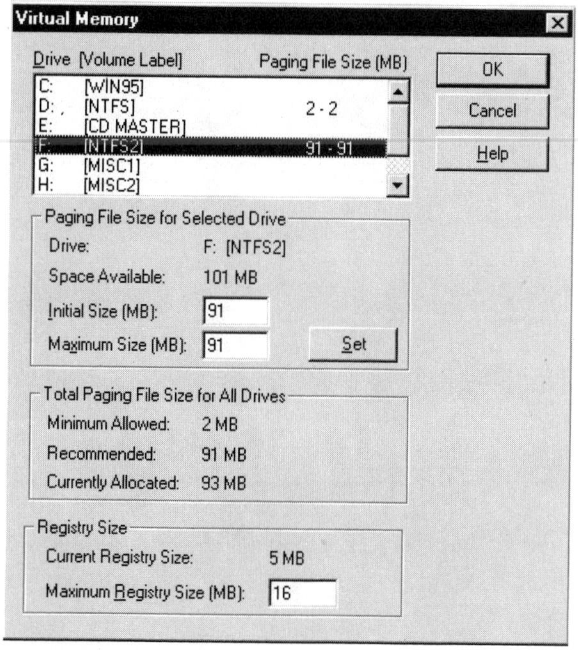

An *asymmetric multiprocessing* (ASMP) system assigns specific threads to a specific processor, which could lead to wasted processor time if one processor is waiting for a thread that is not being executed. An example of asymmetric multiprocessing is a situation where the operating system is running on one processor and applications are running on the other processor(s). When applications are not running, the processor(s) are sitting idle and not effectively used. Figure 13-2 shows an ASMP system with four processors. As you can see, processor 1 is being used for the operating system and processor 3 for an application. Processors 2 and 4 are not being used; they are being wasted. By contrast, in a *symmetric multiprocessing* (SMP) system, available processors are used as needed. Windows NT supports SMP, which allows it to distribute application needs and system load evenly across all the available processors.

FIGURE 13-2

Asymmetric multiprocessing

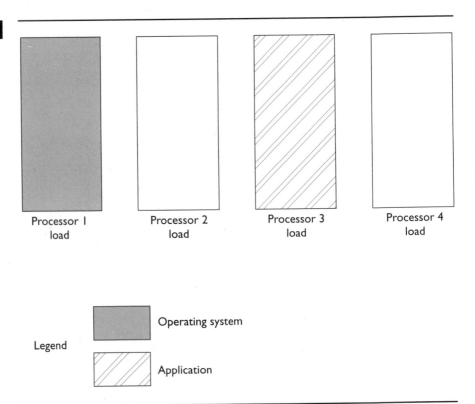

Processor 1 load   Processor 2 load   Processor 3 load   Processor 4 load

Legend

Operating system

Application

Figure 13-3 shows an SMP system with four processors. Each processor is sharing in the load of the operating system and the application.

Multiprocessing systems do not simply double the performance capability of your two-processor system as you might think. There is overhead for resource sharing and scheduling that must be factored in. It is generally accepted that two processors will give you roughly 150 percent the performance of one processor, but this depends on how your system is being used.

As shipped, Windows NT Server supports four processors. If you need support for more than four processors (up to a maximum of 32), contact your computer manufacturer to acquire the appropriate files to support additional processors.

FIGURE 13-3

Symmetric multiprocessing

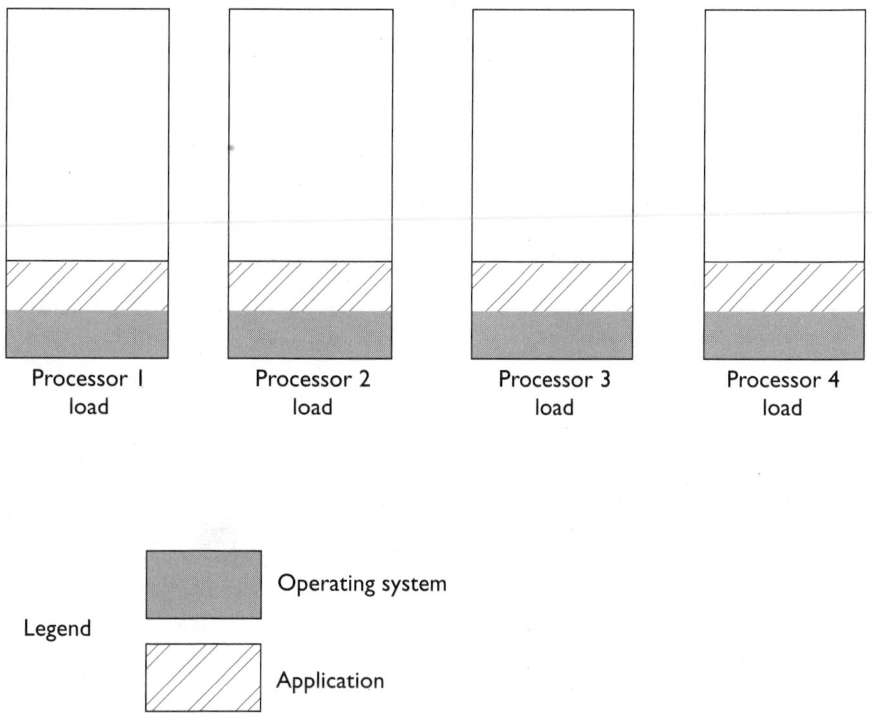

| Processor 1 load | Processor 2 load | Processor 3 load | Processor 4 load |

Legend

Operating system

Application

Many people taking the exam get confused by the number of processors that are supported by Windows NT Server and Windows NT Workstation. Be sure to recognize that NT Workstation, as shipped, supports only two processors, while NT Server supports four.

Thread and Process Prioritization

As discussed earlier in this chapter, a process can be made up of multiple threads that are executed at the same time in a *multiprocessing* system. However, if you look at a *preemptive multitasking* operating system, it only appears that the threads are being processed at the same time. In reality, the threads are processed based upon their priority. Since Windows NT is a preemptive multitasking operating system, there must be a way to manipulate the priorities of the processes and threads. Windows NT always schedules the highest priority thread to run, even if it has to interrupt a lower priority thread. This keeps the processor running the highest priority task.

The priorities within Windows NT are handled in a hierarchical manner, with a number range of 0 to 31 and four base priority classes. Table 13-1 illustrates the four classes and the priority numbers associated with them. Each process starts with a base priority of 8, which is within the normal base priority. The threads of a process inherit the base priority of the process. Windows NT can raise or lower this number by two priority levels, which allows the system to prioritize itself as it is running.

If there are two or more threads running at the same priority, they share the processor(s) by taking equal turns until the threads have finished. Periodically all threads receive a priority boost from Windows NT. This helps to prevent the lower-priority threads from locking onto a shared resource that may be needed by a higher-priority thread. It also gives the lower-priority thread a chance to use the processor.

TABLE 13-1		
Base Priorities for Processes and Threads	**Base Priority**	**Number Range**
	Low	0-6
	Normal	7-10
	High	11-15
	Real-time	16-31

Dynamic applications use priority levels 0-15, while real-time applications operate with the priority levels from 16-31. Examples of dynamic applications are user applications or operating system components that are not critical to the performance of the system; these applications may be written to the pagefile. A real-time application would be a mouse driver that is critical to system performance and therefore cannot be written to the pagefile. Real-time applications must access the processor quite frequently, in order to respond to a real-time event such as a user moving the mouse cursor across the monitor screen.

To start a process with a priority higher than 23, you must be an administrator. This is because a process running at such a high priority dramatically slows the entire system; it changes even a simple task such as moving the mouse cursor into a slow, painful procedure.

As discussed, Windows NT can automatically change the priority of processes as they run. For example, if you bring an application to the foreground, the operating system automatically raises the priority level of the running processes to make sure that it responds to your requests quickly. Priorities 0-15 only have the processor for a time slice, whereas priorities 16-31 use the processor until completed or until a higher priority needs the processor. Later in the chapter you'll learn how to optimize application responsiveness in a variety of ways.

Caching Disk Requests

Windows NT Server improves the performance of your system through disk caching which is controlled by the *disk cache manager*. The disk cache manager helps by reducing the amount of I/O traffic to your hard drive. It does this by storing frequently used data in physical memory rather than having to read it each time from your hard drive. Reducing the amount of I/O increases your system performance.

When a new process starts, the cached memory is changed because the process acquires a working set, thereby reducing the amount of RAM for caching. Windows NT is designed to maximize the usage of physical memory; memory not being used by a process is used by Windows NT for disk caching to improve performance.

It is not possible to manually configure cache size since that is determined by all the applications that are running on the system. The best way to optimize the size of the disk cache is to have as much physical memory as possible in the system. This gives Windows NT sufficient resources to manage itself optimally.

Network Tuning

All networks are not created equal, nor does each Windows NT Server have the same mission on every network. That means that each machine must be tuned for the job it is going to perform. We will discuss two methods to perform network tuning via the Network applet in the Control Panel. The first method is to choose the appropriate optimization setting for the Windows NT Server service. Figure 13-4 shows the four possible settings that can be applied. Depending upon which option you choose, the amount of memory allocated to the server service can differ dramatically.

Options for NT Server service optimization are:

■ Minimize Memory Used, which can handle up to 10 users simultaneously using Windows NT Server. You should not use this option on a file server unless the network is very small.

FIGURE 13-4

Server service optimization levels

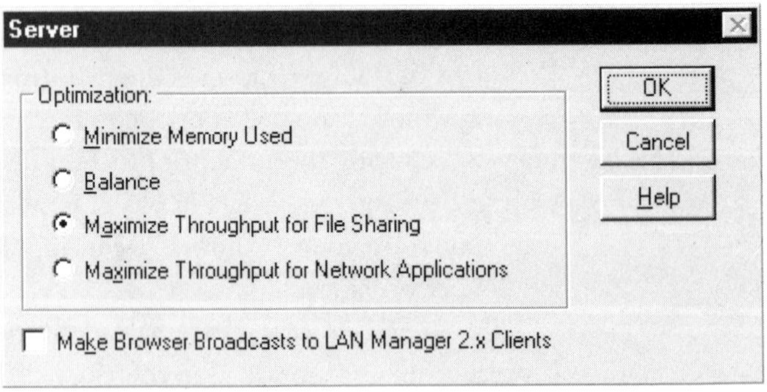

- Balance, which serves up to 64 users and is useful for departmental servers.

- Maximize Throughput for File Sharing, which is for 64 or more users. When you choose this option, access to the file cache has priority over user application access to memory. It also allocates as much memory as is required for file sharing. This option is the default setting.

- Maximize Throughput for Network Applications, which is for 64 or more users. This option allows users' application access to have priority over file cache access to memory. This setting is a good choice for servers that run primarily network applications.

The second way to perform network tuning is to set the binding order based upon the protocols most used on your network. If the protocol used on the machines that you will connect to is first in the binding list, then the average connection time decreases. However, changing the binding order of the server service does not impact server performance. The Server service listens on all protocols and responds when it gets a connection request regardless of the binding order. Figure 13-5 shows the Bindings tab from the Network applet.

Network Interface Card

Choosing the correct network interface card (NIC) for your system can substantially increase system performance. You should choose a NIC that will take advantage of the full width of your system's I/O bus. For example, compare the performance of a low-bit card and a high-bit card: an 8-bit NIC card on an ISA bus transfers data at 400KB, while a 32-bit NIC on a PCI bus transfers 1.14MB in the same time period.

In most situations the self-tuning that Windows NT performs on itself and the network tuning you perform will be sufficient to have an optimally configured system. However, if self-tuning or network tuning does not solve your problem, you will need to turn to other methods of optimization such as the Task Manager or the Performance Monitor.

FIGURE 13-5

Bindings tab from the
Network applet

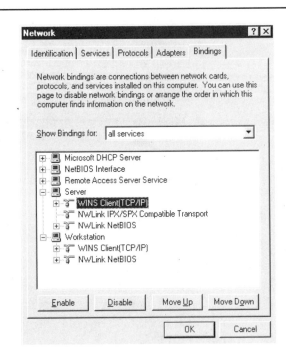

CERTIFICATION OBJECTIVE 13.02

Optimizing Applications

It is possible that an application will not be as responsive as you need it to be. This may be caused by another application that creates a bottleneck or it may indicate a need to change the performance boost assigned to foreground applications. This section describes how you can optimize applications by using the Windows NT Task Manager.

Windows NT Task Manager

The Windows NT Task Manager is a useful tool for short-term monitoring of your system. It can be extremely valuable in detecting an application or

Windows NT service that may have become a memory or CPU (central processing unit) bottleneck. The Task Manager enables you to review applications, processes, and performance statistics in your NT Server at any given moment.

The Task Manager contains three tabs:

- Applications
- Processes
- Performance

The Application and Processes tabs list everything that is running on your system. The Performance tab provides a summary of the overall system by listing CPU and memory usage, as well as other performance information such as the number of threads that are running. An application is listed under the Application tab and also listed in the Processes tab—along with other processes such as Windows NT services and drivers. Figure 13-6 displays the Task Manager's Processes tab. One current process is consuming more memory than it should, thereby slowing the system. Can you identify it?

If you said that LEAKYAPP.EXE looks like it is using more memory than it should, you are correct! This is just one way that the Task Manager can help you quickly identify bottlenecks within your system.

Now it is your turn to start up the Task Manager and take a look at what is happening in your own system. Exercise 13-2 helps you to start up a few applications and look at all three tabs under Task Manager, in order to identify bottlenecks in your own system.

EXERCISE 13-2

Viewing Applications, Processes, and Threads

1. Using your right mouse button, click once on your taskbar.
2. Select Task Manager from the pop-up menu.
3. Click the Start button and select Programs | Accessories | Notepad.
4. Click the Start button and select Programs | Accessories | Clock.
5. Select the Applications tab on the Task Manager. You should see the two applications that you just started. To the right of the application's name, you should see "running." If one of the programs had stopped responding, you would see "not responding" instead.

FIGURE 13-6

Windows NT Task
Manager

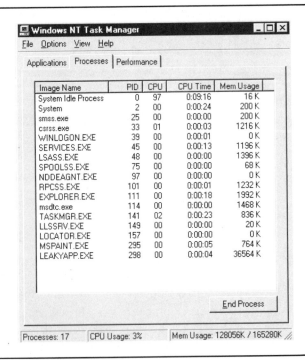

6. Select the Processes tab on the Task Manager. This displays all the processes currently running on your system. The majority of processes listed are Windows NT services or drivers, with the exception of the two applications you just started. The Processes tab is very useful in helping you to determine the CPU usage and memory being consumed by each process.

7. Select the Performance tab on the Task Manager. This screen shows you the total number of threads that are currently running in your system.

8. Close the Task Manager.

Later in the chapter you will use the Windows NT Task Manager to change the responsiveness of processes that are running, but first let's look at how changing the foreground application affects performance characteristics.

Foreground Application Performance Boost

You can change the responsiveness of the foreground application by adjusting the Application Performance Boost slider. Figure 13-7 shows the Performance tab from the System Properties screen. As indicated by the hash marks under the slider, there are three possible slider settings that will boost the foreground application. The Maximum setting increases the foreground application by two priorities. If you have an application that started with a priority of 8 and have the slider in the Maximum position, it will raise it to a priority level of 10 as long as the application is in the foreground. The middle setting increases the priority of the foreground application by one level. With the slider set to the None position, the foreground and background applications run with the same priority level. Exercise 13-3 shows how to change foreground application priority levels.

FIGURE 13-7

Performance tab from
System Properties screen

EXERCISE 13-3

Changing the Responsiveness of Foreground Applications

1. Right-click the My Computer icon.

2. Select Properties from the pop-up menu.

3. Select the Performance tab.

4. Move the slider from Maximum to None.

5. Click the OK button.

6. Answer Yes to restart your system and enable the changes to take effect.

Be sure to set the Application Performance Boost slider back to Maximum after you have finished experimenting with the None setting.

If you have several applications running and you want them all to operate at a high priority level regardless of which application is in the foreground, you can adjust the behavior of Windows NT by manually changing the applications while they are running or before they start.

To manually change the priority of an application that is already running, you utilize the Task Manager as discussed earlier in the chapter. Priority levels changed with the Task Manager remain in effect as long as the process is running. Figure 13-8 shows an example of changing the priority for TCPSVCS.EXE. Exercise 13-4 shows you how to use the Task Manager to change the priority of an application that is already running.

EXERCISE 13-4

Changing the Priority of a Running Process

1. Click the Start button and select Programs | Accessories | Notepad.

2. Using your right mouse button, click once on the taskbar.

3. Select Task Manager from the pop-up menu.

4. Select the Processes tab.

5. Locate NOTEPAD.EXE and click it with your right mouse button.

6. Select Set Priority from the menu. Notice that this process is currently running at Normal priority.

7. Select High from the menu. Notepad is now running at High priority.

FIGURE 13-8

Changing the priority of a
process using the Task
Manager

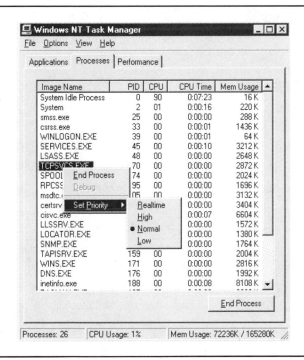

If you want to start a process at a different priority from what it would
normally have, you can start it from a command prompt using one of the
switches listed in Table 13-2. Exercise 13-5 shows you how to start a process
with a priority other than normal.

TABLE 13-2

Command Line Switch
Settings to Change
Process Starting Priority

Switch	Priority Level
/LOW	4
/NORMAL	8
/HIGH	13
/REALTIME	24

EXERCISE 13-5

Starting Processes with Other than Normal Priority

1. Click the Start button and choose Programs | Command Prompt.

2. Type **start /low clock**. Your clock will start at a low priority level.

3. Type **start /high clock**. A second clock will start at a high priority.

4. Type **start /realtime clock**. A third clock will start at a higher priority.

5. Use your right mouse button and click once on the taskbar.

6. Choose Task Manager from the pop-up menu.

7. Select the Processes tab and see that three different clock processes are running.

8. Select the View menu and choose Select Columns.

9. Place a mark in the Base Priority box. This shows you the priorities for all processes that are currently running.

10. Check each CLOCK.EXE and see that each is running at the priority that you specified from the Command Prompt.

11. Close the Task Manager and each instance of the clock.

12. Close the Command Prompt.

CERTIFICATION OBJECTIVE 13.03

Performance Monitor

The Performance Monitor is a tool, included with Windows NT 4.0, that tracks the usage of resources by the system components and applications. By tracking different components of your system it can greatly help you to see what is degrading the performance. The Performance Monitor can be used for a variety of reasons including:

- Identifying bottlenecks in CPU, Memory, Disk I/O, or Network I/O
- Identifying trends over a period of time
- Monitoring real-time system performance

- Monitoring system performance history
- Determining the capacity the system can handle
- Monitoring system configuration changes

The Performance Monitor is used to establish a baseline of your system. A *baseline* is a snapshot of your system under normal operating conditions and a yardstick to measure future abnormalities. When you start Performance Monitor, as with any application, you use a portion of processor time to run the program. If you turn on the switch that allows disk monitoring, that task will minimally affect I/O for the hard drive(s). This should, in essence, have no effect on the results of the measurements you are taking. Figure 13-9 shows the Performance Monitor just after it has been started. Exercise 13-6 shows you how to start the Performance Monitor on your system. It is best to make sure

FIGURE 13-9

Performance Monitor screen

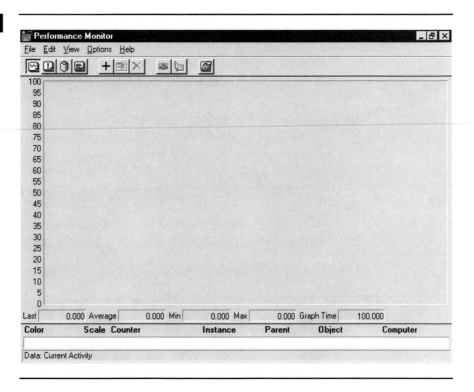

that your hard drive has finished all startup processing before starting the Performance Monitor. This ensures that your results do not include any of the startup processing.

EXERCISE 13-6

Starting the Performance Monitor

1. Click the Start button.
2. Select Programs.
3. Select Administrative Tools.
4. Select Performance Monitor.
5. Leave the Performance Monitor running to complete the remaining exercises in this section.

Performance Monitor utilizes three different types of items to view the system. They are *objects, counters* and *instances*.

- *Objects* are system components such as memory, processor, or disk. See Table 13-3 for other objects.

- *Counters* are specific features of objects; for example, the %Processor Time is a counter for the processor object. Objects can contain many different counters.

- An *instance* is a single occurrence of a counter activity. For example, if your system has two processors, you have two instances of the process counters.

Measurements are always occurring throughout the processes running on your Windows NT system—with the exception of the disk counters, which are turned off by default. The Performance Monitor is the tool that displays this measurement, based upon the objects you choose.

Counters are incremented each time an object performs its functions. For example, each time the processor services a request from an I/O device, the interrupts/sec counter would be incremented.

Many of the counters are used by Windows NT so that it may monitor itself and perform self-tuning for maximum optimization. Table 13-3 lists several of the objects that can be measured with Performance Monitor. This list is not inclusive and your applications may be written to let the system monitor their performance via objects.

The Performance Monitor can display the following views:

- Chart
- Alert
- Report
- Log

The following sections describe these four views and explain where each can be useful in monitoring your system.

	Object Name	Description
TABLE 13-3 Description of Objects Measured by Performance Monitor	Browser	Monitors browser activity for the domain or workgroup to include elections and announcements.
	Cache	Monitors the disk cache usage.
	LogicalDisk	Monitors hard drive partitions.
		Monitors the subpartitions of an extended partition.
	Memory	Monitors memory usage and performance for both physical and virtual memory.
	Paging File	Monitors the usage of pagefiles.
	PhysicalDisk	Monitors a hard drive that contains one or more partitions. This object can be used to monitor the whole drive instead of individually monitoring partitions.
	Process	Monitors all processes that are running on the system.
	Processor	Monitors each processor in the system.
	System	Monitors counters that affect all hardware and software in the system.
		Monitors all processors on the system as a group.
	Thread	Monitors all threads running in the system.

Creating a Performance Monitor Chart

A Performance Monitor chart measures the objects that you designate; it reflects the current activity with a real-time look at the counters chosen. Once you create a display with the counters you want to view, you can save the counters into a file on a regular basis so you don't have to rebuild the display each time. Figure 13-10 shows the Add to Chart dialog box.

As Figure 13-10 indicates, you can vary the color, scale, width, and style of each counter that you add to the chart. When Performance Monitor is started, it uses a default scale. However, if you are viewing more than a single counter, you may want to use a different scale for each counter in order to see the data clearly.

Figure 13-11 shows the chart options available in Performance Monitor. The Chart Options dialog box allows you to customize your charts and change the manner used for updating chart values. Some of the items you can change include the time interval that is used for graphing information from the counters and changing the display from a graph to a histogram.

A chart like that shown in Figure 13-9 shows the activity of each object, counter and instance that is being monitored. The scale on the left of the chart is displayed by default and always starts at zero. The scale can be changed if your activity goes above one hundred. The default time interval is set to one second for each counter. Table 13-4 describes the other values displayed by the Performance Monitor chart.

FIGURE 13-10

Add to Chart dialog box

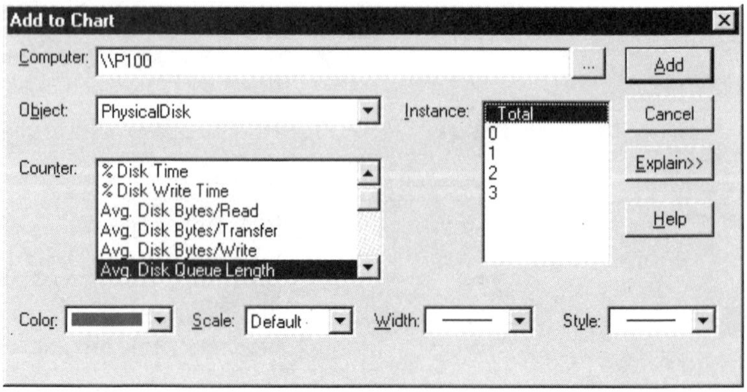

FIGURE 13-11

Chart Options dialog box

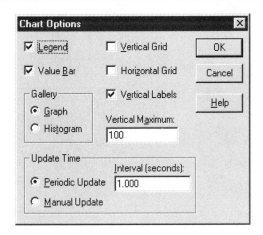

Creating a Performance Monitor Alert

A Performance Monitor Alert tracks events and notifies a user or a computer depending on the parameters you set. You can set the alert log to monitor several counters; an alert is triggered when a threshold setting is reached. Two options that allow you flexibility in defining alerts are the Alert If and Run Program on Alert. Figure 13-12 shows the Add to Alert dialog box.

exam
ⓦatch

A program might not work correctly when you use Run Program on Alert because Performance Monitor passes the Alert condition as a parameter to the program. If it does not work correctly, you should create a batch file to run the program and call the batch file from Performance Monitor.

TABLE 13-4

Performance Monitor
Chart Value Bar
Descriptions

Value	Purpose
Last	Displays the counter's value during the last poll
Average	A running average of the counter during the chart's history
Minimum	The minimum value of the counter during the chart's history
Maximum	The maximum value of the counter during the chart's history
Graph Time	The total amount of time it takes for a complete chart to be created across the screen

FIGURE 13-12

Add to Alert dialog box

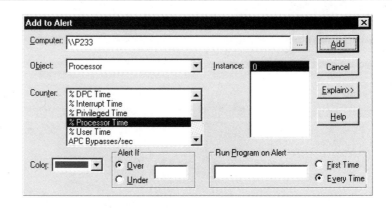

Figure 13-13 shows the alert options that are available in Performance Monitor. The Alert Options dialog box allows you to customize your alerts by switching to Alert view, logging the event in the application log, changing the update time, and sending a network message to a user account or a computer on the network. The messenger service must be started before the network message will function.

FIGURE 13-13

Alert Options dialog box

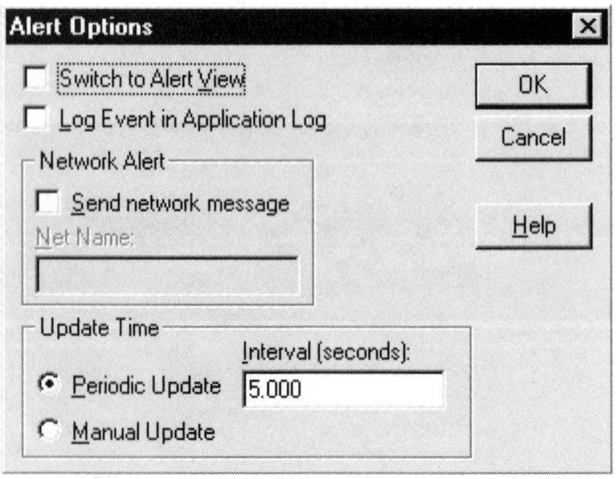

Creating a Performance Monitor Report

The Report view lets you display constantly changing counter and instance values for selected objects. Values appear in columns for each instance. You can adjust report intervals, print snapshots, and export data. For example, you could create a report on all the counters for a given object, then watch how they change under various loads. Figure 13-14 shows the report options available in Performance Monitor. As you can see, the only option available with the Report view is the update time. It can be updated either periodically or manually.

Creating a Performance Monitor Log

Log files, which are in binary format, provide a way to save the counter information and then later run it through the Performance Monitor application. They enable you to track counters over a long time period and provide a very reliable method for documenting your system's performance. Figure 13-15 shows a log view that is monitoring several counters. The log file is set to collect data every 5 seconds and store it in a file called D:\TEMP.LOG.

One advantage of using a log file, instead of extracting information live from the system, is the ability to adjust the start and stop times that will be displayed. It is important to note that you cannot move around the log file while logging is occurring. However, you can use the Time Window option from the Edit menu to change the starting and stopping points by moving the

---

FIGURE 13-14

Report Options dialog box

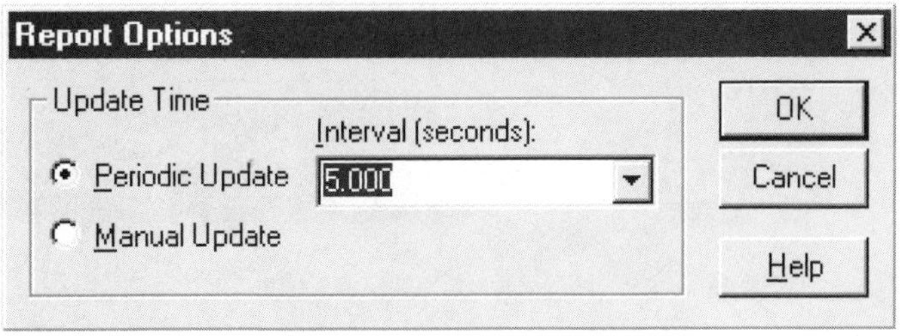

FIGURE 13-15

Performance Monitor
showing Log view

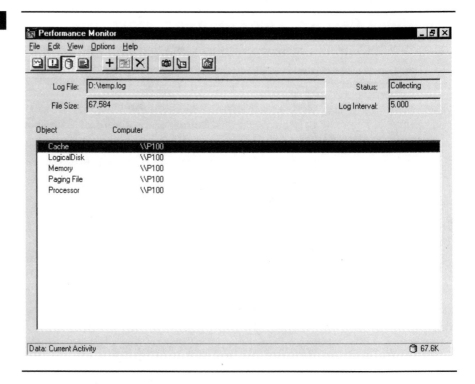

corresponding end of the time interval slide bar as illustrated in Figure 13-16. It is also possible to use bookmarks to change the start and stop points.

FIGURE 13-16

Input Log File Timeframe
window

FIGURE 13-17

Log Options dialog box

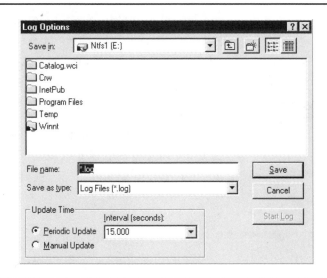

Figure 13-17 shows the log options that are available when viewing a saved log file. Within this window you can change the update time, the log filename, and also start and stop logging. Exercise 13-7 gives you a chance to create and view a log file on your system.

EXERCISE 13-7

Create a Log Where Recorded Metrics Are Stored

1. Select the View menu and choose Log.
2. Select the Edit menu and choose Add to Log.
3. Select Processor and click the Add button.
4. Select LogicalDisk and click the Add button.
5. Select Memory and click the Add button.
6. Click the Done button.
7. Select the Options menu and choose Log.
8. Name the log file as TEMP.LOG.
9. Change the interval to 5 seconds.
10. Click the Start Log button. You can see that the Status changes to Collecting to let you know it is collecting data for the objects you chose. Collect data for one minute before continuing to the next step.

11. Select the Options menu and choose Log.

12. Click the Stop Log button.

Now use Exercise 13-8 to review the log file just created.

Viewing Logs

1. Select the Options menu and choose Data From.

2. Click the Log File radio button.

3. Click the ellipsis and choose the location where you stored the TEMP.LOG file in Exercise 13-7.

4. Click OK.

5. Select the View menu and choose Chart.

6. Select the Edit menu and choose Add to Chart.

7. Select Processor from the Object drop-down list. Notice that the only objects available are those that you chose to be logged in Exercise 13-7.

8. Select %Processor Time from the Counter scroll-down list.

9. Click the Add button.

10. Select Memory from the Object drop-down list.

11. Select pages/sec from the Counter scroll-down list.

12. Click the Add button.

13. Click the Done button. The chart displays statistics from the log file in chart format for your analysis.

Now that you have seen the different views available in Performance Monitor, let's look at how it can help you enhance your system's performance.

Performance Monitor Capabilities

It is important to monitor all actions that may cause bottlenecks in your system. In the following sections you will use Performance Monitor to examine processor performance, disk drive performance, and memory performance. As you will see, things are not as they always appear at first. The suspected culprit may in fact be disguising the real bottleneck.

Processor Performance

Normally the processor is the fastest component in your computer; it tends to waste a lot of time waiting for other processes. The processor is usually not the bottleneck in a modern system unless you are using applications that are graphics- or math-intensive. However, you may want to measure the performance of your processor to ensure that a bottleneck is not present, especially if your processor pre-dates the Pentium family.

When monitoring processor performance, there are three important counters to observe:

- Processor:%Processor Time
- Processor:Interrupts/sec
- System:Processor Queue Length

Processor:%Processor Time

This counter indicates how busy the processor in your system is. There is no need to be alarmed if your processor has spikes of 100 percent; this is expected in some situations, such as when starting up an application. However, a bottleneck can occur if your processor is so busy that it does not respond to service requests for time. If you are experiencing a consistent processor load of 80 percent or more, you have a processor bottleneck. Exercise 13-9 leads you through the steps necessary to add the counter to the Performance Monitor.

EXERCISE 13-9

Adding Processor:%Processor Time to the Performance Monitor

1. Select the Edit menu and choose Add to Chart.
2. Select Processor from the Object drop-down list.
3. Select %Processor Time from the Counter scroll-down list.
4. Click the Add button.
5. Click the Done button to close the Add to Chart window.

Let your system sit idle for a few seconds, then open up any application such as Notepad. What happens to your Performance Monitor chart? You should see quite a bit of %Processor Time measurement being recorded as the application starts up.

Processor:Interrupts/sec

The Interrupts/sec counter measures the rate of service requests from I/O devices. If you see a significant increase in the value of this counter without an equal increase in system activity, then a hardware problem exists; in other words, a component is not working properly. This counter should not normally be above 1,000; however, an occasional spike above 2,000 is acceptable.

System:Processor Queue Length

This counter, which monitors the number of threads that are asking for processor time, is an important indicator of system performance. Each thread requires a certain number of processor cycles. If the demand for processor cycles exceeds what the processor can supply, a long processor queue develops. Such a queue degrades system performance. You should never have a sustained processor queue that is greater than two. If you do, there are too many threads waiting for the processor and the processor has become a bottleneck.

Processor Performance Troubleshooting

Once you have determined that the processor in your system is causing the bottleneck, do not automatically go out and buy a new processor. There are other parts of the system you can check first.

- Check to see if the processor only becomes a bottleneck when a certain application is running. If so, then find a new application to replace it (if feasible). Screen savers, especially OpenGL screen savers, are very processor intensive.

- Check to see if you are using low-bit network or disk adapter circuit cards. An 8-bit card will use more processor time than a 16-bit card, and a 16-bit card will use more processor time than a 32-bit card.

Using a 32-bit card will provide the most efficiency for your system since it will transfer the most bits of data on each transfer from the card to memory.

After checking these items, if you still have a processor bottleneck, you may have no other choice but to replace the processor in your system. If your mainboard supports multiprocessing, add another processor.

Figure 13-18 shows a processor bottleneck caused by a screen saver. The %Processor Time counter is the white line. As you can see, the screensaver kept the processor in use 100 percent of the time, which would prevent other tasks from operating efficiently.

Processor utilization at 100 percent caused by a screen saver

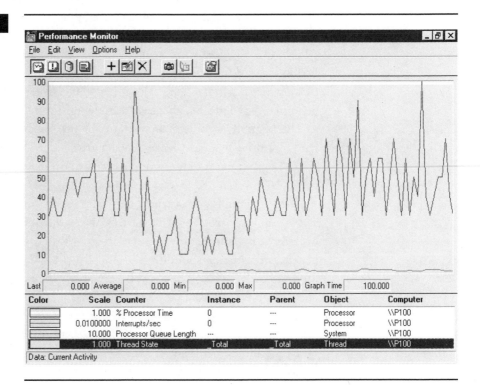

Disk Drive Performance

The I/O capacity of the disk drive is usually the first resource to reach its limit and create a bottleneck on your system. The hard drive in your system participates in everything from booting your system and loading applications, to storing and retrieving data from your hard drive and pagefile. With your hard drive involved in all these processes, you can see that the speed of your drive can impact the performance of your system.

The first sign that you *may* have a disk drive bottleneck could be the amount of time that the disk drive indicator stays illuminated. However, this should be verified by using the Performance Monitor. If Performance Monitor shows sustained periods of disk activity above 80 percent, then a disk drive bottleneck is present. Keep in mind that the disk drive may not be the root cause of the bottleneck: you will need to investigate further to make a final determination.

Table 13-3 showed you a sampling of objects that can be monitored with Performance Monitor. Remember that there were two objects related to disk drive performance, *LogicalDisk* and *PhysicalDisk*. The LogicalDisk object measures performance at a much higher level than the PhysicalDisk object does.

The LogicalDisk object can measure the performance of a partition of a hard disk drive that has been assigned a drive letter such as C: or D:. A good use of LogicalDisk is to monitor which partition may be busy due to a particular application.

The PhysicalDisk object measures real transfers to and from actual hard disk drives, not just partitions. You use this object when you want to isolate differences in performance between drives in your system or if you want very detailed information about the performance of a specific drive. In looking for disk bottlenecks it is best if you start first at the PhysicalDisk. After you identify a PhysicalDisk that has a bottleneck, you isolate the LogicalDisk on that physical disk drive; then, if necessary, you determine which application on the logical drive is generating the I/O activity.

To monitor either LogicalDisk or PhysicalDisk performance you must enable the disk drive performance counters by running the Diskperf utility. These counters are disabled by default because they degrade overall system performance by interrupting the processor during I/O. The counters should only be enabled when you want to monitor disk performance and should be immediately disabled when monitoring is complete. When you enable the counters, Diskperf installs the Disk Drive Performance Statistics Driver that actually collects the data for Performance Monitor, as well as a high-precision timer that times each disk drive transfer. The driver and timer have been measured to take between 1 percent and 2 percent of overhead on Intel-based processor systems.

In order to run the Diskperf utility you must belong to the Administrators local group. Exercise 13-10 shows you how to enable the disk drive performance counters.

EXERCISE 13-10

Enabling the Disk Drive Performance Counters

1. Click the Start button.

2. Select Programs.

3. Select Command Prompt.

4. Type **diskperf-y**.

5. Press the RETURN key. A message states, "Disk performance counters on this system are now set to start at boot. This change will take effect after the system is restarted."

6. Restart your system.

exam
ⓦatch

You must use diskperf-ye to monitor a physical drive in a RAID set. Using diskperf-ye installs the Disk Drive Performance Statistics Driver low in the disk driver stack so that it can see individual physical disks before they are logically combined.

When monitoring disk drive performance there are five important counters to observe:

- ■ Memory:Pages/sec
- ■ %Disk Time (applies to both LogicalDisk and PhysicalDisk objects)
- ■ Disk Bytes/sec (applies to both LogicalDisk and PhysicalDisk objects)
- ■ Average Disk Bytes/transfer
- ■ Current Disk Queue Length (applies to both LogicalDisk and PhysicalDisk objects)

Memory:Pages/sec

This counter watches pages that are swapped and written to your disk drive. Remember that the virtual memory of your system is kept in a file named PAGEFILE.SYS that is located on your disk drive. If you monitor this counter and the %Disk Time counter, you will see how much the PAGEFILE.SYS affects the overall performance of your system. The Memory:Pages/sec value should be <5.

%Disk Time

The %Disk Time counter shows the amount of time the disk drive is busy. It can be a broad indicator on whether your disk drive is a bottleneck. If you use this counter in addition to the Processor:%Processor Time counter described earlier, you can see if disk requests are using up your processor time. The %Disk Time value should be <50.

Disk Bytes/sec

The Disk Bytes/sec counter shows you how fast your disk drives are transferring bytes to and from the disk. The larger the value, the better. This is the primary measure of disk throughput. Exercise 13-11 shows you how to add this counter to Performance Monitor.

EXERCISE 13-11

Adding LogicalDisk:Disk Bytes/sec to the Performance Monitor

1. Select the Edit menu and choose Add to Chart.
2. Select LogicalDisk from the drop-down list.
3. Select Disk Bytes/sec in the Counter scroll-down list.
4. Click the Add button.
5. Click the Done button to close the Add to Chart window.

If you have more than one disk drive, copy a few large files from one disk drive to another disk drive while you monitor the Disk Bytes/sec counter to see the speed at which your drives are performing.

Average Disk Bytes/transfer

The Average Disk Bytes/transfer measures throughput of your disk drive. The larger the transfer size, the greater the disk drive efficiency and system execution speed.

Disk Queue Length

This counter shows how much data is waiting to be transferred to the disk drive. It counts the number of requests, not time. It includes the request currently being serviced and those waiting. A disk queue of more than two may indicate that the disk drive is a bottleneck.

Now that you have completed your measurements, it is time to disable the disk drive performance counters so they do not degrade system performance. Exercise 13-12 shows you how to disable the counters.

EXERCISE 13-12

Disabling the Disk Drive Performance Counters

1. Click the Start button.
2. Select Programs.
3. Select Command Prompt.
4. Type **diskperf-n**.
5. Press the RETURN key. A message states, "Disk performance counters on this system are now set to never start. This change will take effect after the system is restarted."
6. Restart your system.

Disk Drive Performance Troubleshooting

If you have determined that the disk drive in your system is causing the bottleneck, do not go out immediately to buy another disk drive. There are some other parts of the system to check first.

■ Check to see that you have plenty of physical memory in your system. By having as much physical memory as possible you increase the amount of disk caching and reduce the amount of paging to the hard drive. This will increase the performance of your system immensely. Normally when you increase physical memory you also increase the size of the pagefile, especially if you write a dump file when the system crashes.

■ Check to see if you can move your PAGEFILE.SYS file from your system partition to another available partition.

■ Check your disk drive controller card. If you have a card that transfers in 8-bit or 16-bit increments, you will see a drastic improvement by switching to a 32-bit controller card. If possible, make sure that the 32-bit controller card is a bus mastering, direct memory access (DMA) controller rather than a controller that uses programmed I/O. Programmed I/O uses the processor to set up disk drive transfers. A bus mastering DMA controller uses the disk drive controller to manage the I/O bus and the DMA controller to manage the DMA operation. This frees the processor for other uses.

If you have determined that you do need another disk drive and you plan to add it to your existing disk drive configuration, place the drives on separate I/O buses to ensure maximum performance potential.

Figure 13-19 shows an example of a situation where a faster disk drive is needed. The white line displays %Disk Time at a sustained rate of 100 percent. The black line is the Current Disk Queue Length, which has had a maximum of 5 items in the queue with an average of about 2.5 items.

Memory Performance

Memory can contribute significantly to system bottlenecks; some claim it is the most common bottleneck you will encounter. Windows NT is a virtual memory operating system, which combines two items: physical memory and space on the disk drive (PAGEFILE.SYS). Data is stored on the disk drive until needed, then moved into physical memory on demand. In such a scheme, data that is not being actively used is written back to the disk drive. However, if a system has too little physical memory, data must be moved into and out of the disk drive more frequently—which can be a very slow process. Data pages that have recently been referenced by a process are stored in

FIGURE 13-19

Disk drive performance
at 100 percent

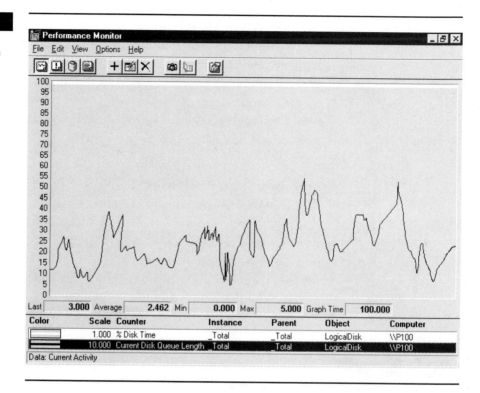

physical memory in a *working set*. If the process needs data that is not in the working set, it will create a *page fault* and the memory manager will add new pages to the working set.

The first step you should take in investigating a suspected memory problem is to measure the amount of paging that is occurring. There are four important counters you should use when you investigate a memory bottleneck. They will indicate how often processes have to look outside of their working set to find data they need. The four counters are:

- Memory:Pages/sec
- Memory:Page Faults/sec
- Memory:Pages Input/sec
- Memory:Page Reads/sec

Memory:Pages/sec

This is the primary counter used to detect a memory bottleneck. It measures the number of requested pages that were not immediately available in physical memory and had to be accessed from the disk drive, or had to be written to the disk to make room in physical memory for other pages. If this value has extended periods where the number of pages per second is greater than five, memory may be a bottleneck in the system.

Memory:Page Faults/sec

This counter measures the number of times that data is not found in a process' working set. This includes both *hard page faults*, in which additional disk drive I/O is required, and *soft page faults,* in which the pages are located elsewhere in memory. If your system repeatedly fails to find data in the process' working set, then the amount of memory is probably too limited. The best indicator of a memory bottleneck is a continuous, high rate of hard page faults. Exercise 13-13 shows you how to add this counter to Performance Monitor.

EXERCISE 13-13

Adding Memory:Page Faults/sec to the Performance Monitor

1. Select the File menu and choose New Chart. This will clear any counters set during previous exercises.
2. Select the Edit Menu and choose Add to Chart.
3. Select Memory from the Object drop-down list.
4. Select Page Faults/sec from the Counter scroll-down list.
5. Click the Add button.
6. Click the Done button to close the Add to Chart dialog box.

Memory:Pages Input/sec

This counter is used to see how many pages are retrieved from the disk drive to satisfy page faults. This counter can be used in conjunction with Memory:Page Faults/sec to see how many faults are being satisfied by reading from your disk drive and how many may be coming from elsewhere, such as other locations in memory.

Memory:Page Reads/sec

This counter reflects how often the system is reading from your disk drive due to page faults. If you sustain more than five pages or more per second, you have a shortage of physical memory.

Memory Performance Troubleshooting

Once you have determined that the memory in your system is causing the bottleneck, you may decide to add physical memory. Although it never hurts to have as much physical memory as your system can handle, there are some things you can check within your system to alleviate the problem.

- Check to see if you have any drivers or protocols that are running but not being used. They use space in all memory pools even if they are idle.

- Check to see if you have additional space on your disk drive that you could use to expand the size of your pagefile. Normally, the bigger the initial size of your pagefile the better, in performance terms.

Figure 13-20 shows an example of three memory counters discussed in this section. The white line is the Page Faults/sec, which is the total page fault rate during this measurement; it averages 81 per second. One hard fault won't slow down your system so that you would notice it. However, a large ratio of hard page faults to soft page faults would slow down your system so that you could notice a performance hit. The black line is Pages Input/sec; it measures the hard page faults by counting the number of pages that have to be taken from the disk drive to satisfy the fault. The area between the white and black lines shows the number of soft page faults during this measurement. (Recall that a *soft page fault* is a page that is found elsewhere in physical memory, such as cache memory.) The dark gray line is the Page Reads/sec, which is the number of times the disk drive had to be read to satisfy a page fault.

Now that you have seen what Performance Monitor can do, let's look at some other monitoring tools available in Windows NT Server.

Memory measurements
from Performance Monitor

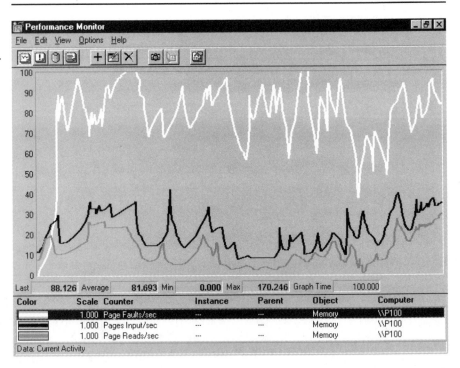

FROM THE CLASSROOM

You Too Can Have Fun and Gain Human Potential with Performance Monitor

We tell students they can find out almost everything they want to know about their NT Server performance just by using Performance Monitor. On its face, this is a true statement. In the classroom, mostly due to time constraints, we give them a few simple exercises to demonstrate the power and potential of Performance Monitor. But there is much more

to this tool than can be covered in a few short classroom drills. Students want to become more familiar with Performance Monitor when they get back to work. Here are some ideas.

First, establish a baseline of performance before you put your server into production. It is most helpful to know what the no-load performance characteristics of your server are.

FROM THE CLASSROOM

Save the performance information that you collect every time you run Performance Monitor. Even more important than the absolute performance of your server is its relative performance over time—in comparison to its no-load baseline.

When you run Performance Monitor, always measure the same core objects and counters. You can add other objects and counters as necessary to measure specifics, but always include these core objects and counters so that you have a consistent frame of reference. We suggest that you select objects and counters

from the categories of CPU, memory, disk and network. The objects and counters you select really depends on your configuration, but choose some from all four categories and include them in every test.

Remember the disk performance counters are disabled by default, and you want them that way for normal operation. Enable them at the command line by running "diskperf-y" and rebooting. Don't forget to disable them when you are done. The command is "diskperf-n" and reboot.

—*By Shane Clawson, MCT, MCSE*

CERTIFICATION OBJECTIVE 13.04

Event Viewer

The Event Viewer, located under the Administration submenu, lets you examine various events generated by audited user actions or the Windows NT system, services, and applications. Figure 13-21 shows an example from the Event Viewer.

Log Files

The Event Viewer can display three separate logs. The log you open depends upon the type of items you need to view.

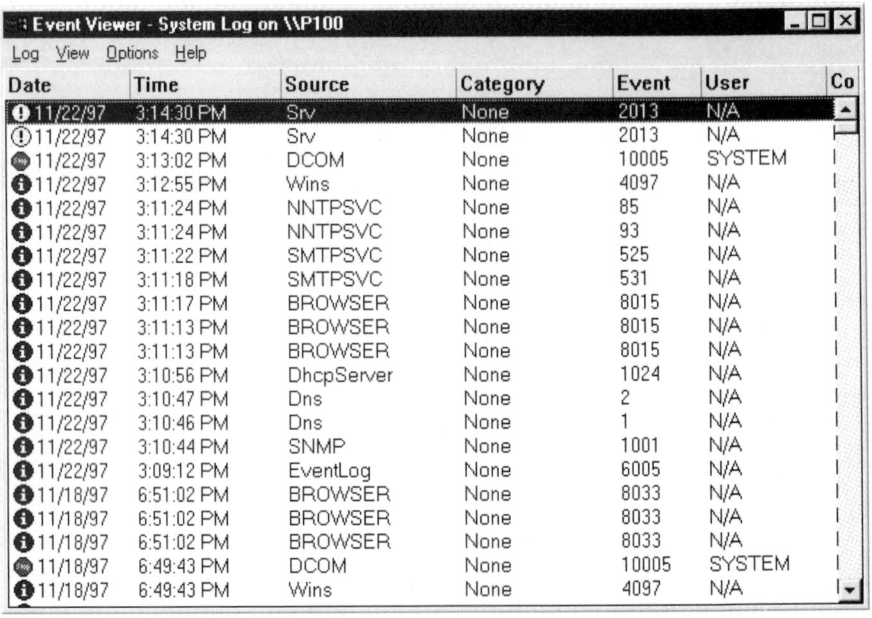

FIGURE 13-21

Event Viewer

- The **System Log** contains events that are provided by the Windows NT internal services and drivers.

- The **Security Log** contains all security related events when auditing has been enabled.

- The **Application Log** contains events that have been generated by applications.

By default, each log file is a maximum of 512 kilobytes in size and overwrites events older than seven days. However, these parameters can be reset by changing the Maximum Log Size and Event Log Wrapping options in each of the three individual log files. The maximum size of the log can be changed in 64 kilobyte increments. The three Event Log Wrapping options are: overwrite events as needed; overwrite events older than 'number' days; and do not overwrite events (clear log manually).

Event Log files may be saved in three different formats: Event Log file with the .EVT extension, text file with the .TXT extension, or a comma-delimited text file with the .TXT extension. The .EVT file is a binary file that can be read only by the Event Viewer utility. Any ASCII editor can read the text files. If you save the log file, the text description will be saved regardless of the format in which you save the file. However, the hexadecimal data will be saved only if you use the .EVT format.

Log File Events

There are five types of events recorded in the various logs. A unique icon identifies each event type, so that you can rapidly locate the type of event you are seeking. Table 13-5 describes each of the event types.

TABLE 13-5	Icon	Event	Description
Types of Events Displayed in the Event Viewer		Error	A significant problem has occurred; for example, a service may not have started properly.
		Warning	An event has occurred that is not currently detrimental to the system, but it may indicate a possible future problem.
		Information	A significant event has occurred successfully. For example, a service that starts successfully may trigger this type of event.
		Audit Success	An audited security access attempt was successful. For example, access to an audited directory was granted.
		Audit Failure	An audited security access attempt was not successful. For example, a login attempt failed.

Log Event Details

Events can be seen in greater detail by using the mouse to double-click on an event or by highlighting the event and choosing Detail from the View menu. The Detail dialog box displays a text description that may help in analyzing the event. Hexadecimal information may also be provided, depending on the event. Figure 13-22 shows the event details for an event from the System log.

CERTIFICATION OBJECTIVE 13.05

Windows NT Diagnostics

Windows NT Diagnostics (also called WinMSD) has several tabs that contain a great deal of information about your Windows NT Server system. Figure 13-23 shows Windows NT Diagnostics just after it has been started.

FIGURE 13-22

Event Detail from the System log

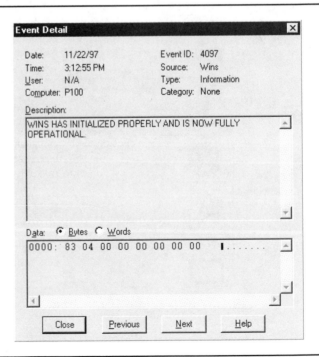

FIGURE 13-23

Windows NT Diagnostics
opening window

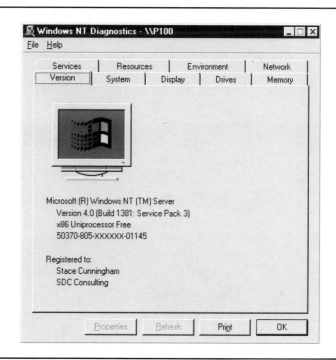

Version

The Version tab shows the NT version number, build and type, CPU architecture, and multiprocessor support. The serial number and the name of the registered user for this copy of Windows NT are also displayed.

System

The System tab shows system-level information about the hardware, including vendor ID, Hardware Abstraction Layer (HAL) type, BIOS date, and a description of the CPU(s).

Display

The Dsplay tab shows the video BIOS date, display processor, video resolution, quantity of video RAM, vendor, Digital to Analog (DAC) type, and driver type and revision.

Drives

The Drives tab provides a tree display that can be sorted by drive letter or drive type for each logical disk drive. Selecting any drive brings up a Properties window that shows information such as the drive letter, serial number, disk space available and how much disk space is in use. A File System tab on the Properties window gives information about the file system being used, including the maximum number of characters in a filename. The File System tab also shows whether the case will be preserved in filenames, the support of case-sensitive filenames, support for Unicode in a filename, file-based compression, and security preservation and enforcement.

Memory

The Memory tab shows in-depth details on memory utilization in your system to include the total number of processes, handles, and threads in use. This tab also displays the total amount of physical memory and the pagefile space available and currently in use.

Services

The Services tab displays information on all services and devices on your Windows NT Server. Highlighting a selection and selecting the Properties button brings up a Service Properties dialog box for the service or device. The information includes the executable file associated with the service or device, the start type, the user account with which it is associated, and any error associated with it. Also displayed are the service flags, which indicate whether it will run in its own memory space, whether it is a kernel driver, and whether it can interact with the Windows NT desktop. A Dependencies tab shows you if the highlighted choice depends on another service or device. If it does depend on another service or device, that information may help you in troubleshooting why the service or device failed to start.

Resources

The Resources tab displays information about hardware resources, including Interrupt Requests (IRQ), I/O ports, Direct Memory Access (DMA), physical memory, and device drivers. If you select an item, it displays a dialog box to indicate the associated device driver, bus, and bus type. A check box on this tab allows you to choose whether you want resources owned by the NT HAL to be displayed on the list.

Environment

The Environment tab displays all environment variables and values. It can display either values for the system or values for the local user for user-specific entries.

Network

The Network tab provides a great deal of information including the number of logged-on users, transport protocols that are in use along with the media access control (MAC) address of each transport, internal network settings, and system statistics which include server bytes sent, hung sessions, and many others.

Now that you are familiar with all the tabs offered by Windows NT Diagnostics, use Exercise 13-14 to see how your system is functioning.

| EXERCISE 13-14 | **Using the Windows NT Diagnostic Tools** |

1. Click the Start button.
2. Select Programs.
3. Select Administration Tools.
4. Select Windows NT Diagnostics.
5. Select the Drives tab.
6. Click the + to the left of local hard drives.

7. Double-click the C: drive.

8. Select the File System tab. Observe the statistics that are applicable to the drive.

9. Click the OK button.

10. Select the Services tab.

11. Highlight Server and click the Properties button. Observe the server flags that are applicable to the server service.

12. Select the Dependencies tab. Notice that the server service has group dependencies on TDI (transport driver interface).

13. Click the OK button.

14. Click the OK button to close Windows NT Diagnostics.

CERTIFICATION OBJECTIVE 13.06

Network Monitor

The Network Monitor is an outstanding tool for monitoring the network performance of your system. The Network Monitor that comes with Windows NT Server will only display the frames that are sent to or from your system. It will not monitor your entire network segment. A *frame* is an amount of information that has been divided into smaller pieces by the network software to be sent out across the wire. A frame consists of the following items:

- The source address of the system that sent the frame.

- The destination address of the system that received the frame.

- The header for the protocol that sent the frame.

- The actual data that was sent.

The Network Monitor is not installed by default when you load Windows NT Server. It is implemented as a network service. Exercise 13-15 leads you through the steps needed to install Network Monitor on your system.

EXERCISE 13-15

Installing the Network Monitor

1. Click on the Start button.
2. Select Settings.
3. Select Control Panel.
4. Double-click the Network icon.
5. Select the Services tab.
6. Click the Add button.
7. Select Network Monitor Tools and Agent from the scroll-down list.
8. Click the OK button.
9. The setup program prompts you for a path from which to install the files. Insert your Windows NT media so the appropriate files can be copied to your system.
10. Click the Close button. You will then be prompted to restart your computer. When your system restarts, the Network Monitor will be available from your Administrative Tools folder.

When you start the Network Monitor, it displays an empty capture window like the one shown in Figure 13-24.

Now that Network Monitor is installed, let's capture some data to see what your system is doing on the network. Exercise 13-16 shows you how to capture data from your system. The exercise works best when performed on a system that is on a busy network.

EXERCISE 13-16

Manually Initiating a Data Capture

1. Click the Start button.
2. Select Programs.
3. Select Administration Tools.
4. Select Network Monitor.
5. Select the Capture menu.
6. Select Start. Let the Network Monitor run for about one minute or so before continuing with the exercise. Depending on your network, you may see a lot of information or very little.

FIGURE 13-24

Network Monitor when
first started

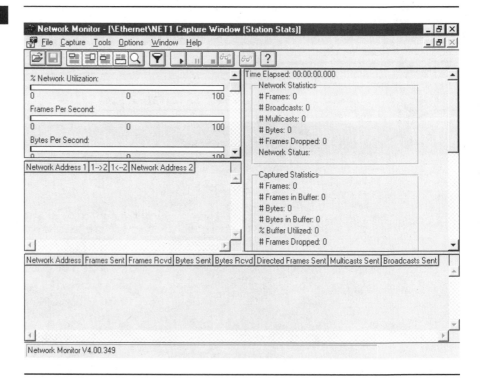

7. Select the Capture menu.

8. Select Stop and View. A Capture Summary of all the frames that were captured is displayed.

9. Double-click the first line of the Capture Summary. Two additional windows, the Detail and Hex windows, are displayed. Figure 13-25 gives an example of these two additional windows.

10. Click the + next to FRAME. Details such as the Time of Capture and Capture frame length are displayed.

11. Select the File menu.

12. Select Exit.

13. Select No when prompted to save the capture.

FIGURE 13-25

Capture window from
Network Monitor

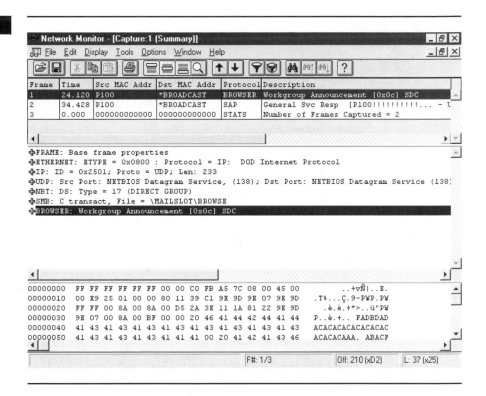

As you can imagine, there is a lot of valuable information to be gleaned
from a Network Monitor capture. Remember, however, that Network
Monitor can be a huge security risk as you or anyone else with access to the
Administrative Tools group will have the ability to analyze frames sent to or
from your Windows NT Server. It would not be a good situation if someone
were able to capture e-mail that was meant for only you. Fortunately, a couple
of precautions exist to help control security. First, the Network Monitor that
comes with Windows NT Server cannot be operated remotely; you must be
physically present and logged in at the server in order to use it. Second, special
passwords for capture and display can be set in such a way that only the people
who know those passwords can use the Network Monitor. Exercise 13-17
shows you how to set these passwords for your system.

Setting Network Monitor Passwords

1. Click the Start button.

2. Select Settings.

3. Select Control Panel.

4. Double-click the Monitoring Agent icon.

5. Click the Change Password button. The dialog box shown in Figure 13-26 displays.

6. Type and confirm a password in the Display Password block.

7. Type and confirm a password in the Capture Password block. It can be the same password you placed in the Display Password block if you want to allow full capture capability with only one password.

8. Click the OK button. You now have password protection for Network Monitor. To verify that the password is working, you can start up Network Monitor to see it prompt you for a password.

FIGURE 13-26

Network Monitoring
Password Change
dialog box

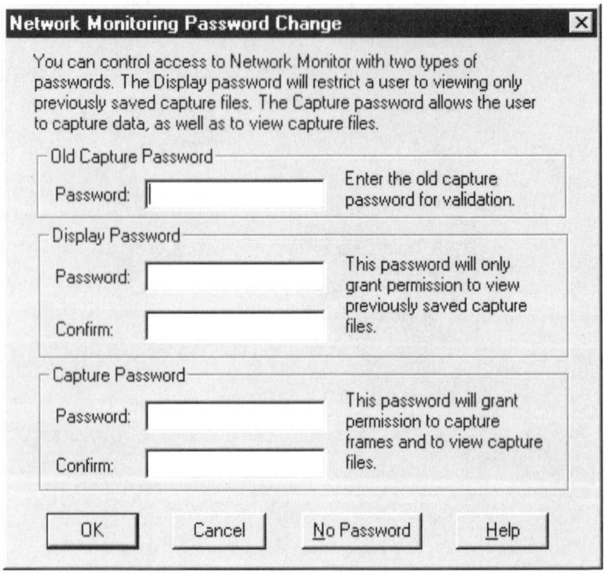

Network Monitoring Password Change

You can control access to Network Monitor with two types of passwords. The Display password will restrict a user to viewing only previously saved capture files. The Capture password allows the user to capture data, as well as to view capture files.

Old Capture Password

Password: | | Enter the old capture password for validation.

Display Password

Password: | | This password will only grant permission to view previously saved capture files.

Confirm: | |

Capture Password

Password: | | This password will grant permission to capture frames and to view capture files.

Confirm: | |

OK   Cancel   No Password   Help

CERTIFICATION SUMMARY

To optimize your Windows NT system, it is important to use all the available tools to improve performance capability. Windows NT assists you in this endeavor by providing counters for every object that the operating system can measure. You can ask Windows NT to use the counters for automatic self-tuning or you can tune performance manually with Performance Monitor.

Some of the self-tuning that Windows NT performs automatically are thread and process prioritization, caching disk requests, multiprocessing capability, utilization of multiple pagefiles, and techniques to avoid fragmentation of physical memory.

It is possible to optimize applications by using the Task Manager to manually change an application's response. You can also change the priority level of foreground applications by using the Performance tab of the System Properties screen.

The Performance Monitor tool shipped with Windows NT allows you to be very granular when investigating the performance of your system by measuring individual objects and counters. The Performance Monitor displays in real-time what is occurring within your system and helps you to rapidly isolate a bottleneck. Performance Monitor can also be used to send alerts when thresholds have been met or to log data for long-term monitoring of your system.

A bottleneck is some element of your system that prohibits it from operating at peak efficiency. The three main areas to target in looking for a bottleneck are processor performance, disk drive performance, and memory performance.

The Event Viewer is a useful tool that helps you monitor security events, application events, and system events. Other useful monitoring tools are contained in Windows NT Diagnostics, which allows you to see many parameters of your system, and the Network Monitor, which allows you to detect network traffic sent and received by your system.

Performance tuning a Windows NT system is an ongoing process that starts with finding and resolving the most significant bottleneck. After resolving the most significant bottleneck, you locate the next most significant bottleneck and repeat until you resolve all possible bottlenecks.

TWO-MINUTE DRILL

❑ Performance tuning Windows NT Server is the art of taking your existing configuration and maximizing its performance to achieve the optimal outcome.

❑ You know you have a bottleneck if one resource has a high rate of use while other resources have relatively low usage.

❑ To locate a bottleneck in your system you must evaluate a set of metrics based upon the number of requests for service, the arrival time of the requests, and the amount of time requested.

❑ NT Workstation, as shipped, supports only two processors, while NT Server supports four.

❑ The first way to perform network tuning via the Network applet in the Control Panel is to choose the appropriate optimization setting for the Windows NT Server service.

❑ The second way to perform network tuning is to set the binding order based upon the protocols most used on your network.

❑ The Task Manager enables you to review applications, processes, and performance statistics in your NT Server at any given moment.

❑ The Performance Monitor is a tool, included with Windows NT 4.0, that tracks the usage of resources by the system components and applications.

❑ Performance Monitor utilizes three different types of items to view the system. They are *objects, counters* and *instances*.

❑ A Performance Monitor chart measures the objects that you designate; it reflects the current activity with a real-time look at the counters chosen.

❑ A Performance Monitor Alert tracks events and notifies a user or a computer depending on the parameters you set.

❑ A program might not work correctly when you use Run Program on Alert because Performance Monitor passes the Alert condition as a parameter to the program. If it does not work correctly, you should create a batch file to run the program and call the batch file from Performance Monitor.

❑ The Performance Monitor Report view lets you display constantly changing counter and instance values for selected objects.

❑ The Performance Monitor log files, which are in binary format, provide a way to save the counter information and then later run it through the Performance Monitor application.

❑ You may want to measure the performance of your processor to ensure that a bottleneck is not present, especially if your processor pre-dates the Pentium family.

❑ The I/O capacity of the disk drive is usually the first resource to reach its limit and create a bottleneck on your system.

❑ You must use diskperf-ye to monitor a physical drive in a RAID set. Using diskperf-ye installs the Disk Drive Performance Statistics Driver low in the disk driver stack so that it can see individual physical disks before they are logically combined.

❑ Memory can contribute significantly to system bottlenecks; some claim it is the most common bottleneck you will encounter.

❑ The Event Viewer, located under the Administration submenu, lets you examine various events generated by audited user actions or the Windows NT system, services, and applications.

❑ Windows NT Diagnostics (also called WinMSD) has several tabs that contain a great deal of information about your Windows NT Server system.

❑ The Network Monitor is an outstanding tool for monitoring the network performance of your system.

SELF TEST

The following questions will help you measure your understanding of the material presented in this chapter. Read all the choices carefully, as there may be more than one correct answer. Choose all correct answers for each question.

1. What type of network interface card should you use in a system that has a PCI bus?

    A. 8 bit

    B. 16 bit

    C. 32 bit

    D. 64 bit

2. Your network has 73 users who will be using Word from your Windows NT Server. What is the optimum setting for the server service?

    A. Minimize Memory Used

    B. Balance

    C. Maximize Throughput for File Sharing

    D. Maximize Throughput for Network Applications

3. Your network uses a combination of two different network protocols. You place the least used protocol at the top of the binding order for the server service. Will it decrease server performance?

    A. Yes

    B. No

4. (True/False) Messenger service does not need to be started in order for an alert to be sent from Performance Monitor.

5. The Event Viewer log size can be changed in _____ increments.

    A. 16 kilobyte

    B. 32 kilobyte

    C. 64 kilobyte

    D. 96 kilobyte

6. What tab of the Windows NT Diagnostics screen would you use to determine the dependencies for a device on the system?

    A. Resources tab

    B. System tab

    C. Services tab

    D. Environment tab

7. (True/False) The Network Monitor that comes with Windows NT Server can be used to collect data for your entire network segment.

8. When the /HIGH switch is used to launch an application from the command prompt, at what priority will the application start?

    A. 24

    B. 13

    C. 7

    D. 4

9. While using the Processor:%Processor Time counter in Performance Monitor, you see it spike to 100 percent when starting an application, but then it drops to 43 percent. What do you need to do?

   A. Upgrade to a faster processor.

   B. Increase the size of your pagefile.

   C. Add more physical memory to your system.

   D. Nothing, the system is performing within acceptable parameters.

10. Windows NT divides memory into _____ pages.

    A. 2KB

    B. 4KB

    C. 8KB

    D. 16KB

11. Windows NT Server supports _____ processors.

    A. 1

    B. 2

    C. 3

    D. 4

12. (True/False) It is not possible to change the priority of the foreground application so that it will run at the same priority as all background applications.

13. How many levels can Windows NT automatically adjust the priority of an application?

    A. 4

    B. 3

    C. 2

    D. 1

14. You suspect a disk drive is creating a bottleneck within your system. You use the LogicalDisk:%Disk Time counter to take measurements but have a consistent reading of zero. What is the problem?

    A. The disk drive no longer functions properly.

    B. Disk drive performance counters are enabled.

    C. The wrong object counter is being used.

    D. Disk drive performance counters are disabled.

15. Multiprocessing supported by Windows NT is _____ .

    A. asymmetrical

    B. symmetrical

    C. both asymmetrical and symmetrical

    D. neither asymmetrical or symmetrical

16. (True/False) Using two processors in your Windows NT system will double its performance capability.

17. Where does Windows NT perform automatic self-tuning optimizations?

    A. Thread and process prioritization

    B. Asymmetrical processing

    C. Swapping among multiple pagefiles

    D. Caching disk requests

    E. All of the above

18. The cache system used by Windows NT is
    ____ .

    A. static

    B. fixed

    C. dynamic

    D. inert

19. What utility is used to enable the disk drive performance counters?

    A. Perfdisk

    B. Diskenable

    C. Diskperf

    D. Enabledisk

20. (True/False) The Task Manager cannot be used to change the priority of a thread.

21. Performance Monitor shows that you have a disk drive bottleneck. What action(s) could alleviate this problem?

    A. Create a RAID 5 set using Disk Administrator

    B. Add more physical memory to the system

    C. Use an 8-bit disk drive controller card

    D. Buy a new processor

    E. All of the above

22. Performance Monitor indicates that you are encountering a memory bottleneck. What action(s) will eliminate it?

    A. Increase the size of PAGEFILE.SYS

    B. Add a new high-speed controller card

    C. Unload any drivers that aren't in use

    D. Decrease the size of the L2 cache

    E. All of the above

23. (True/False) Hard page faults are more detrimental to system performance than soft page faults.

24. (True/False) Once you have manually performance tuned your system you will never have to do it again.

25. (True/False) Disk drive performance counters should only be enabled when monitoring disk drive performance.

26. What would you use to change the priority of an application that is already running?

    A. Performance Monitor

    B. Performance tab from System Properties

    C. /REALTIME switch

    D. Task Manager

14

Troubleshooting

CERTIFICATION OBJECTIVES

14.01   Installation Problems

14.02   Configuration Errors

14.03   Disk Problems

14.04   Troubleshooting RAID Problems

14.05   Printing Problems

14.06   Remote Access Service Problems

14.07   Network Problems

14.08   Permission Problems

14.09   Server Crashes

14.10   Using Microsoft Resources

W ouldn't life be wonderful if you could install a network operating system and never have to worry that it might fail to work correctly? In years of dealing with a varied number of operating systems, we have never encountered one that didn't need coaxing at some point in time. Windows NT Server is no exception, so it is very important that you learn to troubleshoot various problems that can occur.

The chapter begins with installation problems and configuration errors that you may encounter. Disk problems can be frustrating to troubleshoot—especially when dealing with a RAID configuration. Next we examine problems that you may see with printers and Remote Access Service. Then, because network problems can be very difficult to isolate, we describe some of the more common problems that can occur, including problems with permissions. Of course, no chapter on troubleshooting Windows NT Server would be complete without a discussion of server crashes—better known as the "blue screen of death."

There are a variety of resources available to help you keep your Windows NT Server system operating smoothly. The final section of the chapter describes the most important of these resources.

When troubleshooting any problem, a logical approach works best. You need to look at what is working and what isn't. Then you need to study the relationship of the things that do and don't work. Check to see if the things that don't work have *ever* worked on the system. If they once worked, check to see what has changed since the last time they worked.

CERTIFICATION OBJECTIVE 14.01

Installation Problems

You may encounter difficulties during Windows NT Server installation, but with proper planning most of these problems can be avoided. One common cause of installation problems is trying to use hardware that is not on Microsoft's Hardware Compatibility List (HCL). The HCL is a compilation of computer systems and hardware that have been tested for compatibility with Windows NT. Before installing any hardware, you should check to make sure that all your hardware is on the HCL.

Here's one reason why it's important to comply with the HCL. The first part of a Windows NT Server installation is referred to as *character-based Setup* or *text-based Setup*. During this phase Windows NT Server performs an in-depth examination of your system, and it is vital that the information gathered by Windows NT Server is accurate. Windows NT Server may have problems identifying controllers and settings if your system uses proprietary parts that do not meet industry standards. If Windows NT Server gathers incorrect information, your installation will probably fail at some point. Incorrect detection is a common basis for a hardware or configuration problem. Because Windows NT Server has been designed to communicate with specified hardware, compatibility problems are more likely to be critical than they might be under a different operating system.

The second part of a Windows NT Server installation is referred to as the *graphical mode*. When the graphical mode starts, Setup is running under the Windows NT Server operating system.

Table 14-1 lists some of the problems you may encounter during installation of Windows NT Server.

Windows NT Server ships with two utilities to support the installation process—NTHQ and SCSITOOL.

NTHQ is an NT utility that identifies what hardware is installed in your computer, including PCI, EISA, ISA, and MCA devices. NTHQ inspects your computer for hardware incompatibilities without installing the operating system. It also helps to determine whether the hardware is on the HCL. Exercise 14-1 shows you how to make a floppy disk for NTHQ.

EXECISE 14-1

Creating a NTHQ Floppy Disk

1. Change directory to the X:\Support\HQtool directory of the Windows NT CD-ROM. (Replace X with the drive letter of your own CD-ROM drive.)

2. Insert a floppy disk into your A: drive.

3. Run the MAKEDISK.BAT file.

TABLE 14-1

Installation Problems and Possible Resolutions

Installation Problem	Possible Resolution
Media errors	Try other media or another method such as a network installation.
Not enough disk space	Use the Setup program to format an existing partition to create more disk space or remove existing partitions and create new ones that are large enough to install into.
Setup finds no hard drives on your computer	Scan the drive for viruses. If the Master Boot Record is infected, Windows NT Server may not see the hard disk drive. If the hard drive is SCSI, use SCSITOOL to obtain SCSI information. Check to see if there is a valid boot sector on the drive. Check that all SCSI devices are properly terminated.
Setup hangs during text-based Setup while copying files to the hard drive	Use a different Hardware Abstraction Layer (HAL). Make sure Setup is not using reserved memory.
The Dependency service failed to start.	Return to the Network Settings dialog box. Verify that the correct protocol and network adapter are installed, that the network adapter has the proper settings, and that the computer name is unique on the network.
While rebooting from text mode to graphical mode, you receive the error message, "NTOSKRNL.EXE is missing or corrupt"	Edit the BOOT.INI file and change the partition number for Windows NT Server. The BOOT.INI file is discussed in depth later in the chapter.
Non-supported SCSI adapter	Boot your computer under another operating system that can read from the SCSI adapter and CD-ROM drive, then run WINNT.EXE from the I386 directory.
During graphical mode Setup, the screen hangs at random intervals—either during file copies or between screens	This usually indicates problems with computer interrupt conflicts, video, or the SCSI bus.

4. Restart your computer while the disk is still in the floppy drive. NTHQ runs automatically and creates a file named NTHQ.TXT that lists all the hardware detected.

5. Review each device that is listed as not compatible. If a device is not compatible, make sure that you have the third-party driver for that device or else remove the device before you install Windows NT.

SCSITOOL currently reports information for only Adaptec and Buslogic SCSI adapters. You create a SCSITOOL floppy disk just as you created the NTHQ disk. The tools used to create a SCSITOOL floppy disk are located in the X:\Support\Scsitool directory. (Again, replace X with the drive letter of your own CD-ROM drive.)

After you have successfully installed Windows NT Server, you may encounter other problems during normal operation. We'll examine some typical problems, starting with configuration errors you may run into.

CERTIFICATION OBJECTIVE 14.02

Configuration Errors

Configuration errors can be very frustrating when you are attempting to troubleshoot your system because there are many areas where something could go wrong. In this section you will discover how to fix your system when it has a boot failure, the purpose of the LastKnownGood configuration, and how to use your Emergency Repair Disk.

Boot Failures

Boot failures can take many different paths that lead your system to failure. Anything from a corrupted boot file to a bad video driver can prevent your system from booting successfully. The following paragraphs will explore a few of the possibilities when dealing with boot failures on systems that do not use RAID. Later in the chapter, we'll tackle RAID problems.

First, you need to ensure that you have a Windows NT boot floppy in case one of the boot files for your system ever gets deleted. A boot floppy can help you get your system back up quickly and it may enable you to copy the missing or corrupt file back to your hard drive. You must use a boot disk that has been formatted on a Windows NT system.

Exercise 14-2 takes you through the steps in creating a Windows NT boot floppy for an Intel-based machine.

EXERCISE 14-2

Creating a Windows NT Boot Floppy for Intel-Based Machines

1. Log on as Administrator and select My Computer.

2. Right-click on 3 ½ Floppy (A:) and select Format from the menu.

3. Make sure you have a blank floppy disk in the drive and click the Start button.

4. Acknowledge the warning by clicking the OK button.

5. When the format completes, click the OK button.

6. Copy the following files to the newly formatted disk: NTLDR, NTDETECT.COM, BOOT.INI, NTBOOTDD.SYS (if your system uses NTBOOTDD.SYS), BOOTSECT.DOS (if your system is multiple-boot enabled).

7. Reboot your system with the boot floppy you just created. It is better to try it now and make sure it works properly than to need the disk and find it does not work correctly.

Table 14-2 shows some common symptoms and boot error messages. While the Windows NT boot disk can save you from several boot problems, it will not solve them all.

Using the LastKnownGood Configuration

What happens if you load a new device driver that does not function correctly and it stops the system from booting correctly? Do you have to reload Windows NT? Let's hope you answered with a resounding NO! You can get

TABLE 14-2	Symptom	Boot Error Message
Common Boot Error Symptoms and Messages	If the NTLDR file is missing, this message appears before the Boot Loader Operating System Selection menu.	BOOT: Couldn't find NTLDR Please insert another disk.
	If NTDETECT.COM is missing, this message appears after the Boot Loader Operating System Selection menu.	NTDETECT V4.0 Checking Hardware... NTDETECT failed
	If NTOSKRNL.EXE is missing, this message appears after the LastKnownGood prompt.	Windows NT could not start because the following file is missing or corrupt: %systemroot%\system32\ntoskrnl.exe Please re-install a copy of the above file.
	If BOOTSECT.DOS is missing in a boot loader configuration, this message appears after the Boot Loader Operating System Selection menu when the second operating system is attempted to be booted.	I/O Error accessing boot sector file multi(0)disk(0)rdisk(0)partition(1):\ bootsect.dos NOTE: BOOTSECT.DOS stores partition information that is specific to that system. You cannot use BOOTSECT.DOS from another system.

around this problem by reverting to the *LastKnownGood configuration.*
LastKnownGood is the configuration that was saved to a special control set
in the Registry after the last successful logon to Windows NT. Instead of
reloading the entire operating system you can restart the computer without
logging on, then select LastKnownGood during the boot sequence. This will
load the previously known good control set, and bypass the bad device driver.
LastKnownGood can also be initiated if Windows NT has a fatal error at
boot time. Exercise 14-3 leads you through the process of booting using the
LastKnownGood configuration.

EXERCISE 14-3

Booting Windows NT with the LastKnownGood Configuration

1. Start Windows NT Server.
2. When the BOOT.INI displays the OS menu, select Windows NT Server.

3. A message displays, telling you to press SPACEBAR for the LastKnownGood. Press the SPACEBAR immediately, because you only have a few seconds to make this choice before it disappears.

4. Select "L" to choose the LastKnownGood configuration from the Hardware Profile/Configuration Recovery menu.

5. Press the ENTER key to confirm your choice. After the system boots it displays a message confirming it loaded from a previous configuration.

The LastKnownGood configuration will not help you in all situations. For example, LastKnownGood cannot solve problems such as user profiles and file permissions, which are not related to changes in control set information. Nor can it solve startup failures caused by hardware failures or corrupted files.

So, while the LastKnownGood configuration may save the day in some situations, like the Windows NT boot floppy, it will not work in all cases. Another tool you'll need is the Emergency Repair Disk.

Using the Emergency Repair Disk

The Emergency Repair Disk (ERD) can be used to restore a Windows NT system back to the configuration it had the last time you updated your Emergency Repair Disk. This disk can repair missing Windows NT files and restore the Registry to include disk configuration and security information. To create an ERD you use the Repair Disk Utility. Figure 14-1 shows the Repair Disk Utility after it has been started.

FIGURE 14-1

Repair Disk Utility screen

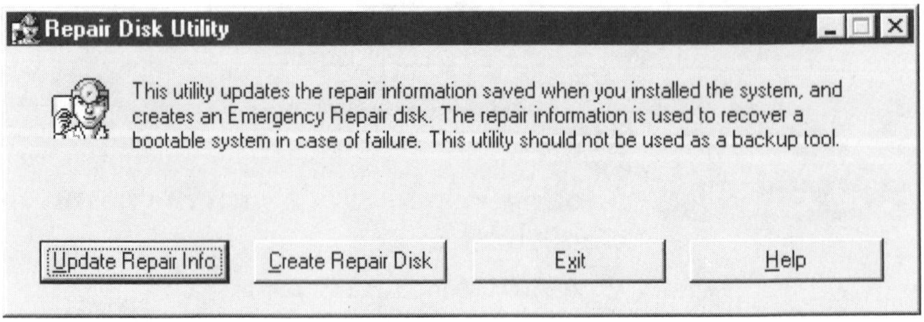

Repair Disk Utility

This utility updates the repair information saved when you installed the system, and creates an Emergency Repair disk. The repair information is used to recover a bootable system in case of failure. This utility should not be used as a backup tool.

| Update Repair Info | Create Repair Disk | Exit | Help |

If you choose the Update Repair Info button, the Repair Disk Utility will overwrite some of the files located in the %systemroot%\Repair directory. After the %systemroot%\Repair directory has been updated the program prompts you to create an Emergency Repair Disk. The disk it creates is the same as if you had chosen the Create Repair Disk option.

If you choose the Create Repair Disk button, the Repair Disk Utility formats the disk, then creates the ERD. This will occur whether you use a prior ERD or a new one. Exercise 14-4 shows you how to create an ERD.

EXERCISE 14-4

Creating an Emergency Repair Disk

1. Log on as Administrator.

2. Select Start | Programs | Command Prompt.

3. Type **rdisk** in the prompt window.

4. Choose the Update Repair Info button.

5. After the program updates your %systemroot%\Repair directory it prompts you to create an ERD. Insert a disk and select OK.

6. A message is displayed as the configuration files are being copied. After the files are copied to the disk, choose Exit.

If you look at the files on the ERD, you will notice some of them end with the characters ._. This indicates that those files have been compressed. You can decompress them using the expand utility that comes with Windows NT.

exam
ⓦatch

The Security Account Manager (SAM) and Security files are not automatically updated by rdisk. To update those files you need to use the /S switch in conjunction with rdisk.

Now that you have an up-to-date Emergency Repair Disk, it is time to use it in the Emergency Repair Process. The Emergency Repair Process is needed when your system will not function correctly and using the LastKnownGood configuration does not solve your problem. This process requires the original installation disks used when you first installed Windows NT Server. You also need the ERD that you created in the last exercise. Please note that ERD's are computer-specific, so don't get them mixed up if you have several systems. Exercise 14-5 shows you how to complete the Emergency Repair Process.

Using the Emergency Repair Disk with the NT Setup Disks

1. Start your system using the Windows NT Setup boot disk.

2. Insert disk 2 when the system prompts you for it.

3. When the first screen appears, press R to start the Emergency Repair Process.

4. Four options are displayed on your screen. Follow the on-screen instructions to select *only* the option Inspect Registry Files.

5. Select the Continue (perform selected tasks) line and press the ENTER key.

6. Windows NT will want to perform mass storage detection; go ahead and let it do that.

7. When the system prompts you, insert disk 3 and press the ENTER key.

8. Press ENTER to skip the Specify Additional Mass Storage Devices step.

9. When the system prompts you, insert the ERD you created in Exercise 14-4.

10. Several choices are displayed on your screen. Select *only* the DEFAULT (Default User Profile) choice.

11. Select Continue (perform selected tasks) and press the ENTER key.

12. The system copies the correct data back to your Windows NT Server partition. Once the data has been copied, remove the ERD and press the ENTER key to restart your system.

It is vital that you regularly update the system repair information in the %systemroot%\Repair directory on your disk drive and remember to create and maintain an up-to-date Emergency Repair Disk. Your system repair information needs to include new configuration information such as drive letter assignments, stripe sets, volume sets, mirrors, and so on. Otherwise, you may not be able to access your drive in the event of a system failure.

The Event Viewer

As you recall, the Event Viewer was described in Chapter 13. It is worth mentioning again here because it can be an immense help in troubleshooting your system—especially when server services do not start. Figure 14-2 shows an example from the System log. The first red flag you encounter deals with Service Control Manager. By showing the Event Details for that log entry, as displayed in Figure 14-3, you can see that the network adapter driver service failed to start. Based upon the error you received, you can quickly isolate the malfunction.

Windows NT Diagnostics

The Windows NT Diagnostics tool was also discussed in Chapter 13. It is one of the most overlooked tools for troubleshooting Windows NT systems. Windows NT Diagnostics enables you to view currently loaded device drivers, IRQ values, and much more. It also provides a view of detected hardware, including the processor that is in your system. Best of all, it can be used over a network to examine a remote system. This works because Windows NT

FIGURE 14-2

System log from the Event Viewer

Date	Time	Source	Category	Event	User	Computer
12/13/97	6:26:53 PM	EventLog	None	6005	N/A	P233
12/13/97	6:26:54 PM	Service Control Mar	None	7000	N/A	P233
12/13/97	5:38:36 PM	EventLog	None	6005	N/A	P233
12/13/97	5:38:37 PM	Service Control Mar	None	7000	N/A	P233
12/13/97	5:20:31 PM	EventLog	None	6005	N/A	P233
12/13/97	5:20:32 PM	Service Control Mar	None	7000	N/A	P233
12/5/97	12:02:00 AM	EventLog	None	6005	N/A	P233
12/5/97	12:02:02 AM	Service Control Mar	None	7000	N/A	P233
12/4/97	11:38:28 PM	EventLog	None	6005	N/A	P233
12/4/97	11:38:29 PM	Service Control Mar	None	7000	N/A	P233
12/4/97	11:30:08 PM	EventLog	None	6005	N/A	P233
12/4/97	11:30:09 PM	Service Control Mar	None	7000	N/A	P233
11/28/97	5:10:00 PM	EventLog	None	6005	N/A	P233
11/28/97	5:10:01 PM	Service Control Mar	None	7000	N/A	P233
11/20/97	11:00:57 PM	EventLog	None	6005	N/A	P233
11/20/97	11:00:59 PM	Service Control Mar	None	7000	N/A	P233
11/19/97	11:33:10 PM	EventLog	None	6005	N/A	P233
11/19/97	11:33:11 PM	Service Control Mar	None	7000	N/A	P233
11/19/97	11:09:21 PM	EventLog	None	6005	N/A	P233
11/19/97	11:09:23 PM	Service Control Mar	None	7000	N/A	P233
11/19/97	10:55:33 PM	Service Control Mar	None	7026	N/A	P233
11/19/97	10:55:24 PM	EventLog	None	6005	N/A	P233
11/19/97	10:55:25 PM	Service Control Mar	None	7000	N/A	P233
11/19/97	7:04:41 PM	Service Control Mar	None	7026	N/A	P233
11/19/97	7:04:31 PM	EventLog	None	6005	N/A	P233
11/19/97	7:04:32 PM	Service Control Mar	None	7000	N/A	P233

Event Viewer - System Log on \\P233

Log   View   Options   Help

Event Detail for the Service
Control Manager error

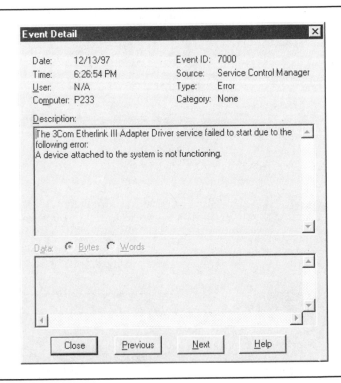

Diagnostics is actually reporting information from the Registry. Figure 14-4
re-acquaints you with the main Windows NT Diagnostics screen.

CERTIFICATION OBJECTIVE 14.03

Disk Problems

It is possible that you will successfully log on to your system before
encountering an error of any type. This section will consider how to
troubleshoot disk problems of this nature. Let's start with a situation
where a volume is displayed as Unknown in Disk Administrator.

FIGURE 14-4

Windows NT Diagnostics
Version tab

Unknown Volume

If you have created and formatted a volume with FAT, but you can no longer access files on it, and Disk Administrator displays the volume as Unknown, the Partition Boot Sector (PBS) for the volume might be bad. The PBS can be corrupted by viruses. Corruption problems can also occur if you have a dual-boot configuration with Windows 95 and you use the Windows 95 Fdisk.

If you have created and formatted a volume with NTFS, but you can no longer access files on it, and Disk Administrator displays the volume as Unknown, the PBS for the volume might be bad, permissions for the volume may have been changed, or the Master File Table (MFT) is corrupt.

Extended Partition Problem

If a logical drive within an extended partition becomes corrupt within the partition table, Windows NT will not be able to access that volume, or any volumes that follow it on the disk. It might be possible to rebuild an extended partition when it becomes corrupt by using a sector editor or partition table editor.

It is more likely on a Windows NT Server that at some point in time you will encounter RAID problems. The next section describes some errors you are likely to encounter.

CERTIFICATION OBJECTIVE 14.04

Troubleshooting RAID Problems

The procedure for detecting and recovering from errors for software fault-tolerant volumes is comparable for both mirror sets (RAID 1) and stripe sets with parity (RAID 5). Windows NT Server's response to the problem depends upon when the problem occurred and whether the loss is due to failure of a *member* of a set or the failure of the *system* partition. A member of a RAID 1 or RAID 5 set is one of the physical disk partitions that make up the set.

If a member disk that is part of a mirror set or a stripe set with parity fails during normal operation, it becomes an orphan. When the fault-tolerant driver (FtDisk) determines that a disk has been orphaned, it directs all reads and writes to the other disk(s) in the set. Figure 14-5 shows the window that is displayed when Windows NT Server detects a fault-tolerant problem during normal operation.

During system initialization, if Windows NT Server cannot locate a member partition in a mirror set or a stripe set with parity, it logs a severe error in the Event Log, marks the partition as an orphan, and uses the remaining partition(s) of the RAID 1 or RAID 5 sets. The system continues to function by using the fault-tolerant capabilities built into the RAID volumes.

FIGURE 14-5

FT Orphaning dialog box

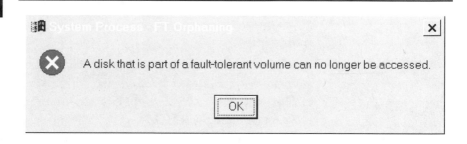

The process of orphaning a partition does not occur during a read operation—only during a write operation. This makes sense, because a read operation does not change any data on the disk.

Regenerating a Stripe Set with Parity

When a member of a stripe set with parity fails, you can continue to use the computer to access all the data. However, you will see a system degradation because it will be regenerating the data in physical memory as the data is needed.

Once a new member drive has been added, you can return the computer to its normal RAID 5 configuration by regenerating the data for the orphaned member. (Specifically, it is reconstructed from the parity data on the remaining members.) Once regenerated, the data is once again available on disk and need not be regenerated in physical memory. The following steps indicate how you would regenerate a stripe set with parity if the need arose.

1. Open Disk Administrator and select the stripe set with parity.

2. Select an area of free space of the same size or larger on the new drive.

3. On the Fault Tolerance menu, choose the Regenerate command.

4. Quit Disk Administrator and restart your computer.

After you restart the computer, the FtDisk reads the information from the stripes of the remaining members and re-creates the data of the orphaned member that was removed to the new member. Your system can be used while the reconstruction is occurring as the process occurs in the background. If you open Disk Administrator, the message in the status bar is: Stripe set with parity [INITIALIZING].

It is possible that you may receive the following error message when attempting to reconstruct a RAID 5 set: The drive cannot be locked for exclusive use. You will receive this error if Disk Administrator does not have exclusive access to the RAID 5 set. You might receive this message if PAGEFILE.SYS or some other system service is accessing the disk. You must move the pagefile to another partition and shut down these services to successfully regenerate the stripe set with parity.

Fixing a Mirror Set

If a *member* of a RAID 1 set fails, the fault tolerance driver directs all I/O to the remaining drive in the mirror set.

When a *member* of a mirror set fails you need to take the following steps:

1. Break the mirror set (as described in Exercise 14-6) so the remaining partition is exposed as a separate volume.

2. Then, unless it has been done automatically, assign to the *working* member the drive letter that was previously assigned to the complete RAID 1 set.

3. Assign the *failed* partition a different available drive letter.

4. Use free space on any other disk drive to create a new mirror set if it is needed. After the computer is restarted, data from the good partition will be copied to the new member of the RAID 1 set.

Exercise 14-6 shows you how to break a RAID 1 mirror set. In order to perform this exercise your system must be set up with a mirror set.

EXERCISE 14-6

Breaking a Mirror Set (RAID 1)

1. Log in as Administrator and start Disk Administrator.

2. Select the mirror set (usually drive C:), then choose Break Mirror from the Fault Tolerance menu.

3. Choose Yes when prompted for confirmation. Notice that the mirrored partition receives the next available drive letter.

4. From the Partition menu, choose Commit Changes Now.

5. Choose Yes when prompted for confirmation.

6. Choose OK when a message box tells you that the Emergency Repair Disk should be updated.

7. Select Exit from the Partition menu.

8. Start Windows NT Explorer and choose the drive that was created when the mirror set was broken. It is an exact duplicate of the drive it had mirrored.

9. Exit the Windows NT Explorer.

Fault-Tolerant Boot Disks

All the procedures just described work fine—as long as you're dealing with a *member* of a RAID set. The story changes when the failure involves the *system* partition on the primary physical drive. In that case, you need to use a fault-tolerant boot disk to restart your system. This boot disk is the key to recovery in case of a physical disk failure and you should create this disk *immediately* whenever you mirror the boot partition of a Windows NT Server. Creating the fault-tolerant boot disk uses the same procedure that you used to create the boot disk in Exercise 14-2—with one exception. In this case, you must modify the Advanced RISC Computing (ARC) path in the BOOT.INI so it points to the mirrored copy of the boot partition. This is why it is very important that you have knowledge of ARC names. Let's review the ARC naming convention so you have a better understanding of the layout of the BOOT.INI file.

ARC Naming Convention

The ARC naming convention comes from the RISC world. It is useful in identifying partition information on multidisk/multipartition machines. For instance, look at Figure 14-6.

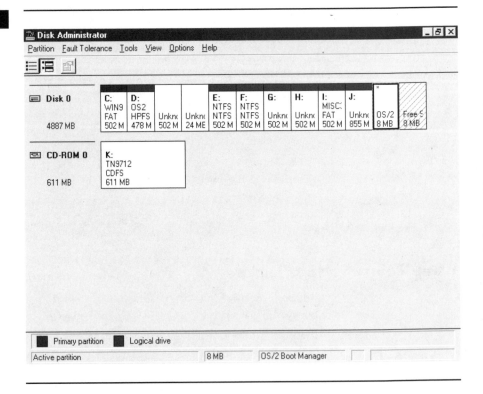

FIGURE 14-6

Disk Administrator showing the disk layout of a particular machine

If we look at the BOOT.INI for this machine, we see:

```
[boot loader]
timeout=15
default=multi(0)disk(0)rdisk(0)partition(6)\WINNT
[operating systems]
multi(0)disk(0)rdisk(0)partition(6)\WINNT="Windows NT Server
Version 4.00"
multi(0)disk(0)rdisk(0)partition(6)\WINNT="Windows NT Server
Version 4.00 [VGA mode]" /basevideo /sos
multi(0)disk(0)rdisk(0)partition(7)\WINNTWS="Windows NT
Workstation Version 4.00"
multi(0)disk(0)rdisk(0)partition(7)\WINNTWS="Windows NT
Workstation Version 4.00 [VGA mode]" /basevideo /sos
C:\="Windows 95"
```

From this we can see the boot partition is on partition number six. But what is all this other stuff? Let's look and see.

SCSI(n) or Multi(n)

A SCSI controller that has its resident BIOS disabled uses the SCSI ARC name. All other controllers (both IDE and SCSI controllers with their BIOS enabled) are listed as *multi*. The numbers that follow SCSI or multi start counting with 0. In the example shown previously, the multi(0) indicates it is the first controller (either IDE or SCSI with the BIOS enabled).

If your BOOT.INI does not list the SCSI ARC name, then NTBOOTDD.SYS is not used.

Disk(n)

Disk is always part of the ARC name, but it is only actively used if SCSI is listed as the first word of the ARC path. If Disk is actively used, then the SCSI bus number is used here. It starts counting with 0. If you have multi in the first space, then Disk will always be 0.

Rdisk(n)

Rdisk indicates the SCSI LUN (Logical Unit Number) when SCSI is the first word in the ARC path, or the ordinal number of the disk if it is multi. Remember the counting here also starts with 0.

Partition(n)

This is simply the partition number on the disk. The important thing here is that the counting starts with one! In Figure 14-6, even though the OS/2 Boot Manager is at the physical end of the drive, it is counted as the number one partition since the system boots from it, then it moves up in count from the C: drive.

To put this all together, if we have the following ARC:

```
multi(0)disk(0)rdisk(0)partition(6)\ WINNT="Windows NT
Server Version 4.00".
```

it is either an IDE controller or a SCSI controller with the BIOS enabled. It is the first controller on the system. Disk (0) in this instance is ignored. Rdisk (0) means that it is the first drive on the system. Partition (6) means that Windows NT Server is located on the sixth partition.

Please note that if changes are made to the system, and this section of the BOOT.INI is not updated, then Windows NT will not load on the next boot.

In case you were wondering about the "unknown" partitions shown in Figure 14-6, they are valid paritions that are unknown to Windows NT 4 Server because it does not recognize OS/2, Linux, or FAT32 partitions.

\ path

The path listed in the BOOT.INI is simply the path to the location of each operating system.

If the *system* partition in a mirror set no longer functions, then the mirror set cannot be booted. However, the data is not lost. It can be recovered because the *boot* partition, where the system files are stored, is still accessible as long as you have a fault-tolerant boot disk. To recover a mirror set, you would need to perform the following steps.

1. Replace the bad drive

2. Boot the system with your fault-tolerant boot disk that loads Windows NT Server from the mirrored partition.

3. Break the existing mirror.

4. Re-establish the mirror to the new drive.

5. Reboot the system without using the fault-tolerant floppy disk.

CERTIFICATION OBJECTIVE 14.05

Printing Problems

It can be very difficult to troubleshoot Windows NT Server printing problems. The process can become complicated because of the many variables involved in printing and the diverse number of clients and print devices that Windows NT Server supports. Some general guidelines that can help isolate printer problems are given here.

1. Check the printer port and cable connections to the computer. Verify that the printer is online. It is amazing how many times a printer is "down" simply because it is offline.

2. Verify that the printer has been selected from within the application.

3. Verify that the correct print driver is being used. You may want to reinstall the print driver just to be sure.

4. Try printing from another client system using the same server. If you can print from a different client system, the print problem is located on the troubled client. If you can't print from a different client, the problem is on the server.

5. Verify that there is enough hard disk space on the drive where the spooler is located. If necessary, move the spooler or increase available hard disk space.

6. Try to print using another application. If the problem occurs only with certain applications, check the appropriate subsystem.

7. Print the document to a file and copy the output to a printer port. If this works, your spooler is the problem. If this doesn't work, the problem is related to the driver or application driver.

Table 14-3 lists some of the more common printing problems you may encounter.

CERTIFICATION OBJECTIVE 14.06

Remote Access Service Problems

This section describes troubleshooting techniques to be used with Remote Access Service (RAS).

TABLE 14-3

Common Printer
Problems and Solutions

Problem	Solution
Disk drive starts thrashing and print job never completes.	Out of hard disk space for spooling. Either create more room or move the spooler to another partition.
No one can print to the server; there is a job at the server that will not print and it cannot be deleted.	The print spooler is stalled. Go to Services from Control Panel, stop the spooler service, and then restart it.
The print job does not print completely or comes out garbled.	Incorrect printer driver is being used. Replace it with the correct printer driver.
A printer has stopped functioning, but people are still printing to it.	Add the Universal Naming Convention name of the replacement printer to the port on the printer that stopped functioning.
Applications running on the system seem to be slowing down the printing process.	The spooler priority is not set high enough. Adjust the PriorityClass Registry entry contained in HKEY_LOCAL_MACHINE\System\CurrentControlSet\Control\Print.

If you have a Dial-Up Networking (DUN) client that has difficulties being authenticated over RAS, the first thing you should try is to change the security option on both the server and client to "allow any authentication including clear text." Because of the wide variety of DUN clients that are available, the clients may not support the same encryption methods that Windows NT Server supports. Switching to the "allow any authentication including clear text" option allows you to try the lowest authentication method on each side. If you have success with that setting, you can start increasing the authentication options to reach a determination of the highest level of authentication that can be used between the client and server.

If a DUN client is having problems with authentication over Point-to-Point Protocol (PPP), a PPP.LOG file can be a very handy way to troubleshoot the problem. The PPP.LOG file is not enabled by default. To enable the PPP.LOG file you need to change the following Registry entry to a 1.

```
\HKEY_LOCAL_MACHINE\System\CurrentControlSet\Services\Rasman
\PPP\Logging
```

The PPP.LOG file is stored in the %systemroot%\SYSTEM32\RAS folder. An example of a PPP.LOG file follows.

```
<PPP packet sent at 12/25/1997 20:25:46:933
<Protocol = LCP, Type = Configure-Ack, Length = 0x19, Id =
0x2, Port = 0
<C0 21 02 02 00 17 01 04 05 F4 02 06 00 0A 00 00
|.!............|
<03 05 C2 23 05 07 02 08 02              |...#.....  |

>PPP packet received at 12/25/1997 20:25:46:943
>Protocol = LCP, Type = Configure-Ack, Length = 0x16, Id =
0x1, Port = 0
>C0 21 02 01 00 14 02 06 00 00 00 00 05 06 00 00
|.!............|
>04 A0 07 02 08 02                       |......    |

FsmThisLayerUp called for protocol = c021, port = 0
LCP Local Options-------------
     MRU=1500,ACCM=0,Auth=0,MagicNumber=1184,PFC=ON,ACFC=ON
     Recv Framing = PPP,SSHF=OFF,MRRU=1500
LCP Remote Options------------
MRU=1524,ACCM=655360,Auth=c223,MagicNumber=0,PFC=ON,ACFC=ON
Send Framing = PPP,SSHF=OFF,MRRU=1500
LCP Configured successfully
<PPP packet sent at 12/25/1997 20:25:46:943
<Protocol = LCP, Type = Identification, Length = 0x14, Id =
0x2, Port = 0
<C0 21 0C 02 00 12 00 00 04 A0 4D 53 52 41 53 56
|.!........MSRASV|
<34 2E 30 30                  |4.00     |
```

Another log file that can be very useful in troubleshooting RAS, especially if it is a modem problem, is the DEVICE.LOG. The DEVICE.LOG captures the initialization information between the system and the modem. The DEVICE.LOG contains entries that show RAS issuing the initialization string, the modem echoing the command, and the modem responding with OK. This can be very helpful if RAS cannot dial or if it returns hardware-related errors.

Like the PPP.LOG, the DEVICE.LOG is not enabled by default and must be turned on by changing the following Registry entry to a value of 1.

```
\HKEY_LOCAL_MACHINE\System\CurrentControlSet\Services\Rasman
\Parameters\Logging
```

The change will not take effect until RAS has been stopped and restarted. After restarting RAS the DEVICE.LOG will be created in the %systemroot%\ SYSTEM32\RAS folder. An example of a DEVICE.LOG file follows.

```
Remote Access Service Device Log 12/14/97 19:24:06
---------------------------------------------------
Port Handle: 108 Command to Device:
Port Handle: 108 Command to Device:ATS0=1
Port Handle: 108 Echo from Device:ATS0=1
Port Handle: 108 Response from Device:
OK
```

After the "Response from Device" line you should see a positive response from the device. If the DEVICE.LOG does not show the modem responding, you probably have RAS configured for the wrong modem or the modem has a hardware configuration problem.

CERTIFICATION OBJECTIVE 14.07

Network Problems

We could easily fill an entire book with information on troubleshooting network problems! They can be the toughest type of problem to troubleshoot because there are so many components where something can go wrong. Worse yet, the path causing the problem may not be active when you arrive to troubleshoot the problem. Table 14-4 lists some of the more common problems and their solutions.

Table 14-4 mentions using Network Monitor to help solve some network problems. Network Monitor, as described in Chapter 13, has some built-in

	Problem	Solution
TABLE 14-4 Common Network Problems and Solutions	Adapter cable loose	Check to make sure the network cable is plugged into the network adapter card. This might sound obvious, but it happens more than you might think.
	Network interface card failure	Check the Event Viewer System log for errors related to the network adapter, the workstation, and the server components. If you are using TCP/IP, use PING to determine if the system is getting out on the wire.
	Protocol mismatch	If two machines are active on the same network but still cannot communicate, it is possible they are using different protocols. Use the Network applet from Control Panel to determine which protocols are in use on each machine. Keep in mind that NetBEUI is not a routable protocol so it will not transverse any routers on your network.
	System on IPX/SPX network cannot communicate	Make sure the system is using the correct frame type.
	External network problem	If the hardware on the local system is functioning correctly and you are using TCP/IP, use PING to attempt to isolate the problem. Attempt to PING in increasing distances until you see a problem. You may want to use Network Monitor to help locate congestion and broadcast storms.
	System on a TCP/IP network cannot communicate outside the local subnet	It is using the wrong gateway settings.

limitations. The Network Monitor that ships with Windows NT Server does not support promiscuous mode. Promiscuous mode allows the capture of any packet that goes over the wire, whether it was intended for your machine or not. The version of Network Monitor that comes with Windows NT Server can capture *only* packets sent from or to one of your server's network cards. If you need to monitor traffic on all of your network you will need to use a different tool. The Network Monitor that comes with Systems Management Server (SMS) *does* support promiscuous mode.

CERTIFICATION OBJECTIVE 14.08

Permission Problems

The biggest problem with permissions is shared permissions versus local permissions. When you share resources on an NTFS partition, you limit remote access by combining two sets of permissions—the network share permissions and the local NTFS permissions. All shared permissions except for No Access are evaluated by accumulation and all NTFS permissions except for No Access are evaluated by accumulation. Then the system looks at both the shared result and the NTFS result and uses the most restrictive. The most effective permissions are those that are the most restrictive. Table 14-5 demonstrates this concept.

exam
ⓦatch

If you encounter a permission problem with a network share, be sure to verify the effective permissions for the user.

TABLE 14-5		Assigned Permissions	Joe's Permissions
Share Permissions versus Local Permissions	Share Permission for C:\Stuff	Everyone: Read Joe: Change	Change (RXWD)
	Local NTFS Permissions for C:\Stuff	Everyone: Read Joe: Read	Read (RX)
	Effective Permissions for Joe		Read (RX)

Taking Ownership of a Resource

It is inevitable that someone will lose access to a resource. Of course, this can only happen if you are using the NTFS file system. Assuming you have Administrator privileges, you can easily solve the dilemma by taking ownership of the resource and then sharing it (with full control) to the person who needs access so they can gain ownership of the resource. This action normally occurs when someone leaves an organization. Exercise 14-7 shows you how to gain ownership of a resource and then allow someone else to take ownership of it. In the exercise Steven is the person who quits the organization and Marissa is the new employee.

EXERCISE 14-7

Taking Ownership of a Resource

1. Log on your system as Administrator and create two new user accounts named Steven and Marissa.

2. Log off the system and log back on as Steven. Create a folder named StevenTest and set the permissions so only Steven has access to it. This folder will be the one that Marissa needs to access in order to retrieve valuable data.

3. Log off the system and log back on as Marissa. Try to access the StevenTest folder.

4. Log off the system and log back on as Administrator.

5. Open Windows NT Explorer and right-click the StevenTest folder.

6. Select Properties and choose the Security tab.

7. Select the Ownership button.

8. Select the Take Ownership button. The system prompts you with a dialog box stating that one or more of the items is a directory. Click the Yes button.

9. Select the Permissions button and give Marissa full control of the StevenTest folder.

10. Select the OK button.

11. Select the OK button.

12. Log off the system and log back on as Marissa.
13. Access the StevenTest folder and follow steps 5-8 to gain ownership of the folder.

Server Crashes

Server crashes are the worst thing that can happen to your Windows NT Server—especially if it is the Primary Domain Controller (PDC) in your network and you have no Backup Domain Controllers (BDC) to fall back on. This section describes how to use the System Recovery Utility and Task Manager to assist you when your system crashes.

System Recovery Utility

Windows NT features a Recovery utility that can perform selected tasks in the event of a STOP error. You configure the recovery options on the Startup/Shutdown tab of System Properties, which is shown in Figure 14-7.

Most of the Recovery options are self-explanatory; however one option is worth singling out. Automatically reboot allows your system to quickly return to normal operation after a system crash and eliminates the need to reboot manually.

The most important part of the Recovery utility to use for troubleshooting is the option Write debugging information to. When this option is checked and a STOP error occurs, the entire contents of memory are dumped to the pagefile. When your system restarts, this information is copied automatically from the pagefile to the filename you specified in the Recovery option block.

Since the entire contents of your system's memory are dumped to the pagefile, the pagefile must be as large as the amount of physical memory installed in your system. So, a system that has 64 megabytes of physical memory needs to have a pagefile that is at least 64 megabytes. One other

FIGURE 14-7

System Recovery
options on the System
Startup/Shutdown tab

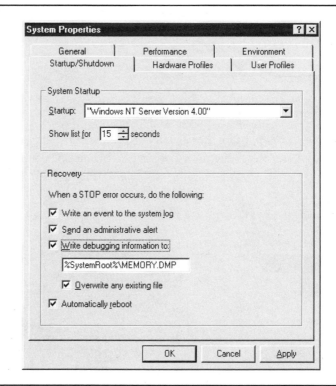

caveat is that the pagefile must be located on the boot partition. Exercise 14-8
gives you a chance to configure your system for memory dumps.

EXERCISE 14-8

Configuring for Memory Dumps

1. Select Start | Settings | Control Panel.

2. Double-click the System applet and select the Startup/Shutdown tab.

3. Under Recovery, select the Write debugging information to box.
   You may either accept the default path and filename or pick one of
   your own.

4. If you want the next memory dump to overwrite any file that has
   the same name, select the Overwrite box. If you leave this block

unchecked, Windows NT will not write a memory dump file if a file with the same name already exists.

Task Manager

At this point the Task Manager should be very familiar to you. Let's look at one more function that it can perform to help in troubleshooting your system. It has the capability to end a task that may be causing your system to hang. Under normal operating conditions you will see the word "Running" in the status column, as shown in Figure 14-8. If a task is no longer responding then the words "Not responding" are in the status column. Exercise 14-9 leads you through the process of shutting down a task.

FIGURE 14-8

Applications tab of the
Task Manager

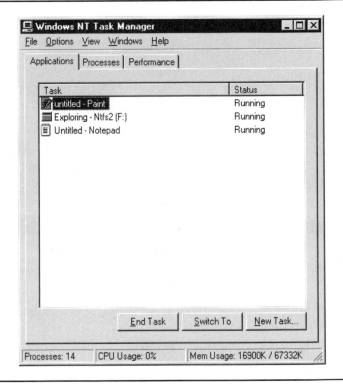

Shutting Down a Task with Task Manager

1. Use your right mouse button and click once on the taskbar.

2. Select Task Manager from the menu.

3. Click on the Start button and select Programs | Accessories | Paint.

4. Click on the Start button and select Programs | Accessories | Clock.

5. Click on the Start button and select Programs | Accessories | Notepad.

6. Select the Applications tab on the Task Manager. You will see the three applications that you just started; to the right of each application is its Status.

7. Let's assume that the Clock application has run rampant and is using 100 percent of the CPU; it needs to be shut down. Click on Clock to highlight it, then click the End Task button.

8. In a real situation when a task is not responding, you would receive a message that explains the task is not responding and asks if you would like to wait. Click End Task.

9. Close all remaining applications that are running.

10. Close the Task Manager.

STOP Error—the "Blue Screen of Death"

The words "blue screen of death" are about the worst thing you can tell someone about their Windows NT Server. The blue screens are actually text mode STOP messages that identify hardware and software problems that have occurred while running Windows NT Server. The reason for producing the blue screen is to visibly alert users to the fact that an error message has been generated. The blue screen is intended to provide information to help in troubleshooting the problem, rather than allowing the system to fail in an "invisible" manner. As shown in Figure 14-9, the "blue screen of death" consists of a STOP message, the text translation, the addresses of the violating call, and the drivers loaded at the time of the STOP screen. If you have configured your system to write debugging information, it will also generate that file.

FIGURE 14-9

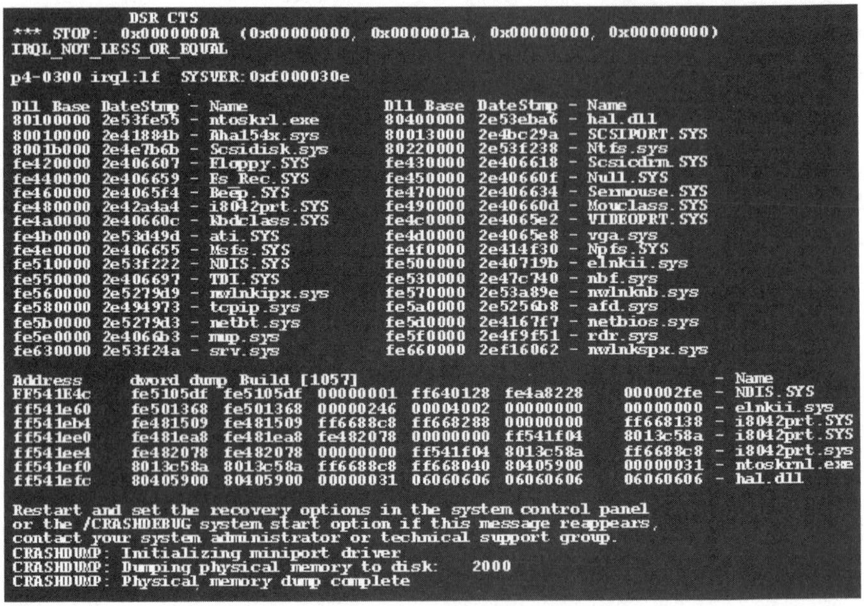

A typical "blue screen of death"

```
                     DSR CTS
*** STOP:  0x0000000A  (0x00000000, 0x0000001a, 0x00000000, 0x00000000)
IRQL_NOT_LESS_OR_EQUAL

p4-0300 irql:1f   SYSVER: 0xf000030e

Dll Base DateStmp - Name             Dll Base DateStmp - Name
80100000 2e53fe55 - ntoskrl.exe      80400000 2e53eba6 - hal.dll
80010000 2e41884b - Aha154x.sys      80013000 2e4bc29a - SCSIPORT.SYS
8001b000 2e4e7b6b - Scsidisk.sys     80220000 2e53f238 - Ntfs.sys
fe420000 2e406607 - Floppy.SYS       fe430000 2e406618 - Scsicdrm.SYS
fe440000 2e406659 - Es Rec.SYS       fe450000 2e40660f - Null.SYS
fe460000 2e4065f4 - Beep.SYS         fe470000 2e406634 - Sermouse.SYS
fe480000 2e42a4a4 - i8042prt.SYS     fe490000 2e40660d - Mouclass.SYS
fe4a0000 2e40660c - kbdclass.SYS     fe4c0000 2e4065e2 - VIDEOPRT.SYS
fe4b0000 2e53d49d - ati.SYS          fe4d0000 2e4065e8 - vga.sys
fe4e0000 2e406655 - Msfs.SYS         fe4f0000 2e414f30 - Npfs.SYS
fe510000 2e53f222 - NDIS.SYS         fe500000 2e40719b - elnkii.sys
fe550000 2e406697 - TDI.SYS          fe530000 2e47c740 - nbf.sys
fe560000 2e5279d9 - nwlnkipx.sys     fe570000 2e53a89e - nwlnknb.sys
fe580000 2e494973 - tcpip.sys        fe5a0000 2e5256b8 - afd.sys
fe5b0000 2e5279d3 - netbt.sys        fe5d0000 2e4167f7 - netbios.sys
fe5e0000 2e406Gb3 - mup.sys          fe5f0000 2e4f9f51 - rdr.sys
fe630000 2e53f24a - srv.sys          fe660000 2ef16062 - nwlnkspx.sys

                                                       - Name
Address      dword dump Build [1057]
FF541E4c     fe5105df fe5105df 00000001 ff640128 fe4a8228   000002fe - NDIS.SYS
ff541e60     fe501368 fe501368 00000246 00004002 00000000   00000000 - elnkii.sys
ff541eb4     fe481509 fe481509 ff6688c8 ff668288 00000000   ff668138 - i8042prt.SYS
ff541ee0     fe481ea8 fe481ea8 fe482078 00000000 ff541f04   8013c58a - i8042prt.SYS
ff541ee4     fe482078 fe482078 00000000 ff541f04 8013c58a   ff6688c8 - i8042prt.sys
ff541ef0     8013c58a 8013c58a ff6688c8 ff668040 80405900   00000031 - ntoskrnl.exe
ff541efc     80405900 80405900 00000031 06060606 06060606   06060606 - hal.dll

Restart and set the recovery options in the system control panel
or the /CRASHDEBUG system start option if this message reappears,
contact your system administrator or technical support group.
CRASHDUMP: Initializing miniport driver
CRASHDUMP: Dumping physical memory to disk:      2000
CRASHDUMP: Physical memory dump complete
```

Even though the "blue screen of death" can look intimidating, in most cases you need to use only a small amount of the displayed data to help determine the cause of the error. The further interpretation of STOP errors is beyond the scope of this book.

FROM THE CLASSROOM

Troubleshooting to Fix Actual Problems (What a Novel Idea!)

We have many opportunities to see students and clients troubleshoot real live problems. It can really be an interesting experience. We have probably learned most about what to do—and what not to do—as we watched our clients try to troubleshoot problems. We are always amazed at how thoroughly students can "hose" (that's technical talk for "render inoperable") their classroom computers! And even when the instructors have no idea what is wrong or how

FROM THE CLASSROOM

to fix it, they must restore the machine, so that the students can continue the class exercises. In these cases, we tell the students not to worry—in the Saturday makeup class (the one that starts at 6:00 A.M.) we'll show them how to not do what they just did.

Not surprisingly, the most critical part of troubleshooting is to *identify the problem*. Many people waste countless hours troubleshooting issues that are not the real problem or not even related to the problem. This is the number one "gotcha." To identify the problem, you first have to collect information—even before you begin to act. For example, let's say data is continually corrupted on your hard drive. What is the problem? In an actual case, we watched a client troubleshoot the drives and the controller, even to the extent of replacing both several times, without ever fixing the "problem." The real problem was that memory was being used for write cache. The original drive and controller were good.

A closely related tactic is troubleshooting the symptom rather than the problem. This is the number two "gotcha." In one vivid example (and our personal favorite), a user called to say they were unable to connect to a remote server. To address this problem, the technician repeatedly connected their own computer to the remote server. Now most of you just said, "Well, what's wrong with that?" But the

technician was troubleshooting the symptom (the user could not connect to the server), not the problem. They found out it was possible to connect. So what? How did that help the user? And did that help find the problem? You're probably saying, "At least they eliminated the 'server is down' issue." But was that an issue? If the server were down, you would have much more evidence than this single user's complaint. In this case, we finally checked the System log on the user's computer and found that the protocol did not initialize, because the adapter drive failed to bind, because the NIC had failed. The failure of the network card was the "problem." The user's inability to connect to the server was only a symptom.

One huge "gotcha" is breaking the rule to "change only one thing at a time." When troubleshooting any problem, change only one simple variable. Study the effects of that change. If there is no change, reset that variable to its original state, change another variable, and re-test. This step-by-step approach lets you isolate what went wrong so you'll be able to correct it. But just as important as correcting the problem is *learning* from the experience. When technical people are surveyed and ask to identify the most important factor in successful troubleshooting, more than half say that prior experience with the problem is the most helpful piece of information they need. You get prior

FROM THE CLASSROOM

experience by successfully fixing the problem. That means you *learned* what was wrong and what you did to fix it. If you changed multiple variables and the problem went away, you did not learn what the problem was—or even what you did to fix it! The next time the problem occurs, you won't know any more than you did before.

Good Luck! Just remember—troubleshooting can be fun!

—*By Shane Clawson, MCT, MCSE*

CERTIFICATION OBJECTIVE 14.10

Using Microsoft Resources

Having access to a variety of troubleshooting resources will make your life much easier when dealing with Windows NT Server. This section describes some resources that are available to you.

Microsoft Web and FTP Sites

Microsoft maintains World Wide Web (WWW) servers and FTP (File Transfer Protocol) servers that can provide you with updated drivers, current product information and more. The WWW address is www.microsoft.com and the FTP address is ftp.microsoft.com. The FTP site allows anonymous logons, so feel free to explore the site.

Microsoft Service Packs

Microsoft periodically issues a Service Pack to fix bugs that have been detected in the Windows NT operating system. At the time of this writing the latest service pack issued was Service Pack 3.

Obtaining a Service Pack

The latest Service Pack can be ordered by phone from Microsoft or obtained from their FTP site. The FTP address for Intel-based machines is ftp.microsoft.com/bussys/winnt/winnt-public/fixes/usa/nt40/ussp3/i386.

Service Pack Pre-Installation

There are several measures you should take to prepare your system for installing a Service Pack.

- Back up the entire system, including the Registry
- Update the ERD
- Save the disk configuration
- Disconnect users, exit applications, and stop unnecessary services

Installing a Service Pack

Another thing you need to do before installing a Service Pack is to read the README.TXT file that comes in the archive to see what bugs have been fixed and if there are any peculiarities that may affect the installation on your system. Installing a Service Pack is not a complex task. There are only a couple of decisions that need to be made; if in doubt, it is wise to err on the side of caution because a Service Pack can render your machine inoperable. Exercise 14-10 shows you how to install Service Pack 3.

EXERCISE 14-10

Installing a Service Pack

1. Obtain Service Pack 3 (nt4sp3_i.exe) via FTP from ftp.microsoft.com/bussys/winnt/winnt-public/fixes/usa/nt40/ussp3/i386. Save the executable file to a folder.

2. Select Start | Programs | Windows NT Explorer and open the folder where you stored the Service Pack archive.

3. Double-click the nt4sp3_i.exe file. The executable starts extracting files to a temporary location and automatically starts UPDATE.EXE. After the files have been extracted, you see a Welcome screen that explains

the procedure. It is wise to follow the instructions about updating your ERD and backing up all system and data files.

4. Click the Next button to display the Software License Agreement. Read it and click the Yes button.

5. Service Pack Setup prompts you to pick the type of installation desired. Make sure the "Install the Service Pack" radio button is selected and click the Next button.

6. The next screen asks you if you want to create an Uninstall directory. As always, it is wise to err on the side of caution. Make sure the "Yes, I want to create an Uninstall directory" radio button is selected and click the Next button. If you do not create an Uninstall directory you will not be able to use the Uninstall feature of the Service Pack.

7. The next screen tells you that the program is ready to install the Service Pack. Click the Finish button to complete the process. The Service Pack will change only those files that were originally set up on your system.

Reapplying a Service Pack

Do not delete the Service Pack archive from your system because any time you change hardware or software on the system you must reapply the Service Pack. When you reapply it you also need to tell the program to create a new Uninstall directory.

Removing a Service Pack

You may find that the Service Pack does not function correctly on your system. If this happens you will need to remove it from your system. Keep in mind that you can only uninstall the Service Pack if you originally installed the Service Pack with the Uninstall directory option selected. Exercise 14-11 shows you how to remove a Service Pack from your system.

EXERCISE 14-11

Removing a Service Pack

1. Select Start | Programs | Windows NT Explorer and open the folder where you stored the Service Pack archive.

2. Double click the nt4sp3_i.exe file. The executable starts extracting files to a temporary location and automatically starts UPDATE.EXE. After the files have been extracted, you see a Welcome screen that explains the procedure.

3. Click the Next button to display the Software License Agreement, then click the Yes button.

4. Service Pack Setup prompts you to pick the type of installation desired. Select the "Uninstall a previously installed Service Pack" radio button and click the Finish button.

5. When your system restarts, the UPDATE.EXE program replaces the files that were updated by the Service Pack with the files from the previous installation.

The Knowledge Base

The Knowledge Base contains support information developed by Microsoft Product Support Specialists for problems that they have solved. We cannot stress enough the value that the Knowledge Base can provide. It is often the first place we will look when faced with an unusual problem. If we are having this problem there's a good chance that someone else has already encountered it. The Knowledge Base is available in many different places. It can be accessed on Microsoft's WWW site, the TechNet CDs, and Resource Kit CDs.

TechNet CD-ROM

The TechNet CDs are an invaluable tool for supporting any Microsoft product. We have already mentioned the TechNet CDs in earlier discussions of troubleshooting. There are more than 1.5 million pages of technical documentation available on the TechNet CDs—along with drivers, updates, and Service Packs. TechNet is available by yearly subscription and delivers new CDs to you every month as they are updated.

Resource Kits

The Resource Kits contain detailed information that is an in-depth, technical supplement to the documentation included with the product. Resource kits also come with a CD that is full of very useful utilities. Resource Kits can be obtained from your local dealer; they are also included on the TechNet CDs.

Help

Windows NT Help is just a few mouse clicks away. Help is available in three different contexts. You can use the Contents tab in Help to find topics grouped by subject, use the Index tab to find specific topics listed alphabetically, or use the Find tab to search for information by typing in a subject, title, specific word or phrase. Figure 14-10 displays the Help Index tab. Exercise 14-12 gives you an opportunity to use Help to find a specific phrase.

FIGURE 14-10

The Index tab of Help

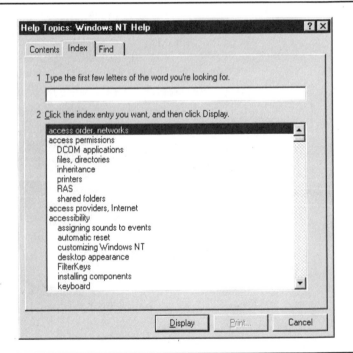

EXERCISE 14-12

Opening Help Files

1. Select Start | Help. The Help Topics window is displayed.
2. Select the Index tab and type **netwo** in dialog box 1.
3. The words "network adapter" are highlighted in dialog box 2.
4. Double-click "network adapter" to see the Topics Found dialog box.
5. Double-click "To install a network adapter" to receive help on that topic.
6. Close Help after you read the information displayed.

CERTIFICATION SUMMARY

When you install Windows NT Server it is essential to verify that your hardware is on the Hardware Compatibility List. Installation errors can occur either during the text-based mode or the graphical mode of Setup. Windows NT Server comes with two utilities that can help identify hardware prior to installation—NTHQ and SCSITOOL.

Troubleshooting configuration errors can be a frustrating process. Problems can include a variety of boot failures in which you may need to use the LastKnownGood configuration or the Emergency Repair Disk. Other tools available to help with troubleshooting Windows NT Server are the Event Viewer and Windows NT Diagnostics (WinMSD).

Disk problems can cause difficulties even after you are logged on to your system. Two of the most common errors are encountering unknown volumes and extended partition problems.

If you have a fault-tolerant configuration, you may have to recover from a RAID problem. These problems affect both RAID 1 and RAID 5 sets. Regenerating a stripe set with parity will reconstruct the data from the remaining members to a new drive. The method you use to fix a mirror set depends on whether it is the member or system partition that no longer functions correctly.

Printing problems can be difficult to troubleshoot because of the many variables involved. Two particularly complicating factors are the number of diverse clients supported by NT Server and the number and variety of print devices supported. One of the most common printing problems is running out of hard disk space for the spooler.

Remote Access Service troubleshooting for Dial-Up Networking clients can be improved by enabling two log files via your Registry—PPP.LOG and DEVICE.LOG.

Network problems can be very tough to troubleshoot because there are many components where something can go wrong. Some of the more common malfunctions include protocol mismatches between systems and the use of incorrect frame types on an IPX/SPX network. Permission problems often become a problem when you create a share on the network that uses NTFS. You have to be cognizant of not only the share permissions but also the NTFS permissions. In some situations you may need to take ownership of a resource to clear up an existing security and permission problem.

System recovery can actually help in troubleshooting by providing a dump of your physical memory that can be further analyzed when appropriate. If you have an application that stops responding, you can use the Task Manager to shut it down. The STOP error, better known as the "blue screen of death," identifies hardware and software problems that have occurred. The "blue screen of death" can be very intimidating and is something that no one who deals with Windows NT looks forward to seeing. It reflects that a serious problem has occurred, but it does provide a good deal of information to help you find out what caused the STOP error.

There are many resources available to help you keep Windows NT Server running successfully. One of the most valuable is the Microsoft Service Pack, which is issued periodically after a significant number of bugs have been fixed. Service Packs can be obtained from the Microsoft FTP site. Installing a Service Pack is not an especially complex task, but you should make a backup of your system and examine the README.TXT file before you begin the installation. Other resources available include Microsoft's World Wide Web and FTP sites, the Microsoft Knowledge Base, the TechNet CD subscription, and the online Help files included with Windows NT.

TWO-MINUTE DRILL

❑ One source of installation problems is trying to use hardware that is not on the Hardware Compatibility List (HCL).

❑ Boot failures can take many different paths to lead your system to failure.

❑ Ensure that you have a Windows NT boot floppy, in case one of the boot files for your system is ever deleted.

❑ LastKnownGood is the configuration that was saved to a special control set in the Registry after the last successful logon to Windows NT.

❑ The Emergency Repair Disk (ERD) can be used to return a Windows NT system to the configuration it had when you last updated the ERD.

❑ The Security Account Manager (SAM) and Security files are not automatically updated by rdisk. To update those files you need to use the /S switch in conjunction with rdisk.

❑ The Event Viewer can be an immense help in troubleshooting your system.

❑ Windows NT Diagnostics enables you to view currently loaded device drivers, IRQ values, and much more. It provides a view of detected hardware and can be used over a network to examine a remote system.

❑ The procedure for detecting and recovering from errors for software fault-tolerant volumes is comparable for both mirror sets (RAID 1) and stripe sets with parity (RAID 5).

❑ When a member of a stripe set with parity fails, you can continue to use the computer to access all the data; however, you will see a system degradation.

❑ As with a RAID 5 set, if a *member* of a RAID 1 set fails, the fault tolerance driver will direct all I/O to the remaining drive in the mirror set.

❏   Printing problems can become complicated to resolve because there are a number of variables involved in printing , as well as a diverse number of clients and print devices supported by Windows NT Server.

❏   If you have a Dial-Up Networking (DUN) client that is having difficulty being authenticated over RAS, the first thing you should try is to change the security option on both the server and client to "allow any authentication including clear text."

❏   Use Network Monitor to help diagnose some network problems.

❏   The biggest problem encountered with access problems is shared permissions versus local permissions.

❏   With Administrator privileges you can easily solve access problems by taking ownership of the resource and then sharing it (with full control) to the person who needs access so they can gain ownership of the resource.

❏   Windows NT features a Recovery utility that can perform selected tasks in the event of a STOP error.

❏   Task Manager can end a task that may be causing your system to hang.

❏   The "blue screen of death" are actually text-mode STOP messages that identify hardware and software problems that have occurred while Windows NT Server is running.

❏   Accessing a variety of Microsoft Resources can make your troubleshooting much easier when dealing with Windows NT Server.

SELF TEST

The following questions will help you measure your understanding of the material presented in this chapter. Read all the choices carefully, as there may be more than one correct answer. Choose all correct answers for each question.

1. Which of the following is a valid ARC path?

   A. Multi(0)disk(1)rdisk(0)partition(0)\ winnt="Windows NT Version 4.0"

   B. Multi(0)disk(0)rdisk(0)partition(5)\ winnt="Windows NT Version 4.0"

   C. scsi(0)disk(1)rdisk(0)partition(3)winnt= "Windows NT Version 4.0"

   D. scsi(0)disk(2)rdisk(0)partition(4)\winnt "Windows NT Version 4.0"

2. What files are required to be on a Windows NT boot disk for a non-SCSI, Intel-based machine?

   A. NTLDR

   B. BOOT.INI

   C. NTBOOTDD.SYS

   D. OSLOADER.EXE

   E. NTDETECT.COM

3. You are sent out on a trouble call and told that the system hangs since the user added a new video driver. What would you do?

   A. Use the Emergency Repair Disk to replace the Registry

   B. Boot the system with a Windows NT boot disk

   C. Reboot the system and choose the LastKnownGood configuration

   D. Reload Windows NT Server on the system

4. Your system has 128 megabytes of physical memory and you have set the System Recovery to write debugging information to %systemroot%\memory.dmp. What else needs to be done to ensure that the debugging information will be saved?

   A. Your pagefile has to be at least 128MB

   B. Your pagefile has to be smaller than 128MB

   C. Your pagefile has to be located on a partition other than where Windows NT Server is installed

   D. Your pagefile has to be equal to the size of your boot partition

5. Paul has been fired and his replacement, Ann, needs to access the 4th quarter report that is located in a folder that belonged to Paul. How will Ann be able to access this folder?

   A. Have Ann log on to the system and take ownership of the folder

   B. Have Paul come back to work so he can give Ann access to the folder

   C. Have an Administrator log on the system and assign ownership of the directory to Ann

D. Have an Administrator log on and take ownership of the folder, then give Ann full control of the folder

6. To update your Emergency Repair Disk you would type _____ from a command prompt.

A. fdisk

B. rdisk

C. ERD

D. update

E. repair

7. (True/False) A Service Pack can be easily removed from your system even if you do not have the uninstall folder.

8. What causes the "blue screen of death"?

A. a STOP message

B. a HALT message

C. a SEVERE message

D. a CRITICAL message

9. The Partition(n) portion of an ARC name starts counting with _____

A. 0

B. 1

C. 2

D. 3

10. A system you have been sent out to troubleshoot will not boot. You attempt to use the LastKnownGood configuration and it does not correct the problem. What would you do next?

A. Format the drive and reload Windows NT Server

B. Use the Emergency Repair Disk for that system

C. Use your Windows NT boot disk to replace a missing script file

D. Use the Emergency Repair Disk for the neighboring system

11. (True/False) The SAM and Security files are automatically updated when you use the Repair Disk Utility.

12. (True/False) The fault-tolerant boot disk must be used if the member drive of a mirror set is orphaned.

13. The fault-tolerant driver detects an orphaned drive on your RAID 5 set. What is the result?

A. The system will be shut down automatically

B. Data will be corrupted

C. The system will continue functioning with no system degradation

D. The system will continue functioning with some system degradation

14. What would cause a system on a network that uses the IPX/SPX protocol to not communicate with any other systems on the network?

A. The IPX/SPX protocol has not been installed

B. TCP/IP is not functioning correctly

C. The frame type is incorrect

D. The default gateway is incorrect

15. A user attempts to print but the print job never completes and the hard drive thrashes a lot. What could be causing this to happen?

A. The print spooler is stalled

B. The print spooler has run out of hard drive space

C. The print spooler priority is set too high

D. The printer has not been installed

A

Self Test
Answers

Answers to Chapter 1 Self Test

1. _____ multitasking is the ability to run several applications at once.
   Preemptive. This is one of the ways applications are multitasked. The other way is called cooperative, or non-preemptive.

2. A _____ is the smallest unit for processing.
   Thread. This is a small code of execution that belongs to a process. Threads inherit the priority of the process that spawned them, but can have their own priorities adjusted.

3. What is the maximum number of processors that Windows NT can support through OEM versions?
   D. Windows NT comes with support for four processors out of the box, but OEM solutions have support for up to 32 processors.

4. When system policies are in place, what file will be in the Netlogon directory?
   D. NTConfig.pol. When this file is present in the Netlogon directory it overwrites the users' registry settings with the policies that you specify.

5. Which is not a RAS security feature?
   D. Restricting access to certain phone numbers. There is currently no way of denying access to a user at a certain phone number.

6. What would be the first step in the replication process if I placed my file to be replicated in this directory? C:*systemroot*\SYSTEM32\repl\export
   B. The file would not be replicated because it is not in a subdirectory. You must place a directory under the C:*systemroot*\SYSTEM32\repl\export path in order to have it be replicated.

7. Which levels of fault tolerant RAID does Windows NT support?
   1, 5. RAID levels 1 and 5 are fault tolerant. RAID level 1 is disk mirroring, and RAID level 5 is disk striping with parity.

8. (True/False) RAID level 5 uses a dedicated drive that holds parity information for fault tolerance.
   False. RAID level 5 has the parity information striped across each of the drives. RAID level 4 uses a dedicated parity drive.

9. (True/False) Environment subsystems are run in the User mode.
   True. Environment subsystems are run in User mode; their calls must be translated to Kernel mode when they need to communicate with a hardware device.

10. HAL stands for _____ _____ _____.
    Hardware Abstraction Layer. The HAL lies at the lowest level of the Windows NT Executive between the hardware and the operating system.

11. Which is not a component of the Windows NT Executive?

    C. This is not a member of the Windows NT Executive. The NT Kernel is responsible for creating and scheduling the threads.

12. What is the size of the pages that are swapped in and out of memory by the Virtual Memory Manager?

    B. 4 kilobytes. The memory pages are 4 kilobytes because it would take too long to swap a large number of small pages to and from the disk as needed.

13. With a linear 32-bit address, the address starts at zero, then increments in what size block?

    A. 1 byte. The address continues in one-byte increments until the physical memory is used up.

14. How much virtual memory does the 16-bit addressing scheme support?

    C. 256 MB. Multiplying 2 to the power of 16 gives the number of bits. A 32-bit addressing scheme results in 4GB of virtual memory (multiplying 2 to the power of 32).

15. How are 16-bit applications run by default in Windows NT?

    D. By default, 16-bit applications run in the same memory space, preemptively multitasked with applications outside of the VDM. However, by default the 16-bit applications are cooperatively multitasked with other applications that are running in the same VDM.

Answers to Chapter 2 Self Test

1. Huey's boss wants him to install Windows NT 4.0 Server onto some legacy hardware. What choices does Huey have to install Windows NT 4.0 Server?

    B, C. Windows NT 4.0 Server can only be installed on hardware that meets the minimum hardware requirements of 486/33, 16MB of RAM and 120MB of hard disk space

2. Elliot wants to check the HCL before he installs his Windows NT 4.0 Server. Where can he find the HCL?

    A, B. He can find the HCL on Microsoft's Web site, Microsoft Tech-Net, Windows NT Server CD-ROM, and on CompuServe.

3. J.D.'s wants to install a protocol to connect up to a client-server database on a Novell NetWare 3.11 server. What must be installed in order for him to use the database?

    B. To connect to the database located on the Novell NetWare server, all that needs to be installed is NWLink (IPX/SPX).

4. Milton wants to let his users connect to a Hewlett-Packard printer that has a HP-Direct Jet card installed. What protocol should he have installed on his server in order for his users to access the printer?

    B. To connect with the Hewlett-Packard Printers, you need to have the DLC protocol installed on your server.

5. What new functionality does the Task Manager provide in Windows NT 4.0?
   B. The new functionality of the Task Manager is that you can now view your server's memory and processor usage as well as look at application and thread status.

6. Steve S wants to convert his server's boot partition to a secure file system that enables auditing and transaction logging. What file system should he use?
   C. NTFS is the secure file system designed for Windows NT that enables auditing and transaction logging.

7. Michael has never used Windows NT 4.0 Server before and is required to create some new printers for his job. What utility will help Michael to do his job?
   D. Since he has not used Windows NT before, he can create printers using the new Administrative Wizards tool.

8. Paul and Laurie are building a Web server on their Windows NT 4.0 Server. What new components are included?
   C, D. Information Server and Index Server are now included with Windows NT 4.0. Internet Information Server is a high-powered Web server and Index Server is a Web-query tool used alongside Internet Information Server.

9. Convert the following Long File Names to the MS-DOS 8.3 standard. (This is a common question on many of the Microsoft exams.)

   A. Account~1.doc **B.** Expense~1.xls **C.** Expense~2.xls **D.** Mikefav~1.doc

10. (True or False) Symmetric Multiprocessing (SMP) takes advantage of the multiple processors in your computer by having each processor share the work load.
    True.

11. (True or False) The version of Network Monitor included with Windows NT 4.0 Server allows the user to capture network packets from any computer on the network.
    False. The version of Network Monitor included with Windows NT 4.0 Server only allows you to capture packets to and from your server.

12. (True or False) Regedit.exe allows you to set security permissions on individual keys of the registry.
    False. Regedt32.exe is the registry editor that allows you to set security permissions on individual keys.

Answers to Chapter 3 Self Test

1. What is the file to start the installation process that you type at the command prompt on a DOS machine?
   C. The Setup and Install programs do not exist in Windows NT Server 4.0. winnt32.exe is used to upgrade from previous versions of Windows NT

Workstation and/or Server. DOS machines use winnt.exe.

2. You want to install Windows NT Server 4.0 and have all available security options accessible. What file system type do you want to choose during the installation?
C. HPFS and FAT32 are not compatible with Windows NT Server 4.0. Using FAT does not let you take advantage of all available security features built into Windows NT Server. The appropriate choice is NTFS.

3. How many PDC's can a domain have?
D. There can be only one PDC per domain and each PDC can only be master of one domain.

4. Your server name is SERVER, and you share with the Windows NT 4.0 Server installation files is called NTCD. What do you type at the command prompt to connect to the network share when using a network boot disk?
A. In answer B the switches are the wrong ones. In answers C and D the commands do not exist.

5. You promote your BDC to a PDC while the PDC is off the network. What will happen if you reinsert the old PDC into the network?
A. The administrator must demote the former PDC in Server Manager. If this is not done, the netlogon service will not run

and the computer will not be able to participate on the network.

6. What switch do you use to re-create the setup boot floppy disks?
D. The switches in answers A, B, and C do not exist with winnt.exe.

7. What method allows you to install across the network successfully on an MS-DOS workstation?
D. The ntsetup.exe and setup.exe files mentioned in answers A and C do not exist. In answer B, winnt32.exe is for upgrade purposes only. On a DOS machine you need to run winnt.exe.

8. In which subdirectory on the Windows NT 4.0 Server CD-ROM are the installation files for an Intel machine located?
C. The paths in answers A, B, and E do not exist. The path in answer D is for a non-Intel platform. The appropriate subdirectory is \i386.

9. You have a BDC you want to make a member server. What do you have to do?
A. The only change that can be made in a server role is promoting a BDC to a PDC. To change either a PDC or a BDC to a member server, you must reinstall Windows NT Server.

10. Which switch tells setup not to look for or create the floppy disks when starting setup?
C. The /B switch tells setup to bypass and not create the floppy disks during

installation. This is the switch most commonly used during network installations.

11. You need to set up and configure three new BDC's for your WAN. What is the quickest and most efficient way to do this?
    C. Just as there can be only one PDC per domain, so can each PDC only be master of one domain.

12. You are setting up a new Windows NT server on the network. This server will be a member server in the Finance department. You want to name this computer for the department where it is located. All servers, domain controllers, or non-domain controllers are set up and named in this fashion. The Finance department already has a BDC installed. What problems will you run into with this installation?
    C. You will create duplicate computer names if you stick to the normal naming process for servers in this organization.

13. What is the default network protocol for Windows NT?
    A. Answers B, C, and D are valid network protocols for use with NT, but they are not the default selection.

14. You have installed Windows NT Server 4.0 and now want to set up fault tolerance on your hard disk. Which of the following fault-tolerance methods can the system files be part of?
    A. Answers B and D do not provide fault tolerance. Answer C is not an allowable

fault-tolerant method of dealing with system files. However, system files can be placed in a mirror set (a RAID level 1 setting).

15. A machine in your organization was formerly a Windows NT server. Now you find that you need this machine as a extra workstation. While logged on locally to the machine, you open the Disk Administrator and try to delete the main system partition. What will happen in this instance?
    D. Because Windows NT Server 4.0 and Disk Administrator are running from the partition you are trying to delete, you will get an error message.

16. When installing Windows NT Server, you selected Per Seat licensing. You find now that you should have chosen Per Server. What can you do in this instance?
    C. When Per Seat is selected, you cannot change the licensing. Your only option is to reinstall Window NT Server 4.0.

17. When installing Windows NT Server you selected Per Server licensing. You find now that you should have chosen Per Seat. What can you do in this instance?
    B. The Licensing option in Control Panel lets you make a one-time change from Per Server to Per Seat licensing.

18. You are installing a multiboot system containing Windows 95, Windows NT Server, and Windows NT Workstation. You want to be able to share files and data among the three operating systems. What

file system should you choose?

B. Windows NT is not compatible with HPFS or FAT32 files, so that rules out answers C and D. Windows 95 cannot read NTFS, which rules out answer A.

19. You are upgrading from Windows NT Server 3.51 that was installed with default settings. You want to maintain the icons, desktop settings, and basic Windows NT information. How would you accomplish this?

    C. winnt32.exe is the correct installation file to use in this scenario, which rules out answer A. The default directory to Windows NT Server 3.51 is WINNT35, which eliminates answers B and D. Answer E therefore cannot be correct.

20. What Server Manager menu do you open to get the option to promote the BDC?

    A. The Promote to Primary Domain Controller command is on the Computer menu. The other menus do not play a role in the promotion process.

21. You are getting ready to start the installation process and decide to boot from the CD. When you put the CD in the CD-ROM drive and boot the machine, the computer still boots from the hard disk. What is a possible cause of this? (Select all that apply.)

    A, C, & D. Choice B is incorrect because the NT 4.0 Server CD is bootable.

22. Where is the SETUPMGR utility installed by default?

    A. SETUPMGR was introduced with NT 4.0 Server but it is not installed by default. You could probably download it, but the URL supplied in answer D is fictitious. SETUPMGR is on the Windows NT CD-ROM, so that is the easiest way to obtain it.

23. You've just installed a new server in a domain. You've verified that there are no evident errors on bootup. You check the domain name, and the name on the PDC matches the name on the server. You verify that you have a valid username and password. For some reason you cannot connect to the network. You check the Protocols tab in Network Properties on the new server and see the information shown in Figure 3-18. You check the same tab on the PDC and see the information shown in Figure 3-19. Why won't the computers communicate?

    B. The protocols that are loaded on two different computers must have at least one match and corresponding configuration information within the protocol (for example, subnet mask and frame type).

24. You are installing a BDC and encounter an error when the computer is being added to the network. Why is this happening?

    C. The username and password must have the ability to add computers to the network in order to install a BDC.

25. You are installing Windows NT Server to be a member server. This machine is a

dual-boot machine with Windows 95 OEM Service Release 2 already installed on it. You install Windows NT 4.0 Server in its own partition. You make sure to install the Windows NT partition as a FAT partition so Windows 95 can access the information on it. When you are in Windows NT you cannot access the drives that contain the Windows 95 information. You open Disk Administrator and see the screen shown in Figure 3-20. After reviewing the information in Disk Administrator, what conclusion do you reach?

D. Windows 95 is not compatible with HPFS, so answer B is not correct. The other two answers, A and C, are not correct because you installed Windows NT Server into its own partition.

26. You have just installed Windows NT Server and realize you forgot to install Windows Messaging. Now you want to add it. What icon do you open in Control Panel (see Figure 3-21) to do this?

   B. The Add/Remove programs icon opens a window that has a tab for Windows NT Setup. You use this tab to add and remove basic components in Windows NT.

27. Which switch tells setup not to check for free disk space on floppy disks when creating them?

   B. The /C switch tells setup not to check for disk space on floppy disks.

Answers to Chapter 4 Self Test

1. You have two SCSI drives, each with a 2GB partition and its own disk controller. You want fault tolerance and you want to be able to continue to use one of the drives should the other fail. What type of fault tolerance should you use?

   B. Disk duplexing is just like mirroring, except it uses two controllers.

2. You have an NT Server computer. You install the client Network Administration Tools on your Windows 95 computer. How can you remotely manage file and directory permissions?

   B. When you install client-based Network Administrator Tools you get a Permissions tab on the Properties page using Explorer.

3. You have two network cards you want to configure with TCP/IP in the same server. How can you do this?

   B. On a multihomed computer you need to use fixed IP addresses. DHCP can only configure on card.

4. You have NetBEUI and TCP/IP installed on your server. Most of your clients have TCP/IP installed on their systems as the default protocol. You've noticed that clients with TCP/IP as the default protocol take longer to connect to your server. How can you fix the problem?

A. You need to move TCP/IP higher in the binding order so the server will try to connect using TCP/IP first.

5. Your users have a mandatory profile with a .man extension assigned. They are logging onto the system for the first time, but the server with the mandatory profile is offline. What will happen?
B. In order for users to log on, they must have access to the mandatory profile.

6. You are creating a stripe set with parity on four disk drives, each with 100MB partition. What's the largest size stripe set with parity you can create?
B. The largest stripe set you can create is 400MB, although the maximum amount of data that can be stored is 300MB.

7. You are creating a stripe set with parity on four disk drives, each with 100MB partition. What's the largest amount of data that can be saved to the stripe set with parity?
A. Same explanation as previous question.

8. You have four hard disks. Drive 1 has 100MB of free space, Drive 2 and Drive 3 each has 200MB of free space, and Drive 4 has 500MB of free space. What's the largest size stripe set you can create?
C. The largest stripe set is 600MB. You might have chosen D because you wanted to use all the disks. However, if you only use the three disks that have more available free space, you can get a larger stripe set.

9. What service should you use to provide IP address configuration information to Windows clients?
C. DHCP assigns IP addresses and configuration information.

10. What are the required parameters for a TCP/IP configured server in a routed environment? (Choose all that apply.)
A, B, C. You need to have an IP Address, subnet mask, and default gateway to communicate in a routed environment using TCP/IP.

11. How would you install Win95 over a network? (Choose all that apply.)
A, B, C. You can make an installation share using the Network Client Administrator tool, then create an install startup disk. Finally you boot the computer at the client, using the install network startup disk.

12. You have four physical disks, each with 250MB of free space. You want to create a stripe set. What will be the largest stripe set you can create?
D. You can use the full 250MB from each partition to create a 1000MB stripe set.

13. You are administering a Windows NT Server computer from a Windows 95 client computer. You install client-based Network Administrative Tools on the Windows 95 computer. You want to share a CD-ROM that is attached to the Windows NT Server computer. What must you use on the Windows 95 computer to do this?

A. Server Manager is the only way to share folders remotely on a server.

14. You configure a stripe set without parity on three physical disks. One of the disks fails. What can you do to recover data that was stored on the stripe set?
D. The only way to recover from a failed stripe set *without* parity is to use a previous saved backup.

15. Your network uses NWLink IPX/SPX Compatible transport protocol. Half of the client computers use 802.3, the other half use 802.2 frame type. You are adding a Windows NT Server computer to the network. This server has one network adapter. What must you do on the new server so it can communicate with all the clients?
C. If your network uses more than one frame type, you must specify which frame types you want use. If your network has only one IPX/SPX frame type, you can use Auto Detect.

16. Your server has six disks, each with two partitions. On the first disk are the boot and system partitions. How can you optimize the pagefile?
A. By spreading the pagefile across all disks except the first (because it has the boot and system partitions which create a lot of I/O) you can increase the pagefile's I/O time.

17. What is the startup value of a boot device in the registry?

A. The startup value 0 forces the device to start up as soon as the kernel is initialized.

18. What is the file name of a mandatory profile?
C. Using the .MAN extension makes the profile read-only so the user can't change it.

19. You want to use WINS on your routed network as the only way for name resolution across the router. Your clients consist of 100 Windows 95 computers, 50 Windows NT Workstations 4.0, 3 NT Servers 4.0, and 5 LAN Manager 2.2c for MS-DOS clients. Will this work?
C. LAN Manager 2.2c doesn't support WINS.

Answers to Chapter 5 Self Test

1. You would like to create a template called USER_TEMPLATE for making new user accounts easier. What is the correct way to do this?
C. Copy the USER_TEMPLATE account and enter the new user information. The copy command is used by selecting Copy from the User menu, or pressing F8. This will not copy the username, full name, or password.

2. The manager for the Sales department has left the company. He has an immediate replacement. What is the best way to give

the new user access to the resources the previous manager had?

B. Rename the previous user's account with the new user's name. Instruct the user to change the password at next logon. This is the reason accounts should be disabled when users leave a company.

3. Members of the Human Resources group have a mandatory user profile. Everything was fine for each user until one day, the server that holds the mandatory user profile went down. What will happen when a user from the Human Resources group attempts to log on?

   B. The locally cached profile is used. This is assuming the user has had a successful logon to the domain before. If the user has never logged on to the domain before, the default user profile from the local machine is used.

4. A user calls you and tells you he just received a message about his account expiring. What should you do to give him access again?

   C. Set a later date for the expiration of the user account in the Account Information dialog box in User Manager for Domains. You can also select the Never option in the Account Expires portion of the Account Information dialog box.

5. (True/False) Everything in the User Environment Profile dialog box is optional.

   True. You can specify user profiles, logon scripts, and home directories for users in the

dialog box. It is reached by clicking the Profile button in User Manager for Domains.

6. What is the default location to place logon scripts?

   D. WINNT\SYSTEM32\REPL\ IMPORT\SCRIPTS. This is so the Replication service can replicate the logo scripts to the other domain controllers in the domain.

7. What is the difference between local and global groups? Choose all that apply.

   B, D. You cannot create global groups on Windows NT Workstation. You cannot place local groups in global groups. The only rules pertaining to nested groups is that only global groups can be placed in local groups. You also do not physically have to be on a domain controller to create global groups if the administration tools are installed.

8. (True/False) To create a new local group in User Manager for Domains, you would select New Local Group from the File pull-down menu.

   False. Select New Local Group from the User pull-down menu to create a new local group, not the File pull-down menu.

9. The _____ global group is a member of the Administrators local group on every Windows NT computer in the domain by default.

   Domain Admins. This is to enable the administrator, or members of the Domain

Admins group to administer the entire domain, and all of the Windows NT computers in the domain.

10. A user would like to log on to any computer in the network and see the same desktop. How do you go about doing this?
D. Assign a UNC path to the profile for the user's account. This creates a roaming profile that can also be changed back to a local profile.

11. You are going to shut down the server for repairs, but before you do you need to disconnect users. Which utility is the best way to accomplish this?
B. Server Manager. You will be able to see which users are attached to resources on the computer, and have the option of disconnecting one or all of the users.

12. Where do you adjust the Log On Locally setting?
B. Select User Rights from the Policies menu in User Manager. None of the other options exists. You also can adjust the Access This Computer From Network setting.

13. (True/False) You can audit a user's attempt to change his password.
True. This is under the User and Group Management event portion of the Auditing dialog box.

14. When Windows NT logs a user on, what is the name of the policy file it automatically looks for and applies for the user?
D. NTCONFIG.POL. If you select the Automatic update mode, the policy file

should be located in the default folder, which is the NETLOGON folder.

15. Which action is not possible in Server Manager?
D. Shutting down a remote computer. It is not possible to shut down another computer remotely using Server Manager.

16. (True/False) The WINDOWS.ADM System Policy Template file is for options that are common to both Windows 95 and Windows NT.
False. The COMMON.ADM template is for options common to both Windows 95 and Windows NT 4.0 machines. The WINDOWS.ADM contains settings specific to Windows 95.

Answers to Chapter 6 Self Test

1. The _____ creates security access tokens, authenticates users, and manages the local security policy.
A. The LSA is the heart of the security subsystem.

2. What maintains the database of all user, group, and workstation accounts?
B. The SAM is actually a hive in the registry that has all user account information.

3. NT supports which of the following logons? (Choose all that apply.)
A, B, C, D. All four of these are types of NT logons.

4. Why must you press CTRL-ALT-DEL to log on to NT?
   C. Pressing CTR-ALT-DEL activates the winlogon process and shuts down all other programs. This ensures that a password capture program won't operate on NT at logon.

5. Which of the following are objects? (Choose all that apply.)
   A, B, C. Almost everything is an object in NT, but it has to be capable of being managed by the operating system. The OS does not manage a keyboard.

6. A _____ is used to uniquely identify each user account.
   A. The security identifier is unique to every user. This is how NT distinguishes between users.

7. If you delete a user account how can you get it back?
   A. Once you remove the account the SID is destroyed and can never be re-created.

8. Which tool should you use to share a folder on a remote computer?
   B. Server Manager is the only tool that allows you to share files remotely on the network.

9. User JesseS belongs to the local group marketing. The permissions on the file dictionary.doc are as follows: JesseS has Change(RWXD) permission and the marketing group has No Access permissions. When user JesseS tries to read the file what access will he be granted?
   D. No Access is processed before any other ACE. Processing stops as soon as No Access is identified.

10. Which ACE does NT process first?
    D. AccessDenied must be processed first to ensure that users denied access don't get to the files.

11. User MaryS is assigned to the local group sales. Mary has Read permissions for all files on your system. The group sales has special permissions of write on all the files in the folder called reports. If Mary requests Read and Write permissions at the same time what will happen?
    C. Access permissions are cumulative. Each ACE is processed until enough permissions are given.

12. If you want to limit the people who can access a folder on your system while they are using the console, how must your hard disk partition be formatted?
    A. NTFS is the only file system on NT 4.0 that allows file and folder permissions.

13. Why is there a special utility to secure the boot partition of RISC computers?
    C. Because FAT doesn't allow file permissions, the tool is required to ensure that only administrators can have access to the boot files. RISC systems can have other partitions formatted with NTFS.

14. What command allows the user to change file permissions from a command shell?
C. The other answers aren't even commands.

15. If you want to audit access to files stored on your NTFS formatted hard drive, what must you do first?
A. Remember you must turn on auditing before you can audit anything. Although the audit button appears on the file's properties, nothing happens until you turn it on.

16. If you change a user's rights on a domain controller, which of the following statements are true?
B. Domain controllers maintained a common SAM database; therefore, all rights are reflected on all domain controllers.

17. Who is the owner of a new file on a FAT partition?
D. NTFS is the only file system on NT that has owners.

18. Who is the owner of a new file on an NTFS partition?
C. NT users discretionary access to control permissions to files and folders. Owners are responsible for securing the files they own. You become an owner whenever you take ownership or create a new file.

19. (True/False) Only administrators can give someone ownership of a file.
False. Ownership can only be taken, NEVER given away.

20. When moving a folder from drive c: to drive d: what permissions will the folder have? (Assume both drives are formatted with NTFS.)
B. When you move a file between partitions, NT actually copies the file then deletes the original. The new copy of the file inherits the parent folder's permissions.

21. Which file systems support Share level security?
D. Share level security is supported by all file systems on NT. File and folder level permissions are possible only with NTFS.

22. Which one is NOT a type of share permission on an NTFS partition?
D. This may have tricked you. There are only four share-level permissions—no matter what type of file system it's on.

23. How can you share a folder on the network to allow everyone to read, write, and execute files, but not delete any files?
D. To share files with more granularity, you can assign NTFS permissions to the same files to control access. You'll need to be familiar with this for the test.

24. Which of the following are negative results from auditing all file object accesses on your system? (Choose all that apply.)
A, B, C. Auditing file access takes time away from your CPU and it causes your hard disk to log the actions.

25. What auditing function must be turned on to allow you to audit writes to your NTFS directories?
B. It's pretty simple—you just need to know Table 6-7.

26. User RyanB is given share level access of Full Control to share SalesRPT; however, the NTFS permissions are set to Read for the group sales. RyanB is a member of the group sales. When she connects to the share SalesRPT what type of access will she have?
B. Although she has Full Control at the share, her file permissions only allow her to Read. Remember the most restrictive permissions always take precedence when share permissions are combined with file and folder permissions.

27. User MarcieJ is a member of Domain Users. She attempts to log on to a domain controller at the console, but she can't be validated. Whenever she tries to access the server through the network she connects without any problems. What is the most likely cause of this problem?
D. MarcieJ is only a Domain User, and by default Domain Users can't log on to a domain controller. If you need her to log on locally, you should add that right to her account.

Answers to Chapter 7 Self Test

1. Domain A trusts domain B. What needs to be done so that the administrator in domain A can be an administrator of domain B?
D. Adding the global group Domain Admins from domain A into domain B's local group Administrators properly assigns

groups. Remember: users into global, global into local, local gets permissions.

2. You changed the ReplicationGovernor on a BDC to a lower value. What effect does this have? (Choose all that apply.)
A, B. Reducing the ReplicationGovernor on a BDC limits the available bandwidth for synchronization by lowering buffers and frequency of calls to the PDC.

3. You have two domains, Sales and Marketing. You want all users in both domains to have access to a resource in the Sales domain. You also only want to use one group to manage access to the resource. What three steps must you perform?
A, D, F. First you create a one-way trust so that users can get from Marketing to Sales. Then create a local group in Sales. Finally, add all users to the local group you just created. It doesn't follow to add users to global groups then global groups to local, but you may see this type of question on the test. You really need to understand how groups and users accounts work through trust relationships.

4. Ten scientists each work on their own computer. Each user is responsible for security and backing up of their own computer's information. When they need to share information they must ensure only the intended person has access. Which model should you use?
D. A workgroup works best in this situation. There isn't a need for sharing data

among all scientists, so a central server isn't necessary. A workgroup allows each scientist to secure his own information.

5. Which variable in the registry do you change to slow down replications of accounts?
   A. The ReplicationGovernor controls the buffers and frequency of replication.

6. User Sally in domain A needs to access a share in domain B. Domain B trusts domain A. What needs to be done to let Sally access the share? (Choose the best answer.)
   B. You might want to choose A, but it isn't the best answer (although it works). The best answer follows the guideline: users into global, global into local, local gets permissions.

7. In a corporate office you have 150 users with five servers in a centralized office. MIS wants to keep complete control of user accounts and resources. Which model should you use?
   A. A single domain is the best domain to choose for centralized management of user accounts and resources.

8. In a corporate office you have 2000 users spread out over three buildings. MIS wants to keep complete control of user accounts, but wants the departmental manager to control local resources. Which model should you use?
   B. The master domain is best for centralized management of user accounts and decentralized management of resources.

However, if you get more than 40,000 users you'll need to use the multiple master domain model.

9. Domain Production trusts domain Sales. You create a local group in domain Production. What can this group contain? (Choose all that apply.)
   A, B, C, D. The only thing that can't go into the local group would be other local groups.

10. What's the maximum number of trusts available in NT 4.0?
    D. NT 4.0 can support an unlimited number of trusts. You may need to increase the amount of nonpaged pool memory or add physical RAM to get more trusts, but the limit of trusts in endless.

11. What's the total recommended number of domain controllers for a single domain with 10,000 users?
    D. This might have tricked you. Did you choose C? The reason it is six domain controllers is because it includes the PDC. If I asked what is the recommended number of BDCs the answer would be five.

Answers to Chapter 8 Self Test

1. In order for replication to fully function, what computers need to be running the Directory Replicator service?
   D. To fully function, both the export server

and import computers need to be running the Directory Replicator service.

2. (True/False) It is best to replicate files that are modified by several people on a daily basis.
   False. The best files to replicate are read-only files.

3. What is the purpose of My Briefcase?
   D. You use My Briefcase to track relationships between file versions on different computer systems so you can keep them synchronized.

4. A company has asked you to consult for them. They have decided they want to use logon scripts for half of their users. The company has more than one domain controller that is validating users. How can you make sure that the logon script will be available for the users who require it?
   A. Place the logon script on the export server and set the other validating domain controllers as import computers.

5. (True/False) By default, the netlogon share is %systemroot%SYSTEM32\REPL\EXPORT.
   False. The netlogon share is %systemroot%SYSTEM32\ REPL\IMPORT.

6. The Directory Replicator service account is used by the_____ .
   A, C. The service account is used by both the export server and import computers.

7. The PDC in your domain becomes overloaded each time it notifies the BDC's of changes in the user account database. What parameter should be changed in the Registry?
   C. The PulseConcurrency should be decreased to control the maximum load placed on the PDC.

8. (True/False) The ReplicationGovernor parameter is used by the PDC.
   False. The BDC's use the ReplicationGovernor parameter.

9. A new vice president has arrived at your company and you create her user account. How can you make sure it gets replicated out to all seven of the validating domain controllers quickly?
   D. Synchronizing the entire domain from the PDC will quickly get the vice president's account to all the BDC's.

10. (True/False) By default, a full replication of the user accounts database occurs every five minutes.
    False. A partial replication occurs every five minutes.

11. What is the default import directory path?
    C. The default import path is %systemroot%SYSTEM32\REPL\ IMPORT.

12. While managing exported directories, you see that the Script directory has Yes under the word Stabilize. What does this mean?
    C. It indicates that the files will be exported after waiting two minutes or more after changes have been made.

13. When you create the service account for use by the Directory Replicator service, what group(s) does it need to belong to?
B, D. The Directory Replicator service account needs to belong to the Backup Operators and the Replicator groups.

14. It will take you approximately 30 minutes to make changes to several files located in your Script export directory. What can you do to prevent replication from occurring until you have completed your work?
B. You should place a lock on the Script directory so that it does not get exported until you have finished your changes.

15. The default size of the change log is _____ .
D. The default size of the change log is 64KB.

Answers to Chapter 9 Self Test

1. What are two advantages of the EMF data type? (Choose two.)
B, C. EMF files return control of the application to the user more quickly because it spools to the spooler then it becomes a background process to print. EMF files can also be printed on any printer because the print process renders the document according to the printing device selected.

2. What are the two types of print processors shipped with NT?

A, C. These are the only two types of print processors supplied with NT. Vendors can make other print processors if needed.

3. If you want to add an HP JetDirect networked printer to your computer, what two things must you do?
A, C. To use an HP JetDirect card you must have DLC installed on your system. Since DLC uses MAC addresses to print, you also need to print a test page to identify the MAC address of the JetDirect Card. Also note that DLC is not a routable protocol.

4. You shared an HP LaserJet 5 on an NT server for everyone in your department to use. When users try to connect to the printer using Windows 95 they get the following error message: "The server on which the printer resides does not have a suitable driver installed. Click on OK if you wish to select a driver to use on your local machine." What should you do to prevent users from receiving this error message?
C. Like Windows NT, Windows 95 supports point and print; however, you must have the proper driver installed. Print drivers aren't independent of hardware platform and operating system. You must have a separate driver compiled for each operating system and hardware platform.

5. (True/False) A local printer must have a port on the local computer.
True. A local printer is just that—local; therefore it must have a local port. A local

port can be a serial port, parallel port, or a network-enabled port.

6. You want to set up a printer pool using two printers. Neither printing device can use a common driver. How can you enable both printing devices to be in a printer pool?
D. In order to set up printer pooling, all printers must use the same print driver.

7. Your boss needs to print to her secretary's printer, but she doesn't want to wait for her print job behind anybody else's print job. How can you share the printer and give your boss a higher priority?
A. You need to create two different printers so you can assign a different priority to each.

8. User JamieS sent a print job to an NT print server. When he went to the printer to pick up the print job he noticed a 200-page report was printing out. He didn't want to wait on his print job, so he printed the document on a different printer. Because JamieS is environmentally conscious, he doesn't want to waste paper printing the first print job. How can he delete the first print job? (Choose the best answer.)
A. Since he is the creator owner of the document, he can delete his own print job. B would also work, but it isn't the best solution.

9. To what group(s) must you add users so they can manage other people's print jobs? (Choose all correct answers.)
A, C. Administrators and Power Users can manage other users' print jobs. Creator

Owners can only manage their own print jobs.

10. Drive C: has 10MB of available disk space on it. Drive D: has 300MB of disk space available. Windows NT is installed on Drive C: which is almost out of space. Sometimes when you print your computer locks up and you need to restart your system. What should you do to prevent this problem in the future?
C. The printer spool file is probably causing the hard drive to fill up, thus causing the system to lock. Moving the printer spooler to Drive D: should alleviate the problem, although the limited available disk space on Drive C: may still cause problems with other applications.

11. Print jobs are stuck in the queue. What is the best thing you can do to fix the problem?
C. Stopping and restarting the spooler service is the best answer because it keeps the other server services up and running. B would probably fix the problem, but it would take longer and it would stop all other server services.

12. You want to allow a printer to be used only during normal working hours (9:00 A.M. to 6:00 P.M.). What is the best way to implement this requirement?
A. The Scheduling tab is the proper way to limit printer use. The tab enables you to select the hours when the printer is available, not the hours when it's unavailable.

13. What command do you use to print to a
    UNIX print server?
    B. The proper format is lpr -S <server
    name> -P <printer name> <filename>

14. (True/False) NT can act as a UNIX
    print server.
    True. After you install Microsoft TCP/IP
    Printing, you can set up NT to allow UNIX
    clients to print to it.

Answers to Chapter 10 Self Test

1. (True/False) Windows NT will successfully
   migrate all NetWare file attributes with the
   Migration Tool for NetWare.
   False. NetWare has a number of extended
   file attributes that are not supported on
   NTFS, and are therefore not migrated.

2. Which of the following functions are
   features of GSNW?
   C, D. NetWare file and print services can
   be connected to, used, and shared to
   Microsoft Networking clients by Windows
   NT Servers with GSNW.

3. Microsoft Services for NetWare includes
   which two products?
   B, C. File and Print Services for NetWare
   and Directory Services Manager for
   NetWare are the two components of
   Microsoft Services for NetWare.

4. (True/False) Loading two network
   redirectors on client PCs is the only way

users can access both Windows NT and
NetWare servers.
False. A Microsoft Networking client can
access NetWare files and printers through a
Windows NT Server with GSNW enabled,
and a NetWare client can access a Windows
NT server that has FPNW enabled.

5. What is the name of the group that must be
   created on the NetWare server for GSNW
   to operate?
   D. A group named NTGATEWAY must be
   created on the NetWare server, and the
   gateway account must be a member of
   that group.

6. (True/False) GSNW and FPNW do not
   create much load on the server, or traffic on
   the network.
   False. FPNW requires Windows NT Server
   to emulate a NetWare server, which is a
   significant burden on the system. Copying a
   file via a GSNW gateway share requires the
   file to be copied over the network twice, first
   to the gateway server and then to the client.

7. (True/False) The Migration Tool for
   NetWare allows you to copy users and
   groups, but account policies cannot be
   migrated.
   False. Account policies on the NetWare
   server can be transferred by selecting the Use
   Supervisor Defaults option on the Defaults
   tab in the User Options dialog box.

8. (True/False) Remote users cannot access
   gateway shares when they dial in through
   RAS.

False. GSNW gateway shares are available to dialin users, just like native Windows NT shares.

9. (True/False) An unlimited number of gateway shares can be created on a Windows NT Server with GSNW.
False. Each gateway directory share requires a drive letter on the server, so the number of gateway shares on each Windows NT server is limited to 26 minus the number of physical drives.

10. (True/False) NetWare file permissions are an effective way to restrict GSNW users from accessing each other's data.
False. The only file permissions that will be in effect for gateway users are the permissions assigned to the gateway account.

11. (True/False) NWLink is not necessary for GSNW if the NetWare server is using TCP/IP.
False. All of the NetWare connectivity tools for Windows NT Server rely on the NWLink protocol. NWLink cannot be removed from the Windows NT computer without first removing the NetWare tools.

12. (True/False) Permissions cannot be set on gateway shares, so security is greatly compromised when using GSNW.
False. Setting permissions on gateway shares is very similar to setting permissions on native Windows NT shares. The only difference is the location of the Permissions button for directory shares.

13. Passwords for migrated accounts can be set to which of the following with the Migration Tool?
A, B, C, D. The Migration Tool allows all four options to be exercised.

14. (True/False) The Migration Tool can only copy entire volumes; you cannot select specific directories to be migrated.
False. The Migration Tool allows you to specify which directories you wish to migrate from a NetWare server.

15. (True/False) Windows NT and NetWare offer pretty much the same functionality, and there isn't much reason to choose one over the other.
False. Windows NT and NetWare are different in almost every way, including the type of hardware they support.

Answers to Chapter 11 Self Test

1. Which of the following configurations are valid using Windows NT RAS?
C, D. Windows NT RAS is not supported as a SLIP server. However, RAS supports both SLIP and PPP in Dial-Up Networking.

2. When you select 'Require Microsoft encrypted authentication' what authentication methods are used to achieve connectivity?

B. By specifying 'Require encrypted authentication' as your encryption setting, you are only permitting MS-CHAP authentication to occur.

3. Users are complaining about the difficulty of connecting to your RAS server. From the information you receive, you determine that the problem may be hardware-related. What actions should you take? (Choose two.)
C, E. Enabling the DEVICE.LOG file is accomplished by turning it on in the HKEY_LOCAL_MACHINE registry path. The file is stored in \<winnt_root>\ SYSTEM32\RAS.

4. Which of the following files can be modified to add RAS support for a non-supported modem?
D. You can add an entry in the MODEM.INF file to provide support for an unsupported modem. Remember, the DEVICE.LOG file provides information to help troubleshoot your modem and RAS.

5. When configuring a port for RAS usage, which of the following are true?
A, B, C. RAS allows the following scenarios when configuring ports: Dial out only, receive calls only, or dial out and receive calls allowed.

6. Which protocols are supported by RAS?
B, C, D. RAS supports the NetBEUI, IPX/SPX, and TCP/IP protocols.

7. Which of the following security features are available when using RAS?

A, C. RAS supports callback and DES encryption. MD5 can only be negotiated by Microsoft Dial-Up Networking clients.

8. You have three Windows NT Servers with the Remote Access Service installed on three different TCP/IP network segments. Windows NT workstations dial into these servers. What method would you use to minimize time required to resolve NetBIOS names?
B. Local LMHOSTS files on users workstations are the simplest way to resolve TCP/IP addresses to NetBIOS names. Installing an LMHOSTS file on the server will only assist the server in resolving NetBIOS names. Windows NT workstations cannot be configured as WINS servers.

9. What new option has been added to the Windows NT 4.0 logon dialog box?
C. The option to logon via Dial-Up Networking is new to Windows NT 4.0.

10. What is true of using PPTP?
B. Lower transmission costs are one benefit of implementing PPTP as most network integration issues can be absorbed into local ISP's.

11. With PPTP filtering enabled, which of the following does a Windows NT Server 4.0 RAS accept?
B. When PPTP is enabled, only PPTP traffic is allowed. TCP/IP, IPX/SPX, and NetBEUI packets tunnel within PPTP.

12. Your RAS server has two internal modems. Remote users report that when they try to dial in to the RAS server, they are being disconnected immediately. How can you diagnose this problem?

    A. DEVICE.LOG is created by enabling it in the registry.

13. What utilities can you use to grant users permission to log in to your RAS server?

    A, B. You can grant Remote Access Service permission to users using the Remote Access Admin utility or User Manager for Domains.

14. You have a RAS server to which Windows 95 clients dial in. They have Client for Microsoft Networks and IPX/SPX installed. You also have a Netware server from which you want to allow these users to access resources. What should you install on the Windows NT RAS server?

    B. Gateway Service for Netware (GSNW) running on Windows NT Server allows access to Netware resources on a Netware server to Microsoft client computer.

15. You have been providing Multilink remote access ability to your users for the last six months without problems. When your manager insisted that you implement tighter security, you chose to implement callback security. Now users complain about dramatic drop in speed when they connect to RAS? Why is this happening?

    C. If a client uses a Multilink-enabled phonebook entry to call a callback-enabled RAS server, when the callback is made only one of the Multilink devices will receive the call.

16. Identify three ways you can manually start and stop RAS.

    A, C, D. The Remote Access Server service can be started and stopped from a command prompt, the Remote Access Admin program, and the Services program in the Control Panel.

17. You want to provide Internet connectivity to your corporate LAN. What should be implemented to help secure your server from Internet-related threats?

    A. When you implement a RAS gateway to the Internet, PPTP is implemented to provide a secure tunnel. By enabling PPTP filtering, you effectively disable all other protocols on the adapter making the connection to the Internet, reducing the security threat.

Answers to Chapter 12 Self Test

1. In order to successfully back up your Windows NT Server you need to use

    _____ .

    A, C. To successfully back up your Windows NT Server you need backup software and tape media with a tape drive.

2. (True/False) Windows NT Backup can
    back up to floppy disks.
    False. Windows NT Backup utility can only
    back up to tape.

3. You need to back up the registry on your
    PDC to tape without taking it offline. The
    tape drive is located on your BDC. What
    must be done to perform the backup?
    D. A tape drive must be added to the PDC
    so that you can successfully back up the
    registry to tape.

4. To make a full backup of your entire
    partition you would use a _____ .
    E. A normal backup is another name for a
    full backup.

5. You have one tape drive located on your
    PDC. It is responsible for backing up a
    BDC and 18 client machines. Through
    careful monitoring, you have found that the
    backup is interfering with users getting their
    work accomplished (it has not been
    completed when they start work). What can
    you do to ensure that backup is done before
    users arrive at work?
    C. Add a tape drive to the BDC and split
    the load on the backups so that it can
    complete before the users arrive at work.

6. You need to back up 30 gigabytes of data
    from your network. What type of medium
    would be best to use for this backup?
    D. DLT is currently the only tape media
    available that can hold this much data.

7. (True/False) A differential backup marks
    files as having been backed up.

False. A differential backup does *not* mark
files as having been backed up.

8. (True/False) It is possible to complete
    backups for one year using only nineteen
    tapes.
    True. Yes, it is possible to complete one
    year's worth of backups using only 19 tapes.

9. A user is attempting to back up a partition
    but the system does not allow him to back
    up everything. What could be the problem?
    C. The user can encounter problems if he
    does not have permissions to a file or
    directory. To alleviate this condition, he can
    be added to the Administrators or Backup
    Operators groups.

10. If your backup strategy consists of
    completing backups for one year using
    nineteen tapes what type of method(s)
    should be used?
    A, E. A combination of normal and
    incremental backups should be utilized for
    this backup strategy.

11. You can successfully back up the entire
    partition on your system; however, you run
    into difficulties when you try to restore the
    partition. What can cause this problem?
    D. You will not be able to restore unless you
    have the right to Restore Files and
    Directories. This is separate from the
    Backup Files and Directories user right.

12. It is recommended that you have ____
    complete backup sets in case of tape failure
    or loss.

B. It is best to have three complete backup sets on hand.

13. (True/False) You should not store the tape backups off-site as this causes a delay if you need to use them for restoration.
False. Backups *should* be stored off-site to protect the integrity of your data if something should happen at your system(s) location.

14. (True/False) The Windows NT Backup utility cannot back up all the files on your system.
True. The Backup utility cannot back up the pagefile.sys, registries from remote machines, or files that have been locked by an application.

15. You want to back up only your complete registry. What tool should you use?
C. REGEDIT can be used to back up your *complete* registry. REGEDT32 will only back up individual registry keys and Disk Administrator will only back up the SYSTEM key.

Answers to Chapter 13 Self Test

1. What type of network interface card should you use in a system that has a PCI bus?
C. PCI is a 32-bit bus and you should use a network interface card that can take advantage of the full bus.

2. Your network has 73 users who will be using Word from your Windows NT Server. What is the optimum setting for the server service?
D. Since your users are using an application from your server, you should maximize it for network applications.

3. Your network uses a combination of two different network protocols. You place the least used protocol at the top of the binding order for the server service. Will it decrease server performance?
B. No, it will not decrease server performance because the server service listens on all protocols and responds when it makes a connection regardless of the binding order.

4. (True/False) Messenger service does not need to be started in order for an alert to be sent from Performance Monitor.
False. The Messenger service needs to be started or else the alert message will never be sent.

5. The Event Viewer log size can be changed in _____ increments.
C. The log size can be changed in 64KB increments.

6. What tab of the Windows NT Diagnostics screen would you use to determine the dependencies for a device on the system?
C. The Services tab shows what dependencies exist for a device on the system.

7. (True/False) The Network Monitor that comes with Windows NT Server can be used to collect data for your entire network segment.
False. The Network Monitor that comes with Windows NT Server can only monitor the server it is installed on.

8. When the /HIGH switch is used to launch an application from the command prompt at what priority will the application start?
B. Table 13-2 illustrates the four switch possibilities and their associated priority level.

9. While using the Processor:%Processor Time counter in Performance Monitor, you see it spike to 100% when starting an application, but then it drops to 43%. What do you need to do?
D. The processor becomes a bottleneck only if the sustained utilization rate is 80% or higher.

10. Windows NT divides memory into _____ pages.
B. Windows NT uses a 4KB page size to help avoid fragmentation of memory.

11. Windows NT Server supports _____ processors.
D. As shipped, Windows NT Server supports four processors. If you need to support more processors you need to contact your computer system manufacturer.

12. (True/False) It is not possible to change the priority of the foreground application so that it will run at the same priority as all background applications.
False. It is possible to make the foreground application equal to background applications by moving the slider to None on the Performance tab of System Properties.

13. How many levels can Windows NT automatically adjust the priority of an application?
C. Windows NT can automatically raise or lower priority by up to 2 levels.

14. You suspect a disk drive is creating a bottleneck within your system. You use the LogicalDisk:%Disk Time counter to take measurements but have a consistent reading of zero. What is the problem?
D. You must enable the disk drive performance counters prior to using either the LogicalDisk or PhysicalDisk Objects.

15. Multiprocessing supported by Windows NT is _____ .
B. Windows NT supports symmetrical processing so that it can effectively share the load among all the processors.

16. (True/False) Using two processors in your Windows NT system will double its performance capability.
False. Overhead for resource sharing and scheduling between two processors prevents

system performance from doubling; the improvement is normally more like 150 percent.

17. Where does Windows NT perform automatic self-tuning optimizations?
A, C, D. Windows NT adjusts thread and process priority, swapping among multiple pagefiles, and caching disk requests as part of its self-tuning optimizations.

18. The cache system used by Windows NT is _____ .
C. Windows NT uses a dynamic cache so that it can adjust itself for maximum performance.

19. What utility is used to enable the disk drive performance counters?
C. Diskperf is the utility used to enable and disable the disk drive performance counters.

20. (True/False) The Task Manager cannot be used to change the priority of a thread.
True. Task Manager can change the priority of processes, not threads.

21. Performance Monitor shows that you have a disk drive bottleneck. What action(s) could alleviate this problem?
B. Adding more physical memory to a system can alleviate a disk drive bottleneck by minimizing the amount of paging to the disk drive if physical memory is low.

22. Performance Monitor indicates that you are encountering a memory bottleneck. What

action(s) will eliminate it?
A, C. If your pagefile is too small it can appear to be a memory bottleneck. Unloading unused drivers will free memory that the system can use.

23. (True/False) Hard page faults are more detrimental to system performance than soft page faults.
True. Hard page faults indicate that additional I/O has occurred, and soft page faults indicate the data was located elsewhere in memory.

24. (True/False) Once you have manually performance tuned your system you will never have to do it again.
False. Performance tuning your system is an ongoing process.

25. (True/False) Disk drive performance counters should only be enabled when monitoring disk drive performance.
True. The disk drive performance counters degrade overall system performance by interrupting the processor during I/O. They should only be enabled when you are using them to measure disk drive performance.

26. What would you use to change the priority of an application that is already running?
D. The Task Manager can change the priority of an application that is running. If you stop and restart the application it will be back to the original priority.

Answers to Chapter 14 Self Test

1. Which of the following is a valid ARC path?
   B. The only choice that fulfills ARC naming requirements is B.

2. What files are required to be on a Windows NT boot disk for a non-SCSI, Intel-based machine?
   A, B, E. The other two files are used for SCSI systems and RISC-based machines.

3. You are sent out on a trouble call and told that the system hangs since the user added a new video driver. What would you do?
   C. Reboot the system using the LastKnownGood Configuration with the original video driver.

4. Your system has 128 megabytes of physical memory and you have set the System Recovery to write debugging information to %systemroot%\memory.dmp. What else needs to be done to ensure that the debugging information will be saved?
   A. The pagefile has to be at least the same size as physical memory so that it can dump everything from memory to the pagefile for debugging.

5. Paul has been fired and his replacement Ann needs to access the 4th quarter report that is located in a folder that belonged to Paul. How will Ann be able to access this folder?
   D. An Administrator will have to take ownership of the folder, but by giving Ann full control she will be able to access the folder and take ownership for herself.

6. To update your Emergency Repair Disk you would type _____ from a Command Prompt.
   B. You would type **rdisk** from a Command Prompt to update your ERD.

7. (True/False) A Service Pack can be easily removed from your system even if you do not have the uninstall folder.
   False. If you did not create an Uninstall folder, you will not be able to easily remove the Service Pack.

8. What causes the "blue screen of death"?
   A. A STOP message will cause the "blue screen of death".

9. The Partition(n) portion of an ARC name starts counting with _____.
   B. The partition(n) starts with a count of one.

10. A system you have been sent out to troubleshoot will not boot. You attempt to use the LastKnownGood configuration and it does not correct the problem. What would you do next?
    B. You should use the ERD for that system to try and fix it.

11. (True/False) The SAM and Security files are automatically updated when you use the Repair Disk Utility.
    False. You must use the /s switch with rdisk if you want to back up the SAM and Security files.

12. (True/False) The fault-tolerant boot disk must be used if the member drive of a mirror set is orphaned.

False. The fault-tolerant boot disk only needs to be used if the failure involves the system partition. Your system will boot on its own when the member partition has failed.

13. The fault-tolerant driver detects an orphaned drive on your RAID 5 set. What is the result?

D. The system will continue to function; however, it will have some system degradation as the data from the orphaned drive will have to be regenerated in physical memory as it is needed.

14. What would cause a system on a network that uses the IPX/SPX protocol to not communicate with any other systems on the network?

A, C. If the system cannot communicate with other systems on an IPX/SPX network then make sure the protocol has been installed and that it is using the correct frame type.

15. A user attempts to print but the print job never completes and the hard drive thrashes a lot. What could be causing this to happen?

B. The spooler has run out of disk space. You need to create more room or move the spooler to another partition that has more room.

B

About the CD

CD-ROM Instructions

This CD-ROM contains a full web site accessible to you via your web browser. Browse to or double-click **index.htm** at the root of the CD-ROM and you will find instructions for navigating the web site and for installing the various software components.

Electronic Book

An electronic version of the entire book in HTML format.

Interactive Self-Study Module

An electronic self-study test bank linked to the electronic book to help you instantly review key exam topics that may still be unclear. This module contains over 300 review questions, the same questions that appear at the end of each chapter. If you answer a multiple choice question correctly by clicking on the right answer, you will automatically link to the next question. If you answer incorrectly, you will be linked to the appropriate section in the electronic book for further study.

Sample Exams

Demos from market-leading certification tools vendors, including Self-Test Software's PEP, Transcender's CERT, VFX Technologies' Endeavor, BeachFront Quizzer's BFQuizzer, and Microhard Technologies' MCSEQuest. These exams may be installed either from the "Exams and Simulations" web page or from Windows Explorer. See the following for instructions on either type of installation.

From the Web Page

Internet Explorer users will be prompted to either "open the file" or "save it to disk." Select "open the file" and the installation program will automatically be launched, installing the software to your hard disk. Follow the vendor's instructions. The software will be installed to the hard disk. Once installed, you should run the programs via the Start Programs taskbar on your desktop.

Netscape Navigator users will be asked to "save as..." the setup file. You should save it to a folder on your hard drive, then click on it in Windows Explorer to launch the installation. Follow the vendor's instructions. The software will be installed to the hard disk. Once installed, you should run the programs via the Start Programs taskbar on your desktop.

From Windows Explorer

You can also launch the installation of any of these programs from Windows Explorer by opening the "Demo Exams" folder on the CD. Each vendor's installation program is inside the designated folder. Click on the appropriate SETUP.EXE file and then follow the vendor's instructions. The software will be installed to the hard disk. Once installed, you should run the programs via the Start Programs taskbar on your desktop.

C

About the
Web Site

Access Global Knowledge Network

As you know by now, Global Knowledge Network is the largest independent IT training company in the world. Just by purchasing this book, you have also secured a free subscription to the Access Global web site and its many resources. You can find it at:

http://access.globalknowledge.com

To acquire an ID to use the Access Global web site, send e-mail to access@globalknowledge.com and type **Access ID Request** in the subject field. In the body of the message, include your full name, mailing address, e-mail address, and phone number. Within two business days you will receive your Access Global web site ID. The first time you visit the site and log on, you will be able to choose your own password.

What You'll Find There. . .

You will find a lot of information at the Global Knowledge site, most of which can be broken down into three categories:

Skills Gap Analysis

Global Knowledge offers several ways for you to analyze your networking skills and discover where they may be lacking. Using Global Knowledge Network's trademarked Competence Key Tool, you can do a skills gap analysis and get recommendations for where you may need to do some more studying (sorry, it just may not end with this book!).

Networking

You'll also gain valuable access to another asset: people. At the Access Global site, you'll find threaded discussions as well as live discussions. Talk to other MCSE candidates, get advice from folks who have already taken exams, and get access to instructors and MCTs.

Product Offerings

Of course, Global Knowledge also offers its products here—and you may find some valuable items for purchase: CBTs, books, courses. Browse freely and see if there's something that could help you.

Glossary

Reprinted by permission of Global Knowledge Networks, Inc. Copyright © 1998 American Research Group, Inc.

10Base-2   An Ethernet topology using thin Ethernet coaxial cable, also known as Thin Ethernet or thinnet.

10Base-5   Also called thicknet, this form of cable was once commonly used for backbones in Ethernet networks. It is now being replaced by 10Base-T.

10Base-T   An Ethernet topology that uses unshielded twisted pair cable. 10Base-T has become the most popular Ethernet cable, because many buildings are already wired for 10Base-T, it is inexpensive and easy to work with, and if the cable specifications are CAT5, it can transmit data at 100Mbps.

access permissions   Access permissions set your rights and privileges to manipulate files and directories. Depending on your permissions, you may or may not be able to copy, delete, or otherwise manipulate files and directories on the network.

Account   An account or user account provides access to the network. It contains the information allowing a person to use the network, including user name and logon specifications, password, and rights to directories and resources.

account restrictions   Restrictions on an account determine when and how a user gains access to the network.

acknowledgment (ACK)   A packet of information sent from the recipient computer to the sending computer, for the purpose of verifying that a transmission has been received and confirming that it was or was not a successful transmission. Similar to a return receipt.

active hub   A hub device used in a star topology to regenerate and redistribute data across the LAN. Unlike a passive hub, the active hub requires electricity. See also hub, and passive hub.

adapter   A network adapter card, also called a network interface card, transmits data from the workstation to the cable that connects the machine to the LAN. It provides the communication link between the computer and the network. See also Network Interface Card.

administrator account   The account used to administer the settings on an NT Server and network. This account is created during install and has unlimited access to the server. Care must be taken when logged into a server as an administrator, because administrator access rights include the ability to shut down the server or erase critical data.

alias   A name used to reference a person, or group on a computer system. Mail aliases are a common use of the alias feature. When an alias is used, the computer system still recognizes a person by a user name, but an alias can be set so that people can send mail or other information using the alias name instead of the user name.

analog   A continuous, non-digital data transmission usually associated with telephone communications.

AppleTalk   The set of network protocols used by Macintosh computers.

archiving   A process that allows you to move old files off the file server to preserve disk space for new files. If the old files are later needed, they can be unarchived and retrieved. Archived data can be saved to CD-ROM, WORM, or tape.

ArcNet (Attached Resource Computer Network)   A bus network topology that is similar to token ring, in that it uses a token to transmit data across the network. ArcNet transmits data at 2.5Mbps and can run on coaxial, twisted-pair, and fiber optic cable.

ASCII (American Standard Code for Information Interchange)
A representation of standard alphabetic and other keyboard characters in a computer-readable, binary format.

Asynchronous Transfer Mode (ATM)   A packet-switching network technology for LANs and WANs that can handle voice, video, and data transmissions simultaneously.

ATM   See Asynchronous Transfer Mode (ATM).

Attachment Unit Interface   A connector on a NIC used to connect a cable to the card. Frequently used with coaxial cable.

attributes   The characteristics of files and directories. On networks such as Windows NT, attributes are set by the administrator, and define the rights for users and groups to manipulate files. On a stand-alone system, the main user can set file attributes. Attributes affect whether a file can be opened, copied, deleted, executed, modified, or otherwise manipulated.

AUI   See Attachment Unit Interface.

back door   Used by system administrators to access the network at an administrator's level, if something happens to the network administrator's home account. This provides a means to rebuild the administrator's account, or otherwise fix the network.

back up   The process of saving files to a separate location, usually an offline storage location, such as tape.

backbone   The main cable that connects file servers, routers, and bridges to the network.

backup   Copies all of the files on a network to some form of offline storage. Backups should be performed nightly, and full copies of the backup should be stored off-site.

Backup Domain Controller (BDC)   A computer that contains a backup of a domain's security policy and domain database, maintained by the NT server. Serves as a backup to the primary domain controller. A BDC is not required but is recommended.

bad sector   A damaged or non-working area of a hard disk. If data has been saved to that area, it cannot be accessed.

bandwidth   The capacity to transmit data across a communications link. Bandwidth is usually measured in bits per second (bps).

base I/O address   The address that identifies a hardware device to the computer.

baseline   The baseline captures the activity on the network on a normal day. This can be used to compare future readings for diagnostic purposes.

BNC (British Naval Connector)   Also known as a barrel connector, the connector type used in 10Base2 (thin Ethernet) networks to connect two cable segments, creating a longer segment.

bootup   The process a computer executes when powered up is known as bootup. This includes the files that initialize the hardware, and the starting of the operating system.

bridge   A hardware device that connects two LAN segments of either the same or different topologies.

buffer space   A reserved portion of RAM that provides room for the storage of incoming and outgoing data.

bus   A network topology that connects all computers to a single, shared cable. In a bus topology, if one computer fails, the network fails.

cache   An area in memory that duplicates information to provide faster access.

CD-ROM   A device, similar to a musical compact disc, that stores data.

client   A machine used to access the network.

client/server network   A network architecture, based on distributed processing, in which a client performs functions by requesting services from a server.

coaxial cable   A cable used in networks, consisting of a conductive center surrounded by a layer of insulation and a non-conductive outer layer.

command line   A character mode interface for computer applications that relies on commands instead of a graphical interface to process information.

compression   A mathematical technique that analyzes computer files in order to compress them to a smaller size. Most backup systems, and many file servers, compress files to provide increased storage capacity.

computer virus   A computer program built to sabotage or destroy a computer or network.

concentrator   A device that connects workstations to the path of the file server. Concentrators typically have 8 – 12 ports into which workstations attach.

conventional memory   The memory below 640K. If you have room, your LAN drivers are loaded in conventional memory.

CSU/DSU (Channel Service Unit/Data Service Unit) A piece of hardware that sits between a network and a digital telephone line, to translate data between the two formats. CSU/DSUs are most commonly used to attach a network router to a T1 or other digital telephone line.

DAT (Digital Audio Tape) A hardware option for tape backup. Some are 4mm while others are 8mm.

Database Management System A software application that manages a database, including the organization, storage, security, retrieval, and integrity of data in a database.

DBMS See Database Management System (DBMS).

differential backup Backing up only the files that have changed since the last backup, this differs from a full backup, in that a full backup saves all files regardless of when they changed. A differential backup differs from an incremental backup, in that archive attributes are not reset.

directory path The path to a directory on a file system, including the server, volume, and other names leading to the directory.

directory tree The file structure, including directory and subdirectory layout below the root directory.

disk mirroring Provides redundancy by mirroring data from one hard drive to another. If a crash or other problem occurs on the active drive, Windows NT automatically begins to use the backup drive, and notifies you of the switch.

distributed-star A combination of a bus and star topology used by ARCnet.

DLC (Data Link Control)   A method that allows token ring-based workstations to connect to IBM mainframes and minicomputers. It has also been adopted by printer manufacturers to connect remote printers to print servers, which is how Windows NT uses DLC.

DLL   See Dynamic Link Library (DLL).

DLT (Digital Linear Tape)   A hardware solution for tape backup and storage that allows multiple tapes to be loaded into the system, providing unattended backups and easy access for keeping data in online storage.

DMA (Direct Memory Addressing)   Matches an area in memory with an area on the NIC, so that when information is written to memory, it is copied to the NIC and vice versa.

DNS   See Domain Name Service (DNS).

Domain Name Service   DNS is a hierarchical name service that translates host names to IP addresses. It is used with TCP/IP hosts.

domain   A set of workstations and servers, on a network, that are administered as a group.

driver   Coordinates the communications between hardware and the computer. For example, it is a driver that allows a LAN adapter or other card to work.

Dynamic Host Configuration Protocol (DHCP)   Designed by Microsoft to handle IP address ranges through temporary assignments of addresses, DHCP provides automatic IP address allocation to specific workstations.

Dynamic Link Library (DLL)   A module of executable code that is loaded on demand. Used in Microsoft Windows products.

edge connector   The portion of an expansion board inserted into an expansion slot when the card is seated in the computer. The number of pins, and the width and depth of the lines, differ depending on the various types of interfaces (i.e., ISA, EISA, PCI, Micro Channel).

EIDE (Enhanced IDE)   EIDE is a disk drive interface that can support up to four 8.4GB drives.

EISA (Extended Industry Standard Architecture)   A standard for the PC bus that extends the 16-bit ISA bus (AT bus) to 32 bits EISA; also provides bus mastering.

electronic mail (e-mail)   Mail messages transmitted electronically from one network user to another, or across the Internet.

emergency startup disk   Provides a bootup option for Windows NT if the server will not boot from its hard disk.

encryption   An algorithm that hides the contents of a message, or other file or communication, by deliberately scrambling the elements that compose the item. The item must then be decrypted to its original form before it can be read.

Ethernet   The most popular LAN network topology.

event logs   Log files containing the system events, including security and application events.

Explorer   The file system navigation tool for Microsoft's Windows 95 and NT 4.0 operating systems.

FAQ (Frequently Asked Questions)   Appear in specific areas of bulletin boards and web sites, and contain answers to questions about a product or service that are frequently asked. These are used in newsgroups to cover questions that have appeared often.

Fast Ethernet   Ethernet provides 100Mbps data transmission.

FAT (File Allocation Table)   Originally the layout of a DOS disk storage system. In Windows NT, a FAT is a NT Server volume that is accessible by DOS and that is using the DOS file storage system instead of NTFS.

fault tolerance   A computer system that is resistant to hardware problems and software errors is said to be fault tolerant.

FDDI (Fiber Distributed Data Interface)   A very fast and expensive fiber-based network access method. FDDI provides 100Mbps network access.

fiber-optic cable   Instead of electrical impulses, fiber-optic cables move light. This type of cable is built around conductive elements that move light, not electricity. For most fiber-optic cables, the conductive element is most likely a form of special glass fiber, rather than copper or some other conductive metal. The beauty of fiber-optic cable is that it is immune to electronic and magnetic interference, and has much more bandwidth than most electrical cable types.

file server   A network computer that runs the network operating system and services requests from the workstations.

file system   The network operating system's rules for handling and storing files.

firewall   A hardware or software solution that protects a computer system from external intrusion. Firewalls have become more instrumental on computer systems as access to the Internet has grown more popular.

full backup   A complete copy of all the data on the network. These should be run frequently, and at least one current copy should be stored off-site.

gateway   A device that connects two or more dissimilar computer systems. Gateways can be electronic or software devices, and are becoming more common as the need for cross-platform communications increases.

GB   The abbreviation for gigabyte, which is treated as equivalent to a billion bytes.

Hardware Abstraction Layer (HAL)   A translation layer between the NT kernel and I/O system, and the actual hardware.

HCL (Hardware Compatibility List)   Lists all the hardware tested by Microsoft that works with NT. Check this before purchasing hardware.

host   A server that is accessed by clients. In a TCP/IP network, any computer connected to the network is considered a host.

hot-swappable parts   Parts that can be replaced without shutting down the system.

hub   The device used in a star topology that connects the computers to the LAN. Hubs can be passive or active. See also passive hub, active hub.

incremental backup   Backs up all the files that have been changed since the last backup. The file is not replaced on the backup, it is appended to the backup medium.

interference   Noise that disturbs the electrical signals sent across network cables.

intruder   Any person trying to break in to a network.

IP (Internet Protocol) A common protocol that sets up the mechanism for transferring data across the network. Usually seen in TCP/IP.

IPX The native transport protocol for Novell's NetWare. It is also available in the Windows NT environment.

ISA (Industry Standard Architecture) The bus used in most PCs since it was introduced in 1985.

Kbps See kilobits per second.

kilobits per second (Kbps) A data transfer speed of 1,024 bits per second.

lag The slowing of network performance usually caused by increased demand for available bandwidth.

LAN (Local Area Network) Consists of any two or more computers joined together to communicate within a small area, usually not larger than a single building.

LAN driver Provides the information to allow the NIC to communicate with the network.

legacy system An existing system that either needs updating or is no longer capable of maintaining required performance.

load The amount of data present on the network. Also known as network traffic.

log off (or log out) The procedure for exiting the network.

logical printers Created by NT, logical printer capability allows you to set a single print definition that can be serviced by multiple physical printers.

log on (or log in)   The procedure for checking on to the network so that you can access files and other network information. When you have access to the network, you are said to be logged on. When you exit the network, you log out.

loopback test   A test which allows a NIC to talk to itself to see if it is working.

MB   megabyte

Mbps (megabits per second)   Used to measure throughput or communication speed. A communications rate of 1,048,576 bits per second.

media filter   Used on token ring networks to change the type of media from Type 1 (shielded twisted-pair) to Type 3 (unshielded twisted-pair) or vice versa.

mirroring   The process of duplicating data so that if one system fails, another can take its place.

modem   A device used to translate digital signals from the computer into analog signals that can travel across a telephone line.

multi-disk volume   A storage system that uses multiple hard disks connected with the OS, so that they act as a single entity with a single drive name/letter.

multistation access units (MAUs)   MAUs are the central hubs in a token ring LAN.

multithreading   The process that allows a multitasking operating system, such as Windows NT, to multitask the threads of an application.

NDIS (Network Driver Interface Specification)   A network device driver specification, NDIS provides hardware and protocol independence for network drivers. A benefit of NDIS is that it offers protocol multiplexing, which allows multiple protocol stacks to coexist in the same host.

near-line backups   These backups differ from offline backups, in that they are kept on devices connected to the network for faster restoration of files. They require more effort to restore than accessing a file from a hard disk, but less effort than restoring a file from an offline backup.

NetBEUI (NetBIOS Extended User Interface)   A transport layer driver that is the Extended User Interface to NetBIOS. It is used by Windows NT and other operating systems to deliver information across a network. NetBEUI cannot be routed.

NetBIOS (Networked Basic Input-Output System)   A networked extension to PC BIOS. NetBIOS allows I/O requests to be sent and received from a remote computer.

NetWare   Novell's network operating system.

network   Two or more computers linked together so that they can communicate.

network adapter   See network interface card.

network infrastructure   The physical equipment that hooks computers into a network. This includes the cables, hubs, routers, and software used to control a network.

Network Interface Card (NIC)   The card that allows the computer to communicate across the network. The network cable attaches to the NIC.

network map   A detailed map of information about what's on the network. Includes an inventory of machines and other hardware, a map of cable layout, and other information to document the network.

Network Operating System   An operating system that permits and facilitates the networking of computers. Windows NT is one.

NIC   See network interface card (NIC).

node   Each device on a network is an individual node. It can be a workstation, a printer, or the file server.

NOS   See Network Operating System.

NT File System (NTFS)   The file system used by Windows NT. It supports large storage media, and file system recovery, in addition to other advantages.

NTDETECT   The hardware recognition program used by Windows NT.

offline backups   Backups that are kept offline. They are removed from the operation of the server and require the medium, usually tape, to be loaded in order to restore.

off-site storage   A place in a separate location from the file server, used to store backup tapes. A complete backup should always be kept off-site.

online backups   Backups that are stored online so that they are immediately available.

overhead   The control attached to packets transmitted across a network. Overhead data includes routing and error-checking information. Overhead also refers to the bandwidth used to sustain network communications.

packet   A unit of data transmitted across a network as a whole.

packet burst   Used in IPX when a packet burst-enabled source sends multiple packets across a network without waiting for an acknowledgment for each packet. Instead, one acknowledgment is sent for the group of packets.

partition   A logical division on a physical hard disk that is treated as though it were a separate hard disk.

passive hub   A hub device used in a star topology that connects machines to the network and organizes the cables, but does not regenerate or redistribute data.

password   The key to access the network during logon.

patch   A program that edits the binary code of another program to insert new functionality, add more capability, or correct a bug in the earlier release. Patches provide software updates in between full releases of the program.

PCI (Peripheral Component Interconnect)   A PC local bus that provides high-speed data transmission between the CPU and a peripheral device.

peer to peer network   A network in which any machine can serve as the server or as a client. These networks are used to allow small groups to share files and resources, including CD-ROM drives, printers, and hard drives.

Performance Monitor   A utility that provides performance information about your network to help you locate bottlenecks, determine which resources are too taxed, and plan upgrades to the system's capacity.

permissions   Sometimes called rights, permissions regulate the ability of users to access objects such as files and directories. Depending on the permissions, a user can have full access, limited access, or no access to an object.

platform   A type of computer system (e.g., Intel x86, or UNIX).

Point-to-Point Protocol (PPP)   A communications protocol that provides dial-up access to a network. It's commonly used to connect to the Internet.

PostScript   Defined by Adobe Systems, PostScript is a page description language. A printer must be PostScript-compatible in order to print PostScript files; otherwise, reams of garbage code prints.

POTS (Plain Old Telephone Service)   The standard analog telephone system, like the one used in most houses.

PPP   See Point-to-Point Protocol.

preemptive multitasking   A method of multitasking that has the capability to prioritize the order of process execution, and preempt one process with another.

Primary Domain Controller (PDC)   The NT Server running the master copy of the WINS service for an NT domain. It contains the domain's security policy and domain database. It handles synchronization with the Backup Domain Controller.

print queue   The line that handles printing requests and supplies files to the printer in their proper order. From the British word queue meaning line.

print server   Controls network printing, and services printing requests. Print servers can be hardware devices or a software solution.

properties   Object descriptors set in the Windows NT naming system or Registry, depending on the type of object.

protocol   A set of rules of formatting and interaction, used to permit machines to communicate across a network. Networking software usually supports multiple levels of protocols. Windows NT supports several protocols, including TCP/IP and DLS.

QIC (Quarter Inch Cartridge)   A tape cartridge format common for backup tapes.

RAID (Redundant Array of Inexpensive Disks)   A disk mirroring scheme that duplicates data across several disks, creating a fault-tolerant storage system. A RAID system can maintain data integrity as long as one disk has not failed.

RAM (Random Access Memory)   Short-term storage memory, physically residing in the computer on memory chips. Since computer applications use RAM in their processing, the amount of RAM in a computer is a major determinant of how well the computer works.

RAS (Remote Access Server)   A Windows NT server configured to use the dial-up service to provide remote access.

redirector   Also called a requester, a redirector is software that accept I/O requests for remote files, and then sends the files to a network service on another computer.

Registry   The Windows NT database that stores all information about the configuration of the network.

Remote Access Server   See RAS.

Remote Access Service   The dial-up service in Windows NT that allows users to access the network remotely by telephone lines.

rights   Authorizes users to perform specific actions on a network. Similar to permissions.

ring   A network topology that connects the computers in a circular fashion. If one computer fails, the complete network fails, so this topology is rarely used.

root   The top level of a directory structure, above which no references can be made.

router   A device that connects more than one physical network, or segments of a network, using IP routing software. As packets reach the router, the router reads them and forwards them to their destination, or to another router.

RPC (Remote Procedure Call)   A request sent to a computer on the network by a program, requesting the computer to perform a task.

scaleable   The capacity to change with the network. As requirements change, a scaleable network can grow or shrink to fit the requirements.

script   Used to describe programs, usually those written in an interpreted language, as opposed to a compiled language, because the instructions are formatted similar to a script for actors.

SCSI (Small Computer System Interface)   A high-speed interface used to connect peripherals such as hard disks, scanners, and CD-ROM drives. SCSI allows up to seven devices to be lined in a single chain.

Security Accounts Manager (SAM)   The application that handles the assignment of rights and permissions to users, groups, resources, and other objects in Windows NT.

Serial Line Interface Protocol (SLIP)   A TCP/IP protocol that provides the ability to transmit IP packets over a serial link, such as a dial-up connection over a phone line.

server   The computer running the network server software that controls access to the network.

server mirroring   Duplicating a complete server to reduce the demand on the main server.

services   Options loaded on computers allowing them to help each other. Services include the capability to send and receive files or messages, talk to printers, manage remote access, and look up information.

share   A setting to make resources such as printers, CD-ROM drives, or directories available to users on the network.

shell   A program that provides communication between a server and a client, or a user and an operating system.

shielded twisted pair   A twisted pair cable that has foil wrap shielding between the conducting strands and the outer insulation.

SLIP   See Serial Line Interface Protocol.

SNA (Systems Network Architecture)   The basic protocol suite for IBM's AS/400 and mainframe computers.

SNMP (Simple Network Management Protocol)   Used to report activity on network devices, SNMP is a popular network monitoring and control protocol.

star   A network topology, in which separate cables connect from a central hub to individual devices.

stateless   The most efficient type of network communication, a protocol that needs no information about communications between sender and receiver.

subnet masking   Used in TCP/IP communications, the subnet mask allows the recipient of IP packets to distinguish the Network ID portion of the IP address from the Host ID portion of the address.

swap file   An area on a disk that allows you to temporarily save a program, or part of a program, that is running in memory.

Switched Multimegabit Data Service (SMDS)   SMDS is a 1.544Mbps data service that supports many common LAN architectures.

Synchronous Optical Network (SONET)   A fiber-optic network communications link, SONET supports rates up to 13.22Gbps.

system administrator   Manages the network. It is this person's responsibility to ensure that network functions are running smoothly—for example, that backups are complete, network traffic is running smoothly, and drive space is available when needed.

T-1   A widely-used digital transmission link that uses a point-to-point transmission technology with two-wire pairs. One pair is used to send, and one to receive. T-1, also written as T1, can transmit digital, voice, data, and video signals at 1.544Mbps.

T-3   Designed for transporting large amounts of data at high speeds, T-3, also written as T3, is a leased line that can transmit data at 45154Mbps.

T-connector   A device used in Thin Ethernet cabling to connect the cable to the NIC.

TCP/IP (Transmission Control Protocol/Internet Protocol)
An industry standard set of protocols used to connect computers within a network, as well as to external networks such as WANs and the Internet. TCP/IP is the most widely-used networking protocol and can be used to connect many different types of computers for cross-platform communication.

TechNet   The technical support CD-ROM published by Microsoft. It includes thorough information about Windows NT and other Microsoft products.

Telnet   A TCP/IP network service that allows a computer to connect to a host computer over the network and run a terminal session.

template   A template is a partially completed object, designed to help you start a task. Windows NT Server provides templates to help the new administrator configure objects and complete other tasks.

Thick Ethernet   See 10Base-5.

Thin Ethernet   See 10Base-2.

throughput   A measure of the rate at which data is transferred across a network measured in bits per second (bps).

token   An electronic marker packet, used in ArcNet and FDDI networks, that indicates which workstation is able to send data on a token ring topology.

token ring   A networking topology that is configured in a circular pattern and circulates an electronic token on the ring to pass data.

topology   The physical configuration of a network, including the types of cable used. Common topologies include bus, ring, and star.

transceiver   A device that allows you to connect a NIC for one medium (cable) to another medium. Most commonly used to translate thin or thick Ethernet to unshielded twisted pair.

Transmission Control Protocol/Internet Protocol   See TCP/IP.

trust relationship   Used on NT networks with multiple domains, trust relationships occur when users from one domain are given permission to access resources from another domain without having to log onto that domain explicitly.

twisted pair   A cable type in which conductive wires are twisted to help reduce interference. There are two types of twisted pair: shielded and unshielded.

Uninterruptible Power Supply   See UPS.

unshielded twisted pair   A twisted pair cable that does not have any shielding between the conducting strands and the outer insulation.

UPS (Uninterruptible Power Supply)   A battery backup system commonly used on file servers to protect in times of power outages.

URL (Uniform Resource Locator)   The URL provides the address to a document on the World Wide Web.

user account   An account on a network designed for a particular user. Based on user account options, a person has access to specific files and services. See account.

User Manager   What you use to create users and groups, assign passwords, and control access rights to files, directories, and printers.

User Profile Editor   What you use to set several user options.

user   Any person who accesses the network.

username   A name used by a user to log on to a computer system.

volume   A logical division of a disk on a Windows NT file server.

WAN (wide area network)   While a LAN is a network where all machines are in close proximity to each other—usually in the same building—a WAN is extended over longer distances, ranging from a few miles to across the world. TCP/IP is the primary WAN protocol and was developed to provide reliable, secure data transmissions over long distances.

Windows Internet Name Service   See WINS.

WINS (Windows Internet Name Service)   The Windows NT service that provides a map between NetBIOS computer names and IP addresses. This permits NT networks to use either computer names or IP addresses to request access to network resources.

wireless networking   A network configured to use communication techniques such as infrared, cellular, or microwave, so that cable connections are not required.

workgroup   A group of users who share files and resources on a network. Members of a workgroup usually have related job functions. For example, they may be in the same department.

workstation   The client machine used to access a network.

WORM (Write Once, Read Many)   An optical storage medium that only permits you to write to it once, but allows you to read from it many times. CD-ROM drives are basically WORM devices.

INDEX

A

Absolute performance (server), 553

Access Control Entries (ACEs), 239, 241-244

Access Control Lists (ACLs), 239, 241-244

Access Global web site, 652

Access masks, 241

Access permissions. *See* Permissions

Access Through Share Permissions dialog box, 262-263

Access tokens (security tokens), 239, 246

Access validation, 241

Account Information dialog box, 191

Account lockout, 238-239

Account Operators group, 199

Account policy, changing, 201-203, 238

Account Policy dialog box, 202, 239

Accounts, user and group, 182-200

ACEs, 239, 241-244

Active partition, changing, 156

Active Server Pages, 43

Add Printer Wizard, 43

Add Users and Groups dialog box, 252, 262, 309

Administration
  RAS, 453-454
  of the registry, 169
  of a remote NT Server, 221-226
  of user groups, 193-196

Administrative Wizards, 16, 35

Administrator account, renaming, 47

Administrators local group, 198

Advanced user rights, table of, 257-258

Alert Options dialog box, 536

Alerts (server)
  managing, 301-302
  Performance Monitor, 535-536

Answers to self tests, 617-645

AppleTalk, 62

Application Log, 554

Application performance boost, 526-529

Application Performance Boost slider, 527-529

Applications
  optimizing, 524-530
  removing, 148
  viewing, 525-526

Applications tab of Task Manager, 600

ARC naming convention, 587-589

Architecture of Windows NT, 16

ARCserve for Windows NT, 506

Asymmetric multiprocessing (ASMP) system, 6, 518

AT command parameters, 495

Audit events, table of, 267

Audit Policy dialog box, 267

Auditing
  activating for events, 266
  of attempts to take ownership, 266-270
  capabilities of RAS, 447-448
  enabling, 204-205
  of events, 266-271
  of printers, 376
  top three mistakes in, 270-271

Automating backups, 491-496

Average Disk Bytes/transfer, 547

B

Backup browser, 167

Backup Domain Controllers (BDCs), 10, 107, 283, 333

    per number of workstations, 284

    problems installing, 108-109

    promoting to PDC, 304

    synchronizing with PDCs, 304-305, 334

Backup drive configuration, 499

Backup Files and Directories right, 476

Backup Operators group, 199

Backup plan (one-year) using media rotation, 471

Backup protection, 472-474

Backup schedule, 468-469

Backup software, 467-468

Backup strategies, 464-474

Backup utility. *See* NT Backup

Backups, 463-510. *See also* NT Backup

    automating, 491-496

    common media types, 466-467

    documenting, 473-474

    hardware for, 466-467

    hardware selection and purchase, 467

    interface type, 467

    partition, 488-489

    registry, 501-503

    single vs. multiple, 464-465

    storage of, 472

    third-party, 504-506

    types of, 469-470

    unattended, 496

    using media rotation, 471-472

Baseline (system), establishing, 531, 552

Basic user rights, table of, 256-257

BDCs. *See* Backup Domain Controllers

Binding order setting, 523

Bindings tab (Network dialog box), 524

Blue screen of death, 572, 601-602

Boot disk/floppy

    creating, 576

    fault-tolerant, 587-590

    re-creating, 87

Boot error symptoms and messages, 577

Boot failures, 575-580

boot floppy (NT)

    creating, 576

    re-creating, 87

Boot loader, changing to MS-DOS, 115

Boot partition, 71, 156

Boot process, 79

Boot.ini listing, 588

Bottlenecks (performance), 513-514

    detecting, 513

    eliminating, 514

Browser elections, 168-169

Browser types, 167-169

Budget factor (in backups), 465

C

Caching disk requests, 521-522

CACLS, 254

Callback security (RAS), 9, 445-446

Canon BJC-4100 Device Settings tab, 378

CDFS (CD-ROM file system), 54

CD-ROM adapters, adding, 150

CD-ROM drives
 adding, 150
 sharing, 84
CD-ROM installation of NT Server, 78, 94-95
CD-ROM in this book, instructions for, 648-649
Central NT File Server network share, 83-84
Centralized profiles and policies, 7-8
Challenge Handshake Authentication Protocol
 (CHAP), 446
Change log, explained, 333
Character-based Setup, 573
Characterization data file, 355
Chart Options dialog box, 535
Client Administrator, 79-83, 164-166
Client configuration information, setting,
 136-137
Client install files, 81
Client protocols, NT-supported, 164
Client Services for NetWare (CSNW), 61, 391,
 397
Client-based network administration tools,
 copying, 166
Clients (NT), 164
Client-to-server connectivity, NT/NetWare, 390
CMD file
 automating use of, 494-495
 creating, 492-494
Command line
 connecting to NetWare services with, 411
 directory permissions from, 253-254
 sharing a directory from, 263
Compact Disk File System (CDFS), 52
Compatibility of hardware and software, 47-51
Complete trust domain model, 294-295
Completeness factor (in backups), 465

Components for final installation, choosing,
 91-92
Compressed files, moving and copying, 57-58
Computers, adding or removing, 302-303
Configuration errors, 575-582
Configuring
 clients, 136-137
 DHCP options, 137
 dial-up networking clients, 449-452
 Directory Replicator service, 325
 GSNW, 403-409
 an ISDN adapter for RAS, 439
 migration to NT, 415-420
 netlogon service, 310-312
 NetWare Server (with GSNW), 405
 network protocols, 130-145
 NT, 129-180
 NT to avoid problems, 137-138
 NWLink, 393, 395-396
 peripheral devices, 145-154
 printers, 365-378
 RAS network settings, 439-443
 RAS ports, 438-439
 RAS security, 443-448
 RAS server with IPX/SPX, 442-443
 RAS server with TCP/IP, 440-442
 a scope, 135
 the system for memory dumps, 599
 WWW Service on IIS, 141-145
Connecting
 to a NetWare directory, 410
 to a NetWare printer queue, 410-411
 to NetWare services with the command line,
 411
 to NetWare services with Explorer, 409-411

to a remote printer, 363
to a shared resource, 265
Connectivity, remote, 425-461
Container objects, 240
Control factor (in backups), 465
Control Panel, 127, 146-150
with GSNW icon, 403
Licensing option, 74
restricting options, 212-213
Cooperative multitasking, 4
Copy backup, 470
Counters (in Performance Monitor), 532
CSNW, 61, 391, 397

D

Daily backup, 470
Data backup
with NT backup, 489-490
recommendations, 51
Data Link Control (DLC), 62
Data page storage, 548
Data type for a printer, changing, 357
Defense Advanced Research Projects Agency
(DARPA), 60
Deleting
a computer from a domain, 303
vs. disabling a user account, 207-208
FAT partitions, 111-113
NTFS partitions, 113
a partition, 157-158
a user account, 187
Demand paging, 24-25
Demoting a recovered PDC to a BDC, 304
DES encryption, 448

Desktop
customizing, 213
sharing a directory from, 260-261
Detailed plan of server, 44
Device drivers, 26
DEVICE.LOG file, 455, 593-594
Devices
configurable, 172
configuring, 145-154
NT-supported, 49
DHCP, 40, 130, 134-137
DHCP Relay tab (TCP/IP Properties), 134
DHCP scope, creating, 136
Diagnostics, improved in NT 4.0, 37
Dialin information, modifying, 192
Dialin Information dialog box, 192
Dialin Information screen, 445
Dialing Properties screen, 450
Dial-Up Networking (DUN), 9, 432, 456
configuring clients, 449-452
for NT and Windows 95, 426-427
Differential backup, 469
Digital to Analog (DAC) type, 557
Digital Audio Tape (DAT), 466-467
Digital Linear Tape (DLT), 466
Direct Memory Access (DMA), 548, 559
Directory
preventing from being exported, 329
sharing from the command prompt, 263
sharing from the desktop, 260-261
Directory compression, 58
Directory path, 12
Directory permissions (shared), 259-263
assigning, 264-265
changing, 251-253

setting gateway, 408
Directory Permissions dialog box, 252-253
Directory replication, 11-12, 318-333
　export directories, 326
　import directories, 328
　verifying, 329
　viewing status of, 332-333
Directory Replicator account, adding, 321
Directory Replicator service, 11, 319, 323-329
　configuring, 325
　starting on export server, 326-327
　starting on import computer, 327-329
　startup parameters, 324
Directory Services Manager for NetWare
　(DSMN), 398
Directory structure, replication and, 341
Disabling the default username, 272-273
Disabling vs. deleting a user account, 207-208
Disabling the Shutdown button, 273
Disabling a user account, 186, 207-208
Disconnecting a user session, 299
Disconnecting a user on a shared directory, 300
Discovery process, 107
Discretionary access, explained, 249
Discretionary access control list (ACL), 240
　delete request allowed, 244
　deleted request denied, 243
Disk Administrator (NT 4.0), 154-166
　backup drive configuration, 499
　backups, 498-501
　on dual boot machine, 126
　launching, 155-156
　restore disk/drive configuration, 500-501
　showing disk layout, 588
Disk Bytes/sec counter, 546

Disk cache manager, 521
Disk drive performance, 544-549
　disabling counters, 547
　enabling counters, 545
　troubleshooting, 547-548
Disk duplexing, 13
Disk mirroring, 13, 162
Disk performance counters, 553
Disk problems, 582-584
Disk Queue Length counter, 547
Disk requests, caching, 521-522
Disk striping, 13-14
Disk Time counter, 546
Diskperf utility, 545
Display adapter, changing, 147-148
DMA controller, 548
DNS (Domain Name System), 3, 36, 131-132
DNS tab (TCP/IP Properties), 132
Docked configuration, 38
Documenting backups, 473-474
Domain account database, 444
Domain Administrator, 200
Domain Admins global group, 200
Domain B trust relationships, identifying, 289
Domain computing, 283-284
Domain concept vs. workgroup model, 284
Domain controllers, 105
　planning for, 45-46
　synchronizing, 336
　types of, 283
Domain files and replicating system, 333
Domain Guests global group, 200
Domain logon, 237
Domain master browser, 167
Domain model, 45, 106, 282

Domain model showing server roles, 106

Domain Name System (DNS), 3, 36, 131-132

Domain strategies, 291-296

Domain structure, 45

Domain synchronization over a slow WAN link, 336-337

Domain trusts, managing, 285-298

Domain Users global group, 200

Domains (NT 4.0), 105, 281-316

    adding, 288

    adding computers to, 302-303

    advantages over workgroups, 284

    four types of, 45

    setting up, 45

    trust relationships between, 285-290, 296

    trusted and trusting, 237

dReplicator account

    group memberships, 320

    New User dialog box, 320

Drive letter assignment, 161

Dual-boot installation, 72

Dual-boot machine, Disk Administrator on, 126

DUN clients, 432

DUN (Dial-Up Networking), 9

    configuring clients, 449-452

    for NT and Windows 95, 426-427

DUN Monitor program, 455-456

DUN session

    initiating, 452

    status of current, 456

Duplexing, 162

Duplicate names, 118

Dynamic applications, priority levels, 521

Dynamic Host Configuration Protocol (DHCP), 40, 130, 135-137

E

8mm tape backup, 51, 467

Electronic version of the book, 648

Emergency Repair Disk (ERD), 501, 578-580

    contents, 42

    with NT Setup disks, 580

Emergency Repair Process, 579

Enabling auditing, 204-205

Encrypted data authentication and logons (RAS), 446-447

Enhanced Metafiles (EMF), 358

Environment subsystems, 20-21

ERD files, 42

Error messages, improved in NT 4.0, 39

Ethernet frame type, configuring, 394-395

Event auditing, 266-271

Event Detail dialog box, 270

Event log file formats, 555

Event Log Wrapping, 554

Event Viewer, 447-448, 455, 553-556, 580-581

    log files, 553-555

    types of events, 555

Exam samples on the CD-ROM, 648-649

Executive Services (System Services), 2, 19-20

Export and import directories, 12, 323

Export server, 321-323, 326-327, 329

Extended partition with logical drives, creating, 158

Extended partition problems, 584

Extended partitions, 156-159

Extending a volume set, 159-160

F

FAT (File Allocation Table), 52-54

FAT file system, 52-54

FAT files, characteristics of, 53-54

FAT partitions

> converting to NTFS, 56
>
> deleting, 111-113
>
> removing NT from, 114-115

FAT-32 file system, 53

Fault tolerance, 9-14, 73-74, 161-163

Fault-tolerant boot disks, 587-590

Fault-tolerant driver (FtDisk), 584

Faulty media, 117

FDISK main menu, 76

FDISK menu (Windows 95 version), 112

FDISK.EXE, 75-77, 154

File attributes, 57, 416

File Auditing dialog box, 269

File compression, NTFS runtime, 56-58

File objects, 240

File options, configuring for migration, 419

File permissions (NT)

> when copying or moving, 250
>
> NetWare file rights into, 416

File and Print Services for NetWare (FPNW), 392, 397-399

File requests, 48

File Server, creating a network share, 83-84

File system configurations, 71-72

File system permissions, setting, 206-207

File systems (Windows NT), 52-59

File Transfer Protocol (FTP) server, 15

Filenames, truncated, 59

File-level permissions (NTFS), 247

Files

> migrating to NT, 415
>
> moving and copying in NTFS, 57-58
>
> ownership of, 248-249
>
> replication of widely used, 340

Folder share level permissions, 260

Folder-level permissions, 247-249, 260

Folders, ownership of, 248-249

Foreground application performance boost, 526-529

FORMAT utility, 75, 77

Formatting a partition, 158-159

FPNW, 392, 397-399

Fragmentation of physical memory, avoiding, 514-515

Frame types

> adding to NWLink, 396
>
> configuring Ethernet, 394-395

Frames, 560

Friendly names, 75

FT Orphaning dialog box, 585

FtDisk, 585

FTP (File Transfer Protocol) servers (MS), 604

Full audit capabilities, 447-448

Full drive backup, 478

Full synchronization, 334

G

Gateway directory share, creating, 406-407

Gateway printer share, creating, 407

Gateway Service, configuring, 406

Gateway Service for NetWare. *See* GSNW

Gateway share permissions, setting, 407

Gateway shared resources, accessing, 408-409

Gateway shares to NetWare directories, 405

Gateway shares to NetWare print queues,
    creating, 407

Global groups, 199-200, 208, 305-306, 309
    creating, 200, 307-308
    vs. local groups, 193-194
    setting up, 307-308

Global Knowledge Network, 652

Glossary of terms, 653-676

Gopher server, 15

Graphical mode, 573

Graphics device interface (GDI), 353, 355

Group administration strategies, 194-195

Group Memberships dialog box, 193

Group memberships for dReplicator account, 320

Group options, configuring for migration, 418

Group Priority window, 212

Groups (group accounts), 183, 192. *See also*
    Global groups
    administration of, 193-196
    assigning rights to, 255-258
    creating and managing in User Manager, 196
    within groups, 195-196
    local and global, 208, 305-309
    local and global guidelines, 306
    local vs. global, 193-194

GSNW, 391, 399, 401-413
    configuring, 403-409
    configuring NetWare Server, 405
    configuring preferred logon, 403-405
    enabling the gateway, 405
        installing, 402-403
        security issues, 409
        using, 396-397
        using RAS with, 409

GSNW icon added to Control Panel, 403

Guest group, 198

GUI setup, information gathering, 90-92

H

Hackers, preventing, 238

Hard disk
    planning configuration, 70-78
    preparing for installation, 75-78
    recommendations, 51
    requirements, 46
    space recommendations, 51

Hard page faults, 550

Hardware
    for backups, 466-467
    compatibility, 47-49
    compression, 485
    for NT Backup, 475-476, 485

Hardware Abstraction Layer (HAL), 18, 557

Hardware Compatibility List (HCL), 48-49, 427,
    572-573

Hardware profile support, 38-39

Hardware profiles, 170-171

Help files, opening, 609

Help Index (NT), 608

Help (NT), 608-609

High Performance File System (HPFS), 53

Hive (registry), 172-173

Hold mismatched documents, 372

Hot fixes, 12
HP JetDirect cards, 363-364
HP Laserjet 5 Device Settings tab, 377
HP Network Port Print Monitor, 360
HP-GL/2 plotter driver, 356
Hpmon.dll, 360

IIS (Internet Information Server), 14, 139-145
IIS WWW Service, 141-145
Import computers, 321-323, 327-329
Import and export directories, 323
Incremental backup, 469
Index Server (with IIS), 15, 43
Index tab of Help, 608
Information gathering (GUI setup), 90-92
Inherited permissions, 250
INI files, 169
Input Log File Timeframe window, 538
Install New Modem screen, 435-436
Installation boot disks, re-creating, 87
Installation files for client installs, 81
Installation (NT Server 4.0), 69-127
    friendlier, 38
    hard disk preparation, 75-78
    methods, 78-105
    on a network, 79-87
    planning, 33-68
    on RISC-based computers, 96
    troubleshooting, 117-118, 572-575
    unattended, 98-105
    upgrade from previous version, 96-98
Installation process, network share, 85-86

Installation Startup Disk, creating, 80
Installation utilities, 573
Installing BDCs, 108-109
Installing and configuring NWLink, 393-396
Installing and configuring RAS, 434-443
Installing GSNW, 402-403
Installing Network Monitor, 561
Installing NT Networking, 92-94
Installing printers, 361-364
Installing a RAS device, 435
Instances (in Performance Monitor), 532
Integrated Drive Electronics (IDE), 467
Internet, RAS support of, 427
Internet Information Server (IIS), 14, 139-145
Internet Service Manager (ISM), 140-141
Internet Service Provider (ISP), 428
Interrupt Requests (IRQs), 37, 559
I/O traffic reduction, 521
IP Address tab (TCP/IP Properties), 131
IPX network number, 395
IPXROUTE command, 394, 442-443
IPX/SPX-compatible transport, 61-62, 130,
    393-396, 432-433
ISDN adapter, configuring for RAS, 439
ISDN (Integrated Services Digital Networks),
    427-428

Keep documents after printed, 372
Kernel, 19
Kernel mode, 2, 17-18
Kernel mode vs. User mode, 17-18
Knowledge Base, The, 607

L

LastKnownGood Configuration, 576-578

Lease duration, setting, 136

Licensing, Per Server vs. Per Seat, 73

Linear 32-bit address, 25

Load balancing among servers, 318

Local groups, 196-199, 208, 305-306, 309
  creating, 197, 307-308
  vs. global groups, 193-194
  setting up, 307-308

Local logon, 235

Local printers
  creating, 361-362
  default permissions, 375

Local Procedure Call (LPC) facility, 20

Local profiles, 171, 215

Local registry backup, 484

Local security authority (LSA), 236

Local vs. share permissions, 596

Lock out after unsuccessful logon, 238

Log event details, 556

Log files
  creating, 537-540
  Event Viewer, 553-555
  viewing, 540
  where recorded metrics are stored, 539-540

Log Options dialog box, 539

Log options (NT Backup), 485-486

Log view of Performance Monitor, 538

Logging options in the Migration Tool, 420

Logical drives, 156, 158

LogicalDisk object, 544

LogicalDisk:Disk Bytes/sec, 546

Logon authentication, 235-238

Logon hours, setting, 189-191

Logon script path, 338-339

Logon scripts, 220, 338-339

Logon Workstations dialog box, 190

Logons, types of, 235

Long File Names (LFN) capabilities, 58-59

lpr command, 360

M

Macintosh print processor, 359

MaintainServerList parameter (registry), 168-169

Manage Exported Directories dialog box, 330

Manage Imported Directories dialog box, 331-332

Mandatory user profile, 217-218

Master browser, 167-168

Master domain, explained, 291

Master domain model, 291-294

Master file table (MFT), 250, 583

Maximize Throughput for File Sharing, 523

Maximize Throughput for Network Applications, 523

MD5 encryption, 448

Media rotation, 471-472

Member servers, 45, 109, 208

Memory dumps, configuring for, 599

Memory organization (NT), 23-26

Memory page, 515

Memory paging, counting, 549-551

Memory performance, 548-552
  counters, 549-551
  troubleshooting, 551

Restrict Access to..., 484-485
review full catalog of backup, 478
Schedule service, 492
selecting files for backup, 477-481
span multiple tapes, 478-479
Tape Name option, 482
Tapes window, 479
verification and logging, 479-480
Verify After Backup, 483-484
Verify After Restore, 488
NT boot floppy
creating, 576
re-creating, 87
NT Diagnostics (WinMSD), 222-223, 556-560,
581-582
Display tab, 557
Drives tab, 558
Environment tab, 559
Memory tab, 558
Network tab, 559
opening window, 557
Resources tab, 559
Services tab, 558
System tab, 557
Version tab, 557, 583
T domains. *See* Domains (NT 4.0)
T Executive Services, 2, 19-20
T file systems, 52-59
T migration from NetWare. *See* Migration to
NT
Hardware Compatibility List (HCL), 48-49,
27, 572-573
Help, 608-609
Networking, installing, 92-94

NT Server. *See also* NT
absolute and relative performance, 553
administering remote, 221-226
crashes, 598-602
CD install, 78
CD-ROM installation, 94-95
determining usage, 44-45
emulating NetWare, 392-393
as Gateway to NetWare, 391-392
hardware recommendations, 51
installation methods, 78-105
installing, 69-127
installing GSNW on, 402-403
introduction to, 1-29
migrating NetWare server to, 417-420
minimum requirements, 50
multi-modem adapters with, 428-429
NetWare comparison, 389
network installation, 79-87
new features of 4.0, 34-44
overview, 2-16
performance tuning, 512-524
properties, 297-298
roles, 105-111
self-tuning mechanisms, 514-522
service optimization levels, 522
service optimization options, 522-523
NT Server alerts, managing, 301-302
NT Server Manager. *See* Server Manager
NT Server names, 46
NT Setup program, 88-90
NT Setup Wizard, 90-94
NT subsystems, 20-23
NT system registry. *See* Registry

Memory:Page Faults/sec counter, 550
Memory:Pages Input/sec counter, 550-551
Memory:Pages Reads/sec counter, 551
Memory:Pages/sec counter, 546, 550
Microkernel, 19
Microsoft object security terms, 240
Microsoft Proxy Server, 14
Microsoft resources for troubleshooting, 604-609
Microsoft Service Packs, 604-607
Microsoft SQL Server, 14
Microsoft Web and FTP sites, 604
Migration to NT
configuring, 415-420
configuring file options, 419
configuring user and group options, 418
data first/users second, 400
NetWare server to NT server, 417-420
source and destination servers, 417
transferring volumes and files, 415
via two redirectors on clients, 401
users first/data second, 400-401
using Migration Tool, 397, 414-420
Migration Tool for NetWare, 397, 414-420
Minimize Memory Used, 522
Minimum requirements to run NT Server, 50
Mirror set (RAID 1)
breaking, 586-587
creating, 162
fixing, 586-587
recovering, 590
repairing damaged, 162
Mirroring, disk, 13, 162
Modem Properties, General Tab, 436

Modems
adding, 152-153
in logical bundles, 428
Modular NT architecture, 2
Monitoring. *See also* Performance Monitor
disk drive performance, 544-548
network, 560-564
processor performance, 541-543
resources in use, 301
server alerts, 301-302
users, 298-299
Moving and copying files (NTFS), 57-58
MS-CHAP, 446
MS-DOS
changing boot loader to, 115
setting as default operating system, 115
MS-DOS subsystem, 22
Multiboot system, 71
Multilink (RAS), 428-429
Multi-modem adapters with NT server, 428-429
Multiple master domain model, 293-294
Multiple backups, 464-465, 473
Multiprocessing (NT), 517-519
Multiprocessing system categories, 6, 517
Multiprocessor support, 6-7
Multitasking, 4
cooperative (non-preemptive), 4
preemptive, 3-4
My Briefcase
adding documents to, 342-343
with additional file information, 344
enabling, 342
first initialized, 342
using to synchronize files, 341-344

N

Naming conventions, 46, 74-75

NetBEUI, 60, 137-138, 431-432

NetBIOS, 60, 137-138

Netlogon service (NT), 237, 309-312

  configuring, 310-312

  Pulse option, 310-311

  PulseConcurrency option, 311

  PulseMaximum option, 311

  PulseTimeOut1 option, 311

  PulseTimeOut2 option, 311-312

  Randomize option, 312

  ReplicationGovernor option, 312

Netlogon share, explained, 339

NetWare connectivity

  NT Server emulating NetWare, 392-393

  NT Server as Gateway to NetWare, 391-392

  options, 390-393

  planning, 388-401

  with two redirectors on each client, 390-391

NetWare directories

  connecting to, 410

  gateway shares to, 405

NetWare directory rights, 415

NetWare file attributes, 416

NetWare file rights, 416

NetWare print queues

  connecting to, 410-411

  gateway shares to, 407

NetWare redirectors, removing, 402

Netware Router Information Protocol (RIP), 432

NetWare Server. *See also* GSNW; Migration to NT

  configuring, 405

  Directory Services Manager for, 398

dynamic link libraries (.DLL files), 411

File and Print Services for, 397-398

integration, 387-424

migrating to NT Server, 417-420

migration strategies, 398, 400-401

and NT Server comparison, 389

NetWare services

  connecting to with command line, 411

  connecting to with Explorer, 409-411

NetWare utilities, 412-413

NetWare-specific applications, 411-412

Network Boot Disk, creating, 81-83

Network cards, recommendations for, 51

Network Client Administrator, 79-83, 164-166

Network client installation disk set, making, 165

Network client protocols, NT-supported, 164

Network Configuration screen (RAS), 447

Network dialog box, Bindings tab, 524

Network drive share distribution files, 85

Network installation of NT Server, 86-87, 79-87

Network installation startup disk, making, 165

Network installation switches, 87-94

Network Interface Cards (NICs), 11, 523

Network interface printing devices, 363

Network logon, 213

Network Monitor, 35-36, 560-564, 594

  Capture window, 563

  data capture initiation, 561

  installing, 561

  Password Change dialog box, 564

  setting passwords, 564

  started, 562

Network Neighborhood icon, 209-210, 222

Network printers

  problems printing to, 364

  sharing, 362

Network problems, 594-596

Network protocols, configuring, 130-145

Network settings, 213

Network share

  creating, 83-84, 205-206

  creating using Server Manager, 265

Network share installation process, starting, 85-86

Network Startup Disk Configuration, 82

Network tuning, 522-524

Network-enabled backup software, 467

New Global Group dialog box, 308

New Local Group dialog box, 197, 308

New Phonebook Entry wizard, 451

New Printer Folder, 43-44

New user account, creating, 185-186

New User dialog box for dReplicator account, 320

New User window, 185

Noncontainer objects, 240

Nonpaged pool size vs. physical memory, 291

Non-privileged processor mode, 17

Normal backup, 469

NT. *See also* NT Server

  architecture, 2, 16

  configuring, 129-180

  configuring to avoid problems, 137-138

  installing on RISC-based computers, 96

  migrating to using Migration Tool, 414-420

  multiprocessing capabilities, 517-519

  removing, 111-115

  removing components, 148

  removing from a FAT partition, 114-115

  supported NetWare commands, 413

  supported NetWare utilities, 412-413

  transport protocols shipped with,

  unsupported NetWare utilities, 4

NT Backup, 474-503

  alternate path, 486

  Append or Replace, 483

  automating a backup, 495-496

  automating use of .CMD file, 4

  Back Up Local Registry, 484

  backing up data, 489-490

  backup and recovery schemes,

  Backup Set Information optio

  Backup Type option, 482

  catalog from a tape backup, 4

  control restoration destinatio

  creating a CMD file, 492-49

  Drives window, 474

  files not backed up with, 48(

  files not restored with, 481

  hardware compression, 485

  hardware for, 475-476

  information for a local driv

  information for a remote d

  limitations, 496

  log options, 485-486

  of NTFS or FAT partitio

  options, 481-486

  parameters, 493

  performing a backup, 48

  permissions to perform

  Restore to drive, 486

  Restore File Permission

  Restore Information w

  Restore Local Registry

  Restore options, 486-4

  restoring data from ba

690

NT Telephony API (TAPI), 449
NT 3.51, upgrading to NT 4.0, 96-98
NT Upgrade, 96-98
NTBACKUP.EXE. *See* NT Backup
NTFS, 52, 54-58
    converting a FAT partition to, 56
    deleting partitions, 113
    file security, 55
    file-level permissions, 247
    folder-level permissions, 247-248
    implementation issues, 55-56
    moving and copying files, 57-58
    partitions, 56
    permissions problems, 596
    runtime file compression, 56-57
    security, 246-258
NTHQ floppy disk, creating, 573, 575
NTHQ utility, 573, 575
NWLink transport protocol, 61-62, 393-396
    adding frame types to, 396
    installing and configuring, 393-396
    IPX/SPX-compatibility, 130
    IPX/SPX Properties dialog box, 394-395

Object security terms (MS), 240
Objects
    classes of, 240
    container and noncontainer, 240
    Microsoft use of term, 240
    in Performance Monitor, 532-533
Off-site storage of backups, 472
One-way trust relationship, 286-289
Open resources on the server, 301

Optical-magneto disks, 51
Optimizing applications, 524-530
Orphaned disk, 584-585
Orphaned partition, 585
OS/2 subsystem, 23
Owner dialog box, 269
Ownership attempts, auditing, 266-270
Ownership of files or folders, 248-249
Ownership of a printer, 376-377
Ownership of a resource, 597-598

P

Packet-switching networks, 428
Page faults, 549-550
Page (memory), 515, 549-551
Pagefile drive, modifying, 150
Pagefiles, multiple, 515-517
PAGEFILE.SYS, 515-516, 546
Paging file, splitting, 148-149
Paging (memory), counting, 549-551
Partial drive backup, 478
Partial synchronization, 334
Partition Boot Sector (PBS), 583
Partitions, 73-74
    backing up, 488-489
    boot and system, 156
    changing the active, 156
    deleting, 157-158
    extended and primary, 156-159
    formatting, 158-159
    orphaned, 585
    restoring backed-up, 491
Pass-through authentication, 237, 310
Passwords, 46

Path to export directory, 12
PBXs (Private Branch Exchanges), 449
PDC (Primary Domain Controller), 10,
    106-107, 283, 333
    demoting to a BDC, 304
    promoting a BDC to, 304
    protocol setup on, 125
    synchronizing with BDCs, 304-305, 334
Peer-to-peer networking, 282
Per Server vs. Per Seat licensing, 73
Performance
    disk drive, 544-549
    foreground application, 526-529
    memory, 548-552
    processor, 541-543
Performance bottlenecks, 513-514
Performance Monitor, 530-553
    capabilities, 540
    Log view, 538
    memory measurements, 552
    objects measured, 533
    Processor Time, 541-542
    processor utilization chart, 543
    starting, 532-533
    uses for, 530-531
    views, 533
Performance Monitor Alert, creating, 535-536
Performance Monitor chart
    creating, 534-535
    value bar, 535
Performance Monitor log, creating, 537-540
Performance Monitor report, creating, 537
Performance Monitor screen, 531
Performance tab, System Properties, 527
Performance tuning, NT Server, 512-524
Peripheral devices, configuring, 145-154

Permissions
    changing with CACLS, 254
    for a directory, 251-253, 259-265
    file system, 206-207
    folder share level, 249, 260
    for gateway shares, 407-408
    inherited, 250
    NetWare directory rights into, 415
    NTFS, 247-248
    to perform a backup, 476
    on print queue gateway shares, 408
    printer, 266, 374-375
    for printer objects, 374-375
    problems with, 596-598
    RAS, 444-445
    and security, 239-246
    for shared directories, 259-265
    user, 208
    viewing and changing, 250-253
    when copying and moving files, 250
Personal (roaming) user profile, 8, 171, 216-217
Phonebook entry, defining, 450-452
Physical disk failure, 587
Physical memory, avoiding fragmentation of,
    514-515
Physical security, 47
PhysicalDisk object, 544
Planning
    hard disk configuration, 70-78
    NetWare connectivity, 388-401
    NT installation, 33-68
Point and Print, 43
Policies
    centralized, 8
    system, 36-37
Policies tab (User Properties), 210

Policy File mode, 211

Policy order, 212

Port Usage Configuring screen, 439

Port usage for RAS, configuring, 438-439

POSIX subsystem, 23

PostScript print driver, 356

Potential browser, 168

PPP (Point-to-Point Protocol), 430

    Multilink dialing, 429

    NT protocols over, 431-432

PPP.LOG file, 592-593

PPTP (Point-to-Point Tunneling Protocol), 37, 428, 432-433

    advantages of, 433

    establishing a connection, 433

    filtering, 448

    installing on a server, 433

Preemptive multitasking, 3-4

Preferred logon (GSNW), configuring, 403-405

Primary partitions, 156-159

Print directly to printer, 372

Print drivers, 355-356

Print jobs, 360, 378-379

Print model (NT), 353-356

Print monitors supplied with NT, 359-360

Print Operators group, 198-199

Print Processor dialog box, 358

Print processors, 357-358

    SFMPSPRT, 359

    WINPRINT.DLL, 358-359

Print queue

    explained, 352

    setting queue gateway share permissions, 408

Print requests, 48

Print router, 356

Print spooled documents first, 372

Print spooler, 356-357

Printer auditing, 376

Printer Auditing screen, 376

Printer graphics driver, 355

Printer interface driver, 355

Printer permissions

    default, 375

    table of, 266

    types of, 374-375

Printer Permissions dialog box, 375

Printer pool, creating, 369

Printer pooling, 368-369

Printer priorities, enabling, 371

Printer problems, 591-592

Printer Properties

    Device Settings tab, 377-378

    General tab, 365-367

    Ports tab, 367-369

    Scheduling tab, 369-372

    Security tab, 373-374

    Sharing tab, 373

Printers, 352

    changing default data type for, 357

    connecting to remote shared, 363

    configuring, 365-378

    installing, 361-364

    ownership of, 376-377

    priority setting, 369-371

    security for shared, 265

    sharing on a network, 362

    troubleshooting, 379-381

Printers folder, accessing, 361

Printers utility, 226

Printing, 43-44, 351-386

Printing devices, 352
Printing to network printers, 364
Printing problems, 590-591
Printing process overview, 354
Printing software, 352
Printing terminology, 352-360
Printing a test page, 367
Prioritization of threads and processes, 3,
    520-521
Priority levels for applications, 521
Privileged processor mode, 18
Process management models, multiple, 4
Processes, 5
    base priorities for, 520
    changing priority of running, 528-529
    changing starting priority of, 529
    prioritization, 520-521, 528-529
    starting various, 530
    viewing, 525-526
Processor Interrupts/sec counter, 542
Processor mode
    non-privileged, 17
    privileged, 18
Processor performance, 541-543
Processor Queue Length counter, 542
Processor recommendations, 51
Processor Time counter, 541
Processor utilization chart, 543
Profiles
    centralized, 7-8
    system, 36-37
Programs, 4
Promiscuous mode, 595-596
Promoting a BDC to a PDC, 109-110, 304
Promotion/demotion process, server, 109-110
Protocols (NT), 59-62, 138

configuring network, 130-145
    setup on new server, 124
    setup on PDC, 125
Proxy Server (MS), 14
PSTN, RAS support of, 427
Public Switched Telephone Network (PSTN),
    427
Pulse synchronization, 335
PulseConcurrency synchronization, 335
PulseMaximum synchronization, 335
PulseTimeout1 synchronization, 335
PulseTimeout2 synchronization, 335

Quarter-Inch Cartridge (QIC), 466

R

RAID (Redundant Array of Inexpensive Disks),
    13, 161
    fault tolerance, 9-14, 73-74, 161-163
    problems with, 584-590
    RAID 1 and 5 support, 13-14
RAM (random access memory), 514
Randomize synchronization parameter, 335
RAS Multilink, 428-429
RAS PPTP, 432-433
RAS (Remote Access Service) Server, 37-38,
    426-429
    administering, 453-454
    built-in, 8-9
    callback security, 445-446
    configuring network settings, 439-443
    configuring port usage, 438-439
    configuring security, 443-448

connection protocols, 430

encrypted data authentication and logons, 446-447

encryption selections, 447

features, 8

full audit capabilities, 447-448

with GSNW, 409

installing and configuring, 434-443

and IPX, 432-433

IPX Configuration screen, 442

and NetBEUI, 431-432

NetBEUI Configuration screen, 432

Network Configuration screen, 440

permissions for user accounts, 444-445

PPTP filtering, 448

problems with, 591-594

removing/uninstalling, 437-438

Setup screen, 438

support for connections, 427

support of LAN and WAN protocols, 427

TAPI features of, 449-450

and TCP/IP, 431, 440-442

TCP/IP Configuration screen, 441

third-party security host support, 448

troubleshooting, 455-456

use of Event Viewer, 447-448

RAS server with IPX/SPX, configuring, 442-443

RAS server with TCP/IP, configuring, 440-442

RAS session, disconnecting, 454

Raster driver, 356

RAW (FF appended) data type, 359

RAW (FF Auto) data type, 358-359

RCONSOLE command, 413

Read-only information, replication and, 318

Real-time applications, priority levels, 521

Rebooting during upgrade, 97

Recovered PDC, demoting to a BDC, 304

Recovering a mirror set, 590

Recovery utility (NT), 598-599. *See also* NT Backup

Redundant Array of Inexpensive Disks. *See* RAID

Registry, 169-173

backups, 501-503

data types, 173

editing, 169-170

finding a word in, 170

hierarchy, 172-173

MaintainServerList parameter, 168-169

restoring, 503

subtrees, 172

Registry Editor (regedit.exe), 41-42, 502-503

Registry keys, setting, 271-273

Registry mode, 211

Relative performance, server, 553

Remote Access Admin program, 453

Remote Access Manager, 454

Remote Access Permissions screen, 445

Remote Access Protocols, 430-434

Remote Access Service. *See* RAS Server

Remote connectivity, 425-461

Remote logon, 237

Remote NT Servers, administering, 221-226

Remote printer, connecting to, 363

Remoteboot client information, viewing, 166

Removing NT, 111-115

Removing NT applications, 148

Removing NT components, 148

Removing NT from a FAT partition, 114-115

Renaming a user account, 187-188

Rendering, explained, 357

Repair Disk Utility screen, 578

Repairing a damaged mirror set, 162

Replication

    and directory structure, 341

    managing, 329-332

    preventing premature, 330

    to replicate or not, 340

    system and domain files, 331-341

    of system policy files, 338-339

    user accounts database, 333-338

    of widely used files, 340

Replication of files, speed of the link and, 340

ReplicationGovernor (Netlogon), 312, 336

Replicator group, 199

Report Options dialog box (Performance
  Monitor), 537

Resource domains, explained, 291

Resource Kit (NT Server 4.0), 454

Resource Kits (MS), 454, 608

Resource servers, 208

Resources

    access to, 597-598

    centralized, 7-8

    connecting to shared, 265

    managing, 181-231

    ownership of, 597-598

    shared, 259-266

Resources for troubleshooting (MS), 604-609

Resources in use, monitoring, 301

Restore disk configuration, 501

Restore drive configuration, 500

Restore Files and Directories right, 476

Restore options, 486-488

Restoring a backed-up partition, 491

Restoring data from backups, 490-491

Restoring the registry, 503

Rights. *See also* Permissions

    assigning to users and groups, 255-258

    user, 203-204, 208

RISC-based computers, installing NT on, 96

Roaming (personal) user profile, 8, 171, 216-217

Run Program on Alert, 535

Running processes, changing priority of, 528-529

S

SAM database, 234, 236, 245

Sample exams on the CD-ROM, 648-649

Scalability, 6

Schedule service (NT Backup), 492

Scope, configuring, 135-136

Screen saver, processor utilization of, 543

SCSI adapters

    adding, 150-151

    incompatible, 117

SCSI LUN (Logical Unit Number), 589

SCSI (Small Computer Systems Interface), 467

SCSITOOL utility, 575

Seagate Backup Exec for Windows NT, 504

Security, 46-47, 105, 233-279. *See also*
  Permissions

    with GSNW, 409

    guidelines, 44

    implementing, 239-246

    Microsoft terms for, 240

    NTFS, 246-258

    RAS, 443-448

    RAS callback, 445-446

    for shared printers, 265

    share-level, 259-266

Security Access Manager (SAM), 234, 236, 245
Security descriptors, 240
Security hosts, third-party, 448
Security ID (SID), 245-246
Security Log, 554
Security model components, 234-235
Security model (NT), 234-239
Security tab (user properties), 251
Security tokens, 239, 246
Security warning message, adding, 272
Self Test answers, 617-645
Self-study module on the CD-ROM, 648
Separator files (NT-provided), 365
Separator Page dialog box, 366
Separator page for print jobs, 365-367
Serial Line Internet Protocol (SLIP), 430
Server Manager, 223-225
    creating a network share, 265
    export server functions from, 329
    launching, 297
    Promote to PDC, 111
    using, 297-305
Server Operators group, 198
Server promotion, 109-111
Server roles, 105-111
Server-based (roaming) profile, 216
Service Advertising Protocol (SAP), 432
Service Control Manager error, 582
Service optimization options, NT Server,
    522-523
Service Pack 3, 604
Service Pack 2, 43
Service Packs (MS), 43, 604-607
SESSION command, 412
Setup Manager (SETUPMGR), 98-105

Advanced Options window, 102-103
    Computer Role tab, 99
    General Setup Options, 98-100
    Networking Options area, 101-102
Setup program, 88-90, 573
Setup Wizard, 90-94
Share names, 75
Share permissions
    vs. local permissions, 596
    types of, 259-260
Shared directory
    from the command prompt, 263
    from the desktop, 260-261
    permissions, 259-265
Shared printers, 362
    connecting to, 363
    default permissions, 375
    security, 265
Shared resources, 259-266
    accessing gateway shares, 408-409
    connecting to, 265
    disconnecting a user from, 300
    managing, 300
Share-level security, 259-266
Sharing a computer's CD-ROM drive, 84
Sharing tab (User Properties), 260-261
Shiva Password Authentication Protocol (SPAP),
    446
Shutdown button, disabling, 273
Shutting down a task with Task Manager, 601
Single domain model, 291-292
Single vs. multiple backups, 464-465
16-bit applications, 22
Size factor (in backups), 465
Skills gap analysis, 652

Slashes, in naming conventions, 75
SMP support, 49-50
Soft page faults, 550
Software compatibility, 47, 49
Software requirements, researching, 46
Special Access dialog box (NTFS), 55
Speed factor (in backups), 465
Spool print documents, 371-372
SQL Server (MS), 14
Stac Replica for Windows NT, 505
Stand-alone server, 109
Start menu options, 213-214
STOP error, 601-602
Storage of backups, 472
Stripe set with parity, 163
    creating, 163
    regenerating, 585-586
    repairing damaged, 163
Stripe sets, creating, 160
Stripe sets without parity, 160
Striping data, 13-14
Striping with parity, 162-163
Subtrees (registry), 172
Symmetric Multiprocessing (SMP), 6, 49-50, 518-519
Synchronization control, 335
Synchronize Entire Domain command, 336
Synchronize With Primary Domain Controller command, 336
Synchronizing BDCs with PDCs, 304-305, 334-337
Synchronizing domain controllers, 336
Synchronizing files using My Briefcase, 341-344
System Default profile, 215

System files, deleting from a FAT partition, 114-115
System Log, 554, 581
System partition, 70-71, 156, 587
System partition failure, 587
System policies, 36-37, 201-214
System policies and profiles, 36-37
System Policy Editor, 8, 209-212
System policy files, replicating, 338-339
System Policy Template file (.ADM), 211
System Properties, Performance tab, 149, 527
System recovery, 598-599
System recovery options, 599
System registry. *See* Registry
SystemAudit, 241

T

Tape backup drives, 51, 149-150
Tape device, 149-151
Tape device driver, 151
Tape drive error detected dialog box, 475
Tapes window from NT Backup, 479
TAPI features of RAS, 449-450
Target Workstation Configuration, 82
Task Manager, 524-526, 600-601
    Applications tab, 600
    changing process priority, 529
    improved, 39-40
    tabs, 525
Tasks, 5
TCP/IP
    advantages of, 60-61
    configuring, 130-145
    and RAS Server, 431, 440-442

Memory:Page Faults/sec counter, 550

Memory:Pages Input/sec counter, 550-551

Memory:Pages Reads/sec counter, 551

Memory:Pages/sec counter, 546, 550

Microkernel, 19

Microsoft object security terms, 240

Microsoft Proxy Server, 14

Microsoft resources for troubleshooting, 604-609

Microsoft Service Packs, 604-607

Microsoft SQL Server, 14

Microsoft Web and FTP sites, 604

Migration to NT

    configuring, 415-420

    configuring file options, 419

    configuring user and group options, 418

    data first/users second, 400

    NetWare server to NT server, 417-420

    source and destination servers, 417

    transferring volumes and files, 415

    via two redirectors on clients, 401

    users first/data second, 400-401

    using Migration Tool, 397, 414-420

Migration Tool for NetWare, 397, 414-420

Minimize Memory Used, 522

Minimum requirements to run NT Server, 50

Mirror set (RAID 1)

    breaking, 586-587

    creating, 162

    fixing, 586-587

    recovering, 590

    repairing damaged, 162

Mirroring, disk, 13, 162

Modem Properties, General Tab, 436

Modems

    adding, 152-153

    in logical bundles, 428

Modular NT architecture, 2

Monitoring. *See also* Performance Monitor

    disk drive performance, 544-548

    network, 560-564

    processor performance, 541-543

    resources in use, 301

    server alerts, 301-302

    users, 298-299

Moving and copying files (NTFS), 57-58

MS-CHAP, 446

MS-DOS

    changing boot loader to, 115

    setting as default operating system, 115

MS-DOS subsystem, 22

Multiboot system, 71

Multilink (RAS), 428-429

Multi-modem adapters with NT server, 428-429

Multiple master domain model, 293-294

Multiple backups, 464-465, 473

Multiprocessing (NT), 517-519

Multiprocessing system categories, 6, 517

Multiprocessor support, 6-7

Multitasking, 4

    cooperative (non-preemptive), 4

    preemptive, 3-4

My Briefcase

    adding documents to, 342-343

    with additional file information, 344

    enabling, 342

    first initialized, 342

    using to synchronize files, 341-344

N

Naming conventions, 46, 74-75
NetBEUI, 60, 137-138, 431-432
NetBIOS, 60, 137-138
Netlogon service (NT), 237, 309-312
    configuring, 310-312
    Pulse option, 310-311
    PulseConcurrency option, 311
    PulseMaximum option, 311
    PulseTimeOut1 option, 311
    PulseTimeOut2 option, 311-312
    Randomize option, 312
    ReplicationGovernor option, 312
Netlogon share, explained, 339
NetWare connectivity
    NT Server emulating NetWare, 392-393
    NT Server as Gateway to NetWare, 391-392
    options, 390-393
    planning, 388-401
    with two redirectors on each client, 390-391
NetWare directories
    connecting to, 410
    gateway shares to, 405
NetWare directory rights, 415
NetWare file attributes, 416
NetWare file rights, 416
NetWare print queues
    connecting to, 410-411
    gateway shares to, 407
NetWare redirectors, removing, 402
Netware Router Information Protocol (RIP), 432
NetWare Server. *See also* GSNW; Migration to NT
    configuring, 405
    Directory Services Manager for, 398

dynamic link libraries (.DLL files), 411
File and Print Services for, 397-398
integration, 387-424
migrating to NT Server, 417-420
migration strategies, 398, 400-401
and NT Server comparison, 389
NetWare services
    connecting to with command line, 411
    connecting to with Explorer, 409-411
NetWare utilities, 412-413
NetWare-specific applications, 411-412
Network Boot Disk, creating, 81-83
Network cards, recommendations for, 51
Network Client Administrator, 79-83, 164-166
Network client installation disk set, making, 165
Network client protocols, NT-supported, 164
Network Configuration screen (RAS), 447
Network dialog box, Bindings tab, 524
Network drive share distribution files, 85
Network installation of NT Server, 86-87, 79-87
Network installation startup disk, making, 165
Network installation switches, 87-94
Network Interface Cards (NICs), 11, 523
Network interface printing devices, 363
Network logon, 213
Network Monitor, 35-36, 560-564, 594
    Capture window, 563
    data capture initiation, 561
    installing, 561
    Password Change dialog box, 564
    setting passwords, 564
    started, 562
Network Neighborhood icon, 209-210, 222
Network printers
    problems printing to, 364
    sharing, 362

Network problems, 594-596

Network protocols, configuring, 130-145

Network settings, 213

Network share

creating, 83-84, 205-206

creating using Server Manager, 265

Network share installation process, starting, 85-86

Network Startup Disk Configuration, 82

Network tuning, 522-524

Network-enabled backup software, 467

New Global Group dialog box, 308

New Local Group dialog box, 197, 308

New Phonebook Entry wizard, 451

New Printer Folder, 43-44

New user account, creating, 185-186

New User dialog box for dReplicator account, 320

New User window, 185

Noncontainer objects, 240

Nonpaged pool size vs. physical memory, 291

Non-privileged processor mode, 17

Normal backup, 469

NT. *See also* NT Server

architecture, 2, 16

configuring, 129-180

configuring to avoid problems, 137-138

installing on RISC-based computers, 96

migrating to using Migration Tool, 414-420

multiprocessing capabilities, 517-519

removing, 111-115

removing components, 148

removing from a FAT partition, 114-115

supported NetWare commands, 413

supported NetWare utilities, 412-413

transport protocols shipped with, 138

unsupported NetWare utilities, 413

NT Backup, 474-503

alternate path, 486

Append or Replace, 483

automating a backup, 495-496

automating use of .CMD file, 494-495

Back Up Local Registry, 484

backing up data, 489-490

backup and recovery schemes, 498-503

Backup Set Information option, 481-482

Backup Type option, 482

catalog from a tape backup, 480

control restoration destination, 479

creating a CMD file, 492-494

Drives window, 474

files not backed up with, 480-481

files not restored with, 481

hardware compression, 485

hardware for, 475-476

information for a local drive, 482

information for a remote drive, 483

limitations, 496

log options, 485-486

of NTFS or FAT partitions, 476

options, 481-486

parameters, 493

performing a backup, 488-490

permissions to perform a backup, 476

Restore to drive, 486

Restore File Permission, 487

Restore Information window, 487

Restore Local Registry, 487

Restore options, 486-488

restoring data from backups, 490-491

Restrict Access to..., 484-485

review full catalog of backup, 478

Schedule service, 492

selecting files for backup, 477-481

span multiple tapes, 478-479

Tape Name option, 482

Tapes window, 479

verification and logging, 479-480

Verify After Backup, 483-484

Verify After Restore, 488

NT boot floppy

creating, 576

re-creating, 87

NT Diagnostics (WinMSD), 222-223, 556-560, 581-582

Display tab, 557

Drives tab, 558

Environment tab, 559

Memory tab, 558

Network tab, 559

opening window, 557

Resources tab, 559

Services tab, 558

System tab, 557

Version tab, 557, 583

NT domains. See Domains (NT 4.0)

NT Executive Services, 2, 19-20

NT file systems, 52-59

NT migration from NetWare. See Migration to NT

NT Hardware Compatibility List (HCL), 48-49, 427, 572-573

NT Help, 608-609

NT Networking, installing, 92-94

NT Server. See also NT

absolute and relative performance, 553

administering remote, 221-226

crashes, 598-602

CD install, 78

CD-ROM installation, 94-95

determining usage, 44-45

emulating NetWare, 392-393

as Gateway to NetWare, 391-392

hardware recommendations, 51

installation methods, 78-105

installing, 69-127

installing GSNW on, 402-403

introduction to, 1-29

migrating NetWare server to, 417-420

minimum requirements, 50

multi-modem adapters with, 428-429

NetWare comparison, 389

network installation, 79-87

new features of 4.0, 34-44

overview, 2-16

performance tuning, 512-524

properties, 297-298

roles, 105-111

self-tuning mechanisms, 514-522

service optimization levels, 522

service optimization options, 522-523

NT Server alerts, managing, 301-302

NT Server Manager. See Server Manager

NT Server names, 46

NT Setup program, 88-90

NT Setup Wizard, 90-94

NT subsystems, 20-23

NT system registry. See Registry

TCP/IP Properties
    DHCP Relay tab, 134
    DNS tab, 132
    IP Address tab, 131
    WINS Address tab, 133
    WINS Routing tab, 135
TCP/IP-related protocol services, 134, 165
TechNet CD-ROM, 607
Templates, 211
Terms, glossary of, 653-676
Test page, printing, 367
TEXT data type, 359
Text-based Setup, 573
32-bit linear address, 25
Thrashing, 25
Threads, 3, 5-6, 515
    base priorities for, 520
    prioritization, 520-521
    viewing, 525-526
Thunking, 22
Time slice (thread), 3
Transmission Control Protocol/Internet Protocol.
    See TCP/IP
Troubleshooting, 571-615
    configuration, 575-582
    disk drive performance, 547-548
    disk problems, 582-584
    installation, 117-118, 572-575
    memory performance, 551
    MS resources for, 604-609
    network problems, 594-596
    permissions problems, 596-598
    printers, 379-381
    printing, 590-592
    processor performance, 542-543

RAID problems, 584-590
RAS problems, 455-456, 591-594
server crashes, 598-602
True multiprocessor support, 6-7
Truncated filenames, 59
Trust relationships (domain), 192-193, 285-290, 296
    explained, 285
    identifying on domain B, 289
    managing, 285-298
    number of, 290
    terminating, 289
    using, 289
Trusted domain, 237
    adding, 288
    concept, 285
Trusting domain, 237, 288
Tuning
    network, 522-524
    NT Server, 512-524
Two-way trust, 287

U

Unattended backup, 496
Unattended installation, 98-105
Unattended installation answer file, 103-104
Unattended setup, and UDF, 104-105
Undocked configuration, 38
Uninterruptible Power Supplies (UPSs), adding, 153-154
Uniqueness Database File (UDF), 104-105
Universal Naming Convention, 75
Universal print driver (unidriver), 356
Unknown volume, 583

Upgrade installation, 96-98
UPS Control Panel Applet, 153
User accounts, 182-188
    assigning rights to, 255-258
    copying, 186
    configuring for migration, 418
    creating, 185-186
    deleting, 187
    deleting vs. disabling, 207-208
    disabling, 186, 207-208
    disconnecting, 300
    local group, 198
    managing, 207
    migrating to NT, 414
    monitoring, 298-299
    RAS permissions for, 444-445
    renaming, 187-188
User community, 44
User Default profile, 215
User directories, creating, 188
User Environment Profile dialog box, 189
User Manager, 183-193
    creating and managing groups in, 196
    icons, 184
    with Username accounts, 319
    window, 255
User mode, 2, 17-18
User mode vs. Kernel mode, 17-18
User Profile options, 214
User Profiles, 7-8, 171, 214-220
    copying, 219-220
    creating roaming, 216-217
    managing, 218
    shortcuts, 218-220
    types of, 171, 215-218

User Profiles tab, 219
User rights, 208. *See also* Permissions
    modifying, 203-204, 258
    table of advanced, 257-258
    table of basic, 256-257
User Rights Policy dialog box, 203, 256
User session, disconnecting, 299
Username, disabling the default, 272-273
Users. *See* Groups; User accounts

Verification (backup protection), 472-473
Virtual DOS Machine (VDM), 4, 22
Virtual memory, 24, 514
Virtual Memory Manager (VMM), 20, 24, 514
Virtual Private Networking (VPN), 433
VOLINFO command, 412
Volume sets, 159-160
    creating, 159
    extending, 159-160
Volumes and files, migrating to NT, 415

Web Browser and Web-ification, 43
Web-based administration, 43
Windows 95, 3, 166
Windows NT. *See* NT
Windows NT Server. *See* NT Server
Winlogon
    changing the security notice, 272
    disabling the Shutdown button, 273
    process, 236
WinMSD, 556-560

Winnt.exe or Winnt32.exe switches, 88
WINPRINT.DLL, 358-359
WINS (Windows Internet Name Service), 3, 36
    Address tab (TCP/IP Properties), 133
    advanced configuration options, 140
    configuration options, 139-140
    renewal interval, 139
    Routing tab (TCP/IP Properties), 135
Win16, 22
Win32, 21
Wizards, Administrative, 16, 35
Work environment, 44
Workgroup model, 282, 284
Workgroup model vs. domain concept, 284

Workgroups, 282
Working set of data pages, 549
Workstations, 3, 166, 284
WWW servers (MS), 604
WWW Service
    Advanced tab, 145
    configuring, 141-145
    Directories tab, 143
    Logging tab, 144
WWW Service tab, 142

X

X.25 networks, 427-428

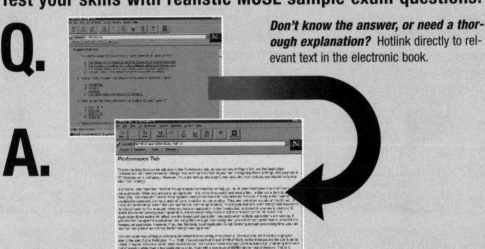